MW01448860

Petra's Legacy

Perspectives on South Texas
Sponsored by Texas A&M University–Kingsville
Timothy E. Fulbright, General Editor

Petra V. de Kenedy

PETRA'S LEGACY

The South Texas Ranching Empire of Petra Vela and Mifflin Kenedy

*Jane Clements Monday
and Frances Brannen Vick*

Texas A&M University Press
College Station

Copyright © 2007 by Jane Clements Monday and Frances Brannen Vick
Manufactured in the United States of America
All rights reserved
First edition

The paper used in this book meets the minimum requirements
of the American National Standard for Permanence
of Paper for Printed Library Materials, z39.48-1984.
Binding materials have been chosen for durability.
∞ ♻

Library of Congress Cataloging-in-Publication Data

Monday, Jane Clements, 1941–
   Petra's legacy : the South Texas ranching empire of Petra Vela and Mifflin Kenedy / Jane Clements Monday and Frances Brannen Vick.—1st ed.
       p. cm.—(Perspectives on South Texas)
  ISBN-13: 978-1-58544-614-8 (cloth : alk. paper)
  ISBN-10: 1-58544-614-9 (cloth : alk. paper)
   1. Kenedy, Petra Vela, 1823–1854. 2. Women ranchers—Rio Grande Valley—Biography. 3. Kenedy, Mifflin, 1818–1895. 4. Ranchers—Rio Grande Valley—Biography. 5. Ranch life—Rio Grande Valley—History—19th century. 6. Rio Grande Valley—Social life and customs—19th century. 7. Married people—Rio Grande Valley—Biography. 8. Rio Grande Valley—Biography. 9. Texas, South—Biography. 10. Brownsville (Tex.)—Biography. I. Vick, Frances Brannen, 1935– II. Title.
  F392.R5M665 2007
  976.4'405092—dc22
  [B]

2007007775

*To my beloved husband Charles,
our children Kimberly, Lauren, Julie, Buddie, Jennifer, and Adam,
and our precious grandchildren, who are our legacy.*
—Jane Clements Monday

*For my children Karen, Ross, and Patrick,
Who have made my life a song.*
—Frances Brannen Vick

Contents

Preface ix

Prologue 1

Chapter 1
1823–54: "Into Her World"—Petra's Story 7

Chapter 2
1823–54: "Into Her World"—Mifflin's Story 24

Chapter 3
1855–60: Forging a Life in Brownsville 46

Chapter 4
1860–62: War Clouds Gather 76

Chapter 5
1863: War Closes in on the Rio Grande Valley 98

Chapter 6
1864–65: Chaos along the Rio Grande 117

Chapter 7
1866: Home Again 141

Chapter 8
1867–68: "Woe to Brownsville! Woe to Matamoros!" 153

Chapter 9
1869–71: "¿*Quién Viene?*" 171

Chapter 10
1872–74: One Foot in Brownsville, One in the Wild Horse Desert 189

Chapter 11
1873: Politics, Bandits, and Hard Economic Times … 199

Chapter 12
1874: Railroads and Cattle Drives … 215

Chapter 13
1875: Leander McNelly and the Texas Rangers … 223

Chapter 14
1876: The Apple of His Father's Eye … 236

Chapter 15
1877–78: "A Fiend in Human Form" … 245

Chapter 16
1879–80: Last Days at Los Laureles—The Laurel Leaf Ranch … 263

Chapter 17
1881: To the Body of Christ—Corpus Christi … 272

Chapter 18
1882: La Parra—The Grapevine Ranch … 280

Chapter 19
1883: They Were Always There for One Another … 289

Chapter 20
1884: Farewell to Santiago … 305

Chapter 21
1885: Goodbye to Petrita … 336

    Epilogue … 348
    Notes … 359
    Bibliography … 405
    Index … 417

Preface

Francis E. Abernethy once wrote that folklorists follow historians "like gleaners—or cotton strippers in West Texas," collecting "the leavings from academic historians," all the tales and songs and traditions that the historians allow to fall between the cracks. Sometimes the historians lose the spirit of the story in doing so.[1] The story of Petra Kenedy and most Tejanas must be told like those gleaners because so many facts of their lives and their families have fallen between the cracks of history. Thus we have at times gone outside the mainline historical sources to find more of the story. However, as can be noted from research of various historical events, and as new material comes to light, sometimes the historians get the details right, and sometimes they don't, which adds to the problem of writing this history of the Kenedy family and of Petra.

It has been said that there is no history, just people. This remarkable family stepped onto the stage of history and molded it in their own way. They made history. They were major players from the frontier settlements in northern Mexico in the 1820s, through the Mexican War, the establishment of Brownsville, the U.S. Civil War, the trail drives and development of one of the great cattle ranches, the expansion of the West, the settling of the Wild Horse Desert, and on to helping bring the railroad to South Texas, catapulting commerce in the United States and Mexico into the twentieth century.

Many have written about these events, but the women seemed to be missing. We wanted to know what role the women played. We knew that Petra was special but we had no idea how important she was until her story began to unfold. The dearth of material on Petra made the piecing together of her life a real challenge. We began with newspaper reports, the writings of historians and folklorists of the region, and the histories of Mifflin Kenedy and Richard King. Then we found the treasure trove of primary material—letters and court documents—that gave us a real sense of Petra's family. Through the letters the happiness, conflicts, marriages, births, deaths, tragedies, and conquests came to life on the stage of history. We wanted to surround this family with the environment in which they lived so that the reader could taste, feel, and smell their world. We researched diaries, letters, and other written accounts from those times to provide this added dimension.

One of the problems with researching the Kenedy history is that a number of the papers are still restricted and unavailable. Our hope is that someday they will be made available and new insights can be added to this story. Everyone who has read about Mifflin Kenedy and Richard King knew they were partners but through their letters we found that the two were closer than brothers, sharing a deep personal relationship and sharing the same dream of Manifest Destiny. Through their letters and other historical accounts we were able to shed new light on their business dealings with each other and the rest of the world as events swirled around them. To paint the background in which these people lived we have used materials from the Brownsville Historical Association's publication *Tidbits* and from their collections. Brownsville and Corpus Christi newspapers flesh out the people of the area at that place in time.

It is impossible to understand this family without having a deep appreciation of both cultures—Mexican and Anglo—in which they lived. We are indebted to Homero Vera for his help in bridging the gap between the cultures and in helping us to move in both worlds. He provided extensive research into primary documents in archives in Matamoros and Mier that added valuable unpublished material to help understand Petra's life and her background. He is one in a million and we are very grateful to him.

Our information had to be correct, as found in the available resources. We appreciate Bruce Cheeseman for his unparalleled knowledge of these people and this period of Texas history. To understand this family and their legacy it is necessary to understand the depth of their faith and the role it played in their lives and in the lives of their descendants. Our deep appreciation goes to Father Francis Kelly Nemeck, OMI, for his advice and his generosity in sharing his knowledge of the Kenedy family history, their faith, and of La Parra.

We consulted with many people. You all know who you are and we thank you from the bottoms of our hearts. This history would have been much harder to write without the informative work that Mary Margaret McAllen Amberson and James and Margaret McAllen did in *I Would Rather Sleep in Texas*. Mary Margaret Amberson is herself one of the legacies of the cross-cultural unions that made the area so rich.

We spent hours researching and working in the depths of the "stacks" surrounded by books, newspapers, and microfilm, but all along the way generous people with warm smiles encouraged us. Thanks go particularly to the Raymondville Historical Association and Community Center and their former director Max Dreyer and current director Clark Allen. We thank the Corpus Christi Library and particularly Ceil Venable. Many people in the Corpus Christi church also came to our assistance—Monsignor Thomas Meaney and

PREFACE   xi

Michael Howell, Father James Harris, Cy Richards, Geraldine McGloin, and Sister Irvena Gonzales. At the Corpus Christi Museum we are particularly indebted to Lillian Embree for the hours she spent transcribing the 1873 and 1874 Kenedy records. We appreciate the help of former archivist Patti Murphy, Jessanine Guerra, Don Zuris, and Richard Starkey. Spohn Hospital and Sammie Grunwald were also very helpful. The Museum of South Texas and the Boot Hill Museum in Dodge City generously shared photographs. Thanks to Judge Ricardo Hinojosa for his help in Edinburg.

In Brownsville, Texas, our research started with and was inspired by Chula T. Griffin, who has been by our side from the very first. She encouraged us and "rounded up" the forces to aid our searches. Thanks to Bill Young and the staff of the Brownsville Historical Association and their director, Priscilla Rodriquez.

Several researchers aided us and we value their willingness to help get the story right and to add to the depth of the research. Gratitude goes to Homero Vera, field historian for Texas A&M–Kingsville; Nancy Tiller, cartographer; and to Steve Harding of Harding Design; Barbara Rutz, researcher for the Chester County Historical Association in Pennsylvania; Johnnie Jo Dickinson of Dickinson Research; J.D. Dickinson for providing Masonic research; Letty Vera; and Ann Froelich. We are also grateful to Alexander Stillman for his help with the Stillman-Kenedy relationship and for sharing his drawings and extensive knowledge of valley history. We appreciate Jack Turcotte for his insights into the Kenedy's history.

We also had help in our church research from Father Bob Wright, Father B.G. Mokarzel, and Martha Santillan at the Oblate School of Theology in San Antonio. Sylvia Probst, assistant to Sr. Joan Marie Aycock, archivist, at the Ursuline Convent in New Orleans, Louisiana, filled us in on information there.

Perhaps the best part of researching this book has been the opportunity to meet Petra's descendants. We met with them from Brownsville to San Antonio, Laredo, Dallas, Seguin, and Colorado. They are proud of their heritage and eager that their family's story is told. We share their pride in Petra and her family. Thanks to Rosa Putegnat's descendants Mary Huebscher, Patsy Reneghan, Rosita Putegnat, Jesse (Sam) Thornham, Patrick Thornham, and Ed McGoohon. Thanks to Luisa Dalzell's descendants Susan Hefley Seed and Janis Hefley. Thanks to Concepción's descendant Rosa María Rodríquez de Swisher and to María Vicenta's descendants Marty Heaner and Michael Hamilton. Petra would be proud of all of them.

We are thankful for the cheering section of Charles Monday and all our family and friends; their encouraging calls, their listening to countless stories of the manuscript progress, and their sharing the "down" moments as well as the "up" moments kept us going. Our good friends Jane Roberts Wood, Marilyn Manning, Joyce Gibson Roach, and Judy Alter have been there all the way encouraging us. A special thanks goes to Gayla Christiansen and of course Mary Lenn Dixon for believing from the beginning that Petra's story was one that needed to be told. They, Dawn Hall, and Thom Lemmons have been a joy to work with; we are fortunate to have them by our side.

This journey has now come to an end. It started almost a decade ago when Jane Monday discovered Petra while working on her book with Betty Colley, *Voices from the Wild Horse Desert*. Monday first collaborated with Carolina Crimm, Darla Morgan, and Betty Colley to tell Petra's story. We are grateful to each of them for their contributions and for caring that Petra's story be told. At a later stage, Jane continued the journey with Frances Vick, who joined the quest, conducting her own research as her interest grew in different aspects of the story, and they finished the journey together. Jane wrote the original draft, passing the chapters back and forth, Jane and Frances adding and subtracting material in an effort to bring readers an accurate history. Here is the story of Petra's legacy. We hope you will find these lives and the events that swirled around them as exciting and incredible as we have.

—Jane Clements Monday, Huntsville, Texas
—Frances Brannen Vick, Dallas, Texas

Petra's Legacy

Prologue

> There is a woman at the beginning of all great things.
> —LAMARTINE

When Mifflin Kenedy came into Petra Vela's world through marriage—rather than she into his—sparks flew and a change was ordained for Texas. She became Mifflin's wife, mother of their children, and matriarch of one of the most powerful families in Texas. He became one of the most successful frontier capitalists and the patriarch of three generations of Kenedys. Little has been written about these two in spite of the fact that their lives touched most of the major historical people and events that affected Texas and Mexico for nearly forty years, from 1846 to 1885. Petra and Mifflin were major influences in the founding of South Texas, and their legacy continues to the present through their descendants' contributions to their communities and through their philanthropic efforts.

In examining the lives, events, and personalities in Texas and Mexico during the years in question, there were very limited sources for Petra's life. Researching women's history for this period is difficult at best. Very few primary documents are available from Anglo women and even less from Mexican women. There are few diaries or letters, but it is to be hoped that more of this information will emerge to fill the void. Tejana history is similar to a woven tapestry, comprised of personal family information, census data, newspaper reports, church documents, letters to and from the families and businesses in the area, and the mores of the time. Petra's story first emerged from such a background. Then more personal letters and documents were found and Petra stepped out of the shadows and onto the stage of history.

When Petra was young the land on which she lived was part of Mexico for as far as one could see. There was no United States for miles and miles and miles. Then the foreigners began to come from the north, south, and east. They also came from overseas to this windswept land that bordered the great river, the Río Bravo, in northern Mexico. First they came in small numbers by horseback and wagon. Then they came in larger numbers by boats, and they began to settle and farm the land. Many purported to accept the Catholic faith and even to speak the Spanish language. The settlers wanted more land, and soon they started a revolution and declared independence from Mexico. In

1836 the foreigners fought and won the land that became the Republic of Texas, the land stretched from the Río Bravo, whose name became the Rio Grande, north to the Sabine River. They brought new languages, food, dress, weapons, and a continued desire to possess more and more land. Petra's family and others had owned land along the Río Bravo since before most of the United States had been settled. This had long been their land, which they had wrested from the indigenous people, and they had worked hard at making it their home.

By 1854, when Petra and Mifflin married, the land had changed, and more changes were to come. Petra had no idea that she and her family would play a major role in those changes. Petra's husband Mifflin would own one of the largest ranches in the United States and would help to develop the cities of Brownsville and Corpus Christi; he and his friends also would control the politics up and down the Rio Grande. He would help develop one of the first railroads in South Texas, connecting the rich agricultural land to the rest of Texas and the United States and into Mexico. When war came again and split the country into North and South, Petra would have family members fighting on both sides of the war, and the war would also provide the means to make her family's fortune. A son would become involved in the French Intervention in Mexico and die before an execution squad of French Imperialist soldiers. Her family would help tame the Wild Horse Desert and produce some of the finest cattle in the world. As the family developed their ranching empire her sons would lead cattle drives up the trails to the railheads of the Midwest. One would be tracked down and shot by the legendary western lawmen Wyatt Earp and Bat Masterson. Her accomplished daughters would marry prominent men up and down the river as well as in Corpus Christi and would play leading roles in Texas society.

Petra and Mifflin could not have come from more different backgrounds. Petra was from Mier, Mexico, a land that had been settled by José de Escandón in 1749. Petra's family had been among the original families that settled the town of Mier. Américo Paredes writes that within these Spanish settlements, "social conduct was regulated and formal, and men lived under a patriarchal system that made them conscious of degree . . . with the 'captain' of each community playing the part of father to his people." It made for a very cohesive group with clanlike characteristics.[1]

The elite landowners—with large ranchos—lived in spacious flat-roofed houses that served as forts as well as homes. The smaller landowners lived in smaller homes and worked their smaller herds, but they differed from the elite only in the size of their landholdings, not in the way they lived and in their philosophies and culture.[2] Petra's home was more modest than the larger haciendas, but her family was actively involved in ranching. Her immediate family established two ranches, named Veleño and Santa Teresa. Santa Teresa was located north of the Río Bravo in what is now Starr and Hogg counties and consisted of two leagues, or approximately 8,856 acres. The headquarters had a two-story structure complete with gun ports for protection. The Veleño ranch also consisted of two leagues and was located north of the Río Bravo on the Santa Gertrudis coast along the Lagarto Creek near the Nueces River.[3]

In the home, no matter how wealthy, the wife and mother managed the education, morals, manners, and most of all, religious training of the children. Petra fit that matriarch role in her home. She was described as warm and energetic with a spirit of love that dominated her nature. Her peers viewed her as "notably handsome of tall and commanding figure, united with the grace in bearing and winning manners." Added to these attractions, she possessed a "clear, keen and incisive intellect, and was a brilliant and vivacious talker."[4] Another unusual aspect of Petra's society, which came from Spanish law, was the ability of the women to inherit land along with their brothers. There was no primogeniture as far as inheritance went, so Petra inherited land from her father, making her even more attractive in a country where land ownership defined wealth and opportunity. Perhaps Petra's finest attribute, however, was that she filled her life with acts of charity, which were often done in secrecy and silence.[5]

Petra came from what Jovita González calls "the effervescent Latin temperament of the Mexican people," with the settlers of Mier called "small in number but of good quality and well to do."[6] According to Abbé Domenece, the families of Mier were physically distinguishable from people in other villas because they had fairer skin; both sexes were "strikingly handsome [with] features that were regular, delicate, and of a decidedly noble cast." They also spoke Spanish "more pure, correct, and less corrupted with Indian words and phrases."[7] Jovita González's writings from her in-depth research into the Spanish Mexican culture on the border, at a time when very few were doing so, is highly revealing, particularly in the area of women's history.

Donald Chipman and Harriett Denise Joseph point out that women in colonial Texas were "historically faceless." They "bore children, washed and mended clothes, swept chapels and helped their husbands," but that would hardly give a complete picture of the many contributions of women.[8] The same would be true of Petra's time. These two historians gained insight into colonial Latinas by examining lawsuits, estate settlements, wills, petitions, and other legal instruments. They discovered, along with learning of daily circumstances, privileges and obligations, that the women understood clearly their rights by law—privileges and rights that were alien to Anglo American women. They also made observations that opened doors to a better understanding of Petra. They pointed out that Spaniards, unlike Anglos, were more "fatalistic than introspective." Thus they would not keep diaries "agonizing over matters of conscience," "express[ing] doubts about their importance as individuals," or "los[ing] sleep over the propriety of their actions."[9] Chipman and Joseph also noted the inability of many of the Spanish to give their exact age, which certainly carried over to Petra and her daughters, as can be seen later. The year of birth might be given, followed by "poco más o menos."[10]

Petra has been presented as everything from the daughter of a governor to a poor ranch girl turned laundress. Research indicates she was probably somewhere in between. No proof has been found that she was a laundress; she was, instead, listed as head of an independent household in the 1850 census. In that same census Mifflin was listed as living in a boarding house with twenty-three other men. Petra was not descended from a bishop or a governor; the possible reason for the confusion is in the interpretation of a document. In the document that verified don Gregorio Vela's Mexican land grant, Santa Teresa, in 1848, the wording seemed to imply he was the interim governor of Tamaulipas: "citizen Gregorio Vela of that vicinity was interim constitutional governor of the state, on the date that is verified." This statement upon close examination actually referred back to Mr. José Antonio Fernandez y Yzaguirre, who was mentioned earlier in the document, but it could easily have been misinterpreted, as evidently it was.[11]

What is important is that Petra was a remarkable young Mexican woman of Spanish descent who had an enormous effect on her family and country, epitomizing the successful uniting of two cultures to create a new vibrant generation to help settle the land known as Texas.

The blending of the two cultures challenged Petra throughout her marriage to Mifflin because she and he were very different. Petra was a faithful church-going Mexican Catholic with a Latin heart. Mifflin was a Quaker, a denomination that is—on the surface at least—as near to the opposite end of the religious and societal spectrum from Catholicism as it is possible to get. Mifflin's religion emphasized simple living and restraint. Her education and upbringing was staunchly Catholic on the Rio Grande border; his was resolutely Quaker in eastern Pennsylvania. Petra would remain a committed Catholic all her life. Mifflin would remain a Quaker in the depths of his soul all his life.

Mifflin was born into a modest family on June 8, 1818, at Downington, Chester County, Pennsylvania. His mother, who had charge of the children's religious upbringing, was a member of the Society of Friends, which rejected ritual, formal sacraments, formal creed, a priesthood, and violence.[12] His father was an Irish immigrant and may or may not have been a member of the Society of Friends. It is very likely, however, that he was born Catholic but did not practice Catholicism. Coatesville, where Mifflin grew up, was only thirty-eight miles from Philadelphia and was said to contain people who were reserved and quiet—modest, good, and fine.[13] He emulated these attributes and assimilated them and always adhered to his Quaker roots. Mifflin was characterized as learned, quiet, and reserved, and although he left home to make his fortune he stayed in close touch with his family. The thread of commonality between Petra and Mifflin was love of family.

Mifflin Kenedy, the "quiet Quaker," almost always ended up in a leadership role. As a businessman, he drove a hard bargain even though he was a negotiator, and he liked "loud, brash, on-the-edge men, like King," but he did not seek credit for his own efforts.[14] However, he was indeed an empire builder. Without Mifflin Kenedy there would be no King Ranch; Mifflin brought Richard King to Texas. The Kenedy story is the other half of this great story that has never been told. Throughout their lives Mifflin served as a partner, confidant, business advisor, and most of all friend to Richard King; and King served likewise to Mifflin.

The ever-careful Mifflin would not have married Petra Vela just because she had the dark flashing eyes of a señora. She would have had to fit into his scheme of assimilation into the "older" culture along the border. Mifflin knew what he wanted and was determined to achieve it. "Family and extended family meant everything, and land meant everything and the river was only a river" as far as assimilation of cultures.[15] On the one hand, Mifflin would have seen Petra as "a strong independent woman of pleasant appearance, heritage, character and devotion."[16] Petra, on the other hand, married a man who could provide her and her children security, safety, and opportunity even though their lives would be filled with both happiness and tragedy.

Petra, with a deeply religious character, may have done much to modify the character and aims of a practical man of the world, absorbed in the labors and cares that beset the road to wealth. It was said that Mifflin Kenedy entered with the ardor of a greathearted gentleman into all his wife's charitable designs and projects.[17] The pairing of the attractive, vivacious, and religious Petra with the reserved personality and brilliant business acumen of Mifflin would lead to the establishment of a charitable foundation and a trust that continues to contribute millions of dollars to worthwhile causes throughout Texas.

The Kenedy saga is epic in scope. Steamboats, war, and the millions made as a result of the war, revolution, livestock raising and rustling, trail drives, gunfights, railroads, and the blending of two cultures in one family—the saga has it all. This is also the story of the age of Manifest Destiny and its impact on the family and the area.[18] And it is the story of a Tejana who could hold her own with two successful men from two different cultures—Luis Vidal and Mifflin Kenedy—one a successful Mexican military man and the other one of the most powerful Anglo men in South Texas and beyond. Finally, it is the story of the role that religion played in Mifflin and Petra's lives, stabilizing them in times of loss and distress, becoming an important bond between generations, and in the last analysis leaving a legacy that is incalculable in its importance.

Tejanos were the original founders of Texas. These Tejano families are Texans who lived and served under all six of the Texas flags. They came originally from the five Mexican municipalities of Laredo, Guerrero, Mier, Camargo, and Reynosa, all settled by Escandón. They founded the ranch towns scattered across the Wild Horse Desert. They came before the area was part of Texas or the United States. They established the foundation of the American ranching industry. By virtue of the Treaty of Guadalupe Hidalgo they became American citizens. Although the Mexican settlers became Texans and American by treaty they retained their strong cultural and family links to their original settlements of Las Villas del Norte located on the southern bank of the Rio Grande.[19]

That was the Vela family story and Petra's. Petra Vela first had children with a dashing military officer; then she married an American, with whom she also had children, who had come into her world with the U.S. Army and stayed to make his fortune. All of Petra's children were Tejanos. Her children are Petra's heritage. This is the story of Petra, Mifflin, and the children and their place on the stage of Texas history.

Today Petra's descendants from Luis Vidal have established their own legacies and married corporate executives, become philanthropists, ranchers, business owners, educators, and military leaders. They are living throughout Texas and are leading citizens in their communities. Petra and Mifflin's descendants left their fortune, later supplemented by oil and gas revenues, to The John G. and Marie Stella Kenedy Memorial Foundation and The John G. Kenedy Jr. Charitable Trust when they failed to produce heirs. These charitable institutions are using the money to help educate, provide medical treatment, and support Texans of both Mexican and Anglo heritage through charitable contributions counted in the millions of dollars. It seems we have come full circle. Petra would heartily approve.

CHAPTER 1

1823–54: "Into Her World"—Petra's Story

The small wood-frame St. Mary's Catholic Church was cool inside on this tenth day of May 1854. The hot Texas sun was beating down on the city of Brownsville and the adjacent Rio Grande. A thin layer of dust covered the city outside as candlelight reflected a soft glow on the group gathered in front of the altar. Father Jean Marie Casimir Verdet, the local pastor and head of the small group of French Oblate missionaries in the Rio Grande Valley, was there to perform a ceremony that would eventually affect the lives of thousands of Catholics and future Texans of all denominations. Standing before him were Doña Petra Vela de Vidal and Mifflin Kenedy, who had come to be married. Petra was thirty-one years old and Mifflin thirty-six.

For years a shroud of mystery has surrounded the woman known as Petra Vela de Vidal Kenedy. During her lifetime, Petra and her family were an integral part of the changes that occurred along the borderlands between Texas and Mexico during the second half of the nineteenth century. As the dramatic events of those years unfurled in a panorama along the border, Petra and her family played leading roles on the stage of history.

Petra Vela was born in Mier, Mexico, on January 31, 1823, although she always altered her age to appear two years younger and listed her date of birth as 1825.[1] Her family was of frontier stock and had been in northern Mexico for six generations. They had deep roots in the soil of Mexico, but originally the Vela family came from Catalonia, Spain, to the New World.[2] Petra was descended from Francisco Vela, rancher and military captain, who was born about 1625, probably in Cuencamé, Nueva Vizcaya (Durango, Mexico); when he asked that a brand be registered in his name, he certified that it was one that belonged to his father in Cuencamé. Francisco arrived in Cerralvo, Nuevo Leon, around 1645. A small garrison had been established at Cerralvo in 1629

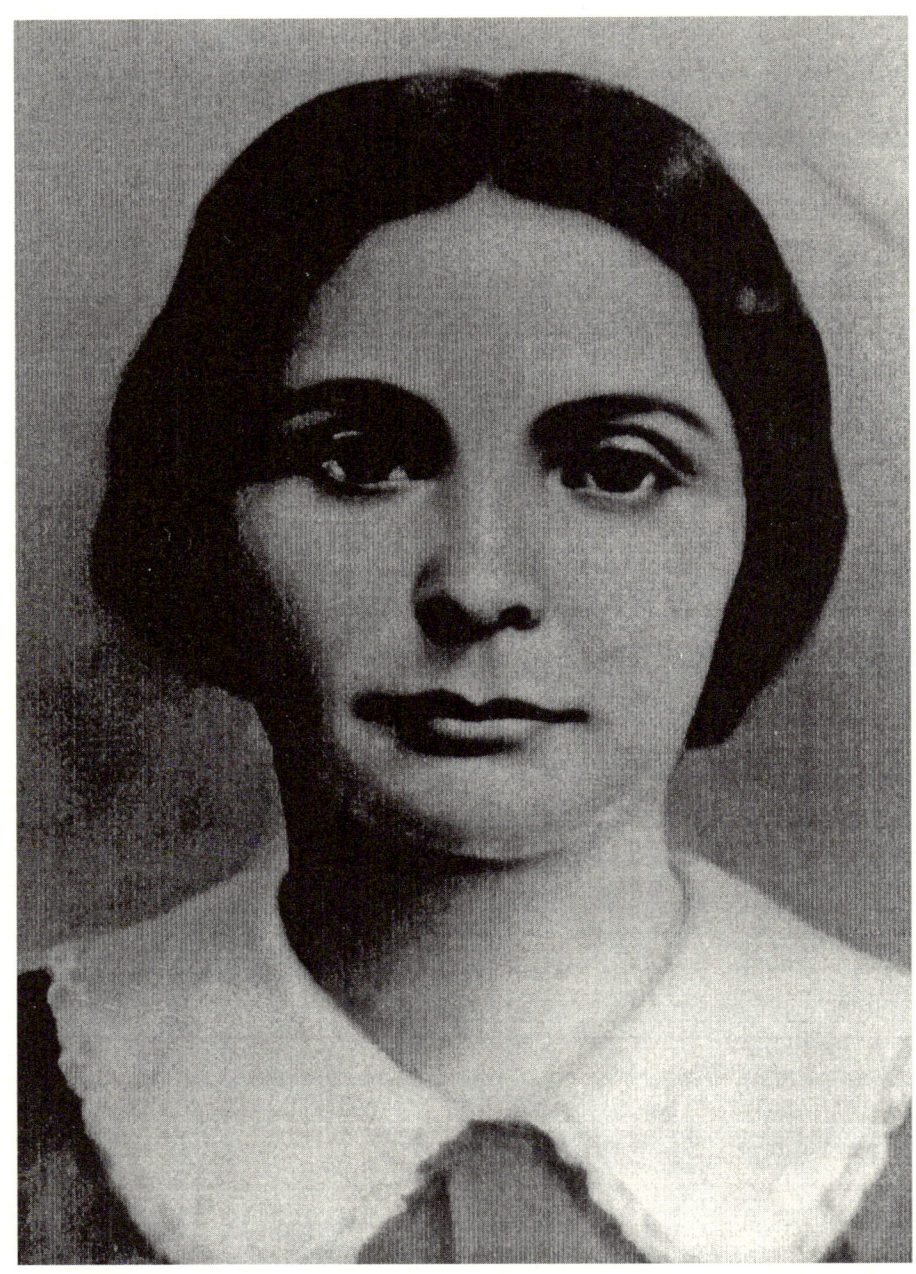

One of the earliest pictures of Petra Vela, who captivated Luis Vidal and later Mifflin Kenedy with her large eyes and vivacious personality. Courtesy of Jesse (Sam) Thornham, Joe Thornham, McGoohan families.

to serve as protection for the people in the area who had moved there when silver mines were discovered during the late 1500s.[3]

Francisco's brand was registered in his name in Cerralvo on May 9, 1665. Later, on May 25, 1685, he applied for a land grant. The application reads in part: "Lieutenant [Francisco Vela] resident of Cerralvo. . . . I say that it has been nearly forty years since I came into this Realm, being at the time a bachelor. Later I married in Saltillo and then came to settle in this section . . . it being on the frontier of the enemy, I have served in all actions and expeditions against them, and as soon as they could bear arms my five sons have served whenever necessary to the royal service . . . for which I have not been paid, and because I am poor and obligated with family, and in need to support them."[4] On May 25, 1692, he gave power of attorney to collect his yearly military pay. This same power is recorded in his name 1696 through 1699. He spent his entire adult life in the Cerralvo district, working his cattle and performing his military duties. It is difficult to get more information on this family because the Cerralvo records have been lost and the family did not become "wealthy and influential" until the 1700s.[5]

The fighting skills of these Spanish soldiers had been honed over the seven centuries of warfare, from 711 to 1492, with the Muslims over the Christian-Muslim frontiers. Soldiers soon ranked along with lawyers and priests in Spanish society. In fighting for their homeland and their religion, both their homes and their religion became uniquely "vital and intense," and whetted their appetite for expansion. They saw themselves on a crusade to spread Spanish culture and religion to the New World. The king of Castile licensed an entrepreneur, or *adelantado,* to "push forward the frontiers of Christianity." These warriors were willing to risk all their capital because success would bring titles of nobility, land, and governmental powers as well as the spoils of war that would accompany conquest. The *adelantado's* rewards could be great and so could the rewards for any young warriors persuaded to join him.[6] No doubt by this means the Velas were persuaded to join the "crusade" to the New World to improve their lives and their status.

The story is written that when Francisco Vela first started to move north to the frontier in 1645, on his journey to Cerralvo he stopped in Saltillo and met a blonde, nearly redheaded, lady who enchanted him, and he promised to return for her. Apparently he did and his family was begun, but first he offered his services to Governor don Martín de Zavala where he registered his brand and signed his name, showing he was educated, and thus registering the Vela name, which means "watchful, on guard," in Latin, apropos of his military career perhaps. With the registered brand and his few horses, he could work for the governor and slowly build up his horse herd, which he needed for his patrolling, and then start a herd of cattle and apply for a land grant.[7] These soldiers were spread out over the territory, usually in pairs, but sometimes alone, which gave rise to the "one man, one rebellion" saying that prevailed two hundred years before the Texas Rangers' "One riot, one Ranger." The soldiers had to furnish all their own arms and mounts, were paid once a year, and they had to raise and keep a horse herd to fulfill their military obligations.[8]

Four of Captain Francisco Vela's sons were Francisco, Santiago, Domingo, and Lázaro. No record can be found of the fifth son he mentions.[9] Petra's great-grandfather was Lázaro, the great-grandson of one of those sons, born around 1721 in Cerralvo.[10] The family had made significant progress through hard work on the frontier and had acquired property and social standing. In 1753 Lázaro was listed in the census as a Spaniard married with six sons/daughters and a herd of mares, ten tame horses, and two hundred goats/sheep. He had married María Antonia García. Their daughter, María Gertrudis Vela, married Juan Pantaleón de Ysaguirre. The priest of the parish and of the Church of the Immaculate Conception of Mier City recorded a sad occurrence about this daughter on August 12, 1789: "I, Fray Pedro Maldonado y Zapata, as Minister of this Town and this sacred Church of the Parish in my charge, give ecclesiastical major burial in a plat [*sic*] of five pesos, the body of doña María Gertrudis Vela, Spanish, originally of the Town of San Gregorio de Cerralvo, but of this town since a child, she being the legitimate daughter of don Lázaro Vela and doña María Antonia García, married to don Juan Pantaleón de Ysaguirre, Spanish. She did not receive sacrament because of the distance and the violence with which she died from the bite from a poisonous snake. She was forty years of age."[11] Apparently in his grief, the husband had gone to great lengths to be sure the details of his wife's birth, her lineage, and how she died were included, which was rarely done in these reports.

The Spanish records for this group meticulously follow the standards set earlier. The term "hidalgo" means "son of someone," and is the lowest rank of minor nobility, but the term indicates a place in society held by people who have won standing, that is, a man of property and one with special responsibilities. He could bear his own arms and the title was bestowed for special services to the Crown or the Church. The title "don" was to be used before the given name, such as an English knighthood carries the title, "sir." It could also be hereditary and could come from either parent. Holders of the title or right were expected to honor the idea of noblesse oblige. In time it became a courtesy rather than a title. However, in the early records, there are listings without "don" and "doña," so it meant something at that time. For example, the 1757 Census lists don Diego García with his wife María Salinas—no doña before her name.[12]

When José de Escandón, a wealthy Spanish count, brought other families to settle the *villas del norte*, Petra's ancestors made the short trek north to the

Rio Grande to acquire more land. This land was awarded to colonists chosen for hardiness and worthiness, and with the Crown's endorsement and support several villas were established.[13] Francisco Vela and his descendants' hard work had finally paid off. Escandón gave each rancher, including Lázaro Vela, a grant of land, rectangular shaped, called a *porción* (portion) consisting of at least 4,000 acres that included a narrow front on the Rio Grande, which allowed a greater number of them to have access to water. With this water the settlers were capable of producing farm crops as well as ranch livestock. These original *porciones* quickly became the symbol of social rank not only to the original pioneers but also to their descendants in the twentieth century.[14]

The 1757 Census of Mier, just four years after the founding of the city, includes the Velas—Head of Family, don Lázaro Vela, and Wife, doña María García. They had seven children. The family names of grantees in 1767 include several members of the extended Vela family with nine total grants—five in Revilla, two in Mier and two in Camargo.[15]

Lázaro was granted *porción* 57 in the jurisdiction of Mier on the Rio Grande in what is now Starr County, Texas. In the Mier census of 1782 and 1790, Lázaro and his wife, María Antonia García, were living on his ranch named Rancho La Gloria.[16] These *porciones* were awarded to the settlers on the basis of how long they had lived in the area as well as their financial ability to support crops, build homes, and protect themselves against Indian raids. Petra's family settled and ranched in these difficult lands for what historian Armando Alonzo calls the central theme to Tejano history—the importance of land to "the settler's way of life and identity."[17]

These ranchos were founded in a dry desertlike region, full of Indians, sinewy cattle, mustangs, swarms of rattlers, and thousands of prickly pear cacti. Petra's grandfather, Nicodemus, followed his father's lead and in 1807 acquired two leagues of land near present-day Live Oak County on the west bank of the Nueces River. This ranch was known as Veleño, which he purchased for 300 pesos.[18] Petra's father, Gregorio, following in the family tradition, purchased his ranch, named Santa Teresa and located north of the Rio Grande, on March 25, 1836, for 70 pesos. His land was two leagues.[19] His grandson and namesake John Gregory Sr. wrote in a deposition that his mother's father, José Gregorio Vela, was a large rancher and landowner in Texas and Mexico. He also said his mother's people were from Spain and settled in Mier, being one of the forty families that came as colonists to that place.[20]

Gregorio's land was two leagues, a league being equal to three statute miles of land. The Spanish were very precise about ownership of land, and don Gregorio followed the established procedure of claiming his land. Don Cayetano López, mayor and judge of the villa of Camargo, and don Gregorio Vela, with

Ruins of Santa Teresa Ranch, built by Petra's father, don Gregorio Vela, who "threw water, cut grass, pulled weeds, and threw dirt in all four wind directions," and claimed his land in 1836. Courtesy of John Martindale Heaner, descendant of Petra and her daughter María Vicenta.

witnesses Juan Villarreal and Antonio Morales, arrived at Santa Teresa on April 28, 1836. Judge López gave Gregorio the legal title to two leagues of land, approximately 8,856 acres. Don Gregorio "threw water, cut grass, pulled weeds, and threw dirt in all four wind directions," and claimed his land.[21] He would have been what Armando Alonzo defined as a "primitive settler," meaning one who had been there more than six years.[22] In going out to the remote frontiers to settle their ranches the Velas were courageous. Lázaro was one of the earliest ranchers on what is now the Texas border. Nicodemus moved to the frontier of the Nueces River, and Gregorio also ranched north of the Rio Grande during times of Indian raids on these ranches. Gregorio would pay for it with his life. The settlers were constantly under attack by Indians looking for livestock, horses, and supplies.[23]

While Gregorio was receiving title to his land, events were occurring to the north that would change the ownership of all of the land between the Nueces and Rio Grande. The Alamo in San Antonio, Texas, had been attacked by President Santa Anna of Mexico and had fallen on March 6. Santa Anna was at this time marching east toward the Sabine River and the United States to capture the remnants of Gen. Sam Houston's army and the officers of the interim Texas government that declared their independence from Mexico only six weeks before on March 2. In a week's time, Santa Anna would be defeated on the battlefield of San Jacinto on April 21, 1836, and surrender Mexico's claim to the land that Gregorio had just acquired. Although he did not know these changes were in the wind, he and his family would live with the consequences for the rest of their lives.

Petra's birthplace of Mier was one of the old *villas del norte* on the Rio Grande, and its citizens in the 1830s were descendants of José de Escandón's original land grantees. When the rancheros set out to build their ranchos, most of the homes were built of rock or stone, with flat roofs. These homes may have been monotonous and uninteresting looking from the outside, but they were the center of border culture and refinement.[24] The large hacienda owners have been compared to French owners of villas, Swiss owners of chalets, and Americans of the Old South on their plantations. The second rung of this economic and social ladder could be compared to the plain-folk Anglos of East Texas.[25] This group could be characterized as the middle class. Petra's family belonged to this group of people, although they did have a stone house in town and other assets. Very few were wealthy in this society, which promoted the rise of the rancheros who were "resolute, hardworking, and pragmatic in outlook."[26]

Settlers, servants, and other workers lived on the land and worked together, in a rather egalitarian society. The highest level was the large landholders, high government officials, and merchants. Rancheros, administrators and artisans

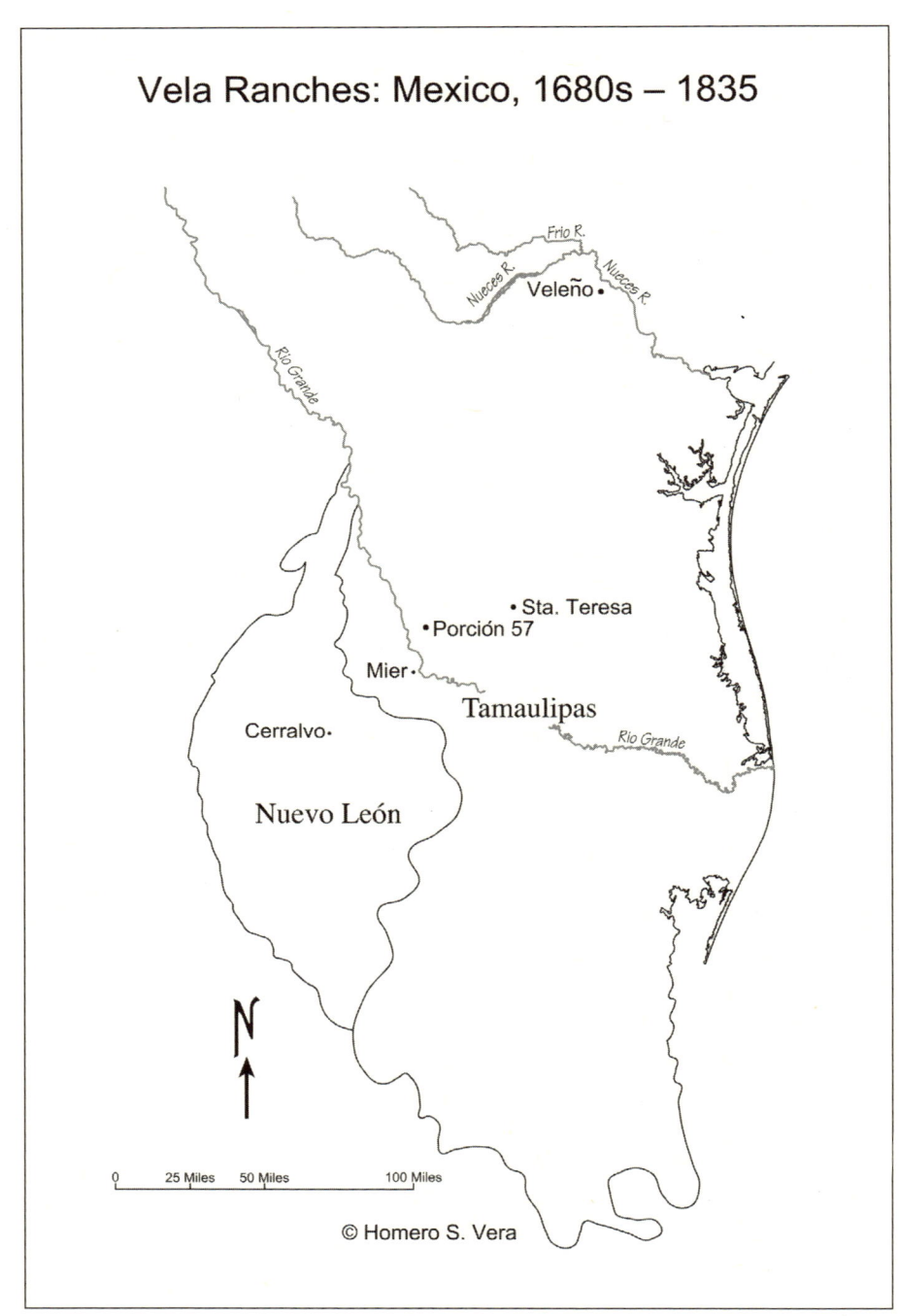

Map of Vela ranches: Mexico, 1680s–1835. Nancy Tiller, cartographer.

were the next level. The servants and Indians were the lowest level. Since many land grants were issued, the Rio Grande Valley identified strongly with the ranchero society. Most important to all these ranchero families were the traditional values of love, honor, and respect for the family members. They were egalitarian in matters of property rights and in dealings with outsiders as well as with one another.[27] This was the society and culture that Petra was born into and the society and culture in which she believed. It provided the roots from which Petra's devotion to her family and church grew and became a mainstay the rest of her life.

Petra's father, Gregorio, brought suit against his father, Nicodemus, May 24, 1826, for his share of his mother's estate, which provides a glimpse into the status of Petra's family. Her grandmother, María Gertrudis Ramirez, the daughter of José Antonio Ramirez and María Catarina Vela, was born in 1761. Her father Antonio was granted *porción* 67 of the jurisdiction of Mier in 1767, known as Rancho de Sabinitos or "small cypresses." María Gertrudis married Petra's grandfather, José Nicodemus Vela, and they had two sons, José María Vela, who died, and José Gregorio Vela, born in 1775. María Gertrudis died December 23, 1821, at the age of sixty, in Mier, two years before Petra's birth. After her death, Nicodemus, who was almost seventy, married for the second time. He and María Isabel Vela had one son, José Andrés, born two weeks after Petra. Gregorio feared he would lose his inheritance to his father's new family and brought suit against his father. He was the sole heir to his mother's estate since his brother had already died. For the court case, Nicodemus prepared a list of assets acquired during his marriage to María Gertrudis.[28]

The inventory shows that the Velas were not only ranchers, they also "rented" out breeding stock. They had a ranch in the common land of the villa of Mier, with tilled fields, fencing, and with *jacales* (small huts) for the workers who tended the land for them. In addition, María Gertrudis had place settings of silver, each piece weighing 2 3/4 ounces, large silver plates, each weighing 17 ounces, and a larger silver plate with cuttings on the edges (decoration perhaps) weighing 2 marks (17 1/2 ounces). This silver is of interest because it leads one to speculate about the family story of Petra arriving in Brownsville with a trunk of silver. Instead of silver coins in the trunk, she may have been carrying her grandmother's silver, which makes more sense, and now with the inventory from the grandmother, is even plausible. María Gertrudis also had two "bulk crosses," which were probably statues of Christ on the cross and one statue of Mary, as well as one picture on linen, among other household items. Petra's family surrounded her with the elements of her church and provided financial stability and the foundation for her deep religious faith. The listing of the livestock includes eight mares and one stallion, nine horses broken to ride, thirty-one breeding cows, eight one-year-old cows, and eight two-year-old cows, fourteen young bulls of one to two years, twenty young bulls of one year, two tame mules, and one stud donkey.[29] The composition of the stock appears to represent breeding stock for both horses and cattle. Since purchasers came from all over northern Mexico and deep inside the Wild Horse Desert, the Vela's stock must have been of high quality.

In addition to the above livestock, Nicodemus and María Gertrudis had livestock "rented" out to ranchers from as far away as Bejar (Béxar). For example, don Ventura Garza de Bejar had four hundred sheep rented from the Velas and doña Josefa Garza de Bejar also had four hundred. According to several pages of such transactions, there seems to have been about 2,700 sheep, 285 goats, six cows, eight calves, and one mule rented out. Gregorio's parents had established a comfortable estate and Gregorio was determined not to lose his rightful inheritance under the law. After the judge had heard the case he determined that Gregorio's portion was the stone house in town, some of the silver, part of the ranches, and the livestock, along with other assets. Gregorio would take care of the funeral arrangements of his mother, and made a promise to the most holy Virgin of Agualeguas for fourteen masses to be said in his mother's name. From the total amount, one-fifth was to be given to the grandchildren of doña Gertrudis Ramirez, each to be given 98 pesos, 5$^{1}/_{2}$ granos. In all, Gregorio would receive 2,941.5.8 pesos in cash, in addition to the other material goods.[30]

Gregorio married twice, first to María Josefa Moreno on November 2, 1795, in Mier. They had six children before she died sometime between 1809 and 1811. The widowed Gregorio married María Josefa Reséndez of Mier on January 30, 1812, and they had eight children including María Petra. Petra was baptized February 3, 1823, at the Parroquia de la Immaculada Concepción church at Mier. Her *padrinos* (godparents) were Sr. Juan Antonio Alba and Sra. María Josefa García.[31]

In 1821, two years before Petra's birth, the commander of the eastern provinces of the interior sent orders to the city council of Mier for parents to enroll their children, at least those of six to ten years, in school. The courses taught were arithmetic, algebra, grammar, spelling, and geography. The schooling was paid for by contributions from the citizens. In the municipality 2,304 men could read and write and 1,396 women could read and write.[32] Thus Mier showed a definite interest in education. Nicodemus, for example, contributed one yearling bull, three goats, four sheep, and four ewes in 1827 for taxes to the school system.[33] Petra's correspondence indicates an articulate individual with a good command of the language and excellent penmanship, reflecting her education.[34]

The land around Mier proper was so unsuitable for farming that most of those living in the city supported themselves by trading hides of cattle and sheep from their ranchos to the Indians in exchange for salt. In order to get their goods to market they put them on flat barges or mule train to Monterrey.[35] Some of them also took their stock to market in the interior to sell.[36]

Traditional towns like Mier were laid out with a plaza in the center with streets crossing at right angles and an open space in the middle. The east side of the plaza was reserved for the church buildings like the cathedral or chapel. The west side had government buildings such as the customs house or municipal offices. The towns had their own commons, common pasture, and rental lands for municipal revenue. A judge typically oversaw the social welfare and administrative needs of the citizens.[37] Escandón, early on, encouraged the settlers to live in the towns and travel out to their ranchos so that the communities could grow and develop a sense of a common history.[38] Jovita González describes these town homes as being small compared to the owners' ranch homes, but they had a large *sala* (living room) and patio for entertaining and were made of stone, with grilled windows. A corral for the horses and quarters for the servants were in the rear.[39] Petra's grandmother's home is described similarly in the inventory after her death. The house, constructed of stone and with a wooden roof, was located on the street that runs out of the plaza toward the north in a straight line from the jail, with a living room and another room fronting the east. A *jacal* was used as a kitchen and was probably connected to the house with a roofed walkway. The size of the lot in varas was 20 across the front and 40 to the back, which would be a lot of approximately 55 feet by 111 feet.[40] This is possibly the house Petra grew up in and which gave her access to the schools that provided her education.

Not much is known about the first fifteen years of Petra's life, but she grew up in a community that observed patriotic and church holidays. Citywide events celebrated Constitution Day, the Feast of Corpus Christi, Christmas, Holy Thursday and Good Friday, the Feast of San Felipe de Jesus, the Feast of the Virgin de Guadalupe, and the newest holiday, Diez y Seis de Septiembre, in honor of Mexico's independence.[41] Petra and her family would have relied on the staple foods of the region, including frijoles (beans), tortillas, *menudo* (stew), *cabrito* (goat), tamales, and *chiles* (peppers). In addition they would have added beef, venison, chicken, eggs, cheese, and milk when available.[42]

One type of entertainment was the fandango, or dance. According to ritual, the young women sat on benches on either side of the dance hall waiting for the music to start and then they selected their dancing partners from the line of prospective men. Petra, at the age of fifteen, would have been considered a woman. After the dance the gentleman led his partner to a table in the corner of the room to indulge in delicacies that included pastries and coffee. Often the young woman would wrap her sweets up in a piece of cloth to take home to share with her family the next day.[43] It may have been at one of these fandangos in Mier that Petra first met the dashing lieutenant, Luis Vidal.

Lieutenant Vidal had been transferred to Matamoros in January of 1837 to join the Northern Battalion of the Mexican Army, which had been defeated with Santa Anna in Texas the previous April. The thirty-seven-year-old lieutenant met the fifteen-year-old Petra Vela and she moved with him to Matamoros. There is still mystery surrounding their meeting and relationship, with no definitive information identified. It is doubtful that she knew that Luis was already in the process of becoming engaged to and marrying Manuela Andrade y Castellanos. Manuela was reportedly from a well-placed family in San Cristóbal de Las Casas, the capital of Chiapas in southern Mexico. Her family's position would possibly be an asset to his military career.[44]

The 1842 Census of Matamoros taken on April 27 has provided a new insight into Petra and Luis and their surroundings. Petra and Luis were living in a military compound probably located a few blocks east of the Plaza de Hidalgo in Matamoros. When Luis was transferred to Matamoros in 1837, the city was a study in intrigue and conflict. Matamoros's history was changed dramatically by three hundred revolutions and wars between 1824 and 1867. Between 1821, when Mexico established her independence from Spain, until 1884, a period of sixty-three years, Mexico had fifty-five presidents, two emperors, and one regency. This turmoil surrounded Matamoros and her development. Matamoros was a struggling village named the Congregation of Refugio until two years after the revolution when it was raised to the dignity of a port, and in 1826 its name was changed. Matamoros was named for a Mexican patriot, priest, and general, Mariano Matamoros, who was a leader in the War of Independence in 1812.[45]

In the 1842 Census, Luis was listed as forty-one years old, a captain, and married. Petra was listed as eighteen years old, single, and a servant. This reference adds to the mystery surrounding the couple. Luis does not marry Manuela until six months later, and Petra is listed as single. So to whom was Luis married at the time? In the compound there was one other officer, Lt. Col. José María Reynosa, who is listed as single living with a single woman, Francisca de Paula Zelaya, and she is listed as a *sirvienta*.[46] During this time there were three levels of servants: the *sirvienta* who was the keeper of the house or the one who was in charge of the other servants, the *criada* who raised the children, and the *domestico* who did the chores.[47] The term *sirvienta* may also have been used as a category when none other existed on the census form to explain a single non-family female member in the household. The military compound housed only officers and, interestingly, a merchant named Charles Stillman, listed as twenty-five years old, single, and living in the third block. Petra and Luis lived in the same block, although not next door. It is very likely that Petra and Charles were friends during this period. Later it may have been Charles who introduced Petra to Mifflin Kenedy, or perhaps Petra acted as a liaison between Mifflin and Charles. Another officer living in the compound was Capt. Miguel Saragosa (Zaragoza) who was married to María de Jesus Seguin, a relative of Juan Seguin. Their son Ygnacio (Ignacio) is listed as thirteen years of age. This young man grew up to be the famous general and hero of the Battle of Cinco de Mayo in Puebla. He is celebrated today as one of Mexico's most famous heroes.[48]

Petra and Luis seem to have lived comfortably with the other residents of the compound, and Petra's contacts were extensive. Another officer in the compound, in the fourth block, was Col. Juan Nepomuceno Ramirez and his wife Gertrudis Salinas. This couple stood with Petra and Luis as *padrino* and *madrina* for their daughter at her baptism the previous year, and must have been close friends to both Petra and Luis to assume roles as godparents to Rosa. Rosa's baptismal record showed that she was the "natural" daughter of don Luis Vidal and doña Petra Vela. Colonel Ramirez and his wife must have accepted the situation to have consented to stand as godparents to Rosa. Luis accepted responsibility and paternity for each of their children and each bore his name.[49] Luis and Petra had eight children: Luis in 1837, Vidal in 1838, Juana in 1839, Luisa in 1840, Rosa in 1841, Adrian in 1845, María Vicenta in 1846, and Concepción in 1849. In the 1842 Census only Luisa, two years old, and Rosa, eight months old, are listed.[50] The older children may have been with their relatives in Mier because later they are listed as being in Petra's household and in school in the 1850 census.

Luis's family was probably of highborn creole stock who had supported the Mexican independence movement. Because of this support Luis was honored with an appointment to the elite Mexican Military Academy, the equivalent of West Point. The Mexican military protected its officers from marrying below their station and required them to complete a lengthy marriage application process that had to be signed off on by all their superior officers, introducing politics and advancement into the marital process.[51] For twelve years Luis maintained two families. He may have been promising to marry both young women and had children with both of them before he finally married Manuela on October 9, 1842. At their wedding one of the witnesses was His Excellency, the Governor of the Department and Commandant General of the Army, don Ygnacio Barberena.[52] It appears that Petra lost the matrimonial battle to the other woman with a more influential background, and perhaps the marriage was an arranged one. Yet she may have known the situation all along, since it was the accepted way with officers at the time, and, because she truly loved Luis, she was willing to accept it so that she could be with him when she could. Although the marriage to Manuela must have been a deep hurt, Petra did not let it destroy her or her love for Luis and their children. This could have been one of the trials that forged Petra into the Texas-Mexico frontier pioneer that she became.[53]

During Petra's time with Luis, she and her family received a severe blow. In 1846 Petra's father, don Gregorio Vela, was killed by Indians. His grandson John Gregory Kenedy Sr. would later explain that his grandfather, José Gregorio Vela, was mistakenly killed by Indians seven miles west of the present site of Roma in Starr County. The Indians belonged to Chief Castro's band.[54] The Mier church archives listed his burial on November 26, 1846. His death certificate reads:

> In the cemetery of this parish of the villa of Mier on the 26th of November, 1846, I interim priest Presbyter don José Luis García gave a major ecclesiastical burial with a procession to the cemetery for 5 pesos the skeletal remains of don Gregorio Vela, widower. Because he was killed by the barbarous Indians in the countrysides of this jurisdiction, he didn't leave a will or receive any sacraments, and to certify I sign. Don José Luis García.[55]

For most of Luis's military service he was stationed in northern Mexico and spent much of the time with Petra when she wasn't visiting her relatives in Mier, Durango, and Monterrey. Luis's military records reflected his accomplishments as an officer: he was cited for coming to the defense of the integrity of the National Territory in December 1839 in Matamoros when a group of rebels were trying to obtain the independence of the northern Mexican states against the centralist Mexican government. Luis participated in the raids on San Antonio in 1842. He had accompanied Gen. Adrian Woll, a French soldier of fortune employed by Mexico, who attacked San Antonio on September 11, 1842, and seized the town and held it for ten days. His military record stated that during the battle Lieutenant Colonel Vidal bore himself with honor even having his horse shot out from under him. General Woll nominated him to receive the Cross of Honor for his devotion to duty and military service. Luis had played an important role in the attack and was promoted to Brevet Colonel, a rank given for performance in the field. During his career he was listed as a lieutenant, captain, and a colonel.[56] After the troop withdrawal, the Tejanos, fearing the wrath of the returning Anglos, fled toward the Rio Grande for protection, carrying whatever was left from the "rapacity" of the Texans.[57]

In a strange twist of fate, Petra played a role in the war, too.[58] The Texas Mier Expedition invaded Mexico in 1842. This expedition was an answer to the Mexican raids into Texas and San Antonio that Luis Vidal had been a part of that so enraged Texans. The Texans' expedition was doomed to failure and on December 19, 1842, Alexander Somervell ordered his men to retreat. Some of the men refused to retreat and under William S. Fisher and Thomas J. Green started toward Mier to plunder the town. The men successfully entered Mier without opposition on December 23 and requisitioned the supplies they wanted but could not get them back to the river. They made arrangements for them to be transported to the Texas camp across the river on December 24 and took the *alcalde* (mayor) with them to ensure compliance.[59]

The supplies did not come and on Christmas Day Fisher learned that Mexican Gen. Pedro de Ampudia and his troops had arrived at Mier and prevented the delivery of the supplies. That afternoon 261 Texans crossed the river to get their supplies and fought until the afternoon of December 26, though they were outnumbered ten to one. Hungry, thirsty, and their powder almost exhausted, they surrendered that afternoon.[60]

The Texans were held in Mier as captives. Those who survived were later marched to Matamoros and then to Mexico City. After an escape attempt on the march, President Santa Anna ordered that they be executed. Governor Mejía of the state of Coahuila refused to obey the order; the government then ordered that every tenth man be executed. In this incident the men were forced to draw from a sack of white and black beans, with a black bean meaning execution.[61]

In later years, the Requiem Mass said for doña Petra Kenedy in Brownsville was reported in the *Brownsville Herald* on March 17, 1885, and told of her story at Mier, where she ministered to the sick and wounded Texans. "Her self-imposed devotion to the duties of nurse, of the suffering and destitute prisoners, won the lasting gratitude of many a bearded and broken-down veteran, who in after years . . . loved to tell of her kindness to the 'enemy,' in that far-off time of trial and suffering."[62]

Gen. Thomas J. Green in his *Journal of the Texian Expedition against Mier*, wrote, "I visited the church that evening to see our wounded and carried them a quantity of bandages. All appeared to be cheerful though most of them were badly and several mortally wounded. In the same building 136 of the enemy's wounded were stretched out on the floor, many of whom had been shot in the head. It was a horrible sight. Most were wounded in the head and breast and many died the first night."[63] Since Luis was in charge of receiving the prisoners it was not surprising that Petra was at the church that night nursing the wounded.[64] She must have been a soothing presence for the wounded as many of them suffered and died while far away from their families. Petra would have gone from one stricken man to another by candlelight, providing water to their parched lips, whispering words of comfort in their ears, and speaking softly about God's mercy and forgiveness in their last moments on earth.

There are several references throughout Petra's life to her skill in helping ill people. General Green's publication was in Mifflin's personal book collection with Mifflin's name on the inside in his own handwriting. Through the years, Mifflin must have heard about Petra's role that night from some of the veterans who had firsthand knowledge of the events recorded in General Green's book.[65]

Luis retired from the army in 1845. Before his retirement and the beginning of the Mexican War he had probably removed Petra and the children to the interior for their safety. Their son Adrian, who the family said was named for Gen. Adrian Woll, under whom Luis served, was born in Monterrey, Concepción in Mier, and María Vicenta in Chihuahua. Luis died in 1849 in Jalapa, just outside Veracruz, of *vómito*, which must have been the result of contracting Asiatic cholera in the epidemic in early 1849.[66] Cholera was described as "The Destroying Angel." Physicians at the time seemed to think that once you had it there was no hope of survival. The sinking was rapid. There were intervals free from pain and when the collapse came the patients often died calmly in complete possession of their reason.[67]

After his death, Petra, either pregnant with María Vicenta or with a very young baby, and the rest of her children returned to her family's home in Mier. Spanish Mexican society in Texas granted widows a special stature, both legally and socially. They had legal privileges and social acceptability not accorded to abandoned women or unwed mothers. Thus many who claimed widowhood, as apparently Petra did, could have been either abandoned married women or unwed mothers. There may even have existed unwritten rules among Spanish officials that the term "widow" be used as a euphemism, since Spanish census records indicate such a pattern.[68]

Petra would have known about Luis's death through her many military contacts made over the years she lived with him. She would have inherited her share of Gregorio's estate upon his death in 1846, so she would have had some means of support. Such apparently was not the case for Manuela. A translated letter indicates that Manuela died "in the most of misery, in a vestibule (*zahuan*) without the least resource for food or medicines." Her three sons "became orphans [and] have been placed in the house of the poor" in Aguascalientes. The only relative in the city was doña Josefa Vidal, sister of their deceased father, and she was "a widow with needs herself." Sr. Gen. don Manuel Zavalo is asking in the letter that the military orphans have a guardian appointed. The letter was written July 10, 1851.[69]

Petra decided to start a completely new life and packed up her Vidal children and moved to Brownsville. Upon crossing the border she sometimes used Petra Vela, as she did in the census of 1850, and sometimes she used Petra Vela de Vidal, as she did on the marriage certificate with Mifflin, which matched the name of her children. The Spanish phrase for a child born out of wedlock is *hijo* or *hija natural,* literally meaning "natural son or daughter." There is a touching, if not romantic, saying about such children: "*Un hijo natural es el fruto del amor, no de la ley.*" That is, a natural child is the progeny of love rather than the law.[70] Luis and Petra's three boys and five girls were perhaps the offspring of such a love.

In Brownsville, Petra probably had many friends from her years in Matamoros, and she could see many possibilities in this growing community. Her descendants said she made the move so her children could be educated. They also said she was in business in Brownsville and that she helped to take care of her ranches. The other family story is that Luis had given her a chest of silver to support her and the children.[71] As mentioned, the chest of silver was possibly María Gertrudis's silver. However, none of this has been proven except for the educating of her children, that María Gertrudis did have silver, and that Petra had enough money to establish her home. The 1850 Texas census records for Cameron, Starr, and Webb counties show Petra Vela as twenty-six years old, and head of an independent household. At this point her three older children were still in the household along with their five siblings. Education was important to Petra and she had enrolled her four oldest children, Luis, Vidal, Juana, and Luisa in school.[72] Sometime in the next few years, Petra would lose these three oldest of her eight children, perhaps to the cholera or yellow fever that frequently plagued the river towns.

Chapter 2

1823–54:
"Into Her World"—Mifflin's Story

Mifflin Kenedy *came from an entirely different culture* and religion than Petra. His mother, Sarah Starr Kenedy, was a devout member of the Society of Friends, a Christian sect founded in England about 1650 by George Fox. The Society of Friends had such distinctions as plainness of dress, amounting almost to a uniform, and "plainness of speech," especially illustrated by the uses of "thee" and "thou" rather than "you," expressions Mifflin used in letters to his mother. The religious education of the children was turned over to Sarah. Mifflin, who was born June 18, 1818, had two sisters, Phebe Ann and Sarah Josephine, and two brothers, George Fairlamb and Elisha Jeffers, plus two other siblings, Mary and John H., who died in infancy.[1] His father, John Kenedy, was an Irish immigrant and probably born into a Catholic family.[2] However, there is no evidence he was a practicing Catholic, thus he was willing to have his children raised as Quakers. This Catholic connection may also have been the reason Mifflin was willing to have his children raised as Catholics.[3]

Mifflin was educated in public schools except for the short time he spent in the boarding school of Jonathan Gause, a famous Quaker educator. Mifflin taught school during the winter before his sixteenth birthday.[4] In the spring of 1834, he sailed as a cabin boy on the *Star of Philadelphia,* bound for Calcutta, India. He returned to teaching school in Coatesville, Pennsylvania, in the spring of 1836, then worked in a brickyard in Pittsburgh from 1836 to 1842. He was able to secure a position as a clerk and then as an acting captain on the steamers servicing the muddy waters of the Ohio, Missouri, and Mississippi rivers.[5] Mifflin, always the opportunist, even at an early age, saw the promise for river traffic. America was moving west, cities were growing along the river ways, and gold would soon be discovered in California. Water transportation

John Kenedy, Irish immigrant father of Mifflin Kenedy, who died in 1840 in Pennsylvania. Courtesy of Raymondville Historical Museum, Texas.

was the way to go for both people and goods, and he capitalized on the "golden days" of steamboating. Mifflin heard the sound of the whistles up and down the river, coming from the new steamboats that were built to provide better housing for their passengers, some even going to three decks or more.[6]

While Mifflin was away, tragedy struck his family back in Pennsylvania. He was twenty-two when he lost his father, similar to Petra who had lost her father at twenty-three. Mifflin's father John, a mechanic, died at the end of 1840. His will was dated December 11, 1840, and probated January 11, 1841, instructing that his daughters Phebe Ann and Sarah Josephine were to be

Sarah Starr Kenedy, Quaker mother of Mifflin Kenedy, who provided safety for her grandsons—Tom, James, and John—in Pennsylvania during the Civil War, where they continued their schooling. She received help from her son Mifflin all her life and died at the age of ninety-one in Pennsylvania. Courtesy of Raymondville Historical Museum, Texas.

apprenticed until seventeen and then have one year at boarding school, while his son Elisha Jeffers was to be instructed in farming until fifteen, then one year at boarding school.[7] Sarah Kenedy on September 9, 1844, petitioned the Orphan's Court for a guardian for her minor children because "her husband lately died." Alexander Mode was appointed as their guardian.[8] Elisha would later join Mifflin in Texas to also work on the Rio Grande. After John's death the family continued to occupy the little house on Main Street between Second and Third avenues.[9]

From 1842 to 1846, Mifflin sailed as a clerk or substitute captain on the *Champion*, plying the Apalachicola and Chattahoochee rivers in Florida. The *Champion* was built in 1842 in Pittsburgh and was the favored river steamer, noted for her excellent speed. This vessel, along with many others, spent the off-season engaged in trade or sailing along the Mississippi.[10] While in Florida on the *Champion* Mifflin met Richard King. When they met, King was nineteen and Mifflin twenty-six. King had stowed away on a ship when he was eleven, escaping an apprenticeship to a jeweler in New York City. He was from Irish immigrant stock, with icy blue eyes in a dark, handsome face and was gregarious and prone to action. Mifflin was taller and slender, with a quiet demeanor and studied ways.[11] They formed a firm friendship that would last their lifetimes, each complementing the other and bringing strength to the relationship.

War brought these two good friends to the Río Bravo. After Texas won independence from Mexico in 1836 and joined the United States in 1845 there continued the dispute of whether the Nueces River, as the Mexicans claimed, or the Rio Grande, as the Texans claimed, was the boundary between the United States and Mexico. During the period between 1836 and 1845 many changes came to the land where Petra had lived and that for generations before had belonged to Mexico. The Mexican people in Texas became Tejanos, or Texans of Mexican descent. Spanish was no longer the single language, and they had to adapt to the new politics and economics of the dominant culture. Failing to adapt would exclude them and lead to failure. At the same time they strove to maintain their Mexican traditions and cultural identity.[12]

This boundary dispute led to the Mexican War, and the result would double the size of the United States. President James Polk tried to settle the problem by offering Mexico $40 million for the purchase of California and New Mexico; he also attempted to settle the boundary line along the Rio Grande. The Mexican government refused to entertain the offer and President Polk sent Gen. Zachary Taylor (who would become president) to Corpus Christi, Texas, and then ordered him to advance to the mouth of the Rio Grande.[13]

When General Taylor arrived at Point Isabel at the entrance to the Rio Grande he built Fort Polk as a supply base, and by March 28 his forces began to construct Fort Texas opposite Matamoros. During this time, heavily armed bandits attacked one of Taylor's wagon trains. The twelve men, three women, and four children in the wagon train were ordered to strip off their clothing. The men pleaded with the bandits to spare the women and children. The bandits refused and bound the captive's hands, raped the women, slit their

Earliest known picture of Mifflin Kenedy (r.) and Richard King (l.), by daguerreotypist Woodbridge from Columbus, Georgia. On the back is the inscription, along with a lock of hair, "Papa's lock of hair. Picture on left is Papa—Capt. King." The handwriting is that of Alice King. The daguerreotype was located in the vault at the King Ranch Main House at Santa Gertrudis. It was possibly taken on King's wedding day, where Mifflin stood as his best man. If so, King was thirty years old and Kenedy was thirty-six. Or it could have been taken in Columbus, Georgia, between 1843 and 1846, when both men were working steamboats on the Chattahoochee and Apalachicola rivers. In that scenario, King would have been twenty to twenty-three and Kenedy twenty-six to twenty-nine years of age. Courtesy of Museum of South Texas History, Edinburg, Texas.

throats, and threw them into the arroyo.[14] Violence such as this incited increased hostility along the border.

On April 23, 1846, Mexico's president declared a state of defensive war and President Polk responded on May 9 by announcing to a joint session of Congress that a state of war existed. General Taylor advanced up the Rio Grande and into Mexico while Gen. Winfield Scott approached Mexico by way of Veracruz. The Mexicans were eventually defeated and the war officially was over with the signing of the peace treaty at Guadalupe Hidalgo on February 2, 1848. In the treaty, the United States gained California, Arizona, New Mexico, and the Rio Grande boundary for Texas, as well as parts of Utah, Nevada, and Colorado.[15]

At the beginning of the war, in the spring of 1846, while taking the *Champion* back for repairs to Pittsburgh, Mifflin met Maj. John Saunders of the U.S. Army, an engineer who was securing boats for use by the army on the Rio Grande during the Mexican War. The army was in need of both river pilots and steamers. Kenedy was convinced to join the war effort and was employed to assist Saunders as a commander on the *Corvette*. He also helped him procure the *Whiteville*, the *Rough and Ready*, the *Brownsville*, the *Hatchee Eagle*, the *Major Brown*, the *Colonel Cross*, the *Mentoria*, and the *Grampus*.[16] On July 2, Kenedy, with a Masters Certificate, sailed the *Corvette* to New Orleans. On August 6, he left for the Rio Grande and Texas, arriving there in late August. He soon wrote his friend Richard King to join him.[17] Steamers could serve the river for 220 miles from the mouth of the river at the Gulf of Mexico to the city of Camargo. Captain Kenedy began piloting the *Corvette*, transporting supplies and men for the U.S. Army up the Rio Grande to a spot opposite Matamoros. Young Captain Kenedy soon made his mark by making the trip from the mouth of the river to Camargo in three days despite delays caused by accidents to the paddle wheel and fog on the river. The trip normally took four to six days and the river talk was all about this new young captain.[18] By the end of 1846 the army was operating twenty steamers on the river.[19]

In May 1847, a year after Kenedy's arrival on the Rio Grande, Richard King arrived in Boca del Rio at the mouth of the Rio Grande, and Mifflin went to meet his friend. When King took his first look at this land called Texas he must have wondered why he had come. The scene could not have been drearier. There was nothing but sand blown into small hills and not a blade of grass to been seen anywhere. A few board houses were set among the sand dunes and not much more.[20] The wind blew constantly across the sands and bit into their eyes and body. Neither Mifflin nor King could have known that in fifteen years they would run the blockade for the Confederacy through these very waters, transporting millions of dollars of goods under the nose of the U.S. Army they were now working for.

On June 13, King reported for duty on the steamer *Colonel Cross* as one of three second pilots with a salary of $60 a month. By June 30, King transferred to the *Corvette* under Kenedy, as First Pilot with a salary of $120 a month. The *Corvette*, built originally for passenger service in the East, was considered a luxury ship. The government had paid $1,600 for her, which was the most paid for any steamer on the Rio Grande. Her biggest asset was that she satisfied the requirements of light draft, needing only twenty inches when not loaded and thirty inches when loaded.[21]

On November 17, Captain King, by then the master of the *Colonel Cross*, transported the victorious General Taylor from Camargo to Matamoros on his way back to New Orleans.[22] Shortly after the New Year, on February 2, 1848, Helen Chapman arrived at Point Isabel. Her husband, Maj. William Chapman, would become the quartermaster responsible for the food, clothing, and equipment for the troops at Brownsville. He would also be given the job of building the town of Brownsville and deciding on who got the contracts for river commerce and supplies. He became very important to Kenedy's and King's financial interest. Helen's letters home have provided invaluable information about life on both sides of the Rio Grande during this chaotic time.[23]

After the war Kenedy and King decided to stay on the Rio Grande and put down their roots in Texas rather than return east. They both scrambled to find jobs, and they began to adapt to their new home. Captain Kenedy went upriver toward the town of Roma. In the *American Flag* issue of November 29, 1848, an advertisement ran promoting the new town. It stated that the town was situated on the east bank of the Rio Grande between Camargo and Mier. The land was rich and would support cane, cotton, and tobacco. It was also good for raising stock and had stone quarries for buildings; river transportation was available four-fifths of the year. The advertisement was signed by M. Kenedy and P. H. Prout, agents for Justo García, José María García and others. Mifflin was already aligning himself with the Matamoros merchants.[24]

During the war, in 1846, the U.S. Army had been interested in how far up the Rio Grande the steamboats could navigate and how much area could be opened up for trade. In October, under the command of Lt. Bryan P. Tilden Jr., the *Major Brown* was sent up the Rio Grande to see how far it could go with troops aboard. During the journey the boat stopped often at ranchos to take on mesquite wood for the boilers. The citizens were happy to see them, especially after Lipan Indians carried off five small boys in a raid. The troops were welcomed up and down the river and finally made it to Laredo. By then the hills had grown rocky and the passage over the rapids more difficult. The boat became stranded for over a year before it could come back down the river.[25] From that experience it was determined that Roma, on a high bluff overlooking the Rio Grande, would become the head of the navigation on the river. Mifflin once more had made the right decision in promoting the town and its potential for trade.

King moved to the shantytown of Boca del Rio at the mouth of the Rio Grande and ran a flophouse and grogshop near the Quartermaster Corps Headquarters, waiting for the chance to purchase the *Colonel Cross* and become her peacetime owner.[26] In April of 1848, King was able to buy the *Colonel Cross* for $750 because of the cholera that was sweeping the area and also because many people were leaving for the gold mines in California. Kenedy continued to invest with Matamoros agents who wanted to bypass the monopoly Henry Davis had at Rio Grande City on the trading routes to Monterrey, Saltillo, and Zacatecas.[27] The land along the Rio Grande that Petra and her family had known for generations was changing forever. The war had brought immigrants from all over the Unites States and the world. They had come to fight and now they were staying to make their fortunes.

Charles Stillman, a future partner of Kenedy and King, was ahead of the game. He had purchased massive properties of the Garza grant north and northwest of Matamoros from the children of the first wife of José Narciso Cavazos. The sellers had no legal right to make such a sale since their father had remarried and the heirs of his second wife, led by the eldest son, Juan N. Cortina, inherited the land from their father upon his death. Cortina would carry on a guerrilla war over this issue for twenty-six years along the border. Nevertheless, Stillman started a town company and began to sell lots. He and his partners Samuel Belden and Jacob Mussina had purchased the land for $10,000 and they sold lots for from $150 to $1,000 apiece. Stillman had purchased the ferry, established the warehouses, and bought river craft and land to establish his town. It would be named Brownsville after Maj. Jacob Brown who had lost his life during the Mexican War.[28]

On June 17, 1848, word was received in Matamoros, with a roar of artillery and ringing of church bells, that the treaty of peace between Mexico and the United States had been signed.[29] Major Chapman was charged with the task of building a new fort across the Rio Grande and selected the site and constructed Fort Brown. He was the quartermaster at the fort until mid-1852 when he moved to Corpus Christi. With the erection of the military buildings the future of Brownsville was secure.

In December of 1848, Mifflin led his first expedition to the annual fair in San Juan de los Lagos, Jalisco. By now Mifflin was fairly competent in Spanish, which was essential if he was going to compete in the markets and on the river. At Zacatecas, his partners, Capt. James Walworth and Samuel Belden, decided to sell their wares and dissolve the partnership. Shortly thereafter, Captain Kenedy, always the shrewd businessman, purchased another stock of goods and headed for Monterrey. After making money on these expeditions,

Kenedy returned to the Rio Grande as captain of the *Troy*, owned by Samuel Belden.[30]

In 1849 both Kenedy and King continued to position themselves in their new life in the Rio Grande Valley. Meanwhile, Charles Stillman was watching them closely. Stillman did not like competition because it cost him money. He tried to neutralize his competition by either buying them out or driving them out. His steamboat operation was not doing well under the direction of James O'Donnell. King was doing well on the river and Stillman had an idea. He knew that Mifflin was a river captain with the competitive spirit that O'Donnell lacked, so he called Kenedy in for a talk about joining forces to conquer the river trade. The ever-careful Mifflin did not give him an answer right away but instead went to talk to his friend and confidant Richard King. With some negotiating on Mifflin's part, the next year, on March 1, 1850, the three men plus James O'Donnell became company partners in M. Kenedy & Co. O'Donnell was brought in as a sign of loyalty.[31] Charles Stillman was famous for never having his name out front on any of his partnerships and business associations. He always was a major component but he never took a visible role. A very astute businessman, Stillman always kept his own counsel. It is doubtful if anyone ever knew all of his businesses. He was particularly astute in choosing business partners. He knew how to select good and capable men with whom he could work. He permitted them also to make money and when partnerships were dissolved the former partners remained friends with Stillman. Many of them became extremely successful businessmen themselves. He seldom openly participated in politics, but he dealt in the county script, bribed officials when necessary or customary, and did not hold political offices or do any of the front work.[32] The partnership that was formed was one that would monopolize river boat traffic on the Rio Grande and cause Father Domenech to label many of the large merchants and capitalists on the Rio Grande as "the scum of society," men whose greed knew no ends.[33]

M. Kenedy & Co. implemented a three-part business plan to succeed in seizing most of the trade on the river. First the partners bought the *Alamo, Ranchero, Camargo, Paisano, Matamoros #1, Matamoros #2,* and other craft.[34] The company was transporting merchandise from Brazos Santiago to Camargo with Captains King and Kenedy commanding the boats themselves. Each boat had a crew of five officers and handled its own transactions. With the increase in boats it became necessary to establish a central office in Brownsville.[35] Second, King decided to design two new boats—one a larger boat to handle the trade at the mouth of the Rio Grande and the other a smaller vessel to run the river. They designed the two boats, the larger christened *Grampus* and the smaller *Comanche*. Mifflin left Texas to place the order for them in Pittsburgh. Third, the new partners saw the need to build a loading depot at White Ranch near the mouth of the Rio Grande to expedite the transportation and transfer of supplies.[36]

Major Chapman, another entrepreneur, had accomplished his first goal of disposing of some surplus property by holding an auction on April 2 and 3 of 1849. He still had another goal to meet. The army was very interested in supplying the line of forts that had been established up and down the river and in doing it more economically. In 1850 Harry Love, the rugged frontiersman, and Capt. Daniel M. Kingsbury explored the upper reaches of the Rio Grande 967 miles to the north. They found one major obstacle to clear at Brook's Falls, about 150 miles from El Paso.[37] It seemed possible that with some engineering work the Rio Grande, which stretched 1,800 miles from the Gulf of Mexico to present-day Colorado, could be opened up to become the Mississippi of the West.[38]

This idea did not sit well with Stillman and his partners. The way to make their steamboat line profitable was to secure the lucrative government contracts and use them to underwrite low civilian rates to drive out any other competition on the river, which meant that any open bidding had to be stopped. If the river were opened up there would be no way to eliminate other steamboat lines from coming in. While Stillman was laying his plans he introduced Major Chapman to the profitability of real estate speculation. Chapman purchased his first piece of property in February of 1850. He continued to purchase and trade property into 1852 with Stillman's friends and his lawyer Stephen Powers. Chapman changed his mind during this time and ceased to encourage opening the upper reaches of the Rio Grande. Instead he began to push the idea of contracting with M. Kenedy & Co. to transport the army's goods. Friendship and loyalty meant a lot to these men, especially in their business investments. Mifflin made a trip to Washington, which he would do many times on behalf of his business. Following his return the contract was signed on February 10, 1852; it had been awarded without competitive bid.[39] The dream of extending the Rio Grande westward had ended.

In July after a trip to Washington, Kenedy returned to Brownsville to find that his rowdy, rambunctious friend King had been smitten by a young seventeen-year-old preacher's daughter, Henrietta Chamberlain. Mifflin had met Henrietta earlier and King asked Kenedy if he would introduce him to her. The next Wednesday afternoon he did so as she approached them on the sidewalk.[40]

Henrietta's father was Hiram Chamberlain who had just arrived from Tennessee and was going to establish the first Protestant church on the Rio Grande. Helen Chapman did not have a very high opinion of Mrs. Chamberlain but a better one of Henrietta. In a letter to her mother on August 1, 1850, she wrote that Mrs. Chamberlain "had a rather languid, fretful, fine lady air." However, the eldest daughter, Henrietta, was a "bright, intelligent, pretty girl, and the other three were large healthy children, but undisciplined."[41]

In 1850 Mifflin was thirty-two years old and his financial future was beginning to look secure. While Petra, twenty-seven years old, was in her own home in Brownsville, Mifflin was living with twenty-three other men in a dwelling owned by Englishman Thomas B. King and his family. The tenants listed their professions variously as seaman, engineer, laborer, cook, and barber, among others. They came from all over, including Ireland, Scotland, Germany, Italy, Pennsylvania, Ohio, Tennessee, Rhode Island, and Mexico. Mifflin listed himself as a boatman from Pennsylvania owning $2,000 worth of real estate. This census information shows that Petra was not living in Mifflin's home but instead was listed as head of household in her own independent residence. It appears she may also have taken in a boarder. Richard King was also living in someone else's home. He lived in the dwelling belonging to F. R. Taylor with Taylor's daughter and three other people. King listed himself as a boatman from New York with $5,000 of real estate. In the 1850 census King is listed from New York but in the 1860 and 1870 censuses he is listed as being from Ireland.[42]

Mifflin and King were becoming a successful part of the strong trade that developed along the river. Adventurers were buying equipment for their overland travel to the California gold fields and traffic was brisk. Brownsville had grown rapidly from no houses in 1848 to a population of two thousand in 1849.[43] Successful men like Mifflin Kenedy, Richard King, Charles Stillman, Samuel Belden, Humphrey Woodhouse, Francisco Ytúrria, Jeremiah Galvan, and José San Román were making their mark in this young country along the Rio Grande.

M. Kenedy & Co. had to wait until 1852 for their efforts with the big vessel *Grampus* and the smaller *Comanche* to pay off. The company controlled almost all of the water-borne goods into the north Mexican trade.[44] It forced most of the other shipping companies off the river and caused several to seethe and plot against M. Kenedy & Co. Captain Kenedy bought out O'Donnell's interest in the company and the company mounted war surplus cannon on their boats.[45] Their monopoly on the river led not only to financial success but also to the best river information, which was one of their greatest assets.

A very serious problem faced the Tejanos of South Texas following the Mexican War. Many of the original landholders had abandoned their claims during the war and fled to Mexico for safety. They returned to find they were being forced to defend their land titles and were facing newcomers eager to stake their claims to land along the river. Two groups emerged. One group supported the formation of an independent Rio Grande Territory that would give them the authority to decide the land questions because they were fearful that the authorities in Texas would annul their titles. They were called the Separatists, and Kenedy and King supported this group. A second group, the Conservatives, recognized Texas authority over the land between the Nueces and Rio Grande and wanted Governor P. H. Bell to appoint a commission to come and settle the land disputes.[46]

The Conservatives prevailed, and on April 24, 1851, the Bourland-Miller Commission published their schedule for public hearings on land title certifications. The commissioners examined mainly three types of claims: *porciones* land grants that fronted the Rio Grande, large land grants to citizens of Reynosa and Camargo, and grants made after 1824. It was a very difficult process but in the fall of 1851 commissioners William Bourland and James Miller finished their work and started for Austin to file their report.[47]

Bourland took the smaller collection of documents and traveled by land to Austin. Miller took the trunk containing all the original titles that had been presented by settlers throughout South Texas and sailed on the *Anson*. The boat sank in heavy seas off Matagorda and with it valuable documents that could not be replaced. The commission requested that owners produce duplicate documentation but in many cases it was not possible, and this tied up the land disputes so that there was very little available to newcomers. Therefore it was to the advantage of individuals if they could associate with families that did have existing claims to land. This meant that many of the newcomers would be engaged as traders, merchants, artisans, and professionals. Large land purchases came later.[48] Using political chicanery in many cases they also gained power and dominance in government in South Texas and in real estate transactions.[49] Some of these newcomers were fortunate to marry upper-class Mexican women and develop ties with influential Mexican families.

Mifflin Kenedy chose this type of pursuit while his partners Richard King and Charles Stillman chose another path in pursuing the women who would become their lifelong companions. In 1851 King was busy attending prayer meetings and courting Henrietta Chamberlain. Henrietta was attending socials around town. On April 7, a Mrs. Falco was married and Mrs. Chapman reported that it was a beautiful affair, with a magnificent supper of meats, fruits, preserves, cakes, and wine. The younger Miss Chamberlain was bridesmaid.[50]

In May 1851, Henrietta broke her engagement to R. N. Stansbury, opening up the way for a more serious pursuit by Richard King.[51] Stansbury was employed as superintendent of the Sunday School in Brownsville, which had sixteen teachers, seventy-two scholars, and 720 books, as reported by the *American Flag* on January 9, 1850. He was a member of the Methodist church and had been brought up with severe notions of Christian decorum. Helen Chapman reports that at the same time he was lively and social. "The poor

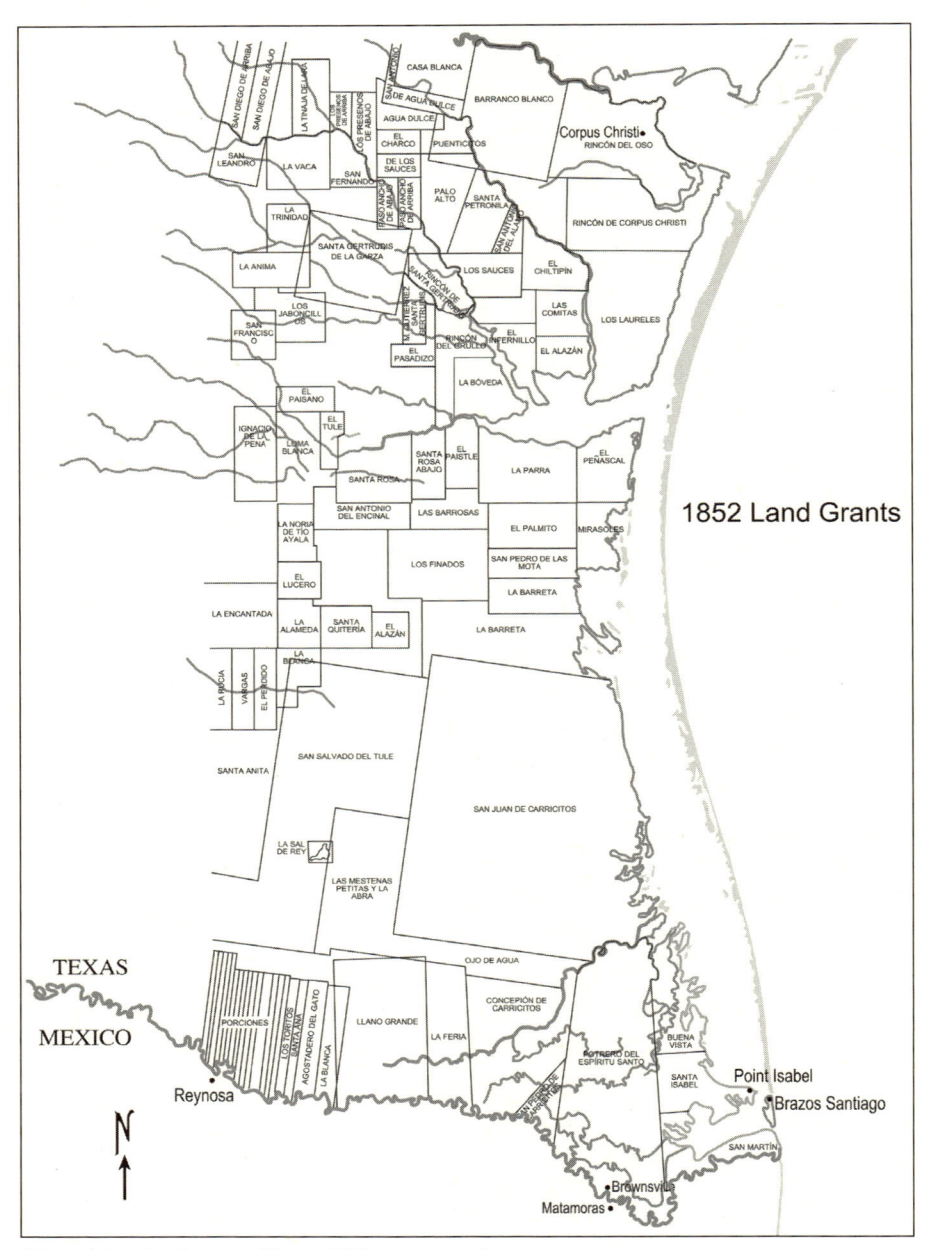

Map of 1852 land grants. Nancy Tiller, cartographer.

fellow is constantly mourning over what he deems his unfaithfulness to his Christian duties, a very tender conscience. It would be more natural for him to compare himself with others, and thereby think himself exalted in piety. He is constantly asked to take a drink, to go to fandangos and other places which his principles compel him to refuse."[52] The Reverend Hiram Chamberlain must have pondered the turn of events when Henrietta rejected the advances of such a religious young man in favor of a rough, poorly educated, drink-prone, good looking, talented steamboat captain named Richard King.

Charles Stillman married Elizabeth (Betsy) Goodrich in 1849 and took her to their first residence above Charles's place of business. It was a brick warehouse at the corner of Twelfth and Levee Street that was later destroyed in the fire of 1857.[53] A family descendant said that the warehouse faced the Rio Grande and the large windows caught the breeze off the river.[54] They later moved into a house built by Henry Miller in 1850. This was one of the first brick residences to be built and the others that followed would give the group the name "the brick house crowd."[55] Charles was the first to marry in his group of friends but others would not be far behind. Petra and Mifflin would be a part of this group along with their neighbors Richard and Henrietta King.

Henrietta King, daughter of Reverend Hiram Chamberlain, chose the rambunctious Richard King over the pious R. N. Stansbury and became the matriarch of the King Ranch. Courtesy of Christus Spohn Health System, Corpus Christi, Texas.

In the 1850s Charles Stillman's Vallecillo mines, between Laredo and Monterrey, produced more than $4 million in silver and lead. On June 9 a son was born to Charles and Betsy and they named him James. He would later take over his father's financial and mercantile empire in New York. In 1872 he turned it into the National City Bank in New York and became one of the most powerful forces in the development of the Rio Grande. James and his associates W. H. Harriman, Jacob Henry Schiff, and William Rockefeller would control most of Texas' future railroads. James's two daughters would marry the sons of his lifelong friend William Rockefeller, the chairman of the board of the Standard Oil Company.[56]

During this time, as is characteristic of most frontier towns, poor law enforcement led to an indifference toward criminal economic transactions, which, combined with ethnic tension and a large number of impoverished citizens, made spiritual leadership necessary and a goal for enlightened citizens. The established churches reflected the mix of Spanish, Mexican, European, French Louisiana, and Yankee cultures represented in Brownsville,

View of levee and ferry, Brownsville. The large steamer in the distance is the Col. Holcomb, *a government transport. The smaller steamer is the* Tampico, *also a government transport. The barge at the edge of the water is the ferry landing. The near line is the wire cable across the river for the use of the ferry. Brownsville Historical Association.*

which made it so different in many ways from the rest of Texas in its cosmopolitan makeup.[57] The Americans gradually absorbed the Spanish customs. Matamoros was Spanish and it was customary for Brownsville citizens to participate in the events in Matamoros and vice versa. The Spanish culture was always cosmopolitan and Brownsville became even more so with additional European influence. Spanish merchants made trips to Spain to buy goods and many of the French merchants made buying trips to the French, English, and German markets. Buying trips to New York and New Orleans were commonplace. The area was an excellent market for French furniture, laces, brocades, and fashions.[58]

The citizens of Brownsville moved past the time of lawlessness and began to establish their homes, businesses, and churches. On February 23, 1850, Hiram Chamberlain organized the First Presbyterian Church of Brownsville. He believed that slavery was not forbidden in the scripture and that the relation of master and slave was a civil and domestic institution in which the church had no power to legislate. He was also an ardent believer in the separation of church and state and dedicated himself to "wake up the attention of Protestants to the errors and evils of Roman Catholicism."[59] However, on June 19 he performed the wedding for a Dr. Prevost and his Mexican bride in the Chapman home. No priest would marry them, since Prevost was Protestant.[60] Mifflin and Petra may have had the same problem that Dr. and Mrs. Prevost had. They may not have been able to solemnize their marriage in the church until 1854 when Father Jean Marie Casimir Verdet would give Mifflin a dispensation for being a Protestant.

Despite the obstacles he faced, Mifflin continued to court Petra. It is not known when Mifflin actually met Petra or how long their courtship continued, and no written record has been found as to why Mifflin chose Petra or vice versa. Among many of the stories that Sarita Kenedy would tell about her grandfather Mifflin was that he had fallen deliriously in love with Petra.[61] Rip Ford wrote, "Kenedy was courting a lady. He may have known her since his days at Roma and she was from a landholding family at Mier." He described Petra Vela de Vidal as a twenty-six-year-old widow and mother of five who possessed an intellect much above the ordinary and who exerted great influence over her countrymen.[62] The *Brownsville Daily Cosmopolitan* described Petra in an article in 1886 as a "notably handsome woman of tall and commanding figure."[63] Whether Mifflin was attracted to Petra for her beauty, wealth, land holdings, or connections is a matter of speculation, but it was probably a combination of all of these.

It is also very probable that the ever-careful Mifflin would have known the facts about Petra, the eight children, and Luis. After all, he had his own resources, surreptitious channels of inquiry, and he would have been careful about whom he married and would not have wanted any legal surprises down the line. He would have wanted to be quite certain that Luis was dead so that the marriage between Mifflin and Petra would not only look legitimate on the surface but would have been so at the core.[64]

Mary Margaret McAllen Amberson, a descendant of Salomé Ballí Young de McAllen, wrote that the landed families "through intermarriage with newcomers, flush with cash from mercantile activity, provided them with the means to maintain their lands and social status, the old Spanish families also strove to maintain their heritage, religion and culture. Marriage with the new immigrants was an opportunity, but not lacking in complexities."[65] Her ancestor María Salomé Ballí de la Garza married Scotsman John Young on November 9, 1853, in Brownsville in a civil ceremony, probably due to the fact that he was a Protestant like Mifflin. John Young was fifty-one and Salomé was twenty-five. John Young listed his worth in the 1850 census as $75,000. John Young acquired an interest in the Santa Anita ranch through his wife and together they would continue to purchase more interest in the Santa Anita as it would become available from other family members.[66] Salomé and Petra developed a special relationship during the early years of their marriages and during the time they spent together in Brownsville. Petra wrote to Salomé in

Spanish in 1883 from Corpus Christi saying, "I am very anxious to see you, Salomé, and you know our friendship has been great and we view ourselves as two sisters."[67]

Other successful merchants were marrying into landed families. Francisco Ytúrria married Felícitas Treviño on December 23, 1853, in St. Mary's Catholic Church in Brownsville. Their marriage in the church would not have been a problem since they were both of the Catholic faith. Felícitas and her brother had inherited the San Martín Grant from their father. Francisco purchased his brother-in-law's interest and so began the Ytúrria Ranch, which is still in the family today, near Brownsville.[68]

Although women's rights were better protected legally in Mexican society, the attractiveness of the American men to the Mexican woman raised in a strict patriarchal society could have been what Jovita González describes in *Caballero:* "Some [of the Americans] had their wives with them in San Antonio . . . and I am told that they treat them like equals, even like queens, and actually defer to them. These men have an ease and a manner about them which, mark well my words, *amigo,* will strike to the heart of more than one of the girls."[69] Could this be what the independent Petra saw in Mifflin in addition to the security he brought? That he deferred to her is clear in his letters, as can be seen later when he must confer with her before ordering china for the new house in Corpus Christi, or making sure her wardrobe is just right for her clothes, or not leaving her side to conduct business when she is ill.[70]

For years the family and writers have listed the wedding date for Mifflin and Petra as April 16, 1852, but no official record has been found to substantiate that. In *I Would Rather Sleep in Texas,* Mary Margaret McAllen Amberson wrote, "Petra, a wealthy widow, married Mifflin Kenedy in 1852 at her family home in Mier, Mexico."[71] At Petra's Requiem Mass in 1886 in front of her lifelong friends, it was stated that she had lived in Brownsville from 1852 to 1868 "with her husband in this city."[72] Tom Lea wrote that in 1853 Richard King, while courting Henrietta, would take her on "a stroll upon a balmy evening under the trees of Elizabeth Street shyly to consider a site for a cottage next door to the home the happy Kenedys had built." He then footnotes this passage with the following: "Mifflin Kenedy and his bride had built a house on Elizabeth Street in 1853."[73] Whatever happened between them and in whatever year, the community seemed to have accepted the new bride into their world.

In 1852 Mifflin assumed the management of Petra's grandfather's ranch, known as Veleño, located on the west bank of the Nueces River. Rip Ford says Captain Kenedy established a cattle ranch at a place he mistakenly called Valenio on the Nueces River.[74] Mifflin, as the patriarch, was now helping to run Petra's affairs. Petra, as the matriarch, in addition to being a homemaker was also the spiritual guide and healer, and responsible for her children's education. Petra would have had daily prayers with her children and seen to it that they attended Mass and went to Confession on a regular basis. Later when she moved to Los Laureles Ranch she would utilize the visiting Oblate Fathers.[75] She would have had an altar, which could have been as simple as a crucifix on the wall before which Petra and her children knelt. Or it could have been similar to the altar set for All Saints Day in *Caballero* where two young women gathered "wild larkspur and oleander blooms and banked them on the table in the *sala* (living room), and set statues and pictures of the saints in a row before silver candlesticks."[76] The altar could also have been made with a sheet hung on the wall with varicolored ribbons—red, yellow, orange, and blue—making arches and arcades. Sprays of cedar and oleander were placed here and there on the "arches." Pictures of saints and angels formed a celestial host, and holy statues, some of wood and some of marble, were placed on the altar table.[77]

Tom Lea wrote that, "As Mifflin Kenedy settled to happy domesticity in a Brownsville house with an attractive bride and a ready-made family of small children, his steam boating partner decided to take a trip." Captain King had decided to accompany his friend Gideon K. "Legs" Lewis to Corpus Christi in May of 1852 to the great Lone Star Fair. This trip overland through the Wild Horse Desert would change Captain King's life and the face of South Texas.[78]

Richard King decided to diversify his holdings and move into the Wild Horse Desert to take up ranching. The decision to try to tame the Wild Horse Desert was not without risk and the possibility of failure. When General Taylor's army crossed this land in 1846 they drank from the flowing stream of the Arroyo Colorado and their throats rasped from the salt. They crossed through boggy *resacas* (old riverbeds), palmetto thickets, and snaggy chaparral and suffered from the shimmering heat.[79]

King and Lewis may have visited with Manuel Ramirez at the Bobedo Ranch. Ramirez possibly interceded for them in the purchase of the Santa Gertrudis Ranch, established in 1853.[80] Some of the contributing factors for these businessmen to diversify their holdings may have been that the Rio Grande during the 1853 and 1854 drought was so low that steamboats could only go above Brownsville with great difficulty and not above Reynosa at all. With boat operations so curtailed King was able to spend much time on developing the Santa Gertrudis.[81]

On May 6, 1853, Charles Stillman bought the Los Laureles Ranch from the heirs of Tomás Paradez of Camargo for $9,500.[82] Mifflin eventually bought this ranch from Stillman, added to it, improved it, and sold it in 1882 for $1,100,000. Stillman entered into a partnership with William S. Gregory to build and stock a ranch on Laureles as well as constructing a salt works. Gregory built a headquarters site in the center of his operations that included

Charles Stillman came to the area when he was eighteen years old and amassed a fortune. According to descendant Alexander Stillman, during the Civil War, as the head stockholder in the City Bank of New York, Stillman loaned President Abraham Lincoln $70 million in gold to finance the Union Army. At the same time, Stillman was running Confederate cotton through the Union blockade. Brownsville Historical Association.

a house, store, barns, pens, and some other buildings near the Corpus Christi to Brownsville road. John Fitch went to work for Gregory and Stillman in 1854. Fitch said that the location of the headquarters at Los Laureles Ranch was built near the ruins of old buildings and pens that appeared to have been constructed many years before. This land would eventually be Petra and Mifflin's home for over ten years.

Betsy Stillman was spending most of her time in New York during this period, and her husband traveled to see her when he could. He obviously missed his family but developed a real zest for ranch life. In 1853 he wrote to his wife in New York, saying "tell Jimmy not to cry for me. One of these days I will roam with him on his big black horse over the wild prairie . . . running down the deer or chasing the wild horses. . . . There [are] nearly one hundred calves in the pen, running after each as I have seen you and Bell. I see you have learned to skate. When you return to your native state (Texas) you can exchange them for a good horse, a rifle, and a knife."[83]

The Oblates returned to Brownsville in 1852 and on March 7, 1853, the Incarnate Word opened its doors for school. Petra now had a place to send her girls; they could continue their education in a religious school, which was important to Petra. However, the facility was simple at best. One Sister wrote that it had the poverty of the Sisters of the Incarnate Word of Bethlehem. There were insects by the million and a clay floor that was kept damp by the small stream nearby. The doors could only be closed by rope since they did not meet for latching. Their furniture consisted of the boxes and trunks they had brought with them. Fortunately, the parish priest of Matamoros, "pitying our distress, sent us four chairs and a table."[84] The rats were so bad they would try to eat the bread at night. With the use of the rocking chair that was sent, the sisters would tie a string to it, place the

The house built in 1850 for Henry Miller and occupied by Charles Stillman and his family. Later it became the Manuel Treviño de los Santos Coy family home. At one time it was the Mexican Consulate in Brownsville, as shown with the Mexican consular seal over the front porch. Brownsville Historical Association.

bread on it, and rock the bread through the night to keep the rats away.[85] The Sisters also feared for their safety in the first few years. Mother Stanilaus told the story of how one night the Indians slipped into the convent and stole their red cloaks. On another occasion they were expecting a postulate from Laredo when they found out she had been captured by the Indians and consumed.[86]

As the sisters described: "From the first day students were numerous and our Mothers were deeply moved by the affection and trust which the girls had for them. The house was very poor. So poor that they had no pepper and they served the priest breakfast and saved their one egg for the Chaplain's breakfast and when the parakeet broke it he [the Chaplain] had only bread and coffee like them."[87] The students noticed the frugality that the Mothers had to live under. Thus one day Luisa Vidal said to her mother, Petra, "Mamma, those ladies must need medicine. Give me some castor oil." And when she had the bottle of oil, she said, "But the poor things must not have anything to make soup with. Give me a chicken, too." Happy with her oil and chicken, she triumphantly brought it to Mother St. Claire.[88] Petra was known for her charity to the church and others, and she passed these traits on to her children.

A portrait of Petra Vela Kenedy, perhaps depicting her wedding day to Mifflin Kenedy. Courtesy of Raymondville Historical Museum, Texas.

While Petra was busy adjusting into the routine and getting her five children situated, she and Mifflin welcomed their first child, Thomas Mifflin Kenedy.[89] Tom was born on April 15, 1853, Mifflin's first son to join an already large family.[90] At the time Tom was born Luisa was thirteen, Rosa twelve, Adrian eight, Concepción seven, and María Vicenta six. Petra's warmth and energetic nature were much needed in this busy household. If reliance can be placed on oral tradition and the impressions of Anglos who came in contact with Tejanos, children were treated lovingly, "with indulgence, and not given too much responsibility." Wealthy parents were even more indulgent, providing their children with such amenities as separate rooms, material goods, vacations, and experiences, as was apparently the case among landholders. This was very different from Protestant Anglo experiences.[91]

Petra and Mifflin had taken different paths to get to this place at this time. They were from two distinctly different cultures and their life experiences had been vastly different. Yet by blending them together they would prove to be stronger and more capable of facing the challenges that lay ahead.

On May, 10, 1854, Petra and Mifflin had their marriage blessed in her church. Father Jean Marie Casimir Verdet, OMI, officiated at the marriage and wrote that Mifflin was an adherent to the sect called the Quakers, "from which impediment I gave dispensation."[92] Mifflin would never become a Catholic but he strongly supported the Catholic churches in both Brownsville and Corpus Christi in honor of Petra. All their children were raised Catholic and Petra's love of the church was passed on from one generation to another.

Present at the ceremony was Rev. Fr. C. Newel, a protestant, as was Edward Downey. He and Margarita García were their sponsors. Mifflin probably felt the need for such at this Catholic wedding. Edward Downey had fought in the Mexican War and for several years after locating in Brownsville he was a clerk for M. Kenedy & Co. He was a lay leader in the Presbyterian Church and one of Petra's grandchildren would be named for him.[93] Margarita García may have been a family member of Petra's or a friend from Roma.

After the wedding Petra and Mifflin presented their one-year-old son, Thomas Mifflin, for baptism. Edward Downey and Margarita García also stood as his sponsors.[94] Mifflin would not have wanted his son to be a *hijo natural* in the records, thus the baptism was performed after the marriage. In the eyes and in the records of the Catholic Church, marriage between the two parents of a child born out of wedlock automatically and immediately makes the child "legitimate." It is possible that Mifflin and Petra were married in Mier in a civil ceremony in April of 1852, because they could not find a priest to marry them in the church since Mifflin was a Protestant.[95] However, no documentation has been found to support this claim. Whether the marriage in St. Mary's Church was the first and only marriage ceremony cannot be stated unequivocally, but it is likely. As Petra and Mifflin stood with their child in their arms surrounded by his half-brother and half-sisters, their family had finally become one.

Chapter 3

1855–60:
Forging a Life in Brownsville

For the next several years *Petra and Mifflin settled* into their new home and doubled the size of their family. Petra also established her place in the emerging Brownsville community and helped the church build one of the finest structures in Texas. During this period Mifflin's company survived a difficult time, maneuvering through drought and competitive pressure to emerge prosperous. Mifflin and King, always looking toward the future, turned their eyes north to the Wild Horse Desert and the beginning of their ranching empires. Mifflin and King were new to ranching, but not Petra. She had been reared in the ranching culture of northern Mexico, but she was now enjoying her life in Brownsville.

Two of Petra's daughter's were beginning to blossom into young women. Luisa was fourteen and Rosa thirteen. Their younger sisters Concepción and María Vicenta were seven and eight. Luisa was enrolled at Incarnate Word School for Girls in 1853 and probably her sisters also. Father Verdet had been appointed Superior of the Sisters as well as the priests. Under his guidance the mission flourished.[1] They laid the cornerstone for the convent on March 25, 1853, and Father Verdet had even put on his working clothes and helped plaster the walls during construction. The Sisters obtained benefactors to help with expenses, and Petra and Mifflin helped with donations, although few, if any, would know if they had. They kept their charity private. When there was a need Petra would find a time when she had Mifflin's ear and make her request. He was not involved in the everyday practice of religion; however, Petra saw to it that he fulfilled his Christian duty by providing monetary contributions when needed.[2]

The Sisters who ran the Incarnate Word School for Girls numbered sixteen by 1857. Twelve of the group had come directly from France and four were

Irish women who had agreed to come to the Texas mission. The Sisters volunteered to travel to a dry, desolate, hot, disease-ridden land where a foreign language was spoken, few resources were available, and minimal outside support could be had. They had to depend on their faith and trust in God and the goodness of such people as Petra and her family to protect them. Petra worked to teach her family the importance of giving to the needy. Time and time again she was described as a benefactor to those in need of charity.[3]

Enrollment grew from sixty to two hundred students in the years between 1853 and 1857. The quality of the instruction was said to be as good as that offered in some of the best schools in the South.[4] The students were instructed in religion as well as secular subjects, with memory work dominating. The intellectual sciences formed the basis of all pedagogy.[5] The Sisters of the Incarnate Word and Blessed Sacrament were educated, well trained, and dedicated to their work. Petra's girls received an excellent education and spoke English, Spanish, and some French.[6]

Controversy and competition was strong between the Protestants and Catholics. The nuns, despite prejudice, provided a quality Catholic education to the children along the Rio Grande. Bishop Odin wrote in 1853 that he knew they faced a challenge from the "local Biblical Society, which made great efforts to proselytize the Mexicans adding that only good schools could counteract this work of proselytizing."[7] Melinda Rankin had come to the Rio Grande as a missionary and teacher and was raising money to open the Rio Grande Female Institute to compete with the successful Sisters.[8] The Sisters had no textbooks as did the Sunday School in Brownsville, which had 720 books along with sixteen teachers and seventy-two scholars.[9] To solve this problem the Sisters printed their own texts with a hand-operated press. They had to be very good in languages to translate from French to English and French to Spanish and sometimes vice versa.[10]

With the girls settled in school, Petra turned to problems with her nine-year-old son Adrian, by Luis. After he lost his two older brothers and sister as well as his father, Petra no doubt threw a protective cloak over Adrian. It must have been difficult for him to adjust to his new family and his place in another culture. He had spent most of his life with his mother and her Vela relatives in Mexico. Adrian was not only the middle child but also the only boy. He likely was very close to his mother and may have felt isolated and jealous when she began a new life with Mifflin and when his half-brother Thomas was born.

Mifflin tried to help Adrian adjust to their new blended family. He became very fond of his stepson, referring to Adrian in a letter to Captain John Wilson as "my boy."[11] Mifflin also tried to provide for his education. In the 1855–56 Brownsville Public School Reports, Adrian Bidel (Vidal) attended school for the term from February 19 to May 4. The name of his patron was Mifflin Kenedy. For the next term from May 5 to September 5, 1855, Adrian, although listed as a pupil, only attended two days.[12] However, five years later in the 1860 Census, Adrian is listed as fifteen years old and still in school.[13]

Adrian likely had language difficulties moving from Spanish, a language he had spoken all his life, to English. Later, when he was an officer in the Union Army, Adrian resigned his commission stating as one of the reasons, "I find myself incompetent to carry on the company books as I do not understand nor have anybody in my company to understand the English language for this purpose."[14] Based on this statement it has been assumed that Adrian had a poor mastery of the English language. However, a letter has been found purportedly written by Adrian in 1863 to Henry Miller, the proprietor of the Miller Hotel in Brownsville.[15] If the letter was written by Adrian in English, it demonstrates Adrian's ability to write in a second language, probably at least at a middle school level, and in attractive handwriting. His early schooling that Mifflin sponsored and Petra insisted on was successful. However, a scribe could have written it. Yet if it *was* written by Adrian then his educational accomplishments might lead to speculation that other reasons of equal or more importance than education led to his resignation.

Adrian's schoolmaster was Mr. Gilbert Kingsbury.[16] He taught writing, spelling, reading, Smith's geography, Mitchell's geography, and arithmetic. Mr. Kingsbury's report to the board of trustees on May 4, 1855, claimed no cases of insubordination or punishment, but complained "his students spoke every modern language except English correctly." Adrian may well have been in this category.

Kingsbury suggested they needed to start classes early and not have a long recess in the heat of the day. He also thought that the teacher should instruct and not have recess. He advised instruction from 8 A.M. until 1 P.M. He complained about many absentees and that he needed new seats because there were five students sitting on six-foot benches designated for three. He also advised against vacations.[17] Adrian was of Spanish descent, as were most of his classmates, and represented the Tejano elite. Mr. Kingsbury expressed a prejudice against mestizos, or Mexicans of mixed blood, as reflected in a letter written in the 1860s. He wrote, "They are of mongrel blood the Aztec predominating. . . . These degraded creatures are mere pilferers, scavengers, and vagabonds downright barbarians but a single removed above the Digger Indians, hanging like vermin on the skirts of civilization—a complete pest to humanity."[18] It must have been difficult at best for Adrian and others to overcome the attitude that Kingsbury possessed and it must have left its mark on many of the children placed under his instruction.

The patrons of the school, whose children were enrolled there, were the

LIFE IN BROWNSVILLE

leading Tejano and Anglo citizens of Brownsville in 1855. Their families would go on to mold the history of the Rio Grande Valley and Brownsville for several generations. Adrian was associating with children from the Putegnat, Ytúrria, Champion, Carvajal, Dye, Glavecke, Longoria, and Kepple families.[19] He and his classmates would be both friends and enemies. Some would fight on opposite sides during the Civil War, but they stayed in this land and their children grew up together.

Mifflin tried to support Adrian, but as he grew older it became difficult. Another child was added each year to the family, and Adrian probably felt pushed out. The girls helped Petra with the younger children and the running of the household, but not Adrian. It was traditional for the children to share in the responsibility of providing for the family. Mexican girls were expected to help "papa" or "mama."[20] Petra stayed close to her girls all their lives and as her own life drained away, they came to her side to take care of her despite their own families.[21] Adrian was different. He was left to himself, and as Mifflin was often away with the pressure of running his various business interests, he had less time for his vulnerable young stepson.

As Adrian grew older, even though he continued in school, Mifflin had him work on the steamboats since it was a busy time. Mifflin could teach Adrian a lot if Adrian would listen.[22] Captain Kenedy was an excellent steamboat pilot, in fact one of the best on the Rio Grande, and he was a good teacher. He knew how to take charge, assume responsibility, steer a straight course, avoid obstacles, meet and beat the competition, and most important, he had the self-discipline needed to be successful. These characteristics were not a part of Adrian's personality. Mifflin started Adrian doing hard physical work, enduring hours of hard labor. Mifflin was reportedly strong enough to throw an anchor overboard. On his trips up and down the river Adrian had the opportunity to learn to pilot the steamboats, but as he grew older he gained a reputation as a habitual gambler and drunkard.[23] Nevertheless, Adrian had the chance to learn the countryside on both sides of the Rio Grande as he traveled its waters, stopping on both shores to obtain wood for fuel. Later, during the Civil War, this knowledge would prove very valuable, enabling him to lead successful raids on cotton trains up and down the river.[24]

Adrian was the son of a Mexican war hero who came to live in the household of a prominent Anglo businessman. His family's roots had been in the soil of Mexico for generations, and he had grown up with the image of his father, Luis, defending his homeland against the Anglo invaders who intended to seize their land. It is not a surprise that Adrian later came under the considerable influence of Juan Nepomuceno Cortina, a folk hero along the Rio Grande for his exploits against the Anglos.

Adrian proved himself a capable and courageous officer like his father, but he was duplicitous and did not hesitate to murder. His fellow soldiers also described him as "vain."[25] He served both the North and the South, deserted from both armies, joined a third and was shot by a fourth. He lived a short and tragic life and had one of the most unusual records in Civil War history.[26] Mifflin and Petra endured challenges and sorrows during their lives where this son was concerned.

Women, like Petra, came to Brownsville, settled down, had families, and demanded changes for a better standard of living. In response, the town's city council passed laws to raise the standard of living and promote safety. Hogs were not allowed to run wild through the city streets. People were not allowed to ride their horses down the newly improved sidewalks, and no one was allowed to bathe naked in the Rio Grande until after eight at night. These offenses were punishable by fines.[27]

Life was changing and Petra welcomed these changes. Brownsville was full of men who were drawn there by the Mexican War and had stayed to make it their home. Buildings were going up every day, goods arriving, steamboats loading and unloading, and everyone seemed to be engaged in useful employment. The number of inhabitants had grown to 2,500 in under two years. The new arrivals came from different countries and backgrounds but all had the same desire to make their fortunes. These families, along with Petra's, formed the backbone of the community. Their expertise lent an international interest and progressive attitude to this desolate land. Men like William Neale were establishing successful businesses such as his stagecoach line that ran from Point Isabel to Brownsville and often carried as much as $100,000 in silver on a single trip.[28] Many of the merchants, like Charles Stillman, Samuel Belden, and H. E. Woodhouse, came first to Matamoros and settled in Brownsville after the Mexican War. Belden fled Matamoros when a Mexican judge fined him $426,000 for illegal trading and seized his store and stock. Others came from different countries, like Jeremiah Galvan from Ireland and George Krausse, an organist, from Germany who established a music store. Some changed their names. Louis Cohen from Poland became Louis Cowen, and Alberto Campione from Italy became Albert Champion. Francisco Ytúrria was of Basque descent and Simón Celaya was also from Spain.[29]

As the face of the land changed and many Anglos and newcomers began to control the major institutions, Mexican culture continued to saturate the border area. Many of the Anglo and European ranchers and merchants became "Hispanicized white men."[30] As this new order developed, Tejanos had to adjust to succeed. Many elected to become active participants in the social process of forging a cultural groundwork that permitted them live in an Anglo American world. They had to adapt, adopt, and socialize to function in the new setting, but they also needed to remain ethnically Mexican in traditions

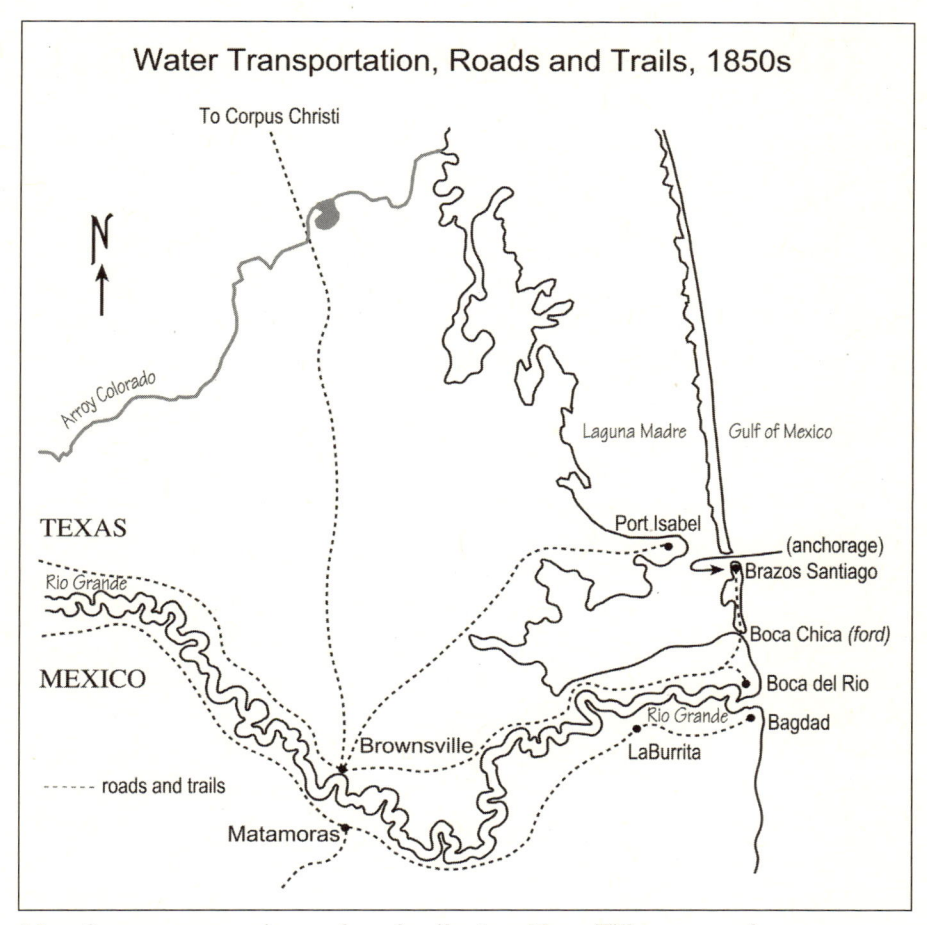

Map of water transportation, roads, and trails, 1850s. Nancy Tiller, cartographer.

and group relationships.³¹ They married and settled down and began to build their city. Brownsville's access to a port and international trade allowed these families to have many of the finer things in life if they so desired. Through all of this change, captains Kenedy and King continued to invest in property and expand their real estate holdings in the Rio Grande Valley.

Charles Stillman, José San Román, Humphrey Woodhouse, Jeremiah Galvan, Richard King, Mifflin Kenedy, and Francisco Ytúrria operated successfully as businessmen because they were their own bankers. The Ytúrria private family bank started in 1853 and operated for a hundred years. All of these men had banking connections in Europe, New Orleans, and New York. Mexican silver money was used almost exclusively during the 1850s and since it was purer than American silver money it brought a premium on the money market.³²

Brownsville's population included both rich and poor. For the poor people, every day was a struggle to survive and provide for their families. Most depended on the wealthier citizens for jobs. These wealthier merchants and tradesmen enjoyed a high standard of living and had access to an amazing variety of goods. The City Hall and Market, the center of Brownsville's community and government, was a large two-story building constructed between 1850 and 1852. Foodstuffs were available from steamers coming from Galveston, New Orleans, New York, and foreign ports. Locals found venison, wild duck, and geese, jacksnipe and other birds, as well as carrots, beets, cabbage, radishes, potatoes, corn, tomatoes, turnips, okra, beans, and pumpkins. Recorded pricing included oysters at $1 per hundred, trout at five cents a pound, and catfish at three cents a pound. Beef cost seven cents a pound. On a typical day Petra and her family were awakened by the gun firing and reveille being sounded at Fort Brown at 6 A.M. The marketplace at the center of the town opened the stalls very early in the morning, and the vendors had already been up for hours preparing their goods, hoping to sell enough to sustain their families.[33]

Petra planned her family's meals, and she or her servant shopped each day, which was required due to the lack of refrigeration. Early in the morning the marketplace was filled with the aromas of ground coffee beans, fresh vegetables, baked breads, and herbs. Shoppers bargained for prices and filled their baskets. The market offered meats and fowl for roasting, and fish. Fresh vegetables, goat cheeses, and fruits filled the stalls with splashes of color and fragrances. Bakeries provided fresh breads and homemade tortillas. Fine European wines and Cuban cigars were brought in for the gentlemen. The women shoppers exchanged the latest news of the day as they made their way up and down the aisles. Typically, the men would have a roll and coffee about nine in the morning at the Market and they too exchanged the latest news. At noon the market bell sounded, signaling lunchtime. The town's shops closed and some people went home for lunch.[34] The poor ate a small meal of rolled tortillas filled with beans or perhaps meat and then rested on a small mat for their siesta. Frijoles (beans) and tortillas were the sustenance of life to the Mexicans, and were served for breakfast, dinner, and supper. These two foods identified the Tejano way of life.[35]

The wealthy merchants went home for a formal dinner starting with soup followed by a plate of seasoned rice or garbanzo beans; roasted *cabrito* (goat), beef roast, beef steak, or fish; and vegetables such as peas or green beans. Fruit was often on the table and flans or custards were served for dessert. The women drank orangeade or lemonade, many times from fresh fruits off the trees in their yards. The men drank wine or had a cordial. A siesta followed during the heat of the day and activity would resume about three in the afternoon. Dinner in the evening was light, consisting of a cold plate and a dessert of custard or flan.[36] Carriers provided household water on a regular basis, or families drew from their cisterns, except during drought when they used street vendors. These street vendors attached a rope to a rolling water barrel and delivered the water throughout town.[37]

A descendant of Petra's daughter, Luisa Vidal Dalzell, contributed the following recipes that have been handed down through Petra's family.

Mexican Rice

Oil to coat a medium saucepan.
- 1 cup rice
- 1 chopped onion
- 1 can whole tomatoes, including juice (adapted to contemporary times)
- 1 cup water

Sauté the onion and rice in oil until light brown. Add tomatoes, smashing in your hands. Add 1 cup water. Simmer on low about 20 minutes.[38]

Mayme Dalzell Hefley's Charlotte Russe Recipe

- 1 pint heavy cream (for filling)
- 1 pint heavy cream (for top)
- 1 cup sugar
- 1 T gelatin
- 1 T vanilla
- 1 cup milk
- 3 eggs (separated)
- 1 pkg. Lady Fingers

Whip cream until stiff—Cream sugar and egg yolks—Dissolve gelatin in milk to simmering, not boiling—Stir dissolved gelatin with yolks and sugar—Stir this into whipped cream—Add vanilla—Last add beaten egg whites—Pour into mold lined with Lady Fingers—Top with whipped cream and sprinkle with glacé cherries.[39]

Clothing, furniture, and household goods were brought in on the boats. Salomé Young McAllen helped with her father's store, Francisco Ballí and Company, which offered a variety of goods, many of them brought by M. Kenedy & Co. steamers. These stores as well as companies like M. Kenedy & Co. maintained their own vaults and often acted as banks, credit agencies, and money exchanges. The store inventory included fabrics, blankets, shirts, denim pants, coats, wool hats, plain leather boots, shoes, sugars, raisins, soaps, candles, starch, liquor, wines, champagnes, tobaccos, coffee, shotguns, clocks, furniture, and many other kinds of household products.[40]

Tejano dress usually reflected the economic circumstance of the individual and family. Some women dressed in loose clothing of cotton material due to the heat. Many wore morning dresses of various colors including the traditional black. A *rebozo,* a silk or cotton scarf about six or eight feet long and two to three feet wide, often covered the head and shoulders. The men often wore white domestic muslin pants that were tight around the thighs and widened around the hem. Their shirts were like American shirts, and often pantaloons were worn displaying buttons and ornaments. The wealthier Tejanos wore pants with rows of jewels or pieces of silver coins down the entire outside seam. A red silk sash was sometimes wrapped around the waist and a serape or blanket worn in cold weather that covered the entire body. The Tejanos found that boots and sombreros were useful and many of the Anglo and European men adopted them as their own.[41]

Petra was in a particularly good situation because Mifflin could see to it that she and the family had what they needed; he could allot the space on his boats without going through a mercantile dealer. The poorer women could not afford to shop at the stores and often made their own clothes and bought cheaper goods at the market. The wealthier women and children's clothes were often made by a seamstress in Brownsville. Fashion magazines such as *Miss Leslie's Magazine* were ordered to learn the latest fashions. Petra received her regular copy of *Miss Leslie's* and made good use of it, especially with her household filled with growing young ladies. Silks and other fabrics as well as some clothes were sometimes ordered from New York and France.[42] Petra's great-granddaughter, Rosa Maria Swisher, shared the story that Mama Petrita sent her daughter Concepción, after she was married, "fabrics, laces, and silks that she ordered from France and Spain. Concepción had a live-in seamstress who made all her gowns and her children's clothes."[43]

Jovita González gives excellent descriptions in *Caballero* of the finery of the wealthier women. The novel's character doña Dolores selected fabrics from a tradesman to be made into dresses for the women of the house. For herself, since she was a widow, there was plain black in silks and wool for afternoon and evenings; for the others, figured calico for morning wear, and a bolt of nun's veiling to be cut into *rebozos* for gifts for the servants. For the young women of the house there was fine striped material of black wool and shiny purple satin, wine-colored silk, self-stripe brown and maroon in satin, silk, and wool. When the young women and doña Dolores prepared for the *baile* at *la Fiesta de Nuestra Señora de Guadalupe,* doña Dolores wore a black lace gown with her hair piled high and adorned with a fanlike comb of jets and brilliants. She wore a jet necklace and earrings and carried a black lace fan. One of the young women was dressed in a wine-colored silk gown and wore a necklace with a dull gold chain and a garnet pendant, garnet earrings, and a garnet ring. Doña Dolores had designed the other young woman's dress from an older dress that had been carefully put back for just such a use. She made it more fashionable in the redesign. The heavy cream lace of the dress fell in a rich cascade from the straight line of the décolleté and covered the upper arm almost to the elbow. A necklace of emeralds set in gold filigree, emerald earrings, and emerald bracelets on each arm completed the outfit.[44] One can imagine that Petra and her teenaged daughters would have had much pleasure in choosing fabrics and dressing for just such occasions.

While Petra was busy with the children, including one-year-old Thomas, and the household, Mifflin was busy with the steamboat business and his new ranching interest. The river level was down due to the drought. If that was not enough of a problem, M. Kenedy & Co. lost a government contract to Capt. James B. Armstrong, a former disgruntled associate. The government regulations had changed and now Major Chapman could not award army contracts without putting out a call for bids, causing captains Kenedy and King to lose a major advantage. Armstrong, along with the help of José San Román and James Grogan, had secured two refurbished steamboats and was able to deliver the service at a reasonable cost. The Mexican merchants up and down the river were delighted at the lower freight charges. It appeared that the expensive monopoly that M. Kenedy & Co. had held over the Rio Grande transportation was over. However, Stillman, Kenedy, and King fought the contract bitterly, with the fight lasting until 1856 when Kenedy & Co. was able to influence the Quartermaster Department to create a favorable loophole for them. The new policy stated that in order to move government stores the contractor had to have a backup boat available at all times. That clause eliminated the other competitors. In 1857, Kenedy, King, and Stillman paid off the owners of the two competing boats and took in John Young and San Román as partners. John Armstrong's estate was later paid $17,000 in 1858 for wrongfully being deprived of his contract.[45] M. Kenedy & Co. managed to solve their problems one way or the other and retained control of the river. They had long known the advantage of cultivating friends in influential positions. The partners practiced the policy of, if you can't beat them, buy them out and eliminate the competition.

In the meantime, Kenedy and King were turning their attention inland to the vast Wild Horse Desert and their new ventures into ranching. Mifflin had been helping to manage Petra's family's ranch, Veleño, since 1852. In later years, Captain Kenedy told Richard Mifflin Kleberg Sr., King's grandson, that it was Captain King who spurred him to turn to ranching as a serious business.[46] Mifflin never developed the passion for the land or ranching like King.

Mifflin was a businessman and was looking for profit. Nevertheless, listening to his good friend, Mifflin became the owner of another ranch at San Salvador del Tule in 1854, which was one of the first ranches in that part of the country.[47] Mifflin's rancho was small, and he managed it from Brownsville by using others to live there and run it for him. The ranch complex probably consisted of a *noria,* or hand-dug stone-lined well, maybe a small church, cemetery, a small store for supplies and provisions for the workers, various storage sheds, a *corral de leña,* or livestock enclosure made of mesquite logs, and a stock tank with an earthen *presa,* or dam. The new ranch was on the San Salvador del Tule grant, sixty-some miles northwest of Brownsville.[48] Kenedy did not become a rancher there but kept supplies on hand for the men he employed.[49] While ranching was new to Mifflin it was, of course, very familiar to Petra because of her family.

Mifflin, like Richard King, James Durst, and others, was buying sheep as well as cattle and horses. Mifflin owned a flock of sheep near El Sal del Rey in Hidalgo County. He began buying merino sheep from his home state of Pennsylvania. Despite losses by fire and drowning en route to Texas, he saved enough sheep to have a flock of 10,000. Mifflin had bad luck with the sheep and he lost 75 percent of the flock before he sold what remained to John McClain in 1856.[50]

Mifflin's good friends King and Lewis were getting established on their new rancho, Santa Gertrudis. The first problem they had to deal with was the lack of water, which they solved by putting a rough dirt dam across the bed of Tranquitas Creek to impound the water when it rained. It became the first engineered improvement from Brownsville to Corpus Christi and the only place where a thousand horses or cattle could be watered at one time.[51] Water was the key to success in this wild land. If you had it you made it, and if you didn't, you failed.

Another problem they had was securing safety from attack by Comanches and Anglo bandits dressed as Indians. In 1854 an outlaw band disguised as Indians attacked both Roma and Rio Grande City along the river, looting the churches and attacking U.S. troops. The citizens managed to catch two of the raiders; they were hanged with their white skin exposed.[52] To provide safety for the ranch, King hired his good friend, and veteran of the Mexican War, Capt. James Richardson to act as his foreman and Capt. William Gregory to help protect the ranch. King and Kenedy followed the practice of having former soldiers and Texas Rangers protect their property and help them acquire property from other landowners. These protectors became very powerful in a land where no other lawmen were available. They were "hired guns," in effect.[53]

King had one more problem to solve; neither he nor Kenedy, who would soon be his partner, knew anything about ranching, cattle, or horses. They were river men. They knew about good anchorages, navigation in difficult currents, and obtaining good headings in high winds, but they knew nothing about raising stock. King solved the problem in a unique way. He traveled to Mexico in 1854 to hire the best horsemen in the world, the vaqueros of northern Mexico who had been handling livestock for generations. Their ancestors had brought the knowledge with them from Spain. The drought became an advantage for King. He wanted to buy cattle and horses on his trip and because of the drought the prices were cheap.[54] He traveled to the village of Cruillas in the foothills of Tamaulipas and made his purchases. He then offered to settle the entire population of the village on his Santa Gertrudis rancho.[55] King probably acquired his vaqueros and their families from the *municipio* (county) of Cruillas and not necessarily from the villa of Cruillas, which is the county seat, since the town is still there. King may have resettled a whole ranch within the *municipio* of Cruillas and not the villa itself.[56] The vaqueros and their families accepted the offer and the resulting *entrada* of more than one hundred men, women, and children with all their possessions piled on yoked oxen, donkeys, and carts started north to the Wild Horse Desert and their new home. They brought their poultry, dogs, and pots and pans.[57] It turned out to be a brilliant decision for captains King and Kenedy, as many of these vaqueros and their descendants stayed on the ranches for the next four or five generations. All ranchers employed Tejano hands when they could get them because of their skills in roping, branding, and handling cattle. The vaqueros taught the Anglo cowboys; both Texas-Mexicans and Anglos understood that.[58]

While Mifflin was busy with his business interests, Petra was involved with an effort dear to her heart—the plans to build the Church of the Immaculate Conception. The Catholic community had a rough start in Brownsville. The first missionary Oblates of Mary Immaculate had arrived in December of 1849. When they criticized the saloons, gambling halls, and houses of prostitution the local politicians told them they were to ignore them. When the Fathers refused to remain silent the community support turned against them. One night they were made the butt of a practical joke when a long cord was tied to the bell of their little chapel and rung from a distance to wake up the priests and their neighbors.[59] In September of 1850 the priests were underfed, ill, disheartened, and recalled to France, only to return in 1852.

King split his time between his rancho Santa Gertrudis headquarters and his Brownsville home, while Mifflin worked out of Brownsville. As 1854 drew to an end, Mifflin and Petra were delighted to hear that Captain King had finally won over the support of Rev. Hiram Chamberlain, and he consented to King marrying his daughter Henrietta. The wedding license was issued on

December 9, 1854, and the wedding took place after the evening service of the First Presbyterian Church on December 10. Henrietta sang in the choir that evening while Captain King waited impatiently for the service to end. After the service, Henrietta, wearing a peach-colored ruffled silk dress with a white silk front trimmed with beading and white baby ribbons on the lace sleeves, came down from the choir to join King in front of her father. Their honeymoon was a trip to the rancho in the new closed carriage that her husband had recently purchased for $400. It took four days to cover the 120 miles, with armed outriders riding alongside the dusty coach. A ranch cook provided meals by a golden fire and guards stood by during the night. Her first few nights of married life were spent under the prairie stars.[60] When she arrived at the small settlement of mesquite corrals, a small blockhouse, and stockade with a brass cannon little did she know that she and her husband would play a significant role in taming the Wild Horse Desert and the development of South Texas.

Back in Brownsville, Petra and Mifflin welcomed their second son to their new home on February 22, 1855. They named him James Walworth Kenedy. James would be called Santiago by his mother and father and later was referred to as Spike on the cattle drives.[61] He grew up to have a daring spirit, and like his half-brother Adrian, had a short and tragic life. He too would be involved with bloodshed and murder. This son, named for an ex-steamboat skipper who was a dear friend of Mifflin's, loved the land and ranching. James Walworth had been his father's trading partner in 1849 when they started into Mexico with mules, wagons, and merchandise to the fair at San Juan de los Lagos. Walworth became a master on a steamboat for Kenedy and King and a partner in the Santa Gertrudis rancho. Captains Kenedy and King warmly respected him.[62]

In April, Henrietta and Richard lost one of their friends and partners in an incident surrounded by scandal. The sudden death of Legs Lewis would also influence Petra and Mifflin's destiny. It was the topic of conversation and speculation from Corpus Christi to Brownsville to Laredo and throughout the Rio Grande Valley. Captain Lewis had first taken King across the Wild Horse Desert and sowed the seed of developing a rancho there. Capt. Legs (G. K.) Lewis had decided to run for Congress when on April 14, 1855, an irate husband shot and killed him. The *San Antonio Herald* reprinted an account from the *Galveston Journal* on April 26.[63]

Dr. Yarrington of Corpus Christi suspected Captain Lewis of improper freedom with Mrs. Yarrington due to letters that he intercepted between the two. He and his wife separated. When Lewis heard that Dr. Yarrington had the letters he went to the doctor's office and demanded them. The doctor refused to give them to him and Lewis came back a second and third time. The doctor then told him if he came back another time he would kill him. Lewis came back another time and was met with a double-barreled shotgun. He lived but a short time after the discharge. Dr. Yarrington wrote a letter to the *Gonzales Inquirer* published April 21 stating that it was his misfortune to kill Captain Lewis but "he had seduced Mrs. Yarrington from me and my children and added insult to injury by continually coming to my house and trying to steal my children from me and force from my possession certain letters which I intercepted addressed to my wife." The *San Antonio Herald* regretted the tragic death of Captain Lewis and in its last line stated, "While the mantle of charity is thrown over his errors, let us drop a tear to the memory of the boy-prisoner of Mier."[64] Captain Lewis had not only survived his imprisonment at Mier but also the death march to Mexico City and the drawing of the black beans. He had stood in that hot dusty plaza as a boy when each of the prisoners was forced to reach into the container and draw out either a white bean or a black one.

Lewis's death presented a special problem for King; it led to Mifflin joining King as a partner in the Santa Gertrudis rancho. Captain Lewis's death, without a will, left his partner King in a bind because his interest in the rancho was put up for public bid a year later on July 1, 1856. King convinced his longtime friend Major Chapman, who was now in Corpus Christi, to bid for the interest in the *rincón*, and he purchased it for $1,575.[65] Chapman was shortly transferred back east by the U.S. Army. He committed suicide on September 28, 1859, at Old Point Comfort, Virginia. King convinced their mutual friend Captain Walworth to purchase Chapman's interest and to become King's partner in the rancho.[66] In less than a year Mifflin was a full partner with King and Walworth at the Santa Gertrudis.

While Petra was busy with the children that summer, plans were being made for the finest building in Texas to be built in Brownsville. Their good friend Father Verdet laid the cornerstone for the new church. The location was at Twelfth Street and East Jefferson. The church was to be built in French Gothic style by Father Keralum, who had been trained in Paris as an architect. Keralum also built new Gothic churches at Laredo and Roma. The Rio Grande Valley was lucky to have a man of his talent serve the Texas mission. Father Pierre Yves Keralum was known for his piety, humility, generosity, and dedication to visiting the scattered Mexican ranches. He was not a good preacher so he spent most of his time in the countryside. He was described as being timid in character but the people were affectionate toward Padre Pederito and said he did much good.[67]

The Oblate Fathers served 150 ranches, and it took months. When the priests arrived at the ranches they conducted marriages, baptisms, and administered communion. The workers sometimes saw a priest only once a year, and perhaps the home altars in South Texas are the result of the isolation from the traditional places of devotion. The altars occupied a space in a room that was dedicated as a center of worship, usually bedrooms, since the altar was a place for nightly devotionals before retiring. The home altar included a crucifix or cross, an image of Christ and usually an image of the Virgin Mary, and candles. A wide range of religious items could also be found: flowers, jars of holy water, *milagros,* a variety of saints, *palma bendita* (a piece of blessed palm from Palm Sunday), and rosaries.[68]

In 1872, Father Keralum was making his last missionary rounds before retirement when he got lost while riding his horse through the chaparral and subsequently died. The dense chaparral (brush in low profile) was difficult to navigate and there were few roads. Food and water were quickly depleted when a person got lost, because landmarks were difficult to spot in the unchanging terrain. Father Keralum was overdue in returning from administering to the far-flung ranches of the area. When his horse was found grazing, a search was launched but the priest was not found. Some ten years later a group of cowboys working cattle in the brush found human remains about forty miles from Brownsville. Since church vessels and gear that priests carried with them on their rounds were found with the remains, they were assumed to be Father Keralum's. However, the cause of death was not ascertained.[69]

In August Father Verdet again conducted a Kenedy family baptism in the small frame St. Mary's Church. This time on August 23, 1855, it was James Walworth Kenedy and his sponsors were Edward Downey and Margarita García as they were for his brother Thomas.[70] Mifflin and Petra's family continued to grow and now they had seven children ranging from Luisa at fifteen to baby James.

Rain returned to the Rio Grande Valley in 1856, and bringing business back for M. Kenedy & Co. Business also improved when Captain Kenedy traveled to Washington, D.C. early in the year to present a letter of introduction to Quartermaster General Jesup that was signed by Texas Senator Thomas Rusk and Congressman P. H. Bell. The letter asked for consideration of Captain Kenedy as an experienced and dependable contractor for transportation of army supplies on the Rio Grande.[71] Mifflin always did the negotiation for the company and was successful in obtaining the contract; in November alone he billed the U.S. Army $16,000 for services. He began to supply the army with mules, horses, and other staples.[72] King was dividing his time between Brownsville and the rancho as his herds grew and the ranch developed. Kenedy was also continuing to work with his ranches and on March 27, 1856, Petra Vela registered her brand in Corpus Christi.[73] Richard King followed suit in 1859, registering his wife's brand before his own.[74]

Livestock Brands

Nicodemus Vela
CD. Mier 1824

Gregorio Vela
CD. Mier 1824

Petra Vela Kenedy
Cameron County
Jan. 30, 1855

Petra Vela Kenedy
Nueces County
March 27, 1856

Doña Petra Vela
Palomas Ranch
Sept. 26, 1871

Mifflin Kenedy
Cameron County
July 19, 1861

Vela brands, including Petra's, and Mifflin Kenedy brands. Courtesy Homero Vera, Kenedy Ranch Museum, Sarita, Texas.

In the early part of 1856, Henrietta and Richard stayed at Santa Gertrudis while their home in Brownsville, next to Mifflin and Petra's, was being constructed. The house was completed and the couple moved in; they were particularly happy because they were expecting their first child in April. Petra and Mifflin were also expecting a baby in April. Neither the Kenedys nor the Kings were active participants in the social life of the "Brick House Crowd," taking more pleasure in neighborly visits among friends and families. The army's musical presentations at Fort Brown, or the evening galas in Matamoros were not their diversions. Petra and Henrietta enjoyed their homemaking duties and their churches and were busy with children. King when not working enjoyed a drink in less formal surroundings than he found in society. Henrietta and Petra had a lot in common during those first few months while expecting their babies. Petra had a lot of good advice for Henrietta as a new mother. On April 17 a daughter was born to the Kings, named Henrietta María. The little girl was named for her mother and grandmother and was called Nettie.[75]

Just four days later on April 21 Mifflin also had good news when John Gregory Kenedy was born. He was named after both his grandfathers, Gregory for Petra's father and John for Mifflin's father. The naming of this grandson after her husband who had died so young no doubt pleased his grandmother Sarah Kenedy. Petra, however, called him Gregorio after her deceased father.[76] He did not use the name John until later in life. Petrita, as Mifflin called her, had now given Mifflin three sons. These three sons plus his five stepchildren certainly surrounded him with the joys and distractions of fatherhood. The neighborhood was brimming with children now and their three boys under four years of age must have seemed like a litter of puppies going everywhere at once.

In the fall, King made a trip upriver and met one of the most famous men in U.S. military history—Lt. Col. Robert E. Lee. He had been sent to the Ringgold Barracks to participate in a court-martial. On the return trip downriver the two developed a warm friendship. Colonel Lee had been on the Rio Grande a decade before when he fought in the Mexican War. Lee made a treasured and lasting impression on Henrietta King, when he, accompanied by younger officers, made a formal call at the King home. The captain was away at the time and Henrietta received the callers.[77]

Robert E. Lee wrote to his wife that, "The King cottage was removed from the street by well kept trees and shrubbery in the yard, among which were several orange trees filled with ripening fruit. Mrs. King's table was loaded with sweet oranges and many other things tempting to the eye." The colonel did not think it proper to be too interested in the food so he tasted nothing. His junior officers complained and told Colonel Lee that they had been in other

Brownsville homes and had been entertained elaborately with cold meats, coffee, tea, fruits, and sweets. Colonel Lee reprimanded them for calling on townspeople in hopes of being asked for supper. Lee visited Santa Gertrudis on several occasions, and Henrietta recalled that he gave Richard the very sound advice of "buy land but never sell."[78]

Colonel Lee had many lonely hours to fill while he was in Brownsville for another court-martial. Often he got up early and walked over from the barracks and had breakfast with Henry Miller, who claimed to flip the best flapjacks in the country. The Webb and Miller Hotel, formerly the Cameron House, sat on the corner of Thirteenth and Elizabeth. It was a two-story hotel considered the best in town. Henry Miller employed the best cooks, evidently from New Orleans, and the cuisine was excellent. A great variety of seafood and game was available and many rowdy and fun dinners were held there, including Richard King's birthday party. The bar was called "Noah's Ark" because elderly cowmen and steamboaters came to sit and spend the time trading stories and whittling away at the furniture.[79] Adrian, as he grew to be a young man, frequented the hotel. He stabled his horses there and ran up large bills from his drinking, billiards, and gambling.[80] Other forms of entertainment that had carried over from the Mexican culture and were found in Brownsville and up and down the river were *fandangos* (dances), billiards, ball games, cockfights, and raffles.[81]

Soon after Nettie was born, Henrietta began traveling back and forth to the rancho with King. Sometimes they were accompanied by armed guards and sometimes not. On one evening late in 1856, as the Kings were making camp, a lone Mexican appeared from the brush; King gave him permission to join them and asked him to gather wood for the fire. Looking up from the blanket on which she sat with the baby, Henrietta suddenly called out, "Captain King! Behind you!" Being the practiced fighter that he was, King grabbed the knife-wielding hand and swung the man to the ground. Instead of killing him King told him to get out and stay out.[82] Henrietta had her own troubles at the rancho, times when she had to think quickly. One day while alone in the *jacal* (wood, mud, and straw structure) used as a kitchen at Santa Gertrudis, she was baking bread, filling the room with wonderful aromas. She had put Nettie in a cradle by the door to catch the cool breeze. As she turned, to her horror she saw a half-naked Indian standing silently by the door. He immediately jumped to the cradle and held a club over the baby while motioning with his other hand toward the bread. Henrietta gave him all the bread he could hold and he disappeared through the door.[83]

Helen Chapman expressed a more sympathetic attitude toward the Indians, stating that they were trapped between the sterile plains of the West and advancing settlements of Americans. Their game was growing scarce, the buffalo had abandoned the dry plains, and they were driven to steal or work for a bare subsistence with no territory to fall back on.[84]

Fortunately for Petra, Mifflin did not elect to try to live on one of their ranchos during this time. It was extremely difficult to take care of children, especially babies, at the isolated locations. The desert was filled with danger from bandits, Indians, and wildlife, and it was a difficult life at best. Mifflin continued to purchase property in Brownsville and owned the block where the church building housing the school was located. In April the schoolmaster announced that the subjects were going well but that he needed to learn Spanish because the Mexican students were frequently the originators of prohibited plans. He reported to the trustees that he had received a letter from Mifflin Kenedy demanding that the building be repaired in fifteen days because the underpinnings were bad and in danger of being thrown down. He estimated the cost of repair at $18. Mifflin was always a tough and exacting businessman.[85] During this period Mifflin Kenedy had built a substantial warehouse on the Rio Grande to handle his and King's upriver traffic. It later served as the first courthouse of Starr County.[86]

Petra and Mifflin lost their friend Father Verdet in 1856. He was there for them at the most important times of their life. He was the celebrant at their marriage and baptized two of their children. He worked with Father Keralum to build the church that they all wanted. He decided to travel to New Orleans to bring back more funds for the church and lumber for the construction. To save money he accepted an offer of free passage from the captain of the *Nautilus*. This proved to be a bad decision because when they stopped in Galveston a hurricane was brewing. The captain, not wanting to lose money by caring for the two hundred head of cattle on board, decided to try to outrun the storm. In order to keep his free passage, Father Verdet stayed with him. The storm overcame them and one survivor said Father Verdet was last seen baptizing the captain and his son before they drowned.[87]

October 23, 1857, was a frightening and happy day in Petra's life. She gave birth to Sarah Josephine Kenedy, and Mifflin had his first daughter. Sarah was born with dark hair and large dark eyes like her mother. She grew up to be called the "Belle of Corpus Christi."[88] However, on the day of her birth a great fire destroyed a good portion of Brownsville. The town was filled with screams, bells ringing, and smoke and heat as cinders descended upon the buildings. The townspeople feared that the entire town would burn. From the first alarm given, the flames made such rapid progress that it was impossible to remove the three hundred kegs of powder stored in the buildings in town. The kegs of powder exploded at once, driving a lurid sheet of flame and everything before it across the intervening alleyway through Mr. Alsback's store and out into Elizabeth Street. With the exception of one clerk, none of the persons who were within those premises were seen again.[89]

The merchants had been storing gunpowder to sell in Mexico, along with guns and ammunition. The fire apparently started in Jeremiah Galvan's store, on Levee Street. The rumors that spread after the fire were that Galvan and a group of friends, which included William Neale, were sitting on small gunpowder kegs and drinking good Irish whiskey. When it got dark they placed a candle on top of one of the gunpowder kegs so they could see. As the evening progressed the candle burned down into the keg and set off the gunpowder. Galvan had all that gunpowder on hand in violation of a city ordinance that forbade the storing of more than one keg of gunpowder in any house in the central section of town.[90] Henry Miller, owner of the Miller Hotel, was blown right through the brick wall of Charles Stillman's counting house, but miraculously survived. Even doors across the river in Matamoros burst open. Flames shot rapidly all the way to Elizabeth Street. Half a block was burned out before citizens, Fort Brown soldiers, and river steamers pumping water were able to get the blaze under control. Considerable financial damage was done. Charles Stillman had the means to recover from his $25,000 loss, but his partner, Samuel Belden, lost his fortune and ended his days as a manager-clerk for Stillman.[91]

Petra, Mifflin, and the children were caught in the middle of the panic. All around them heavy smoke swirled and the sounds of explosions filled the air. Mifflin was at the waterfront trying to keep the fire from spreading and destroying their home. Rumors swirled about how rapidly the fire was spreading and who had been killed. Two of their good friends, Jeremiah Galvan and Charles Miller, were both near the point of explosion and in immediate danger. Their close friend Charles Stillman's nephew Frank North was killed along with many of their other acquaintances.[92] Businesses were destroyed and many more would have been hurt if it had not been for the M. Kenedy & Co. steamers that were able to pump water from the river.[93]

Petra feared for her children's safety. She foresaw the dilemma of protecting her children if they had to abandon their home because she had or was having a brand new baby amid the chaos. Her older girls Luisa, Rosa, Concepción, and María Vicenta helped with Thomas, who was five, three-year-old James, and Gregorio, who was eighteen months. Adrian, who was thirteen, probably joined the other men and boys in the fire brigade and helped on the steamers to pump the water. Petra with the help of her servants and perhaps a midwife welcomed little Sarah to a frightening scene. This day required not only Petra's keen intellect but also her deep religious faith to get her family safely through the ordeal. Some of the family must have carried messages from down on the waterfront as the fire spread and they kept watch on their home. As the fire reached Elizabeth Street, they had to decide whether to stay or leave the house for safer ground. Petra, with the birth of Sarah, was in no position to leave. Staying calm and having faith during this terrifying night would be one of many tests that she would face with resolute spirit and determination. Petra's household and particularly her children looked to her for guidance through that fire-filled night. After the fires were put out and the smoke cleared, Petra and Mifflin could thank their Lord for the safety of their family on that fiery night in Brownsville.

Petra was thirty-five in 1858, with a family of four boys and five girls. Baby Sarah was named for Mifflin's mother Sarah Starr and his sister Josephine, as well as Petra's mother, Josefina. Grandmother and aunt in Pennsylvania were no doubt happy when they received Mifflin's letter telling them they had a little one named for them in Texas. Mifflin and Petra continued to enlarge their family and on April 22, 1859, welcomed their fourth son, John William Kenedy. This was the second son Petra and Mifflin named John after Mifflin's father.[94] Willie, as he was fondly known, was the baby boy of the family. He was a quiet, studious, and sensitive boy who appeared to have many of Mifflin's qualities and characteristics. Petra's household was busy as she tried to give all the children the attention they needed. She now had five boys and five girls with five of the children under six, which must have taxed her boundless energy, even with servants to help. Each child had its own personality, interests, and needs. The demands on Petra to meet their needs, run the large household, and help Mifflin were sizeable. The saving grace was that the older children helped take care of the younger ones and a strong bond of friendship developed between them in this Spanish language household. Perhaps one of Petra and Mifflin's most valuable accomplishments was the blending of the two families. The children developed close ties that would last until Petra's death.

In business, however, Mifflin was surrounded by criticism of his river monopoly, and the tension in the community was growing all around them. On March 13, 1858, a correspondent for the *Nueces Valley* wrote, "the present monopoly lines are getting rich too fast and too much at the expense of the people. They are clever men, but that does not justify them in making everybody else hewers of wood and drawers of water for them." People up and down the river of all economic levels were getting tired of the Stillman, King, and Kenedy monopoly.[95]

The partners of the Brownsville Town Co. transferred their interest to Mifflin Kenedy, acting as a front for Stillman and Belden,[96] which brought more controversy for Mifflin and made him a prime target for the anger of Juan Nepomuceno Cortina. Cortina's mother's land had been sold illegally to the Brownsville Town Co., and he was determined to have his revenge on the participants and all those who had victimized the original Mexican landholders. The Cortina family had split down the middle, with some of the family becoming allies with Mifflin and Stillman and county office holders, and others supporting Cortina. Cortina did not learn to read and write and preferred learning about knives, ropes, firearms, and fast horses. His cousin called him a "desperate contrary fellow." He tasted his people's defeat and felt racial hatred from the time he fought against General Taylor in the Mexican War. He worked for the U.S. Quartermaster trains at $25 a month after the war and although he discharged his duties he had trouble with the teamsters because, "they would not take orders from a Mexican." He quit and left for his mother's land on the Texas side of the river.[97]

Juan Nepomuceno Cortina, in formal attire, one of the most colorful and controversial figures in the history of South Texas. He was from a respected, established family, the grandchild of Jose Salvador de La Garza, the original grantee of the Espíritu Santo grant. In 1859 Cortina and a band of retainers raided Brownsville and held the city for nearly twenty-four hours, during which five citizens were killed. Brownsville Historical Association.

Cortina and Adrian had a lot in common. Cortina had fought against the Americans in the Mexican War just like Adrian's father, Colonel Luis Vidal, who had fought to protect Mexico against the Texans. Both Cortina and Adrian had trouble working for the U.S. Army and felt the sting of discrimination. Later they fought together while the U.S. Civil War and the French Intervention War raged along both banks of the Rio Grande.

During the remainder of the year Brownsville continued to grow. The census of 1858 showed the following breakdown of its citizens: 670 white males between eighteen and forty-five; 387 white males under eighteen; ninety-two white males over forty-five; 634 white females over eighteen; 174 females under eighteen; 436 white females under six; four slaves and twelve people of color believed to be freed black slaves.[98] All of these citizens faced an invisible killer in the fall of the year. It came without sound and struck deadly blows to both rich and poor. The dreaded yellow fever was back and the town began to make preparations to combat the disease. The city council selected a suitable building to be used as a hospital and stated that physicians and necessary medicines be provided; they authorized a draw on the city's treasury to pay for the services. A temporary hospital was constructed as the fever swept up and down the river.[99]

Father Pierre Parisot, who had taken Father Verdet's place, was summoned by telegram to come to Brazos Santiago to treat the "yellow jack." A fellow priest volunteered to go in his place and he contracted the disease and died. Father Parisot rushed to Brazos Santiago to give him the last sacraments. Dr. Watson at Fort Brown reported that the population of Fort Brown was 120 and forty-one had contracted the disease. He stated that the disease had caused a general panic throughout the command and men of temperate habits resorted to liquor to drive away their fear. He believed that it had been more malignant and unmanageable than any before seen.[100] One of the problems the priests and doctors faced was how to tell if someone was dead or in a trance. Not wishing to bury someone alive they came up with a recommendation of how to be sure: Tie a tight string around the little finger and if at the end of an hour it had not turned red or inflamed with blood settling in it then the patient was dead and could be buried without doubt.[101]

Petra's family escaped the epidemic. She had lived on the river all her life and knew the danger the fever brought. She probably lost her first three children to one of the epidemics, and she was fierce in her determination to protect her remaining children. She and Mifflin would have been very careful about whom their children were allowed to come into contact with. They had long periods when they only had other family members for company.

Petra knew about the general treatment prescribed to fight this deadly disease. At the first appearance of the fever a hot and strong mustard footbath was used, followed by twenty-five grains of chamomile and two hours later two ounces of castor oil. Mustard plaster to the hands and feet were to be applied and cold applications to the head and repeated footbaths every two or three hours. At the second stage, chamomile was given every three hours and three grains combined with quinine leaf tea, gum water, or flaxseed tea to be given frequently according to the condition of the patient's stomach. Also one could sponge the body and limbs with warm brandy and lemon juice. A mild enema and general bleeding were inadmissible.[102]

A committee met to secure medicines for the poor and on August 13 the aldermen passed a resolution prohibiting all passengers of a steamship of the Alexander Line, then off Bagdad where the disease was reported, to enter the city. The fever was also reported in Matamoros, and a strict quarantine was set in place to keep anyone from crossing the river. The streets were disinfected with lime, and finally with the arrival of cooler weather the disease disappeared in November of 1858.[103]

The Brownsville Census of 1859 reflected the large Mifflin Kenedy household:

1 white male between 18 and 45
5 white males under 18
0 white males over 45
3 white females over 18
11 children between 18 and 6
8 children under 6
0 slaves
0 free color
1 Qualified Elector

This account of the household included servants and their family members. Since Mifflin's immediate family had only one white female, Petra, over eighteen, it appeared that there were two servants over eighteen. Since they only had ten children of their own, there was one extra child between six and eighteen. Since they had six children under six it appeared that the two extra children belonged to the servants.[104] There are no slaves noted in the census, reflecting good practice of Catholic principles on Petra's side and good practice of Quaker principles on Mifflin's part. Mifflin's business partners, however, did have slaves listed. King had three slaves and one slave house while Charles Stillman had one slave and a slave house.[105]

Petra was sad to hear that her good friend Salomé Ballí Young lost her husband John on May 11. He was a business associate of Kenedy and King's and she and Petra were close friends and worked in the church together. When John Young died he left one-half of his estate to his son John and one-half to his wife Salomé. The next year's census showed that she had $100,000 in real property and $25,000 in personal property including one-sixteenth interest in M. Kenedy & Co. She was one of the 263 wealthiest Texans, and only fifteen of those were women. After John Young's death, Salomé carried on and was known for her strong will and quick temper.[106]

Salomé and Petra were pleased to see the completion of construction for the church they had worked so hard to support. The large Gothic church could seat nine hundred persons.[107] Father Parisot discovered that funds were needed for the purchase of an organ for the newly constructed Immaculate Conception Church. The projected cost of the instrument was $1,450, quite a sum in those days. The ladies of the parish set about to raise the money and were successful in raising $600. They felt sure that given the time they could obtain the entire amount needed for the organ. Father Parisot, however, not wishing to delay in procuring the money, set out on a fifteen-day tour through

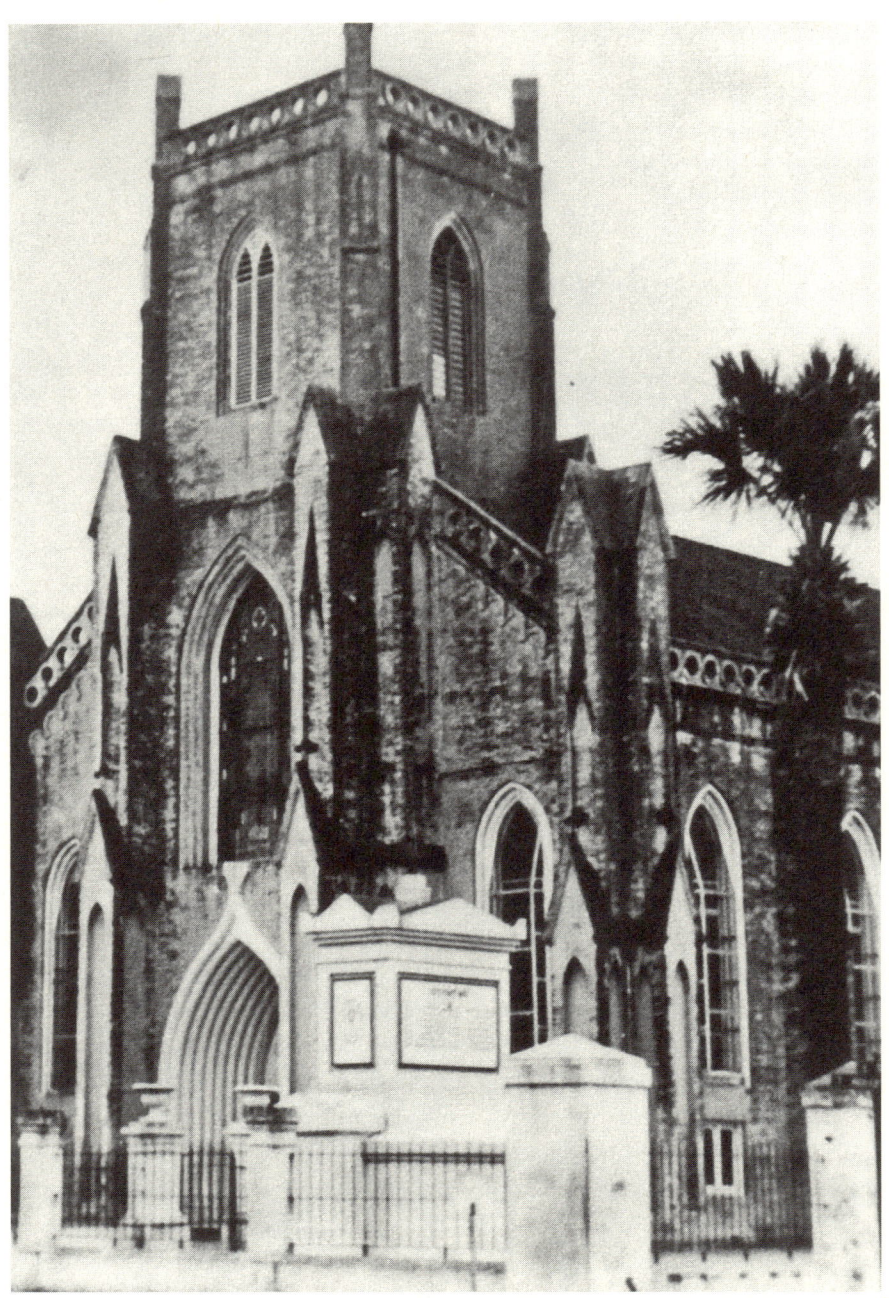

Church of the Immaculate Conception built in French gothic style by Father Keralum who had been trained in Paris as an architect. Father Parisot helped raise money for the church organ by taking tithes of livestock and returning to town driving a herd of cows and calves before him, which he raffled off. Mifflin Kenedy contributed a stained glass window in honor of Petra. John Gregory, Sarah Josephine, and William Kenedy were the first to be baptized in the new church. Brownsville Historical Association.

the countryside where he raised some $1,315 through a unique scheme. The parishioners had little ready cash for the organ fund but most of them had cattle, so Father Parisot took tithes of livestock and returned to town driving a herd of sixty-five cows and calves before him as he rode down Elizabeth Street. He disposed of the cattle at a raffle, which left a small balance due on the instrument. It was soon settled and the organ is in that church today.[108]

Mifflin also did his part. Mifflin Kenedy, the Quaker, in honor of Petra donated a stained glass window.[109] Mifflin was always quick to fund a cause Petra cared about and certainly a cause in which the church was concerned. He knew how strong her faith was and what an important role the church played in her life and by extension, in his. Finally, on June 12, Father Augustine Gaudet blessed the church on Pentecost Sunday. Petra and her family joined with the many other families who had worked so hard to see this day come about; they knelt to give thanks for their church.

On June 21, Petra and Mifflin's three children John Gregory, Sarah Josephine, and William shared the honor of being the first to be baptized in the new church. The children's sponsors joined the family at the altar. John Gregory's sponsors were San Román and Luisa Vidal, his oldest half-sister. San Román had gone from being a competitor in business to being a partner in the last few years and a good friend in the church. Luisa took a special interest in this child named for their grandfather don Gregorio and for John Kenedy. Sarah's sponsors were San Román and her second oldest half-sister Rosa Vidal. A very special relationship developed between Rosa and Sarah as the years went by. William's sponsors were Jeremiah and Mary Galvan. Jeremiah was a business partner of Mifflin's and friend of Petra's through the church. San Román was a Spaniard who had come to Matamoros in 1846 and established a dry-goods firm that extended across the Rio Grande into Brownsville in 1850. He expanded his business into commercial credit, trustee holdings, real estate, and cotton brokerage and thus became a very prominent businessman.[110]

Godparenting, or *compadrazgo,* was a very strong institution among the Tejano ranch families and along the border. The sponsors of the child at baptism—godfather and godmother, or *padrino* and *madrina*—assumed the role as coparents of the child. They promised to train the child in family and Christian values and provide more effective parenting should the case arise in sensitive situations. Godparenting linked the extended families together in a community of loyalties. It was taken as a very serious responsibility. "Friends may fuss at one another, even brothers may have serious disagreements, but when one has stood as godfather for another's child and become a *compadre* to the parents, it is unthinkable that he should so forget his relationship as to quarrel over anything whatsoever."[111] Mifflin and Petra had turned to two of

This magnificent altar graced the interior of the Church of the Immaculate Conception, constructed in 1856–59, until it was removed in the 1960s and replaced with a smaller, simpler altar in keeping with liturgical change enacted by the Second Vatican Council. Brownsville Historical Association.

Mifflin's business partners and friends to assume this important role. They also included two of the children's half-sisters, as they always closed the family circle in unity.

Following the baptism of his children, Mifflin left for New Orleans. In a letter written on July 14, 1859, to Captain Walworth, William Hale in Galveston wrote that Captain Kenedy had just left on the *Grampus* on his way to New Orleans. "Capt. Kenedy has agreed you should be nominated for the House of Representatives and should have talked to you by now. It is imperative that we have protecting laws passed for our region and trust you will serve. You should visit Brownsville soon."[112] This was followed by another letter from Charles Lovinskiold in Corpus Christi to Capt. Richard King at Santa Gertrudis telling him Captain Walworth "should be elected even though he is in Hot Springs for his health. All the Mexicans should be gotten out to vote."[113] Kenedy and King knew the importance of having politicians "in your corner," just as they had put up their partner Legs Lewis to run before Captain Walworth. It was customary for the various ranchers to gather their workers and take them to the polls to see that they voted for their intended candidate. Tejano politicians from wealthy and privileged backgrounds held public office and were often assisted by the lower classes in the political system. They could represent the interest of their supporters but were sometimes limited by the Anglos' political agendas.[114]

Meanwhile, against great protest from the Brownsville citizens, the Rio Grande was left undefended and vulnerable for an invasion in February when General Twiggs withdrew the troops from Fort Brown and from the other facilities up and down the river.[115] Mifflin was gone and Petra was by herself the morning that Cortina, with his hatred of the Anglos for taking land from his family and for other ethnic conflicts, rode into Brownsville with some of his vaqueros for morning coffee. There they saw City Marshal Robert Shears pistol-whipping a vaquero who worked for Cortina's mother. Cortina stepped up to the marshal and asked him, mildly enough, to treat the man more easily. Marshal Shears thereupon started a war. He cursed Cortina, who pulled a gun and shot Shears in the shoulder, mounted, pulled the vaquero up behind him and galloped from town.[116] Cortina spent much of the next few weeks recruiting men, supposedly for the Mexican Army. He also made some overtures to Shears, offering to pay for some of the damages. This was as close as he ever got to an apology. Shears, Glavecke, and others wanted Cortina captured and punished.[117]

Because of this incident Cortina became such a folk hero that one of the first *corridos* (a narrative folksong) to arise in the Lower Rio Grande area—the region now half in Mexico and half in Texas—was of his exploits. The *corrido* was written in the 1850s, under the influence of border conflict with the Anglos. Américo Paredes writes, "all men who, as a corrido puts it, *defendieron su derecho* (defended their right)—were immortalized in songs and legends."[118] This possibly was the first *corrido* written, unless other true *corridos* are discovered and collected in greater Mexico. Cortina is the earliest border *corrido* hero known, whether his exploits were put into *corridos* in 1860 or later.[119] The influence of Cortina upon the Mexicans along the border cannot be overstated. Nor can the influence of the conflicts between the Mexicans and Anglos be overstated. When land was ceded to the United States in 1848, the first Mexicans to become residents were those living in the ceded territories who had been living there for generations. Spotting an opportunity, the North Americans moving into the area in search of riches treated the Mexicans as conquered people, confiscating land as often as not. Thus began the long struggle between cultural differences. The Mexican saw himself and all that he stood for as continually challenging a foreign people who treated him, for the most part with disdain.[120] Folklore, in the form of a *corrido*, contributes to the understanding of the history of people. Attitudes and feelings, undercurrents of emotion in the masses of people, are not recorded in official documents, but may have a profound effect upon events. Illustrating this is the fragment of the *corrido* collected by Paredes describing the event of Cortina's rescue of the vaquero: "The famed General Cortina is quite sovereign and free / the honor due him is greater, for he saved a Mexican's life."[121]

Cortina, or Cheno as he was known, sought vengeance on the large merchants of Brownsville and declared, "The war still exists. I did not sign the Treaty of Guadalupe Hidalgo." He became the hero of the Texas Mexicans and he became their chief.[122] Throughout this time there was a young teenage boy watching the dashing young Cortina, who had been born into a landed Spanish family but spoke the language of the common people and fought for their rights and their dignity. Adrian Vidal must have envied Cortina's spirit and purpose and admired him as a hero like the other Tejanos. After all, Adrian's father had fought to keep the land for Mexico and the original landowners and so was like Cortina. Adrian, like Cortina, would want to adopt what Paredes identified as an ideal pattern of male behavior that developed interculturally along the border and influenced the male self-image. In the language of the ballads, the mounted man with his pistol in his hand, "defended his rights."[123]

Petra was no doubt relieved when everything quieted down. She and the family continued their routine until the evening of September 28. About three in the morning shouts were heard through the streets of Brownsville: "*Viva Cheno Cortina: Mueran los gringos; Viva Méjico.*" As the citizens heard a call for their death they jumped from their beds to see Cortina leading about a hundred men across the river to capture the town. He had no opposition and established himself at the deserted garrison of Fort Brown. He then began to look for his gringo enemies. Petra, knowing that Mifflin and their property were one of Cortina's targets, feared for Mifflin's life and the safety of their businesses. Marshal Shears hid himself and many scrambled for cover. Five citizens were shot, including the city jailer, when Cortina's men let all the Mexican prisoners free. Cortina wanted to burn the stores of his enemies and at daylight was searching the stores on the riverfront for turpentine.[124] The Sisters at the convent shared the fears of the rest of the people until they heard that Cortina with a dash of chivalry had ordered his men to throw a cordon around the convent with strict orders that nuns should not be disturbed.[125]

Cortina had timed his attack with the Mexican Independence celebration in Matamoros that was being held late because of the election, since he knew the noise from the celebration would cover his approach.[126] The men to die in the raid included William Peter Neale, who was fatally struck when shots were fired into the open window of his home. George Morris, town constable, hid under his house but was spotted by one of the raiders after Morris's wife, Luciana, told them he was not home. Morris ran for safety but was shot down and stabbed, the rings cut from his fingers. The raiders took his shoes, horse, several firearms, and $150 from his house. Another victim of the raiders was an unarmed Mexican *carretero,* Clemente Reyes, apparently a victim of being in the wrong place at the wrong time. Marshall Shears escaped death by hiding in a bake oven. Glavecke made it safely to Samuel Belden's store and escaped death,[127] although there were threats of burning down the store.

Cortina particularly hated Glavecke. He was married to his cousin and at one time they had been best friends. A Kentuckian named Somerville hired another friend, Juan de la Luna and Cortina to drive north eighty mules he had bought. The Kentuckian was found dead and Glavecke claimed that after

Somerville's death, Cortina had the mules and sold them to the U.S. Army. There was evidence that Juan de la Luna had killed Somerville, but Cortina had a warrant issued for his arrest although he was never brought to trial. Even John Ford thought that Cortina was innocent.[128] Cortina also resented the influence Glavecke exerted over his mother and brother, particularly in legal and financial matters. He felt Glavecke had a conflict of interest because of his dealings and connections to the Brownsville legal establishment, particularly when it came to handling the estate of his deceased aunt, Feliciana Goseascochea de Tijerina. The feud between the two escalated with Cortina vowing to kill Glavecke on sight.[129]

To end the raid, General José Carvajal and Cortina's cousin Miguel Tijerina and others crossed the river and convinced Cortina to withdraw.[130] Two days later from his rancho, Cortina, surrounded by volunteers who were coming from everywhere, issued a proclamation that "our enemies should not possess our lands." Cortina wanted to drive the hated Americans to the Nueces River and some even said the Sabine River should be the boundary of Texas.[131] Many of them had been jailed and robbed of their property. Cortina told his followers that he had been entrusted to "break the chains of their slavery."[132] More than half of the men who joined Cortina were from below the Rio Grande; however, a few Cortinistas from the north bank of the Rio Grande were influential in the Mexican-Texan community. Teodoro Zamora was chief justice of Hidalgo County and Jesus Ballí was one of the heirs to a large land grant in the Valley. John Ford told Governor Runnels in late 1859, "the whole Mexican population on both sides of the river are in favor of him."[133]

The Cortinistas had taken guns, ammunition, liquor, and several horses from private homes and stables during the raid but there was never any wholesale plunder. Several times during the raid, Cortina told the Mexicans in the community not to fear him; he was only looking for bad Americans to kill. Cortina rode up to Alexander Werbiski's store and when his Mexican wife answered the door she began sobbing in total terror. Cortina told her not to cry, that it was "no night for Mexican tears." One wonders if that is why Petra, wife of the hated Mifflin Kenedy, escaped harm that night.[134]

Brownsville was scared and Mayor Powers began to organize the town's defense.[135] Mifflin helped to organize a civilian group and was elected commander to respond to Cortina. Unknown to him at the time, he was joined by two future sons-in-law—Joe L. Putegnat and Robert Dalzell—as well as his brother Elisha Kenedy who had joined him in Brownsville and was living in his home.[136] Don Cavazos, Cortina's half-brother, also sided with Mifflin's volunteers.[137] Captain Ytúrria organized another company for protection.[138] Two ineffective attempts to raid Cortina's rancho were turned back, and he held Brownsville under his control for more than two months. A letter

The lead vest Mifflin Kenedy wore during the Cortina War. The vest weighs thirty pounds and is on display at the Raymondville Historical Museum, Texas.

from E. Basse in Brownsville to William Hale stated that a cannon had been planted in the principal street. Everyone was carrying arms, expecting an attack. The Mexican authorities said that they could not give assistance unless Tomás Cabrera, Cortina's second in command who had been taken prisoner, was returned. They said that the whole Mexican population was against them and that it was a much more serious affair than people who were not there thought. They felt that Cortina could lead the Mexican population against them.[139]

On Wednesday, November 2, Kingsbury, writing to the Chief Clerk of the Post Office Department, said that the mail could not get through because Cortina was intercepting the carriers and imprisoning them. Cortina was camped not far from town and his men fired on the carriers every night. The parts of town that were built the strongest were used as barricaded forts, and all the families were crowded into that space. The men patrolled every night. Kingsbury had stood duty ten or twelve nights and didn't go the next day because the mail came from Matamoros at sunset. He was arrested and taken to the guard house as a prisoner for his delinquency, until midnight, when the town was attacked and he was released.[140]

Petra and her family, along with the rest of the town, would have been terrified. It must have been very difficult to look after her large household and ten children in such confined quarters. Mifflin was heavily involved in the defense and was gone nearly all the time. He even had a thirty-pound lead vest made to protect him from the bullets.[141] Petra had many concerns for the safety of her family during this period. Supplies were in demand and none were coming in. The steamboat traffic had been shut down as well as any overland supplies. Brownsville was under siege. The citizens had to depend on what they already had in the town. They were used to ordering basic goods in large quantities so they would have had the basics of beans, ground corn, canned goods, and some meat, but supplies would run short as the siege continued.

To add insult to the situation, when the men had gone out to capture Cortina and had been defeated, they had taken two cannon with them, one from Mexico and the other from one of Mifflin's steamers. Mifflin's cannon had not worked and Cortina had taken possession of the other one, which he fired every morning, waking up everyone in Brownsville and letting them know of his close presence.[142] The town was under constant threat of attack while the surrounding countryside was being raided and looted. All the men were on twenty-four-hour duty and shared the watch around the clock.

News coming from the Rio Grande was often alarming and totally untrue. W. A. Miller had issued a sworn statement that appeared in several Texas newspapers saying that "400 crazed Cortinistas . . . had overrun the barricades and seized the town." Every defender was supposedly killed or executed. "Mifflin Kenedy had died gallantly at the barricades and Francis Campbell had been hanged." It was two weeks before the misinformation was corrected.[143] The inaccuracies continued with comparisons being drawn between Cortina and John Brown's raid at Harpers Ferry, Cortina being labeled a "wild Abolitionist plotting with northern radicals" to free slaves in Texas and murder their owners.[144]

During this time, Cortina had his revenge on Mifflin but it was not in Brownsville. Instead he raided his ranch, San Salvador del Tule. In August and September of 1872 a series of depositions before a U.S. Commission were taken in Brownsville to document the losses that occurred during Cortina's raids. The property owners were seeking damages from the U.S. government because it had failed to provide protection. Mifflin and others testified to the damage that he and Petra suffered from Cortina's raid. Viteriano Sandoval testified that he had worked on the ranch under J. F. George who ran the San Salvador del Tule for Captain Kenedy. He said they had about 3,500 head of quality cattle and he could not remember how many horses. He said in 1859 they had branded 1,200 calves and still had two or three hundred more to brand when Cortina and his men came and all the employees ran off because they were afraid. He said he hid in the chaparral near the rancho and saw them carrying off everything they could carry or round up, and he left on the fourth day because his life was in danger.[145] Juan Miguel Longoria worked for Captain Kenedy and said there were a number of fine saddle horses, a drove of mares, and a proof of jacks. He said that Cortina's men destroyed all the provisions on hand to supply the employees and all the goods in a store kept on the rancho such as groceries that had been sent from Brownsville by Captain Kenedy.[146]

Francis M. Campbell testified that he was coming down the Rio Grande in January of 1860 on the steamer *Manchero* when Cortina attacked them at the Solas. He saw a great many cattle on both sides of the river that had Mifflin Kenedy's brands and were in the possession of the thieves who had attacked them. He also saw many hides and horses with Mifflin Kenedy's brands.[147]

Capt. W. G. Tobin of San Antonio and his volunteer Ranger company were the first outside help to reach beleaguered Brownsville, but they have been called a "sorry lot." According to Harbert Davenport, Tobin had one good man, but unfortunately "he fell off a carriage and broke his neck soon after reaching the city." After Tobin arrived, Cabrera was forcibly taken from jail by a mob and hanged. Maj. Samuel P. Heintzelman, who was on his way to Brownsville, would imply that the hanging was by Tobin's men.[148] The night before Major Heintzelman arrived, Colonel Ford testified in 1872, Cortina had dispatched a party of highwaymen to assassinate Captain Richard King. In a letter to William Hale on December 11, 1859, from King's partner James Walworth, Walworth says he is relieved to learn that Captain King and family have not been molested.[149]

With the news of the death of Cabrera, Cortina allegedly retaliated by hanging three men who had been captured in October. Apparently several Americans disappeared into areas controlled by Cortinistas and were never heard from again. The hanging of Cabrera was the act that left little hope for reconciliation in the Cortina War. It would be a bitter guerrilla war from then on.[150]

Finally, after many appeals to the U.S. Army, on December 5 Maj. Samuel P. Heintzelman marched into Brownsville with 117 regulars. There are comments in Heintzelman's journal that the Rangers' reports were exaggerated and that many Ranger crossings into Mexico were unjustified and embarrassing.[151] Also, Rip Ford had been commissioned by the governor as a major of the Texas Rangers and was sent to help.[152] When Ford left Austin he had eight men, two guns, a few pistols, and a little food lashed to their saddles. He had no money because the treasury was empty, but Ford was known for being resourceful. When he arrived in Brownsville he had a company of fifty-three well-armed volunteers equipped with two wagons and supplies.[153] It was a good guess that Ford had stopped by the Santa Gertrudis rancho and Captain King had helped to equip the men.

Together the combined forces attacked Cortina on December 27 outside of town and he moved up the river to Rio Grande City and the Ringgold Barracks on Christmas Day, 1859, for safety.[154] Although Cortina had retreated, everyone, including Mifflin and Petra, knew that he would be back to try to claim his birthright. The fight for the land along the Rio Grande was continuing between the original Mexican landowners and the Anglos from the north. To add to the controversy, internal wars would erupt within the United States and Mexico. In the United States the war was fought between the North and South and in Mexico it was between the French Imperialists and the Juaristas. In the next few years the Rio Grande exploded with fighting, terror, and tragedy that surrounded Petra and Mifflin and their family.

Chapter 4

1860–62: War Clouds Gather

The last five years had been good ones for Petra and Mifflin. The 1860 census gives a snapshot of Petra and Mifflin's home. There were nineteen members of the household. Mifflin was forty-one years old and a steamboat captain with a real estate value of $50,000 and personal value of $50,000. Petra at thirty-four years old was listed as a housekeeper, as was Henrietta King. Petra's children, Louisa, eighteen; Rosa, sixteen; Adrian fifteen; Concepción, thirteen; and Vicenta, eleven, are all in the household. Adrian, Concepción, and Vicenta were listed in school. Her younger children with Mifflin, Thomas, seven; James, five; Gregorio, four; Sarah Josephine, three; and William, one, are all in the household, too. Thomas was listed as being in school. In the household was Mifflin's twenty-one-year-old brother, Elisha J. Kenedy, listed as a clerk. Six servants provided the Kenedy's help. They were all from Mexico. The female servants' ages were fifty-four, eighteen, and eleven; the males were twenty-four, thirteen, and twelve.[1]

Petra's older children would soon be adults, each pursuing their individual interests. The next five years would not be as good for this family as the last five had been. The clouds of war were gathering across the nation and Mifflin and Petra would not escape the sorrow it would bring. They, too, would be caught up in the controversy and conflict as family turned against family and friends took up arms against one another. Their lives would be uprooted and they would have to abandon their home, have their family separated, and suffer the death of a son. It would take all of their resolve, ability, and faith to endure the war that would tear open their country. Petra would rely again and again on her faith as the anchor for her family through these hard times.

After the Cortina raid Mifflin decided to move what was left of his livestock at San Salvador de Tule to King's Santa Gertrudis rancho located one hundred miles inland. After his vaqueros rounded up what was left he found that he only had about one-third of his herds remaining. In January of 1860 his men drove 1,595 cattle and eighty-seven horses to the safety of the Santa Gertrudis. Mifflin was now one of the largest landowners in the county. The 1860 census showed that he owned 180,000 acres in Cameron County, J. N. Cabazos owned 539,000, Richard King 70,848 acres, and Charles Stillman 20,000 acres.[2]

At the end of January in 1860, Petra was worried about the business and what Mifflin and his partners were going to do about the cargo that stacked up all along the river. The boats had not been able to run since Cortina's September raid on Brownsville. All up and down the river the boats needed to pick up cargo and more importantly transport money that had been collected. Cortina's spies were also scattered up and down the river and he soon learned that the steamboat *Ranchero* had been dispatched upriver and that there would be as much as $300,000 aboard when she made the return trip. The lure of money was too much for Cortina, and he prepared to attack the boat at one of the horseshoe bends in the river. Petra and Mifflin had their spies, too, and they prepared for him by taking aboard a unit of army regulars to man the guns. Tobin and Ford with their Rangers were to be on the bank nearby. Cortina attacked on February 4 with about four hundred men and was defeated by the men who defended the boat. Petra was relieved when the *Ranchero* came steaming safely into her mooring slip in Brownsville.[3] Some of the men may have celebrated after their harrowing experience by going to Miller's Hotel or Victor's for dinner. Victor's was a restaurant that was touted for its billiards and saloon, which appealed to the gentlemen. It served excellent foods such as green peas, mushrooms, truffles, French sausages, jellies, French cheeses, claret, and white champagne.[4]

In June Captain Kenedy traveled to Pittsburgh to order two large boats to be used outside the bar in the Gulf of Mexico for loading, and two smaller boats to be used upriver.[5] Mifflin and his partners were reading the signs of a coming war and hearing the cries for secession. They knew that if war did come they would not be able to order any more boats and the Rio Grande might become one of the most important waterways in the nation. Petra was eager for Mifflin to make the trip and return soon because they were expecting another child in August. Captain King and his wife had added another girl to their family April 13, 1858, named Ella Morse King.[6] Henrietta was also expecting again like Petra but her baby was not due until December. On August 7, 1860, Mifflin and Petra welcomed a baby girl named Phebe Ann, after Mifflin's sister.[7] The other brothers and sisters must have been used to having a new baby in the family every year and welcomed her to the group. Petra now had a family of six girls and five boys.

Concepción Vidal married Manual Rodríguez of Laredo in 1860. She was a beautiful young woman with green eyes and auburn hair. She became an accomplished hostess, throwing extravagant parties with imported food and wines. She wore tall Spanish combs, lacy mantillas, and satin gowns. Her family called her Conchita. Courtesy of Jesse (Sam) Thornham, Joe Thornham, McGoohan families, and Rosa Marie Swisher.

Manuel Rodríguez was a rancher and later was the mayor of Nuevo Laredo. He was very helpful to Mifflin Kenedy, strengthening Mifflin's network up and down the Rio Grande. He was also in several business deals with Mifflin and helped him in securing real estate deeds. Courtesy of Jesse (Sam) Thornham, Joe Thornham, McGoohan families.

Life was changing around Petra; sometime in 1860 Concepción married Manuel Rodríguez of Laredo. Concepción, like her mother, chose to marry at a young age. She was about thirteen or fourteen.[8] Petra understood this young daughter and her desire to go with the man she loved, given her experience with Luis, and Mifflin listened to her counsel. Manuel Rodríguez was a rancher and later the mayor of Nuevo Laredo. The couple lived first in Matamoros and then in Laredo.[9] Concepción, called Conchita by her family, was a beautiful young woman and would become an accomplished hostess, throwing extravagant parties with imported food and wine. She would have beautiful silver and gold jewelry, tall Spanish combs, lacy mantillas, and satin gowns. She was petite, had green eyes and auburn hair, perhaps reminiscent of that "almost redheaded" lady who captivated Francisco Vela in Saltillo. Concepción's granddaughter said their home covered an entire block in Nuevo Laredo and had a large Spanish-style entrance for carriages. It was located near the Santo Niño Church and was later destroyed by floodwaters from the Rio Grande. Her granddaughter also said that her father had told her that Concepción was at one time the most elegant lady in the city. She would go to the ballroom at the casino in Nuevo Laredo and take her personal lady to help her change into new attire in the middle of the gala or dance.[10]

According to the granddaughter, Concepción was very young when Mama Petrita married Mifflin, so he was the only father she ever knew and she was very fond of him. Later in their life, after Petra's death, Concepción and Manuel would own three houses and live lavishly. Concepción spoke and wrote English and Spanish.[11] Her schooling was good and she stayed in close contact with her family, naming two of her sons after her half-brothers Santiago and Tomás and two daughters after her mother Petra and half-sister Sarah.[12] Manuel worked with Mifflin in several business deals and helped him in securing real estate deeds. Through Manuel, Mifflin strengthened his network up and down the Rio Grande. When a new person came into the family, he or she was automatically accepted. Another future son-in-law, Joe Putegnat, Rosa's husband, was getting involved in local politics and was a candidate for county treasurer, a position that could also help further the family's influence.[13]

The close of 1860 brought many changes. King decided to form R. King & Co. and consolidate the interests in the Santa Gertrudis rancho. The partners consolidated their interests and the new shares in R. King & Co. were divided three ways: James Walworth, two-eighths; Mifflin Kenedy, three-eighths; and Richard King, three-eighths. These three steamboat captains were now ranching partners.[14] As the talk of war spread throughout Texas, Walworth was elected a delegate to the Texas convention for secession.[15] During this process, Richard King filed a claim in the Nueces district court under the provisions of the act of February 11, 1860. On May 26, 1860, claiming his ownership of the Santa Gertrudis rancho, he stated he had purchased it from Juan Mendiola's heirs, July 25, 1853, for $300. The case was delayed because of the Civil War and not settled, recognizing King's ownership, until July 31, 1868.[16]

Before the end of the year there was a good deal of excitement on Elizabeth Street. On December 3, King moved his family to Santa Gertrudis. Henrietta's father, Rev. Hiram Chamberlain, noted, "This day Captain King commenced packing up for a general move to the Rancho de Santa Gertrudis. I am truly sorry to part with them. But I suppose it is all for the best. This is a world of changes."[17] It was hard for Petra to understand why King moved nine-month-pregnant Henrietta to a remote rancho in the middle of the Wild Horse Desert. Sure enough, it was a problem. On December 15, Richard King II was born in a coach on the way to Brownsville as Henrietta was making a mad dash for help.[18] Mifflin and Petra were happy their friend had a male heir and Petra was thankful that she was not living out at the rancho. It was much preferred to give birth in town where there was access to clean water, a clean environment, midwives, and a doctor if necessary.[19]

Another major change was occurring in the Kenedy household. Luisa, now eighteen years old, was attracting attention from the young men around town. Not only was she attractive but also her stepfather was rich and very influential in the community. Mr. Kingsbury noted in his journal that, "Dalzell is a popular commander, especially with one of the young ladies at Kenedy's."[20] Capt. Robert Dalzell was no stranger to Mifflin and Petra. He had come from County Down, Ireland, to fight in the Mexican War and was in the Quartermaster Corp with Mifflin. He too became a steamboat captain. He also was a one-eighth partner with Mifflin in M. Kenedy & Co. and fought beside Mifflin against Cortina during the recent raids.[21]

On January 31, 1861, the Mifflin Kenedy family again gathered in the new church they had helped to build. This time it was for the baptism of their new daughter Phebe Ann Kenedy.[22] The weather was cold following an unusual major snow and ice storm the previous month. In this tranquil setting Mifflin and Petra presented their young daughter to Father Keralum for baptism.

Phebe's sponsors were Abelardo and Dolores Treviño.[23] Abelardo was from one of the wealthiest families in Mexico. After Charles Stillman left Brownsville following the Civil War Abelardo bought his home and the family occupied it for over one hundred years. Abelardo was the youngest of three brothers and one sister. His brother Manuel Treviño was a businessman who had vast land holdings in Mexico and was involved in the cotton business in Brownsville. He and Mifflin must have had many dealings, and Mifflin became acquainted with the entire family. Manuel later plotted with Porfirio

Lovely Luisa Vidal began attracting attention from the young men around town and married Robert Dalzell when she was eighteen in 1861. Courtesy Susan Hefley Seeds and Janis Hefley, descendants of Petra and Luisa Dalzell.

Díaz in his successful revolution to take over the government of Mexico and was later appointed Mexican consulate. There were stories of a large emerald that was used as a doorstop in Manuel's house. Abelardo continued to be a good friend to Mifflin and Petra and supported the family through the years.[24]

It became vital that Kenedy and his partners be informed of what was happening in Washington and on the East Coast. Information was critical to them. Each of the gentlemen subscribed to different periodicals that reflected their individual interests. Captain Kenedy subscribed to the *Atlantic Monthly*,

Robert Dalzell, Mifflin's son-in-law, became his partner in many businesses and his lifelong confidant. Brownsville Historical Association.

the *Pittsburgh Journal,* and *Miss Leslie's Magazine* for Petra and the girls. Stillman subscribed to the *New York Mercantile Times* and the *Galveston Times.* Hiram Chamberlain subscribed to *True Witness, Galveston Times,* and the *Indianola Courier.* E. J. Davis, future governor of Texas, preferred the Texas publications *Austin Intelligencer, State Gazette, Galveston Civilian,* and the *Galveston News.* San Román favored the *New York Courier, Corpus Chronicle, Galveston News, New York Mercantile Times,* and *Harper's Weekly.*[25]

Texas was soon making news that traveled all over the United States. Texas voted overwhelmingly to secede from the Union on February 1, 1861. By March 21, Rip Ford, who had been given command of the lower Rio Grande area for the Confederacy, had secured all the former Federal posts along that part of the river. A month later Fort Sumter was fired on and the Civil War between the North and South began.[26]

It took a while for the war to touch the shores of the Rio Grande. During the spring of 1861 the Kenedy family experienced both joy and sorrow. On April 29, 1861, their young eight-month-old daughter Phebe died. Only four months after her baptism the family gathered to bury her in the City Cemetery in Brownsville.[27] Again Petra's faith was called on to provide strength to help the family deal with the loss of their little sister and daughter. Petra and the family would have drawn some comfort from the Catholic Church's belief that little ones had a special place in heaven. Tejanos believed that the soul of a baptized but unconfirmed child would go directly to heaven as a little angel, *angelito,* so the death called for celebration rather than sadness.[28] This belief was later reflected in the quote chosen for the family burial plot in Brownsville, "Blessed are the pure in heart for they shall see God."[29] After Phebe, Petra had no more children. It could have been because of age, grief, or medical complications, but when she lost her youngest child there would be no more.

In the spring, Mifflin, Petra, and the family were able to share the joyous occasion of Luisa's wedding to their good friend Robert Dalzell. According to the 1860 census, Luisa was eighteen years old and Robert Dalzell was close to ten years older.[30] The wedding may have been a simple affair since the family was in mourning over Phebe's death. Even as Petra felt the grief over losing one child she would have been delighted that this beautiful daughter had found happiness, and wanted to marry and start her own family.

The women busied themselves preparing a trousseau for the bride. In the novel *Caballero,* Jovita González details the list of things required of the daughter of a don, a "ruling rigid as law." The bride must have six linen sheets with pillowcases to match, embroidered and hemstitched, and a similar set of cheaper cotton material. She should have one wool blanket with the wool carded, spun into thread, and woven by the bride herself. Perhaps Luisa did not do this, as the young woman in the novel did not, much to the distress of the matriarch. Six pillows were needed to match the blanket, which would be set on the floor of various rooms. She would need at least three tablecloths with napkins. For personal items, she would need new linen underwear of petticoats and chemises and ruffled drawers, two bright silk dresses for summer afternoons and two of calico for summer mornings. For winter wear she would need one velvet dress and one of cashmere or merino, and a black and a white mantilla.[31]

Robert Dalzell was a longtime friend and certainly had the financial means to take good care of Luisa. Captains Kenedy and King had offered him a job in 1852 on their steamers following the war. Dalzell had also been a pilot on the river during the war.[32] He was welcomed in the Kenedy household as a worthy suitor for their oldest daughter. He and Mifflin were business partners, and Mifflin often wrote to him through the years sharing personal cares and concerns. He seemed to be the closest male family member to Mifflin. Luisa, or Louisa as she would later style herself, settled down in Brownsville near Petra and Mifflin, their family, and friends. It would have been comforting to Petra not to have Luisa move away. Throughout her life, Petra remained very close to each of her daughters, and they spent a great deal of time visiting in Petra and Mifflin's home.[33]

Another wedding took place later in the summer on July 19, and it was a large and happy affair. Petra's close friend, Salomé Ballí de Young, married John McAllen at the Immaculate Conception Catholic Church in Brownsville. Father Parisot officiated at the ceremony and Charles Stillman and Simon Celaya were the witnesses. After the wedding a grand party was held at the Miller Hotel. John had purchased a thousand cigars from the store for the occasion and freely handed them out at the reception. John had helped Salomé run the store after her husband's death, and now they were starting a new life together along with her young son John J. Young. McAllen presented Salomé with a fine carriage and a team of black horses as a wedding present.[34]

While the social events in Brownsville continued, the war was moving closer. In July, about the same time as the battle of Bull Run, President Abraham Lincoln gave the order to blockade all seaports in the South, including Brazos Santiago on the American side of the Rio Grande. He saw that the Confederacy could be kept alive if it could trade cotton for war materials. Lincoln's problem was that half of the mouth of the Rio Grande belonged to Mexico, and as a neutral country they could not be blockaded. The other problem for the North was that they did not have the ships to accomplish this task, so it was near the end of 1861 before the effects were felt along the Rio Grande.[35] The merchants had problems from the Confederates as well as the Federals because the Confederate government put an embargo on all cotton hoping to force the Europeans to recognize the South in return for allowing the cotton to flow again.[36]

Petra was surprised at how fast they were enveloped in the war. They had to scramble to keep up with all the changes, and Mifflin was involved on several fronts. The recent investment in King & Co. seemed threatened since the price of cattle was down because of the blockades and the difficulty in shipping the cattle east. Two solutions were tried. One was to drive the cattle to East Texas and ship them into the Confederacy, and the other was to sell salt that the Confederacy desperately needed from the salt marshes on the ranch. The three partners each handled different parts of their diversified interests. King took over the management of Stillman's Laureles ranch as well as the Santa Gertrudis rancho. Stillman was busy in Brownsville and Matamoros arranging for the cotton business.[37] Mifflin was in charge of the river transportation and keeping everything moving.

The beginning of 1862 saw the merchants and their families along the Rio Grande positioning themselves as the war escalated. Many of them were making arrangements to leave Brownsville and move their families and businesses to Matamoros for safety. José San Román was one of the first to move to Matamoros in the early 1860s to wholesale cotton to textile firms in New York, England, and Germany to avoid U.S. government authorities.[38] Petra watched as her neighbors began to leave and knew that she and her family would soon have to make some decisions. To add to all of the chaos, France, Spain, and England, seeing the vulnerable state of Mexico and its financially depleted government under President Benito Juárez, had landed troops in Mexico under the pretext of collecting debts the government refused to pay. England and Spain withdrew but France moved to take over Mexico. All of these countries were eyeing the Confederacy, the Union, and Mexico as valuable objects for takeover.[39]

M. Kenedy & Co., under the leadership of its partners, was also making plans. Richard King, along with his family, decided to stay at the Santa Gertrudis and run the land operation that would include both selling supplies to and assisting the cotton caravans that would soon form a solid white line from the Confederate South to the Rio Grande and its ports. The King Ranch was on the route traveled by the wagon trains and was one of the spots where they stopped to replenish their stock and supplies. Charles Stillman was busy arranging their Mexico connections so that they could do business under the Mexican flag. Stillman used Jerry Galvan in Matamoros to ship Confederate cotton to New York for the northern cotton mills, and to England and France. Stillman also used José Morell of Monterrey and Santiago Ytúrria and his brothers Bernardo and Francisco as business associates in Matamoros. At first the ships sailed from Brazos Santiago carrying Confederate cotton to New York and then returned with boots, powder, cloth, coffee, soap, arms, and other supplies. Later when the Union cracked down further, the ships sailed to Havana and Nassau and then on to their ports of destination.[40] Mifflin never agreed with blockade running and certainly not in investing in it. He sent a letter blasting King for using $16,000 of Kenedy's money to buy interest in the steamship *Ike Davis*. Mifflin was a staid, cautious businessman, but he was attracted to reckless daredevils such as King. The two did not always act in concert and when they disagreed it was over money and risk taking.[41] In the meantime, Mifflin was left to run the operations in Brownsville and also Matamoros later in the war. That put Petra and the family in the line of fire and he, too, was thinking of where to send them for safety.

Petra had two reasons to celebrate early in 1862. On January 2, 1862, Petra welcomed her first grandchild into the world. Luisa and Robert honored Mifflin by naming their first son for him. Robert Mifflin Dalzell was born on

The small Mexican smuggler's cove of Bagdad, Mexico, underwent an amazing change during the Civil War. New shanties were built overnight as hundreds of men moved in to load, unload, and operate the boats. Next to the rundown shacks were buildings holding millions of dollars in gold and silver. Note the harbor filled with ships. Brownsville Historical Association.

January 2, 1862, in Texas.[42] The second reason was the success of Mifflin's business. In February in a letter to King at Santa Gertrudis, Charles Stillman wrote, "Yesterday we were all in great glea [*sic*]. Kenedy saw a 100,000 in his vaults, twelve vessels reporting having arrived in the offering with a prospect of shipping 20,000 bales of cotton at 5 per bale and upwards freight would repay running expenses."[43] Petra's family fortune was being made from Confederate cotton, and that wealth would grow into millions in the years to come. For the few wealthy merchants left in Brownsville the high prices would have been something they could handle, but for the poorer people the blockade was causing severe problems. Shoes and boots were in big demand. Flour was selling for two and one half times previous prices, from $5 to $12. Prices were high and it would not be long before household goods disappeared altogether from the market.[44] To make matters worse the soldiers at Fort Brown, as well as the citizens, were suffering a severe drought through the summer. It was so bad that by July 31, the *Fort Brown Flag* reported that "the corn and pastures need rain, the cisterns have evaporated and the Provost Marshall has shut down the whiskey stills."[45]

By February 24, 1862, the cotton merchants found the passage at Brazos Santiago blockaded by Union ships; it was time for the next stage of their plan.

Miller Hotel on East Elizabeth and Thirteenth Streets, Brownsville. Henry Miller began construction of the hotel in 1848, and it was opened for business in 1849. Here Adrian Vidal often enjoyed a good time and stabled his horses. Brownsville Historical Association.

José San Román, Francisco Ytúrria, the Treviño brothers, Mifflin Kenedy, Charles Stillman, Richard King, British consul Louis Black, and Col. Rip Ford held an emergency meeting to decide on how to circumvent the blockade. On Ford's suggestion, M. Kenedy & Co. listed its boats under Mexican registry although they were worried about Mexico's unstable politics. This allowed them to pass through the blockade.[46] On March 11, 1862, Stillman wrote King and told him that their boats would have "turkey buzzard at their masthead in a day or two." He also said, "Affairs look dark ahead. Prepare for squalls and keep your affairs snug as you can."[47]

In late 1862, Stillman wrote his wife Elizabeth, "I am winding up my affairs, commercial affairs, as fast a possible, and placing what funds I can gather together in my friends in Europe, so that in case I should get my head knocked off, you and the children will get a nest egg there."[48]

With all the commerce developing at the mouth of the Rio Grande the small Mexican smuggler's cove of Bagdad underwent an amazing change. Its wharves, protected from the sea and wind, stood stacked high with war goods taken from the vessels offshore and with thousands of bales of cotton waiting to be loaded and taken to Europe.[49] New shanties were built overnight as hundreds of men moved in to load, unload, and operate the boats. The *New York*

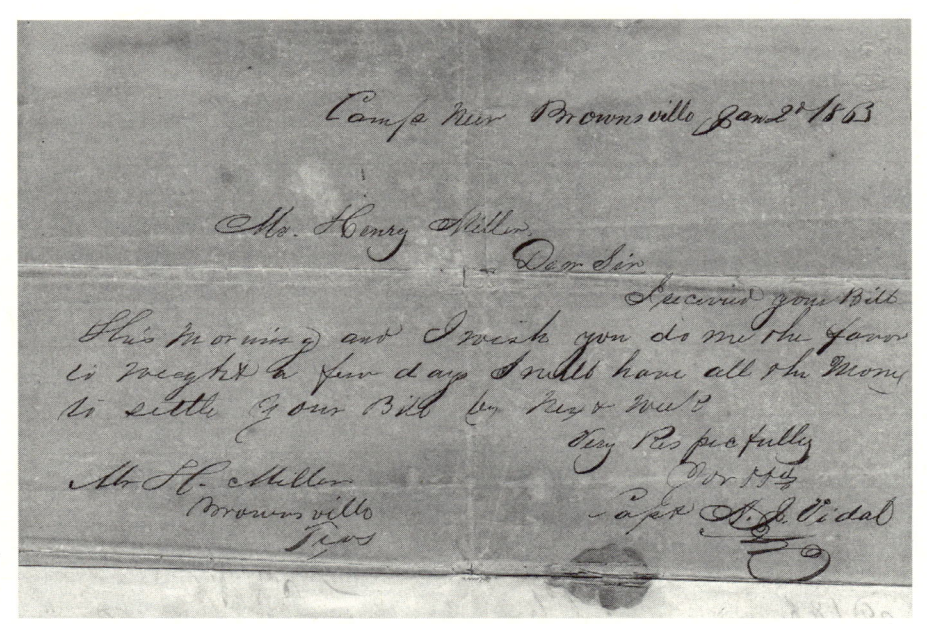

Letter possibly written by Capt. A. J. Vidal to Mr. Henry Miller requesting more time to pay his bill, which would show that Adrian could write in English. However, a scribe could have written the letter. Brownsville Historical Association.

The Putegnat Drug Store, photograph taken in 1904, was one of the first pharmacies in Brownsville, founded by J. L. Putegnat. George Miller Putegnat, second from right, is standing in front of his drug store, carrying on the family tradition of J. L., his father. Brownsville Historical Association.

Rosa Vidal married Joseph Luke Putegnat when she was eighteen, in 1862. After the wedding she took her half-sister, Sarah, who was five years old, home with her and her new husband, as Sarah did not want her godmother and sister to leave. Courtesy of Jesse (Sam) Thornham, Joe Thornham, McGoohan families.

Herald wrote that the town was full of blockade-runners, desperadoes, the worst of both sexes, and houses of drink and worse. All vices thrived in Bagdad. Yet next to these rundown shacks were buildings holding millions of dollars in gold and silver.[50]

The fall of 1862 brought major changes again to Petra's life. In October Adrian joined the Confederate Army in San Antonio as a private. He was in the Confederate Thirty-Third Texas Cavalry, and it was thought that he brought to the cavalry a group of men willing to serve with him. These men were mainly Tejanos and they brought a special skill to the army. They had grown up along the Rio Grande and knew the land and how to travel both by water and land. This skill would be invaluable when the Confederate troops, who were unfamiliar with the land, were trying to cross the miles and miles of desolate prairie that all looked the same. Adrian was later promoted to captain and some speculated it was because he was Mifflin's stepson. A fellow soldier described Adrian as having a dark complexion with hazel eyes and black hair. He said he was a vain trifling fellow without any experience who cared for nothing except gambling and drinking.[51] Evidently his fellow soldiers thought very little of him and would think less of him in the months to come. Adrian was seventeen years old and like most of the boys his age wanted to be part of the action. Adrian obviously enjoyed a good time and spent time at the Miller Hotel in Brownsville. In January 1863, as noted earlier, Capt. A. J. Vidal wrote from Camp New Brownsville, or had a scribe write for him, asking the proprietor, Mr. Henry Miller, for a few days so he could pay his bill in full the next week. If Adrian did write the letter it shows that he was capable of writing in a second language in a competent manner indicating his educational achievement. There has been and still is a question of whether Adrian joined up to serve as a spy for the Union and the Cortinistas or joined the Confederates in good faith. Petra said goodbye to Adrian in 1862 with a heavy heart. During this same month, the port of Galveston fell and the ships off of Bagdad went from twenty to between two hundred and three hundred by late 1864. Bagdad became the only sea outlet the Confederates had.[52]

Many of the Confederate soldiers in the Texas Volunteers were Mexicans who had left their army for better pay, better food, and nicer uniforms. Col. John Ford was experienced and qualified in working with Mexicans; when he was in command the situation was stable. When General Bee took over, however, the Mexicans distrusted him and there was a mutiny. The situation was straightened out, but feelings of distrust remained on both sides.[53]

At the end of the year, Petra's daughter, Rosa, was planning to marry Joseph Luke Putegnat on December 26. Again, one of Petra's daughters was marrying into a well-respected family in Brownsville. Joe's father, John Pierre Putegnat, had moved to Matamoros between 1840 and 1850 and then to

Petra Vela de Kenedy. Brownsville Historical Association.

Mifflin Kenedy photograph found in a locket he had given to Sarah on October 23, 1886.

Brownsville. He made trading trips deep into Mexico and built a large mercantile business. His sons J. P. and J. L. became pharmacists. J. P. practiced in Brownsville and Rio Grande City while J. L ("Joe") operated one of the first pharmacies in Brownsville. His store, Botica del León, was founded in 1860, offering medicines, lumber, paint, turpentine, perfumes, stationery, garden seed, fancy goods, candy, and soda water. J. L. is still recognized in the United States Dispensatory for his research on native drugs and herbs. One of these drugs, Chaparre amargosa, was successfully used at that time for the treatment of dysentery and the various fevers that were common. An interesting legend is connected to the discovery of another herb, guace. The story has it that an

Indian was watching a battle between a roadrunner, or *paisano*, with a rattlesnake. When the snake struck the bird, it availed itself of a nearby herb and then killed the reptile. The Indian later used this herb to treat the bites of snakes and venomous insects. J. L. Putegnat made an extract of the drug, and it was frequently used for the treatment of venomous stings and bites.[54]

At the time of their wedding, Joe was twenty-four and Rosa was probably eighteen because the 1860 census had her age at sixteen two years before. Rosa and Joe, whose father was a French Huguenot, were married at Petra's home since he was not Catholic. Witnesses to the wedding were Jesse Grasham, Mary Gallagher, Mifflin Kenedy, and Elisha Kenedy.[55]

A revealing family story reflects the affection that developed between the half-sisters and half-brothers through the years. At the time of Rosa's wedding little Sarah was five years old. Sarah loved Rosa, who was her godmother, and she did not want Rosa to leave after the wedding. Rosa and Joe's house was just down the street from Petra and Mifflin's at Elizabeth and Ninth Street, so they took Sarah home with them after the wedding. Petra had a Mexican servant called "Aunt Nana," and when Rosa married, Petra wanted Rosa to have her; Aunt Nana stayed with the Putegnat family all her life.[56]

As 1862 came to a close, Petra had seen a dramatic change in her family over the last two years. Her older children had all left the house. Three of her daughters, Concepción, Luisa, and Rosa, were married. Adrian had joined the Confederate Army and was now in the middle of the fighting, and she and Mifflin were surrounded by the turmoil of war. They had lost their baby daughter Phebe and welcomed their first grandchild, Robert Mifflin Dalzell.

CHAPTER 5

1863:
War Closes in on the Rio Grande Valley

Sometime in 1863 Petra and Mifflin decided to send their oldest three sons to Pennsylvania to stay with Mifflin's mother and sister and continue their education in a safer environment. Salomé Ballí de Young McAllen and her sons went to New York for safety in 1864, so things were heating up enough in the war for concern to grow.[1] Tomás (Thomas) was ten years old, Santiago (James) eight, and Gregorio (John Gregory) seven. The boys needed to be in school and Mifflin knew they would receive a good education in Pennsylvania. Even though they would not be completely out of the war in Coatesville they would be in Quaker country and, he hoped, removed from most of the conflicts. Brownsville schools closed as the northern army successfully blockaded the mouth of the Rio Grande on the Texas side and began to move troops toward Texas to take over the last transportation outlet left to the Confederacy.[2]

John Gregory later wrote in a deposition that before he and his brothers, Thomas and James, left for Pennsylvania, he went downtown and watched as the Brownsville men who joined the Confederate Army filed through the Washington Street Gate, marching east to war. He also said that he and his brothers spent four years in Pennsylvania, from 1864 to 1868.[3] He made no mention of his mother, of Sarah, who was six years old, or Willie, who was four. Petra, Sarah, and Willie must have stayed with Mifflin in Brownsville until it became unsafe; they then moved to Matamoros with him during the last two years of the war. John wrote that they left via New Orleans, traveling up the Mississippi and Ohio rivers to Cincinnati and by rail to Philadelphia. According to John, a Mr. Rowe accompanied the boys.[4] This may have been Mr. E. D. Rowe, who had been involved with Captain King in marketing mules in New Orleans. He would have been familiar with the boats and routes from Texas up the Mississippi.[5] Mifflin could not have accompanied them because of fear of arrest as a prominent Confederate supporter. By the time the boys started up the Mississippi, Union forces had secured the river after the battle of Vicksburg in the summer of 1863. The boys passed through the city of Cairo, Illinois, at the confluence of the Mississippi and Ohio rivers. During the war, Cairo had become a major Civil War medical center and the success of the Union Army had sent a steady stream of about 14,000 Confederate prisoners there awaiting assignments to northern prisons.[6]

Petra knew that war might surround her boys in the North and could only hope they would be safe. She knew there were no guarantees that Pennsylvania would not be engulfed in the war. The Battle of Gettysburg in Pennsylvania commenced on July 1, 1863, approximately seventy-five miles from Coatesville, with some of the fiercest fighting in the war. From July 1 to 3, there were 25,000 casualties for the North and 28,000 for the South.[7] Petra had no way of knowing how long the war would last or when she would see her sons again.

Petra was aware that she would miss an important part of their formative years, and that they would be going into a Quaker household from her strong Catholic home. They were still little boys when she said goodbye to them but she was afraid when she saw them again they would not only be older but changed in many ways. Petra's children had been raised in a multicultural world. They spoke both Spanish and English fluently and many of their friends were Mexican and American, Tejano and Anglo. The food they ate, their church, their clothes, and their friends were all products of the bicultural home she and Mifflin had established and the society in which they lived. Now she and Mifflin were sending them into a different culture, of which the boys knew nothing, and into a land that was also involved in the war but with sympathies on the Union side. Petra and Mifflin felt strongly about their sons' education, and that commitment in addition to the danger at home drove them to make this difficult decision. They shared their sorrow and worry as they said goodbye to the boys, encouraging them to write but knowing that letters were going to be difficult to send. The boys would have to draw strength from one another and from the love of their family. As hard as it must have been for Petra to send her small boys off into unknown and dangerous waters, they, in turn, were probably excited about an ocean voyage, a steamboat trip up the Mississippi, and about seeing the cities and countryside of their father's homeland.

In Pennsylvania, Mifflin's mother Sarah (Sallie) and his sister Jo (Sarah Josephine) welcomed them. In 1863 Coatesville was called a "beautiful and healthy village" located in the great Chester Valley on the east bank of the Brandywine River. This agricultural valley was described as a land of "milk and honey."[8] What a contrast this provided for the three boys, coming from the dusty barren land surrounding the Rio Grande during a time of drought. The boys arrived in the midst of a business boom in a town with fine schools, a handsome town hall, two banks, churches, and a dry goods store. The town was thriving and putting in a new water system for its citizens.[9]

Mifflin's family accepted the responsibility of the boys and enrolled them in school. Mifflin's mother had raised sons, but the presence of three young boys was perhaps a bit overwhelming, especially with the war surrounding them. Life was very different for the young boys as well. They were living in a Quaker household where even the English language was spoken with a different accent and phraseology, which was hard to understand. Spanish was not spoken at all and the clothing, food, and religion were different. The boys did have one another for company but they must have spent many lonely hours wishing for their family back home and hoping for a letter bringing news from Texas. John Gregory said that he saw trains coming through Coatesville transporting Confederate prisoners. The ladies of the town were kind to the prisoners and distributed bread and food to them.[10] John and his older brothers knew that their father and his friends had supported Texas secession and were working actively to supply the Confederate troops in the field. They also knew that some of the prisoners on the trains might be from Texas or even Brownsville.

The boys attended public school in Coatesville from 1864 until 1868.[11] The Township School Board had declared that the schools would be kept open eight months during the 1866 school year allowing for school two months before and six months after the harvest. They also levied a tax of four mills on the dollar for school purposes and two mills for building purposes and were in the process of building a new and larger schoolhouse.[12]

Back at home, Adrian was the only young man in the immediate family to join the Confederacy and fight for the South. Mifflin's new son-in-law, Joe Putegnat, had two brothers, John P. and William, who had been in military school in Victoria, Texas, when the war started. They left school and joined the Confederate Army as artillerymen. John P. was captured by the Federals and transported to the Elmira prison in New York. Putegnat and nine others succeeded in tunneling out of prison. To decide how far they needed to dig, Putegnat tied a thread to a stone, and by cautiously throwing it so guards would not see him, he hit the fence. The thread was slowly drawn back and measured and the distance measured was sixty-eight feet. They began the tunnel from their tent, using a knife and their hands for the digging. Putegnat was the only one with an extra shirt so his shirt was used as a sack to take the dirt away. The tunnelers overcame the obstacles of foul air as the tunnel lengthened, and of straightening the tunnel when they discovered they were slanting it: They were all right-handed and because they were lying on their left sides to dig they were going toward the right instead of straight to the fence. On the morning of October 6 the tunnelers reached their goal and sent word back that they had struck a post in the fence. After surfacing on the other side of the fence, the men went out in pairs, Putegnat picking up two stones on the way out. J. P. eventually returned to the southern lines.[13]

Matamoros and Bagdad continued to be extremely important to the survival of the Confederacy. The supplies that arrived through the port were its lifeblood. One ship named the *Will O' the Wisp* was unloading its cargo when it was discovered that on board were thirty-seven barrels and 190 kegs of gunpowder and 89,000 percussion caps not listed on the ship's inventory. The kegs of gunpowder were found in bags of shoes and large cases marked "clothing."[14] Robert Kingsbury reported that everything in Matamoros was extremely expensive and housing very hard to find. The Union was now turning its full attention to Texas, and the Union blockade was tightening around the Rio Grande. He said that on March 10 a Federal transport had arrived at the mouth of the river with a Col. E. J. Davis and a Col. W. W. Montgomery; two hundred Confederate deserters went aboard. He also reported that the Confederate dollar was down to twenty cents in value.[15] Shortly after, on April 1, 1863, Col. A. J. L. Fremantle of England observed seventy merchant ships off of Bagdad.[16] When men like Colonel Fremantle visited Brownsville and Matamoros they were entertained and courted because everyone was in the business of making money. Confederate Gen. Hamilton P. Bee, commander of Fort Brown, frequently entertained his English guests with cocktail parties, formal dinners, and fandangos in Matamoros. Colonel Fremantle wrote that he had gone to a cocktail party with General Bee that lasted for an hour and a half and some of the drinks had five or six different liquids in them. Prussian Consul Oettling invited Colonel Fremantle to a fandango in Matamoros. He said they started about 9:30 P.M. and continued until daylight. The setting was decorated with paper lanterns, and benches were placed in a square to allow for dancing in the center. Surrounding the benches were gambling tables and drinking booths. The crowds mostly conducted themselves in a formal manner, exceptions being some Texans who came from Brownsville.[17]

Colonel Fremantle was also treated to a trip to the Santa Gertrudis rancho while he was in the United States. In the spring he traveled there from Matamoros. In his journal he said that Mr. and Mrs. King had gone to Brownsville but at the ranch General Bee's wife greeted him. General Bee may well have placed her there to be out of harm's way. Fremantle described her as "a nice lively little woman, a red-hot Southerner, glorying in the facts that she had no Northern relations or friends, and that she is a member of the Church of England."[18]

Plaza de Hidalgo in Matamoros, Mexico, with the cathedral and Mexican customs house in the background. During the Civil War many Confederates lived in Matamoros during the Union occupation of Brownsville. Brownsville Historical Association.

During the spring of 1863, while some of the people were engaged in entertaining, Petra watched as Mifflin struggled to get bales of cotton into Mexico while King kept the cotton moving through the drought-stricken Wild Horse Desert. Once the cotton reached the Rio Grande it was ferried across the river on flatboats operated with a series of pulleys and wheels. Two-wheeled oxcarts, three bales per cart, provided transportation down the river road to Bagdad, where it was transferred to vessels waiting to take it to foreign ports.[19] M. Kenedy & Co. had been made the sole suppliers to the Confederate forces, and they were paid in bales of cotton. The contract called for 3,000 bales of cotton to be delivered to the company to cover the cost, but until that cotton could be secured and sold Mifflin would have to make heavy advances for the supplies.[20] It was helpful and financially beneficial that the government contract allowed them and their agents to use conscripts in the transportation of the cotton. Mifflin, ever the businessman, and his partners were making a fortune. Cotton sold in the interior of the Confederacy for a few cents a pound and in Matamoros for about fifty cents. During the course of the war Stillman, King, and Kenedy received a commission equal to 2.5 percent of the gross value of the goods they hauled to the Nueces Strip and Rio Grande Valley and another 2.5 percent to deliver and store it in Matamoros, and they were paid in gold. Additionally, the partners were the suppliers to Fort Brown and received a 15 percent profit on the supplies they delivered. This profit was paid by their right to five hundred bales of cotton per month, and the men profited by about

$60,000 per month each and avoided the use of Confederate currency. Stillman, because of his shrewd investments, became one of the wealthiest men in the world by the end of the Civil War.[21]

By 1863 the price was up to eighty cents in gold to the merchants purchasing cotton to ship to England and the United States' eastern coast.[22] One contract dated May 1, 1863, between M. Kenedy & Co. and Major Charles Russell, quartermaster for the Confederate Army in Brownsville, agreed to furnish the company no fewer then five hundred bales of cotton per month in exchange for supplies for about 2,000 troops. The five hundred bales of cotton at that time were worth $125,000. Wagons piled high with cotton were coming from all over the South and leaving the Santa Gertrudis rancho heading for the border and Mexico. The supplies for the troops came into Matamoros and then had to be loaded back on the carts and sent back the way they came, to the Confederacy. In order to pass inspection at the customs house in Matamoros some creative labeling was employed. Cases of Enfield guns were labeled "hollow-ware," kegs and barrels branded "bean flour" were gunpowder, percussion caps became "canned goods," and cargoes of lead were labeled "bat metal."[23] It was an innovative method of slipping goods to the Confederacy, but it was only a matter of time until the Union moved to stop this lifeline.

The Union was winning on the battlefield with victories at Gettysburg and Vicksburg, which cut into the Confederacy, but the failure of the blockade in Texas kept the Confederacy alive. The ability to trade cotton for war materials was a big problem for the North, with wagon trains of cotton from plantations in Arkansas, Louisiana, Texas, and perhaps some states east of the Mississippi moving in long lines on what became known as the Cotton Road.[24] The Mexicans called it *la época del algodón*, "the time of the cotton."[25] Cotton was being shipped from Matamoros to New York as well as to Europe, which continued throughout the war. Confederate Gen. Hamilton Bee said that pistols and carbines could be bought in New York and shipped to Matamoros, an extreme irritant to Union generals.[26] In addition to this, with French control in Mexico there would be a European power on the border of Confederate Texas. It seemed to Union strategists the best way to prevent this was to occupy Texas.[27]

Adrian was now a captain in the Confederate Army and was stationed at Boca del Rio with orders to guard the mouth of the Rio Grande. Among the men he had recruited to fight with him were members of the Garza family, one of the earliest families in Cameron County. Remigio Garza and his sons Juan and Santos Garza fought for the Confederacy around Brownsville in Adrian's company.[28] In June of 1863, Adrian wrote that his men were without supplies. He reported his company was "entirely destitute of camp necessities" and asked headquarters in Brownsville for kettles, iron pots, and spades. Five days later he asked for one Sibley tent and hats, shirts, pants, and fifty pairs of shoes.[29] Ironically, his stepfather was in charge of supplying the army. The family story is that Adrian appealed to Mifflin for the things he wanted and when he did not get them he appealed to Petra and got them.[30]

Despite the lack of supplies, Adrian displayed courage and daring and received praise for his bravery in the capture of a Federal gunboat and its crew in July.[31] What happened between July and October has been and still is an unsolved mystery. Adrian decided to desert the Confederate Army and turn traitor. He did not just leave the army but planned an attack with his men on Brownsville and Fort Brown. Some believe that Adrian became disenchanted with the Confederates due to a lack of supplies and support and looked for a better deal, which came in the form of an offer of gold from the Union sympathizers in Mexico if he would join their cause.[32] John Haynes had received a commission as a colonel in the Union Army with the assignment to raise a company of cavalry to fight the Confederates across the river in Texas and to pay them in gold.[33] Others felt that Adrian was an arrogant, self-indulged man who could see that the Confederates were losing and simply wanted to be on the winning side. It could well have been admiration for Cortina, whose influence would only be known later, and Vidal may have also been in communication with the Union naval commander blocking the coast.[34] Whether it was bribes or admiration for Cortina, the mutiny was the final straw for General Bee.[35]

For two reasons, General Bee had good cause for anxiety. He had reported that the Mexicans could not be trusted, and that if Matamoros fell to the Union, *guerrilleros* would immediately flock to their side. He was worried about a "large and effective force of a race embittered against us by real or imaginary wrongs."[36] Second, the Union Army had finally decided that they had to shut down the flow of cotton and supplies through the Rio Grande outlet, and Gen. Nathaniel P. Banks, commander of Union operations in Louisiana, had devised a plan to draw the Confederate troops away from the Rio Grande to East Texas while he moved troops down to Texas to seal the mouth of the river. At the time, General Bee only had 1,200 men to defend the entire river, and the Confederate command kept reducing his forces.[37] During this time some of the Confederate forces under Col. James Duff at the mouth of the river crossed the river in an unauthorized mission and kidnapped E. J. Davis, the future governor of Texas, and Capt. W. W. Montgomery. They brought the prisoners to Texas and hanged Montgomery for the murder of a respected Tejano, Isidro Vela. Judge Vela was a strong Confederate supporter and county judge of Zapata County in 1860.[38] General Bee managed to save Davis and return him to Mexico, but Bee knew that the *renegados* wanted revenge for that act. Then Cortina, always sensing an opportunity, reappeared in support of the Juaristas, became "General" Cortina, and supported the Union cause. On October 26, Duff's cavalry was recalled and General Bee was left with only nineteen men to defend Brownsville and the millions of dollars' worth of Confederate cotton and supplies.[39] This set the stage for Adrian's next move.

Because of his depleted force, Bee sent D. H. Dashiell and Private Litteral to Boca del Rio to order Vidal and his men back to Fort Brown to help defend Brownsville. A report came back to Bee that Vidal and his men had deserted and that with the help of the Union sympathizers in Mexico were going to attack Fort Brown that evening. Bee disregarded that rumor because the young captain had always obeyed orders and he had faith in his abilities. He probably would have been unprepared for the attack except for the heroic efforts of Private Literal. Vidal and his men had received Dashiell and Literal into their group and then turned on them. They killed Dashiell, who was the Texas adjutant general's son, and shot Literal in the mouth. Adrian's pent-up anger and resentment of the Anglos and Confederates must have come bursting forth. Literal managed to escape, rode to Fort Brown, and warned General Bee of the impending attack by Vidal and about one hundred men. He could not talk because of his ghastly wound and had to scribble his story on several scraps of paper. He managed to convey what had happened when he and Dashiell had delivered the message to Vidal. They had joined Vidal and his men and they started toward Brownsville. About two miles down the road Vidal had stopped the group and ordered that they prepare supper. A fire was started and Adrian invited the two men to have a drink with him. Suddenly, without warning, Vidal and his men opened fire.[40] Meanwhile, Adrian and his men rode toward Brownsville, fully intent on capturing the fort and shouting, "Death to the Americans." The attack was probably meant to be a duplication of Cortina's raid. However, the *Vidalistas* passed only within a mile of Brownsville.[41]

General Bee wasted no time and sent a man to call back the three companies that had departed, formed a local militia, and mobilized two large artillery pieces to prepare for the attack.[42] Bee sent Lt. Jack Vinton and ten men to engage Vidal, and they did so and fought him to within one mile of town. Vidal, realizing that the private had probably reached the fort and was able to warn them of the attack, decided not to attack Brownsville.[43]

Adrian led his men to Ramireño, a rancho in the next bend of the river. An account published in a Laredo newspaper years later, in 1891, related the story of what happened next. At the rancho, Vidal captured a cow and was in the process of slaughtering it for his men when the owner, Mr. Jeff Barthelow, who knew Adrian and his family well, tried to stop him. Mr. Barthelow had been the sheriff of Cameron County. Adrian shook hands warmly with him and then signaled to his men to tie him up and walked him into the woods. His men then ransacked the house, demanded money and arms, and took his young son's saddle. A neighbor named Antonio Cruz, the young son's godfather, came and asked them to give the little boy's saddle back. They answered by stabbing him, tying his hands, and turning him into the woods. Meanwhile, Mrs. Barthelow was waiting for her husband to return when a young Mexican boy came running out of the woods crying for her to escape, as Vidal had murdered her husband and Antonio Cruz, and would soon be there to kill her, too. He told her to flee to the ferry crossing and he would try to find a boat. She snatched up her baby and other children and ran toward the water. When he returned to her she asked the boy how her husband had died. He told her that Vidal and his men had told Barthelow that he was an American and had brought to justice some of their friends many years ago and he must now hang. Since Cruz was his companion, they said, he must hang, too. They then chased Barthelow up and down the woods, inflicting cruel blows with swords, then prepared a rope to hang him. He asked them to take off his hat so he could pray to God for his wife and little ones. They told him they were also going to hang her and the children, and they did hang both men. That is when the boy ran to tell her to flee.[44]

While Mrs. Barthelow was huddling near the ferry location, Mr. Pierce Randolph and his wife came upon her. They were from Ohio and were traveling from Brownsville to Nueces County when they heard the crying of the children. They decided they would try to help her find a boat, and if they couldn't find one then they would take her with them as far as the Santa Gertrudis rancho where they would be safe. Mr. Randolph left his wife Amanda with the Barthelow children and he and Mrs. Barthelow and the young Mexican boy set off to look for a boat. Amanda turned around in surprise when she heard the trampling of a horse and saw a Mexican riding toward her. She told the Barthelows' young son to run for help and to find Pierce. The man identified himself as "Vasquez, the outlaw, and an admirer of beauty." He then seized Amanda and threw her up in the saddle and galloped off, leaving the two little ones screaming at the top of their lungs. On his return Pierce was frantic that his wife was gone. He saw a cloud of dust coming and thought it must be Adrian and his men. It turned out that it was Capt. Matt Nolan and a company of Texas Rangers on their way to Brownsville. They had passed the Mexican with a bundle in front of him but had no idea that it was a woman. They immediately left to rescue her. When Vasquez saw them coming, he threw Amanda into the river. All the Rangers jumped into the water and pulled her from the river, dripping. They reunited her with her husband and she appeared to be fine.[45]

When Captain Duff and his cavalry arrived back in Brownsville on October 29 in answer to General Bee's summons, he was ordered to go after Adrian Vidal, who used to be in his company. Capt. Richard Taylor left in fast pursuit and when he arrived at the ford upriver he was only minutes behind the *Vidalistas* as they crossed into the safety of Mexico. He could see a large body of Texas Unionists waiting for Adrian and his men on the Mexican bank of the Rio Grande. General Bee immediately wrote Gov. Manuel Ruiz of Tamaulipas demanding that he assist in capturing Adrian and his men. The governor wrote Bee saying he would send men out to capture him and later reported that Cortina had captured some of the *Vidalistas*. Bee was not convinced that Cortina did this and thought that Adrian was actually working with Cortina and was hiding out in Matamoros. He soon realized that Cortina had instigated the entire affair.[46] Vidal was called "wild and reckless," "daring," a "crazy young man."[47] He was surely all of those things.

Many different people could have hidden Adrian in Matamoros. Mifflin had his offices there and probably had already moved Petra and the younger children to Matamoros for safety. There were the Unionists who encouraged him to desert in the first place. He was not given up or captured and soon a more important development made his capture less important. On November 1, 1863, in the middle of a Gulf storm, twenty-six boats carrying nearly 7,000 Union soldiers appeared at the mouth of the Rio Grande. As soon as the Union forces were spotted trying to make the difficult landing on Texas soil, the rumors began to fly that the Union troops were at Brownsville's doors. None of this was true but General Bee, who had been told in case of an enemy landing that he must evacuate Brownsville and allow no supplies or cotton to fall into Union hands, began preparing for retreat, organizing a wagon train with tentative plans to ship the cotton to Matamoros by steamers. On November 3, Bee, in a panic, cut short the loading of his supply train, dumped his siege guns into the river, and prepared to order the military installations and supplies burned.[48]

Charles Stillman wrote his wife, Elizabeth, "It was a hot and awful sight, men, women, children screaming and flying to the other banks of the river for safety." More than four hundred Unionists hissed and cursed the Confederates from the other bank of the river. "Peril was around me on all sides," Bee wrote.[49]

Then Bee and his staff had an excellent dinner at Henry Miller's and drank an abundance of champagne and told Mr. Miller that he had better get all the carts he could hire and go to the commissary stores and take whatever he chose in payment, for they had no money. They returned to the garrison and the order was given to fire the quarters. They did and soon the fort was on fire. Bee then ordered the long rows of cotton to be fired, as he had not completed making arrangements for their transport. Soon the town of Brownsville was engulfed in fire and smoke as Bee and his men beat a hasty retreat north toward the Wild Horse Desert.[50]

The townspeople were in a complete panic. The roads to the ferry were quickly filled with women and children screaming and rushing toward the waterfront with hastily gathered possessions. Mr. William Neale hurried his wife and children to the ferry. A strong south wind was blowing and the ferry was covered with black smoke and was barely visible. Everyone was trying to get into the boats and the men were crowding the women and children out of the way. Mr. Neale knew the danger because 8,000 pounds of gunpowder were stored less than a hundred yards from the ferry. He snatched up a double-barreled shotgun and threatened everyone until the women and children were in the boats. He had all of them safely in the boats when the explosion came that shot firebrands into the air and started fires all along the waterfront.[51] M. Kenedy & Co. was one of the buildings that caught fire, and before the night was out two city blocks, the fort, and the cotton on the levee were all destroyed. Mayor Dye, along with volunteers, was able to keep the entire town from burning, but the next night Brownsville was filled with murderous and drunken riffraff sacking and running unchecked through the town, killing people in the streets and looting stores.[52] Gen. José María Cobos and a group of his men helped to stop the fire and the looting and restore order in the burned-out town. When Union General Banks arrived in town he found it necessary to declare martial law to restore order. In a very short time General Cobos crossed to Matamoros, joined forces with Cortina, defeated Governor Ruiz, assumed the governorship, decided to side with the Imperialists, and was executed by Cortina who then assumed the governorship. Such was Mexican politics at the time.[53]

Rip Ford and the other Confederate leaders were embittered by Bee's seemingly cowardly retreat and thought a deeper conspiracy was perhaps behind Bee's quick exit. Confederate Quartermaster Russell had been taking bribes from a number of Mexican firms for Confederate cotton and the fire was partially set to cover his theft.[54]

After Adrian crossed into Mexico he joined Cortina and his men. General Banks, after securing Brownsville for the Union, crossed to Matamoros on November 17 to visit with Cortina. There he discovered the Confederate traitor Adrian Vidal and Union sympathizer J. L. Haynes with Cortina. It appeared that Vidal and Cortina were helping Haynes recruit men up and down the river to join John Haynes's cavalry. He wanted to use them to break up the cotton traffic on the Mexican side of the river.[55] Adrian may have been using this opportunity to strike back at Mifflin and to declare his long-felt loyalty to his real father's homeland of Mexico.

October and November were difficult times for Petra and Mifflin. Their

The Putegnat house was the headquarters in Brownsville for the Federal troops, shown here with Federals on the porch. Originally constructed in Point Isabel and used as the first customs house in that port, it was moved to Brownsville and relocated at Elizabeth and Ninth streets, remodeled, and enlarged. Brownsville Historical Association.

son had deserted from the Confederate Army, murdered D. H. Dashiell and Jeff Barthelow, severely wounded Private Literal, joined forces with their archenemy Cortina, and was being courted by Union forces as a result. In addition, a large quantity of cotton and Mifflin's Brownsville office had been lost to fire, and thousands of Union soldiers were on their way to occupy Brownsville. However, there was one moment of joy when Petra again became a grandmother. A son was born to Rosa and Joe Putegnat on October 3.[56]

Before leaving Brownsville, the Confederates had secretly notified the Sisters at the Incarnate Word and Blessed Sacrament about the plans to fire the fort, so they were not totally shocked when the explosion came. Most people left Brownsville; one priest wrote, "Our nuns could now go about the city without breaking their vow of enclosure." Although this was exaggerated, the nuns worried about the uncertain turn of events. Sister Ephrem summed it up, "During the Civil War in the United States, we were almost the only women in Brownsville, the panic being so great that nearly everyone had left the city. Divine Providence watched over us and every mark of respect was shown us by the generals of both armies who on visiting offered us all kinds of provisions." The officers sought accommodations for their wives at the convent since the school was closed and there were no appropriate accommodations for women in Brownsville. The Sisters complied, which was a wise decision. The

Pontoon bridge across the Rio Grande, constructed under the command of Gen. Thomas Sedgwick, who had been sent to the border to prepare to drive the French and Austrians out of Mexico if Benito Juárez should be unable to break their power. Sedgwick marched a force to Matamoros and remained there a week to protect the U.S. Consulate and all foreigners while the rival Mexican factions fought. The bridge was dismantled when his forces were withdrawn. Brownsville Historical Association.

commanding officers placed a guard around the convent and the Sisters were left in peace.[57]

Father Parisot and the Oblate Fathers faced new challenges with the Federal occupation of Brownsville, just as the Sisters had. The Father said that they tried to be as gentle as lambs with their new masters. The Oblates were suspected of being Confederate sympathizers by the Union forces because all the Oblates were French. Since France was one of the main foreign countries buying cotton from the Confederacy, anyone of French extraction was suspect.[58]

Father Parisot had to make a sick call twelve miles from the city and applied to Maj. Fred Starck, the post adjutant general, for a pass. He got the pass and on his way to make the call was stopped four times. He later asked Major Starck about that. Starck replied that the Union officers had been told that the priests were the staunchest adherents of the Confederacy and they were watching them closely. Father Parisot had an ingenious way of dealing with his new masters. He carried chewing tobacco in his pockets. Tobacco was scarce in those days, yet Dr. C. Macmanus would supply him with chewing tobacco, which he would cut into quids and distribute out as he passed through the men. His trips to the hospitals were made a lot more easily.[59]

Mexico itself was in the throes of its own civil war: the French Imperialists against the native Mexican Juaristas. The French Imperialists were generally sympathetic to the Confederacy, while the Juaristas generally favored the Union. This was another reason why the French Oblates were considered Confederate sympathizers. In reality, the Oblates tried their best to remain officially neutral in regard to both civil wars. In order to minister, the Oblates had to work with and through whichever side was occupying the area at the time. No doubt each Oblate and each Sister had his or her opinion about the war, but for the sake of their ministry, they had to keep it to themselves and remain outwardly neutral.[60]

The Sisters and Oblate Fathers were not the only people to adapt to having an army in town. When Union Gen. Nathaniel Banks moved into Fort Brown, citizens like Judge Bigelow, Jerry Galvan, Stephen Powers, and Mayor George Dye, who was an avid Union man, took the oath of allegiance to the Union. Mayor Dye's wife and daughters were Confederate sympathizers and refused to take the oath. They verbalized their support for the Confederacy until it became intolerable and Gen. N. J. T. Dana, commanding the Union Army in the Valley, issued an order banishing them to Mexico. They were accompanied by a squad of police guards to the river and there they shook hands with their father and husband and left for Matamoros with their heads high.[61]

Charles Stillman again demonstrated his ability to be on the right side at the right time. Stillman's friend George Brackenridge arrived in Brownsville as a United States Treasury agent in July of 1863. Brackenridge had previously come to Brownsville in 1861 without any money, met Charles Stillman, began shipping cotton to him, and made a great deal of money. For some reason he defected to the Union in 1863 and went to Washington.[62] Was it incidental that he went to Washington or did he and Stillman plan this action? It was logical for him to be assigned to Brownsville because of his knowledge of the area and the cotton trade. Once there he called on Stillman in Matamoros and invited him to come to Brownsville and meet with General Dana. General Dana had seized Stillman's Santa Rosa Ranch, but Stillman had his agents bid for it at public auction and get it back. To avoid further loss of property, Stillman swore an oath of allegiance to the Union and got most of his property back by the middle of 1864.[63] Englishman William Neale had a different kind of problem. The Union officers needed lumber to build additional barracks at Fort Brown so they began to tear down his hotel and stagecoach stop to obtain it. He appealed to the general as an English citizen and they were made to stop the destruction of his property.[64]

Richard King's Santa Gertrudis Ranch was the major Confederate cotton depot in Texas and was raided by the Federals in December of 1863. The Federals hoped to kill or capture King; however, King was away from the rancho, scouting with Capt. J. J. Richardson. Francisco Alvarado, his trusted kineño, was killed in the raid instead. Brownsville Historical Association.

Mifflin and Petra were not so lucky. Mifflin refused to cross over and take the oath of allegiance, so their property was confiscated for the use of the Union Army and officers.[65] Cortina also got another shot at revenge toward Mifflin. Cortina had played in the political confusion in Mexico between the Juaristas and Imperialist and had managed to become the interim acting governor of the state of Tamaulipas, which included Matamoros. In that capacity, since M. Kenedy & Co. boats were under the governor's jurisdiction, he made a gift of three steamers, the *Matamoros,* the *Mustang,* and the *James Hale,* to General Banks for use by the Union Army.[66] When Cortina presented the boats he also arranged to be reunited with his mother, from whom he had been estranged since he deserted his wife in 1860 to go to Mexico. His mother, being the matriarch of her family, met the general, now governor, across from her ranch on the Mexican side of the river. As they met, the son handed his mother his riding crop, and as he knelt before her, in the presence of his officers, she whipped him across the shoulders. Then the chastised son arose and embraced his mother. As Américo Paredes points out, a strong woman could command as much respect as the father in a family.[67]

The Union was unable to completely shut down the cotton traffic even though they occupied Brownsville. King diverted the cotton upriver, where Maj. Santos Benavides, a Confederate hero, was protecting the crossing. General Dana did not quite understand river politics and sent Col. Edmund J. Davis and his men upriver to close the crossing. Some of the men were dispatched on Mifflin's steamer *Mustang,* which had been generously turned over to him by Cortina. It seemed, however, that the *Mustang* made very slow progress. Col. John Black reported when he returned to Brownsville that the officers of the *Mustang* were "capable and accommodating gentlemen in their line of business—yet these gentlemen were in the hire of the Mexican 'owners' who still operated under orders from a staunch Confederate by the name of Mifflin Kenedy." He also reported that these gentlemen were certainly passing on any military information they acquired while on these voyages. Mifflin's network was still proving successful. Very little cotton was confiscated during this campaign because the Confederates knew of the plans and had moved the cotton crossings upriver to Laredo and Eagle Pass.[68]

Mifflin and Petra had more bad news ahead of them before the year was out. Adrian, seeking to further his career, decided to join the Union Army. He was like a rebellious teenager, doing everything he could to strike back at his parents and declare his independence. He could be full of machismo "with his pistol in his hand."[69] Shortly after the Federal Army occupied Brownsville, Adrian J. Vidal, late of the Confederate Army, appeared at the Union Army office and said he was prepared to raise a company for the Federals. He was mustered into the service of the United States and commissioned a captain on November 26, 1863. In November and December hundreds of Mexican Texans, many influenced by Vidal, also joined the Union Army. Vidal's company was attached to the First Texas Cavalry and known as Vidal's Independent Partisan Rangers. Gen. N. J. T. Dana reported, "Vidal's command has been mustered in, armed and equipped to the number of 89 men for one year." Many of Vidal's men, having served with their captain in the Confederate Army, continued their rough and rowdy ways in the Federal ranks. In early December 1863, a brawl broke out in the company in which a private was mortally wounded. General Dana promised to make an example of the murderer.[70]

Adrian had wasted no time after the Union secured Brownsville and after General Banks's visit to Matamoros on November 17. By November 18, Adrian had crossed over to Brownsville and was ordering a $1 breakfast, a $9 dinner with claret, and a $1 supper at the Miller Hotel. From November 18, 1863, until December 6, he ate one or more meals a day at the hotel. On two occasions he entertained another guest with a bottle of wine and dinner. Then, from December 7, his name is missing from the hotel ledger until December 29, 1863. Perhaps this is the time when his men got into a brawl and were disciplined. At the end of December Captain Vidal returned to the hotel and was charged with an $89 bill for stabling five horses for varying times ranging from twenty-two days to two days.[71]

Petra and Mifflin personally felt the next move made by the Union. The Union decided they must close down the major Confederate cotton depot in Texas, the Santa Gertrudis rancho. Their partner Captain King had moved his family there, including his father-in-law Hiram Chamberlain, believing it to be a safe haven. From there he had continued to direct most of the cotton that was delivered to the Rio Grande, and Mifflin helped to ship it out of Mexico.

Mifflin Kenedy was King's partner in the Santa Gertrudis and felt the sting of the raid.

On December 22, 1863, that all changed when the Santa Gertrudis was raided by Union troops as an important depot for cotton wagons on the way to Brownsville. King had been gone from the rancho for several days when the raid occurred, scouting with Capt. J. J. Richardson and thirteen others in pursuit of a "band of robbers with a drove of beeves; and to see if there were any Yankees on the Rio Grande."[72] The party that attacked the rancho consisted of about eighty men, half Anglo and half Mexican. One of the kineños, Francisco Alvarado, was killed when shots were fired into the house. King had charged Alvarado to keep his family safe when he left. He had been lying on a cot near the front door so he could protect the family. When he heard the shots splintering the wall of the house he flung the door open to tell the soldiers not to fire that there was family in the house. He was hit and dropped dead in the doorway. Union soldiers thought they had killed King and were disappointed when they saw they had shot the wrong man. Francisco was one of the most trusted kineños and had been on the Santa Gertrudis rancho from the very first. He had helped to build the first *jacales* on the rancho, and he had been there when Henrietta was first brought there as a bride by Captain King.[73]

The soldiers ignored the very pregnant Henrietta and her elderly father, who wrote in his report that the Federals began to thoroughly search the house, "not sparing the ladies' trunks and apartments. We were plundered of every thing they could carry away, even to the covering of our beds, and many articles of wearing apparel." They rounded up horses and mules for a drive and all adult males who were caught, many of them kineños, were taken prisoner, including captains James D. McCleary, John Brown, W. D. Gregory, and Almond Dix. They came to take Henrietta's father Reverend Chamberlain as well, to which he responded, "You don't want me, an old man of sixty-seven and a minister of the Gospel." The lieutenant said he would have to speak to Captain Speed, who later told Chamberlain to "tell Captain King that if one bale of cotton were removed or burned, he would hold him responsible with his life." The soldiers stayed at the ranch two days, until Christmas Eve, when "friends came to our aid, and on Christmas morning, with Mrs. King and all her family, we left that once pleasant home."[74]

Henrietta King would never forget that Christmas Day. She had no idea if Captain King was alive or dead or when she would see him again. Early that morning, without him beside her, she loaded the family into a coach. She looked out at the destroyed home they had worked so hard to build together and the fresh grave of their friend Francisco Alvarado who had given his life to protect her. There was a great sadness in her as she left her rancho in the middle of the Wild Horse Desert not knowing if she would ever see it again. She traveled to a friend's house in San Patricio and there on February 22, 1864, she gave birth to their son. This strong woman who had helped to settle the land between the Nueces and Rio Grande defiantly named their new son Robert E. Lee King.[75]

When King returned to the Santa Gertrudis he reported to Col. A. G. Dickinson, commanding San Antonio, Texas, that the rancho was "entirely abandoned, in fact a complete wreck," that he had no place he could call home, and he was busily engaged in gathering horse stock, which had been scattered to the four winds, so that it would not fall into the hands of the enemy and robbers.[76]

Mifflin and Petra felt helpless and angry as they learned what happened to the rancho and to their best friends Captain King and Henrietta. The Union had now taken their Brownsville property and their steamers, and had raided their rancho. It was indeed a difficult time for them as the year came to an end. The only bright spot was the baptism of Joseph Louis Putegnat, their new grandson, on December 26, 1863. The family gathered again that day in the church in Brownsville and Father Parisot conducted the baptism. The sponsors for Joe and Rosa's baby were Fulgencio San Román and Petra Vela Kenedy.[77] The network of old friends was still there for business and for the family, and alliances through godparents remained strong.

Petra stood in her church holding her new grandson and pondered all the changes that had come so quickly in her life. She only had Sarah and Willie at home now. Her daughters were married and seemed happy but she regretted that Rosa and Luisa and their two families had to desert their homes due to the war. Petra and Mifflin's home and their Brownsville warehouse were now occupied by Union officers. She had one son in the Union Army who was being hunted as a traitor by the Confederates and three sons far off in Pennsylvania. She held the hope for the future in her arms but all around her were the fears of the present.

CHAPTER 6

1864–65:
Chaos along the Rio Grande

The year 1864 found the towns on both sides of the Rio Grande in total confusion. Union officers and troops occupied Brownsville, and most of the citizens had fled to Matamoros for safety. Petra and Mifflin were surrounded by friends and family who were now living in Matamoros, which was full of Union sympathizers, Confederate supporters, and foreign merchants hoping to make money in the cotton trade. The town and surrounding area were caught up in the battle between the French Imperialists who wanted to acquire Mexico and the Juaristas who wanted to return the land to the Mexican people. Texans divided their loyalties between the two groups. Confederates tended to support the Imperialists. Union supporters usually lined up on the Juaristas' side and with Cortina.[1]

The Confederates were not standing still after the fall of Brownsville. The Texas government called on their most able warrior, John "Rip" Ford, to again come to their rescue and take back Brownsville and control of the river. On December 22, 1863, Ford received orders to return to the Rio Grande, and by December 27 he was on the move. It took him a while to get equipment but by February 1864 he was in position to fight.[2]

In January Gen. Francis J. Herron took over the Union command in Brownsville. Across the river Cortina declared himself the governor of Tamaulipas and placed himself in charge of the military. Fighting broke out in the town, and the sitting governor, Albino López, was shot while trying to board the ferry to cross to Brownsville to safety.[3] Petra and Mifflin were trying to avoid getting caught up in this conflict.

The Valley was also suffering from a terrible drought, which brought hot dusty winds and hundreds of fleas and mosquitoes.[4] In February, Major Rogers wrote, "you cannot imagine how desolate, barren, and desert-like this country is, not a spear of grass, nor a green shrub, with nothing but moving clouds of sand to be seen on these once green prairies."[5] Around water holes, hundreds of domestic animals lay dead, their flesh drying in the sun. The only water for the movement of troops or wagon trains was from wells, as the Nueces River was dry for miles. It took hours to draw enough water from a well to satisfy the thirst of a regiment of men or a caravan of wagons.[6] Mifflin and King were attempting to manage not only their own stock at Santa Gertrudis but also the wagons trying to make their way south with cotton for the border. It was a grim time for anyone having to be in the Wild Horse Desert.

Maria von Blücher, the wife of the surveyor Mifflin and King often used, was also having a difficult time during this period. She wrote home to her family in Europe from Corpus Christi that the Confederate dollar was only worth ten cents in silver. She said she was drinking coffee made from acorns, without milk, and using moldy flour and bacon, which is what they ate daily. She said the drought was so bad that the cattle and sheep were dying in masses and it was not difficult to see 10,000 a day on the Nueces River and in the creeks. The animals were so weak that when they reached the swampy banks they could not get out and died there.[7]

The priest in Brownsville had a difficult time under the new Federal rule. Father Clos wrote in 1864 that the country was ruined and they had suffered much. He said the priests were virtual prisoners in Brownsville, and could not leave without a passport; consequently, children died without confession.[8] Adding to the difficulties was an epidemic of smallpox that raced along the river and swept through Fort Brown on January 21, 1864.[9] In response to this threat a young officer, Lt. F. E. Starck, the post adjutant, issued an order from Col. Henry Bertram, commander of the post, that all streets, alleys, and grounds would be swept every morning and that no garbage would be allowed to accumulate but would be picked up by army wagons. The first offense would be a fine of $10, with half going to the enforcement; the second offense would be met with imprisonment and hard labor.[10] This young Union officer would soon play a major role in Petra's life.

In the midst of this confusion the United States Consul in Matamoros, Leonard Pierce, had a problem. He had collected duties and fees amounting to about $1 million and was afraid he would lose the money to one side or the other or even to looters. He requested that General Herron give him protection until he could move the money to Brownsville. Pierce wrote that people were fighting among themselves on the border and in states of the interior. President Juárez was on his way to establish his headquarters in Matamoros and expected protection from the United States.[11] Cortina had an opportunity to solidify his connection to Juárez when it was learned that the French had ordered troops to Bagdad to prepare for an attack on Matamoros. Cortina helped to fortify the area against attack and sent money to Juárez to help win his favor.[12]

During this time, Adrian Vidal was able to court and win the affections of a young lady. He was nineteen, good looking, and a captain in the Union Army with his own company of cavalry. Since the Confederates had withdrawn from Brownsville he was no longer a hunted man and was viewed as a hero by the Unionists. The girl he convinced to become his wife was Miss Ana Marie de Chavero. The Brownsville *Loyal National Union Journal* reported on March 5, 1864, "Our prominent townsman, Captain A. J. Vidal, having convinced himself that it was not good to be alone, has taken unto himself as a life companion the accomplished and beautiful Miss Ana M. de Chavero."[13] The certificate of marriage from the Immaculate Conception Church in Brownsville attested that Adrian Vidal son of Luis Vidal and Petra Vela and Ana Ma. Martínez Chavero daughter of Demetro Martínez Chavero and Guadalupe Rodríguez were married on February 27, 1864, with Father Pierre F. Parisot officiating. Again, Father Parisot was presiding over a Kenedy occasion. The witnesses were Juan M. H. Tasgain, Francisco Goma Rodríguez, R. Cabanas, and Abelardo Treviño.[14] Mifflin's good friend and associate Abelardo Treviño and some of the other witnesses could have been members of Adrian's cavalry. Adrian settled down with his new wife and divided his time between her and his army duties. In May he was attacking cotton trains up and down the river in an attempt to stop the Confederate flow of cotton. These trains could well have been his stepfather's or those of his stepfather's associates. The knowledge gained when he was running the steamboats for Mifflin was invaluable to him. He knew the land, the crossings, and the river. He also had the contacts to gather information needed by the army. Adrian was at last becoming a military hero like his father, and in so doing perhaps striking a blow against his stepfather and the gringos.

After Richard King was sure his family was safe, he became an aggressive fighter. He grew a beard, became a private in the Confederate Army under Captain Richardson, and kept the cotton, horses, and supplies rolling for the Confederate soldiers. Mifflin was in Matamoros finding supplies for the army and furnishing Captain Ford with vital information.[15] Mifflin was the quiet man behind the scenes, in charge of affairs. King wrote to Ford from Santa Gertrudis, welcoming him back to South Texas and assuring him of ample amounts of beef and other foodstuffs for his men.[16] On March 12, 1864, Col. Santos Benavides turned back a Union force that had driven to Laredo, and moved to join Ford downriver.[17]

The editor of the *New York Herald* wrote on March 1, 1864, that eight to ten capitalists in Brownsville and Matamoros and their supplies to the rebels had done more to sustain the southern cause than eight to ten rebel regiments.

These men had provided half the supplies to Lee's men in Virginia and they had made millions by treason. They had sold town lots, controlled the ferries, owned the steamboats, which carried 150 million importations a year, and controlled elections.[18]

Ford was worried about his family, and in April he decided to send his wife, in the company of Abelardo Treviño's brother Manuel Treviño and his wife, to Matamoros for safety. When Mrs. Ford arrived at Matamoros she received very courteous treatment from none other than Juan Cortina. Colonel Ford had shown courtesy to Cortina's mother in the past and Cortina was returning the favor. Mrs. Ford's father and sister still lived in Brownsville, and her sister crossed over to Matamoros to warn Mrs. Ford not to come to Union-occupied Brownsville. The United States provost marshal had been sent to their house to find out when Mrs. Ford would arrive and her sister felt that they had every intention of arresting her.[19]

The cotton trade proceeded at a frenzied pace, and Kenedy, King, Benavides, and Ford were becoming the lifeline of the Confederacy. Joe Kleiber, an earlier settler and drugstore owner, ordered one hundred carts to run from Mexico to Alleyton, Texas, close to Houston, loaded with saltpeter, sulfur, and lead. These carts would return loaded with Confederate cotton headed for Matamoros.[20]

Meanwhile, María Vicenta Vidal, Petra's last unmarried daughter by Luis, was attracting a great deal of attention among the young Union soldiers. Vicenta was eighteen years old. Lt. Frederick Edward Starck, a Union officer serving as the post adjutant at Fort Brown, won her hand. Fred Starck was from New York, and his father, Carl, was an oboist in the New York Philharmonic Orchestra. He also had been an accompanist for the famous singer Jenny Lind.[21]

Before coming to Brownsville in 1860, Fred had been in the U.S. Army at Fort Davis, Texas. This post, nestled in a narrow canyon with walls two hundred feet in height, was home to the "Camel Corps" while Fred was there. The army had been experimenting with these animals as beasts of burden to carry heavier loads, as they did not need as much water to travel as did other animals, but the Civil War ended the project. From there Fred went back east and volunteered in 1862 in Iowa in the Union Army, which led to his assignment in Brownsville.[22]

Fred and Vicenta's wedding on April 2, 1864, was attended by most of his fellow officers. B. F. MacIntyre described Vicenta as, "a hansome [sic], fascinating, and rich young Mexican lady of this place. The ceremony came off on Saturday evening and was a grand affair, many of our officers being present."[23] Fred evidently had made some powerful friends during his career. The day before the wedding Maj. Gen. John A. McClernand, who had recently been made commander of the 13th Army Corps, arrived in Brownsville with the intention of meeting with Governor Cortina and jointly reviewing the Union troops.[24] The Union was obviously intent on securing Governor Cortina's support in helping to stop the Confederate cotton trade. The next day, April 2, he stood as one of Fred Starck's attendants, along with Col. James Klegiom, M. C. Garber, Capt. W. M. Clapp, and Capt. S. B. Morey. Father Parisot officiated at the ceremony, and since both were Catholics the service could be held at Petra's church. It is doubtful whether Mifflin or Petra attended due to threat of arrest. Vicenta's family was represented, though, in a special way. As the priest conducted the service, Fred slipped a simple but large gold ring on María Vicenta's finger. This ring was made from gold that Mifflin had provided. The ring remains in the family to this day.[25] Two days later Governor Cortina arrived on the parade grounds accompanied by Major General McClernand and, according to McIntyre's diary, the review was the finest and most successful ever witnessed.[26] After the review the U.S. and Mexican principal officers retired to Miller's Hotel for a grand dinner accompanied by live music.

María Vicenta Vidal (Nene) was attracting attention among the young Union soldiers. The one who won her hand was Lt. Frederick Edward Starck. B. F. MacIntyre described Vicenta as "a hansome [sic], fascinating, and rich young Mexican lady of this place." Her wedding ring was made from Mifflin Kenedy gold and is still in possession of her family. Courtesy of Michael W. Hamilton, Petra and Vicenta Starck descendant.

Now Petra had a son and son-in-law who were officers in the Union Army. At the same time, Mifflin was doing everything he could to defeat the Union Army and drive them out of Texas. Because of this division, Petra was deprived of participating in either Adrian or María Vicenta's weddings. Life was very difficult and complicated for Petra as she worried about the safety, happiness, and well being of her family. All of her adult children were married, three of the young boys were in Pennsylvania, and only young Sarah and Willie were left at home with her. Just as the wind constantly changes direction as it blows across the Rio Grande, Petra's life was going to change again.

On May 30, Adrian resigned from the Union Army. There has been a great deal of speculation on why he took this action. Rosita Putegnat, Petra's great-granddaughter, said the family believed that Adrian was acting as a double agent.[27] If *his* word is taken, it was because he was encountering racial slurs, having a difficult time with the paperwork, and wanted more time with his family in Brownsville.[28] He wanted to spend more time with his new bride and if the army continued to send him on raiding parties he would be away from her often. Perhaps the prejudice Adrian and his men encountered from the Anglo Union soldiers played a more important part in his resignation than his

Photograph believed to be of Frederick Edward Starck, in an apparently local Brownsville uniform. Fred was from New York, where his father was an oboist in the New York Philharmonic and accompanist for Jenny Lind. One of Starck's attendants at the wedding was Maj. Gen. John A. McClernand, Commander of the 13th Army Corp. Courtesy of Michael W. Hamilton, Petra and Vicenta Starck descendant.

ability to deal with the English language. It must have been difficult for Adrian and his men to fit in with the northern soldiers who looked down on them. Col. John L. Haynes, who may have recruited Adrian in the first place, was commander of the First Texas Cavalry and recommended that his resignation be accepted. General Herron, taking Haynes's recommendation, passed the paperwork on to New Orleans. On July 9, 1864, Adrian's request was approved and the captain was issued an honorable discharge.[29]

Unfortunately, the order came too late. Adrian had become impatient and left the U.S. Army on June 19 before his discharge reached Brownsville, making Adrian a deserter. Prior to Adrian leaving the army, most of his Partisan Rangers had fled across the river to Mexico. In the four months before Adrian's desertion fifty-three men had deserted the company. Weeks after Adrian's flight another eighteen men left the company on a march from Brownsville to Brazos Santiago. Only twenty-three men of his original group served until the end of the war with the Union Army.[30]

On June 27, 1864, B. F. McIntyre gleefully recorded, "We are enjoying a variety of almost daily excitement—Capt Videlle [sic] the deserter from the 2d Texas was reported in town at an early hour this morning. Two dwellings one of which was his brother-in-laws residence (Adjt Starcke) were surrounded by guards and after a thorough search it was supposed he had vamoosed the city or most probable had not been here at all. I understand Officers and soldiers are instructed to shoot Videlle if found in the city. I do not think this little affair will add anything to the felicity of Lieut Starcke and family."[31]

MacIntyre had grumbled earlier about Adjutant Starck in his diary on June 3, "Post Adjutant Starck made himself particularly obnoxious to a number of our men today by having them regularly detailed to clean his dwelling, scrub the poarches [sic], clean out his privy and stable, and other things of a like character which will not redound to the Adjutants popularity and which was disgraceful employment to the soldier and equally so to an officer asking it."[32]

Adrian had many people concerned about him, including Rip Ford. Ford

Col. Rip Ford protected the cotton trade for Kenedy and King and fought the last battle of the Civil War by defeating Union forces at Palmito Hill. He was a help to Kenedy and King during Reconstruction as well. Courtesy of Corpus Christi Library.

had known him and his family for years and knew that the young man had a great deal of ability and knowledge of the land. On June 20, 1864, Ford wrote Brig. Gen. J. E. Slaughter in Houston from his headquarters on John Young's ranch forty miles above Brownsville, "Vidal has crossed the Rio Grande with some sixty men, armed, mounted, and equipped; but for the rise in the river

400 others would have gone with him, carrying with them ten wagons and teams."[33]

Adrian and his Partisan Rangers may have been better informed than the Union Army about what was happening along the river. General Herron was concerned about building a narrow gauge railroad from the dock at Brazos Santiago to White Ranch to ease the problem of transporting supplies for his troops.[34] He was not watching his back upriver as Rip Ford prepared his attack on the Union soldiers. Adrian and his men were well aware of these activities from their information network and they began to desert. Interestingly, rather than wait for his discharge, Adrian chose to leave the army just six days before Ford's victory at Las Rucias. He may well have known the attacks were coming and that he had better leave quickly because he had deserted the Confederate Army and was labeled a traitor by them. The last thing he wanted was to be caught by them in a Union uniform.

Adrian fled to María Vicenta's house, which placed her new husband, Capt. Frederick Starck, in a bad position when they accused him of harboring a deserter.[35] Eighteen more of Vidal's men left the Union Army on July 28, just two days before Colonel Ford marched in and took possession of Brownsville.[36] Like Adrian, these men were not eager to be on the losing side in this war, and they all had been well equipped for their next adventure. Adrian went to Mexico for safety and again joined with Cortina's forces fighting against the French Imperialists.[37] He now was a deserter from both the Union and Confederate armies. He needed to stay out of Texas because he could be arrested by either side or shot on sight as a traitor.

Some of Adrian's men were not as lucky as he and were caught trying to desert. On June 17, it was reported that twenty-seven soldiers of the Texas Cavalry had deserted in the past week, and an infantry guard had been posted around their camp with an order to shoot the first one to approach their line. Then two days later an order to solve the problem was issued; the remaining Texas Calvary with the exception of a few were ordered to Point Isabel and from there to New Orleans. One Texas Calvary man, Pedro Garcia, was caught trying to escape and was court-martialed and sentenced to be shot.[38] The execution of the deserter was held on June 22, 1864, at 4 P.M. The entire regimental force, accompanied by the post's brass band, was assembled in Washington Square as the cart holding the victim, accompanied by a priest, was brought in. The coffin was placed by the open grave where the victim kneeled on it after the priest administered the last rites. A blindfold was offered, which he refused, and the word was given and a dozen rifles fired simultaneously, all aimed at his breast. The columns were forced to walk past the grave and view the gory corpse to see what happened to a deserter.[39]

Ford won a decisive victory on June 25 at Las Rucias and drove his opponents across the Rio Grande. Ford, with his superior knowledge of the land, attacked and withdrew and attacked and withdrew until the Union forces moved all their troops back to Brownsville. Ford advanced to within eleven miles of Brownsville on July 21 and to the outskirts on July 25.[40] General Herron, needing supplies, decided to move his troops downriver out of Brownsville and toward the mouth of the river, closer to his supply lines.[41]

Shortly after the execution, the Union Army made plans to evacuate Fort Brown and pull back to the mouth of the Rio Grande. Fred Starck was evidently very disliked by the men, which may have been due in part to his association with Adrian, or it could have been the age-old dislike for higher-ranking officers. On July 7, Lieutenant McIntyre noted that he was happy to learn that Lieutenant Starck had vacated his office as post adjutant.[42] The Union dependents were also planning to leave, including María Vicenta. It must have been difficult for her to leave her family, friends, and home to travel to Louisiana with her husband. The military authorities were offering free passage to all citizens wishing to leave. On July 23, General Herron stated he had 250 refugees, two hundred sick, and a number of ladies that would immediately go to New Orleans.[43] The army did move to replace Father Parisot's store of bricks they had confiscated to use in their defense works and noted that they had all been replaced except the 150,000 in the kiln.[44] The retreat was a nightmare in the July heat. The soldiers suffered sunstroke and the ambulances were overflowing. The road was strewn with overcoats, blankets, and clothing. To make matters worse the Rio Grande had overflowed and sometimes they were marching in two to three feet of mud.[45] After reaching New Orleans things did not go well for Fred and María Vicenta. They had a son, F. J. C. Starck, born in Baton Rouge on May 3, 1865, and two weeks after that María Vicenta became seriously ill. Fred requested an emergency leave to take his wife home to Brownsville to be near Petra and Mifflin. Their baby died in Brownsville on September 22, 1865, and was buried there.[46]

Rip Ford and his men rode into Brownsville on July 30 to reclaim the town for the Confederacy. Captain Ford was ill from a fever and he had to be helped to mount his horse, but he would not give up. Almost immediately the cotton trade began in earnest again. M. Kenedy & Co. was back in business with much of the work left to Mifflin and King. They were still ferrying the cotton across to Matamoros and then down the Mexican side of the river because the Union forces still controlled the Texas side of the lower Rio Grande. Cortina was still governor of Tamaulipas and they had worked out a cooperative agreement with him to transport the cotton.[47]

At the end of June, a new force came on the scene that changed everything. The French arrived in large warships and landed their marines in Bagdad to take over the border trade. The French government had enthroned Austrian

Archduke Maximilian as the emperor of Mexico. The elected president of Mexico, Benito Juárez, was hiding in the mountains near Durango. Cortina, as wily as a fox, realized the winds of change were blowing again and approached the Union Army through U.S. Consul Leonard Pierce Jr. He offered to capture Brownsville and turn it over to the Union if he would be made a brigadier general in the U.S. Army.[48]

Colonel Ford was well aware of Cortina's plan to capture Brownsville for the Union, and on September 3, 1864, Ford said, "Cortina hates Americans, particularly Texians. . . . If he could cut his way through our lines, plunder our people, and get within the Yankee lines it would be a finale he would delight in."[49] Ford worried that Cortina would succeed in this effort and on the night of September 6 sent his wife and children to the convent in Brownsville even though they had only been united since July when he recaptured the city. The next morning Mrs. Ford came back to the house at an early hour and announced she was not going back to the convent but she was going to "share the fortunes of my husband," as did many women.[50]

The Federals did not like the idea of Cortina being a brigadier general in the U.S. Army and refused his offer. When this did not work, Cortina had to think quickly. Gen. Tomás Mejía arrived with 2,000 troops and was moving toward Matamoros to take over for the French Imperialists. As usual, Cortina had a plan. He told Capt. Mifflin Kenedy that he would see the last piece of his army's artillery destroyed before he would let the Confederates have them. He then contacted Colonel Ford with a different story. He asked Ford to come to Matamoras and greeted him with a big hug; they talked about Ford purchasing Cortina's weapons before General Mejía arrived with his army. They set a price and time for Ford to come over and meet Cortina and purchase the weapons. General Mejía was scheduled to arrive the next day. During the meeting a messenger came and announced that the French Imperial Guard was entering the city. Ford left immediately and escaped back to Brownsville before he was caught in the trap that Cortina had arranged. Cortina was left without options so he joined forces with General Mejía and the Imperialists. At the same time, he sent a note to Juárez saying that he was doing this only because it was expedient and he would rejoin Juárez when possible.[51]

Where did this leave Adrian? He was fighting with Cortina and now Cortina had given his loyalty to a foreign army trying to occupy Adrian's country of Mexico. He could not cross the Rio Grande into Texas to join either the Confederate or Union armies. He probably elected to join Servando Canales, one of Cortina's colonels. Canales and his followers crossed over the Rio Grande to Brownsville for safety, and Adrian waited until they came back into Mexico to join him. Canales and his men reorganized upriver as Juaristas to fight for Mexico.[52] This is probably where Adrian went during the winter of 1864 and spring of 1865. He was good at guerrilla warfare and was an asset to the Juaristas. This forced Adrian to be separated from his new bride. He and Ana were now expecting their first child in late summer. By February 1865, Cortina had officially abandoned the Imperialistas to join forces again with the Juaristas, as he had promised.[53]

The Rio Grande Valley was a shambles at the beginning of 1865. The Union was in control of Boca Chica at the mouth of the Rio Grande on the Texas side and the French were in control of Bagdad on the Mexican side. The Confederates controlled Brownsville and the French controlled Matamoros. Benito Juárez was hiding in the mountains and his Juaristas, including Adrian, were conducting guerrilla warfare on his behalf up and down the river. Matamoros was to the Confederacy what New York was to the Union in feeding and clothing the two armies. The city itself, though, bore the burden of war. Rents soared from $10 per month for a large house to $100 for a small 12-by-14 foot room.[54]

Ford had arranged with the French to allow cotton to be shipped, and the one thing that did not change was that the cotton brokers were making a fortune in the trade. Both Mifflin and King made enough money in gold from the cotton trading that they had plenty of money to carry them through the reconstruction period and to develop the Santa Gertrudis rancho.[55]

During February of 1865, Mifflin wrote King in Houston concerning his continued involvement with blockade-runners. On February 2 he wrote to King telling him he did not want to become involved with the blockade-running business. He declined the opportunity and wrote that if he or Stillman or Walworth drew out the funds like he did that the business would have to stop for want of means. Mifflin told King that he thought it was undoubtedly proper to let the matter rest until he came to Matamoros. He then told him he was sorry to see him put his money into the blockade-running business.[56] The next day Mifflin was still upset enough about the issue to write King again, "With regard to the blockade running business, you are old enough to judge for yourself & do not require a guardian. You appear to forget there are others in the concern."[57] On the thirteenth, Kenedy wrote King again to tell him that Fort Fisher had fallen and Wilmington, North Carolina, had closed. He then wrote, "The blockade running is about wound up & weather [sic] you thank me for the advice or not, I advise you to let it alone."[58]

As Mifflin and King were very close throughout their lives, a letter of February 3, 1865, from Mifflin to King reveals a personal side of Mifflin rarely seen. He told King that he was sure King realized their ideas were different at the present time regarding their business but that he had the best intentions in regard to King's interest. He also told him that he was sure that he did not like the remarks he had made in yesterday's letter of February 2. He continued, writing that he knew King was aware of his family relations and that there was no improvement and that he wanted to divide up their business and leave the country. He wanted to talk to King personally for a few hours because he was afraid that the large cash advances would make it difficult to successfully terminate the business.[59] At one point he told King that he was not overburdened with friends and he knew he stretched his letters out too long. Mifflin was clearly despondent. The future of the Rio Grande Valley and his businesses were in doubt because of the end of the war and Union occupation. His family relations were growing more complicated with Adrian's erratic behavior, with the children divided by marriages to Union and Confederate sympathizers, and with the responsibility that was placed on him by all the family members. When Mifflin reached this low point he turned to his lifelong friend for understanding and assistance just as King would turn to him in his times of need. They might disagree but they were always there for each other.

In the same letter, Mifflin wrote to King that Ford has just come in and informed him that Gen. James E. Slaughter, commander of Confederate forces at Brownsville, would abandon Brownsville and that many people were deserting the cause. He doubted that they could find five hundred fighting men they could call on if they had too. He signed his letter "Respectfully and truly yours, M. Kenedy."[60]

Throughout February Mifflin continued to write King, keeping him informed of events at the border. On February 6, Kenedy wrote King that General Slaughter advised him to tell King to move as much of the ranch property as possible to a safe place. He also wanted King to send the cotton from the Sabine to Houston and use the blockade-runners, but Stillman had not yet approved that move.[61] On February 15, Mifflin wrote that the federal government refused to acknowledge the French Empire in Mexico and that the English and French ministers in Washington had asked for their passports. Mifflin felt uneasy about the peace and quiet on the frontier.[62]

Mifflin wrote King on March 27 that their steamer *The Cora* was taken by the blockade at Brazos on Friday morning March 24 at 7 A.M. He informed him that he had registered the steamer *Camargo* in the name of Santiago Ytúrria.[63] Then on March 31, Mifflin wrote King that he had just received intelligence of the death of Captain Walworth on March 15. He also told him that he did not consider Brownsville safe, since "it was becoming more insecure everyday not only from the common enemy but from its demoralized and disorganized defenders."[64]

Word of Lee's surrender on April 9, 1865 was slow reaching the Rio Grande. The news was faster reaching John in Pennsylvania. He wrote in later years that when the news of the end of the war came to Coatesville there was a big celebration all over the county with bonfires in the hills and firearms being discharged.[65] It was very different for the Confederates along the border. Reportedly, some of Ford's men read about the surrender on May 1 when a copy of the *New Orleans Times* arrived by steamer. On April 20, Mifflin Kenedy in Matamoros received a New Orleans newspaper that had been sent by his partner, William Hale, reporting the surrender. On April 21, Kenedy wrote to Hale from Matamoros telling him that the paper had arrived and King was sending it to Gen. John Bankhead Magruder. Even though it is sure that Ford must have known about the surrender, defeat came slowly to the Rio Grande. Ford was protecting the cotton trade for King and Kenedy and did not relish facing defeat and Union occupation.[66] King was back in Matamoros by April 26, 1865, and expressed most of the Confederates' feelings. He wrote to Capt. Green Hall aboard the *Three Marys* in Tampico, Mexico, regarding the Confederate surrender, "Every body here is blue & despondent."[67] Greed could not keep its ugly head from rising up, and the Union wanted the bales of Confederate cotton stacked on the wharves at Brownsville. They planned to attack the town and seize them. Ford gathered his men on May 13 and, rallying for one last fight, met the Union forces at Palmito Hill, causing them to retreat. This was the last battle of the Civil War.[68]

Many of the Confederate soldiers, vowing never to live under Union rule, rode into Mexico to fight for the Imperialists. Many of them feared they would be imprisoned or hanged for treason.[69] Kenedy and King also acted quickly. The Confederacy owed them $237,000 on unpaid advances for cotton. They asked for at least a partial payment of $150,000 to be paid to M. Kenedy & Co. based in Matamoros. Special agent W. M. Perkins in Matamoros was authorized by Gen. E. Kirby Smith, Confederate commanding general at Trans-Mississippi headquarters, to release the payment.[70]

On April 22, 1865, John in Pennsylvania went down to the train station in Coatesville to see President Abraham Lincoln's funeral train pass. An article written in the *Village Record* said that the citizens gathered at the railroad station to pay reverence to the body of the martyred president, who had been shot in Washington on April 14 and passed away the morning of April 15. "The old flag again was unfurled but draped in black. Slowly the train approached and Mr. James Penrose, a leading citizen called 'All hats off' and at once our heads were uncovered as the train slowly passed us. The coffin holding the body of Mr. Lincoln was visible to the crowd—it rested on trestles that lifted it up to uncurtained windows."[71]

Now that the war was over, Petra hoped she and her family could establish their home again and settle into a peaceful life. Little did she know that one of the greatest tragedies of her life would occur in the next few months. Mifflin, Petra, and the family were living in Matamoros because the Union soldiers still occupied their home and warehouse in Brownsville. Life was

A young John Kenedy was educated first in Pennsylvania, then briefly in Brownsville, and then at Spring Hill College in Mobile, Alabama. Courtesy of Raymondville Historical Museum, Texas.

difficult and dangerous for Mifflin and Petra in Matamoros. Mifflin wrote that they were in a state of siege and had no communications except from the mouth of the river by water. He said forty or fifty of Cortina's men had dashed into the town's market square the night before, killing five or six men.[72] Gen. Ulysses S. Grant was so concerned about the border rebels that he sent top officer Maj. Gen. Philip Henry Sheridan with 25,000 troops to Texas to stop the cotton trade and handle the rebels. When Sheridan arrived in Texas in May of 1865, he was sorely disappointed to find almost all the rebels had crossed to Matamoros, taking their arms and valuables. None of the rebels, including Captain Kenedy or Captain King, wanted to be there when they marched in. The immediate peace that Petra hoped for was not to be. The war and its aftermath on the border "cooked a slumgullion stew of many bad bloods, of Rebels against Yankees, of Imperialists against Juaristas, of white men against Negro Union troops, of gringos against greasers."[73]

On June 29, Mifflin, in Matamoros, wrote to King in Camargo requesting he come to Matamoros as quickly as possible so they could take care of their affairs. Mifflin felt that they had committed no crimes but they could be tried for treason like thousands of others and they needed to return to their country.[74]

The northern soldiers who were sent to Texas were not prepared for the country they found themselves in. One soldier described his "short" walk of 150 miles from Brazos to Rio Grande City in May of 1865. He said he saw various kinds of snakes, and that they killed twelve rattlesnakes. He described millions of lizards, many mosquitoes, and creeping things like tarantulas and poisonous spiders. Above all were the "horned frog" of Texas, which had "six or eight horns on its head and the body and tail like a crocodile." The birds were of the "gayest hues." The only water available to drink was from the Rio Grande, which was so muddy that if a saucer was filled with it the bottom could not be seen.[75]

A longtime friend of Kenedy and King's came to their rescue in this uncertain time. Shortly after the war ended, Col. Rip Ford had won the respect of the Union officials, and they had visited him in Matamoros. He served them eggnog and took them on a tour of Matamoros. They felt they could trust him and he would be someone they could work with to help restore order. Ford arranged for the Union officers to come to Matamoros one Sunday morning; they attended Mass and a military review with Gen. Tomás Mejía presiding. Colonel Ford showed them every courtesy.[76] When Maj. Gen. Frederick Steele arrived in Brownsville in the summer of 1865 he sent for Ford to come to the American side. Captain Kenedy, Captain King, Felix Blücher, and others accompanied Ford. They discussed the best way to restore order to the area and facilitate the taking of the oath of allegiance to the United States. General Steel said the best way to reconstruct a state was to use its leaders to bring the people back to their allegiance. Ford was appointed commissioner of paroles for the Confederate troops in the area.[77] It probably did not hurt that Colonel Ford had a family connection with the U.S. Army in Lt. Richard Strong, one of the Federal commander's staff officers, who was Mrs. Ford's cousin. He was a clever gentleman, and aided communication between General Steele and Colonel Ford. Ford prevailed on every Confederate he found in Matamoros to accept a parole, return to his home, and become a good citizen of the United States. He argued that the South needed them if they were going to restore its commercial affairs.[78] Since Mifflin and King both had more than $20,000 dollars worth of property, they had to apply for special amnesty and be pardoned directly by the President of the United States.[79]

While Mifflin was working to obtain their amnesty papers so they could return home, Petra worried about Adrian and her boys in Pennsylvania. She had not seen the boys in over a year and could hardly wait until she could get settled in her home again and they could return to her. Adrian was fighting with the Juaristas against the Imperialists and she knew he was in constant danger.

Kenedy and King tried to consolidate their business interests. In April of 1865, Walworth had died, leaving all of his estate to his widow, Jane Walworth. Kenedy and King moved quickly. In a letter from Richard King in Matamoros to Reuben Holbein in Corpus Christi on May 3, 1865, King wrote that the heirs of Captain Walworth were demanding a settlement of his estate, making it necessary for Holbein to report as soon as possible with all books, papers, and accounts for the purpose of making a report on the rancho affairs. He also wanted to know the condition of charges on all cotton belonging to R. King & Co. He said evidently the Juaristas had gone back to Monterrey. He ended with, "As usual nothing is sane, 'Nothing true but Heaven' which is far from this degree of latitude."[80]

The Union would have loved to intercept those reports of cotton sales, but they did not, and by May 6, Kenedy and King paid Mrs. Walworth $50,000 cash for her interest in M. Kenedy & Co. and R. King & Co.[81] Mifflin was very concerned with money during the month of May. He wrote a letter to William

Hale in Houston on May 15 saying that after all the amounts drawn on the accounts for blockade-running and steamers that there was not much left. Kenedy told King,

> I want you to go to Houston to meet with Hale. I have now to my credit with San Román about $100,000, about $60,000 of this belongs to Hale. I can draw from San Román about $50,000. I have then a special deposit in his hands $1,000,000 more. I will have from necessity to use this deposit. Beverhard & Co. are in advance to us over & above each sales $90,000, so I cannot expect anything from them for a long time. My means then is about $150,000 including the special deposit, and I wish to use as little of that as possible. With the whole advanced on the King & Co. contract, the amount taken by Mr. Hale when he left here, what you & he have drawn for, & the funds placed in San Antonio & Galveston to your credit, & the expenses on the King & Co. contracts, all amounts to $540,000. I only mention this to give you an idea of what amounts you have yet in the country.[82]

The key words addressing their scarcity of cash were "in the country." Much of their money was stashed elsewhere, particularly in England, for safekeeping.

On May 15, Kenedy wrote Hale, "The drain I have been subjected to at the time you were here and since you left—to say nothing of other large amounts drawn from me for other purposes—what you have spent on blockade running and the steamers, there is not much more to drain on, and I beg of you to touch me lightly. I have thought for a long time you and Capt. King did not understand the situation."[83] On May 16, Kenedy told King, who was at Los Conchos, that after they paid Mrs. Walworth her $50,000 he would have no more than $50,000 in available funds. He told him that he had the special account of one million dollars but that he would need that for expenses already obligated.[84] By May 31, 1865, Kenedy wrote Stillman to inform him that the Union army was in control of Brownsville and the town was in shambles. He also told him he was more afraid of the trouble brewing between the Imperialist and Liberals than he was of facing charges of treason across the river in the United States.[85]

While Mifflin was busy getting his affairs in order, the Imperialists had captured Adrian, it was said, on his way to confer with Cortina. The "colorful and impulsive" Adrian became one of the victims of the vicious war on the Rio Grande. He was court-martialed and found guilty of being a traitor and guerrilla spy, fighting for the Juaristas against the French Imperialists.[86] He was executed on June 14, 1865, at Camargo. Mifflin wrote about his death in a letter to Capt. John Wilson in Tampico, Mexico, on June 30,

> I write with a heavy hand, as my boy has been shot at Camargo. As bad as he is, I would have saved him if I could, but my efforts have failed. Adrian was taken prisoner by the Imperial forces when they reached Camargo, tried and condemned as a guerrilla capt. and spy of Cortina, and was shot on the morning of the 14th of this month. He died at 20 years, one month and five days old, and to all appearances less concerned than any one present. He took the bandage from his eyes, and faced the guard, requesting them not to shoot him in the face which was not complied with. He requested his body to be sent to his mother. My brother being at Camargo at the time with the *Alamo*, he has brought him down, and is buried here in Matamoros. I used powerful means to save him, but could not succeed.[87]

Many questions surround Adrian's death and what the "powerful means to save him" meant. A letter written from A. A. Champion to Max Dreyer stated that when the Federalists retook Brownsville two weeks before Adrian's death, the Brownsville newspaper moved to Matamoros. It picked up an item from the *Matamoros Monitor* and published it on June 21, 1865, saying that there had been a guerrilla attack on Capt. Jeff Kenedy's (Captain Elisha Jeff Kenedy, Mifflin's brother) steamboat *Alamo*.[88] Since Mifflin's letter indicates that neither he nor Petra were at the execution, it is possible that Mifflin sent his brother up to Camargo with a great deal of money to try to bribe the Imperial officials to let Adrian go. We do know that Mifflin, even then fearing Adrian's execution, had written to Messrs. J. W. Lock & Co. at Camargo on June 10, 1865, to say that he had sent on the *Alamo* $5,000, "which my brother will hand to you. He has other funds which he may turn over if you need them. I could get no one here to send to Laredo. Please make any arrangements you think best in regards to any cotton that may have been turned there."[89] This letter appears to be in regard to the shipment of cotton, but it does put Mifflin's brother in the area at the same time of Adrian's death, on the *Alamo* and with money. It may have indeed been about cotton or that could be a cover for the attempted bribe. According to family lore, Petra offered to pay a ransom in gold equal to her beloved son's weight if they would spare him, but since he fought with the rebels it did no good.[90]

Three stories relate Elisha Kenedy's experience in trying to free Adrian. One is that Captain Elisha ("Jeff") Kenedy did succeed in getting Adrian on board and that the Imperialists boarded his boat and took him off at Camargo.

Steamboat captain and brother to Mifflin Kenedy, Elisha Jeffrey Kenedy, failed to rescue Adrian Vidal from the Imperialist forces in Mexico, who henceforth executed Adrian. Brownsville Historical Association.

Another family story is that Adrian had robbed a Greek merchant's mule train traveling from Brownsville to the Mexican interior. As luck would have it, that merchant was on Captain Elisha's boat and spotted Adrian. He managed to get word to the French soldiers and facilitated Adrian's capture.[91] A third is that Elisha successfully boarded Adrian and had started downstream when the boat caught on a sandbar, allowing the Imperialists to board and recapture Adrian. Max Dreyer, a descendant of Elisha's, said that the family story really was that Mifflin was angry with Elisha for allowing Adrian to be captured and blamed him for many years to come.[92] In a letter from Hubert Davenport to S. L. Gill, dated January 20, 1953, Davenport wrote that he had talked to George Scanlan, a Brownsville old timer, who told him that Capt. Mifflin Kenedy arranged to have Bidal [sic] secreted aboard his brother's boat. By reason of navigational problems, Captain "Lisha" was compelled to touch the Mexican bank of the river, where the Imperialists could and did search the boat, recaptured Vidal, and placed Captain "Lisha" under arrest. Capt. Mifflin Kenedy considered his brother's landing on the Mexican riverbank a grievous fault.[93] Mifflin was not in Camargo because on June 13 he wrote to Hiram Chamberlain Jr. at Santa Gertrudis from Matamoros, telling him to take care of the property as best he could and to carry out the instructions Captain King had left him. If he needed help he was to call on James J. Richardson for advice, as he knew the Captain's views and wishes.[94] Since Mifflin was in Matamoros on June 13, he could not have made it to Camargo on June 14, the day Adrian died.

Adrian died alone in a hot dusty plaza, without either of his parents, yet he remembered his mother at the very end and asked that his body be shipped to her. No doubt Mifflin suffered Adrian's loss almost as strongly as Petra. This difficult and complex son had been a problem from the moment Petra married Mifflin; Adrian had never adapted to the Anglo world. Instead, his world was Mexico. He fought and died for Mexico's independence and freedom. He did not waver in his belief in his native country and stayed by his convictions even though it cost him his life.

Mifflin and Petra removed Adrian from the *Alamo* and buried him in Matamoros. Later they moved him to the family burial plot in Brownsville.[95] His tombstone in Brownsville's old cemetery reads (translated from the Spanish):

Here lie the remains of
Adrian Vidal.
May he rest eternally in peace.
Born May 9, 1845.
Died in 1865 at the age of

20 years, one month and five days.
His parents, wife, daughter, & sisters
Dedicate this monument to his memory.

The use of the phrase "his parents" in this context would indicate Petra and Mifflin. It is touching that Petra included Mifflin in a very delicate way, at a very sensitive time. This gesture shows that Petra herself saw Mifflin as a "father" in some significant way to her Vidal children. Concepción Vidal's descendant, Rosa Swisher, wrote "Mifflin was the only father that she [Concepción] had ever known and she loved him dearly."[96] Correspondence indicates through greetings, salutations, and content that Mifflin was very fond of his stepchildren and step-grandchildren. In the case of Adrian's daughter, Mifflin referred to her as "my dear granddaughter."[97] Petra could have avoided the issue by writing simply "his mother, wife and daughter," yet she chose deliberately though subtly to include Mifflin. After Mifflin and Petra's deaths the family moved the family graves in the old cemetery to the new cemetery in Brownsville, but left Adrian behind. Today Adrian's grave is in a plot in the old cemetery, separated from his mother, whom he remembered at the time of his death.[98]

As Petra was grieving, Mifflin continued trying to put their business affairs in order. In July he wrote to William Hale, saying that Union authorities had seized all his property and were renting it out.[99] He had this letter hand delivered by don Manuel Rodríguez, Mifflin's stepson-in-law. Mifflin turned to Concepción's husband as a valued family member. When he needed someone he could trust, Manuel was a logical choice because as a Mexican citizen he would have a good chance of getting through the soldiers along the border. He sent a letter to Messrs. Robinson in Pittsburgh liquidating a debt of $4,886.28 and sent payment in British pounds.[100] He wrote Hiram Chamberlain Jr. at Los Conchos Ranch, advising him to resist any group that came to take the horses and cattle to sell to government butchers.[101] He wrote to Messrs. Robinson again in Pittsburgh to obtain letters of recommendation to President Johnson for amnesty.[102] He was handling all of his and King's correspondence, and on July 14, 1865, they both crossed the Rio Grande and were treated well.[103]

As soon as the last battle of the Civil War had been fought, King and Kenedy began to try to put back together M. Kenedy & Co. The ranching enterprise of R. King & Co. had to wait until they took care of their river interest. After Stillman and Walworth were out of the picture, the boats needed attention. First they had to get the boats from behind the wartime fronts of Mexican ownership, and new boats had to be purchased to make their new operations efficient. They also had to again develop good relationships with the military administration and the new Reconstruction regime. Kenedy and King were able to buy back the *Matamoros, Mustang, James Hale,* and the *Señorita,* that the Union army had confiscated. Some of these boats had little use left, so the partners ordered specially designed boats at Pittsburgh. The four new steamboats were the *Antonio, Eugenia, Tamaulipas,* and *Camargo,* and they were on the river by late 1865. They arranged to charter the *Tamaulipas* to the United States Quartermaster, sell the *Antonio* and *Eugenia* to the Imperialist forces, and retrained the *Camargo* for their own use.[104] Captains Kenedy and King were back on the river in force.

August brought bittersweet joy to Petra. On August 17 in Brownsville, Ana Adrianne Vidal was born, two months after her father had been killed in June.[105] She was named for her father and mother. The entire family enveloped this baby and her widowed mother. In Adrianne, Petra saw Adrian and a way to continue to love him and his new family. On September 4, another family event occurred; George Mifflin Putegnat, son of Joseph Putegnat and Rosa Vidal, was baptized by Father Parisot. The godmother was Louisa Vidal de Dalzell and Mifflin Kenedy was the godfather.[106] The arrival of these grandchildren gave Petra's life renewed hope for the future.

By August, King was back in Matamoros. Mifflin wrote to James J. Richardson at the Santa Gertrudis rancho on August 22 of King's whereabouts and spoke of going up to the rancho soon in company with Major Blücher.[107] On September 15, 1865, Kenedy and King signed the oath of allegiance to the United States. They were glad to have reestablished their citizenship. Now they could proceed with getting their pardons and getting their property back from the government. On the same day that they took the oath of allegiance, King wrote Maj. Gen. Giles Smith, asking respectfully for the possession of his home. He said that he knew his home was not in good repair and he needed to work on it to bring his family back from San Antonio where they had gone for safety after Henrietta had given birth to Robert E. Lee King in San Patricio.[108] A day later, on September 16, Mifflin wrote from Matamoros to Maj. Gen. Giles A. Smith at Brownsville, "Being desirous of returning with my family to Brownsville, I beg leave to apply to you for possession of my dwelling house situated on the corner of Elizabeth & Ninth streets and the lot in the rear of same on which is my servant's quarter and stable being corner of Ninth and Washington streets in order that I may resume my residence in this place."[109] Some U.S. government officials were not particularly pleased that King and Kenedy were going to be back in business so soon. Maj. Gen. Giles Smith, commander of Fort Brown, turned King's letter over to W. W. Gamble, the customs house collector, since the property was "abandoned." Maj. E. P. Durell of the Twenty-Eighth Illinois Volunteers, on November 29, 1865, asked for permission to appropriate Richard King's "abandoned" property as a telegraph office.[110] Maj. Giles Smith also received a letter from Ytúrria on August 31, requesting as a citizen of Mexico and resident of Matamoros that his property be returned. Since he was a Mexican citizen his request could be dealt with much more simply and faster.[111]

Mifflin, writing from Matamoros to Charles Stillman in New York on October 19, said he would be in Washington in about a month and that he might need then to obtain ten to twelve thousand dollars. He could send it to him at Pittsburgh, Pennsylvania.[112] Later, in a letter of April 7, 1866, Mifflin wrote that he went to Washington on November 25, 1865 to secure the pardons for King and himself.[113]

It is interesting to read parts of Richard King's Petition for Pardon and to analyze the reasoning he and Mifflin used:

> His Excellency The President of the United States
>
> Your Memorialist was then, at the commencement of the War, attending to the management of the stock on the Rancho, and was consequently called on by the Confederate Authorities, for the contribution or sale of large numbers of beeves, mules and horses, and was thereby placed in such a position as to be compelled to determine promptly what course he should take. His partner, M. Kenedy, then in charge of the Steamboats on the Rio Grande, was also exposed to similar requisitions; and both were thus obliged to decide whether they would abandon their moveable property, or remain in the State under the new organization. They were not politicians, but simply under the new organization. They were not politicians, but simply Steamboat men and stock raisers, who by a lifetime of industry had accumulated this property and desired to preserve it honorably for their children. They did not anticipate a long war, but felt persuaded that it would soon close under some amicable arrangement, and they decided, therefore, to remain and protect what they would otherwise lose.
>
> After thus deciding to remain, they felt it their duty to act honestly and sincerely as citizens of the seceeding [sic] Government under whose protection and laws they came; and they did so during the War, but without any feeling of hostility or enmity to the citizens of the Northern States or to those who took a different course: on the contrary, on every occasion in their power, they assisted and protected individual citizens of the United States who needed their aid: as a matter of business they invested their surplus means in cotton in Texas and exported it by the Rio Grande; and they were induced to take several contracts to supply the Confederate Forces on that River

Robert and Luisa Dalzell's residence, which was being built when the lumber for construction was stolen. Brownsville Historical Association.

and in Western Texas. Their motive for taking these contracts was not so much to obtain profit (because they actually proved unprofitable) as to ensure protection to their property on and near the Rio Grande during the war. The Confederate troops posted there not being designed originally to oppose the armies of the United States, but to preserve order on the Mexican frontier. Not withstanding all these efforts, a large portion of their stock was appropriated by both parties during the war, or dispersed; and they were obliged to sell their Steamboats then belonging to M. Kenedy & Co. to W. I. Galvan, who transferred them to the United States at the time of the occupation of the Rio Grande by Gen. Banks. Their losses have thus been very heavy and they desire to collect and preserve what remains of their property.

That in all their acts during the war, they have not been influenced by motives of hostility to the United States; and on the contrary sincerely desired at the commencement, that secession could be prevented; but being compelled either to remain in Texas or abandon everything, they thought it right to remain, and in that case, felt it their duty not to deceive their old friends and associates by taking a doubtful or insincere course—but to give their candid concurrence to the measures of the new Government.[114]

At the end of 1865 the banks of the Rio Grande once again rang with gunfire. War was raging in Mexico between the Juaristas and the Imperialists and would continue for two more years. Bandits were everywhere. They robbed the bishop of Monterrey as he paid a visit to Brownsville, asking his blessing as they did. Father Parisot was attacked on his way to Bagdad, and his assailant was caught and executed even though Father Parisot appealed to General Mejía to release him.[115] In October the U.S. soldiers at Clarksville, many of them black, were upset at their lack of blankets and clothing; when a severe norther hit about sixty of them marched on Brownsville where Mifflin's son-in-law, Captain Dalzell, had his new home under construction. On October 8 the soldiers killed a saloon owner and ransacked the town for clothes and lumber to protect them from the cold. At the corner of Eighth and Elizabeth, they began to carry off the Dalzell's lumber. Rosa Vidal Putegnat's brother-in-law, William Putegnat, was bayoneted in the forehead and seriously wounded while attempting to stop the soldiers.[116]

Petra's grief and unhappiness had filled the past year. She and Mifflin had been unable to save their troubled son Adrian from death, but at least they had his young widow and daughter to look after. Petra had been separated from her three small sons and longed for their return. Petra and Mifflin's home and business property had been seized and lived in by the Union soldiers, and she had lived amid constant danger and turmoil. Her faith had been tested.

CHAPTER 7

1866:
Home Again

Violence escalated at the mouth of the Rio Grande *in January of 1866, and Petra's good friend, Father Parisot, was caught in the middle of it. On January 5, 1866, the Union troops at Clarksville, who were newly mustered out of the army and waiting for transport, turned their frustrations across the river. Three hundred troops crossed the Rio Grande and attacked Bagdad. In what is known as the "Bagdad Raid," the mostly black soldiers killed the justice of the peace, damaged buildings, and left twenty people dead. On hearing about the trouble, Father Parisot bribed a boatman to take him to Bagdad. He landed and retrieved a large number of church goods that had been stored in the warehouse. On his third trip he had a large statue of St. Joseph on board when a Mexican officer stopped him, demanding to know what he had in the boat. The officer detained but did not guard Father Parisot. As the rain worsened he covered himself with a rubber coat, and when the guard did not return, he pushed off and returned to Clarksville, crediting St. Joseph with his safe return.[1] In another story of the event, the priest is delegated to go out to the ship to bring back a beautiful statue of St. Joseph for the church. All arrangements were made but the priest tired of waiting and placed the statue on the boat and started with his load. When the guards saw the boat pulling out they began to fire on the priest, who hid behind the statue, which saved his life.[2]

Petra gave thanks that her friend was safe, and others undoubtedly said thankful prayers at the church. While Petra was waiting for their home and possessions to be returned so they could move back to Brownsville, Mifflin was stabilizing their business affairs. The steamboat business was in trouble up and down the river. The Union troops were downsizing and many people were leaving after the conclusion of the war. The cotton business had diminished

Father Parisot, OMI, who was close to Petra and her family. Brownsville Historical Association.

and there was little private freight to haul. Again, Mifflin and King turned to their old standby—the army—and they once again secured the U.S. Army's freight-hauling business.[3] It was a credit to their political and negotiating skills that these two ex-Confederates landed on their feet and in control of that contract.

Kenedy and King knew they had to play tough to protect their interests. Gen. Philip H. Sheridan had built a small narrow-gauge military railway in 1865 from the sea anchorage at Brazos to the riverboat terminal at White Ranch, posing the possibility of replacing the need for Kenedy & Co.'s "outside boats." Mifflin first employed the usual technique of buying up the competition. They bid $60,000 for the railroad, but were outbid by the firm West & Chenery, who bid $108,000. Then Mifflin and King had to take harsher measures. The firm of West & Chenery did not know that Kenedy and King owned both the terminal facilities at White Ranch and the land that the terminal of Brazos Santiago was built on. The firm had bought a railroad with no place to go and thus turned their purchase back over to the government.[4] Mifflin recognized the opportunities that railroad transportation could bring and on October 1, 1866, Kenedy and King received an exclusive charter from the Texas legislature to build a railroad linking Brownsville to Brazos Santiago. Mifflin ran into strong opposition from Charles Stillman, who thought the railroad would hurt his company's wharfage and ferry rights as well as the steamboat business. He was able to stall and keep the company from proceeding with the project. The merchants up and down the river were again being charged the high fees they had previously paid to M. Kenedy & Co. due to their monopoly. From 1850 to 1870, Kenedy and King operated twenty-five steamers on the Rio Grande. These steamers used huge quantities of wood from cypress trees, which have since almost totally disappeared, that once grew in profusion along the banks of the river. Sentiment against Kenedy and King continued to build until 1870, when it erupted into an all-out fight between M. Kenedy & Co. and the merchants.[5]

During this time Petra was involved with a movement seeking to relocate southerners to Mexico and Latin American countries. The movement developed in answer to the desolation and starvation that existed after the Civil War across the South. The banks were ruined, railroads destroyed, the money worthless, and much of the South lay in waste. Glowing accounts in periodicals attested to the advantages of moving to these countries. The Confederate currency was worthless and no other was available, and there were no laborers to cultivate the land, which could not be sold because there was no one to purchase it. Mexico and Latin America seemed an option for the discouraged Confederates. Matthew Fontaine Maury, a Virginian, had been writing about the benefits and advantages of Latin America and comparing the Amazon Basin to the great valley of the Mississippi for twenty years before the Civil War. Many turned to the idea of fleeing and settling in a foreign land. A plan had been underway about the same time as Lee's surrender in April of 1865. The Confederate diplomatic agents received a grant on April 27, 1865 from Emperor Maximilian of Mexico to organize in St. Louis the American and Mexican Emigrant Company. Gen. J.B. Magruder, the chief of the land office, arranged for opening land offices in the southern states and in California. Heads of families were to be offered 640 acres of land, single men were to receive 320 acres, and there would be freedom from taxation for one year, freedom from military service for five years, and religious toleration.[6] Yet the Maximilian government in Mexico believed that the sturdy landholders would offer support against the general population led by Benito Juárez.[7]

Among the leaders in this movement were several Confederate generals: J.B. Magruder, Cadmus Wilcox, James E. Slaughter, Sterling Price, E. Kirby Smith, J.B. Clark (former senator from Missouri), and governors Henry Wallace of Louisiana, Governor Reynolds and former governor Polk of Missouri, and former governor Isham G. Harris of Tennessee. Some of the leading Texans were generals W.H. King, W.P. Hardeman, H.P. Bee, Joseph Shelby, former attorney general George Flournoy, A.W. Terrell, Governor Pendleton Murrah, colonels D.S. Terry, Phil Luckett, and M.T. Johnson, and most surprising of all—and the only woman noted among this powerful group of men—Mrs. Mifflin Kenedy.[8] These movements were never very successful but exemplified the frustration of the defeated Confederacy and its supporters in the years following the war. Although little is known about Petra Vela Kenedy's involvement, it is interesting that she is listed as a leader along with the generals, colonels, governors, and senators. Petra's vast network and contacts in Mexico may well have been an advantage in their negotiations.

Finally, Petra's frustrations ended and she could rejoice in March 1866 when she and Mifflin were able to move back into their home in Brownsville. Mifflin maintained his office in Matamoros while he closed down some of his businesses. He wrote a letter from there on April 7, 1866, to Capt. L.G. Aldrich at Natchez, Mississippi, telling him that he and King had surrendered in November and he had gone to Washington and secured their pardons on November 25. He wrote that he was glad to be a good citizen and that he and King were now both living in Brownsville again. He said he had only been

Mifflin Kenedy dissolved M. Kenedy & Co. and established King, Kenedy & Co.

moved over about a month and went on to document some of the losses that he and King had suffered during the war. They had lost 5,600 bales of cotton, which had been seized by the Federals, and they hoped by course of law to have some 4,000 bales returned. Their ranch, Santa Gertrudis, had lost a great deal of horse stock. He said he and King were both back on the river working to restore that business and they had the government contract from Brazos Santiago to Ringgold Barracks. They still had two steamers on the Mexican side and ten steamers on the Texas side, since they had bought four from the government. He told Aldrich that King was now the managing partner and did not have much idle time.[9]

In this letter Mifflin explained the new arrangement that had led to dissolving M. Kenedy & Co. and starting King, Kenedy & Co. The new firm had been established to deal with the withdrawal of partner Stillman, who was returning to New York, and partner Walworth, who had died. In 1866, Charles Stillman suffered a stroke that paralyzed his left arm, and upon his return to New York his son James built on the wealth his father had acquired, investing money to start the National City Bank of New York. King, Kenedy & Co. had a capital stock of $250,000, and its new ownership was divided as one-fourth to Mifflin and King and one-eighth to Robert Dalzell and Joseph Cooper. One-twelfth also went to Francisco Ytúrria, Jeremiah Galvan, and Artemus Brown, who had helped them with the cotton trade during the war.[10]

At this point Mifflin was bringing into his business his new son-in-law, Robert Dalzell. Mifflin had been instrumental in bringing Dalzell to Texas during the Mexican War as a steamboat captain, and now as Luisa's husband he was a member of the family. Mifflin would continue to rely more and more on Dalzell as a business partner. On April 13, Mifflin had his son-in-law Dalzell dash from Brownsville to Brazos Santiago to catch a steamer for New Orleans to see about government surplus steamers that were to be sold. Dalzell barely made it in time and had to jump on board as the steamer was leaving the wharf. With the four steamers he bought, the company had all they could use.[11]

Joe Putegnat, the other son-in-law, and Rosa were also moving into the social scene. The Englishman James Horrocks wrote about a party that was held at the house of the Putegnats on October 22, where twenty people had a champagne supper and played round games. The party was held to celebrate the wedding of Belle Green, "a very handsome girl." Horrocks had stayed on after the war and in 1866 landed a job with Mr. Kingsbury in the collector's office. He wrote to his brother that he was on good terms with most of the respectable men in Brownsville, four of whom were worth over a million dollars. He referred to King, Kenedy, & Co. as the "richest firm in Brownsville."[12]

On April 9, Mifflin wrote William Robinson in Pittsburgh to tell him that the *San Román* had arrived in fine condition. He complained that a large warehouse and office were in the government's control and that the ranch had suffered greatly. They had been raided by the Confederates, Mexican thieves, Texas thieves, and by the Federals. He then told him that "success depends on the peace and quiet of Mexico or another war, that would bring our large steamboat properties into full service."[13] Mifflin was not to get his wish; Mexico neither saw peace nor a full-scale war but stayed in a state of chaos for the next few years.

On April 10, Mifflin wrote Charles Stillman, "the machine here is now in running order, under active management of Captain King, assisted by Elisha Kenedy, and from this time forward I will devote my time to closing up our old affairs."[14] It appears that Mifflin was moving toward his expressed desire to wind up his affairs in Brownsville and move on to something else. Mifflin was always a businessman first and perennially looking for the next opportunity to make money. Mifflin's longtime friend John Ford had these words to say about Mifflin: "after an acquaintance of forty years with Captain Kenedy, I have never known him to desert a friend or to quail before an enemy. He has been candid and outspoken, despising the arts of concealment and disguise. He has been a man of success, but that success has been the outcome of good sense and integrity. That he possesses talents of a high order none can deny. Let the man who writes of him after he has passed away speak of his mental acquirements. Let him do justice to a man who has made his mark in a country where thousands have failed to succeed and who never resorted to the arts of a flatterer."[15]

Mifflin had his family on his mind as well as his business. In a letter written on April 9 to his mother, a personal side of Mifflin was revealed as he reverted back to his Quaker roots with the use of "Thee" and "Thou". He expressed his concern that they were all well taken care of financially, using his London bank accounts to provide the money. He told her about her other son, Elisha, his wife Petra, and inquired about his boys. Mifflin wrote that he was "sending a note of exchange drawn on myself on Messrs Des Fag & Co. of London England for 200 pounds sterling to give it to Abraham Gibbons [president of the bank] and he will send it forward for Thee." The money was for the "purpose of furnishing the house or some part of it as Thee may deem best." Mifflin continued to help them with the house and its maintenance. He then wrote,

> Thee will recollect Jo was to place herself in this matter. We are well. I moved from here to Brownsville about a month ago. My wife will visit you this summer—the exact time I cannot yet tell. . . . I have been very busy since my return having made three visits to New Orleans. We are getting our affairs into shape again and all is working well. Elisha is now Captain of the *Jose San Roman* the boat that Robert Dalzell built at Pittsburgh. . . . Has Jo not time to write— direct one to Brownsville, Texas—kind remembrances to Esquino

Valentino and Family and all Friends—Same to the children, not forgetting Jo and say to her write.

With the hopes this may find you all in good health, and that God in his Infinite Goodness will bless and protect you are the prayer of Thy—Ever Affectionate Son, M Kenedy.[16]

The month of May brought an occasion for celebration for Petra. The bells that Mifflin had funded for the church were to be dedicated. Father Parisot was a never-ending force in trying to improve the church and the community. The church had been badly damaged when General Bee withdrew and the powder exploded. The locks and windowpanes were broken and the church was badly cracked by the blast. He had to raise money for the repairs and was distressed that his church did not have bells.[17] He came up with an idea to hold a concert in order to raise money to fund the purchase of the bells. This would certainly be easier than rounding up cattle, as he had done before. The singing groups were put together and they began practicing. Father Parisot called on Captain Kenedy one morning to request that his daughter's name be placed on the program. The captain expressed his belief that the child was too young to sing in public, which Father Parisot met with the statement that she was already very proficient in her part.[18]

Father Parisot said that Captain Kenedy

> went to his desk and handed me a draft for $2,000 in gold, saying, "Father, this is to buy a chime of three bells for your church." I was so astounded at the generosity and magnificence of the gift, that I could not find words to express my gratitude. I merely said, "O Captain, what good news for Brownsville! Allow me to go immediately, and communicate this extraordinarily happy event to my fellow Priests." Then giving the Captain a warm shake of the hand, I departed. I had gone but a few steps along the sidewalk when he cried out: "Father, come back," Quick as lightning the thought flashed into my mind, that the draft was but a joke. When I returned to the office, the Captain received me with a hearty laugh and said: "Father, you have become so excited that you have forgotten your hat and cane," and in fact it was true; I had started for Brownsville, without either hat or cane. I was somewhat ashamed of this predicament and it was some time before my mind recovered its equilibrium.[19]

The bells were now in place, and were to be dedicated on May 20. The three bells were blessed and given the names of Jesus, Mary, and Joseph. The *padrinos* who signed the church record on the occasion were Captain Mifflin and Petra Vela Kenedy, Nestor Maxan, Sofia Rivadulla, Ignace E. Rock, Felipa H. Tijerina, and Sarah J. Kenedy. It was quite a tribute to young Sarah at age nine to be listed as a *madrina* for this occasion. Petra was very proud as she watched her young daughter participate in the program. Mifflin through his generosity continued to honor his Petrita and bring her joy.[20]

The nuns at the Incarnate Word and Blessed Sacrament were also very busy; they were determined to enlarge their facility. Following the war, Sister Ephrem gave this account: "Mother St. Ange had a large house built, south of the original one, for classrooms, art rooms, etc. . . . It was a hundred feet long, with all the conveniences that were possible to procure then. It had galleries closed with blinds. On the north side there was another building, the first floor of which was for the chapel; the second, for the novitiate; the third was for the novices to study art. In front of the chapel there was a smaller building for a parlor and the priest's room. Until then the chaplain took his breakfast in the cellar." Sisters and students alike were very pleased with the added facilities, which made living and working much more pleasant. It would seem indeed that the community was entering an era of progress. Many boarding students were attracted to the school, and enrollment of day students continued to increase.[21]

Mifflin continued to be frustrated with the federal government and took matters into his own hands. On June 16, he wrote a letter to Mr. Charles Worthington in Georgetown, Washington, D.C.,

> Enclosed you will find bill for part of the warehouse on the corner of Elizabeth and 11th St. occupied by the U.S. as warehouse from December 1, 1865 to June 1866. The site was occupied by the Custom House here, previous to Dec. 1, 1865—but I cannot make any claims as my pardon here dates from November 25, 1865. . . . Mr Hopkins informs me that the goods stored in the building have been confiscated property. . . . If you cannot get the bill allowed as sent, you will please settle the rent at whatever you think it is worth, so as to close the affair up to the first of June. The house is still occupied by the Custom House. I have possession of the balance of the building and it is now in fine order. The whole building is 120 × 80 feet divided into three rooms and a passage of 10 feet running through the center. It is fireproof, except doors and windows—they being of wood. Inside is a cistern underground containing 24,000 gallons of water. Should the government desire to rent the whole house I will rent it for $350 per month—you are aware it is the safest and best warehouse in Brownsville. There is a fine office in the building 30 × 25 feet.[22]

Mifflin wanted the government to either pay up or get out. Some of the Federals were not very happy with Mifflin and his partners and were suspicious of their friendly relationship with certain federal officials. Customs inspector T. M. Balsiones wrote Hon. F. Cummings, office inspector of customs at White's Ranch, Texas, to complain that the *Tamaulipas No. 2,* one of Kenedy and King's boats, was operating in an irregular and clandestine manner without paying proper duties. He said that she was delivering six cases of valuable medicines that weren't taxed. He also went down to Clarksville to check out how some people had come into possession of a quantity of good cigars, and he was reprimanded because he tried to investigate the matter.[23] He had not yet learned how business was conducted in this part of the world.

The war along the border changed again on June 24 when General Mejía and the French army surrendered Matamoros to Carvajal and Escobedo and left for Bagdad and then Veracruz. The French had left the Rio Grande Valley. This did not bring peace, because the victors then turned on each other. The forces finally joined together in 1866 to get rid of the French and on June 19, 1867, a year later, Escobedo's army executed Emperor Maximilian, Gen. Tomás Mejía, and Miguel Miramon at El Cerro de la Campanas, near Querétaro.[24] John Ford related that at one point in the war General Mejía had saved General Escobedo, and he thought poorly of Escobedo for having Mejía executed. General Escobedo, according to Ford, explained that the night before the execution, General Escobedo entered the room occupied by General Mejía. He told him to go to a certain point, at a certain hour, and there he would find a man on guard, in whom he could confide. From that point he would be conducted to where he would see a horse already saddled. "Mount him and save your life." General Escobedo said he was astonished when Mejía, a noble old Indian, remarked: "No, I will stay and die with the Emperor."[25]

Mexican nationalism owes a great deal to the French occupation during the reign of Maximilian. The people of the northern frontiers and parts that had been taken from Mexico by the United States had started feeling nationalism by the end of the 1830s, stirred up by the daily conflict between the "quietism of the Mexican and the power, the aggressiveness, and the foreign culture of the Anglo American." The conflict was expressed almost immediately in folkloricisms, such as in terms for North Americans, "gringo," for example.[26] This labeling can even be found in Petra, the mother of half-Anglo children, when in her letter to Salomé she refers to the possibility of her sons marrying *gringritas* when she prefers them to marry Mexicans who can speak Castilian.[27] Although she may soften it by adding "*ita,*" it is still a pejorative term. Spanish dictionaries define *gringo* as "foreigner," and to speak in *gringo* is to talk gibberish, be a barbarian in the ancient Greek sense. Only during the last century has it come to mean American.[28] The French, although not contentious enough to warrant labels, still gave rise to nationalism in Mexicans who resented an invasion from yet another country.

After the French left, Father Parisot, ever undaunted, heard that the Juaristas had assumed control and two local priests were imprisoned. When the priests refused to give up the keys to the church, the military denied them food and water. Father Parisot, hearing about their predicament, hurried across the river and appealed for their release. When their freedom was denied he presented the officials with a church key; the priests were freed and Parisot hurried them to Brownsville and safety. Only later did the officials find out that they had been given the wrong key.[29]

Petra departed on July 3, taking Sarah and Willie north to see their grandmother and the family; María Vicenta possibly accompanied her. The children were probably excited about taking a real ocean voyage and traveling up the Mississippi. Mifflin would have booked them first class passage so they could enjoy the steamboat to its fullest. Mark Twain wrote about what they might have seen along the way—the low shores, the ungainly trees, and the "democratic buzzards" along the lower river. As the boat reached the upper river there were islands, bluffs, woods, and villages. Crowds of people would have greeted them along the way as they pulled into the towns with the whistle blowing and flags flying.[30] When they boarded the train to Coatesville they would have had the chance to see the green hills and valleys where their father grew up. Best of all, when they pulled into the station their brothers would be waiting for them. Petra was happy to see her young sons because it had been over two years since they left. John Gregorio was now ten, James, or Santiago, was eleven, and Tom was thirteen. Their younger brother, Willie, was now six years old; he had only been three when they left Brownsville. Sarah was now nine and she had been only six then. It was a joyous reunion when Petra held her boys and they could again play with their younger siblings.

On the way home they probably went through New York City because their father had written Charles Stillman that he might see them in New York. Their stay was not a very long one because Mifflin said the children were back on September 6.[31]

The newspaper in Coatesville published a piece in 1895 on Mifflin, and in it they described a visit by Petra. She was a "young Mexican woman in whose veins the blood of the Hidalgos was flowing," and who when she walked about town with "modest dignity" accompanied by her servant was of interest not only because of the stories of her fabulous wealth but also because "she wore a Spanish mantilla of black lace which rested upon her head with native grace."[32] It is possible that the "servant" was María Vicenta, who traveled with her mother perhaps to get her mind off of the loss of her baby after his birth in

Baton Rouge and death a few months later. Also she would have been an excellent interpreter for her mother. The oral history in the family is that María Vicenta went to Pennsylvania at one time.[33] The article also noted that Mifflin had sent his mother drafts "which the bank officials were only too glad to honor."[34]

This must have been a difficult trip for Petra in one way since she did not speak English. It is most certain that she understood it but was not comfortable speaking it. For a usually vivacious talker who was warm and friendly it may have been difficult to fit into this society. That Mifflin sent her and the children without him is a mark of his confidence in her ability to take care of herself and their children in a completely unfamiliar environment.

By September, Kenedy and King were able to turn their focus to the ranch they now jointly owned. Despite their large stock losses during the war, they were still the most prominent ranchers in South Texas. They had 84,000 cattle and 5,400 horses to manage.[35] Bandits and thieves were rampant, and on September 16 Richard King at the Santa Gertrudis was writing to General Getty requesting additional protection and offering, if they would send men, to help them become familiar with the roads and towns.[36] Disenfranchised Anglo Confederates and Mexicans who resided on both sides of the river launched raids across the Rio Grande Valley.[37] Mifflin in Brownsville wrote King at the ranch on September 23, 1866, telling him he was glad to hear of the safe arrival of King and his family at the ranch. Mifflin appeared to be a little frustrated with King and his management style. He wrote that he was telling him to spend $10,000 on the ranch however he deemed necessary, but he did not understand not having a plan. He said that if King wanted to sell the ranch as he had indicated then he does not understand the expenditure of the money even though he said the horse stock was not in proper condition. He concluded by asking King to send him his definite plans for the future in regard to the rancho.[38]

After the Civil War the U.S. military was issuing large contracts for beef. The future for cattle was bright, and many people were looking for ways to get into the cattle business. Cattle were selling for between $8.50 and $14 a head and there was little expense involved. Sheep sold at $1 to $1.75 per head and goats at $1.50 per head.[39]

Meanwhile, in Matamoros the two Juarista factions led by Servando Canales and General Escobedo were in conflict over control of the town. The U.S. government was watching the situation carefully, and General Sedgwick at Fort Brown was able to obtain a truce between the two groups.[40] In a letter on September 6 to Mr. F. J. Parker in Austin, Mifflin in Brownsville wrote, "The river is very high, higher than it has been since 1846. Ford is in one of the forts in Matamoros with some 1,411 men. I don't know exactly whose interest he is in, but it would not surprise me to see him in command of Matamoros. Get the rail charter."[41]

The end of October was a sad time for Henrietta King because her father, Hiram Chamberlain, was gravely ill. Mifflin once again was there to support the King family any way he could. On October 27, Mifflin wrote King at the rancho that Mrs. King and Reverend Chamberlain had arrived safely. He said the Reverend was better but that there was little hope for him.[42] Then the next day, on the twenty-eighth, Mifflin wrote that Mr. Chamberlain was getting weaker and that Mrs. King was holding up, "Yet I am afraid next Sunday when I write you, I will have to announce to you his death."[43] On November 2, Mifflin wrote King, "Mr. Chamberlain died yesterday at 7:30 A.M. and was buried today at 2 P.M. I have been there much of the time."[44] Mifflin had stepped in for King and taken care of his family during this time of grief. On November 4, Mifflin wrote that Mrs. Chamberlain, Nettie, and Mrs. King were doing as well as could be expected and that Mrs. King hoped to start for the rancho on the seventh or eighth but they were having heavy rains and she might not get off in time.[45] After Reverend Chamberlain's death, Mrs. Chamberlain went east to live, taking her daughter Adelia and her youngest son Edwin with her. The other Chamberlain boys, Hiram Jr., Bland, and Willie went to live at the Santa Gertrudis and work for Captain King. Edwin soon joined his brothers and the captain often grinned and referred to his children's "half-uncles."[46]

By the end of November the businesses of Mifflin and King were straightened out. On October 1, they had obtained the charter from the Texas legislature to build a railroad from Brazos Santiago to Brownsville, which they never built but prevented others from doing. Mifflin was again writing to King on November 18 telling him he was enclosing $20,000 to be divided up, $10,000 for the rancho and $10,000 for his individual account. He reminds King that he does not want to hear, "What has become of the money?" again. Mifflin evidently had received King's plans for the rancho and in the same letter he writes that he does not think that the plans King says will cost $50,000 can be done for that amount, that he thinks it will take nearly $100,000.[47]

Petra ended her year with the baptism on December 26 of her newest granddaughter, Rosa Elisa Putegnat, the daughter of Rosa and Joseph. Father Parisot gathered the family before him as he baptized the newest member of the Kenedy family. Her sponsors were Willie Kenedy and María Vicenta Vidal de Starck.[48] The children continued to support one another and the family unit remained strong.

CHAPTER 8

1867-68: "Woe to Brownsville! Woe to Matamoros!"

Mifflin, Petra, members of their family, and their friends assumed leadership roles in trying to reconstruct Brownsville. After the war, over a thousand soldiers on the Rio Grande left the army and many of them stayed along the river. Cameron County, which included the city of Brownsville, needed to reorganize. Mifflin served on the Brownsville City Council with Stephen Powers, Adolphus Glavecke, Alexander Werbiski, Henry Miller, and Robert Shears. These men were all ex-Confederates or Southern sympathizers, but their mayor, Josiah Moorhead, was a Union man, and he presided. The group was chosen to maintain peace between the two political forces of the Reds and the Blues.[1] Edward Downey, Mifflin and Petra's good friend, served as county judge, and Mifflin and Petra's son-in-law, Fred Starck, served as county clerk. In February of 1866, Mifflin served with John McAllen and a son-in-law, Robert Dalzell, on the Cameron County grand jury. This group met throughout the year mainly to hear cases concerning cattle theft, which was a significant problem throughout the Rio Grande Valley.[2]

As 1867 began, Mifflin also served on the district court. John Ford said, "Captain Kenedy was foreman of two Grand Juries. John S. Ford, at the request of Judge (John Charles) Watrous of the Federal court, also acted as foreman of a grand jury. Every proper effort was made to execute the laws and to bring the offenders to justice. More than seventy offenders were convicted and sent to the penitentiary. The fact of Captain Kenedy's agreeing to serve two terms on the grand jury had a good effect on the citizens. All felt assured that

St. Joseph College was started by Father Parisot, who collected and stored 300,000 bricks during the Civil War when buildings were being torn down. John Gregory attended St. Joseph College and probably his brothers did, too. Brownsville Historical Association.

he would not indict anyone without guilt. His name to an indictment was esteemed a rather clear proof of guilt."[3]

March was a good month for Petra and the family. On March 2, Julia Dalzell was born and Petra welcomed another granddaughter. Two and a half weeks later she welcomed another grandson. Frederick Edward Starck was born to Fred Starck and Vicenta. This child was especially dear to his parents and grandparents because of the loss of Fred and Vicenta's first little boy and because of Vicenta's serious illness the year before. The older daughters and their husbands, Willie and Sarah, and the grandchildren surrounded Petra and Mifflin. But three of their children were still away. Sometime during 1867 or early 1868 Mifflin and Petra welcomed home Tom, James, and John Gregorio from Pennsylvania; the family circle was complete at last. The boys told stories of the time they spent in the North and stories of the Civil War from a Union perspective. They eagerly greeted their old friends, met the new family members, and settled down. In 1868 John and probably the other boys attended St. Joseph College, which had been established in 1866 by the Oblates in Brownsville.[4]

On May 30 a dispute arose between Mifflin and John McAllen and his wife Salomé Ballí. In 1859 John Young, Salomé's first husband, had purchased half of the Las Mesteñas grant, or twelve leagues, for $1,500, from Mifflin Kenedy. Mifflin had bought the land in 1854 and 1855 from Vicente Hinojosa. Young had aggressively sought to buy up as much of Las Mesteñas as possible. At Young's death in 1859 he left his interest to his wife and minor son John J. Young. Mifflin claimed that Young sold the land back to him and that on May 30 he had a contract drawn stating that Young had sold the land. Salomé and John McAllen swore that the signature of John Young on the original contract was a forgery. B. Bigelow, Jeremiah Galvan, and Robert Hughes had witnessed the signature. Many court proceedings followed, including a claim by the Kenedys that Salomé had filed a protest to the document, which, according to her, she did not. The case ended with a default judgment because she did not take action on the protest, thus giving the land to the Kenedys. Mifflin thought he owned the land and gave his interest to his son Thomas in 1885 in a settlement of the estate following Petra's death. Thomas sold the property and the McAllens continued to proceed with their oppositions. The case was not settled until 1908, when the McAllens received half of the Las Mesteñas grant.[5]

During the summer a dreaded visitor appeared again along the Rio Grande. A yellow fever epidemic hit and almost one-third of the people in Brownsville succumbed. Petra and her family escaped the fever but many were not so lucky. The epidemic started when a man arrived on horseback from Indianola in July; he was taken ill the next day. Within thirty-six hours he had died, and within ten days the city resembled 1854. For days and weeks the streets were deserted except for the physicians driving rapidly from house to house in the death-laden air. Petra had not only her household to worry about but also those of her daughters and the grandchildren. Two resident physicians died as the town fought once more against its enemy.[6]

October was both a sad and terrifying month for Petra. She lost her first grandchild, Rosa Eliza Putegnat, who had been born on December 26, 1866, and died on October 1, 1867.[7] The death of this child would have been doubly difficult for Petra because she was almost exactly the same age as her baby Phebe when she lost her. Petra could not help but relive the grief she and Mifflin had shared when they had to bury their baby, and now she needed to comfort Rosa who was expecting another child in the near future. Petra and Rosa were again consoled by their belief that when God's little angels die after they have been baptized, but before their confirmation, they go straight to heaven to be in God's embrace.[8]

Less than a week after the baby's death a terrifying event occurred along the Rio Grande. On October 7, Father Parisot said, "For three days previous an Irish woman had foretold the destruction of the twin cities of Brownsville and Matamoros, crying out in the streets, 'Woe to Brownsville, Woe to Matamoros.' She was looked upon as a crazy woman and locked up in jail as a disturber of the peace." Father Parisot continued, "a dark and heavy cloud appeared in the North. When it burst, a strong wind arose and the rain poured down in torrents. Through the day the wind became stronger and stronger. In the evening it became more violent. The hammer was heard all over the city. The doors and windows were fastened and barred: everything forebode a terrible calamity."[9]

Mother St. Ange from the Sisters of the Incarnate Word and Blessed Sacrament Convent and School wrote a letter to France describing in detail the events of October 7 and 8:

> The hurricane was preceded by three weeks of rain that fell in torrents, by sudden changes in the atmosphere, by a certain physical discomfort impossible to define. At seven in the morning a strong wind began to blow from the north, accompanied by a freezing rain. The day was so dark that we could scarcely see to sew. The rain penetrated everywhere, forming a kind of frozen sleet. The day passed silently and sadly, and the evening seemed to foretell a stormy night. About seven P.M. balls of fire were seen in several directions in the air, vivid lightnings pierced the heavens in every direction, and fear reigned everywhere.
>
> After taking all possible measures for security of the house we went to bed, but we had scarcely done so when we were obliged to get up. The wind from the north blew so furiously that in spite of all our precautions the windows began to break and the water to come in torrents. Again, we fought against the wind, nailing boards against the openings but the sleet cut the faces and arms of the Sisters, rendering it impossible for them to continue. Besides, it was useless, as the wind tore off the boards a soon as they were nailed. We tried to protect the sanctuary with mattresses, but it was a useless endeavor—the water overflowed every thing. "What shall we do, Mother," asked the Sisters. "Nothing, we cannot fight against God. Let us go and pray."[10]

Sisters and children groped their way to the chapel in utter darkness. There, close to the tabernacle, they knelt in prayer, with arms outstretched in the form of a cross, asking God to spare them. The storm subsided for a short time, and everyone thought the worst was over. Suddenly, however, the winds raged with ever-greater force, overturning buildings and leveling everything in their path. The Sisters returned to the chapel to continue their supplications, which they and the children kept up for two and a half hours.[11]

At last, there seemed to be an end to the storm, and the Sisters, completely exhausted, let their hands drop to their sides but remained in the chapel until daylight. Only then was it discovered that two young girls were missing. Terror-stricken, some of the Sisters went in search of them. With difficulty they made their way to what was left of the dormitory. There lay the children fast asleep, in a pool of water. With grateful hearts the Sisters carried them to the chapel, the only part of the building offering a safe

Brownsville after the hurricane of 1867, which significantly damaged the entire Rio Grande region. The unroofed two-story building on the left was the Iron Building, which served as headquarters for King, Kenedy & Co. Brownsville Historical Association.

refuge. Father Parisot wrote that one minute later, the dormitory came down with a tremendous crash.[12]

Finally, the full extent of their losses made its impact on the Sisters. What they saw as they ventured forth to view the damage was enough to shake their faith, but their reaction was a spontaneous prayer of resignation. That night of horror had wiped out fifteen years of savings, and they still owed $10,000 francs at 18 percent interest on the last building project. Parents rushed to the convent to remove their children, giving praise that they were safe. The children did not return for a while though, because yellow fever broke out again in the town three or four days later. The loss of revenue was a blow to the sisters. The Oblate Fathers were quick to come to the Sisters' rescue, and seeing them without a home offered them space in a building that was being erected for St. Joseph's College.[13]

The *Daily Ranchero* summarized the storm by saying, "In the short space of twenty-four hours, commencing on Monday morning, October 7, a belt of country nearly one hundred miles in width, embracing Brownsville, Matamoros, Brazos Santiago, Clarksville, and Bagdad, was the theater of every storm known. The last three named towns were completely wiped out while

Brownsville and Matamoros suffered heavy losses in life and property. Convent and school were a total loss, but the lives of the Sisters and children were saved miraculously. The solid ornament and palatial structure, the Catholic convent, crumbled away to ruins."[14]

The *New York Times* ran the headlines "Brownsville, Bagdad and Brazos Destroyed." The *Brownsville Courier* gave the full details of the awful hurricane on the Rio Grande:

> On the 7th of the present month the long heated term was put on end by a refreshing norther which sprung up about eight A.M. and continued with more or less violence until about nine o'clock P.M. when it assumed a rotary motion, striding with a fearful fury from north-northeast and momentarily increased to the violence of the most dreadful tornadoes of the tropics. We have seldom had occasion in our journalism to describe an occurrence so vivid in terrors and so prolific in destruction. There is not a habitation which has not felt the terrible force of the storm. The scene on the river was frightful to behold. All our steamers are partially or totally destroyed. *Tamaulipas 1* and *2* have their upper works and cabin destroyed and the *Matamoros* drifted down the river and is now lying at the point wrecked.
>
> Matamoros: the destruction at Matamoros was still greater than at Brownsville. Whole squares of edifices are mere ruins and it is estimated that 1,500 homes have been destroyed. It is estimated that twenty-six persons were killed. There is not a house left in Bagdad and only three houses left in Clarksville. At Brazos de Santiago some of the people escaped to the sand dunes and have nothing left but such clothes they had on and have no provisions. Mr. Kelly states that the Negro soldiers who went to the sand-hill during the storm returned and the next day robbed and pillaged such property as could be carried off. They broke open four safes and killed one guard. Shortly after dark yesterday the whole population of Brownsville was called to the levee by the shrill whistle of the *Tamaulipas No. 2* coming from the rescue of the Bagdad people. It is impossible to describe the scene with everyone talking at the same time, inquiring for his own particular relations or friends.[15]

Petra and her family escaped injury, but once again a Kenedy baby made its appearance during a traumatic moment in Brownsville history. Sarah Kenedy had been born during the fire in 1857. Mary Louise Putegnat, the daughter of Rosa and Joe Putegnat, was born October 10, just two days after the hurricane had passed through and while everyone was in the midst of trying to clean up the destruction. The family was glad that the baby was there and healthy since Rosa's baby had died only nine days before.[16]

Once again the Kenedy and King steamboats had come to the rescue. They had helped to put out the big fire in 1857 and now, although the boat was damaged, the crew of the *Tamaulipas No. 2* had managed to keep her afloat and rescue those stranded by the storm. They found places for them to stay and helped feed and clothe them. Petra's son-in-law, Robert Dalzell, was building a spacious building in Brownsville when the hurricane struck. After the storm he and Luisa donated the use of the building for a fund-raising benefit for St. Joseph Academy.[17] Father Parisot said, "the church was saved due to the heroic effort of Father Manuel who in the midst of the falling bricks placed a ladder against the large window above the entrance door. Had this window been burst open by the fury of the wind, the church would have been doomed to complete ruin. The only damage done was the demolition of two turrets and the tower roof, which was carried off in one piece to a neighbor's yard two hundred feet distant from the church. Nearly all the poor Mexicans' huts were down. A collection of $4,500 placed in the hands of the Priests for distribution, helped considerably in rebuilding the poorest districts of the city."[18]

King had already moved his family to the Santa Gertrudis, so they were all fine. Yet he was upset to hear they had lost four steamers—*Antonio, Enterprise, El Primero,* and *Camargo* were all sunk. Also the military railroad and the terminal at White's Ranch were destroyed. King viewed the damage as a clear signal to quit the river and turn his attention to ranching. Mifflin soon agreed and they began to consider how to run their rancho.[19]

After the storm, the community tried to recover as the area fell into an economic depression.[20] To add to their troubles, a few days after the storm yellow fever broke out again. During this time Kenedy and King had come to an important decision. They decided to draw up a partnership agreement for the purpose of the division of their herds. The steamboat business was on the decline, and early in the year they had been running only one boat on the river.[21] Good friends like Uriah Lott were leaving the river. He had relocated to Corpus Christi where he established a business; by 1871 he had three sailing vessels transporting wool and hides to New York.[22]

Kenedy and King's problem in dividing the herds was how to calculate the quantity of stock on their 146,000 acres. The number and value continued to fluctuate. At the same time it was difficult to account for the improvements to the ranch buildings and debts and credits from old and new projects. They knew that a careful inventory was needed and that it would take time. They wanted a sound business approach to the conclusion of their partnership with no hard feelings.

Kenedy and King had very different management styles and it was now time for the good friends to develop their own cattle operations. To accomplish this purpose, on November 5, 1867, they signed a plan for the division of their herds:

> The cattle shall be gradually gathered and driven to the rancho at Santa Gertrudis or any other convenient rancho ... belonging to the firm and there divided as fast as collected by each partner ... taking an animal alternately and placing his own brand there on, and so continuing until all of said cows have been gathered: the horses, mules, jacks, and jennets shall be divided by taking the manadas and remudas two at a time as nearly as possible of equal value and allotting them to the respective parties who shall draw lots for the first choice ... the sheep, goats, and other stock shall be divided into two lots of each kind of equal value and the parties shall draw lots for the first choice; provided also that it is distinctly understood that neither party shall use any of the original or present brands of the stock belonging to the partnership, as his own after but shall have a new and distinct brand to be put on his share respectively at the time of division.[23]

The year ended quietly for Mifflin and Petra. Mifflin and King had started the process of division and Mifflin focused his eyes north instead of south for his next adventure. The Wild Horse Desert and ranching would now demand most of his time. Petra's family responsibility continued to grow. On November 20, Frederick Starck was baptized at the Immaculate Conception Church. The church still had not fully recovered from the hurricane damage it received, but repairs were being made. Petra stood at the front of the church and held her young grandson as a sponsor during the baptism.[24] Less than a month later, the family ended the year with the baptism of Rosa and Joe's daughter, Mary Louise Putegnat. This time Father Manuel, the priest who had saved the church, conducted the baptism. This little girl's sponsors were Concepción and her husband Manuel Rodríguez.[25]

As soon as Bishop Claude Marie Dubuis heard of the tragedy wreaked by the hurricane he hurried from New Orleans to Brownsville to see the ruined convent buildings for himself. After seeing the ruins, a businessman approached him to find out if he would take the Sisters away. The Bishop told him he did not think he had any choice but to do just that since they had no home. The businessman said, "It is necessary that you leave them, because we can no longer do without them." Then the man asked him how much land would it take to rebuild, and inquired, if the land were donated, whether he would rebuild and let the Sisters stay. The Bishop, respecting the man's goodwill, said he thought fourteen lots would be a minimum required for the present needs and future expansion. Bishop Dubuis, having no money, turned to the Lord in prayer to ask him for help in solving the problem. With confidence in God and a good deal of faith he contracted with Mr. George Moore, a local builder, to erect the buildings for $20,000 dollars. The contract was signed on February 24 and the first installment of $5,000 was paid.[26]

The second payment was due in thirty days and the Bishop wrote a draft due in thirty days and wrote Archbishop Odin in New Orleans asking him to please cover it. He told him he would be there to explain, but slow boat service delayed him and he arrived in New Orleans on the day the draft was due. He found the Archbishop in a state of consternation because he did not have enough gold to pay the draft and the payment was due at noon. Bishop Dubuis went to Mass and when he returned he opened the mail and there was a check for $5,000 payable on the Rothschild Bank of London. The benefactor's name was withheld, requesting only that Bishop Dubuis say a Mass for the benefactor. This action would have been characteristic of the manner in which Mifflin operated, but the identify of the benefactor was held secret as requested. Later that day Bishop Dubuis discovered another anonymous gift of $50, which was enough to pay for his return trip to Brownsville.[27]

Meanwhile, John Gregory was enrolled at St. Joseph College as his brothers probably were, too. St. Joseph College was established because of Father Parisot's energetic leadership. During the war, when buildings were being torn down, Father Parisot obtained permission to save the materials he could from the buildings so they could be used in the construction of a college. He was able to collect and store 300,000 bricks. Some of the materials were appropriated by the Union troops but most of them were returned before they left. Despite the setback, he was able to open the college, and although small it offered a sound education.[28] Father Parisot also attempted to repair and expand the church. The ladies of the church, including Petra and her daughters, most assuredly, held a fair that lasted four days in order to raise money for the Gothic groined ceiling for the church. They successfully raised $3,400. The ladies' husbands had no choice but to contribute generously after all of their hard effort to make the fair a success. Father Parisot not only took care of the church in Brownsville but also several of the smaller chapels in the area.[29]

One Sunday he returned after being out for a week and found the church crowded and the priest sick in bed and no one to conduct Mass. He cleaned up and having no sermon prepared, used the text "Seek ye first the kingdom of God and His justice, and all these things shall be added unto you." Mr. Jerry Galvan was so moved that he wanted to do something for the church. He gave the Father enough gold to buy twelve large chandeliers. Father Parisot ordered them from Paris; their four hundred lights were a magnificent spectacle.[30]

Captain Wainwright had decided to rebuild Fort Brown because it had deteriorated; the army housed soldiers all around Brownsville. He built new infantry barracks, a hospital, and between forty to seventy other buildings. This construction helped the town and its craftsmen.[31] Later that year, in November, a new young doctor arrived. Dr. Arthur E. Spohn was a U.S. Army surgeon, having charge of military quarantines that helped combat yellow fever in Galveston, Corpus Christi, and Brownsville. He requested permission to treat patients at Santa Gertrudis. He met Richard and Henrietta King, who were rebuilding the ranch after the chaos of the Civil War, and won their confidence. He continued to provide them medical service when he could. He spent two years in Mier, Mexico, with the army, and utilized a tourniquet for bloodless operations that later was used as a standard field instrument by armies all over the world. It is very possible that Spohn knew some of Petra's family while he was in Mier. Little could Mifflin or Petra know that someday this brilliant young surgeon would become their son-in-law when he married their Sarah.[32]

Petra and the family were busy helping wherever they could in the reconstruction efforts. Petra was also very busy at home, and finally her family was reunited. Tom, James, John Gregory, Sarah, and Willie lived at home. The children attended school, but they kept Petra and the household busy with their various needs. Mifflin was also making adjustments; he put his son-in-law, Robert Dalzell, in charge of the steamboat business. King was concentrating all his efforts at Santa Gertrudis and Mifflin wanted to turn his attention there also.[33]

On May 31, 1868, Kenedy and King moved to dissolve R. King & Co. and signed an instrument titled "Articles of Agreement and Settlement between R. King and M. Kenedy," setting forth how they would equitably divide all the land and assets of the company. Three days later, on June 3, 1868, Mifflin Kenedy became an independent rancher. He purchased twenty-six leagues of land—the Laureles grant—from Cornelius Stillman, who had bought it from his brother Charles in 1864. Cornelius wrote terms of the sale that called for the making of three notes "each for the sum of 2,061 pounds, 17 shillings and 4 pence, payable one, two, and three years after date," payable by Kenedy.[34] The British money probably indicated that Kenedy was using his profits from the Civil War that he had banked in London.

The Laureles purchase was tied up with the association among Stillman, King, and Kenedy and their friendship. The original appropriation of 10,848 acres was granted to the Rey and García families of Mier in 1807. They established a ranching operation on it until the Indians drove them off in 1814. Sixteen years later, on October 16, 1830, the Rey and García heirs sold the property for $2,000 to Tomás Paradez of Camargo who attempted to build a rancho. Paradez described the property: "*Es habitado de variedad de animales,*

Drawing of the original Los Laureles, built by Charles Stillman in the 1840s. A modest but gracious house, Los Laureles was designed in the late Georgian style. The carpenters were shipwrights. Drawing by Alexander Stillman, 2006.

como son venados, jabalíes, caballada mesteña, víboras" (It is inhabited by a variety of animals such as deer, javelinas, wild horses, and snakes). Paradez and his family were apparently driven off the land during the Texas Revolution.[35]

Charles Stillman purchased the Rincón de Los Laureles from Tomás Paradez on May 6, 1853, for $9,500. Stillman entered into a partnership with William S. Gregory to run the ranch and construct a salt works. Gregory built the headquarters on a site near ruins of old buildings and pens. The headquarters was also near the old road leading from Corpus Christi to Brownsville. Gregory built a house, store, barns, pens, and other buildings for the ranching operations. Stillman and Gregory operated the ranch for nine years, from 1853 to 1862. Stillman estimated that he put about $20,000 into it during that period.[36]

When the Civil War broke out Gregory joined the Confederate forces and Stillman chose to end the partnership. After the war Gregory went to work for Richard King. Stillman empowered Richard King to take control of the property and oversee the partnership liquidation. At this point Richard King tried to purchase the property from Stillman, but he refused to sell it to him. On April 14, 1862, Stillman wrote King, "I am prepared to sell you the land and

*"Los Laureles"
Southeast Side*

Drawing of the original Los Laureles from the southeast side. Drawing by Alexander Stillman, 2006.

stock as it is, but under the present state of our political affairs, have no hope that such is possible. As the property has cost me now some twenty odd thousand dollars, it stands me in hand to look after it." Then he upset King by sending his brother Cornelius and Joe Turner to run the ranch and salt works.[37]

Stillman later heard that King was upset and wrote him saying he regretted not knowing he wanted it. He went on to say that "affairs look dark ahead. Prepare for squalls, and keep and settle your affairs as snug as you can before we are stampeded. If I in any way have acted amiss regarding your views, it has been unintentionally." Then on August 25, 1864, Charles Stillman sold Laureles to his brother for $10,000. Cornelius operated the ranch for another four years before selling it to Mifflin in June of 1868.[38]

Why Stillman did not sell the ranch to King in 1864 instead of to his brother is a puzzle. The war was at its peak, and King was on the run from the Union army. Perhaps he could not make the sale at that time, or perhaps Cornelius liked the ranch by then and wanted it for himself. Charles was winding up his affairs at this time and planning to return to New York. Now that Kenedy and King were ending their partnership, Mifflin had to have another ranch, and it may be that Mifflin and King decided this ranch would be perfect for Mifflin. Mifflin turned Los Laureles into one of the greatest ranches in the United States, acquiring the adjoining land grants of the Rin-

Photograph of Los Laureles house, showing the addition that was made by Mifflin and Petra. Courtesy of Alexander Stillman.

cón de Corpus Christi, El Chiltipin, Las Comitas, El Alazan, and El Infernillo, which expanded the ranch to over 240,000 acres.[39]

In a deposition given by Mifflin Kenedy on September 27, 1872, he was asked if he bought the Rancho "Los Laureles" from Cornelius Stillman, and he answered that he had. Mifflin then stated that he was supposed to take possession of 10,000 head of cattle but that they fell short and he only received 6,000 head.[40]

Mifflin wasted no time in getting started with his ranch. He registered his laurel leaf brand, chosen because of the laurel trees on the property and the ranch's name.[41] Mifflin registered his brand November 20, 1868, while Petra had registered hers twelve years earlier on March 27, 1856.[42] Mifflin then fenced 131,000 acres and thus created a milestone in the development of livestock ranching. He did so using heavy posts and three-plank fencing across the throat of the peninsula that formed the Laureles grant. This became the first fenced range of any real size west of the Mississippi.[43]

Kenedy and King never liked the open range and free grazing that many ranchers advocated. Mifflin took the same businessman's approach to ranching as he did with his other ventures. He and King believed that in order to

When the house on Los Laureles was moved, the vault under the fireplace used for hiding money and valuables was discovered. Courtesy of Alexander Stillman.

have an efficient operation a rancher needed to control the land, and the only way to do that was to fence it. A fenced range allowed a rancher to control the grass and water, as well as the breeding program by keeping out strays. The fence also put up a legal barrier to notify trespassers and thieves that the property was private, which in the open prairie became very important. The creosoted cypress posts and hard pine planks had to be ordered and shipped from Louisiana and then hauled out to the ranches by wagon. King was also beginning to fence, but because his property was not located on a peninsula like Kenedy's it was much harder to fence.[44]

On June 14, Mifflin was in Brownsville and wrote to Maj. Felix Blücher in Corpus Christi saying that he would be in Corpus by the end of the month. Major Blücher was a surveyor and probably wanted some work from Los Laureles. He stated, "there was little business with a prospect of a dull, dull, dull summer ahead."[45] But Felix Blücher was not finding life quite as dull any more, since he had nearly lost his life the month before Mifflin's letter arrived in Corpus Christi, according to a letter Blücher's wife wrote home to her family. On May 24 he had drunk too much and didn't come home for several nights, but evidently he had made it home that night. Mrs. Blücher was awakened by a loud crash. Her husband had fallen out of the first floor window during the night. He had managed to get to his feet and struggle as far as his office, where he was prostrate for two weeks. He seemed to recover and by the time Mifflin wrote was fully restored.[46]

One of the methods by which Kenedy and King and other large landholders expanded their ranches and businesses was with control of credit services. José San Román, Mifflin Kenedy, Richard King, Charles Stillman, Humphrey Woodhouse, Jeremiah Galvan, Santiago Ytúrria, and the Treviño brothers monopolized the credit, or money lending, making it difficult for smaller merchants to stay in business.[47]

In June, Petra was involved in a land transaction herself. She continued the process of conveying her interest in her family's land to family members. The document was agreed to on March 27, 1854, but not witnessed until June 1868, and not filed until March 31, 1875. She gave her interest in "the Rancho Veleño or Beleño, *sobre el* Rincón de San Pedro, at or near the mouth of the La Garto Creek, or Arroyo de la Garto on the West bank of the Nueces River in Nueces County, and containing four square leagues more or less; also the Rancho de Santa Teresa, where there is a well of fresh water; also the Rancho of San Antonio Viejo, where there is another well of fresh water; also to a *Porción* of land lying between the town of Roma and the Alamo and fronting the Rio Grande called the Rancho de Ramirez," to her uncle Andrés Vela; her sisters Nicolasa Vela, Gertrudis Vela, Juliana Vela, Casilda Vela; the only child of her deceased brother, Pablo Vela—Faustina Vela; to William Cox, only child of her deceased sister Francisca Vela; and to Wenceslado Garza, only son and child of her deceased sister Antonia Vela. That this land had water made it even more valuable.[48] Thus Petra was turning over her interest in more than 26,000 acres to her family members from her part of the inheritance. It indicates some of the wealth she brought to her marriage with Mifflin. There were twenty-six Velas listed as owners of land grants in 1836. One of these grant holders was Petra's father, Gregorio. The others were Petra's relatives. Gregorio's mother was a Ramirez. There were twenty-four Ramirez land grants in 1836 that were confirmed by the Republic of Texas. The Vela land grants alone totaled 170,922 acres. Add the Ramirez grants, the de la Garza and the Resendez grants from the women in the family tree, and there were hundreds of thousands of acres owned by Petra's Spanish relatives in 1836. They created ranches, raised livestock, built stone cabins/forts with gun ports for protection against Indian raids, and built houses for the wives and children in Revilla and Mier.[49] Petra's family was rich in land and family heritage.

At the same time, Mifflin was helping his Pennsylvania family financially. In 1867, Sarah Starr Kenedy was a signer upon the application for the establishment for the Borough of Pennsylvania. Probably with Mifflin's help in the same year she purchased the Joel Thompson property, where she lived until she died in 1884.[50]

The most difficult part for Petra in moving to Los Laureles was what to do with the children. The children had just been reunited after their separation during the Civil War, and now less than a year later she was facing the decision to send the children to boarding schools or not. There were no schools at Los Laureles and the children were growing up and needed to be educated. They would have to be boarded at a school and the question was where they would get the best education. For the boys the decision was made to send them to Spring Hill College in Mobile, Alabama. Petra insisted on a Catholic school and Mifflin agreed. After being in Pennsylvania she felt that the children must not only be educated but also receive a good grounding in their Catholic faith.

Spring Hill College was a small Jesuit boarding school with an excellent reputation. Mifflin may well have known of it from his steamboating days in his early career.[51] "Jesuits" is the popular term for The Society of Jesus, founded in the mid-1500s by St. Ignatius of Loyola. The Jesuits are a worldwide order of the Catholic Church noted for their missionary zeal and their first-rate institutions of learning. Following the Ignatian tradition, Spring Hill College emphasized loyalty to the Church and humble service to others, especially the less fortunate. These principles may have influenced the Kenedy children, and their children, in turn, to establish the Kenedy Memorial Foundation and the Kenedy Trust to benefit the Church and the poor in South Texas.[52]

Later, Mifflin's two grandsons, John Kenedy Jr. and George Mifflin Kenedy, would enroll in Spring Hill, too.[53] While John Kenedy was at Spring Hill in 1873, his classmates were William and Arnaud Turcotte from New Orleans. Their father Joseph Turcotte operated a lucrative transport shipping operation from one side of Lake Pontchartrain to the other. They introduced John to their sister, Marie Stella, and John and Marie Stella would marry on January 30, 1884.[54]

Petra also knew how dangerous life in the Wild Horse Desert could be; the isolated ranches were easy prey to bandits who tortured, murdered, and burned out ranch families. Travel in the area was equally dangerous; Texas vigilante groups and bandits conducted guerrilla warfare throughout the area from 1865 to 1878.[55] As much as Petra hated to let the children leave, she would not put them in harm's way. Also, some of their friends and family had attended Spring Hill. Their son-in-law Robert Dalzell had gone there as well as William Kelly, Francis Ballí, and Thomas O'Connor in Victoria, Texas.[56]

Petra and Mifflin decided to send Sarah to the Ursuline Convent in New Orleans. Sarah had dark, curly hair, a round face, and heart-shaped lips that usually turned up in a smile. She also had a beautiful voice. The Catholic Dimonds publication in Corpus Christi said, "Sarah's education was at the

Ursuline Convent in New Orleans for nine years. She was charming in manner, engaging in conversation, gifted pianist, mistress of French, Spanish and English. She was an ornament to any society and Corpus Christi recognized it."[57]

Petra readied the children for a fall departure. For some reason James did not accompany the other boys and would go the next year. The children took a steamship from Brownsville to New Orleans, where they were collected by the officers of the college and taken to Mobile aboard the Pontchartrain Railroad. The Spring Hill records report that Captain Kenedy's children enrolled at Spring Hill College on October 18, 1868. They were Thomas Mifflin, age fourteen; John Gregory, age eleven; and William, age nine. John Kenedy was enrolled in 1868 as Gregory because his mother called him Gregorio after her father. By 1872 John had dropped the Gregory and went by the name of John Kenedy. When the boys arrived they had received the sacrament of Confirmation in the Catholic Church but they had not received their First Sacrament of Holy Communion. The Sacrament was performed at Spring Hill College at some point during their seven academic years there.[58]

When the Kenedy children enrolled, the college offered three courses. The Preparatory Course usually lasted one year and was intended to prepare the students for the more advanced level. It comprised reading, writing, arithmetic, and elements of the languages they would learn. Then they would choose to enter either the Classical Course or the Commercial Course. The Kenedy boys enrolled in the Commercial Course. The first, second, and third years of grammar, English grammar and composition, history, mathematics, and Christian doctrine were taught first. This was followed by three years of poetry and general literature, rhetoric, advanced mathematics, evidences of religion, and the graduating year of mental and moral philosophy, which included chemistry, physics, astronomy, natural history, and the completion of higher mathematics. To this was added bookkeeping, penmanship, French, German, Spanish, and Italian for the Commercial Course.[59] For this education Mifflin paid $434 dollars for tuition, and room and board for each of the three boys. There were 105 boys enrolled at the college in 1868.[60]

In moving to Los Laureles, Petra not only had lost her younger children to school but she also was going to have to leave her older daughters and their families, including her grandchildren. She knew she would travel back and forth frequently, they would come to see her, and they would be in touch almost daily through Mifflin's dispatches, but it was not the same. She did most of her traveling in a Concord stagecoach made in 1852. The trip to Laureles was 160 miles and it took forty-eight jolting hours. Laureles was only twenty-two miles from Corpus Christi, so it was no wonder that she and Mifflin would travel there for supplies. Petra also knew she would miss the friends she had made through the years, but the other big loss in her life would be her church. She and Mifflin had been married in the old church and helped to build, repair, and add to the new church. Much of her life had been centered in the church and now she would have to find a new church home and she would be isolated, inhibiting her ability to get to Mass or devotions.

Petra had faced many difficulties and challenges in her life but this move was daunting. Mifflin needed her if he was to be successful. She had been brought up in a ranching family and understood what it took. Her Spanish language and understanding of Mexican culture was also an advantage for him. Together they would have to work hard to make their new ranch a success.

Chapter 9

1869–71: "¿Quién Viene?"

Petra and Mifflin committed to moving to Los Laureles Ranch in 1869. For a number of reasons it was the time to leave Brownsville. The firm of King, Kenedy & Co. was now virtually dissolved. Charles Stillman had moved to New York. The other partners had found new involvements, and the businessmen of Brownsville began to sit back while the more aggressive merchants of Corpus Christi and San Antonio bid for leadership and control of the steamship trade.[1] Kenedy and King had lost much of their influence on the Rio Grande. The railroad they had acquired a charter for was not being built, and many merchants were upset by both their monopoly of the river trade and their high charges. The Reconstruction government was difficult to deal with, and the hurricane had destroyed a number of their boats and facilities.[2]

In January, Kenedy and King employed one hundred men to begin the process of rounding up and dividing their stock.[3] Mifflin, in a deposition on August 28, 1872, before a commission in Brownsville, was seeking to recover the money he had lost from the theft of his cattle between 1866 and 1869 due to lack of protection by the government. As of August 20, 1866, he and King had their stock on the Santa Gertrudis rancho and several other ranches. They had "84,000 head of beef cattle, five thousand four hundred head of horse stock, seventeen thousand sheep, five hundred hogs, and four thousand goats."[4] In the latter part of 1868 they deemed it to be in the interest of the parties to dissolve the partnership because of the depredations on their property by armed bandits coming over from Mexico and carrying off their stock. In the deposition Mifflin stated:

> We commenced the division about the first of January 1869, and concluded on November 11, 1869. They were branded for me at the

Rancho de Los Laureles, twenty-five thousand head of cattle, they were branded for Capt. King at Rancho Gertrudis twenty-three thousand six hundred and sixty four head of cattle. Captain King got the balance of the cattle on the prairie the expense of rounding them up being so great and that made a total of 58,664 on hand. As to the sheep, hogs, and goats the firm makes no claim. The firm sold about one thousand head of beeves and five hundred and seventy head of horses and mules. With their natural increase from 1866 to 1869, we lost one hundred and eight thousand three hundred and thirty six head of cattle at ten dollars per head. We lost in the same period three thousand three hundred and twenty eight head of horse stock valued at sixty dollars per head. Our loss from 1866—total is 2,480,160 for all livestock loss to Mexican raiders. There is no security for life or property since 1859. Juan Nepomuceno Cortina on Sept. 23, 1859 entered the town of Brownsville, Texas, broke open the jail and liberated the prisoners, and murdered five of its citizens. He planted the Mexican flag on the U.S. reservation near where the flag staff of Fort Brown now stands.[5]

For his own ranch, Mifflin chose the Laurel Leaf for his brand to be used on his newly divided cattle. The original grant was named Rincón de Los Laureles, "Corner of the Laurels," so Mifflin chose the brand.[6] King chose the running W. In Spanish the brand is called the *Viborita*, or the Little Snake. King may have chosen the brand because of the location in the Wild Horse Desert and the symbolism of the snake, but there may be a more practical explanation. King had purchased the Santa Gertrudis from William Mann, who had a wavy initial M as one of his brands. King may have simply turned the brand upside down to form the wavy running W. The brand made a shape that was hard to alter by rustlers and was good looking on the side of his cattle; it almost came alive as they moved, like a little snake.[7]

Kenedy and King entered the cattle business at a propitious time. The Civil War had depleted the beef stock in the northern states, while the untended cattle in Texas had multiplied on the Texas prairies. The railroads had reached toward the west, and stockyards and packing plants were springing up in Kansas City and other towns as the rails stretched westward. Mifflin and Richard intended to complete the link between the thousands of head of cattle in Texas with the stockyards in Kansas. From Kansas the beef would go by rail to urban markets in the east. During the reconstruction years a $5 steer in Texas was a $20–$40 steer in Chicago, making cattle drives valuable for the ranchers who could put them together.[8]

Kenedy and King's major problem was protection against cattle theft and the resulting loss of revenue due to lack of government protection. They needed to devise their own methods to protect not only their stock but also their families. King elected to always travel with armed vaqueros and gunmen.[9] These armed vaqueros carried .30–30s and side arms and rode the finest horses in the Wild Horse Desert. They wore Mexican sombreros, bandoliers with spare cartridges across their chest, and large knives on their hips.[10] King carried a shotgun loaded with buckshot because when he shot he wanted results.[11]

Legend holds that King rode with hundreds of guards and his own private rangers. Although the reports were exaggerated he usually traveled with about half a dozen men. His expenses for the men he traveled with even included money for whiskey. King had learned that his safety on the road depended on his ability to ride with speed. He set up stage camps at about twenty-mile intervals along the length of the road. Each camp was guarded, and fast horses and strong mules were kept ready in the corral for his relays. He said later, "I had to travel fast. My life depended on it." Due to Santa Gertrudis's isolated location, King carried large amounts of currency to meet his payroll. In order to hide his money he devised a steel box that he built inside his coach; the only people who knew about it were his wife, Henrietta, and his office manager, Reuben Holbein. King was never successfully robbed.[12]

King also had to protect his home and family. For years he had maintained a band of Kineños—men of the King Ranch—commanded by their foreman, Capt. James Richardson, to protect his property. He also kept a brass cannon, which he had used in the Civil War on his boat, at ranch headquarters, loaded and ready to go. Lookouts atop the commissary on a high hill could see for miles on the prairie. He purchased thirty stands of Henry rifles and a large supply of ammunition so that his men were always ready.[13]

Petra and Mifflin encountered the same problems at their ranch. They had to provide for defense and to protect themselves on their long road trips back to Brownsville. Rip Ford said that Captain Kenedy had less exposure to the vengeful feelings of the raiding Mexicans because of Petra. "She possessed an intellect much above the ordinary and exerted great influence over her countrymen. It was natural for her to shield her husband as well as she could against the men who were systematically robbing the Texians and murdering those suspected of opposing them."[14]

One of Petra's descendants tells the story that Petra would travel from Brownsville to the ranch under heavy guard with the payroll each month. Near San Pablo Ranch close to San Pedro, bandits held them up. A newspaper feature tells of Mifflin and of the calm courage of his Mexican wife:

En route from the ranch to Brownsville, the coach stopped in the dense chaparral for the night. The impenetrable brush made travel by night extremely perilous, notwithstanding the presence of an armed escort of half a dozen true and tried plainsmen to guard the party from harm. Late in the night when the party was wrapped in peaceful slumber, between the yelps of the coyotes and the nighthawk's screech, the watchful Captain detected the sound of moving brush. He quickly and quietly awakened his men and warned them to prepare for trouble. With a gun in hand he challenged the sound with the well-known Mexican martial cry, "*¿Quién viene?*" meaning literally translated, "Who goes there?" "*Paisanos*," meaning "Your countrymen," came the reply. Although Captain Kenedy was a cool determined man who didn't know the meaning of fear, he wasn't altogether at ease with the intricacies of the Spanish language. Kenedy scenting danger met the reply with "*Pase*" meaning to order them to "Pass on." Instantly, a dozen highwaymen stepped out into the opening. The guards immediately covered them. The assailants evidently hadn't expected any resistance after receiving the seemingly hospitable invitation to enter. About this time, the Captain's wife, who had been comfortably resting in the bottom of the coach, jumped down and rushed to her husband and exclaimed, "No, no, *mi capitán*, you do not mean for them to pass; you mean for them to retire." With this her sharp eyes quickly but carefully scanned the faces of the amazed desperadoes. Recognizing one of them, she called out in her native tongue, "Look you, sire; go away from here at once, or when I arrive at Brownsville, I will tell your mother of your shameful conduct." This clever ruse worked. The desperadoes instantly disappeared into the chaparral.[15]

It also shows the power of the mother over her children. If this story is true, and it has been told many times, these men feared the wrath of their mothers should they be caught in acts of which the mothers disapproved. Petra knew this.

Years before, Mifflin realized the need for good transportation for Petra and the family, as well as for himself, if they were going to be traveling long distances in dangerous territory. He drew up plans for an elaborate stagecoach and sent them to New Hampshire. There, a famous wagon maker built the coach. The stagecoach's nameplate bears its construction year, 1852. It had been sent to New York and then to the mouth of the Rio Grande aboard a three-masted schooner. It was delivered to Captain Kenedy, and the Concord

Petra's Concord coach with her monogram on the door led an adventurous life and was known as the most famous coach on the Rio Grande border. Petra traveled back and forth from Los Laureles to Brownsville each month under heavy guard with the ranch payroll. Courtesy Corpus Christi Museum of Science and History.

coach started its adventurous life; it became known as the most famous coach on the border. On another occasion, Captain Kenedy and a party of friends were returning from the interior of Mexico to Brownsville. On a dark night, as the coach was cautiously winding its way down the steep mountains from Monterrey, it was attacked by bandits. Before they could chase off the attackers, don Castillo, a highly respected citizen of Matamoros, fell back against the great cushions of the coach with a fatal bullet from an enemy's gun.[16] To illustrate how difficult coach travel was, Alfred Neale, a descendant of William Neale who owned the stagecoach line, described the trip from Corpus Christi to Brownsville. The passengers would have to carry enough edibles to last the entire trip. They would also have to travel with the curtains drawn in the heat of the summer to protect themselves from sandstorms, whirlwinds, and swarms of mosquitoes.[17] The formal dress of the time included layers of petticoats and stockings, even in summer.

On the night of February 4, 1869, Petra and Mifflin did not know that their sons were in grave danger in Alabama. That night the boys had gone to prayers and retired for the evening. The *Mobile Times* of February 5 vividly described the boys' experience:

> At a quarter to twelve, the smell of smoke and dazzling light caused one of the student infirmary patients to hobble to the window. Immediately, he screamed "fire" and the infirmarian taking in the situation in a glance, rushed to ring continuously the big college bell. The prefects and teachers were at once on the scene which presented on the south side dense clouds of flame and smoke and a mass of burning buildings on the north.
>
> The pupils were aroused and every precaution was taken to prevent panic among the inmates. The terrible element had already made such headway that it was only by presence of mind and careful management that the whole household was saved, without hurt or accident, in the clothes they had on or in the blankets and covering they seized, and with nothing else besides. The entire College building was utterly destroyed. When we reached the scene this morning nothing but smoking and rocking walls, crumbling from time to time with a dull crash, remained to what yesterday had been a splendid and valued adjunct to the educational facilities of the South. The furniture, library, chemical and physical apparatus, laboratories, and the clothing and personal effects of both teachers and students were entirely consumed, with scarce a vestige left.
>
> When first discovered the fire was issuing in full blast, filling all the passage ways with smoke and thrusting its darting tongues through the windows. Many were obliged to leap or climb from the first gallery after they had been directed through the thoughtful courage of the Fathers to seize hurriedly all the clothing they could reach. This was a fortunate provision for the clothes-room was in flames and the temperature was below freezing point. When safe the boys fell to work with a will endeavoring to rescue what they could, and had to be ordered to desist. Fifteen barrels of flour were alone saved from all the valuable possessions of the Institution.[18]

As dawn came that morning the Jesuit Fathers provided for the needs of the ill-clothed pupils. Father Montillot recalled Grand Coteau, Louisiana, an institution that had been recently closed. He arranged to have it reopened and transferred the students there. They left for New Orleans by train and traveled to Baton Rouge by boat and to Grand Coteau by three mule carts.[19]

One of the priests, Father Yenni, lost a violin of irreplaceable value in the fire. On leaving his home in Tyrol he had received the violin from his father as a parting gift. He had so much talent that he was allowed to keep the Cremona violin and play it even in the Novitiate. He made good use of it at Spring Hill. Many people attended his concerts in order to hear him perform. People would even come to hear him practice outside of class. Having a fear of fire, he normally placed his violin within close reach before going to bed, but the night of February 4 he had left it in the music room. His friends replaced the Cremona with the best violin procurable, but his loss could not be totally appeased.[20]

In April the boys were back at home with Mifflin and Petra. Petra was delighted to have her sons home and to know they were safe. She had given many thanks that they had been delivered safely from the fire that night. They could so easily have perished in the cold snowy night away from all their family. Petra was glad also, though, that they were receiving such a good education and instruction in her faith.

William and John Gregory would return to the newly built Spring Hill College in the fall, but Tom would not go back with them. This time James would enroll with his brothers. After spending the year after the fire with Father Yenni, both John and William enrolled in music classes at Spring Hill.[21] When the boys returned home they found they had a new nephew. John Peter Putegnat had been born on March 8 to Rosa and Joe. He was baptized by Father Parisot on June 12, with his uncle Thomas Kenedy and Adrian's widow Anita Chavero de Vidal as his sponsors.[22]

Politics changed drastically along the border after the Civil War when the Reconstruction government took control. William Neale was elected mayor of Brownsville on August 17, 1866, and for nearly three years ran an efficient municipal government. Then in March 1869, everything changed. Maj. Gen. E. R. S. Canby, commander of the 5th Military District with headquarters in Austin, arbitrarily removed Neale and replaced him with Edward Downey. On June 5 the eight city commissioners were "disqualified" by Maj. Gen. J. J. Reynolds. The elected commissioners, James Browne, A. Glavecke, Alexander Werbiski, N. Champion, Petra's son-in-law J. L. Putegnat, George William, Henry Miller, and Josiah Moorhead, were summarily replaced by Joseph Hopkins, Petra's other son-in-law Fred Starck, William Scanlan, Jerry Galvan, M. de Llano, F. H. Pierce, Juan Pecina, and J. L. Rudolph.[23]

Petra's son-in-law, J. L. Putegnat, had been a Confederate supporter, and her other son-in-law, Fred Starck, had been a Union officer. Petra was used to having family members on both sides of issues, but it created some tense feelings. Later, this divisiveness may have been a contributing factor to a family split.

John McAllen was also finding it difficult to work with the new government. On November 4 he wrote, "The City fathers are all government appointees and not elected.... They don't care how private parties suffer, they can make their own laws to suit the time as they are supported by the bayonets at Fort Brown."[24]

Captain King provided his own protection for his ranch, but there were issues. Roberto Villarreal, a descendant of some of the first vaqueros who worked for Mifflin Kenedy, said, "the issue of land acquisition is closely connected to the Texas Rangers."[25] Walter Prescott Webb explains that a Mexican after 1848 was "victimized by the law." The old landholding families found their titles in jeopardy. If they did not lose in the courts they lost to their American lawyers; Mexicans suffered in their persons and in their property.[26] The law was enforced principally by the Texas Rangers who, it was said, furnished the "fortune-making adventurers" with services that were not forthcoming from the U.S. Army or the local sheriffs. Among the Mexicans of South Texas, the official Texas Rangers are known as the *rinches de la Kineña*, or Rangers of the King Ranch, in accordance with the belief that the Rangers were the personal strong-arm men of Richard King and the other "cattle barons."[27]

Villarreal also told a story about Mifflin and land he later acquired for his La Parra ranch. He fenced Mrs. Tijerina's pasture because she had a big lake on her property and he needed the water and did not pay her for it. She could not get to the water and so had to sell him the rest of her land. On March 5, 1872, Doña Eulalia, Cortina's cousin, bought one league of land from Rafael Garza Ramirez in the La Parra land grant in Cameron County. The league consisted of 4,428 acres and bordered on the north with Los Olmos Creek. The acreage was located on the western boundary of the La Parra grant. Eulalia named her new ranch La Atravesada for the natural hill that traversed her land. Not long after she moved onto the ranch, Encarnación and Atanasia Morales, with their children, arrived from Brownsville and became her trusted workers. In 1875, "La Atravesada was hit by a band of Anglo vigilantes seeking revenge for the Nuecestown raid. They came into the recently opened commissary and shot and killed Encarnación's oldest son Guadalupe when he opened the door. The owner of the store, a half Anglo and half Mexican named Henry was also killed and Encarnación Morales was never seen again."[28]

After this, many of the Mexican ranchers were killed and many families moved back to Mexico and gave up their property. Many of these ranchers could not overcome the problems of titles never legally recognized; lawlessness; changing boundaries such as rivers, trees, and dried-up creeks; tracts not properly divided among heirs; language difficulties in English courts; and trespassers or squatters. Doña Eulalia was one of the few to remain on her property. Her husband Esteban Cisneros, a well-respected rancher, died in 1880, leaving her as head of the household. Mifflin Kenedy began buying up the major tracts of land surrounding La Atravesada, and in 1883 three of Esteban's four children, heirs in the deed, sold their interest to Kenedy for $100 each. It took Eulalia seven years, in which time Kenedy had already fenced in her property, but on May 30, 1890, she won her right to live on her ranch for the rest of her natural life and pass her inheritance on to her three daughters. Two of her daughters sold their interest, after her death, to Kenedy. The other daughter sold her interest to G. A. Riskin in 1930 for $16,432. That land is still held outside the Kenedy interest today with full mineral and hunting rights. The only access is through Kenedy Trust property. Doña Eulalia was well respected as a Tejana ranch woman and her husband don Esteban was a leading stockman with ranches from Victoria to Nueces/Cameron County.[29]

In the fall of 1869, Petra again said goodbye to three of her sons and to Sarah. Sarah returned to the Ursuline Academy in New Orleans and John, William, and James went to the newly built Spring Hill College. Thomas did not return. John and William would go another five and six years respectively and James would stay another two. The college was structured and disciplined in those days; the schedule was rigorous. The boys would rise at 5 A.M. and have prayers, study, and breakfast. Classes opened at 7:30 followed by recess at 10:00 and study again at 10:30. Classes resumed at 2:00 and then there was recess and lunch at 4:30. At 5 P.M. there was study until 6:45 when they had recreation. At 7:15 they had supper followed at 7:40 by prayers, spiritual reading, study, and then to their dormitories at 8:30.[30]

John G. took up the flute and Willie, as the family called him, the piano. John earned First Class Honors in English Composition and First Accessit Honors as a flutist. John and William were, for the most part, good students and their appreciation of music, as an extracurricular pursuit, made them more rounded.[31]

October brought trouble for King. On October 12, 1869, Nestor Maxan, a Brownsville lawyer, wrote his partner Stephen Powers. Powers was in Hot Springs, Arkansas, seeking a cure for his poor health. Maxan wrote, "day before yesterday, Captain R. King and J. J. Richardson and five other persons came into town and were immediately arrested by order of General Clitz for murder. . . . I attended to their cases and succeeded in persuading the Commanding officer to place them under bond, to appear before the next District Court in the sum of $10,000 each. We created quite an excitement!" It is not

Sarah Kenedy attended Ursuline Academy in New Orleans while her brothers were at Spring Hill College in Alabama. After her education she was known as the "belle of Corpus Christi." Courtesy of Raymondville Historical Museum, Texas.

John Kenedy attended Spring Hill College in Alabama where he met the Turcotte brothers of New Orleans. John Kenedy had finished his schooling at Spring Hill and went to work for Perkins Swenson and Co. in New Orleans, bankers, and a cotton commission company that Mifflin Kenedy often used. A reason for this employment might be that William Turcotte had introduced John to his sister Marie Stella. Courtesy of Raymondville Historical and Community Center, Texas.

James Kenedy, who loved the land and ranching, attended Spring Hill College in Alabama, but not for as many years as his brothers John and Willie.

known why King and Richardson were arrested, but the news jolted their friends. Maxan worked to control the damage and they were found not guilty.[32]

In November, Kenedy and King had completed their cattle roundup. They finalized their Agreement and Final Settlement of Affairs of R. King & Co., signed it on February 26, 1870, and filed it at the Nueces County Court House on September 21, 1870. The diversity of the real estate they held showed the breadth of these two friends' affairs over the last twenty years. They were determined to split their holdings evenly so that each got what they needed for future operations. Mifflin traded all the Santa Gertrudis as a working unit, with one parcel of Corpus Christi town property and some odd pieces on the Rio Grande frontage for six parcels of Brownsville town property and three tracts of pastureland unrelated to the Santa Gertrudis. They divided the livestock, land, cash, debits, and credits, including two slaves who had worked on the ranch before the Civil War ended and had subsequently been lost. They managed to dissolve the partnership with no loss of respect for each other or diminishing of their friendship. Years later Mifflin would tell Richard Mifflin Kleberg, a grandson of Richard King's, "Your grandfather and I had lots of fights. Always on the same side."[33]

In January of 1870 the Republican Edmund J. Davis was elected governor of Texas. A former member of the Blue Party in Brownsville, he had bad memories of his time there in the U.S. Army. He had filled the county and city offices with Blue Party members to the dismay of the Red Party members like Mifflin and King. The new mayor was Frank Cummings, for whom there was little respect, and the old city council, including Jerry Galvan, was replaced by Republicans. John McAllen wrote, "A fellow by the name of Slikum [Ferdinand Schlickum] which kept a little book store during the last of the war was the man Davis selected and in order to do this they threw the seat of Cameron and Hidalgo out . . . [Robert B.] Kingsbury is first justice of Cameron Co., he turned Radical and run [on] the Hamilton ticket which had the majority on this frontier . . . few of the old settlers are here. The war has made grate changes."[34]

Rip Ford was so upset that as the editor of the *Brownsville Sentinel* he lashed out at the new government and lost his right to vote for a while. Later in the year McAllen wrote again, "We hear great talk about railroads but they have not commenced. Davis is not popular with the people, he is keeping a brache [sic] open and flooding us with carpetbaggers for the cause. I don't care for what principle he may have in this but let him take hold of good men, let them belong to any party in place of the men he has selected. If you were here you would not associate with any of the crowd in Brownsville. . . . King and Kenedy have both left Brownsville and are on their ranchos."[35]

Mifflin and King had definitely left Brownsville at just the right time. The 1870 census showed that Mifflin was fifty-two years old and that the Kenedy family in Nueces County, which is now Duval County where the Laureles ranch was located, had real property or real estate worth $21,000 and personal assets worth $139,000. Petra was forty-seven years old. Sarah, thirteen, was the only child listed at home. Since the census was taken in August she may have been home between school terms in New Orleans.[36] The Wild Horse Desert was a very lonely and unsafe place to be. This piece of land between the Nueces River and the Rio Grande for years had been referred to as "No Man's Land." This name could have been changed to "Every Man's Land" after the

Civil War. It was a wide-open space that invited thieves and bandits with a near guarantee that they would not be pursued.

After the severe winter of 1863–64 thousands of stray cattle had drifted south in search of food. They stayed and multiplied so that the land was filled with unclaimed cattle. They were there for the taking. Raiders came from Mexico and took cattle at will, including the stock that bore brands from established ranches. Anglo raiders also came to the Wild Horse Desert to take advantage of the exposed ranches. There was no law enforcement in the area. The Reconstruction government had abolished the Texas Rangers and the only lawmen were the U.S. troops posted at the garrisons. Rip Ford summed up their position toward protecting the cattle owners by writing, "It might have been that the powers of government remembered the course of Texas during the Civil War, and left her to take care of herself in the emergency brought about by Mexican raiders."[37] Mexican law enforcement was equally bad, and some were soon bragging, "The Gringos are raising cows for me." Their theory was that Mexico had owned that territory and they had a right to take back what was theirs. They called the cattle they stole "nanita's" meaning their grandmother's cattle.[38] It was equally unsafe for the inhabitants of the Wild Horse Desert. In Clarksville, the Kenedy's steamboat agent Mr. Clark was playing dominos one night when a band of outlaws raided the town, walked into his house, and killed the young customs agent with whom he was playing. They had placed him against the wall when one of his young daughters jumped in front of him. They called all the family by name telling them they would not hurt them but proceeded to take everything they wanted out of the house.[39]

By now Petra and Mifflin were accustomed to their nemesis Cortina raising his head whenever there was chaos in Texas. With the lack of law enforcement under the Radical Republican regime, Cortina established himself as "Brigadier General Juan Nepomuceno Cortina, Commander of the Line of Bravo, with the power to make or unmake governors at his pleasure."[40] Many of Cortina's followers were busy rustling Texas cattle, so they were delighted to be under his protection. Not all the thieves took the trouble to drive the cattle over the Rio Grande. Instead they would kill them, skin them, and haul the hides to market, which was considerably easier than driving the cattle. "Many of them used cruel methods including a *media luna*, a scythe-like knife in the shape of a half-moon mounted on a long shaft, handled from horseback to hamstring cattle. The knocked-down animals were sometimes skinned while still alive. Ranchers pursuing hide-peelers would come upon suckling calves bawling by their mothers' raw carcasses still warm and jerking with signs of life."[41] Mifflin was a little more protected than King because he was located farther from the Rio Grande and he had completed fencing his ranch.

Mifflin tried to provide a collective ranchers' effort to stop this thievery. He presided over the first Stock Raisers Association meeting held in 1870. The members' goals were to help one another stave off theft, find and return stolen cattle, bring to trial all thieves caught, and to bring pressure on both state and national governments to provide protection. Kenedy and King strongly supported the organization, and they published the stockmen's registered brands in local newspapers so that there would be no mistake about who legally owned those brands and the cattle on which they appeared. Their enforcement efforts did little good in Mexico, as illustrated by a sign on a Matamoros hide dealer's fence that said, "Shoot the first damned gringo son of a bitch who comes here and attempts to look at a hide."[42]

Kenedy and King found a way to make a profit in tallow factories. After the Civil War, tallow, or cow fat, became an important exportable item. The rancheros who had insufficient capital to set up rendering establishments sold their herds to King and Kenedy, who owned two of the four tallow factories in Nueces County, giving them not only profits but also control of the cattle trade of South Texas.[43]

The two had hoped to maintain their monopoly on the river trade with their steamers and the charter they had from the Texas Legislature to build a railroad between Brownsville and Brazos Santiago or Point Isabel. They did nothing to construct the railroad except buy up some land in the Espíritu Santo grant, which would provide the right of way. Hostile merchants, led by H. E. Woodhouse of Brownsville, took their complaints about Kenedy and King's high freight rates to the Texas legislature. The driving force behind this movement was Joseph Kleiber. He had moved to Point Isabel and married Emma Butler, the daughter of John Rocha Butler, a prominent resident of Port Isabel. Kleiber felt passionately about having a railroad between Port Isabel and Brownsville and wrote to Jacob Mussina in Galveston, "If you want to see the Iron Horse travel over Palo Alto Prairie in your lifetime, now is the time to act." The group traveled to Austin to demand that King and Kenedy forfeit their charter and transfer it to them. The legislature revoked King and Kenedy's charter and granted it instead to a group headed by Simon Celaya, a wealthy businessman and Spanish vice-consul at Brownsville. The group named their officers in their charter granted May 23, 1871: Simon Celaya, president; Joseph Kleiber, secretary; Francisco Armendaiz, treasurer; and H. M. Field, engineer. Other directors were Charles Andre, H. B. Illius, Franklin Cummings, A. R. Erhard, Antonio Longoria, J. Eversmann, Nestor Maxan, S. P. Gelsten, A. Werbiski, Charles McManus, John S. Ford, Henry A. Maltby and Dr. R. Deffendorfer. Joseph Kleiber became responsible for seeing that the railroad was built. This group organized the Rio Grande Railroad Co. and began to build twenty-two and a half miles of track from a dock at

Men working to refill water supply for Rio Grande Train. Built in 1868, it ran between Brownsville and Point Isabel, Texas.

Point Isabel to a station in Brownsville. Kenedy and King were not happy about this event but there was little they could do. Mifflin wanted to stop this group, and filed two obstructive lawsuits against the Rio Grande Railroad Co. preventing them from entering the city limits of Brownsville and keeping them from using the land they owned on the Espíritu Santo grant. At one point during the trial the usually staid Kenedy referred to the plaintiffs as a "Fifth rate, one pilon [sic], dog-powered railroad." He lost both of the suits in court and the railroad was completed in 1871.[44]

Petra often traveled with Mifflin when he went to Brownsville for business, and sometimes she went on her own, either with the payroll or on family business. On August 30 the family gathered there for the baptism of William Putegnat, son of Joe and Rosa, with Father Parisot presiding over the services. William had been born on July 10, 1870.[45]

Brownsville and the Rio Grande were again faced with yellow fever in the following months. On November 24, John McAllen wrote that the port and the Rio Grande had been quarantined for the last three months and they had no communication from the outside world.[46] Not only was it hard on all the inhabitants, but also it was very difficult on the steamship business.

On December 15, the family once again gathered for a poignant ceremony. That day, in the church they had helped build, Ana Chavero Vidal married John Peter Putegnat. It had been five years since Ana lost Adrian to his executioners in Camargo. She had given birth to a daughter three months and three days after his death, on August 17, 1865. Ana had continued to live in Brownsville and had been strongly supported by Mifflin and Petra as well as the rest of the family. She was now marrying Joe Putegnat's brother John and the family was delighted. Joe and Rosa served as sponsors, as well as Nene (Vicenta) Starck and Robert Dalzell. They were joined by Sam B. Kathrens and John Valls, who in 1881 would serve as the U.S. vice-consul for the City and Port of Matamoros.[47] Petra knew now that Adrian's wife and her granddaughter would be well provided for and that they would remain within the family circle.

The family experienced both happiness and sorrow on a regular basis. Shortly after the wedding on January 15, 1871, Rosa and Joe's young baby, John Peter Putegnat, died.[48] This was the second time that Rosa had lost a baby one year old or younger. Petra one more time tried to comfort Rosa and Joe, and this time Ana and John were also there to help. It was particularly hard for them as newlyweds to see this young child that was named for John slip away at such a young age.

The year 1871 brought even more violence across the prairies of the Wild Horse Desert; Cortina's raiders continued to run free across the land. Mifflin, taking a unique approach to the problem, along with prominent lawyer and politician Stephen Powers, sought to have Cortina pardoned for his past offenses in Texas. In return for this pardon, Cortina would use his considerable influence to suppress the raids into Texas. Powers actually managed to get the bill through the Senate to pardon Cortina, but there was such outrage expressed at its passage that the House postponed the bill indefinitely.[49] This enraged Cortina, and the situation worsened. It was reported that Cortina stocked four ranches in Tamaulipas mainly with cattle and horses stolen from Texas. He either appropriated the stock after it was brought across the border or bought it at his own designated price. It was proven that he was filling beef and hide contracts in Cuba and had his men deliver the goods to waiting ships. Cortina got very rich off of the gringos' cows.[50]

In 1870 murders became so common that people were forced to travel with squads of bodyguards. Doña Salomé McAllen was no exception. She always traveled with armed guards and carried her own weapon. On one trip, her niece Joaquina de la Vega accompanied her, and their coach overturned. One of the hatchets they carried on their belts for protection fell and hit Joaquina on the forehead, cutting her and leaving a scar she bore the rest of her life.[51]

It was estimated that during the period from 1865 to 1873, thieves drove more than 100,000 head of cattle across the Rio Grande.[52] Petra was glad that her married daughters and grandchildren were in Brownsville and not traveling the dangerous roads. She and the rest of the family gathered again in their church on December 19, 1871, for the baptism of John Peter Putegnat III, son of Ana Chavero and John Peter Putegnat. Ana now had a little brother for her daughter Adrianne to love along. Father Manuel conducted the baptismal service and the sponsors were Rosa Vidal and John J. Falls.[53] Petra and Mifflin were living through difficult times, and moments like this brought much-needed pleasure to their lives.

CHAPTER 10

1872-74:
One Foot in Brownsville, One in the Wild Horse Desert

Petra and Mifflin experienced two years of transition from 1872 to 1874. They were still involved in Brownsville with their family and business interests. However, the steamboat business was slowly dying, while the cattle business was on the verge of exploding. Thus they had one foot in Brownsville and the other in the Wild Horse Desert at their Los Laureles Ranch.

The decade from 1870 to 1880 would be full of challenges and turmoil for both the Kenedy and King families. During this time they would become two of the largest and most successful ranchers in the United States. They would take thousands of head of cattle up the trail to the Midwest and the railheads for shipment to the East. They would also develop and improve the cattle and open up the Wild Horse Desert for commerce. They did this despite violence, bandits, thievery, drought, and politics.

Bruce Cheeseman described their accomplishments in the following manner. After the division of the ranch, King and Kenedy went on to build two of the most famous ranches in the American West. They revolutionized the economics of South Texas ranching with the introduction of fencing; livestock drives to northern markets; large-scale cattle, sheep, mule, and horse raising; and the scientific breeding and upgrading of livestock. King's access to capital fueled his never-ending expansion in land and livestock that created volume and scale. This allowed King to displace competing ranchers and landowners both Anglo and Mexican and crush his competitors. He believed vehemently in the concept of private property, which was incompatible with the open range. He particularly despised squatters, no matter what race, religion, or creed. He utilized armed force, not always legally deputized, to protect his interest against all outlaw elements.[1]

In Brownsville, Mifflin was upset about the railroad his competition had built and the threat it presented to King, Kenedy & Co.'s monopoly of transportation services along the Rio Grande. In April, Joseph Kleiber, who was running the railroad operations, wrote several letters to Humphrey Woodhouse in New Orleans regarding Mifflin's actions and temperament. On May 6, he wrote, "Kenedy looks terribly blue lately. It makes me feel sorry to see him."[2] Later, on the thirteenth, he told Woodhouse that Kenedy had tried to buttonhole San Román. Mifflin was trying to convince the investors in the railroad that it was not in their best interest. He also complained that the railroad would give the company a monopoly and that they could charge any rates they wanted, which was amusing to everyone but Mifflin because of the monopoly he had held for more than fifteen years.[3]

A most interesting letter was written on April 27 from Kleiber to Woodhouse in which he wrote, "It is reported that Doña Petra is going to lend "El Capitán" her money she has in Europe so as to enable him to build an opposition railroad from Brazos to Brownsville. The Mexicans believe in this yarn. I am told Kenedy makes everyone feel he comes in contact with his ill humor. Old friends turned against him."[4]

This was a difficult time for Mifflin, and Petra did call him "El Capitán," and he affectionately called her "Petrita." M. Kenedy & Co. had made its fortunes often at the expense of its friends. Even so, it was difficult for Mifflin and Petra to see their friends turn against them to make a profit. Petra and Mifflin had known many of these men in the railroad operation for over twenty years. San Román had stood as a sponsor for both John Gregory and Sarah at their baptisms. Nothing was supposed to break this all-important bond between families. Mifflin did not seem to be able to give up on his prospects for Brownsville and continued to seek a strategy to bring another railroad into competition against his enemies.

The cattle business had begun to boom right after the Civil War. Since 1867 cattle had been moving toward Kansas and from there on to the eastern markets by railroad. It was about 1,100 miles from the Santa Gertrudis and Los Laureles to the railheads in Kansas. It took a special breed of cattle to sustain that trip, walking ten to twelve miles a day through both heat and cold and across rivers and mountains and still having enough meat on them to be marketable on arrival. The Texas Longhorn was just that breed. The three-year-old steers were fondly referred to by Texas cattlemen as "roaming $20 gold pieces" because of the price they would bring at the end of the trip.[5] By 1870 the market was right and between 1870 and 1872 King sent about 13,500 cattle

Texas Cattle Trails, 1870-1880s

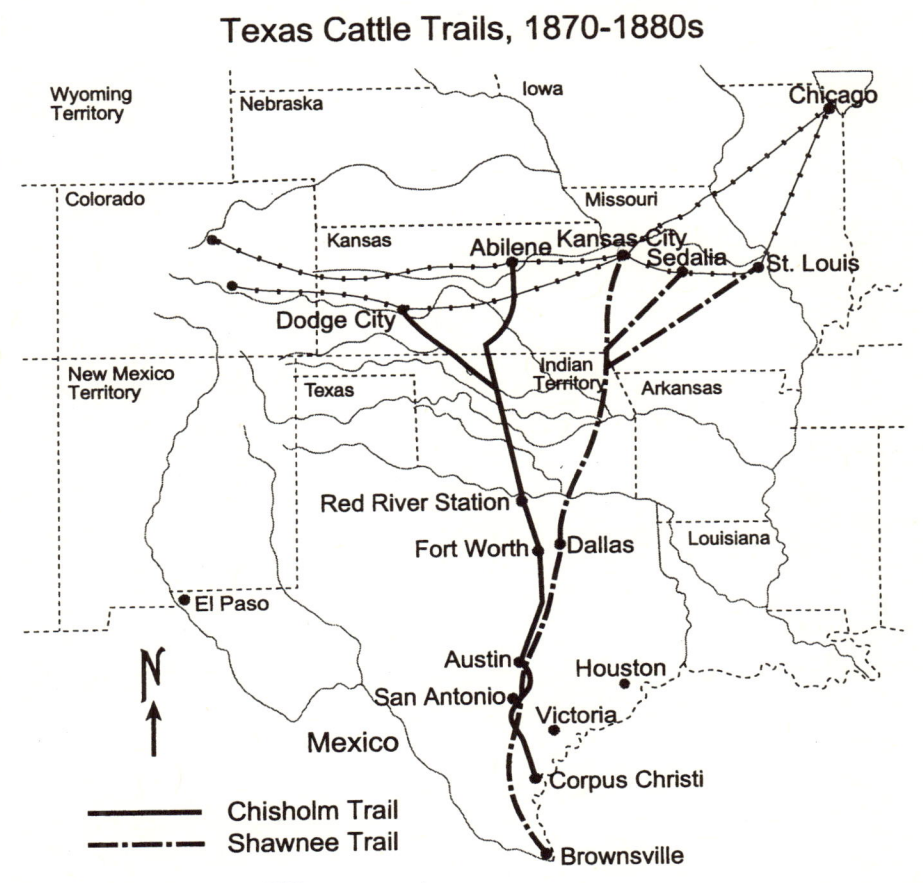

Texas cattle trails. Nancy Tiller, cartographer.

to Kansas and made a good profit.[6] King was further along in his cattle interests than Mifflin because Mifflin was still fighting battles in Brownsville. In March of the previous year King, along with Martha and John Rabb, who were neighbors of Mifflin and Petra's, had sent cattle up the trail.[7]

Richard King was one of the earliest and most successful ranchers to send cattle up the trail. Between 1869 and 1885 he shipped about 70,000 cattle. His trail drivers invested in the herd, which added to their incentive to make the drive successful. As the trail bosses traveled toward Kansas they stayed in contact with King via telegraph.[8] In 1875 Captain King made a net profit of $50,000 on a single herd of 4,737 cattle.[9]

South Texas ranchers mainly used two trails, the Western Trail to railheads in Dodge City, Kansas, and the Eastern or Chisholm Trail to Abilene, Kansas. These trails connected with other trails along the way that led into Colorado, New Mexico, Arizona, Wyoming, and California. The cattle were gathered in late February or March and would feed on the new spring grass on the way north, arriving in late summer. A "road herd" of about 3,000 cattle needed a trail boss; about ten cowboys; a cook in charge of the team, wagon, supplies, and bedrolls; and a wrangler who tended to the remuda, or string of extra horses. It took about six horses per cowboy; for ten cowboys sixty horses were needed.[10]

They usually formed up with the trail boss in the lead, followed by the chuck wagon pulled by mules. To one side of the herd the horse wrangler would bring the remuda along. The point riders would guide the lead steers and the swing riders kept the herd together. The flank riders were farther back, and the drag riders were in the rear. The flank and drag riders caught most of the dust, hence it was not the desirable place to be and the spot usually went to the newest on the crew. About mid-afternoon the cook would pull out in front and begin to make camp at the campsite the trail boss had picked out.[11] The trail rides were long, tiring, hot, dusty, and dangerous. The team faced Indian raids, swollen rivers, lightning storms, stampeding herds, wild animals and reptiles, and the loneliness of hard days and nights in the saddle from dawn to night. However, they were paid well and the trail drives provided employment for many South Texas cowboys.

Owners like Mifflin Kenedy, Richard King, and Martha and John Rabb would have their entire ranching investment for a year on the road. They had to depend heavily on their trail bosses and the vaqueros who handled the cattle. Ranching could bring good rewards, but it could also bring financial ruin. John Rabb died in 1871, leaving his wife to run their cattle business. Not many women were independent ranchers, but Martha was an excellent manager and cattle raiser. On John's death she was left with 10,000 cattle, 3,500 sheep, 450 horses, and a small house they had built in Corpus Christi in 1859. Martha faced dangerous times when the country was filled with rustlers and outlaws. She was involved with the everyday operation of the ranch and continued to buy surrounding land. She built a large ranch, was fond of smoking cigarillos, and became known as the "Cattle Queen of Texas." She too enclosed her land with cypress and pine fencing like her neighbor Mifflin; she put up thirty miles of fence. She later built a beautiful home on the bluff in Corpus Christi and called it the Magnolia Mansion. Mifflin, after Petra's death, bought her previous house for his son John Gregory.[12]

Martha had three sons, Dock, Frank, and Lee. After John's death Martha married a Methodist minister, C. M. Rogers. The sons did not think highly of their new stepfather, especially when Reverend Rogers took a portrait of John sitting on a horse and hung it in the outhouse.[13] Mifflin and Petra's granddaughter, Lillian Starck, married Martha Rabb's son Frank in the late

Frank Rabb purchased the Rabb Plantation, or Palm Grove Plantation, outside of Brownsville, consisting of 20,305 acres. Mifflin and Petra's granddaughter, Lillian Starck, married Frank, whose mother, Martha Rabb, was known as "The Cattle Queen of Texas." The house and six hundred acres now belong to the National Audubon Society. Brownsville Historical association.

1880s and they purchased the Palm Grove Plantation outside of Brownsville, which is now owned by the National Audubon Society.[14]

Petra and Mifflin established their ranch next to the Rabb's ranch. Their land was a mixture of soils and terrain, including sand dunes, brush-covered pastures, salt marshlands, and black-soil prairie.[15] They had a house, store, barns, pens, and other outbuildings on the property. When they arrived at Los Laureles there was already a house; Charles Stillman had built it on the property. The house had a hidden vault in the floor of the fireplace in which to place valuables for protection from robbers. Petra and Mifflin added on to the house as more room was needed, and a large wraparound porch connected the additional structures.[16] Mifflin had also completed fencing their property, so they were safer from rustlers and could contain and therefore improve their herds more easily. In the fourteen years between 1869 and 1882, Mifflin increased the property from 131,000 acres to over 240,000 acres.[17]

Petra took control of the property and the people who worked for them. She knew about ranching and she spoke the language of the workers. She helped in ordering their supplies, providing housing for them, and in many of their daily needs. Their ranch, like others, used the grains, vegetables, and fruit they grew and canned, as well as the chicken, pork, and beef they raised.

They purchased staples like salt, coffee, flour, and sugar.[18] In addition to running the domestic side of the ranch Petra also aided by carrying the payroll and other business transactions to Brownsville. She provided medical care for the workers and those in need. Petra's experience using the native plants and herbs helped produce helpful medicines. Many of the plants at Laureles were familiar to her from her childhood at her father's ranch.

The land produced both helpful and harmful plants. And this was not a welcoming land. In an 1806 survey of the ranch it was described as full of salty lakes and populated with a variety of grasses, mesquite, oak, and laurels of little value.[19] The Spanish dagger, a type of yucca, has sharp points that could inflict painful wounds, and if left untreated could be very difficult to heal. This plant came in handy, though, to help treat snakebites. The Tejanos believed that by jabbing the points into the flesh around the wound and getting the blood out it would permit the point from the daggers to offset the venom of the snake.[20] Another antidote for snakebite was an herb of the acanthus family, which according to one writer every man among the Mexican troops stationed along the Rio Grande was required to carry.[21] The most prominent of all plants on the ranch was the mesquite tree. It has sharp thorns and white flowers that turn yellow. Livestock used it for food and workers used it for fence posts and sometimes to burn. It has bean pods that grow from four to ten inches in length. The adage was that if the trees were heavy with beans it would be a cold winter. Both men and animals ate the beans. A small, flavored ball made of ground beans could sustain a man for a day.[22] Indians made meal from the beans and used it to make bread.[23] During the Civil War when the Confederate soldiers had no coffee they made a substitute beverage from mesquite beans. It was also believed that the mesquite leaves made into tea could cure diarrhea. Vaqueros often put fresh mesquite leaves in their hat to cure headaches.[24] It was believed that chewing mesquite bark could cure colic.[25] This plant grew rapidly and could take over the land very quickly.

Another plant to be found was la retama, a wandering and graceful tree that concealed sharp-toothed thorns, like so many of the plants on the Wild Horse Desert. It has beautiful yellow flowers and teas made from it help cure diabetes. The Anacua tree has a mass of many branches that bear berries that are good for a cough. The lantana plant grows from three to six feet high and was usually avoided. It was called the "rattlesnake bush" because often they were found curled up under the plants.[26]

John Gregory and Willie had returned to Spring Hill College and Sarah was back at the Ursuline Academy in New Orleans.[27] Tom had not returned to Spring Hill and James had stayed only two years. By now Tom was nineteen and James ("Santiago") was seventeen. James liked ranching. Of all the sons, he was the one who liked working the stock and being on the land. However, in the summer of 1872, James found himself in serious trouble while in Ellsworth, Kansas.

On July 20, 1872, James "Jim" Kenedy was playing cards at the Nick Lentz Saloon with Texas cattleman Print Olive, a man with a tough reputation, Gene Lyons, his best friend, and two businessmen. Olive had won several hands when Kenedy questioned the dealing. A violent argument broke out that ended with Olive telling Kenedy he would not play with him and for him to cash in his chips. In spite of a "no gun" law, Olive was wearing his guns, so Kenedy backed down but warned when he left the saloon, "There will be another day!" Olive and Lyons left and were questioned by the city marshal, J. L. Couincell, and sheriff Chauncey Whiteney, who had heard about the fight. They warned that Kenedy was a "bad one." Kenedy had been in Ellsworth for several weeks, and in one account, he had just sold a herd of cattle. Olive said, "if he can't play poker any better than that he'll starve to death." Olive later entered the Ellsworth Billiard Saloon and joined another game. Olive's trail boss, an African American named Jim Kelly, and a Mexican vaquero with the Olive outfit had just come into town and so had not checked their guns. They were outside the saloon watching the goings on in the street and were unaware of the quarrel between Kenedy and their boss. Everyone's attention was on the card game inside when Kenedy walked past the Olive cowboys, went into the saloon, and to the checked guns at the end of the bar. He picked up one and went over to Olive saying, "You S.O.B., now you can cash in your chips!" and began firing. The first bullet hit Olive in the hand, scattering cards, the second hit him in the groin and the third in his thigh. Kelly looked into the saloon and saw Olive falling, with Kenedy standing over him ready to deliver the coup de grâce. Kelly fired through the window and hit Kenedy in the leg, knocking him off balance and giving one of the cowboys time to knock him to the ground. Olive was put on a table and a doctor called for. Two doctors arrived, with the unlikely names of Duck and Fox. They probed the wound in Olive's groin and eventually pulled out part of a watch chain that was imbedded with the bullet. Disgusted with these two, Olive stopped them and a Dr. Minick was sent for. He arrived to pull out two slugs and dress the wounds. Kenedy was taken to jail but escaped and fled to Texas on the old cattle trail, never to return to Ellsworth again.[28]

After James returned home, raids continued on the ranches and everyday life was very dangerous. Mifflin spent $3,000 with the Remington Arms Company to continue to arm his vaqueros so they could protect his property.[29] King was in the process of building about thirty-two miles of fence with guard stations on each of the four sides.[30]

Mifflin had called a Stock Raisers of Western Texas meeting and observed that Texans all along the Rio Grande were thoroughly upset at the condition of things. He said, "If protection was not forthcoming, that the association would form protection against the marauders that might soon repel the acts of vandalism by violence."[31] Finally, the cries from the Nueces Strip (the land between the Nueces and Rio Grande) were heard in Washington. On May 7, 1872, President Grant authorized $6,000 to be used to send a United States Commission to Texas to investigate the bandit and outlaw disturbances. The commissioners were Thomas Robb, Richard Savage, and J. J. Mead. They arrived on the Rio Grande in July of 1872 and heard testimony from July 30 to October 3. During this period, the commissioners received 1,090 depositions from the residents of South Texas and accepted 423 petitions of claims from people living between the Rio Grande and the Nueces River. The amount of losses and injuries they claimed totaled $48,496,235.25.[32]

On August 26, Richard King testified to a frightening incident that he had been involved with in July of 1872. "I left Corpus Christi, in company with George Evans, my driver, and Franz Specht for the purpose of appearing before this Commission. At a point six miles east of my ranch, on the Corpus Christi road, at a place called San Fernando Creek, at about eight o'clock in the evening, twenty-five or thirty shots were fired into the ambulance (coach) in which I was riding, killing Franz Specht.... I do not know who my assassins were, but to the best of my knowledge and belief, they were a party of Mexicans, eight or ten in number.... I have been obliged, for a number of years, to keep quite a number of men, for my protection, at my expense, around my ranch, and in traveling I am obliged to have an escort of those men. Citizens of this frontier are obliged to travel armed always in self defense." Franz Specht was a traveler from Corpus Christi who had by chance asked for a ride to Brownsville. A $600 reward posted by the governor of Texas failed to lead to the arrest of the assassins who, in gunning for Richard King, killed the luckless Specht.[33]

Complicating the problem on the border was the death of President Benito Juárez from a stroke in 1872. His successor, Sebastián Lerdo de Tejada, had relieved Cortina of his post as "Commander of the Line of the Bravo," but Cortina had continued to exercise his control of the border for the next four years. He was later captured by Tejada but escaped and threw his support to Porfirio Díaz in his bid for the presidency.[34]

Kenedy and King spent several weeks in the early fall testifying before the Robb Commission. When Mifflin was giving testimony, "his Laureles Ranch was larger than King's holdings and his influence was equal or greater. Kenedy was troubled by the random violence and killings that accompanied the raids. He pointed to the long stretch of the Rio Grande and demanded better protection from the Rangers or the military. His estimate of losses by ranchers between Brazos Santiago and Roma totaled four hundred thousand head of cattle worth over six million dollars during the previous seven years."[35]

Mifflin testified for about a month, from August 28 to September 27. The cattlemen had placed a good deal of importance on this hearing. It is interesting that when appearing before the commission, King listed his address as a post office box in Corpus Christi, Texas, Nueces County. Mifflin listed his address as a post office box in Brownsville, Texas, Cameron County. The friends had turned their interests in different directions. Mifflin testified in support of the losses suffered by Alex Werbiski and Francis Campbell. He also testified as a partner of R. King & Co. and the $2,486,160 damage they had suffered from 1866 to 1869 at the hands of thieves and bandits. During the testimony he had Santiago Alvarez, Anselmo Longorio, Juan Miguel Longoria, Santos Longoria, Tomás Sandoval, and Vitterian Sandoval testify about Mifflin's losses at his San Salvador de Tule rancho from Cortina's raids in 1859. They also testified that they had helped deliver the 1,595 head of cattle that were left after the raid to Captain King and the safety of the Santa Gertrudis rancho and they bore the brands of VO and VO with a bar above the V.[36]

Justo López, who lived near a popular Rio Grande crossing, swore that he had personally seen 60,000 head of stolen cattle driven across the river. There were very few ranches that did not have claims similar to Kenedy and King's. The claims amounted to 750,000 head of cattle. These claims may have been exaggerated but many were not.[37] All of the Rio Grande Valley ranchers' losses were attributed to Mexican raiders and thieves of all sorts, many associated with Cortina.

The depositions provided an interesting insight into the early ranching endeavors of Mifflin and Petra. Instead of living on the San Salvador de Tule ranch and actively managing it themselves, they had lived in Brownsville and employed Mr. Jacob George to run the rancho. They hired herdsmen and vaqueros to handle the stock. The cows were of good quality and gentle. They had fine saddle horses. Water on the rancho was obtained from wells. The San Salvador de Tule rancho was about forty miles from Brownsville.[38] One of the family ranches, Santa Teresa, is still in the family today, owned by Niceforo Peña, descendant of Gertrudis Vela de Resendez, Petra's half-sister.[39]

The Mexican government was not going to sit by and let these Texans' claims go unanswered. In September they charged a special commission to investigate the same allegations that the United States Commission was investigating. The commission was known as the Comisión Pesquisidora de la Frontera del Norte, or The Commission to Investigate the Northern Frontier. It assembled in Matamoros in September of 1872. They were given the U.S. commission's depositions and came to different conclusions. They found that the thefts were committed not only by Mexicans living in Mexico but also by former Confederate soldiers, Mexicans working with Texas cattlemen, and Indians. They found that Texas served as a refuge for Mexican outlaws. They said the early settlers in Texas were honest but that the newly arrived Texans wanted wealth and would break the law to acquire it. They blamed Texans for buying stolen Mexican stock, and pointed out Brownsville businessmen who dealt in stolen cattle and hides. They also pointed out that most of the raiders were Mexican because most of the population was Mexican. They recognized that Cortina was a bandit but defended him in some cases because he was trying to punish smugglers. They said the Mexican government had reprimanded him. They also stated that Cortina was being used as a "scapegoat" in order to give the American Imperialists the right to invade Mexico and increase their ownership of Mexico to the Sierra Madre.[40]

Neither of the commissions had much effect on the situation along the Rio Grande. The bandits, outlaws, and renegades continued to terrorize both sides of the border. Petra and Mifflin and the other ranchers continued to do the best they could but ultimately realized that they would have to provide their own self-defense.

CHAPTER 11

1873:
Politics, Bandits, and
Hard Economic Times

Danger in every direction surrounded Petra in 1873. She was busy helping run Los Laureles while Mifflin was embroiled in Brownsville's political battles. The unsolved railroad issues demanded a great deal of Mifflin's attention. John Gregory, seventeen, was one year from completing his studies at Spring Hill College. Willie, fifteen, continued his studies at Spring Hill, and Sarah, sixteen, continued at the Ursuline Academy. Tom, twenty, and James, eighteen, were in Texas with Mifflin and Petra. Her married daughters were settled and continuing to add children to the family. The sons-in-law were often involved with Mifflin in his business ventures. Little did she know that this year would hold a personal crisis.

Despite the investigations, cattle stealing continued to escalate along the border.[1] King seemed to be a particular target for Cortina. Cortina had sworn to capture and to hang the owner of the ranch on the Santa Gertrudis and more than once tried to ambush him. The black-bearded Captain King fought back with everything he had. When John S. McCampbell of Corpus Christi, who in 1873 had abandoned his practice of law because of the dangers of travel to attend the courts, was asked about King at his isolated ranch, McCampbell replied with a hint of doubt in his voice: "He thinks he can defend himself."[2] The Tejanos had a different version of the violence. They said that Mexicans were no longer safe on the highways or outside of the towns because they were shot down as if they were savages just because they were Mexicans. Around San Marcos, a San Antonio newspaper said, the trees were bearing a "new kind of fruit"—Mexican cattle thieves hung by so-called vigilance committees organized for self-protection against the rustlers infesting that section.[3]

For a number of reasons the U.S. government did not offer good defense for southern Texas. Only 250 to seven hundred soldiers remained in the area after the Civil War. Communications were slow and many of the federal officials thought that the Texans were exaggerating the violence and their claims. In the meantime, the bandits and outlaws operated at will against the citizens of the Rio Grande Valley.

Captains Kenedy and King were coming to the attention of Corpus Christi residents, and the paper began to carry news about them and their ranchos. According to lore, Corpus Christi was named by the early Spanish explorer Alonzo Alvarez de Piñeda in 1519. The Spanish custom was to name locations for the feast of the day of discovery, and the feast of Corpus Christi, "Body of Christ," fell that year on June 24, 1519 when Alvarez discovered the bay. The town of Corpus Christi, founded by Colonel Henry L. Kinney of Pennsylvania, grew up on the banks of the bay. He came to the area around 1839 and discovered a small Mexican town already there. In 1848 he purchased the land on which Corpus Christi now sits and opened a trading post. About the same time that Colonel Kinney arrived in 1840, John Kelsey came to the area and established a general merchandise store. His correspondence was sent to him at Corpus Christi, Texas, Corpus Christi Bay. The nation first heard of the small town when General Taylor landed his troops in preparation for the Mexican War and spent the winter there from late 1845 to early 1846. Kinney held an organizational meeting of the citizens and petitioned the Texas legislature to organize the government of Nueces County with Corpus Christi as the county seat. The petition was granted and the county government installed on January 11, 1847.[4] The International Fair that he organized in 1852 brought Richard King and "Legs" Lewis across the Wild Horse Desert and prompted Captain King's interest in ranching.

Mifflin published his brands in the *Nueces Valley* newspaper of January 18, 1873. The paper listed his horse and cattle brand, his cattle earmark, and his ranch as Rancho Laureles located twenty-one miles south of Corpus Christi.[5] Mifflin, like all the stock raisers, was publishing these brands throughout South Texas in hopes of deterring cattle rustling. The same paper said that good times were back because the holidays had disrupted trade, but now the hides, skin, and wool sales were increasing daily and the streets were lively again. It also mentioned that Mifflin was busy at his cattle plant in Four Bluff and was slaughtering up to five hundred head of cattle a day.[6]

The February 1 edition had excellent news for the Corpus Christi community. "Dr. Spohn of Laredo and his brother the prominent Physicians and Surgeons are in town. The latter came recently from Mier, Mexico, where he made an enviable reputation in his practice. We learn he intends locating here which if true, we congratulate the people upon the acquisition. Of the former gentleman we simply say that Laredo can't spare him or we should hope to have him locate here."[7] The February 15 edition confirmed that Dr. Spohn had inserted his card. "The experience and excellent reputation of this gentleman in the profession commends him sufficiently to the community."[8] Dr. Arthur Spohn would not only become Petra and Mifflin's physician but also their son-in-law, husband of their daughter Sarah.

Dr. Arthur Spohn was born on April 27, 1847, in Ancaster, Canada. He attended McGill University where he received the practical anatomy award in 1864. His interest in surgery and human anatomy continued through his medical education at the University of Michigan and at Long Island College Hospital in New York where he was an assistant professor of surgical anatomy in 1867. The next year he was sent to Texas as a United States surgeon in charge of military quarantine combating yellow fever in Corpus Christi and Brownsville. While he was in Corpus Christi he started his long association with Captain King and his family. He requested permission to treat patients at the "King's Ranch" which was located forty-five miles from Corpus Christi.[9]

Captain King and Henrietta were trying to rebuild their ranch after the devastation of the Civil War. They were immediately impressed with the twenty-one-year-old physician. The Kings asked that he provide them medical care whenever possible. He served the family for many years. He left Corpus Christi for a two-year stay in Mier, Mexico.[10]

It appears that Dr. Spohn returned to the Corpus Christi area just in time. The February 22, 1873, edition of the *Nueces Valley* newspaper said that they "regretted to state that Captain R. King lies seriously ill at his residence Santa Gertrudis."[11] On February 28, Mifflin received a letter from Mr. Holbein, the bookkeeper at Santa Gertrudis, informing him that he had received a telegram from Henrietta's younger half-brother Willie Chamberlain. He told Holbein that the commissioners were leaving from Ringgold Barracks and heading for Corpus Christi. He did not know if they were coming by land or water, but Mrs. King would do everything possible to make them comfortable.[12]

In March the prairies bloomed and were filled with millions of flowers. The paper said that it was as if "God made them to look at Himself and enjoy, for nobody less than He can see them all."[13] It was a beautiful time for Petra to live on the Wild Horse Desert. In times of drought it was dusty, full of thorny plants, and presented a bleak landscape. Times were good for Petra and Mifflin. The paper bragged that the principal butchers in town were buying their beeves from Captain Kenedy and that was the reason they had good beef now.[14] On March 21, Captain King, obviously recovered from his illness, wrote to Mifflin at Los Laureles and told him that the commissioners had left that morning for San Diego and then to Laredo.[15]

King was in trouble and needed help from Mifflin, his older friend and advisor. King said, "What can you do for me in funds, if not I will have to sell, not having a dollar and twelve miles of fence to build. I have spent more money than I ever hope to [receive] from any of our claims, can we not sell out and quit? Will you or Dalzell and Cooper buy my interest in the boats and property in the river? Let me know. I have been very sick—things are going badly with me in money matters."[16] Mifflin must have thought back to the letter he had written King before they dissolved their partnership, telling him that he thought King's projected expenses of $50,000 for the Santa Gertrudis would cost nearer to $100,000. It was difficult to manage large ranches and many times the ranchers had all their cash tied up and were "land poor." King was in that spot. Mifflin must have helped King with financing because King kept his rancho and completed his fencing

Dr. Spohn was busy in his first month of practice because smallpox broke out in the vicinity of Corpus, which was quarantined. The Corpus Christi paper, which also published Brownsville news, gave the Honorable Mayor credit for prompt action in preventing the smallpox from spreading. Doctors were seeing patients by the score, one doctor vaccinating over three hundred patients in three days.[17] Isolation out on Los Laureles did provide some protection from the dreaded smallpox. The same paper brought news that the railroad in Brownsville was within one and one half miles of Brownsville and near completion. It also reported that a late norther had hit and half of the peach crop had been destroyed and was on the ground.[18]

In April, Petra and Mifflin's good friend Edward Downey came to Corpus. He had been a witness at their marriage nineteen years before in Brownsville. One of Rosa's sons, their grandchild, was also named for him. Mifflin and Petra were delighted at the opportunity to see him again and to catch up on the latest news from Brownsville. He was in town attending the Presbytery. He was the elder from the Brownsville Church, and the paper commented on his general cheerful countenance and how he was always welcomed.[19] The paper carried another announcement of great interest to the town. Mr. Louis de Planque, the French photographer who had been established in Matamoros and Brownsville since 1864, was setting up a studio in Corpus Christi.[20]

King wrote Mifflin on May 2 to catch him up on how he was doing. He said he was sorry that he had not had time to come for a visit at his rancho but that he hoped to soon so they could talk matters over more fully than he could by letter. He said his fence was coming along slowly but he had run out of lumber and today he had received four wagons full so he hoped to be through fencing by July. He described his land as very dry and that if he did not get rain, 1,000 men—well mounted—could not keep the cattle from the water. King said he had received a letter from Cal Rabb in San Antonio saying it was going to cost money to get their case together and that if they would send him $500 he would have it done for them. King said he had no money for this and wanted to know what Mifflin thought about it.[21] The paper confirmed King's progress three weeks later, reporting that Captain King was enclosing a pasture comprised of sixty square miles, or 38,400 acres.[22]

The next month King seemed to be concerned with events in Brownsville and wrote Mifflin saying that he had had doubts for some time about San Román's loyalty. He was getting his horses ready to go to Brownsville and told Mifflin that he would let him know if there was going to be any delay. This time King lectured Mifflin. He told him that there should be no more than 125 to 150 horses sent from Los Laureles and that all the horses front locks and tails should be trimmed because their stock of horses did not look well with long tails. He assured Mifflin that he would do the best he could with them in Brownsville.[23]

In June, the paper covered Mifflin and Petra's rancho extensively. On June 14 they published news that Captain Kenedy of Los Laureles had stopped in the city for a few days and that he was one of the largest stockowners in the West. They also reported that he had enclosed the largest stock pasture in the state. The paper said they had not had the pleasure of knowing Captain Kenedy in person but from the history of his business they could see that he could add as much material wealth to this part of the state as any man in the West.[24] The *Corpus Christi Caller*, not to be outdone by the *Nueces Valley* newspaper, published an excellent description of the Laureles ranch on June 22:

> Laureles Ranch of Captain Kenedy contained 131,000 acres of grazing land. The pasture fence was thirty-six miles in length: thirty miles of heart-pine boards, sawed to uniform length, with cypress posts; and six miles of wire and board. The latter fence was comprised of galvanized wire passing through holes in the posts; winches were attached one-fourth mile apart for tightening wire slack [which Mifflin invented].[25] The pasture contained 30,000 cattle, 5,000 horses and colts and mules, and 2,000 hogs. From ten to twelve thousand calves were branded yearly. An ironbound tank had 2,500 gallons capacity. Captain Kenedy also had four smaller ranches at the time.[26]

The violence continued around Petra, and the entire area outside the cities remained unsafe. In July, Lt. D. H. Floyd, a graduate of West Point, was in Corpus Christi. General Hatch sent Floyd and his company to be stationed at Captain King's Santa Gertrudis rancho to operate against cattle thieves and

Mexican marauders.[27] It was a good thing they were nearby because Dr. J. Crockett on July 6 was murdered fifteen miles from Santa Gertrudis and not far from Petra at Los Laureles. After he had camped for the night, a party of Mexicans passed on the road, and then they returned to kill him, shooting him in the head, arm, and side. Lieutenant Floyd and the 9th Cavalry were sent to investigate.[28]

King worried about the safety of the road between Santa Gertrudis and Corpus Christi. On July 12 he sent Captain John Greer to Chicago and on to Danville, Kentucky, to bring his two daughters back safely.[29] Henrietta enrolled her girls at a school in Kentucky, while Petra had Sarah in New Orleans, because the children were safer away from South Texas. Both Petra and Henrietta made sure that their children were trained in their mothers' religions. Henrietta enrolled Nettie in the Henderson Female Institute, a solidly Presbyterian girls' school near the Presbyterian Centre College for boys that her half-brother Hiram had attended. Nettie enrolled in 1870 and was joined by Ella in either 1872 or 1873, and then by Alice in 1874. Captain Greer returned on July 26 with Misses Nettie, Ella Morse, Alice Gertrudis, and Richard King Jr.[30] Captain Greer and the children had traveled on the steamer *The Yacht* from Indianola and then left by stage for Santa Gertrudis.[31]

Petra was no doubt glad to see an ad in the August 2 paper about her son-in-law Joe Putegnat's business. The advertisement was for a new Texas remedy, Putegnat's Amargosa—"Diarrhea Specific, Warranted Free of Narcotics and Minerals. A certain cure for Diarrhea, Chronic Diarrhea, Dysentery (Bloody Flux), Chronic Dysentery, Cholera, Morbus, Cholera—Infantburn (Summer Complaint), Colic and Looseness of the Bowels. It was prepared by J. L. Putegnat, Brownsville, Texas"—sold in Corpus, Galveston, and New Orleans.[32] It seemed it was good for almost anything that ailed a person.

Mifflin and King had employed former Capt. William Kelly to run their business office and look after their interests in Brownsville while they were on their ranchos. Captain Kelly kept a bound copy of his correspondence with both Mifflin and King from August of 1873 through 1874. He wrote about the commerce along the river, the steamboat business, customer bills, cargo, weather conditions, family news, and most of all about the compelling and often vicious politics that governed Brownsville and the Rio Grande Valley during those years.[33]

On August 13, Captain Kenedy left Brownsville. He and Captain King had been trying to work out some propositions between them and their railroad opponents. They were too far apart and could not come to a conclusion so Mifflin ended it by buying out San Román's interest in the firm of King, Kenedy & Co. for $700 in cash. Captain Kelly felt that losing San Román was no real loss because he had been against them for the last year and it was

Capt. William Kelly had been employed by Mifflin Kenedy and Richard King to run their business office while they were on their ranchos. Kelly kept a bound copy of his correspondence with both Mifflin and King, providing an insight into the personalities of the times and the reality of business and politics along the border. Courtesy of Jesse (Sam) Thornham, Joe Thornham, McGoohan families, Petra's descendants.

dangerous to have him involved with the boats. He informed Joseph Cooper, another partner, that their boats were in first class order and he thought they could compete with the railroad. They were sending Mr. Gomila to New York to try to convince Mr. Morgan to start a line of steamers from New York to Rockport and Brazos in hopes of crippling Mr. Woodhouse and his shipping business.[34]

Yellow fever was raising its ugly head again in New Orleans and the rumors all over the country were that it had reached Texas.[35] Mifflin and Petra worried about their children and grandchildren in the early part of September when they got a telegram from Captain Kelly telling them that Brownsville had been hit by a very severe gale and they had eight inches of rain in twenty hours. With Brownsville being nearly at sea level, the rain was crippling. Petra must have remembered the terrible hurricane of 1867 and worried about the family's safety. Kelly told them that all the telegraph lines along the river had been swept down and that the steamers *San Juan* and *Petrita* had broken their anchors and drifted to the Mexican side, unhurt. The railroad had been severely hurt. The tracks broke in many places and the dirt washed away all along the track. The engine house of the railroad was blown down, falling on one of the locomotives in Point Isabel and bringing down the smoke stack. The board of directors met, needing to raise $30,000 for the repairs, which would probably set them back three months in construction. Kelly urged Mifflin to go to New York and see Morgan personally because he thought he could strike a favorable deal to bring in another line of steamers from New York to Brazos.[36]

Captain Kelly did not know yet that Mifflin was not leaving Texas to go anywhere. Yellow fever worries, business competition, and weather all became insignificant because his Petrita was in trouble. She had developed a large growth in her neck and had become dangerously ill. Captain Kelly wrote Mifflin on September 18 that he was "exceedingly sorry to hear your almost gloomy anticipation of Mrs. Kenedy's health. I trust her strong constitution will carry her through."[37] It is probable that Mifflin and Petra turned to Dr. Spohn to help them in this emergency. He was already a renowned surgeon and was in Corpus, only twenty miles away. They were very lucky to have him to turn to. Ten days later, on September 28, Kelly wrote Mifflin, "I trust that by this time, Mrs. Kenedy has passed through the ordeal of the operation and is now enjoying her usual good health."[38] Petra probably traveled to Corpus Christi to have the operation although Dr. Spohn may have come to Los Laureles. A little more is learned about her operation from Kelly's letter to Joseph Cooper in New Orleans on October 13. He wrote, "Mrs. Kenedy has been dangerously sick. She has had an operation performed on her throat [cutting out a tumor] but she is fast recovering."[39] Petra's tumor must have been large enough to cause great discomfort and concern. The operation and threat of infection were cause enough for worry, but also her prognosis worried Mifflin a great deal. From looking at Petra's earlier photographs, it is likely she suffered from a goiter. A goiter is an enlargement of the thyroid gland, visible as a swelling at the front of the neck. Goiter surgery during the 1870s in the best of medical centers would have been very dangerous. Operating conditions, infection (aseptic surgery was a new concept), hemorrhage, and even vocal cord paralysis were very real concerns. Thyroid surgery would not have been a consideration unless asphyxiation was threatening.[40] Mifflin probably feared that this could be the beginning of a life-threatening disease. Having a surgeon of Dr. Spohn's ability was a true blessing for Mifflin and Petra and they would be grateful for her recovery.

The news of Petra's illness spread to Brownsville. On October 5, Kelly wrote Mifflin, "your several telegrams affording the greatest gratification to your friends and calling forth congratulations and good feelings on all sides came duly to hand."[41] Mifflin had kept them informed of Petra's progress and her friends and his associates celebrated her recovery. Her family also traveled to Los Laureles to be near her. Travel was difficult because the roads were in terrible shape with mud and washouts after the September rains. Kelly wrote Captain King on October 8 telling them that Captain Dalzell and party were expected from Los Laureles on Friday or Saturday.[42] They had been to Los Laureles to see Petra.

Petra's illness did not stop the troubles from swirling around Mifflin's business and the nation during this time. On September 19, "Black Friday" struck on Wall Street, leading to the tightening of credit and plunging prices. The beef market collapsed and many stockmen could not meet their obligations and lost their ranches. It took the market two years to recover and all of the ranchers in South Texas faced tough challenges trying to stay afloat.[43] Kelly wrote to Mifflin on September 28 that they were still under a yellow fever quarantine and there was no sign of it being lifted. He said that they had received dispatches from New Orleans reporting that all the banks and banking institutions had suspended payments to prevent an immediate run and subsequent crash. He had telegraphed Mr. Cooper in New Orleans to tell him what credit they had with Perkins and Swenson & Co. and to check on their solvency.[44] Two weeks later, on October 13, Kelly wrote to Joseph Cooper in New Orleans to tell him that the money panic had not passed. He advised him to draw out any funds he had in the banking institution and to keep his money in his charge for the next year. He recommended United States bonds as the most secure investment.[45]

Petra was better, and on October 8 Kelly heard that she was continuing to improve.[46] This was especially fortunate because for the next three months politics and trouble in Brownsville would demand most of Mifflin's time. In September Kelly wrote Mifflin to tell him that General Hatch, Acting Inspector General, Department of Texas, was inquiring about an agent of the Morgan Line who had delivered to King, Kenedy & Co. government stores, after the Morgan agent had been informed that their contract had expired and Mr. Woodhouse had the new contract. He implied that improper influences had been used on the quartermaster at New Orleans to have it assigned to King, Kenedy & Co. General Hatch said that the quartermaster would take care of his reputation but questioned the company's involvement in another earlier instance when Mr. Armstrong had a government contract for transportation on the Rio Grande and the local inspector condemned his boats and then gave the contract to King, Kenedy & Co. Armstrong had then had an inspector come from Washington; he found that his boats were sound, and Armstrong filed suit against the government. After several years, he won the case and his heirs later collected $13,400. Kelly was asking Mifflin to clarify this because he thought the boats were condemned by a board of army officers and he might need this information. He said the current complaint to General Hatch sounded like Mr. Humphrey Woodhouse, who had dined with Hatch the last day he was there.[47]

The bitterness between Kenedy and King and the railroad group ran deep. Many of Kelly's letters provided news of the group's progress and expressed delight in their failures. On October 5, Kelly wrote that San Román and Celaya and about half a dozen other Mexican investors from Monterrey went out to inspect the damage the recent rains had done to the railroad. They went by hand car and took a squad of men with them to engineer it over the breaks and weak places. They got wet on the way and decided to take an ambulance (coach) back the next day. About twelve that night they came to a large *resaca* (an old river bed).[48] One of the members was seized with a congestive fit brought on by cold and exposure and died in the wagon before they reached town. San Román sat next to him in the carriage and helped bury him on Friday.[49]

Kelly told Mifflin that they had arranged for Russell to run for state senator in their district, which extended from El Paso to Corpus Christi and included the Rio Grande Valley. He also told him that Mariano Treviño Garza was organizing a Mexican club and wanted to know if Mifflin had purchased cattle from him recently.[50] Three days later Kelly wrote to Mifflin urging him to support Galvan for state representative and Russell for state senator because they were the Stockraisers' candidates and supported the hide and cattle laws. Russell had a proven record in the last year acting in his capacity as judge forcing the customs collector to deliver stolen hides to the sheriff and hide inspector. He said without him the hide and cattle laws would have no effect.

Kelly then asked Mifflin to digest all of that and let him know what he thought. He was glad to hear that Petra continued to improve.[51]

Having the hide laws enforced was critical to Kenedy and King if they had any hope of stopping the thieves who were robbing them daily. Kelly provided information that their railroad competitor, Mr. Woodhouse, was also involved with shipping stolen hides and had every reason to want to elect his candidates or officers so they would not interfere in this enterprise. The current hide and cattle inspector, Mr. H. S. Rock, had recently obtained information that H. E. Woodhouse & Co. was in the habit of purchasing stolen hides at night and at other times when the inspectors were not about. They mixed these with previously inspected shipments. When the company had been caught with a hide from Mr. Zamora, who testified he had not sold any hides to them recently and that the one in question had been stolen from him, the company used an outdated bill of sale from January to explain why they were in possession of Mr. Zamora's hide. Kenedy and King feared if Woodhouse and his group elected their candidates they would reopen the stolen hides trade on both sides of the river.[52]

Politics along the river was a product of self-interest and survival. Mifflin and his group needed their people in office to control law enforcement, government contracts, and railroad contracts from Austin. They needed to control all the political offices on the city, county, and state levels. They attempted to win these positions any way they could. Captain Kelly was upset with King and Mifflin because of their lack of involvement in Brownsville's political scene, and on October 19 he wanted to know if Mifflin was reading his letters. He summed up the political situation succinctly, "No greater mistake could be made than to imagine that the coming elections will drift to a desirable issue. Your enemies are numerous, industrious and energetic; your friends few, lukewarm and timid. Instead of taking to the field boldly on our own strength—and under our own name, we are forced to work behind the shelter of devotion to party . . . which restricts independence, and prevents profitable action." He complained that he could not answer the question of what Captain Kenedy or Captain King would do. He goes on to say, "the fight with the Railroad company is in my opinion a political sore now. If they can elect their representatives to the city council, the county offices and the legislature, it will revive the drooping spirits." He also told him that they had taken over the Republican club.[53]

The pressure continued to build through October and into November. Captain Kelly was trying to have the city elections moved from November 10 to the general election in December on the basis that they could not properly provide a correct voter registration list by the November election. He also held an informal citizen's meeting in which they selected a city ticket without regard to party to win enough support to prevail in the election. He assured Mifflin that all the candidates had pledged their opposition to running the railroad to the river, which is what they wanted. The ticket was constructed to conciliate the Mexicans and Republicans.[54]

By the second of November, Kelly had heard from Captain Kenedy and was following his advice to hold numerous caucuses to work out any problems with the slate. The railroad group had gotten into the Mexican club and outvoted the regular members, and the new members had endorsed the railroad slate. He told him, "all the decent citizens were disgusted and their slate would be supported now by the respectable Mexicans and their followers, the custom-house, and by all the other white voters not connected with the railroad."[55] A common practice was to take illiterate Mexicans on the eve of an election to a deserted house or barn and supply them with plenty of whiskey and rations. The next morning they would be marched to the polls and their tickets filled out. In the border regions, newspapers reported, Mexican Americans crossed the Rio Grande on election days with orders to cast their ballot for the chosen candidates.[56]

The biggest problem was the voter's list. The railroad group wanted to use the old list because they had brought in about four hundred migrants from Mexico to work on the railroad and had registered them to vote on the old list. If the election was postponed until the December election, the election board that Kelly was on would have time to strike them all from the voter's list. Kelly told Kenedy that the aldermen were going to submit a resolution to postpone the election. They also had too many men wanting to be sheriff. Glavecke, Browne, Campbell, and Scanlan were all canvassing for the position besides Fields, who was the railroad group's nominee. Kelly wanted Mifflin to use his influence to get Campbell to back out so that they could put up Browne. He again chastises Kenedy and King for holding back on their support as "Ytúrria, Galvan and Dougherty and me are working very hard." He tells him it is hard for their friends when the heads of the concern are not working hard but are keeping the "Steamboat interest" in the background.[57] The next day Kelly informed Kenedy of the agreed-on slate: sheriff, James G. Browne; clerk, Robert B. Foster; presiding justice, Henry Kleiber; justice precinct no. 2, Manual Treviño Garza; justice precinct no. 3, Juan Longoria; justice precinct no. 4, Cornelius Stillman; justice precinct no. 5, Raphael.[58]

The next topic in his letter was money. It was costing the railroad group $300 a day to keep the four hundred migrants on the payroll, and their wages were guaranteed to the thirteenth. The election would be held on the tenth. He tells Mifflin that if they put off the election until the general election on December 2, the opposition would bear the expense of keeping the migrants on the payroll that long. He closed by telling him that they were holding a meeting to address their campaign finances and that only Galvan, Ytúrria, Dalzell, Dougherty, Browne, and Glavecke would be there. He felt sure that Hale and Stillman would have to carry the lion's share of the expense. He would let him know how the meeting went.[59]

The city alderman ordered the election for December 2 but the mayor called for the election as planned on the tenth, and without a revision of the voting list the four hundred Mexicans who had been registered voted. The railroad group promenaded through the town with banners and lanterns and had a large procession the night before the election.[60] The other citizens took no part in the election and a new election was called for December 2; in the interim there were two mayors, two sets of police, and duplicate officers.[61]

In the three-week interim, Mifflin's group had a lot to do. They first had to dispose of Campbell as a candidate because he would split their vote and the railroad group's candidate would be elected sheriff. Finally by November 16 they had convinced Campbell that he would be made Browne's deputy if he would withdraw his name; he did so only temporarily.[62] Kelly's other problem was that Captain King would not support Russell for Senate and was instead supporting Dr. Kearney because of their friendship. Kelly viewed Kenedy and King not supporting the same candidate as very damaging to their cause.

In a November 19 letter to Captain King's accountant, Reuben Holbein at the Santa Gertrudis ranch, Kelly sought to solve a political problem with a unique solution. He explained his problem this way:

> The railroad concern have brought over from Matamoros and caused to be registered as voters of Cameron County some five hundred Mexicans, who in consideration of obtaining work on the railroad have perjured themselves by taking the necessary oaths to entitle them to register. They hoped by those votes to carry both the city and County elections but they knew that on the revision of the registration lists, all those names would be stricken off. The board of revision consists of Justices Stillman, Haynes, Kingsbury and myself, and any three of us form a quorum. The opposition interest therefore sent out writs of injunction restraining Stillman and me from sitting at the board, thereby breaking the quorum, and preventing any revision. Judge Barden granted the writs in Corpus on Sunday the 9th but when they reached here our District Clerk had resigned, and they could not be legally served or issued. When they realized the situation there was "weeping, and wailing and gnashing of teeth in Jericho."

They then sent their man Howell to Victoria with fresh petitions, asking the Judge to direct the clerk of Victoria County (or any other county in his district) to issue the injunctions. If he succeeds in inducing the Judge to do so, and can be back here on or before Saturday their object will be gained and they will probably carry the election—if he can be detained on the road till beyond that day the revision will be complete, and we will have a fair election. . . . Howell is in Victoria today and will probably leave there tonight or in the morning. This may reach you in time to do him a good turn yet.[63]

Howell was taking relays and it would take him about eight days to make the round trip. Evidently he was delayed because the board of revisions met and completed their work before Howell arrived. Kelly wrote Kenedy that he no longer feared Judge Barden's writ. He told him that they had a clear majority of the 250 on the revised list now and that nothing should interfere with their success.[64] On December 7, Kelly wrote that the elections were over and everything was quiet again. Ford and the new council had taken their seats and they were in possession of the city government. He told Captain King that they had been equally successful in the county and district elections. Both Senator Russell and Representative Galvan had been elected. He told him, "this is a great victory for us and a heavy blow to the railroad faction."[65] Earlier he had shared with Mifflin that Russell was disappointed with Captain King and the Nueces vote. Obviously Captain King had complete control at Santa Gertrudis, with the vote coming in Kearney 81, Russell 2.[66]

The opposition tried three different methods to invalidate the results of the election, but with Russell still acting as judge until he was sworn in as senator each of them was dismissed.[67] As usual in politics, it all cost money. Kelly informed Mifflin that the total expense for the election had been $2,580, of which $1,725 had been raised by subscriptions. He said the $885 left would have to be raised by further assessment. He had told him in another letter that King was questioning the amount of money spent; Kelly admitted that he had freely used the telegraph during the elections.[68]

Woodhouse and San Román not only had bad results in the elections, but their railroad and river transportation interests were also not going well. During the fall, their steamboat *Lee* was sunk, and Kelly thought there was a good chance that King, Kenedy & Co. might be called on to fill out their government contract.[69] The company continued to fulfill the contract by using ox carts to take supplies up to Ringgold Barracks. Mifflin and King had troubles on the river also, and on November 23 Kelly wrote to Mifflin and told him that the *Tamaulipas No. 2* had hooked a sunken anchor and a hole had been knocked in her keel on the starboard side. They were able to get the *Petrita* to her and help offload some of the cargo. The majority of the cargo was damaged and Kelly feared that the railroad group would use this as an example of why they could provide safer transportation during the winter months once they were up and running.[70]

By December Kelly was writing Mifflin that he thought the railroad group were badly beaten and more disheartened. The disaster of the *Lee* had brought them to their knees. He had heard that the talk at San Román's had been to try to compromise. He urged Mifflin to come in and quietly try to negotiate behind the scenes. Later he said that the group had decided to stick it out and was raising money to replace the *Lee*.[71]

Shipping along the Rio Grande and out into the Gulf of Mexico was difficult. Captain Kelly relayed a story about Manuel Treviño, who was trying to ship some cattle to Havana in December. The steamer *Truxton* arrived at Brazos on December 5 and did not leave with the cattle until December 16. Because of all the delays, the cattle were driven back and forth several times from the river to Brazos. First the cook came to Brownsville and claimed the captain had treated him badly. The captain and most of the crew were arrested and brought to Brownsville to trial. The investigation showed that the cook had exaggerated and the captain was let go. Then they started to load the cattle again and the condenser was found to be out and in need of repair. The crew refused to go on board because they said the ship was not seaworthy and leaked. The board of surveyors inspected her and discovered a piece of coal had been placed to keep her bilge injection valve open and once it was removed the pumps worked and it did not leak. It was then revealed that the crew was scared and did not want to go to Havana because of the fear of yellow fever. They were ordered on board and sixty head of cattle were loaded. The captain discovered he had no hay and concluded it was necessary for 360 animals to have something to eat on the eight- or nine-day voyage. He sent to Brownsville for twenty bales of hay and loaded the remainder of the cattle. The half-starved and tired cattle and twenty-five horses started their journey. The chief engineer had stated that the ship could not make over five miles in good weather and the cattle would be lucky to make it to Havana.[72]

Although Brownsville was full of ill will it was at least safe. The countryside continued to be dangerous. In November, while Captain Kenedy was in Corpus Christi, Kelly wrote Hiram Chamberlain that there was a rumor of another gang of thieves operating in Nueces County and that Captain King might be in danger. While Mifflin was in Corpus Christi, Petra was left at the ranch in charge; Thomas and James helped. No doubt they had heard the rumors too and had posted extra guards around the headquarters and along the fence line. Kelly wrote that Mifflin had not heard anything alarming from King or from the ranch.[73]

Bitter politics, bandits, and hard economic times reeled around the residents of South Texas. December brought additional worries for the Texas border region. There was a hot contest for the alcalde (mayor) of Matamoros between Cortina and Servando Canales. Cortina won the election and the raids continued. Everyday tensions along the border mounted with talk again of war between Texas and Mexico.[74]

CHAPTER 12

1874:
Railroads and Cattle Drives

At the end of Reconstruction in Texas, Mifflin and Petra were pleased when Richard Coke was installed as the governor in January of 1874. He was interested in providing protection along the border, but it took him a while to get his forces engaged in keeping the peace and stopping the thievery in the Nueces Strip. In the meantime, Cortina's power had never been greater along the border. Adj. Gen. William Steel said, "It is impossible to conceive . . . of the extent of the power of this great robber chief. It is a well-known fact that not only Cortina himself, but even his mistress, gives orders to judges as to their decisions in cases . . . and such orders are obeyed. His armed adherents are said to number over two thousand. . . . The police of Matamoros . . . is [sic] composed entirely of ruffians, ready at any moment to commit murder . . . at his bidding."[1] J. Frank Dobie called Cortina, "the most striking, the most powerful, the most insolent, and the most daring as well as the most elusive Mexican bandit, not even excepting Pancho Villa, that ever wet his horse in the muddy waters of the Río Bravo."[2] These observations by Anglos hold elements of admiration for Cortina—his exploits and the power he held among his people. "Great chief," "most striking," "most daring," "most powerful" are heady observations of the man, and indicate the problems he was capable of causing along the border.

Although it was difficult for Petra to be separated from her married children and grandchildren in Brownsville, it was time to conclude most of their business interests there. Also, Petra's younger children were reaching maturity. They were coming back home and involving themselves in Corpus Christi as well as Brownsville. Thomas was twenty-one and James was nineteen, and both were working at Los Laureles. John was eighteen and had finished his studies at Spring Hill during the year. He left school and went to work for

Perkins Swenson & Co. in New Orleans, bankers and a cotton commission company that his father used often.[3] While at Spring Hill College, John had been classmates with William and Arnaud Turcotte from New Orleans. At some point William Turcotte introduced John to his sister Marie Stella.[4] She may have been a reason why John wanted to go to New Orleans to work.

In the beginning of January, Petra and Mifflin were worried about their good friend Captain King. They received a letter from Kelly in Brownsville telling them that he had received a telegram from Hiram Chamberlain that King was dangerously ill from typhoid fever. Dr. McManus had been sent for. Mifflin left for the Santa Gertrudis to check on his friend and found him recovering slowly.[5] King did not bounce back very well. On February 27, King wrote to Mifflin and told him that "the cattle are being handed over to the Caporals at this time. I expect to send 4,000 head of beeves from 3 years old and up to Kansas." He told him that he still had pains in all his bones and wanted a change in climate. He wanted to sell his part in the company but would prefer selling it to Kenedy.[6] On March 5 he wrote Kenedy and told him he would be traveling to Brownsville in the stage or buggy because it would be easier to travel. He was not well and still had pains in all his bones.[7] Kelly must have pleased King when he wrote him and told him that on March 2 he had sent by mail rider two hundred fine Havana cigars. He said he would send a like quantity by Saturday's conveyance.[8] Kelly was also busy taking care of Mifflin and Petra's children. On May 7 he wrote to Messrs. Perkins Swenson & Co. that they were shipping two trunks to be billed to Captain M. Kenedy with one to be delivered to Ursuline Convent and one to Spring Hill College, Mobile, Alabama.[9] Mifflin did not forget his mother. In January, Kelly wrote Mifflin that Manuel Rodríguez (Concepción's husband) had delivered one sack of Mexican coffee to be forwarded to his mother, Mrs. Sarah Kenedy, in Coatesville. He told him they had shipped it to New York in care of Swenson Perkins & Co. prepaid through New Orleans at the same company.[10] Evidently Petra and Mifflin had introduced her to fine roasted Mexican coffee beans.

Through the spring of 1874 Mifflin and King used their political clout to their advantage to come to a settlement with the railroad group and to dissolve King, Kenedy & Co. for good. They had tried through the fall of 1873 to come to an agreement with their opposition and had no luck. They decided the only way to bring them to their knees was to go into direct competition with them and build their own railroad.

Kelly wrote to Senator Russell on February 4 explaining to him that they wanted to have a bill passed that would let them create a new competing railroad. He thought they could have the road operational in two years.[11] At the end of the month Kelly was delighted because the bill passed the Senate 18 to 5. He wrote to Joseph Cooper in New Orleans and told him, "we are and have been for over two years fighting an opposition that has invested over $500,000 to wipe us out—and that so far, with small means and few friends, we have won the fight."[12] It may well be that this prompt action by Senator Russell directly coincided with a letter written to Captain Kenedy by William Kelly in early January. The letter stated that Captain Robert (Dalzell) and Kelly agreed that they should continue to "retain" Russell on their payroll with extended loans. They had already loaned him $1,000 and wanted to extend with another six-month loan so he would not seek help from "unfriendly" hands.[13]

Kelly, Kenedy, and King continued to try to come to an agreement with the opposition. In April, Kelly again wrote Joseph Cooper to give him an update on the company and the negotiations:

> I write to state the condition of King Kenedy and Co. The business has been losing about 1,100 dollars a month, King and Kenedy have been trying to effect a compromise with the opposition. The opposition owes over two hundred thousand dollars and cannot give it up. This is the offer King, Kenedy, Dalzell and Ytúrria have made and we think the partners will go along. If it doesn't work then a third party like Charles Morgan will come in and buy it. For $100,000 the company will sell the *San Juan* and *Sellers* and the four sailing lighters, they will give one hundred thousand dollars, payable $10,000 at once, $15,000 in 6 months, $20,000 in 12 months, $25,000 in 18 months, and $30,000 in 24 months and 10% of the gross proceeds of the government contract if they keep it without opposition for five years. We have to agree to release them from all suits now pending, guarantee not to use the balance of boats in this trade, or sell them to be bought here, guarantee not to put in the Southwestern railroad charter, and guarantee not to engage in transportation on the Rio Grande, nor by land from Brazos or Point Isabel. In addition, each partner agrees to railroad his freight that is consigned to him.[14]

This agreement would completely remove Mifflin and King from the business along the Rio Grande they had been in for the past twenty-seven years.

It was still not a done deal. Galvan refused to go along with it on Mifflin's side and Kelly was worried that if they did not get the money from Stillman to finance the new railroad that "Brownsville will go into the hands of Woodhouse and the Spaniards with Stephen Powers as chief trickster." Mifflin was in telegraphic correspondence with Stillman on the subject of raising $150,000 on the first mortgage, offering their present steamboat and other property in Brownsville as additional security for the loan.[15] King wrote Mifflin in Brownsville and told him, "I hope you will not leave there until you do something with the Road mess but sell is the only hope for us I think but do the best you can and it will satisfy me. Woodhouse is the best man to deal with."[16] Mifflin was able to bring the negotiations to a close, and on May 2 Kelly wrote to Bernardo Ytúrria in Matamoros and told him to "come to our office this evening at six and bring Don Pancho's power of attorney."[17] On May 8, Kelly wrote to Dalzell in New Orleans to say that the boats would be turned over that day and the crews were discharged on the 3rd. He continued, "I can hardly realize that King, Kenedy & Co. is dead and cannot bear to think of it—much less talk or write about it."[18]

When the crews were discharged, other people, too, had to make adjustments. Kelly wrote to Cooper again on the eighth, "for some time, at least, Brownsville will not suit me to live in and I must seek other fields and other means of living."[19] Kelly changed his mind later and stayed in Brownsville. His stepson, Jesse Thornton, married Petra's granddaughter Mary Putegnat, and they continued to be like family.[20] Mr. Thornton worked with Captain Kelly until the Rio Grande business dried up. Kelly was in a dying business and in less than ten years there would not be enough water in the Rio Grande to sustain the steamboat business. Captain Dalzell was also greatly affected by King, Kenedy & Co. going out of business and had to make a difficult decision. Steamboating was his life. He had been engaged in it for over twenty-five years. He decided in the fall 1874 to move to Galveston and run the *Matamoros* and *Tamaulipas,* which would not be in violation of their agreement to stay off of the Rio Grande. This was particularly difficult for Luisa and the family, but he did not have much of a choice. Kelly wrote to Messrs. Perkins Swenson & Co. in New Orleans that since Dalzell was leaving for Galveston, "the Honorable Edward Downey would be placed in full charge of all of their affairs and fully authorized to sign our name in all matters pertaining to our business."[21]

In the meantime, Galvan offered to buy the *Tamaulipas No. 2* in present condition for $15,000 in coin to be delivered on September 1.[22] Mifflin responded that he had consulted with the interested parties and they did not wish to sell. He did offer to purchase his interest at the same rate. Mifflin was concerned that once Galvan learned Mifflin had leased the *Tamaulipas No. 2* to the railroad group, Galvan would be upset and might try to stop the boat from running.[23] Another piece of business that Mifflin and King needed to wind up was the telegraph line they owned between Brownsville, Clarkesville, and Brazos Santiago. They authorized Mifflin's son-in-law, Manuel Rodríguez, to offer it for sale for $1,500 net cash in Brownsville and to hold the offer open until June 30.[24]

Mifflin and Petra continued to own property in Brownsville, but their focus now moved toward Corpus Christi. Brownsville's loss was Corpus Christi's gain. Mifflin and Petra engaged in helping to build Corpus Christi into a vibrant center of trade. Mifflin became a major force in building another railroad, but this time it went from Corpus Christi to Laredo, bypassing Brownsville and dominating the Mexico trade. Petra was involved with her church again in Corpus and became a major factor in the building of their new facility.

Kenedy and King believed in controlling their politicians and rewarding them well. In January, Mifflin was to meet Judge Russell, the new senator from Brownsville, at the Santa Gertrudis to discuss what they needed in the legislative session in regard to their railroad. They had to advance him money to ensure that he was on the "payroll" for services.[25] By January 24, they had the draft of the bill from Senator Russell in their hands and were ready to send it back with any necessary alterations. In February, Kelly told Russell that he was sorry he had drawn a two-year term but that if he would take care of El Paso they would look out for the river counties from Starr down.[26] Less than two weeks later, Russell had gotten the railroad bill passed and managed to get Governor Coke to appoint Mr. Dougherty to his old judgeship position.[27] On March 1, Kelly congratulated Senator Russell on his good service and talked about how the jail problem was out of hand. He said if they were ever going to build branch prisons outside of Huntsville that they should have one near Brownsville. He thanked him for his own appointment as a notary and told him that Dougherty had left for Laredo with a military escort.[28] By the time Mifflin got to Brownsville on March 22, he had an amendment he needed Senator Russell to take care of. He wanted him to fix the original stock of the new railroad company at $250,000 so that their friends could take it up immediately and not worry about others trying to buy in.[29] They wanted to take good care of their new senator, and on April 4 Kelly wrote Joseph Cooper in New Orleans to deliver a barrel of whiskey to Senator Russell and bill them for $164.[30]

During 1874, Mifflin and King each had their share of misfortunes. The year started with King's illness. Kelly then wrote Mifflin with news that they had no money to spare. With heavy election expenses and advances to Russell, along with other expenditures, they were bare of cash. The year 1874 was a tough one following the crash in 1873. Mifflin and King were both summoned to serve on the Brownsville Grand Jury in March, and Kelly warned them that the judge was very strict and had been known to fine jurors heavily for not showing up on time.[31] While Mifflin went on to Brownsville to head up the negotiations with the railroad group, King stayed behind to deal with their ranching interest.

On March 5, King wrote Mifflin that the horse board was there and he had only sold them eight horses and he feared he could not sell them many more. He had told them that Mifflin had two hundred that would fill the bill. However, he could not figure out what they wanted or how many and he was not sure they wanted to buy horses from this section.[32] Eight days later King wrote Kenedy in Brownsville that Thomas had left home with seventy-one head of horses and would be at the Santa Gertrudis by evening. He told him one of the board members had been sick but he hoped they would be through by Wednesday night with both of their horses. Also he informed Mifflin that they had had fine rains since he left.[33] On the seventeenth, King wrote Mifflin that Tom had arrived there the past Saturday with his seventy head of horses, out of which sixteen head amounting to $1,340 were received. He said more of his horses might have gone but the standard was too big. He told him he would get the check and bring it to him and that Tom was leaving the next day for Los Laureles with the balance of the horses. They would leave Friday and expected to arrive in Brownsville Saturday afternoon and to make hotel reservations at Miller's Hotel for King, Hiram, and Holbein.[34]

The year continued to go badly for the Kenedys and the Kings. In April, King was faced with paying a tax statement of $1,814.32 on $35,646 evaluated at 5 percent.[35] On May 1, King wrote Mifflin to tell him he had arrived about 3 A.M. that morning and found his "stable and camp house burned to the ground—buggies and ambulances are burned—caused by accident—things look much different now than when I left."[36] This put King in further financial trouble; on May 9 he wrote Mifflin and asked him to please close out all unsettled matters before leaving Brownsville. He also asked, "Can you let me have some money—it would be a great help."[37]

Mifflin was also having trouble at Los Laureles. On April 20 he wrote Mr. Jesus Sina [sic] in Matamoros stating, "You are establishing a ranch on the Burros on the land known as Concepcion Corricitas [sic] in the county of Cameron. The land where you are building belongs to me. This is not a friendly act and you have sheep which ruins the land. Cease doing anything on the land . . . I will take all legal means to defend it."[38] Land titles continued to be a problem, but it was helpful to Mifflin and King to get the railroad problem solved so they could begin to receive the money derived from the business.

Petra acted as hostess to travelers, just as Henrietta King did over at the Santa Gertrudis. In a land as sparsely settled as the Wild Horse Desert, shelter was greatly appreciated. Joseph Almond was traveling from his place to Corpus Christi on December 12, 1874. He wrote, "I started on Saturday the 5th about eleven o'clock for the Laureles, went by way of the Banquetti to see Eliff, about a horse but he was not at home. I stayed all night at Jim Merriman's. Started about half past eight on Sunday morning and arrived at Captain Kenedy's just about sundown."[39] Joseph Almond and J. J. Cocke are two visitors documented as staying at Los Laureles, but there must have been many in this wild place. As a rule, no one was turned away.

On July 12, Mifflin received a letter from King saying, "I am now satisfied that your Daughter has come to her sinces [*sic*] at last—I am very glad of it—for you. She handed me the letters to read and in my opinion it is a good letter and all to the point—she cares nothing for him now. She is cheerful and Mrs. Kenedy stood the trip well. Mrs. Kenedy says to me to say to you to telegraph to Rosy [probably Rosa Putegnat] if she has not left Brownsville not to come as she will not be wanted."[40] Sarah was seventeen and had been attending Ursuline Academy in New Orleans. She evidently had some trouble and King had helped in solving this domestic problem, as Mifflin had helped him. Petra was definitely involved and it appeared that her health was good enough for her to travel to her daughter's side.

Mifflin's troubles were not over. In September a big storm blew through and Mifflin said he suffered terrible wreckage. "I am badly damaged but am not alone—over three feet water here—Never have I seen such rain. I have lost fences, say some two or three miles, a new bridge, forty-one feet long that I had just completed forty-eight hours before being swept away, 30–40,000 bushels of salt and one of my salt warehouses 20 × 20 was blown down and some four or five hundred head cattle drowned. Many fine trees down—rabbits, rats, snakes and birds by the thousands drowned—my dam stood the test."[41] Petra was no doubt troubled by the massive damage done to their ranch. The clean-up alone was dreadful and it would be months before the repairs could be completed and the pastures back in working order.

Then thinking of his enemies, Mifflin wrote,

> I regret the Rail Road is badly injured—I have ordered the *Tamaulipas No. 2* put at their disposition and the *Matamoros* brought from Galveston if they want her. King, Dalzell and myself prefer the "Old Settlers" to men not withstanding they have injured us badly in to the congregations of Rats who compose the merchants line—and if the Rail Road people will work together we will do all in our power to help to flax out the opposition—the Road can be put in condition to so stand the test but it will take time and money—I want to extend my hand to expand my domain as I must give all my attention to Ranching—I want to make some trade with Alec if Possible.—I hardly think his Ranch a success—I want to trade him other lands for his in the Alagan—and for his stock in some way—I will give him an advantageous trade and if he can in any way secure me the other position of the Alagan I will pay him well for his services—I have in Brownsville: The Ga—ier property opposite Miller's hotel; The Warehouse property on Elizabeth opposite Miralles; Three lots adjoining Kingsbury; six lots where Kelly lives, and other lots. I have

half league I believe in the Espiritu grant—adjoining so I was told Brownsville on the north and three other grant holdings . . . including ten or twelve leagues in the Mestenes Grant. He can I think select from these—I would like to know if there is any chance of my trading with him—Please inform me again the name of the party who purchased the land in the Chitilpin Grant, opposite the Laureles, and all the data you have about it—you told me once but I have forgotten it—I will make Alejandro an advantageous offer, provided he wants to drop the stock business for my part I will be obliged to stick to it.[42]

Mifflin had every reason to want the railroad people to succeed. They had bought him out over a two-year period and he needed them to be successful so they could meet the terms of their agreement. He also was serious about expanding the ranch. Like everything he did, once he decided on a course he planned to be successful at it. Mifflin had ordered three boxes of hardware for the ranch marked MK in a diamond and he continued to supply his rancho.[43] In October he ordered through the same company in Rockport, Texas, thirteen saddles, one box containing chains, six kegs of spikes, one package of three crosscut saws, and two bundles of gas pipe. He ordered that they be shipped to Flour Bluff, which was the closest water port to the ranch.[44] Mifflin felt complete confidence in his new money manager, Mr. Downey, and told Dalzell that the railroad notes were paid punctually on the seventh. He had given Louisa $342.86 and sent the balance to his credit at Perkins and Swenson.[45]

Mifflin went through a real depression at the end of 1874. He had a rough year facing the closing of his steamboat business in Brownsville, family problems, the downturn in the cattle market, and the destruction at Los Laureles by the violent storm in September. In December he wrote Stephen Powers, "I regret now that I have built a panel of fence, or ever saw a ranch, but it is now too late for regrets and I must make the most of what I have."[46]

CHAPTER 13

1875:
Leander McNelly and the Texas Rangers

On *January 1, 1875, Willie, away at school* in Mobile, Alabama, wrote his father to express his sympathy about the destructive storm that had done so much damage to the ranch at the end of 1874. Willie was sixteen and Mifflin was fifty-three. A gentle and studious boy, Willie took after his father's side of the family, and he adored Mifflin. In the letter he worried about his father and "the disasters that befell you during my stay at home on vacation and the damage done to our ranch." He hoped, "You may live to see your 'Golden Wedding' and gather your children and grandchildren to give them your blessing. I will always think of the great and good father. My love towards you, dear father, cannot be expressed in words. You have well discharged your duties towards all your children. You have worked day and night for them; and for this you have been repaid by Him, from whom all mercies are. I will follow your example all my life and wish you a long and happy life. Love to all. I will one day meet you face to face in heaven—where all your troubles will cease, and where New Years go by without being counted. From your affectionate and loving son, William Kenedy."[1] Willie was now the only son Petra and Mifflin had in school at Spring Hill, where the officials said that "William was a premiere student at Spring Hill College" and had been described as the apple of his father's eye as the youngest child.[2]

Petra was proud of Willie, the baby of the family. He reminded her more of Mifflin than the other boys. James and Thomas, who were now at home with them, had always been daring and independent. They were anything but scholarly and loved attention. John was bright and a good student but was all

Photograph believed to be William "Willie" Kenedy. He was a gentle and studious boy who took after his father. He was called a "premiere student at Spring Hill College," and was described as the apple of his father's eye. Willie died at seventeen years of age on July 7, 1876, in New Orleans.

business and was not as sensitive as Willie. Petra had to be away from Thomas, John Gregory, and James during the Civil War, but Willie and Sarah had stayed at home and Petra had grown very close to both of them. She was proud of Willie's accomplishments at school and of the fact that he was an accomplished pianist. She was even more pleased when John returned home from New Orleans to work for George F. Evans Wholesale Grocery, Hides, and Wool.[3] Petra had a rough couple of years with her illness and it was comforting to have three of her sons back home. She did however worry about their safety on and around the ranch.

There was trouble throughout the Rio Grande Valley and even among the religious communities in Brownsville. On December 8, 1874, Bishop Dominicus Matthew Manucy was ordained at an elaborate ceremony in Mobile, Alabama, as the new Vicar General appointed to Brownsville. This move in the Catholic Church had been several years coming. The Church wanted to strengthen its presence in South Texas. However, this position was not desired by anyone. Two Oblate priests whom Petra knew well and were close to the family—Father Augustin Gaudet, OMI, and Father Pierre F. Parisot, OMI—turned down the position. After his appointment, Bishop Manucy said: "I look upon this as the worst sentence that could be passed on me for any crime. I had reason to believe, if I had been proposed for any See, it was for San Antonio. Brownsville district is a country without resources. The Catholic population is composed almost exclusively of Mexicans—drovers and ladrones. No money can be got out of such people, not even to bury their fathers.—Worst of all, the priests in the country are the Oblates of Mary Immaculate. They most likely own what little property is in the place, and in consequence will be masters over the bishop. All a bishop will be useful for then, will be to ride the circuit like a Methodist preacher, administer Confirmation and be the laughing stock of religious men. A fine prospect for a man who has already spent twenty-four years of his life in arduous duties! . . . Surely if that district or country presented any advantages, one of the Oblates would have been appointed Bishop!"[4]

The missionary journeys on horseback by Fathers Jules Piat and Jean-Marie Clos, two of the Oblates referred to above, illustrate the demanding life they endured in ministering to the inhabitants of the Wild Horse Desert. Both were members of the Cavalry of Christ and each year logged thousands of miles trekking through the vast Nueces Strip wilderness. At each ranch along the way, especially the larger ones, the missionaries would celebrate Mass, catechize the children, conduct services for the dead, baptize the newly born, anoint the sick, witness marriages, and generally visit with the people. The priests on horseback braved bandits and marauders, flash floods, and seemingly interminable droughts; and suffered infestations of ticks, chiggers, fleas, and rashes of all kinds. They abided extreme hunger, thirst, fatigue, and loneliness. Father Piat wrote a friend, "from one July 25 to August 4 I traveled three hundred and thirty miles to Brownsville and back; from August 10 to 24, three hundred more miles to go to Laredo, see our Vicar-Apostolic, and make a few purchases for the chapels I am building, and I am not counting the hundred miles I rode at the beginning of July to visit my district. Every other month I visit those thirty-five or forty ranchos."[5] The priests knew that the Tejanos devotedly prayed and said the Rosary and taught their children their prayers.[6]

The brides and grooms on these ranches, to begin living as a married couple, became espoused through the informal practice called *la tomada de manos*, or "the taking of hands," until the missionary priest could visit and validate the wedding. Petra grew up with this practice, which explains her attitude about her situation with Luis and also with Mifflin. She might well have left her parents to follow Luis with the promise of a wedding when a priest could be found. There was no shame or disgrace attached to this practice. The baptism of children also had to wait for the priests' visit, and it was very important that the infants be baptized before they died, a present danger in the isolated environments of the ranches.[7] The priests were badly needed by these ranchers and their families, and Bishop Manucy was absolutely right about what a tough but necessary life they led.

The bishop's Consecration service was held in Mobile, Alabama, and if Willie was still in school at Spring Hill before his holiday break he probably attended the service. Despite the negative reports about Manucy and by him, energetic Father Parisot went about organizing a welcome for the new bishop. His church, and Petra's family's, the Immaculate Conception Church in Brownsville, was the cathedral designated for the vicariate. A reception committee was set up and $1,500 was raised to finance the ceremonies. The women would decorate the church and the young people were assigned the procession and banquet. The reception committee met the bishop in Port Isabel, where they all boarded the train for Brownsville. The Mexicans were in a fiesta mood and the Anglos, both Catholic and Protestant, were full of civic pride. A few bigots tried to spoil the day's festivities by organizing a masked ball to conflict with the bishop's reception. They sent an anonymous threatening letter to Father Parisot: "Sir, I am delegated to announce that if you attempt to have a procession through the public thoroughfares of our city there is a bullet ready for your worthless carcass and another for your damned Bishop. . . . Remember, sir, that in this grand Republic there is no room for such trash as a Prince sitting on a throne. Bullets are in readiness, look out."[8]

Petra's daughters, sons-in-law, and grandchildren were caught in the controversy and potential danger. The threat did not deter the celebration, however, which was a success. The Mexicans had built a triumphal arch for Bishop Manucy; a band played as the leaders of city government led the bishop to the cathedral and while the bell of the church (which Petra and Mifflin had donated) rang out, the military garrison fired a salvo. The unsympathetic bigots of the town likened the event to dancing the "bolero and fandango."[9] Father Manucy continued to look down on his parishioners, and even when the Sisters of Charity from Mexico arrived in Brownsville seeking sanction he refused to shelter the nuns because he feared the influence the Spanish-speaking nuns would have on the Tejanos. He sent them back to Mexico over citizen protestations.[10]

Even with the discord within Brownsville, people felt much safer there than in the countryside. Throughout the Wild Horse Desert people were leaving their small ranchos and fleeing to the towns for safety. The small owners were losing their lands. Some sold after inherited lands became too small to ranch, some because of the raiders, some due to drought, and often because they did not have access to banks to help sustain them until the rains came, as did the large ranchers like Mifflin and King. The Tejanos lost much of their land to Anglos who used courts and violence to drive Tejanos off their ranchos. The sheriff's auctions were used to claim the ranchos during their absence. Tejanos who did hold on had to defend themselves from Mexican rustlers from across the Rio Grande as well as from Anglo vigilantes who targeted Tejanos in order to get their land. They could fight off the attacks from Mexico but they could not manage the vigilante sweeps from the Anglos.[11]

The Penascal Raid of 1874, or the "Second Cortina War," had been such a raid. For months prior to the raid King and others had complained about the Tejano ranches, including the Atravesada, La Parra, El Corral de Piedra, and El Mesquite, and the Penascal Ranch, which taken together housed about five hundred Tejano men, women, and children. These Tejanos were accused of stealing cattle. A hundred vigilantes made up of Anglos and reportedly some Mexicans from Corpus Christi set out to presumably avenge the murder of four Anglos by Mexicans at a store near Corpus Christi. It has been recorded that one of Mexicans who led the murdering spree at the store was identified by Ranger J. B. Dunn as "Tom Bosquez," said to be Richard King's worker, Tomás Vasquez. After being deputized, the deputies masked and painted themselves and, full of liquor, threw coal oil on the roofs of the houses and stores at the ranches and killed all of the patriarchs plus any other adult males present. The women and children hid in the chaparral. They were greeted in the morning with only chimneys standing. Most of the lands involved in this raid ended up in the King and Kenedy ranches.[12]

Perhaps the most telling part of the loss of Tejano lands, however, came from the legal profession. Reportedly, Stephen Powers and his junior associate, James B. Wells, increased the Kenedy and King ranches through their legal handiwork. They cleared the titles to a large portion of the grants lying between the Nueces and the Rio Grande. These land lawyers were the intermediaries between the land-based Mexican elite and the capital-based Anglo merchants.[13] The lawyers were directed to purchase as many *derechos* (rights) as they could find. The lawyers in turn hired agents to locate people who had undivided interests in land grants. The pressure applied was no doubt intense.[14] Some historians have written that although "gross thievery" of the Tejanos' land is not easy to prove, it is seen that some Anglos did obtain land through "fraud, intimidation and other illegal means."[15] Yet as the old rancheros died, it was difficult to keep the ranchos intact. Sometimes a widow would sell her share, on occasion it would be done to pay taxes and debts of the estate. If the ranch kept running, subsequent probate proceedings eventually led to it becoming a multiplicity of small landholdings. Other than oral histories, it is difficult for researchers to prove illegal acquisitions of land because of the lack of written documentation. Also, some of the records, public and private, are missing.[16]

Kenedy and King and other Anglos were not always safe from the raiders, either. In early February Captain King had a large herd of horses taken from the ranch and several of his men were killed. In November a popular and "inoffensive" American schoolteacher, Billy McMahan, was captured north of Brownsville. The desperados tortured him by cutting off his fingers, toes, wrists, and ears, and finally "severed his legs from his body and left him lifeless."[17]

Surrounded by violence, Kenedy and King continued to try to run their ranches in order to survive financially. King wanted to send 4,737 head of cattle up the trail to Kansas. He chose one of his foremen, Captain John Fitch, to be the cow boss. Fitch and fourteen vaqueros gathered the cattle in February and early March and then divided them into four road herds. Each would travel as a separate unit with their own boss, hands, cook, wagon, and remuda. Fitch took in a partner, A. C. Allen, and they signed a contract with King in which they agreed to pay him $12 a head with the profit divided and all expenses paid from the profit. Fitch hired forty-three men and paid his four foremen $108 a month. Half of the men were vaqueros and half Anglo. The men furnished their own saddles, bridles, blankets, pistols, spurs, leathers, clothes, and bedrolls. They had to buy their own soap, medicine, whiskey, tobacco, and ammunition. The employer furnished horses to ride and food from the cook's wagon, such as beans, bacon, rice, coffee, bread, molasses, pickles, butter, and milk. When they could find them they provided fresh vegetables and chicken. The beef was not to be eaten. They were the profit.[18]

King had employed Mr. J. H. Stevens to broker the cattle and follow the progress of the herd on the trail. King stayed in contact as much as he could through telegraph. The drive experienced stampeding cattle crossing the San Antonio River, heavy rain, trouble with Mr. Allen striking an unauthorized sale, and a difficult selling market, but the cattle were finally sold at Denison, Texas, on July 21 for $18.44 average per head. King's profit from the sale of the 4,710 head of cattle was $61,886.40, less the cost of breeding and raising the stock.[19] King thought so much of Mr. Stevens that he wrote to Mifflin on February 1 to give him a letter of introduction to Stevens.[20] He followed that letter with another on February 3: "Mr. Stevens is coming down to see about driving cattle to Kansas. If you should drive cattle to Kansas I think he would be one of the best men to take them you could find—he went with Mr. Fitch last year for me and he sold the cattle at fair prices—and I found him strictly honest in all matters—he is a good seller and trust worthy man. Why he did not go for me this year is the cattle I send is contracted—and I will not pay two head men is only cause he did not go for me."[21]

Although Stevens did not take the herd up for King he did broker his cattle and got a good price for him. As usual, King was looking out after Mifflin with good cattle advice. King loved ranching and threw himself into it with gusto. His rancho was described in 1874 in the *Corpus Christi Gazette*. The Santa Gertrudis headquarters was built on a hill with a view for about twenty miles around. The complex had a large home, stable large enough to hold fifty to sixty head of stock, houses for the vaqueros, and a picket fence that enclosed several acres of grass and shade trees, resembling a park in the spring. The Captain had expanded his holdings to include not only the Santa Gertrudis containing 78,225 acres but also the following: Rincón de Santa Gertrudis with 15,500 acres;, the Agua Dulce with 33,631 acres, 25 leagues out of the San Juan de Carricitas, 13,284 acres on Padre Island, 15,000 acres on Saus Creek, two leagues at San Diego, and recently Loma Alto and dependent ranchos. The ranch was arranged to be entirely independent and had all the modern appliances of a well-regulated farm. The workers were capable of forging a horseshoe or building a fine house. King employed about one hundred workers to keep the hacienda in good running order. The ranch had six gates with guards at each and comfortable quarters provided for them. He had about 50,000 cattle and he branded about 15,000 calves a year. He had about 6,000 head of horse stock and branded about 1,400 to 1,500 head a year. He continued to upgrade his stock. The ranch kept about 30,000 head of Merino sheep that averaged about four pounds of wool per head a year. Captain King had an unknown number of hogs. Five years before he had purchased 1,000 hogs and turned them out to run wild. There were probably between 5,000 and 6,000 hogs now in his various pastures.[22]

King continued to advise Mifflin on ranching affairs and on January 24 warned him about a man named López who was a thief with four hundred head of cattle with the wrong brands. He had taken the information to the sheriff.[23] Mifflin and King were well on the way to building their ranching empires but at great cost to themselves and others. The danger affected them all and surrounded them with uncertainty day in and day out.

On March 26, Good Friday, the Nueces Strip exploded with violence. A raiding party attacked Nuecestown thirteen miles southwest of Corpus Christi and close to Petra and Mifflin's Los Laureles Ranch. Although Cortina was not physically present it was generally thought that he was behind the raid. About thirty of the armed and mounted Mexicans continued toward

Corpus Christi, stopping at San Fernando Creek to stab two Anglos to death. At Chocolate, two Hispanics were left hanging, apparently because they refused to join the raiding party. About noon the raiders appeared at the ranch of Samuel H. Page, where they looted the house and took the men prisoner. One elderly Hispanic was hanged because he refused to join them. The band robbed any traveler who happened to have the bad luck of being in their way. At Nuecestown they ran into Thomas John Noakes.[24]

They attacked Noakes's store and Noakes shot the first man through the door, Godina, and then escaped to the river by dropping through a hole in the floor and crawling down a ditch he had built for just such purposes. His wife stayed in the store, surrounded by raiders who were setting fires, and she put them out until it was impossible to continue to do so, then she gathered her children and miraculously escaped. The family was not injured, but there was huge monetary loss because all of their possessions had been in the combination store and home.[25]

The raider Noakes shot was taken to Dr. Spohn, who bound up his wounds. Then a mob took him over and finally, after many attempts at finding a place to hang him, managed to hang him from a heavy cross pole that was set from gatepost to gatepost. He stayed there until a priest and local official cut him down.[26]

The ranchers and citizens had had enough, and revenge swept across the strip. Mob law ruled. No Mexican was safe; they were rounded up and killed indiscriminately. Many innocent Mexicans were killed. Word had come to Corpus Christi that five "Mexicans," hanging from a tree, "some distance beyond King's Ranch," were "supposed to belong to a gang of thieves and cutthroats." On the return trip to Mexico the gang had stabbed two Anglos to death and lynched two Hispanics, "evidently the work of the raiders."[27]

The lawlessness from both sides prompted action in the form of a Texas Ranger named Captain Leander H. McNelly. He was described as being able to "ride like a Mexican, trail like an Indian, shoot like a Tennessean, and fight like a devil."[28] Thirty-one years old and a former Rebel with a soft voice and cool temper, he was considered as not knowing the word "danger." He commanded respect from his men and demanded absolute obedience. His men were young and daring and would follow him anywhere.[29]

When Governor Coke took over the Texas government from E. J. Davis he reestablished the Texas Rangers.[30] After the Nuecestown Raid, Sheriff John McClane of Nueces County sent the following telegram:

> "IS CAPT. MCNELLY COMING. WE ARE IN TROUBLE FIVE RANCHES BURNED BY DISGUISED MEN NEAR LA PARRA LAST WEEK. ANSWER."[31]

Captain McNelly arrived with fifty men and immediately moved to disband the Minute Companies who were terrorizing the Mexican population, saying, "you damn fellows have been doing more mischief than the bandits themselves."[32] McNelly wrote to his commanding officer on April 29 that the acts committed by Americans "are horrible to relate, many ranches have been plundered and burned, people murdered, and one of the men told me they had killed eleven people on their last raid." He disbanded all armed bands without authority of the state in hopes of preventing a civil war erupting. He then moved his men south where Cortina was filling a contract for delivery of 3,500 beeves to the Spanish army in Cuba; the ships at Bagdad were waiting to be loaded.[33] This may explain why the raiders had ventured so far north into Texas. Cortina had to fill a large order and his normal raiding areas, including the ranches near the Rio Grande, were not sufficient.

Captain McNelly offset his small number of men by utilizing spies and information from captives. He found out who could be bribed in the outlaw groups and paid them more money for information than the opposition did. He also promised not to interfere with their own outlaw activities.[34] The next tactic he used was brutal. One of McNelly's recruits, Jesus Sandoval, not only spoke Spanish but also knew how to get information from the prisoners. His motivation came from the vengeance he felt because his wife and daughter had been violated and killed by raiders. This red-bearded man with savage blue eyes seemed to go crazy when given a prisoner. After he extracted any information he wanted from them, he would tie them to a tree by their necks. Then he would loop their feet with a rawhide lariat that was tied to his horse. He would slap his horse and the body was torn away from the head. When the Rangers got there he would be looking up and crossing himself.[35]

Kenedy and King actively supported Captain McNelly. On May 1, King wrote to Mifflin and asked him if he could provide some good serviceable horses for McNelly. He told him "most of us are doing so" and that he thought Captain McNelly "is a good man and means business and order."[36] King evidently had enough confidence in McNelly that he made the decision in May not to shift his cattle but to leave them at home that fall, as things were quiet there for the present. King had firsthand knowledge of the network McNelly was establishing in order to stop the bandits. On May 4, King wrote to Mifflin: "Captain McNelly will return from Brownsville today. I think he went on secret service business which he keeps to himself, he is in my opinion a good man and as good as men with him he means to do something I think—have sent two of the boys to the Banquette to fetch horses they will be here today with them if possible. Come up—will keep him here until you come—would take him down but do not like to leave at this time."[37]

McNelly wasted no time. Through his information network he was able to strike at the bandits on the morning of June 12 on the Palo Alto prairie located about fourteen miles north of Brownsville. With only twenty-two men he struck a group of bandits driving three hundred stolen cattle toward Mexico. The Rangers lost only one man and killed all twelve of the bandits. The next day the dead bandits' bodies were displayed on the Brownsville Square as a warning to all the other outlaws that law and order had returned to the Wild Horse Desert.[38] Many Tejanos were angry with this and threatened that Cortina would come and kill the Rangers.[39]

McNelly's next big encounter was in November. It appears that Petra and Mifflin's son James was riding with Captain McNelly by then as one of his rangers. James's Texas Ranger Service Record showed him as a private enlisting on November 3, 1875, and discharging April 26, 1876, with five months and twenty-three days service with pay of $13 a month.[40]

On November 22, 1875, Petra and Mifflin received a telegram from King through Reuben Holbein at King Ranch to Mifflin at Los Laureles. He was worried about the "unfortunate condition of Captain McNelly . . . do not know the problem but they think he could have been betrayed and prepare for the worse." [41]

Petra and Mifflin had to await the outcome of McNelly's next encounter with the bandits to know if their son was alive or dead. Captain McNelly had made the decision to cross into Mexico, without authorization, to Rancho Las Cuevas to retrieve a large herd of stolen cattle. McNelly and thirty men, along with Col. A. J. Alexander of Fort Brown's cavalry, decided on a plan that would leave the military on the Texas side of the river but in support of the Rangers if they were needed. After crossing the Rio Grande the Rangers attacked the wrong ranch by mistake in the early morning fog. With the element of surprise gone and chased by Gen. Juan Flores Salinas, the leader of the Mexican *rurales,* they fought for their lives. With support from the military firing from the Texas side they were able to kill General Salinas and sixteen others in a gun battle near the river. McNeely was then ordered to return to the Unites States. He refused the order and told Porter, "Give my compliments to the Secretary of War and tell him the United States troops may go to hell."[42]

A doctor by the name of Alexander Headley was chosen to deliver a message from the governor of Tamaulipas requesting the Rangers to leave Mexico. Dr. Headley told them they had killed the beloved *alcalde* (mayor) of Camargo and eighty other people. McNeely told him he would not leave without the stolen cattle, and he did not. He negotiated with Headley and returned with about fifty-two head of stolen cattle to Texas soil.[43]

Despite McNelly's efforts, the raiding continued throughout November, with 1,620 cattle being stolen between Ringgold Barracks and Brownsville during this period.[44] James "Santiago" Kenedy was exactly the kind of recruit that Captain McNelly was looking for. He was a good shot, daring, and not afraid of danger. In April of 1876, Capt. L. N. McNelly, Commander of S Troop, wrote the following letter to Captain Kenedy:

> Capt. Kenedy,
> Esteemed Sir.
> I must say that I am very sorry that circumstances make it necessary for your son to leave us. Since he became a member of my company his conduct has been at the most exemplary character, ready, prompt, and gentlemanly doing his duty faithfully and fully winning the respect and confidence of his comrades. He leaves us today with more friends than any other man in my company and what is better, he deserves it.
> Very Respectfully,
> L. N. McNelly[45]

During the year, Kenedy and King continued to wrap up their business interests in Brownsville. At the first of the year they were dealing with two lawsuits, the Gray Suit and the Molina Suit. They had both been appealed to the Texas Supreme Court. The Gray Suit received an adverse ruling and King offered to settle with Gray's attorneys for $1,500 and $2,500. Both were declined and he thought it would take $5,000 to settle it and wanted to know if Mifflin wanted to go to court or seek a settlement. The Molina case had been decided in favor of the Company but was being appealed to the Texas Supreme Court by the plaintiffs. In both cases Mifflin and King turned to Judge Stephen Powers to represent them and were glad that Mr. Maxan was joining him in the Molina case.[46] King also wrote Mifflin about the management fee he had billed to their financial man, Mr. Downey, in Brownsville. In February he wrote to Mifflin and said he had sent the bill for "personal services and expenses incurred for the benefit of the company. (from May 1, 1874–Sept 1, 1875) Many valuable services and expended thousands of dollars besides neglecting my ranch and other important individual business which has suffered many thousand dollars have in consequence of my absences on many occasions attending to the interest and welfare of the above company." The bill was for $5,500.[47]

Kenedy and King also wrote about personal friends and with ranch advice. King had written Mifflin in January to tell him that their good friend William Hale had died. It was a blow to the family because they had only six dollars in their house. They wanted to borrow six or seven hundred dollars from

King and Kenedy until they could recover. King said he had sent Mrs. Hale $500.[48] Mifflin was also concerned with a friend, James P. Horback, and wrote Stephen Powers to see if he would draft a letter to Governor Coke to see if he could help him. He said he had known the man for over thirty years and since he was in trouble he wanted to help him.[49]

Old and new railroad issues had to be dealt with throughout the year. Mifflin and King were already turning their interest toward Corpus Christi, and on March 18 they joined with their friend and former associate in Brownsville, Uriah Lott, to invest in a new railroad. This railroad would run from Corpus Christi, Texas, across the Wild Horse Desert to Laredo, Texas, and bypass Brownsville as a major trade center for Mexican trade. Mifflin invested $10,000 with Lott, and King invested $20,000. The new railroad would be called the Rio Grande Railway (RGRC).[50] Both Mifflin and King knew the importance of rail to move their cattle and other products to the northern markets and also to capitalize on the trade products coming out of Mexico. At the same time, they still had to finalize their old railroad business in Brownsville. Mifflin wrote Stephen Powers in May, bringing to his attention the fact that Woodhouse had not made his railroad payment and he was afraid the would need to file suit but would like to give them a chance to pay first.[51]

Then in August, Mifflin wrote Powers again to discuss the possibility of seizing the railroad's rolling stock. Mifflin told him he would come if necessary but that he had all he could handle.[52] Powers did file, and on September 22 Powers received a letter from Mr. Gomila stating that by October 5 he expected to be able to satisfy the execution of the levy Mifflin had filed which was in the hands of the sheriff of Cameron County on all the property of the RGRC and that he had delivered his bond to the sheriff.[53] Kenedy then instructed Powers on October 22 that if it did not prejudice his claim he desired the sale of the railroad property be postponed until the first Tuesday in December to give them a chance to remit. He then told him he was leaving for New Orleans on the twentieth and would be gone about two weeks. He listed his address at D. L. Kernion.[54]

One reason for going to New Orleans may have been for Petra to seek medical help. Mifflin, late in her illness, mentions trying to get her to New Orleans. On November 24, Mifflin wrote Powers after his return from New Orleans. He was responding to Powers's request that he was needed in Brownsville: "I do not wish to lose any time, and Mrs. Kenedy has been and is still very unwell—and my presence here almost actually necessary and together with the very uncomfortable trip over land and the matters transporting at this time. I telegraphed you on the 20th asking you to advise me once on your return if you still considered as necessary for me to be there."[55]

Petra was ill again and needed Mifflin to be near. The year had been difficult, her health problems continued and James's involvement in the bandit wars was worrisome. She was glad to have John back home, but then she continued to also worry about Sarah. On March 31, Petra filed the deed of property that had been executed back in 1868, gifting her interest in the Vela property to her siblings. Petra's life was difficult at best. She was living in isolation out at the ranch surrounded by bandit hostility. Mifflin's attentions were spread in many different directions, including concerns about the stock, weather, bandits, railroad business, and money. Petra's thoughts must have turned to their earlier days of marriage when the children were young and, like most mothers, she wished she had all her children and grandchildren around her where she knew they were safe from harm.

CHAPTER 14

1876:
The Apple of His Father's Eye

As Petra faced the beginning of 1876 she had no idea she would gain a family member and lose a precious one. The lawlessness continued to surround her and the family on the ranch, everyone living in the Wild Horse Desert lived in terror.

In January, Rip Ford accompanied Captain McNelly to Washington, D.C., to testify before a special committee that included former Union Army generals Banks and Hurlbut. They traveled there to describe the conditions in South Texas along the Rio Grande. The generals were interested in whether or not Captain McNelly thought his unauthorized raids into Mexico represented a declaration of war. Captain McNelly, not backing down for a minute, answered that he thought "he was following a rule of international law where by if a nation was unwilling or unable to restrain its own people from preying on a neighboring country, the affected nation had the right to pursue the offenders."[1] He also informed the committee that he felt the command of his company of troops was not half as hazardous "as that of those men living on ranches."[2] Another source of help besides the United States government would end the lawlessness along the Rio Grande and throughout South Texas. In Mexico, a tough young general named Porfirio Díaz led a revolution to unseat President Sebastian de Lerdo. General Díaz first sought financial backing in Brownsville to carry out his campaign. He arranged a meeting with Captain Kenedy, Captain King, Francisco Ytúrria, and Charles Sterling representing James Stillman, son of Charles Stillman. These men desired two things from Díaz before promising him financing: First, he must back a national railroad that would connect at Laredo, Texas, to the new railroad to be built from Corpus Christi to Laredo, which would allow seamless trade between the two countries. Second, he must promise to get rid of Cortina so he could no longer conduct raids into Texas. Díaz quickly agreed, and a number of Brownsville merchants provided the funding he wanted. John Ford reported that the sum was $50,000, and Cortina's half-brother don Savas Cavazos advanced Díaz the money.[3]

Cortina was a survivor and as usual managed to line up with Díaz and his followers; he helped take control of Matamoros on April 2, 1876. After his victory in Matamoros, Díaz took his troops inland, and by November he had won Mexico.[4] In a letter to Mifflin Kenedy in April, Captain McNelly, who was back in Texas, reported that "the raiding has become less frequent lately, in fact has entirely stopped on account of the cattle thieves having joined the revolutionary forces but we anticipate a vigorous renewal of the raids as soon as General Díaz moves to the interior as it is understood that the raiders refuse to go away from the river towns."[5]

After Díaz assumed the presidency of Mexico, President Rutherford Hayes refused to recognize his government until he controlled the violence along the border. He was not quick to reply, so President Hayes had General Ord continue to pursue bandits into Mexico when necessary. Finally, in 1877, Cortina was arrested by Gen. Servando Canales for disobedience and was condemned to death.[6] Rip Ford had sent a warning to Cortina that his life was in danger: "Do not trust yourself in Matamoros. Sell off everything you have which can be moved." Cortina did not take heed of Ford's warning. When he received it he replied, "That old white-headed American thinks he knows Mexicans better than I do." Ford was proved right when Cortina was arrested. Ford intervened with General Canales, explaining to him that everyone knew the two men were personal enemies, and it would always be a stain on Canales's memory if he had Cortina executed. Ford suggested instead that he send him to President Díaz and let him decide. General Canales followed Colonel Ford's advice; President Díaz kept Cortina under surveillance for nearly twenty years.[7] Cortina, who had terrorized so many for so long was finally removed from the Rio Grande Valley.[8]

Petra was relieved when it looked like Cortina was finally being dealt with. On April 19, James was discharged from the Texas Rangers, bringing him back home to help with their ranching enterprise and to be near to her. Finally she could feel that her family was safer and they could throw all their energy into the Los Laureles Ranch.

The *Corpus Christi Caller* announced on January 26, 1876, that Captain King would be putting 31,000 head of cattle on the road to Kansas. The projected prices were $8 for a one-year-old, $11 for a two-year-old, $15 for a three-year-old, and $20 for a four-year-old.[9] Mifflin confirmed this information when he wrote Stephen Powers in Brownsville on February 8 to tell him that he had just returned from the Santa Gertrudis and that King had been dangerously ill for the last few weeks. Mifflin reported that King was better and that he was busy getting 30,000 cattle on the road.[10] A couple of weeks later, on the twenty-sixth, Mifflin again wrote Powers to tell him that he could not come to Brownsville for court in March. He was putting 10,000 cattle on the road for Kansas, which would require his being there for the month of March. He also told him that he was sending Mr. Downey his power of attorney and that he should continue to try to collect the debt from the railroad group. Even if Woodhouse had gone back on his word the others should not. Mifflin also offered to go to Corpus when needed if that would make communications easier.[11] The *Corpus Christi Caller* reported on February 29, "we are pleased to note the convalescence of Mr. Richard King, now on a visit to our city."[12]

Mifflin decided not to accompany his cattle to Kansas but instead meet them there to facilitate the sale. He was also interested in buying up parts of the Espíritu Santo. He told Powers that he had bought his son-in-law Dalzell's interest for $4,000 and wanted him to be sure that his other son-in-law Starck had it recorded.[13] Again, King wrote to his good friend Mifflin on March 28 to help him out with suggestions on rounding the cattle up and moving them up the road.[14] The *Corpus Christi Caller* reported on March 19, "More Stock for Kansas: Within a few days Capt. M. Kenedy of Los Laureles will commence moving his cattle for the Kansas market. He is fully prepared as rapidly as the stock can be gathered and arranged in herds. They will be moving toward the Nueces. We heard it was his intention to have 5,000 head."[15]

Captain Kenedy wrote to Powers at the end of the month to explain his condition after he finally had the cattle on the road: "I have put ten thousand head of cattle on the road—has drained me perfectly dry." He told Powers that when he got back from Kansas he could count on him to have the means to carry out the arrangements Powers was trying to make for Kenedy on Brazos Island.[16] Like King and the rest of the cattlemen, once the cattle were on the road their financial future was tied up in the successful drive and concluding sale.

In Corpus Christi, Dr. Arthur Spohn was making himself known in both the professional and social circles. In February his ad in the paper announced the organizing meeting for a Medical Association for Western Texas, which would be held on March 1, 1876, for every practicing physician holding a diploma from a known college of medicine.[17] It appeared that Dr. Spohn was equally busy with his social involvement in the community. He helped out the ladies of the Catholic Congregations when they held a comedy, "Rough Diamond," at Market Hall by participating as part of the cast. After the play, benches were cleared for dancing until 3 A.M.[18]

Since Dr. Spohn was a member of the Episcopal Church it may be that he was seeking the approval of Sarah Kenedy by helping out the Catholic women's project. Sarah, with her dark curls and flashing eyes, must have caught his attention during some of the town's socials. Sarah was reported to be "charming in manner, engaging in conversation, a gifted pianist, mistress of French, Spanish, and English. She was an ornament to any society and Corpus Christi recognized it."[19] Sarah, as Mifflin and Petra's daughter, was an exceptionally eligible young woman in society, since she was heiress to one of the fortunes of the Cattle Kings of Texas.

Dr. Spohn was practicing medicine with Dr. Burke. Their office was in Spohn's personal residence.[20] As the months went by he became more and more social, and on April 29 he celebrated his thirty-first birthday at his residence on Mesquite Street. The paper reported that he accepted bouquets of flowers and rich cakes, and then the party adjourned to Mrs. Merriman's for dancing for several hours. He was highly esteemed by his friends, particularly his lady friends.[21] He had become one of the most eligible bachelors in town.

Sarah Kenedy Spohn and Dr. Arthur Spohn married in Corpus Christi November 22, 1876, and set out on a world tour. Sarah was "charming in manner, engaging in conversation, a gifted pianist, mistress of French, Spanish, and English." Courtesy Christus Spohn Health System, Corpus Christi, Texas.

Dr. Spohn continued his professional involvement, and on May 24 invited a *Corpus Christi Caller* representative to watch a bloodless amputation. He had used the tourniquet that allowed for bloodless procedures while in the U.S. Army. A snake had bitten the patient being operated on. Dr. Spohn used chloroform during the procedure, which took about fifteen minutes, and "there were only five drips of blood and loss scarcely perceptible."[22] A story from the Henrichson family relates how beloved Dr. Spohn became to the Corpus Christi community.

> Dr. Spohn was always called in case of emergencies for the Henrichson's. He never spared his horses in coming because he knew it was a grave situation and it was understood that he did lose one of his horses in this call to aid the girl Mayme this time as she was delirious from high fever from Typhoid Fever. He took her to the hospital for three weeks and the father would make the trip to Corpus from the ranch 3–4 times to bring the mother clean clothes and check on Mayme as the mother stayed with her. One day late in the evening

Dr. Arthur Spohn, renowned physician of Corpus Christi and founder of Spohn Hospital. Courtesy Christus Spohn Health System, Corpus Christi, Texas.

when George Henrichson drove up to the ranch he saw his youngest son Comley lying in the end of the trough. At first he thought he was asleep but then realized he was unconscious with high fever. He was about 5 years old and his father picked him up and ran into the house to get a cloth to cool him down while the older boy harnessed a fresh horse. They headed for Corpus with the father holding Comley and the older boy driving. When they got to the hospital, Dr. Spohn took one look at him and turned to the nurse Sally and said, quick get him into the bay to cool him off. Sally said, can't I change my dress first and he said no I will buy you another dress. Sally ran to the bay with him and waded out to meet the waves and balanced him on her knees and bathed his face. Comley opened his eyes and did not know where he was. He later said he went to sleep in the horse trough, looking for a cool place to lie down and the next thing he knew he felt the salt waves hitting him in the face.[23]

In May, Petra welcomed the news that she had three more grandchildren. The Dalzells had a little girl named Mary Josephine, the Putegnats had a boy named Edward, and the Rodríguezes had a boy named Alfredo.[24] All of Petra's children and grandchildren were doing well and were involved in their communities.

The *Evening Ranchero* reported about the Fourth of July celebration held in Brownsville in honor of the nation's one-hundredth birthday. At dawn, a thirteen-gun salute greeted the "glorious day." A procession was formed on Elizabeth Street at about 9:30 A.M. In the parade, fourteen young ladies representing Columbia and the thirteen original states, each wearing a banner and a crown, sat on a platform. The first platform held the original states and the second held the additional states that had been added to the Union. On these two platforms were three of Petra's granddaughters. Miss Irene Dalzell represented New York, Miss Lula Dalzell was Wisconsin, and Miss Julia Dalzell was California.[25]

Corpus Christi also held a celebration on July 4, but it was marred by one event. The *Corpus Christi Caller* reported the firing of a one-hundred-gun salute from the bluff. During the firing of the twelfth round a gun misfired and former district judge Stanley Welch suffered a terrible mutilation of his right arm. Doctors Spohn, Burke and Ansell amputated the arm. The celebration continued with the feeding of 1,000 people followed by toasts and a grand ball at the city hall.[26]

Three days after the fourth, on July 7, a tragedy struck Mifflin and Petra; they would never recover from it. Willie, "the apple of his father's eye," succumbed at the age of seventeen to consumption. He had run a high fever and died.[27] He was buried in New Orleans in a vault that Mifflin purchased in section no. 88 at the Metairie Cemetery on the next day, July 8, 1876, for $100. On March 7, 1890, Mifflin paid the cemetery $250 to move Willie's remains to Brownsville's old cemetery, where he was buried alongside Phebe Ann and Adrian in the Kenedy plot.[28]

Petra, having continuing health problems, turned to her faith to survive the grief from the death of her youngest son. Her three oldest children had been lost to her and then little Phebe and now Willie. Willie was sensitive, intellectual, caring and particularly close to Mifflin. Losing a child is the most difficult thing a parent can do, but to lose one far away when you can't hold or be with the child is particularly difficult. Petra knew that Willie's faith was strong after his training at Spring Hill. She felt confident that he would have utilized that faith as he bravely faced the end of his young life. She could only hope she could also find solace in God's mercy and comfort.

Petra had lost a beloved member of the family and just four months later gained another. On November 22, 1876, Sarah Josephine Kenedy married Dr. Arthur E. Spohn at Petra and Mifflin's Los Laureles Ranch. The witnesses were Sarah's brother John and Mrs. Rachel Doddridge. Father P. de St. Jean officiated.[29] Rachel Doddridge's husband, Perry, had been employed as a clerk with M. Kenedy & Co. in 1852. He had known the Kenedys for twenty-four years, since before Sarah was born. Mr. Doddridge had established the first bank in Corpus Christi in 1871, with his partner Allen Davis. He had been elected mayor of Corpus Christi in 1874 and was also a friend of Richard King's.[30] John Kenedy and his brother-in-law Dr. Spohn would be called on in the years to come to handle many family problems; it was good that John was back in Corpus Christi.

Since Petra and her family were still in mourning over Willie's death, the wedding was not a large social affair in Corpus Christi. Sarah had married one of the most eligible bachelors in Corpus Christi. He, in turn, had married a

Petra Vela Kenedy in a formal pose.

wealthy young heiress who would have the resources to fund his medical research and various trips around the world in search of medical excellence. The *Corpus Christi Caller*, on November 26, reported the wedding and announced that Dr. A. E. Spohn and wife were headed for a tour through the south of France and other parts of Europe.[31]

Dr. Spohn must have been preparing for this occasion when on October 3 he announced that he and Dr. Burke had acquired a new partner, Dr. Hamilton, his brother-in-law, who would be practicing with them in the office at

Photograph of Mifflin Kenedy. Brownsville Historical Association.

Dr. Spohn's home.[32] With the addition of another physician to the practice, Dr. Spohn could more easily be away from Corpus Christi.

Petra was pleased that Sarah's previous personal problems had been resolved and that she had married an accomplished young professional. The year following their marriage Dr. Spohn traveled to New York to take a postgraduate course at Bellevue Hospital.[33]

November found Mifflin dealing with the never-ending job of trying to collect the money owed by the railroad people in Brownsville. Downey had telegraphed him on the sixth to say that his presence was absolutely needed in court in regard to the levy of the Woodhouse property. Mifflin telegraphed Powers on the tenth to say that it was impossible for him to come because his health would not permit it.[34]

On November 26, Thanksgiving Day, Mifflin had something to be thankful for, something that would brighten his world a bit after Willie's death. A grand ceremony took place to start the laying of the track for the new railroad from Corpus Christi to Laredo. The mayor spoke, and there was a demonstration by the fire department; a drill by the Corpus Christi Star Rifles; and fat steers and turkeys were slaughtered, roasted, and served to all the guests. Mr. Uriah Lott drove the first spike for the railroad, which was gilded to look like gold. In fact, the spike looked so real that someone stole it that night.[35] Lott had worked with Mifflin and King in Brownsville before coming to Corpus Christi where he established his own commission and forwarding business in 1871. He chartered three sailing vessels to transport wool and hides to New York. He had convinced Mifflin and King to invest in this railroad project and had high hopes for its success.[36]

Mifflin and Petra were beginning to have a firm foundation in their ranching enterprise at Los Laureles. Their children were also firmly established in both Corpus Christi and along the Rio Grande. As the winds blew across the Wild Horse Desert late at night, Petra could perhaps let her tears flow freely in grief over the death of Willie. Mifflin, because of his Quaker background, tended to keep things inside and remained outwardly calm and resolved. Petra had seen many tragedies in her life but Willie was her fifth child to lose. There never could be anything that filled the void or lessened the hurt of one of her own being lost forever.

Chapter 15

1877–78: "A Fiend in Human Form"

After the turmoil and tragedy Petra experienced over the last several years, it was comforting for her to know that the countryside was safer. At last the ranchers on the Wild Horse Desert could concentrate on delivering their beef to the northern markets. For the first time in a long time three of Petra's sons were at home with her. Tom, James, and John worked at Los Laureles,, which was especially nice after the loss of Willie. Sarah and Dr. Spohn would make their home in Corpus Christi and her married daughters were in Brownsville and along the river. The family seemed to be doing well. The sons-in-law were established; the daughters were involved in community activities and charities; and more grandchildren were being added every year. Petra's daughters and Mifflin's stepdaughters, their children, and their descendants would leave an enduring legacy throughout Texas.

The cattle business saw big years in 1877 and 1878, when thousands of cattle were put on the road toward Kansas. Mifflin wanted to spend his time on the ranch, but the new Corpus Christi railroad was in financial trouble and early in the year two of the investors from Harrisburg, Pennsylvania, came to take a look at their investment. Unfortunately, bandits robbed the investors during the trip. All of their valuables were lost, their carriage was overturned, their horses stolen, and they were left stripped down to their underwear while bound hand and foot and tied to mesquite trees. Needless to say, they were not impressed with Texas hospitality.[1]

Mifflin had to go to New York and raised $250,000 in private placements so the railroad could continue. Many began to call the project "Lott's Folly." It took seven years to build but it was the first railroad to reach Laredo. Díaz's election as president of Mexico opened the door to the industrialization of Mexico and, in many instances, U.S. domination over the Mexican economy.

Díaz encouraged the building of railroads all along the border, and these railroads lined up with the National Railway System that was financed by U.S. banks, such as Stillman's National City, Morgan, Brown Brothers, and First National of New York. James Stillman, as chairman of the board of National City Bank, became one of the "Big Four" U.S. railroad tycoons. Many of his closest associates had ties to the Mexican economy. Joseph Peter Grace of W. R. Grace and Co. controlled the garbanzo bean industry of Sonora; Cleveland Dodge of Dodge and Company was in the mining conglomerates; Cyrus McCormick, president of International Harvester, dominated the Yucatán peninsula trade; and J. P. Morgan was heavily involved in the industrialization of Monterrey. These men's investments set off fears in later years about former President Lerda's warning that the United States would devour Mexico if given the opportunity.[2] An old Mexican lament, usually accredited to Díaz, goes "*Pobre Méjico, tan lejos de Dios y tan cerquito de los Estados Unidos*" ("Poor Mexico, so far from God and so close to the United States"), which might well have expressed the worries of the people.[3]

While tending to the new railroad, Mifflin was plagued throughout the year with trying to collect funds from the railroad people in Brownsville. He wrote Powers in February about trying to collect it, and as late as December 14 was vowing that only at the bitter end would he yield to them a right of way over his land.[4]

In Mifflin's letter to Powers on February 4, 1877, he tells him that he cannot come to Brownsville because he "is preparing to drive a larger number of cattle to Kansas this year and cannot remain in court as it will do injury to my business."[5] Mifflin wrote to Powers on May 10 that he had started his eighth and last herd the Sunday before. He said he had a little less than 18,000 head of cattle and one herd of four hundred mules.[6] John Kenedy confirmed this drive in a deposition in 1877: "I went up the cattle trail to Kansas. Father drove 18,000 head of cattle, horses and mules to Dodge City arriving there on July 4, 1877. In September of 1877, I drove 2,500 head of three and four year old steers to Ogallala, Nebraska, to be delivered to Congressman Randall of Illinois. I delivered the cattle and returned home by rail to Galveston via Omaha."[7]

The end of the bandit raids freed the ranchers to expand their herds, and as long as the cattle prices remained good they took the road to the northern markets. The larger ranchers, like Kenedy and King, had enough cattle to make up their own drives, but many smaller ranchers joined their herds for efficiency.[8] Many of the South Texas ranchers went up the Chisholm Trail, which took them from the Rio Grande at Brownsville past Kenedy's and King's ranches, through Beeville, Gonzales, and Lockhart to Austin or San Antonio. By the time the cattle arrived at Fort Worth there were many other herds that joined them, and the trail was solid with dust and slowly moving steers for as far as one could see. The cattle then moved through the Indian Territory to Kansas. The cattle drives were often dangerous and full of hazards for both men and animals. There were flooded rivers and quicksand to deal with. If a large flood was encountered the herds had to be held until the floodwaters subsided. The cattle could easily get disoriented crossing the river and start to circle back. Natural elements such as lightning or thunder, howling winds in the night, or birds in sudden flight could startle a herd and start a stampede. Once the cattle were scattered it could take weeks to gather them.[9] One of Captain Kenedy's vaqueros on the La Parra rancho lost his life while trying to cross cattle at a river. Marin Acuña was pushing the cattle across the river when he and his horse suddenly disappeared under the water. The horse surfaced but Acuña did not. The other vaqueros thought maybe the struggling horse had hurt him, but by the time they reached him he was already dead.[10]

While on the trail, long, tiring, hot, dusty days with never-ending work faced the cowboys, day in and day out. One of the few pleasures they had on the drive was their grub. A good cook kept the men satisfied, enabling them to work the long, hard hours the drive demanded. The chuck wagon was the cook's kitchen. Charles Goodnight was given credit for inventing the chuck wagon in 1866 to facilitate cattle drives. The chuck wagon was wooden; mules pulled it. Metal bows bent over the bed of the wagon, which was covered with a sheet or tarpaulin that could be fastened down to protect against rain. The rear wall sloped outward and was hinged at the bottom so it could be swung down, to provide a worktable for the cook. The wagon would travel about ten or fifteen miles a day and then the cook would set up camp. The cook started at about three or four in the morning and prepared a breakfast of refried beans, coffee, and bread. Sometimes the vaqueros would eat cooked beans, rice, fried meat, bread, and coffee. The vaqueros ate in shifts so that the cattle were always tended. The cook often mended clothes and served as doctor and banker; he sometimes even held the bets in a poker game. The wagons also carried water tanks from which the men could fill their canteens. The evening meal was the most important. Often the men worked until after dark, then they would sit around the campfire after dinner and sing or tell tales. They would get a cup, plate, and utensils from the chuck wagon and help themselves to some coffee and whatever was cooking in the pot or skillet. They ate wherever they could find a place to sit.[11]

The men observed a universal cowboy's social etiquette: (1) The cowhands ate as they came in instead of waiting for everyone else. It was more polite to go ahead and serve themselves than to have the others stand in line waiting. (2) Even if everyone was there at once, there was no crowding, shoving, rushing, or overreaching. These were not tolerated. (3) The Dutch oven lids were kept away from the sand, and the cowboys were careful to put the pots back on the fire so that the food would be hot for those still to come. (4) A cowboy did not take the last serving unless he was sure everyone else was finished eating. (5) There was no waste. He left no food on his plate. He either ate all the food or scraped it off for the animals and birds to eat. He might put it in the "squirrel can," a can for leftovers that would be fed to animals later. He would then place his dirty dishes in the huge dishpan for washing. (6) It was a breach of etiquette to tie a horse to a wheel of the chuck wagon, or to ride fast into camp so that the wind blew sand in the food the cook was preparing. (7) The men dared not eat until the cook called it ready. (8) If he found the water barrel empty, the cowhand's duty was to fill it. (9) To leave a bedroll unrolled and unplaced was a serious breach of etiquette. This might cause it to be left behind when the cook packed up. (10) Around the campfire, an unwritten law was that a song or fiddle piece or story was not interrupted. (11) A stranger would always be welcome at the wagon and ate with the cowhands. The unwritten code was that he was expected to dry the dishes.[12]

When the cowboys reached the end of the trail in Abilene or Dodge City they were ready for a bath, haircut, and new set of clothes. Then they were ready to celebrate at one of the dance halls or saloons. Most of the cowboys sold their cowponies. Some of them raced the ponies against other cowboys before getting rid of them. They usually took the money and returned home by rail.[13] J. Frank Dobie told a tale about a famous King Ranch vaquero called Ablos whose story he believed was based on the life of Ignacio Alvarado, who lived on the King Ranch. This story illustrated the importance of the man in charge of the valuable herds.

> One spring in the 1880s Captain Richard King of the vast ranch that bears his name had already sent several herds up the trail to Kansas and had the last herd gathered, "shaped up," ready to go. It was made up of big steers, all in the Running W brand, freshly road-branded with the KW.
>
> Ablos, the most efficient and most valued caporal (boss) of the ranch, was to take it. He had been trail boss for years, but now, his outfit all ready, he had not appeared. For a day, two days, three days, the vaqueros loose-herded the steers by the day and held them on be-grounds by night. Still there was no Ablos. It was said that he was away in San Diego (Texas) on a drunk. Young Richard King, very young, was in a stew.
>
> "What on earth," he said to his father, "do you mean by putting up with that old drunkard? Let's place another man in charge and get the herd moving."

"We'd better wait a while longer, I guess," Captain King measured out his words.

"Just an old drunkard," young Richard insisted.

The captain kept on waiting and a day or two later Ablos showed up. "I am ready," he said. He took over the herd and left. The property under his charge was worth many thousands of dollars. He was as much the master of it as a captain at sea is master of a ship. He must rely upon himself. For many weeks he would have no one to report to or account to.

After the herds had been on the trail for two or three months, Captain King and his son Richard traveled to Dodge City, Kansas.

"How did you make the trip?" would be the question asked of each trail boss as he arrived. The first one said: "We had much trouble at the Cimarron. The cattle milled in the water and several drowned." The second one said: "It kept raining and storming all through the Indian Territory. My cattle stampeded every night for two weeks. I am short." Indians had run off the third man's horses, some of them not recovered.

And so it was with each of the half dozen trail bosses. At length Ablos appeared. He had started after the others and had steadily lost time. "And how did you make it through, Ablos?" Captain King asked.

"Oh, *muy bien, Señor.* No trouble anywhere. All was pacific all the way. We came along *despacio, despacio,* slow, slow. I picked up 136 K.W. cattle lost out of other herds. We are 136 cattle long. And look how all the cattle have gained in weight! Look how contented they are!"

Captain King turned to Richard. "Now you know why I wait for that old drunkard Ablos." Years went by. Captain King had died. His son-in-law, R. J. Kleberg was managing the great King estate. Ablos was still the king of caporals. One day a herd was to be moved. Ablos had been notified to take charge of it. The herd was "shaped up," ready to move. No Ablos. One day passed, two days, No Ablos. Then his son appeared.

"My father says to tell you he cannot come," reported the son. "Why?" "He says he is sorry, but he has to stay at home to die."[14]

On July 7, the anniversary of Willie's death, Petra and Mifflin held a requiem mass in his honor. Petra particularly wanted the song "Jerusalem" included. Petra wanted the mass sung in the church in Brownsville where Willie had grown up and been baptized. Here they had attended church together and had stood so many times for family occasions. Willie would never be far from

Petra because she carried him in her heart. It was natural that Petra would hold Willie's mass in Brownsville, but the state of the church in Corpus Christi probably played a role in the decision also.[15]

Bishop Manucy had arrived in Corpus Christi after leaving Brownsville three years before. He found that he "had not whereon to lay his head" because there was no house to accommodate the priest. He found it necessary to build a house so that the mission priests would have a place to stay when they came to town. The priests were constantly in the countryside ministering to the people on ranches and at the missions. The bishop wrote, "out of a population of 1,500 Mexicans in Corpus Christi and eighty families in the ranches outside, there are not ten persons who comply with their Easter duty." The congregation in 1875 numbered about four hundred English-speaking persons. The little church was about twenty years old; the walls were cracking and the tower had been blown off during a storm. Bishop Manucy needed a larger church. It would be another two years before he could build the church he wanted, and once again it would be Petra and Mifflin who would be instrumental in making that happen.[16] The day after Willie's requiem mass in Brownsville, Petra's daughter Rosa gave birth to Susan Catherine.[17]

In August, Captain King had left again for the north and Mifflin was complaining to Powers about the heat, saying that it had been up to 100 degrees for several days in a row.[18] September brought the news of the death of a good friend, Texas Ranger Capt. Leander McNelly, who had been the most effective single factor in stopping the raids. He died of consumption, which he had contracted in the line of duty, on September 4, 1877, at Burton, Washington County. Texas treated him shabbily. When he was too sick to ride, the adjutant general at Austin simply reorganized McNelly's company, omitting his name from the roster and appointing a new captain in his place. He provided no compensation to the dying man, who left a wife and two children. Richard King upon at least two occasions had sent the McNelly rangers a cash bonus as a token of esteem for their work. There is no record that he aided the ranger captain in his final illness or helped the widow later, but Richard King had a decent monument of granite erected over the resting place of "brave Leander H. McNelly."[19]

By October, Mifflin was worrying about the stock because of the heat and hoping for plenty of rain and a very mild winter.[20] At the end of October he was serving on jury duty in Corpus Christi for several weeks and was very busy. He was also trying to handle a touchy situation with his son-in-law, Fred Starck. Starck had been handling the recording of Mifflin's land deeds and had written to complain to Mifflin that Powers was taking care of Mifflin's business rather than he. Mifflin wrote Powers and told him that he was not going to answer the letter but "to gratify the young man's vanity, when the papers are all ready hand them to him, to have duly signed, witnessed and recorded, and say to him to deposit the two thousand dollars at San Román's to my credit and have them to advise me of the same." He then informed Powers that they were having some good rains, which were needed. He passed along the good news that all his "cattle sold from the drive except about two thousand calves—my son Santiago [James] will winter them about 80 miles South of Fort Dodge in the Indian Country—between the Kansas and Canadian [rivers]."[21]

In January of 1878, Mr. Downey wrote to Captain King that he was coming to the Santa Gertrudis by way of Los Laureles. He said he had promised Captain Kenedy he would come to Los Laureles the first time he went to Corpus Christi. He wrote that he regretted that "Mrs. Downey cannot leave home at this time."[22] A description of Sixtus Bluntzer's farm in 1880 that was reported in the *Cureo Record* from an interview might give a good idea of what life was like at the Los Laureles Ranch when Downey visited:

> Hunting rabbits, going down to the river to pick grapes, pecans and plums. Things like the horse collar, the walking plow, the buggy, the wagon, the coffee grinder, wood stove, smokehouse, and the garden. Medicine shelf with supplies of calomel, rhubarb, quinine, salve, Epsom salts, and the old doctor book that was second only to the Bible. You went to town once a month to sell cotton, corn, bacon, hides, cord wood, etc. You would buy cloth like calico, buckskin cloth for jeans, material for shirts, take corn to be ground into corn meal, buy coal oil for lanterns, buy cowhide work shoes, and bullhide for mud boots, buy a barrel of flour, 100 pounds of salt, a barrel of apples, barrel of brown sugar, and a gallon keg of whiskey or any quantity from 3 fingers in a tin cup to a barrel. In the fall there would be hog-killing day to fill the smoke house with sausage, hog's head cheese, pickled hog's feet, bacon, ham, cracklings, lard.[23]

Life on the ranches and farms in southern Texas was all-encompassing. The ranches had to be self-sustaining and able to provide for all the basic needs. They had to provide for the well being of the stock, family members, and workers. It took people with many different types of skills and a lot of hard work to provide all the necessities of everyday life.

One of the ways the Tejano ranch residences were able to carry on their work was in teams. The men might work as teams in fencing crews or windmill repair crews. The Tejana women worked in teams, too. If they needed to make lime they carried large baskets to the creek and gathered scallops or mussels and stacked them in layers for burning. They burned the shells for two days with patties of dried cow manure, reducing the shells to pure white lime. They also worked with the men to make soap for the household cleaning. The men slaughtered a hog or steer and the women gathered the fat in large iron pots and melted it. The tallow produced went into candle molds. Some also went into other boiling pots with lye added and then it was placed into molds and cut into cakes of soap. The women also gathered for quilting bees, which provided companionship as well as a work center.[24]

Tejano children learned at an early age to respect one another and the natural environment. They were taught that to be cruel to small animals like the common horned toad might lead to the animal coming in the night and choking them to death. They learned to say "*Jesús lo ayude*" or "Jesus bless you" when someone sneezed. Many times their parents taught them good manners and hygiene through folk lessons. The families practiced cleanliness in their homes. At night they often entertained their children with ghost stories about hidden gold and moving lights across the chaparral.[25]

Tejano families worked hard but they also took a great deal of pride in their work, and they liked to relax not only at home with their families but also in celebrating religious holidays. They also took pride in their food, and it was delicious. A favorite food of Anglos, barbecue, started with Tejano workers. They would cook a beef head or other cuts of meat over a deep pit of mesquite *brazas,* or embers, until the meat was tender, and that became known as *barbacoa*. The ranchers used the food sources around them, like the pear-shaped fruit of the prickly pear cactus, to make preserves. They also made *buñuelos,* which were favorite sweet breads often made during the holiday season. Wedding cookies and *piloncillo* (caked brown sugar) candy were also made.[26]

Petra had grown up with these traditions, and her children were immersed in them as well. This was their way of life at Los Laureles and later on La Parra Ranch. The ranch families were close and all of them were like extended family. They celebrated births, weddings, religious holidays, and joys, and grieved sorrows and deaths—always together.[27]

Brownsville was caught up in a dramatic scene in early 1878, when Mr. Nestor Maxan, a leading citizen and sometimes Mifflin's lawyer, scandalized the town with his behavior. Maxan, a married man, was involved with a woman who was rumored to sing in the Presbyterian choir and play sometimes in the Fort Brown orchestra, where Maxan also played on occasion. Another gentleman, Miguel de la Peña, a military physician posted in Matamoros, was interested in the same woman. Maxan found de la Peña with the woman and they quarreled; both agreed not to see her again. Later de la Peña saw her walking up Elizabeth Street with Maxan and confronted Maxan in front of his home. Maxan asked him to move elsewhere; they both did and their heated argument continued. Maxan ended up challenging de la Peña to a duel. De la Peña tried to get Dr. Charles B. Combe to negotiate a settlement with Maxan, thus avoiding a duel, but to no avail. Dueling was illegal, but since Maxan refused to change his mind, a time and place was established. Mifflin's business associate, Capt. William Kelly, helped stage the duel in Matamoros at the Garita de las Puertas Veredes, a gateway in the fortifications surrounding Matamoros. Captain Kelly and Dr. Arthur S. Wolf served as Maxan's seconds. Dr. Charles B. Combe and Captain Elijah J. Kenedy, Mifflin's brother, acted as de la Peña's seconds. De la Peña described the scene:

> Maxan, Kelly, and Wolfe were already there and Mr. Kelly called attention to our slight delay. Captain Elijah Kenedy arrived alone in one carriage, Dr. Combe and I were together in another carriage. We were mild and moderate before the combat, on the ground we could only be firm and resolved. There was quite a fresh wind blowing at the time . . . it was at the back of my adversary and full in my face. The seconds each tossed coins to determine where his principal was to stand and who was to call the signal for firing. Captain Kenedy won the former decision and Dr. Combe the latter. Maxan showed himself to be brave and dexterous, he took the usual position and I did the same. We presented our right side to each other and we drew ourselves up and settled ourselves perfectly in our respective places. Maxan's first shot passed near me.[28]

After that shot, de la Peña fired into the air and sought to lay down his arms, but Maxan would have none of it and wanted to continue. Maxan's second shot grazed de la Peña, and again Captain Kelly tried to stop the duel but Maxan refused to give up. They presented to each other again and de la Peña's third shot fatally wounded Maxan. Maxan was taken to H. E. Woodhouse's store. Then, to prevent an international incident, Maxan's body was loaded into a rowboat and crossed to the American side. He was passed through the checkpoint as suffering from a night on the town and his body was delivered to his home and left on the porch. His wife was in shock at his death, as was a good portion of Brownsville. After he lay in state at his home, Father Parisot conducted the services at the Immaculate Conception Church.[29]

Maxan's death left an opening in Stephen Powers's law office, until a young lawyer named James B. Wells filled the position. Jim Wells was born in Texas on St. Joseph's Island and had received his law degree three years before at the University of Virginia. His knowledge of the law and command of the Spanish language made him a natural to handle land acquisition for King and sometimes for Mifflin. Jim Wells also became the political leader of South Texas and held that powerful position for years.[30]

In March, Mifflin indicated that he was busy again getting his cattle ready for Kansas. He also told Powers to secure the balance on a land note by offering all his female cattle and Mrs. K's, thus diagrams of two brands, "as of record in this county."[31] In April and June, Mifflin was concerned about the division of the Espíritu Santo tract and could not firm that up because King had already left for Kansas.[32]

James "Spike" Kenedy, twenty-three years old, had stayed in Kansas to winter the cattle in order to fatten them up and get them ready for next year's sale. On August 17, 1878, Spike was in Dodge City and became involved in the killing of one of the most glamorous and famous women in the West. Up until now there have been several versions of the shooting and Spike's role in it. James Kenedy was also known on the trail as Jim Kenedy, Spike Kenedy, and Santiago Kenedy. The victim's name was Dora Hand. She was thirty-four years old when she came to Dodge City. As one story goes, she was born Fannie Keenan in St. Louis and left home to marry Theodore Hand, a vaudevillian and honky-tonk musician, with whom, as Dora Hand, she appeared in the variety shows of New Orleans and the Mississippi river towns. Fannie continued to use the name of Dora Hand even after she divorced in 1876. Although she had a trained voice, Dora was not a graduate of the Boston Conservatory as has been reported. She sang at Esher's Varieties Theatre in St. Louis, where her best friend, Fannie Garrettson, also sang.[33]

Fannie Garrettson received an offer from the Lady Gay Theatre in Dodge City, probably for better money, so she left, with Dora not far behind. They lived together in a one-room cabin on the south side and performed at the Lady Gay. The entertainment there was to appeal to the cowboys who had just finished a long trail drive and wanted to live it up before they left to return to Texas.[34] Dora was said to be a mixture of wanton and virtue.[35] One of her contemporaries said, "only one thing anyone could hold against her was her after-dark profession, and by Godfrey, I allow she elevated that considerably."[36] Whether sinner or angel, however, when Dora Hand sang the songs of home and mother she captivated her audience totally.[37]

Jim Kelley, mayor of Dodge and proprietor of the Alhambra saloon and gambling parlor, became interested in Dora Hand. He would go by the Lady Gay to hear her sing. She was described as the "Nightingale of the old frontier." Soon Dora was out riding with Kelley on the prairie. Kelley also employed Dora to sing in his saloon for one hour, five nights a week, with the consent of the owners of the Lady Gay. With this added income, Dora helped the poor inhabitants of Dodge.[38]

To Dodge City, Dora Hand was a honky-tonk singer by night, and perhaps a "lady of the night," if some stories are true, and an angel of mercy by day.

James "Spike" Kenedy, the son who most loved ranching and the land, was grievously wounded by the formidable posse of Sheriff Bat Masterson—Deputy Sheriff William Tilghman, Marshal Charley Bassett, and Assistant Marshal Wyatt Earp—while they were in pursuit of Dora Hand's killer. Courtesy of Jesse (Sam) Thornham, Joe Thornham, McGoohan families, Petra's descendants.

Dora Hand, the honky-tonk singer by night and angel of mercy by day, was killed in error by Spike Kenedy. She was buried on Boot Hill. Courtesy of Boot Hill Museum, Inc, Dodge City, Kansas.

One of the stories told of Dora Hand was that when she sang at the Sunday evening services of the First Methodist Church, some of the sinners from the brothels and saloons filled the pews.[39]

On August 17, Spike Kenedy had been losing at blackjack at the Alhambra and in a fit of rage accused the dealer of manipulating the cards. It was the second time James's temper had gotten him in trouble in a Kansas card game. It was a serious charge to make at a gambling house; the man employed to keep things under control tried to quiet Spike. Because Spike was the son of the "second wealthiest cattleman in Texas," Kelley confronted him, and a fight ensued. The older and heavier Kelley soon overpowered Spike and threw him out the door.[40]

Spike was not done, however. He stayed in Dodge long enough to learn Kelley's habits, then he left by train for Kansas City to buy the fastest horse he could find, one that could take him forty miles a day. He rode the horse back to Dodge, conditioning him along the way so he could outrun any pursuit.[41]

It was raining when Spike rode up to Kelley's house on the south side at 4 A.M. on October 4. He fired shots into Kelley's cottage and fled up the river. As he passed the Western Hotel, however, a man ran out and recognized him.[42]

Unfortunately the person murdered was not Jim Kelley but Dora Hand. Kelley was five miles away in the hospital ward at Fort Dodge, recovering from surgery that had been performed after Spike Kenedy left Dodge for Kansas City. Since he was going to be gone, Kelley had offered his cottage to Dora and Fannie. Fannie was asleep in the front bedroom and Dora in the rear. The bullets from Kenedy's gun had not struck Fannie, but had gone through the thin partition that separated the rooms and killed Dora Hand.[43]

Bat Masterson, Ford County Sheriff, assembled a posse consisting of himself, Deputy Sheriff William Tilghman, Marshal Charley Bassett, and Assistant Marshal Wyatt Earp. Spike could not have been pursued by a more formidable group. Deciding that Kenedy was trying to throw off pursuers by fleeing up the Arkansas, the posse headed for Wagon Spring, crossing on the Cimarron and hoping to cut him off. They reached the sod house there at the crossing before Spike. They saw a horseman approaching and recognized Spike Kenedy. When Kenedy was within a few yards of the sod house he spied the posse's horses in the rear and was galloping away when a bullet from Earp's rifle struck his horse. Kenedy leaped free and started to run as the animal went down. Bat Masterson stopped him with a bullet that struck him in the left shoulder and bowled him over.[44]

Spike Kenedy was shocked to discover he had killed a woman and not Jim Kelley. He was brought back to Dodge City and placed in the Ford County

Lawmen: Left to right, top row: W. H. Harris, Luke Short, Bat Masterson. Bottom row: Charley Bassett, Wyatt Earp, McLean, and Neal Brown. Masterson, Bassett, and Earp were in the posse that pursued Spike Kenedy, August 17, 1878. Courtesy Center for American History, University of Texas, Austin, Texas.

jail in the rear of the sheriff's office; Dr. McCarty performed the required surgery in Spike's cell.[45]

Mifflin Kenedy received word of Spike's situation and went to his son. On October 21, he was in Dodge, where he found Tobe Driskill, the Dewees brothers, and several other wealthy Texans waiting to support him with their presence and their money.[46]

Spike Kenedy had been held prisoner for weeks on suspicion of having killed Dora Hand, but there was no formal indictment. On October 28, Dr. McCarty told Judge R. S. Cook that Kenedy would be able to face a "preliminary" arraignment. The judge and doctor went to Sheriff Masterson's office, where Kenedy was brought from his cell. The proceedings lasted a few minutes with no witnesses present. The court record reads: "State of Kansas vs. James W. Kenedy in re killing of Dora Hand, Case dismissed for lack of evidence." Many thought the verdict was bought, particularly after the apparent sudden affluence of several of Dodge City's most famous lawmen. When Wyatt Earp had arrived from Wichita, his funds were so low that he had to ask the mayor for an advance against his wages. Later, when he and his brother Morgan joined the gold rush to the Black Hills, they survived the winter by cutting wood. The following year, back in Dodge again and serving as assistant marshal, there is no record of Wyatt having received an unexpected windfall in addition to his wages. Ten months later, when he arrived in Tombstone, he had enough money to buy an interest in the very profitable Oriental Saloon. Bat Masterson was a gambler, and depending on how the cards ran, was either flush or broke. Shortly after the Spike Kenedy incident, he bought a half interest in the Lone Star Saloon and Dance Hall.[47]

Newspaper articles were less than flattering about the law enforcement officers, Dodge City, and the mayor himself, who was supposed to be the recipient of the bullet that took down Dora Hand. Mr. Ruby wrote to the *Oskaloosa Herald* (Iowa), "the mayor is a flannel mouthed Irishman and keeps a saloon and gambling house which he attends to in person. The city marshal and assistant are gamblers and each keeps a 'woman'—as does the mayor. . . . There seems to be no energy or pride among the citizens as regards improving the looks or comfort of their property and surroundings. They all seem to be reaching for the almighty dollar and a majority of them are not particular how they get it either."[48] This atmosphere may explain Captain Kenedy's success in getting James released, if money did indeed change hands.

Dora Hand's funeral was described as the largest ever held in Dodge City. The prairie schooner that carried her coffin creaked up Boot Hill, followed by dance hall girls and two hundred mounted men. They were there to pay their last respects to a woman who had been a friend to them. The Rev. O. W. Wright used as his text for the funeral a verse from the Gospel of John: "He that is without sin among you, let him first cast a stone at her." "Men who had killed ruthlessly and had seen many die without so much as a look of pity wept for the first time since they were boys as Dora Hand, dance hall singer of wicked Dodge, was lowered into a grave on Boot Hill." Fannie Garrettson, writing from Dodge City on October 5, 1878, speaking of James, declared: "Let him be what he may I know him to be a fiend in human form."[49]

Another story is told of how James was treated during his incarceration.

When Captain Kenedy arrived from Texas, several weeks later, James was still in the hospital at Fort Dodge with a shoulder full of buckshot. He said he had been taken there to protect him from being lynched by the Dodge City residents. He was a man who had taken a life, and no one had taken the trouble to relieve his suffering. Mifflin, shocked at his son's condition, immediately sent to Fort Leavenworth for Dr. B. E. Fryer, one of the most skilled surgeons in Kansas at that time, and with the help of doctors Tremaine and T. L. McCarty of Dodge City, Fryer removed the shattered bones and shot. However, Spike's arm was crippled for life. When Spike recovered he was placed on trial, defended by expert counsel employed by his father. There were no witnesses to the shooting, and as excitement over the murder had died down the accused man was acquitted.[50]

With the help of the above stories and the unpublished letters from Captain Kenedy, the compelling story of Spike Kenedy and the killing of Dora Hand can be put together. The fight between Spike and Sheriff Jim Kelley in the Alhambra Saloon was on August 17, 1878. James returned to Dodge City on October 4 and shot at Sheriff Kelley's house, killing Dora by mistake. Mifflin did make two trips to Dodge City to come to the aid of his son. The first trip was after Spike's shooting. Mifflin arrived from Texas probably about October 21. A week later, on October 28, the doctor stated that Spike was well enough to be brought to trial. Spike was brought out of his cell and within a short time his case was dismissed for lack of evidence. Mifflin and his Texas rancher friends probably represented the majority of Dodge City's cattle business, and that also may have weighed significantly on the decision to release Spike.

On November 8, Mifflin was back at his Los Laureles Ranch in Texas and wrote his lawyer, Stephen Powers: "I expect to go north to see my mother about the middle of the month—I am only waiting for the arrival of my boy from Kansas—He has been tried and acquitted and will leave there about the tenth of this month—I hardly think he will leave at time stated as he is not as well as when tried."[51] It is a good possibility that James's serious wound had become infected or that he had encountered other complications.

While Mifflin and Petra were awaiting Santiago's return from Kansas they had a houseguest. On November 14, J. J. Cocke, the Cameron County surveyor, wrote to Mifflin, saying, "Since leaving your hospitable house I have almost entirely recovered from my sickness, thanks to your kind attention and that of Mrs. Kenedy and Mrs. Starck. I followed your instructions closely with regard to applying the same dies with which you kindly supplied one and the result was most beneficial—The directions you gave me about the road was very accurate and I had no difficulty whatever in regard to it, finding every point just as you explained to me and laid it down on the little sketch you gave me. I feel very much obliged to you for your kindness to me and shall always remember it with gratitude"[52] In spite of Petra's probable frantic worry over Santiago's condition in Kansas, she had been gracious to their guest. Petra once again had the opportunity to use her medicinal skills. She ran a hospitable home, and guests were always welcomed and well taken care of at Los Laureles. Nene (Vicenta) may well have come to stay with her mother, as they all worried about Santiago. First they worried whether he would be convicted and hanged for the murder. Next they worried for his safety in recovery from his wounds and on the road home. It was important for Nene to be at Los Laureles so she could also help her mother and provide companionship while Mifflin was away on his trip east visiting his mother. Mifflin was always careful to provide support for Petra, especially in times of stress, worry, and danger.

Finally, on November 25, Mifflin wrote Powers, "As I telegraphed you yesterday I leave for the north to Kansas City first thence may have to go to Dodge City thence to New York and Philadelphia and return via Washington City—hope to be able to make the trip in a month staying a week with my mother."[53]

On December 17, Mifflin was back in Dodge City, Kansas, and wrote to Powers in Brownsville about Santiago's grave condition:

> I am detained here by the dangerous illness of my son and cannot leave here until the Doctors know we are out of danger. I cannot send the funds to meet the final payment until I get to W. H. and I may be behind the time to pay—1st January next, you will please see that I do not suffer by a little delay—I will pay you in funds at the earliest possible moment.
>
> On my arrival at Kansas City, I met my cattleman Mr. Stevens and Dr. Tremaine, Post Surgeon at Fort Dodge who has attended my son, since he was brought in here 7th Oct. last wounded.
>
> I found that he was much worse than I anticipated. Tremaine desired to consult with another surgeon and I secured the services of Dr. B. E. Fryer medical Director of the Dept. of the Military of the Missouri.
>
> We came on here and as I did not consider him safe here in town and also at the suggestion of the surgeons, I moved him to the hospital at Fort Dodge from below here on the Arkansas.
>
> On the 11th they made an examination under Ether were afraid of chloroform and found head of left arm bone badly shattered. . . . They could not proceed with the examination as he was sinking fast. For some hours he was in a very critical condition and it was with great

difficulty he was reinstated. Several times we thought he was gone. He however recovered and looked bright and on the 14th the operation was concluded using the Ether carefully.

The upper end of arm bone was taken out at the socket and cut off five inches below. He lay ten hours hovering between life and death—the doctors never leaving him a moment and still is in a very critical condition. This evening they express confidence in his recovery but his arm may have to be taken off at shoulder. Eight or ten days will decide this matter—they wish to try every means to save his arm. I cannot leave until the doctors pronounce him out of danger—will leave for N.Y. then to pass a week with my mother, thence to Washington a day or two and home via W.N. soon as possible.[54]

Petra and Mifflin had a lot to be thankful for at the close of the year. James had escaped a conviction and death sentence in the murder of Dora Hand and had survived the near-fatal gunshot wound. He suffered life-long health problems from the injury, but he did heal and returned to them safely in Texas. Petra had come so close to losing another son this year, which would have made two in two years.

CHAPTER 16

1879–80:
Last Days at Los Laureles— The Laurel Leaf Ranch

The *Chester County, Pennsylvania, newspaper* published an article on January 8, 1879, reporting: "Mifflin Kenedy, who left Coatesville a poor boy in 1836, came back the other day to visit his aged mother. He owns a stocked farm of 132,000 acres in Texas and his possessions are estimated at $2,000,000."[1] Mifflin visited his mother and sister and then returned to Texas to find James at home, healing from his wounds.

While Mifflin was away, another tragedy struck the family. Petra's granddaughter, Fred and Vicenta's five-year-old daughter Daisy, was attending a parade on January 13 with her family. The maid let her leave her side and Daisy dashed out into the street and was killed under the wheels of a wagon. The maid was so distraught that she ran away and was never heard from again.[2] It is unknown if Vicenta had returned to her own home and was there when her daughter was killed or if she was still at Los Laureles with Petra. Either way it was a tragic loss for this young mother, her husband, and for the grandmother who had just experienced the near death of her son James.

Mifflin was back at Los Laureles writing Powers that he would not be able to come to court next term because it would be the time for gathering cattle for Kansas: "It will be injurious to me to be compelled to leave here at that time—I cannot see that my presence will do any good—if you need to take testimony can it be done here in Corpus."[3] By August, Mifflin had made an offer of settlement to the Rio Grande Railroad Co. and Mr. J. J. Gomila wrote on the fourteenth to say that they declined Captain Kenedy's offer.[4] The next

Early Texas Railroads

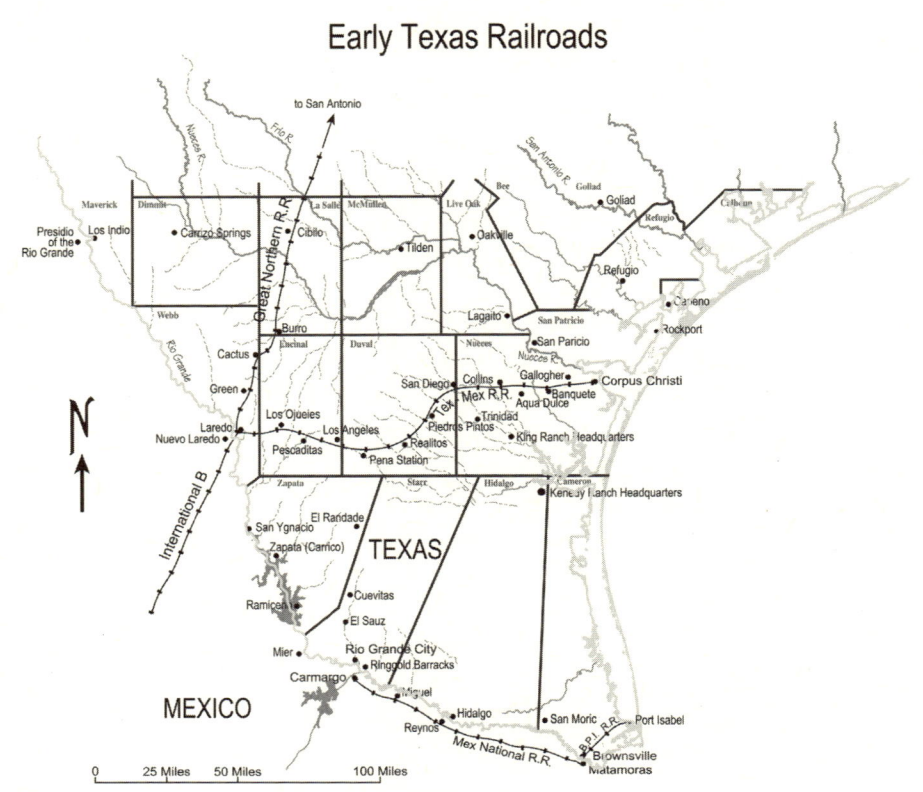

Early Texas railroads map. Nancy Tiller, cartographer.

day Mifflin countered by telegram and then on the sixteenth he again telegraphed, writing, "if the suit is not settled today it cannot then be settled except by the law. I don't want the law suit."[5] The parties apparently came to an agreement at last and on September 21 Mifflin wrote that he was "sending the deed for right of way to the RGRR signed by me and King."[6]

The year 1879 would see Mifflin settle his business with the Brownsville railroad, but his new Corpus railroad was demanding time, too. In February, Uriah Lott signed an agreement with Kenedy and King which gave them control of the railroad company in return for a capital infusion of $112,812.39. Mifflin took over the company's finances and went off to Wall Street to raise more money. He then instructed Lott to build the railroad to Laredo as fast as he could. Uriah was attempting to do just that and in August advertised for 150 laborers and seventy-five teamsters to start construction of the line, promising good wages to good men. In the meantime King began petitioning the general land office in Austin for state bonuses. By the end of the year, 855,680 acres had been granted to the railroad. Many of them wound up behind King's fences.[7]

Building the railroad provided an opportunity to earn a living for many of the cowboys who had lost their work as trail drivers. During the 1880s the work of the cowboy was less needed. The task of fencing was about over and fewer men were needed to handle the cattle. Many of the ranchers were using contractors to take their cattle up the trail. The work was becoming specialized; there were construction teams, roundup teams, and mending teams. On the ranches that employed both Anglo and Mexican hands, many of the Anglo hands were let go because they were paid one-half to two-thirds more than the Tejanos. Meanwhile, the railroads were beginning to change the face of South Texas. The railways would also facilitate production of cotton and other crops since they provided a way to get the produce to market.[8]

In the early 1880s, the little "Tex-Mex" railroad, as it was called, began to function as its owners had hoped. Cattle were loaded and shipped north through connecting lines. Collins Station was built along the line and was only twenty miles from the Santa Gertrudis headquarters and not far from Los Laureles.[9] The distance was a great deal shorter than the eleven hundred walking miles to Kansas. It would take a few years for the railroad cars to replace the trail drives but these small railroads introduced significant changes to the Wild Horse Desert.

Until the railroad was finished the ranching business went on as usual. In the spring, Captain King was preparing to send three herds of cattle to the Kansas market. On April 17, Mr. "Jap" Clark had already started up the road with one herd.[10] By summer the *Galveston Daily News* reported that King was fencing another fifty miles, making a total of 175 miles of fence enclosing 253,000 acres of choice grazing land. The paper also reported that Capt. M. Kenedy was going to "continue his fences across the Agua Dulce to connect with the mammoth pasture fences of his former partner, thus entirely shutting out from others all of what is termed the lower or coast country for a distance of 75 miles from Corpus."[11] The same newspaper reported in September that "Nueces county is one of the largest stock raising and wool growing counties of the state. The fact of the land's being owned in large bodies is seriously detrimental to the interest of its inhabitants and will retard its development until a new system is inaugurated. Richard King owns according to his assessment 236,288 acres of land, 24,000 cattle and 17,500 sheep and his total taxable value for 1880 is $379, 426. M. Kenedy with a total taxable value of $327,000, 225,730 acres of land and 24,000 head of sheep."[12]

Life on the ranches continued to be profitable as well as challenging for Kenedy and King. They dealt with the ups and downs of the cattle industry and everyday life on the tough terrain. In July the paper reported that the largest rattlesnake in the world was killed in the mountains near Brownwood, in central Texas. It was fourteen feet long and had forty-eight rattles.

Ranches, Nueces County, 1879

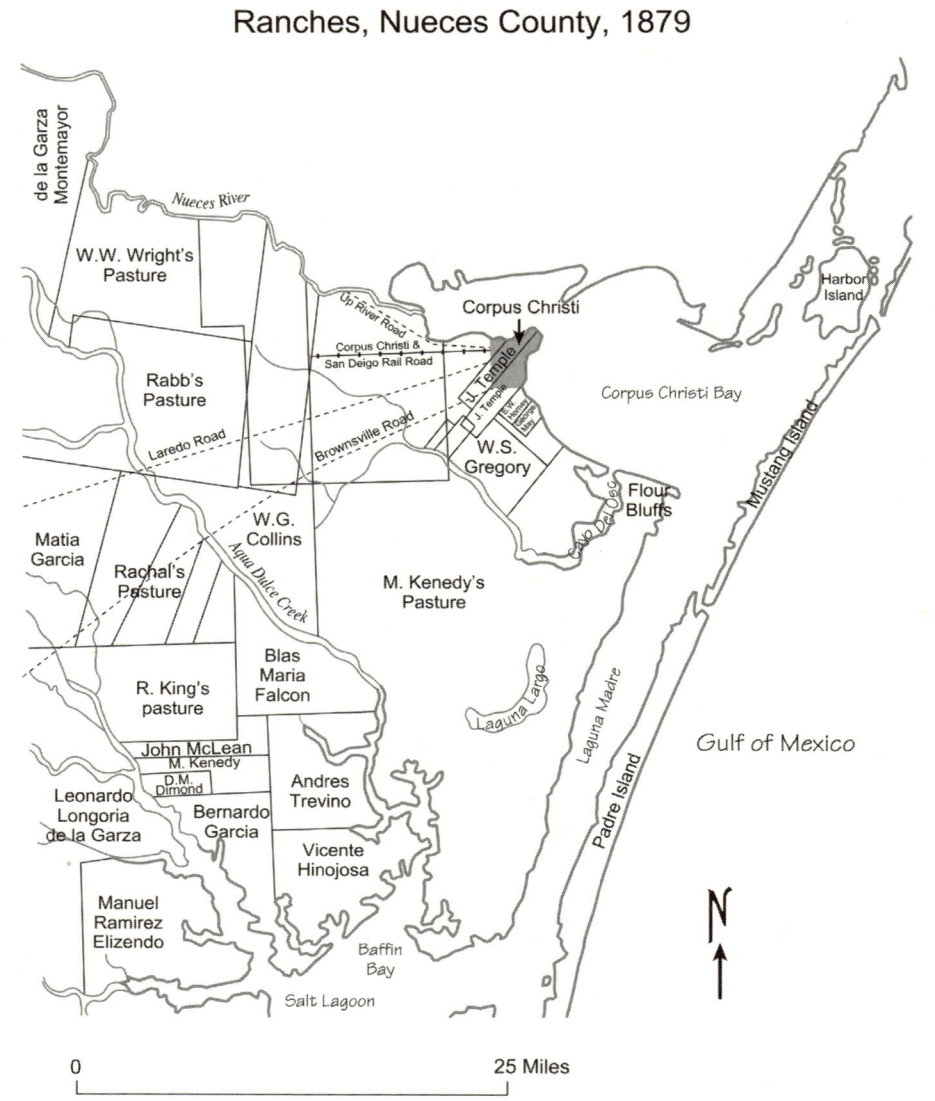

Ranches, Nueces County, 1879, map. Nancy Tiller, cartographer.

Although the rattlesnakes Kenedy and King and their vaqueros encountered daily were not that big, animals of prey and rattlers were constant hazards.[13] Weather was probably the most imminent threat to the ranchers because they could not control it. They were at its mercy. In August another hurricane hit Brownsville and Matamoros; afterward, the towns looked as if they had been hit by artillery fire. The buildings at Fort Brown were torn down and three hundred houses in Matamoros were demolished. The damage was estimated to be over $500,000. The *Galveston Daily News* reported that the storm had moved up through the Nueces Strip and that "the chaparral had been whipped to pieces by the hurricane and the low lands are all under water and [the number of] dead sheep and goats on the rancheros is large. A great deal of game has been killed and Mr. King lost seventeen fine jacks during the storm."[14]

At the end of the year the *Galveston Daily News* reported further about Captain King: "An accident occurred to Captain King last week ... which came near being fatal. At the Arroyo Colorado the entrance to the ferry is abrupt in the descent. Upon entering the stage pitched off the bank and threw Capt. King into the stream where he sank, the stage driver diving down and rescuing him."[15] Henrietta and the family were relieved that he survived the crash and had reason to feel blessed as they celebrated the New Year.

Mifflin always helped his family members when in need; in September he wrote to Powers to tell him that Manuel Rodríguez, his son-in-law, had been to see him in reference to getting some assistance to prosecute his cases against the Singer Manufacturing Company. Mifflin wrote, "I told him I could give him no assistance and no answer, until I was fairly posted of the situation and to hand the papers to you for reviewing. So, Judge, please review so you can give me your opinion when I go—I will be in Brownsville not later than Oct. 11. I desire to assist Rodríguez if he is in the right—He is very poor and has a large family."[16] Manuel and Concepción's wealth came after her mother's death and their inheritance from the settlement of Petra's estate.

The 1880 census provided information about the Kenedy family. In Corpus Christi, Dr. Arthur E. Spohn, physician, was thirty-four years old and was living with his wife Sarah J. Spohn, who was twenty-one (but by her birth date should be twenty-three) and they had a domestic servant, Eugenia Hernandez, who was twenty-four.[17]

The inhabitants of Rincón de Los Laureles, County of Nueces, State of Texas were enumerated on June 29, 1880. The following depicts a snapshot of the ranch Petra and Mifflin had lived on for eleven years. They had built the rancho from a very basic establishment to one of the largest ranches in the United States. The immediate family showed Mifflin Kenedy, sixty-one years old, married to Petra Vela who was fifty-four years old (should be fifty-six by real birth date). In the household were a son who was single, T. M. (Tom), who was twenty-six, and another son J. G. (John), twenty-three. John listed his occupation as sheep raiser. Tom listed his occupation as being on the ranch with the family.[18] It is interesting that James is not listed.

There were 168 people living on the ranch, including vaqueros, housekeepers, overseers, and five servants. T. H. (Thomas), forty-three, lived there and had a four-year-old son named Mifflin and a one-year-old daughter named Petra. They also had Isaac Hodges who was black, forty-six years old, and disabled. They had employed Mr. W. A. Walls, who was a white male twenty-eight years old and a widowed schoolmaster from Canada. The rancho contains 172,000 acres under fence and included more than twenty families of Mexican origin, with forty children.[19]

The census reveals how many people Petra supervised daily. Mifflin managed the ranch and the vaqueros, working with the stock. Petra's job was equally large, managing the domestic staff and their families. She had employed a schoolmaster, not for her children, who were all grown, but for the younger children under her care. She was responsible for the supplies, food preparation, gardens, slaughtering, repairs, and medical needs. They employed five servants to take care of the household needs and multiple cooks to prepare meals. A boatman hauled materials back and forth from the boats that came in through the Gulf of Mexico. Los Laureles was a large operation and kept Petra busy. For instance, in July Mifflin wrote to King to let him know that King's cousins had arrived at the ranch about 3 P.M. and that he had not arrived until about 9 P.M. He told him that Mrs. K. had gone to Corpus to hunt for a cook and sent her regards to Mrs. King, the young ladies, and gentleman.[20] Petra had the staff trained well so they were very capable of receiving guests in her absence.

Workdays on the ranch were long and hard for both the women and men. Kenedy family members, all involved in their own management tasks, and the ranch helpers, worked from daylight to evening. The ranching families did stop work for celebrations throughout the year, though, and most of these were religious holidays. Petra had celebrated these holidays all her life and knew that they were woven into the fabric of home for the Kenedeños ("Kenedy's men") and their families. The religious festivals included the celebrations of Santiago (St. James Day) on July 25, Día de Santa Ana on July 26, St. Peter's Day on August 2, el Día de la Santa Cruz on September 14, All Saints' Day on November 1, All Souls' Day on November 2, and on December 12 the Día de Nuestra Señora de Guadalupe. Most of these holidays were not observed with time off for the ranching families unless a visiting priest was present. In contrast, the days between Christmas and New Year were usually a time of rest for all.[21] The children particularly looked forward to Los Pastores, the story of the shepherds coming to worship the Holy Mother and the Christ child, a Spanish medieval play brought to Texas by priests.[22] These activities must have reminded Petra of her childhood. She provided both religious and academic education for all the children living at the ranch.

Petra had a special coach for her frequent trips back and forth to Corpus

Christi. It was called a "mud wagon," specifically constructed to travel the dusty and sometimes muddy roads. The heavy-duty passenger coach was durable and, in Petra's case, beautiful; this was no ordinary coach. Petra's coach bore her personal crest with her monogrammed initials. This impressive crest also adorned her European china. Mifflin saw to it that Petra had the best of whatever she needed.[23]

Neither Petra and Mifflin nor Henrietta and Richard had ever entertained much or attended society events. Even in Brownsville they had chosen a more personal and close life for their families. This was not the case for some of the other big cattle ranchers. On July 14 a celebration was held at the new Chiltipin Mansion in San Patricio County on Coleman Fulton Pasture Co. land, as reported:

> It is a four-story structure that has taken five years to construct at a cost of $150,000, and is to be thrown open to neighbors and friends. Many guests will spend the night and have brought along an elaborate change of costume for the evening festivities. Some of the ladies' gowns have been ordered . . . from the most exclusive Fifth Avenue shops. The front gate is a mile from the front door. This enormous expanse is a carpet of green grass . . . and imported shrubs and flowers. The word "Chiltipin" has been blocked out . . . by the head English gardener and his five Mexican assistants. There is a wrought-iron fountain surrounded by Duchess de Brabant roses. . . . The driveway is lined with cedars, magnolias, palms, and a privet hedge. Peacocks spread their gorgeous tail feathers. . . . The handsome woodwork . . . the exquisite hand carved marble mantels from New Orleans. . . . The ornate ebony and walnut furniture from New York. [There are] stables [with] a magnificent Kentucky stallion, [and] Jersey cows, hogs, sheep, guinea hens, turkeys, and chickens and the kennels of greyhounds for coon and wildcat hunting. [They have] a blacksmith shop, smokehouse, the dairy, and cement reservoir. They play billiards in the billiard room and sip mint juleps. . . . [They served] barbecued meats, spiced with Chiltipin pepper sauce, enormous trays of grapes, . . . peaches, . . . figs, and plums. . . . The young and old danced on a twelve foot wide cement terrace that completely surrounds the mansion. Two bands furnish music: a Mexican orchestra . . . and Favella's Italian string band from Corpus Christi.[24]

This was a dazzling tribute to the astonishing wealth credited to the sovereigns of the Cattle Kingdom.

Corpus Christi was growing and prospering. The city was attempting to protect its citizens from the dreaded fevers that continued to plague the area. A new ordinance forbade any owner, driver, conductor, or anyone in charge of stage, railroad, or public conveyance to carry anyone sick unless they contracted the illness on the way, and any inn, hotel, tavern, or boarding or lodging house should report afflicted persons within six hours. All physicians were to report them in six hours to the City Health Office.[25]

Mifflin and the employees of Los Laureles were involved with Corpus politics. Mifflin well understood the value of political control, and he always was a part of the political structure wherever he put his roots down. On November 3 the newspaper reported about the elections held the day before:

> Yesterday's election—Beyond the display of a few flags from the store doors, decoration of hacks, delivery wagons and drays in a similar manner there was nothing to indicate the deep feeling which actuated voters. Some trouble was at first experienced in securing clerks for all of the polls but by half past nine all were supplied and voting commenced. Bar rooms were all closed, which effectually barred any unpleasantness from the too free use of the ardent, the bane of election days usually. In the early part of the day, crowds were predominately around the voting places on the bluff but by ten o'clock the arrival of the Kenedy club of 43 members gave to the third ward where they were voted, the air of being the only poll in the city. These voters were accompanied from the Laureles rancho by their employer Capt. M. Kenedy who in person superintended the deposit of their votes. It is the first instance within our recollection that this gentleman has taken so great an interest in election matters, and is indicative of an appreciation of the necessity for more general attention to the selection of local officers. The day passed off quietly.[26]

Mifflin and Petra had made a decision that would affect not only their life but also that of Corpus Christi itself. They moved into town and became a part of Corpus Christi's business and social life. In August an advertisement ran in the newspaper: "Valuable Property for Sale: My residence on the Bluff with two or four lots of ground. The house has nine large size rooms with five brick fireplaces all in perfect order. Brick and front galleries and large underground cistern. D. Dowd."[27] On October 17 the paper announced that "Captain Kenedy has bought the property of D. Dowd on the bluff at a good round figure. We are glad that the Captain is going to be a citizen of Corpus." The paper also reported that Dr. Spohn and Sarah were back in town.[28] Mifflin and Petra were soon to enter into a new phase of their life. From the defined and structured life at the ranch they were going to move into the fluid society of Corpus Christi. Petra knew she was facing health issues, which may be one of the reasons Mifflin wanted to be in Corpus Christi. The move was particularly difficult for Petra because most of her family except for Sarah and sometimes John had settled in and around Brownsville. It seemed she continued to move farther and farther away from her family and her native land of Mexico.

CHAPTER 17

1881:
To the Body of Christ—Corpus Christi

Petra had lived at Los Laureles for eleven years. She loved the land and the cattle. She enjoyed the changing landscape, the plants and the animals. She had grown up on similar land and she was at home at Los Laureles. In the next year she would be moving to town and meeting the challenges of adapting to new friends, to a new home, and a new church. Her heart longed to be back in Brownsville and near her daughters and her grandchildren. Spanish was the language of the ranch and in the family. In Corpus Christi there would be more English expected and used. Petra was fifty-six years old and in poor health. Change came with difficulty and her energy was slowly being drained. Her children were now grown and profiting each in their own way. She wanted some quiet days with Mifflin to share memories of the past and to cherish the present. Petra knew in her heart that the move to Corpus Christi would place more demands on Mifflin's time and that she would see him less. Sarah and Dr. Spohn were there and she would see them more often but they were busy with his medical practice and the Corpus Christi social life. Petra had never enjoyed the social scene, except for church activities. When she moved to Corpus she would again make valuable contributions to her church, and that legacy would continue even after her lifetime. Mifflin carried on her passion for caring for the poor and needy even after her death. In a letter to John written on August 8, 1892, Mifflin wrote that he had been feeding fifty to one hundred people weekly for over six months, through the convent in Corpus Christi.[1] Petra's sons would still be nearby working at the ranch, but her other daughters would be even farther away. There were no grandchildren near Corpus Christi because Tom, James, and John had not yet married and Sarah did not have any children. Her grandchildren were all in

Brownsville so she would not be able to see them as much, watch them grow, or hold them on her lap. With sadness she faced the changes 1881 would bring.

For Mifflin, 1881 was one of the most exciting years ever. His dream of completing the railroad was nearly realized and he looked forward to moving to Corpus Christi. Located on a high bluff, Corpus Christi overlooked a bay that connected to the Gulf of Mexico. In the next four years it would grow to 4,200 citizens. There would be three banks, a customs house, railroad machine shops, an ice factory, carriage factories, several hotels, and Episcopal, Presbyterian, Methodist, Catholic, and Baptist churches.[2] Mifflin had seen the opportunities that Corpus Christi presented and had begun to focus his efforts in its direction. He was ready to make the move and he would soon be an integral part of Corpus Christi's economic changes. He welcomed the challenges ahead and the possibilities for him and his family.

In January, Mifflin and Lott were having difficulty establishing the location of their railroad terminal along the Rio Grande. Laredo was their first choice but the negotiations proved problematic. They went to Laredo in January to see if they could finalize the proposal.[3] The negotiation did not go well at first and on the nineteenth a telegraphic dispatch announced that Lott, King, and Kenedy were having surveyors look at Rio Grande City to see about locating the terminus there because they could not come to terms with Laredo.[4] The negotiations finally were satisfactory to both sides and Laredo became the terminus for the railroad. In the meantime the principal merchants and representatives of the railroad met in Corpus Christi at the Wharf Co. office on the sixteenth to discuss railroad business.[5]

By February news was circulating that the parties holding large interest in the Wharf Stock and Ship Channel were going to sell out to the Palmer-Sullivan Co. and were also looking at buying the Corpus Christi, San Diego, and Rio Grande narrow gauge railroad. This would make a complete package for Mifflin, King, and Lott to offer the eastern investors. They could bring their trade products into Corpus, offload on their own wharf, place them on their railroad to Laredo, and then join up with the Mexican National Railroad there and ship directly into Mexico. On February 27, the newspaper stated, "if all this goes through with the port and road, we must have a great attitude and encourage enterprise and trade to come here."[6]

The economic benefits were boundless, but the wagon and cart industry was against it and afraid that large unemployment would occur if this new transportation system came to Corpus Christi. In April, Mifflin, Lott, and King had arranged everything and Kenedy and Lott sailed for New York. "This time they did not go to beg for money from Wall Street but to cash in their chips. Kenedy negotiated the sale of the narrow gauge railroad to [Jay]

The Texas-Mexican Railroad engine #19.

Gould's arch rival, General William Jackson Palmer, president of the Denver & Rio Grande Railroad, in a cash and stock transaction valued at $5,000,000. Upon closing, Kenedy, King, and Lott took a profit of $483,174.52."[7] Under new ownership, the Texas-Mexican Railway Co. pushed into Laredo on September 1, weeks ahead of their competition, Gould's I. & G. N. Palmer, the new owner of the Texas-Mexican Railway Co., tied his property to the Mexican National Line that is still in operation today. "Mifflin, King and Lott had outflanked their Brownsville rivals. In just one year the new trade route channeled the bulk of the Mexican trade away from Matamoros-Brownsville to Laredo-Corpus Christi, two hundred miles northward. The Brownsville area receded into isolation and recession, which lasted the final twenty years of the nineteenth century."[8]

"Triumphant, Kenedy, King, and Lott were the men of the hour in Corpus Christi. Parties abounded. When the line was completed, General Palmer hosted a gala and toasted the trio: 'Your efforts in the prosecution of the enterprise are unsurpassed in the history of railroad building. Men who can do as much on a little are greatly in the minority.'" The paper announced, "fried oysters were in abundance and the affair closed amid good cheer and the music of champagne corks."[9]

Lott, who for six years had served as promoter, builder, and manager of the narrow gauge, was presented a silver tea service of seventy pieces. He in turn presented King with a bronze sculpture of a ferocious pit bulldog, honoring perhaps the pugnacious tenacity of his mentor.[10] Lott presented Mifflin with a wood and brass telescope inscribed, "Presented to Captain M. Kenedy, Corpus Christi, Texas by his friend U. Lott." This may well have represented the long-range vision Mifflin brought to his many projects. Mr. Lott knew Kenedy and King well, and both gifts seem to reflect the personalities of these unique Texans. Petra was also caught up in the moment and presented Mrs. Lott with a diamond ring, which Mrs. Lott later sold to the Starr's Co. in New York when they fell on hard times.[11]

Not everyone was thrilled about the completion of the railroad in Corpus Christi. Bishop Manucy had started construction on a new church in Corpus Christi the year before reporting that the material was on the ground and the work had begun. In 1881 he reported, "Work on the church progressed slowly, but funds came in still more slowly. A year after the work on the edifice started, the railroad from Corpus Christi to Laredo was finished. This deprived our city of trains of wagons which up until this time came from the interior and provided a living to retail merchants."[12]

Even though Bishop Manucy was depressed over the slow progress of the Corpus Christi church, he was still ministering to the many ranchos spread over the Wild Horse Desert. Two years before he had set about in September to visit about eighty ranches, which he figured would take him over two months. He had left Corpus Christi, accompanied by Father Parisot, with an ambulance loaded with ten or twelve boxes, trunks, and an invalid driver. It took two mules to draw the heavy vehicle through the sand and mud. They had a terrible time traveling and were stuck nearly every day. Father Jalliet and Father Bretault joined them at different ranchos, preparing for confirmations when they arrived.[13]

Bishop Manucy loved to hunt and was an excellent shot. With his old fashioned muzzle-loading musket he almost never missed a shot. He provided meat for the next meal and any extra was shared with parishioners along the way. Sleeping spots were hard to find. At one stop they slept in a schoolhouse with the bishop sleeping on a table two feet shorter than he was and the two priests on school benches. The day before reaching Las Palomas ranch, Father Bretault had gone ahead and prepared the people for the reception of the Sacrament of Confirmation. The people had constructed an altar and decorated it with wildflowers. The bishop's splendid attire impressed them. The older people received communion and the younger children were baptized. From that ranch the clergymen moved on to the ranch of don Juan McAllen. Doña Salomé welcomed them, and they felt like they were back in civilization. That night they slept in soft, clean beds.[14]

When Father Bretault went out ahead to prepare the people to take communion at the various ranchos, he would ask them how long it had been since they last took communion. He would often get answers like, "since the coming of the Yankees," "since the siege of Matamoros," or "since the great fire."[15] One of the fathers' best receptions was at Los Federales ranch. The people there arranged handkerchiefs on long poles along the fences to look like flags. They made a triumphal arch from flowers and green branches. The women were grinding corn for tortillas and they were roasting a kid. A large tent made from hide and blankets sheltered an altar covered with a silk shawl. The altar was decorated with wildflowers and individual small clay saints that had been handed down from one generation to another in the families. Along the walls of the tent hung pictures of steam engines, birds, horses, cows, sheep, goats, and any animal they could find a depiction of; most of the pictures came from newspapers and fashion journals. The service was held and then supper was served with hot tortillas, roast kid, baked chickens, eggs, hot coffee, and rich milk. The feast was good enough for a king.[16]

Although Kenedy and King were busy with the railroad, they still had large ranches to manage. The cattle business was now difficult; one major problem the ranchers faced was drought. All over the Wild Horse Desert the grass was turning brown and the watering holes were drying up. The market for cattle was good but the production was difficult. The very fences that Mifflin and King prided themselves on were now getting in their way; ranchers along the northern routes to Kansas began to also fence their land. Trail bosses were forced to take longer and longer detours, which cost them time and money.[17]

The other problem Texas ranchers faced was a disease called "Texas Fever." No one knew what caused it, but it seemed to arrive at the northern markets when the southern herds appeared at the railheads. In order to protect their own cattle, ranchers along the way would meet the herds with armed guards, forcing them to detour farther around their land. Some of the markets would only accept Texas cattle when there was frost on the ground. A continuing problem was the drought, and both Mifflin and King began to look about them to buy more land that had good water on it.[18]

Mifflin and King continued to up-breed their cattle, hoping to produce cattle that were more marketable. The *Galveston Daily News* reported on January 23, 1881, "the vast herds which heretofore roamed the expanseless [sic] prairies have been considerably thinned out by the continuous annual drives to Kansas and other places. But what they lack in quantity they make up in quality. The continual grading of the longhorn with the best of Durhams, Devonshires, and Herefords had greatly improved the native breed. The building of large pastures throughout the south and west has had a tendency to correct many evils that existed among cattle raisers and improving cattle."[19]

Captain Kenedy and his son John continued to try to improve their stock. Faustino and Guadalupe Morales said that Captain Kenedy had bulls shipped into Alice, where they were picked up from the train and hauled in carts to the ranch. They brought in white-faced cattle and later the red cattle and Brahmas; they slowly got rid of the Mexican longhorns. The native Mexican horses were small and they crossbred them to get larger horses.[20]

As if the drought were not enough to fight, the dry conditions produced fire hazards, which is exactly what Captain King had to face at the end of January. An extensive fire at the Santa Gertrudis burned immense haystacks, destroying several hundred tons of hay that he was storing for winter feeding. He also lost his hay baling equipment. The smoke from the fire was so great it could be seen from Corpus Christi. Many of the older settlers were saying that this was the worst winter ever known in Texas.[21]

Kenedy and King still planned to send cattle north in a spring drive. On March 30, the newspaper reported, "Monday morning a number of cow men were in the city preparing for the Kansas trail. They left the same day for Los Laureles, Captain M. Kenedy's rancho, from which they will leave in about two weeks to take the trail. Six thousand head will go up the western trail under Uncle Henry Stevens."[22] Captain King's recommendation to Mifflin about Stevens had been a good one, and not only had Mifflin continued to trust him with his cattle but he had also asked him to look after James after he had been shot in Kansas.

Young Robert Kleberg, who would marry Alice King and eventually run King Ranch after King's death, wrote a letter to his mother on July 24, 1881, that gave a delightful view of both Captain King and the ranch:

> Captain King had written to come out to see him and to name the day and he would meet me at the road as he lives about eighteen miles from the railroad so I went on the railroad and found him waiting for me at the depot with his carriage. He runs a regular wagon to the depot daily to bring in his mail and supplies but it had no seats. He said his carriage would be there if I notified him. We had a delightful trip out to his ranch—he drove a pair of fine fast horses and in two hours we were at this ranch. He had plenty of ice, wine, and cigars so the heat did not bother us much. At the ranch a table was loaded with good things to eat and drink; he lives like a prince and has a regular French cook. He treats his friends to the best he has. I stayed at his house from Monday until Saturday morning. We rode all day and he showed me his land. He has 1,000,000 acres of land. Near the lakes where the cattle come to drink could be seen as many as 3,000 head at a time. On Saturday morning he set me back to the R.R. depot and furnished with suitable wine and ice on the way. He wants us to attend his legal business for him and I hope we are to find it remunerative.[23]

Cattle were not the only livestock raised in the area. Sheep also had a significant market. Between 1870 and 1880 Corpus Christi was the center of the wool market. But the growth of the cattle industry had the greatest impact in the 1880s, with Corpus Christi becoming an important shipping point for cattle. The city saw the growth of packinghouses, stockyards, and markets for hides, tallow, and other products.[24] King raised sheep and reported in February of 1881 that he had not lost 2,000 head as rumored but more like six hundred head.[25] In July he was able to bring 166 bags of wool to market.[26] John Kenedy had also gone into the sheep business in 1878 and in 1881 decided to sell out to Uriah Lott and J. P. Wilson.[27]

Mifflin, always the businessman, had begun to look for a better and larger ranch than Los Laureles. He had been circulating the news that he would entertain a good price on the ranch and in the meantime had been looking for a suitable ranch to buy in its place. After the sale of the railroad, Mifflin had enough money to make a change. He wanted to sell Los Laureles and buy another ranch with water, which was critical in these times of drought. Mifflin decided to purchase La Parra Ranch.

La Parra was called the "Grapevine Ranch" because of the large grapevines found on it. This ranch was located in the "sands" and was much closer to the coast than Los Laureles. Mifflin would fence all 400,000 acres of this ranch and make it his home base for his cattle operations.[28] On October 19, Mifflin telegraphed Powers to purchase La Parra, San Pedro de las Nietas, Palmito, Mirasoles and La Barretta. La Parra was available at $2,000 per league or 45 cents per acre—$9,840. Mifflin told him to get La Parra because it was the key to all others.[29] On October 29, Kenedy again telegraphed Powers, "La Parra is worth double of the surrounding lands because it has water."[30]

When Mifflin acquired La Parra and fenced it he had the second largest pasture in the United States. On October 29, Mifflin wrote to Powers and Wells to tell them to "buy two leagues in the La Parra at $2,000 if they can as it is the key. Very important to secure Rafael Cisneros and Doña Eulalia—don't fail with them. Now La Parra is the key to all the surrounding lands—$2,000 a league is entirely too much, but as we are now into it, we must buy the balance of the La Parra at the best figures one can, and as soon as possible. In fact the purchase of all ought to be pushed as fast as possible, for as soon as it becomes known I am buying lands will rise."[31] Mifflin was able to purchase La Parra but not without controversy and problems with the surrounding landowners.

The year ended with an extravagant excursion organized by Mifflin, Lott, and King to celebrate the success of their new railroad venture. A ride along the newly constructed railroad to Laredo was organized for the men in the community. The event had been scheduled for September 22 but was postponed because of President James Garfield's death. On September 27, everything was ready. There were 150 invitations issued for the trip from Corpus Christi to Laredo, returning the next day. The coveted invitations included bankers, merchants, doctors, lawyers, judges, scientists, and bishops as well as preachers, deacons, and vestrymen. The well-equipped train included a boxcar loaded with all the necessary ingredients for a pleasurable time. The day dawned bright and hot and the participants decided that a barrel of cold lemonade should be made for the trip. The Roman Punch, as it was called, consisted of lemons, pineapples, and other fruit juices, and additions that were made when Mr. Turner and his group left the beverage to go into the other cars. Someone poured three gallons of Rose Bud (bourbon) and twelve quarts of Champagne into the brew and by the time the train reached its destination all were having a "gleeful" time.[32]

Robert Kleberg, in a letter to his sister, said that the guests were provided with plenty to eat and drink. He said they had over two thousand cigars, forty baskets of champagne, and many other types of liquors. Dr. Spohn played the drums and the Corpus Quartet sang. Robert Kleberg said that when they pulled into Laredo quite a crowd had assembled for the arrival.[33] This trip had been the talk of Texas. Kenedy and King were known throughout the state.

Mifflin looked forward to the New Year and to establishing his new ranch. Petra was busy organizing the move to her new home in Corpus Christi. She already knew that this house would be a temporary one because Mifflin planned to build her one of the finest houses in Texas. The paper reported, "Capt. M. Kenedy has purchased the homestead of M. S. Culver on the bluff south of the railroad depot, for the sum of $25,000. It is one of the few remaining desirable building sites for field slices in the City, and its purchase by the gentleman named cannot fail to be interpreted as a good omen for the future. The confidence thereby manifested should lend encouragement to the weak and faltering."[34] The next few years would be full of plans for their new ranch and their new house. Petra had everything to look forward to and yet perhaps deep within herself she feared she was moving into an alien and unfamiliar world where her future was unsure.

Chapter 18

1882:
La Parra—The Grapevine Ranch

1882 *saw the continuation of the 1881 drought.* There was less water and less grass. Things were not well at the Santa Gertrudis rancho. Young Bland Chamberlain, Henrietta's half brother, was working a pasture in the stifling heat and came down with a fever. Although immediately taken to headquarters, he grew steadily worse. The young man was delirious; he asked for Captain King, who had been like a father to him. When King arrived he walked to the young man's bedside and said, "Bland, do you know who this is?" "Yes," Bland replied, "*El Cojo*" ("the lame one"), and died. That summer Captain King himself was feeling poorly. He stayed tired for too long and could not be refreshed by sleep. His stomach hurt and it was hard to swallow. He had lost his hearty appetite and pain continued most of the time. To kill the pain the Captain used whiskey. He kept on going because he had no other choice, but he knew that something was wrong.[1]

Mifflin, meanwhile, was well and hardy and moving along with plans for his new ranch. He sold Los Laureles to a syndicate from Dundee, Scotland, known as the Texas Land & Cattle Co., Ltd. for $1,100,000 in cash.[2] The ranch consisted of 242,000 fenced acres, 50,000 head of cattle, and 5,000 head of horses, mares, and mules.[3] He had finalized his purchase of La Parra—the Grapevine Ranch—and was busy fencing all 400,000 acres. Care of the ranch was entrusted to sixty men, except during the roundups and other times of need. Part of the ranch was located in the "sands"—sand dunes along the coast of Baffin Bay.[4]

Mifflin's new ranch was twice as big as his previous one, and it had water, which was the most precious asset on the Wild Horse Desert. On March 10, 1882, he formed the Kenedy Pasture Co. He put all the land at La Parra, as well as its cattle and horses into the corporation. He put his holdings at $900,000.

LA PARRA

The first "steamboat" house at La Parra, built on the highest ground at thirty-seven feet above sea level. The house contained four bedrooms: two bedrooms downstairs off the living room and two bedrooms upstairs. Santiago was the first Kenedy to occupy the house and Thomas and John would come and go. Neither Mifflin nor Petra actually lived in this house. Eventually John moved in and took over the ranching operation and probably brought his bride, Marie Stella Turcotte, here to live. This house was later moved three hundred yards to the east when the present house was built. Courtesy Kenedy Pasture Co. Museum, Sarita, Texas.

Each share was worth $1,000 and Mifflin had 96 shares; each of his boys, Tom, James, and John, had one share; and Edwin Mallory, Mifflin's secretary, had one share.[5] The corporation's board of directors included Mifflin Kenedy, Thomas Kenedy, James W. Kenedy, John G. Kenedy, and Edwin Mallory. James was general manager in charge of the operations.[6] Mifflin put his sons on the payroll and expected all of them to help get the family business started. According to the Kenedy Pasture Co. 1882 ledger book, James Kenedy, from February 1 to October 1, was paid a salary of $50 a month. It appears that by October 1 he had accumulated $405 to his credit but in six weeks time, by November 24, he only had $49.15 left. Tom and John were not officially on the payroll until the following year, 1883. The working hands, though, were hired from $12 to $15 per month.[7] The vaqueros' compensation often included lodging and some sort of rationing.[8]

The original La Parra consisted of 23,000 acres; Mifflin soon bought the other Spanish grants contiguous to La Parra. The ten or twelve Spanish grants amounted to close to 440,000 acres and came to be called the Kenedy Ranch. Mifflin moved to build his ranch headquarters at La Parra and chose the exact spot for the ranch house. He chose the highest sand dune, some thirty-seven feet above sea level, where he could see for miles in any direction. Being a man of the sea and a former captain he knew the importance of high ground. The house had four bedrooms, two upstairs and two down, off the living room. The front entrance to the house had a large veranda on the first and second floors. When viewed from the front the house resembled the side of a double-decked riverboat, recalling Mifflin's past. At the time he built the house he also constructed a bunkhouse, barns, carriage houses, dairy, and commissary. James was probably the first family member to occupy the house, as Thomas and John came and went. John moved in when he took over the ranch operations due to James's illness and probably brought Marie Stella there as a new bride. It seems that Petra probably never even saw La Parra due to her illness. Mifflin stayed on occasion when he had ranch business to attend to.[9]

Petra had already become involved with the Corpus Christi church before she made the official move to town. In 1882, Bishop Manucy wrote in more cheerful tones to the Propagation of the Faith:

> The English speaking Catholics of Corpus Christi contributed fully according to their means, but their contributions were far from covering the expense. A Protestant gave three bells, an organ, and the fresco painting that decorated the ceiling. He had contributed over 21,000 francs—more than all the Catholics, who are mostly poor, put in all together. The Church as it stands cost about 75,000 francs ($18,000). . . . The Protestant whom the Bishop writes about was Captain Mifflin Kenedy who had settled at Laureles ranch near Corpus Christi. . . . When he heard that the work had been halted on the church for lack of funds, he and his wife gave not only the items mentioned above, but the amount necessary to finish the building. He had married Petra Vela. . . . She was a friend of the poor and humble, and no one ever left her empty-handed. She gave for the pure and unalloyed happiness she felt in giving. No doubt Mrs. Kenedy exercised a great influence on her husband in the contributions he made toward the Catholic Church in Corpus Christi. They were also generous friends and benefactors of Incarnate Word Convent.[10]

Petra's bells at the church were rung for the first time on Christmas Eve of the year before. She and Mifflin were proud of them, yet little did they know that the next time they would be rung would be in honor of a dear friend upon his death. On February 5, 1882, Judge Stephen Powers died in his home in Brownsville. He was serving as state senator at the time of his death. Powers had come to Texas with General Zachary Taylor in 1847. He moved to Brownsville after the war and along with his law partner, James B. Wells, played a key role in settling land titles and disputed areas between the Nueces and Rio Grande. He had served in numerous elected positions and was a driving force in the Democratic politics along the border.[11] Not only was he an accomplished lawyer and politician but he was also a very good friend of Petra and Mifflin. He handled their legal affairs and also lived near them in Brownsville. Petra was especially fond of him and his family.

Mifflin wrote to his law partner James Wells on February 12, "The death of Judge Powers has cast a gloom or spell over his friends, I am satisfied the same as myself, that they can handle account for—May God pardon his Transgressions is the prayer of a true friend. Please convey my condolences to his family. . . . The Bells, a duplicate of those in Brownsville in the Catholic Church Mrs. Kenedy presented to the Cathedral here and which were rung for the first time last Christmas Eve were rung the second time on February 6 tolling a solemn requiem for our departed friend at 4 P.M. by request of Mrs. Kenedy."[12] Captain King expressed his sentiments also to James Wells, "It is with great regret I learn from Captain M. Kenedy's telegram and your kind letter that my old and true friend Judge Powers has left us which is a great loss to all of us. You must double your energy in all particulars and take his place and stick in all matters which you fill my dear friend's place. There is not a man in this State, less yourself, misses him more than myself. God bless him and his dear family."[13]

King did not let dust accumulate under his feet; he immediately went to Brownsville to make arrangements for Wells to take over his legal work. He arranged for Francisco Ytúrria and Wells to have his power of attorney, enabling them to draw on his account when needed. Wells asked King how

Stephen Powers arrived on the Rio Grande with General Taylor's army and stayed to settle down in Brownsville. He practiced law, becoming an expert in Spanish land grants. Petra was particularly fond of Powers and, upon hearing of his death, had the bells, which had been donated to the church in Corpus Christi by her family, rung for him. Brownsville Historical Association.

often he should report his progress, and King replied, "Young man, the only thing I want to hear from you is when I can move my fences."[14]

King had also realized more than a year before that he needed additional representation in Corpus Christi. During a trespassing case held there, the opposition lawyer, Robert Justus Kleberg, who beat them in court, impressed him.[15] Kleberg was a junior partner in the law firm of Stayton & Lackey in Victoria and had been sent to Corpus Christi to open a branch office for the firm. King hired Kleberg on a case-by-case basis. Kleberg would loom large in the King family in later years. Henrietta King would hire Kleberg in 1886 on a $5,000 retainer to manage her interests, upon the advice and counsel of Mifflin Kenedy.[16]

Mifflin turned to his son James as his general manager to get La Parra into shape. By May, Mifflin was writing James to send him descriptions and drawings of the structures to be built on the ranch. He wanted wood sheds on the north line of fence and wanted them 36 × 8 feet high back and 12 feet high front.[17] A stickler for details, in June Mifflin wrote Captain Hawley, who was working at the ranch, to be sure the fence had two coats of tar. On the same day he wrote to James telling him that he planned to drive 2,800 cattle north from La Parra.[18] A couple of days later, Mifflin wrote James concerning additional buildings he wanted erected. He reminded him to put lightning rods on the barn and caporal houses. He wanted a chicken house built before Frank left and had materials and hands to do it. It needed to be 50 feet long, 12 or 14 feet wide, 10 feet high; tarred planks were to be nailed all around the outside and under the sills. He also wanted a wagon shed 75 feet long, or the same length of the barn, which was 12 feet wide and 8 to 9 feet high, constructed next to the North barn.[19] Interestingly, Mifflin changed the style in which he addressed James in his letters from these early letters. His later addresses went from "to James Kenedy General Manager" to more affectionate salutations.

July was a busy month for Mifflin because he was preparing to visit his mother in Pennsylvania. Petra and her daughter María Vicenta Starck (Nene) were traveling with him. Nene was close to Petra and a great comfort to her. She was there when her mother had health problems or other needs. During the preparations for travel, Mifflin wrote James because he was concerned about the little or no increase of yearlings since last year. He wanted to know, "Where are they?" It was a good question.[20] Mifflin also wrote to Nene's husband, Fred Starck, in Brownsville to be sure that he recorded the deeds to the Kenedy Pasture Company and then mailed them back to him.[21]

On July 7 Mifflin left final instructions with James. He advised him to purchase Cisneros Hinojosa's cattle even if he had to pay as high as $13 per head. He also reminded him if he did purchase them to let Mr. Mallory know so he could place the proper funds with Francisco Ytúrria to meet the draft. He wanted all purchases made in the name of the Kenedy Pasture Co., as it was fully organized. He told him to sign his name as general manager and that he should have enough for this purchase and maybe a few yearlings but to wait on all other purchases until he returned. He told him to send all communication through Mr. Mallory. He added that James had better get the lumber off the beach in case of high water, as it might be lost.[22]

On July 14, James received a letter from Mr. Mallory informing him that his father, mother, and Mrs. Starck had departed Corpus Christi on Tuesday morning by railroad. He also enclosed a letter from John regarding the herd and said he would send all the information he received to him.[23] It may be that John took the cattle up the road and the letter is regarding that herd and its sale in Kansas. A week later the *Galveston Daily News* ran an article by Edmond called "A Texas Stock Rancho—The Kenedy Pasture the Largest in the United States." The article gave an excellent description of La Parra:

> Corpus Christi, July 17, 1882—at 5 o'clock in the morning of the 4th I got aboard the schooner *Night Hawk* bound to Pasadisa Landing, 70 miles down West Bay. In three hours we reached Flour Bluff a distance of 28 miles. Here we found six schooners loaded with fence posts to take to the rancho. There was only about 18 inches of water on the flats so it was slow going and the posts were put on barges and towed over. These flats for about 16 miles are covered with a thick coat of green that grows under the water. The grass will die and float to the shore where it admits an offensive odor. These are great feeding places for fish. We went ashore on Padre to get a barrel of water and reached our destination on the 9th. We entered Baffin Bay which has a large number of shell formations.
>
> Kenedy Pasture is 60 miles from Corpus and 90 miles from Brownsville and has 400,000 acres. It fronts on Baffin Bay and runs back 25 miles and is nearly in the shape of a square and takes 100 miles of fence to enclose it. Captain Mifflin Kenedy is erecting several large dwellings, store-house, stable and cow-houses on the place. It is enclosed with cypress posts 6 × 6, 8 ft. long and coated with thin coal tar and put in the ground 3 feet. He runs the wire through the posts; puts up 5 wires or 500 miles of wire to go around it. Posts are 20 ft. apart.
>
> Captain Henry Hawley is in charge of the working force. I drove over a portion of the pasture in the company with Mr. Thomas Mifflin Kenedy. The grass was so tall that we could not drive faster than a walk. The land is undulating, interspersed with live-oak groves, and fresh and salt water lakes. We saw thousands of wild ducks, cranes, and waterfowl. We killed some fat turkeys and saw large herds

of deer and antelope. Lakes are full of red fish, mullet, trout, black bass, etc.

The Captain has purchased in Northern Texas about 6,000 head of improved stock. When they arrive he will have a little over 8,000. He hopes to put about 12,000 head by January principally Durham. He hopes to have 50,000 head by January of 1885. When he has this pasture enclosed he will have the largest pasture in the United States with the exception of the Maxwell brothers in Mexico [sic].

Captain is 64 years old and a most popular stockman. He commands the respect of all. He is now on a visit to his mother who is within a few months of her ninetieth year. He is associated with his three sons in the Kenedy Pasture Company with a cash capital of $1,000,000 with the power to raise it to $4,000,000. These are all young men and like their father they are full of energy.[24]

On August 13, while Mifflin was away, James wrote to James Wells asking for help obtaining a commission to deputize him so he "could rid the neighboring ranch of undesirable elements." By November James had received his commission and on November 11 he wrote James Wells thanking him for his help in becoming deputized.[25] This was another method the large landowners utilized to remove unwanted elements from the Wild Horse Desert.

On October 6, Mr. Mallory wrote James, "your mother, Mrs. Starck and the Head President arrived by train last night—all well and I recken [sic] pretty well tired out. It's hot and dull here no news—papers full of election news."[26] By November the Kenedy election machine was in full swing. Jim Wells had telegraphed James to have all his men vote. James replied, "I received your telegram asking for assistance on Election. I didn't get it for four days after it arrived being out on the range. I sent every man I could spare to vote at San Jose. All voted Blue Democratic Ticket. 23 all told. I received Sheriff's Commission from Brito a few days ago."[27]

Most of the vaqueros who worked on La Parra had been on La Atravesada before the purchase of the land from Mrs. Eulalia Tijerina; most stayed on to work for Captain Kenedy. The Morales family was well established there. The Moraleses and Buenoses and their descendants worked on the ranch for nearly one hundred years. In addition to Encarnación Morales's sons, stepsons, and sons-in-law, over twenty of his grandsons, two grandsons-in-law, fifteen great-grandsons and seven great-great-grandsons worked for the Kenedy ranch.[28]

In November the tone of Mifflin's letters to James changed dramatically. His letters were addressed to "Dear Son" and closed with "your affectionate father." He told James that he could "buy any cattle that are offered if the figures suit you—say up to twenty five hundred or three thousand. I prefer two-year-old heifers and one-year-old steers. Keep some men so as to make sure we get the fence up." In the postscript he refers to Petra. "Ma wants to go down but don't know if she will go with me yet or not." Petra was considering traveling to La Parra with him but it appears that she did not. On December 1, Mifflin received a letter at La Parra from Mallory, who said he had delivered the telegram that Mifflin sent to Petra. On November 24, Mifflin told James that John had returned home and he did not know yet what he was going to do.[29]

One of the reasons Petra may have stayed in Corpus Christi rather than traveling to La Parra was because the dedication of the new St. Patrick's Church took place in November. Bishop Manucy was the celebrant of the Solemn Pontifical Mass and delivered the sermon. Fathers John Robert, pastor; Claude Jaillet; Edward Smyth; C. Morin; Bishop Mondesdioca of Monterrey; and several priests from Mexico were present in the sanctuary.[30] Petra took pleasure in seeing the church finished, particularly since she and Mifflin had played a large part in making the church a reality.

In December, Mifflin positioned himself to sell La Parra and take the profits, or to borrow money using La Parra as collateral. On December 8, a letter from Teal Cooprerco to Mr. Hicks, Wells, and Rentfro in Brownsville asked for a memorandum on the Kenedy ranch including land, grass, improvements, and stock so that they could put it before their associate before he left London.[31] Then less than a week later Mifflin was back in Corpus Christi and wrote to S. M. Swenson Sons in New York, "Herein I hand you a proposition date July 17th last to the firm of Underwood Clark of Kansas City Mo, for the sale of the Rancho La Parra and dependent ranches. The property of the Kenedy Pasture Co. The proposition of sale, I believe, fully explains itself. Underwood Clark will tender you one hundred thousand dollars on the twentieth of this month according to the propositions, you will please receive it and place to my credit as President and Treasurer. You will not receive it after that date."[32] Then just three days later, Mifflin wrote James that Wilson wanted an extension on buying the ranch and he would extend until October if he would meet his terms.[33] It appears that Mifflin was determined to sell La Parra if he could get the right price for it. This was one of the main differences in Mifflin and King. King had a passion for the land and instructed both Henrietta and his future son-in-law, Robert Kleberg, never to sell. Mifflin was in the ranching business strictly for the money and had no attachment to the land except when it could make him a profit.

Mifflin ended the year in a state of apprehension. King said that unauthorized people were going into Mifflin's pasture. He had heard this news from Frank Gregory. Mifflin asked James to refrain from giving the key to anyone unauthorized.[34] On December 21, Mifflin wrote James to let him know, first, that he had heard from Swenson and no deposit or communication was received from the parties so the ranch sale fell through. Mifflin was also concerned because Frank Gregory had reported that sixteen of King's cows had fresh La Parra brands on them. Gregory had not told King, but had told John. Mifflin then told James that he awaited his answer with much anxiety.[35] Mifflin was looking to James to straighten out an embarrassing situation with King.

Petra and Mifflin attended Christmas Eve services in their new church, from which the peal of the bells they had given could be heard throughout town. They had made a gift that would be enjoyed by the church and community for years to come. On this night Petra and Mifflin had a ranch that was going well and their children were all established. They could give thanks that night for their family, their blessings, and each other.

CHAPTER 19

1883:
They Were Always There for One Another

Close friendship helped *Petra, Henrietta, Mifflin, and Richard* make it through the devastating year of 1883. The drought came close to forcing one of the families to sell a ranch, and illness reappeared. They had always been there for one another over the past thirty years, and in no year did they need the companionship more than in this one.

Both families focused their attention on Corpus Christi and planned to make it their permanent home. In 1883 the town had a population of three thousand people and forty-eight businesses. The town center had Market Hall that offered fresh produce, meats, and household items. The bakery in town delivered fresh bread three times a day for the ladies' convenience. The streets were not in good condition and turned to mud when it rained, making them difficult to navigate. On Mayor Murphy's orders, drainage ditches were dug to the bay to try to correct the problem. He used prisoner laborers; if they refused to work they were given only bread and water to eat. Corpus had no city water utility. Homes and stores used cisterns that filled with roof runoff when it rained. Water could also be purchased from carriers in times of drought, but it could cost as much as 25 cents to a $1 per batch depending its scarcity. The water was shipped in by railroad car from Agua Dulce Creek. The fire department pumped water out of the bay. Kerosene lanterns supplied the town's street lights; a lamplighter lit the street lanterns at sundown and extinguished them at daylight. The Tex-Mex Railroad was two years old and already making a considerable difference in the town's trade.[1]

The citizens of Corpus Christi enjoyed an active social life filled with

Mifflin Kenedy's office in Corpus Christi, Texas, with his neighbor Henrietta King's home in the background. Courtesy Texas A&M University–Corpus Christi, Archives.

entertainment and outings. Boating and yachting was available. Skating could be enjoyed until 10 P.M. and dancing until 9 P.M. at the Bluff City Rolling Skating Club.[2] On August 12, Sarah Kenedy Spohn was the chairperson of a boating excursion to Ingleside, Texas. According to the *Corpus Christi Caller*,

> Bright and early Saturday morning the young people of our city were treated to a grand excursion on the bay to the little village of Ingleside. The promise of ninety degrees in the midday shade could not deter them. In the words of one crusty old bachelor "we are going to fish or heat." At half past six the schooner Four Bluff raised anchor. . . . Mrs. A. E. Spohn acting as chairperson. Billy's Italian band furnished gay music as the westerly breeze caught the sails of the old scow. The "Can't-get-away's" stood on the dock enviously gazing at the departing vessel, consoling themselves with the belief that it would be too hot for pleasure anyway. The party arrived at Ingleside in good time where fishing, dancing, and flirting were the amusements. Few fish were caught, while many noses were blistered. Several bottles were picked upon the beach late in the day bearing the well known marks

of the Bachelor's Club, yet the party arrived intact, saying, "we had a joy time—you don't know what you missed—you ought to have gone, etc."[3]

With fall weather came a whole different list of entertainments. October brought moonlit nights, dancing, and serenading. It also brought oyster season, with all the regular fleet of boats running and all hands employed. The cost was 25 cents a hundred in the shell and 50 cents opened. Oyster houses served a plate of oysters cracked, with sauces, for 15 cents. Later in the fall the ladies of the Episcopal Church hosted a pumpkin pie social; the Knights of Honor gave a Mother Goose Masquerade Ball in December.[4]

The social season ended with a "Brilliant Wedding" at the Episcopal church; the bride was Miss Fannie Mallory, the daughter of Mifflin's faithful secretary, E. Mallory.[5] For the Kenedys, it was a family affair. The bridegroom, J. H. C. White would succeed Mallory as the secretary of Mifflin's Kenedy Pasture Company after Mr. Mallory's death.[6]

Petra and Mifflin supported the church in Corpus Christi as they had in Brownsville. Petra had always fulfilled any need the church had and she raised her children to do the same. Bishop Manucy had been traveling the countryside visiting the ranches again and was back from his trip. During this last trip he had confirmed 734 people, including 254 at San Diego, 370 on the ranches, and 100 at Laredo.[7]

In Brownsville, Petra's son-in-law Fred Starck was complimented in the *Brownville Cosmopolitan* for his untiring efforts on behalf of the children in the Catholic Church for helping make their Christmas celebration a success.[8] Petra and Mifflin found themselves in the paper throughout the year in regard to the building of their new home. Mifflin had started to build her "the finest home in Texas." In March the paper ran an article titled "Capt. Kenedy's New Residence":

> During this week we dropped into the office of Carroll & Iler—architects and builders, and saw drawings of several buildings about to be erected by them in this city. We were shown the drawings and plans of Capt. Kenedy's new dwelling which Carroll & Iler have contracted to build. It will be a handsome house, having all the modern conveniences. It is on the order of an Italian Villa. Situated as it will be on the bluff overlooking the bay and the business portion of our town, it will present a splendid appearance, it will occupy the site of Captain Kenedy's old dwelling which will be removed across the street on the opposite corner. This will be entirely remodeled and will occupy a good view. We were informed by Messrs Carroll and Iler that

work had begun and they will proceed as rapidly as possible weather permitting.[9]

By June the company was true to its word and the Kenedys' old house had been moved, entirely remodeled, and everything arranged for comfort.[10] In the meantime, Petra and Mifflin moved to a rented house while the new house was under construction.

Kenedy and King both had their hands full with the management of their ranches. The drought was now in its third year and was becoming critical. The new year of 1883 had arrived and with it no rain. The pastures were overstocked and could not sustain the large herds' demands. The cattle boom had caused ranches to develop from Texas to Wyoming and Montana, and they were in full swing. Journalists wrote about how to get rich in the cattle industry. These articles captured the attention of investors in England and Scotland, and Mifflin seized the opportunity and sold Los Laureles to a Scottish group. King considered the possibility of selling because his pastures were overstocked, the drought continued, and his health was beginning to fail.[11] Mifflin sought to establish the family business so that his boys would be taken care of and his ranch would prosper.

Tom was thirty years old, James twenty-eight, and John twenty-seven, and none were married. Tom was good looking and liked the high life. He enjoyed ladies, expensive clothes, fine horses, sports, and being the "man around town." In March, Mr. Mallory had to write Tom about his extravagant Lichtenstein Department Store draft for $388.21.[12] James, in contrast, was tough, quick of temper, loved the land, and liked taking the law into his own hands. John was the intellectual; he was also interested in business. Perhaps John was the more mature of the boys even though the youngest. In January, trouble erupted between James and John and lasted almost the entire year. Mifflin ended up right in the middle of the disagreement. On January 11, Mifflin wrote James addressing the letter "Dear Sir" and signing it "M Kenedy Pres. Treas." He wrote that he had received James's letter of resignation as general manager of the Kenedy Pasture Co. He asked him, "to please turn over to John G. Kenedy all and every thing, all money, books, papers, and accounts, and given all the information you possess on all matters and things in the Pasture or pertaining there to in any [way] so as to enable him to prosecute the business of the Company intelligently."[13] James was the son Mifflin thought could run his ranch and the one he had the most confidence in. Mifflin did not turn the management over to Tom, even though he was the oldest. The same day Mifflin wrote to John G. Kenedy, Sec of Kenedy Pasture Co. to tell him James had resigned and he had directed him to turn all things over to him.[14] He then followed those letters with a letter to Francisco Ytúrria in Brownsville informing him that James had resigned and John was now in charge, and he was to pay all his drafts.[15]

Then on January 22, Mifflin wrote a letter to John expressing his change of mind: "It was thought proper for the interest of all concerned to send James W. Kenedy to the La Parra again to take charge of the Kenedy Pasture Company. You will please return over to him and inform all employees of this order. You will resume your duties as delegated to you by him at this time. You will sign your signature as Secretary."[16] What happened to make Mifflin change his mind? The answer may come from a small line in the January 28 edition of the *Corpus Christi Caller,* "James Kenedy of La Parra rancho in City last week."[17] It seems that James had left La Parra and ridden to Corpus Christi to talk with his father, and shortly thereafter Mifflin had reinstated him and demoted John, placing him under James's orders once again.

The next few months did not appear to go well for John. In March Mifflin telegrammed him, "nothing can stop you from laying fence except an injunction served by a proper officer so keep laying fence on the surveyor's line."[18] Mifflin was in the middle of another land and boundary dispute. The La Parra ledger book clearly indicated that John was being treated as a regular employee. During that period, John was charged for soap, starch, oil, chocolate, rope, calico, thread, buttons, coffee, jeans, bleach, cotton needles, and bluing, but no tobacco. The rations for one man at La Parra were: $1^{1}/_{2}$ lbs. sugar, $1^{1}/_{2}$ lbs. beans, 1 lb. coffee, 1 1b. rice, 8 lbs. flour, 2 lbs. bacon.[19] The dispute finally came to a head on August 24. Mifflin wrote to James saying, "I have a letter from John G. Kenedy of the 10th in which he says—

> I was notified by James previous to his departure for Corpus that my services would not be required by him after the first of September next, stating that there was not work enough for two here. I will leave on the 1st Sept turn over books, papers, and cash to him. Now while you were here, you gave me to understand that he was just as anxious to leave as you were to have him go—and that the only thing in the way of his leaving was, that he did not want to leave without a promise from me that I would not count him off in the way of stock and asked you to get an expression from me. I told you I was not making promises of that kind, that he was at liberty to leave if he wanted to, or that you could discharge him of your desires—that you put him where he was (in capacity of clerk only) and you had the right to dismiss him. I told you I would make no promises, but that from my antecedents, genuinely, I thought you could at cost assumed I would—justly by all and that if you and he could not agree, it was best you separate—Now from the tenor of his letter he leaves the impression

on one that he has been discharged—You know if this is so—you told me he was anxious to leave if he could get this promise from me through you—It will need to be a thorough understanding and in writing so there may be no recriminations hereafter. If you discharge him, put it in writing. If his leaving is agreeable, put it in writing and have him sign it.[20]

John did leave and as fate would have it, turnabout is fair play. The day would come when James's family would be dependent on John's good graces.

Mifflin and James had a rough year in the ranching business. In January, Mifflin was trying to find the Mexican title to El Paistle and Las Barrosas. He telegraphed Fred Starck to check with Powers and Wells to see if the title was in the safe and to let him know the results of the search.[21] The next day he sent telegrams again, this time to his other son-in-law, J. L. Putegnat. He told him that he needed the original Mexican grants, and asked him to send the certified copy of the map and field notes of the Mexican survey.[22] Mifflin's old ranch Los Laureles was doing well under its new management. They were putting 16,000 head of cattle on the road to the northern territory, through the Panhandle and Indian Territory, where they would be held and fattened before being put on the market. Four herds would leave their pasture and they would buy from other ranches and take their cattle with them for the spring drive.[23]

In April, Mifflin wrote a letter to John McAllen informing him that "Santiago [James] had just handed me your account of the cattle purchased of you by him totaling $21,655.50. Let me know when you have received my checks and Santiago I believe has also advised you he will take the balance of your steer cattle."[24] Santiago must have spent his time at the McAllen's Santa Anita Ranch doing other things besides buying cattle. Shortly after returning home he told his parents he was engaged to Corina Ballí Treviño, Salomé Ballí Young de McAllen's half-sister. While at Santa Anita, he asked for Corina's hand and was accepted.[25]

On April 26, 1883, Petra in Corpus Christi wrote to Salomé at the Santa Anita Ranch, in Spanish. She expressed to Salomé her hope that Salomé and don Juan and all of the family were enjoying good health. Petra told Salomé that she and the Captain had been ill, but they were better now, but that she had been so ill that she had not seen La Parra yet. Petra told Salomé something very revealing—that she enjoyed better health on the ranch than in Corpus Christi, that the climate in Corpus had done her harm.[26] Apparently Petra missed her life on the ranch.

Petra told Salomé that after Santiago had returned from Santa Anita he had informed her of his engagement to Corina. Petra was very happy because they are "young people from the same town." She is sure Santiago will meet his obligations and "be a good man who can maintain Corina and more with your support." Petra said she wishes all her sons would marry Mexicans as she has a great fear that she will be presented with a "Gringita" who cannot speak Castilian, and what could be worse. She is very anxious to see Salomé and tells her that she knows "our friendship has been great and we view ourselves as two sisters." Petra closes with "we need to ask God to bless them and give them happiness all their life" and sends her greetings to don Juan, Corina, and all the rest of the children on her behalf. She then asks Salomé to please receive her heart as a true friend who will never forget. Petra signed her name Petra V[ela] de Kenedy.[27]

Petra was obviously pleased that Santiago and Corina were engaged. He was the second son to marry. Adrian had married a Mexican and now Santiago would, too. It was very important to Petra for the family to carry on her Spanish heritage and language. Her daughters by Colonel Vidal were all married, and one daughter, Concepción, had married a Mexican. The other two had married Anglos. She must have had confidence that her daughters would see to it that Castilian was spoken in their homes and they would keep their Spanish heritage, traditions, and most of all religion. Their children, she felt, would be brought up as she hoped.

Petra's letter indicates that her education in Mier was a good one and reveals her close relationship with Salomé Ballí McAllen. The letter also shows the closeness of influential Tejana women.

During the year, Mifflin struggled with another land acquisition. On November 12, Mrs. Groesbeck wrote Mifflin that he was offering her too little for the land she had owned for forty-five years. She told him that he had claimed the land under false pretenses and that she had the tax receipts for the past forty-five years. She told him she had been waiting for the day the land would increase in value and she did not know she would have to deal with him. She never thought that he or other men would surround her and then expect her to take what they would offer for the land. She explained that her youngest son was deaf and dumb and that she wanted this money for him so that he could be protected form the world.[28] On December 5, Mifflin received a letter from Mason Carr in San Antonio, who was Mrs. Groesbeck's lawyer, with the settlement terms relative to Mrs. Groesbeck's case.[29]

Even though Mifflin had a rough year, it was nothing compared to the year Henrietta and Captain King experienced. Their son Lee died in St. Louis on March 1. Jim Wells wrote to Mifflin on that day with this account:

> After a pleasant ride I arrived here about three o'clock, to find a sad household. Captain King had just received a telegram announcing the death of his son Lee. He died in St Louis at two o'clock this morning of pneumonia after a few days illness. Upon first intelligence of his illness Mrs. King left Tuesday accompanied by Richard [Jr.] to reach St. Louis tomorrow morning. The Captain and Miss Alice remain here and seem just heartbroken. Mr. and Mrs. Hopkins and Captain Greer are fortunately with them. Do you not think it well for Capt. King and his daughter to join the other members of the family "north"? I mention this to you knowing your long friendship for them and so that after giving it your kind consideration, you may so say to him if you think best.[30]

The following day, Mr. Mallory wrote to John at La Parra to tell him, "before this reaches you, you will likely have heard the affliction which Captain King and family are in on account of the death of Lee in St. Louis. We do not know if Mrs. King and Richard Jr. got there before he died or not. This is a severe blow to Cap. & Mrs. King."[31] The newspaper ran this account:

> The sad news reached our City Thursday of the death of Capt. Richard King's son, Mr. Lee King, at St. Louis of pneumonia. He was born February 29, 1864 in San Patricio county, Texas. He had just completed a liberal education in Northern schools and colleges and supplementing it with a commercial course in St. Louis preparing for a business career in Southwestern Texas—his home. He was an excel-

lent young man with fine qualities of both heart and head. Robust in health, hopeful and joyous in spirit the hope of his father's heart, death spared him not but took him away from loving friends and a dear home. Verify this old Saying "death loves a shining mark" is exemplified in this case. His mother and brother [Richard Jr.] started for St. Louis on receiving the news of his illness and Capt. King and daughter followed a few days later. He will be buried today in St. Louis.[32]

Tom Lea wrote that the death of Lee "stunned the King family. Mrs. King was so stricken she became seriously ill and remained in St. Louis for months. Affairs at the ranch called the captain back immediately and Alice returned with her father. The eighteenth of March, he was sending a letter. 'My Dear Dear Wife. I cannot write with any heart to you. . . .'" Tom Lea continued: "Lee had promised much for the future of the Santa Gertrudis. Lee the staunch boy who went out with the rawhide riders at the cow camps, Lee who knew the livestock, the grass, the water, Lee who loved the range, Lee who—was gone. So was his father's heart."[33] Captain King started drinking more, turning to his "Old Rosebud" heavily. He developed stomach pains that sometimes even the drink would not help.[34]

Petra wrote to Henrietta expressing condolences. She, of all people, understood the grief that Henrietta and the Captain were feeling. Seven years before she had lost her seventeen-year-old son Willie to a fever in a faraway place. Lee was nineteen. The two boys had taken business courses so that they could return home and be useful in their respective family ranching businesses. They both seemed to have been the "apple of their father's eye." These two mothers had lost their sons at such an early age with so much promise ahead. Petra expressed her understanding of this great loss and hoped that with God's help Henrietta and Captain King would be consoled in their grief.[35] Petra well knew that this kind of loss would be carried in their hearts forever.

King was not only stricken with the loss of his son, but he was also facing a financial crisis at the ranch. His funds were depleted and unless his dearest friend, Mifflin, could help him he would not be able to carry on his business. It was a time that tested the friendship of these two men, and again they came through for each other. Devastated by his son's death, King wrote his wife in early April to tell her he was tired of the business and wanted to quit ranching. He began negotiations that would enable him to get out of the business and move to some quiet place.[36]

In the middle of April, King wrote to Henrietta that he hoped Mr. Hancock, who was the agent for the potential buyers, would come up with the payment soon because something must be done. He wanted to know what she wanted to do with her cattle and sheep and advised her to sell and take the cash.[37]

Sometime between the middle of April and the end of June, King had another disappointment. It was later reported in the *New Orleans Times Democrat* that on April 15, 1885, Captain King's asking price for the ranch and its stock had been $6,500,000. The potential buyers came to the Santa Gertrudis in 1883. The price may have been what frightened off his potential buyers but there might also have been another event. Victor Alvarado, a trusted vaquero, related this story:

> These men wished to see the cattle first, then the rest of the stuff. King called his cattle bosses, who at that time were Ramón Alvarado and Jack (Jap) Clark. He told them "Tomorrow morning by nine o'clock, I want a roundup in the Preso de las Tranquitas," and this we did. When King thought that the hour was at hand he went to the lookout of the house with his field glass and saw that everything was ready. He ordered a large stage coach to be hitched so that the buyers could go. He went in his buggy as was his custom. They reached the roundup, but as there were so many in the herd, they had to go in with the vehicles to the middle of the herd. Even this way they couldn't see well. The buyers on the edge of the herd had to climb on top of the coach. In this way they were better able to see. They rode around the herd about an hour. The herd, I calculate, to be of about 12,000 animals. When the buyers wanted to go back to the ranch, King called the bosses, Ramón Alvarado and Jack Clark, and said, in English, to Ramón Alvarado: "Why did you gather such a little herd?" "Señor, you wanted the roundup very early, we didn't have time to gather any more." "Well, tomorrow morning, I want another roundup larger than this in the corner of the Bóvedo." When the buyers heard this, they asked King if he could gather more of a herd than what they saw there, and King said he could give them four or five roundups equal to the one they had. Then the buyers looked at one another and said to King that they didn't want to see any more than that one, it was enough to know they couldn't buy even the herd they saw, much less the land, and they left very sad.[38]

They were no sadder than King at the failure to sell the ranch.

Henrietta was home at the Santa Gertrudis by May 2. She wrote Mifflin, "Dear Friend, At my husband's request I wish to say that it will be a matter of great accommodation to him if you will send him your check for $25,000 by

Thursday's mail as he wishes to leave at once for Brownsville. . . . He is not well tonight so I write this for him. Kind regards to Mrs. Kenedy."[39] On May 3, King wrote Kenedy that he had received the $25,000 check and that he was much obliged and was leaving for Brownsville in the morning.[40] Two weeks later King wrote to Mifflin to tell him that the grass was short and that he had a man there to buy ten thousand head of cattle, five thousand steers of all ages, and also five thousand heifers one or two years and how much it bothered him to sell the females.[41] At the end of May, King wrote Mifflin that Hancock and his associates were coming, and he thought it was probably worthless but asked if he would come for a day; he then sent his kindest regards to Mrs. Kenedy and family. King was also trying to help out Henrietta's half-brother Bland's widow. At the Santa Gertrudis she told Captain King that she wanted to sell Captain Kenedy 150 steers and some heifers to pay off some of Bland's debts. Bland's brother Willie sold them to Lind but she "wanted to sell them to you and she objected to the sale. She came here to get me to write you to see if you wanted them. She said she was holding them in a separate pasture and was waiting to hear from you." He asked Mifflin to let him know at once.[42]

Evidently the sale did not go through and by the middle of June King wrote to Mifflin to tell him that he had written to Mr. James Kenedy and had not had an answer from him about the crossing.[43] A week later he told Mifflin that he had no rain and that "things with me in the cattle line is bad."[44] Mifflin knew his friend was in deep trouble and telegraphed James three days later to see if there was any way they could assist King. He also wanted to know how long "our lakes would last with our own stock." He asked him to see the telegrams sent to John and to answer fully.[45]

A week later Mifflin wrote James about a difficult decision:

> I wrote Capt. King and told him that under the circumstances it would be impossible for us to take any of his cattle. It is hard to see an old friend lose his property but still he has not taken any precautions to preserve it until too late. If we do not have rain before August or September . . . you must take every precaution to protect the stock without injury. . . . I advise you now to make all preparations for water possible—everything now looks to be long and severe drought. It is lucky for us that we got our fence completed in time. . . . King has put 5,000 cattle at Roger's tank and Spohn tells me the tank will last a week. When it is gone those cattle will perish as there is no place for them to go.
>
> I am more concerned about King, than all other things together. I would like to help him, but it is too late. If we attempt it, we would

probably lose his cattle and ours—and both go down together. This cannot be and he ought not to expect it—will go down if you need me—but prefer not to do so.[46]

Two days later Mifflin had taken the matters into his own hands and telegraphed James that in absence of his reply he had today given King permission to turn loose at the Paistle and the Cobos lakes 5,000 head and if he doesn't hear from him to the contrary on Saturday morning he will give him permission to put in 5,000 more.[47] Mifflin could not stand by and let his friend go down. This friendship ran too deep for one to not be there for the other no matter what the circumstances.

By July, King had sold his interest in his bonds to Kenedy and had told him that he did not want to spend any more money on the place as he had always been afraid of being in debt.[48] Then the rains came and the life-giving water bolstered King's spirits. He wrote to Henrietta, "My Dear Wife, We are all well and the grass in the yard is green once more thanks be to God for it." King regained his enthusiasm and began to see his way to continuing on the ranch.[49] King was so happy that on July 4 he had his private battery of four cannon fired not only for greeting a national holiday but also because of the rain that fell on his vast pastures that day.[50] He wrote to Mifflin that he had hopes of more rain and he was sending about three or four thousand more beeves to the Oso to fatten them up for a fall sell; he wanted to know what Mifflin thought.[51] Mifflin wrote James at the end of June to tell him he had a telegram from King and he had not put any cattle in yet but to prepare for them and build the cross fence to keep them separate.[52]

In August, King found it necessary to borrow money from Mifflin and told him he would pay him 10 percent, as "I have to pay others."[53] In October, King reported that the grass was fine and thanked Kenedy. He said he feared he could never repay him for his good business advice and other things.[54] Also in October the newspaper noted, "Captain Richard King was in the city Sunday and returned to his rancho, Santa Gertrudis, the same day. A number of citizens have expressed the wish that the Captain would follow Captain Kenedy's example and build a fine residence in our town. The *Caller* joins in the wish."[55] King was still involved in a number of businesses, including the ice business, in Brownsville. In early September the paper reported, "Capt. Richard King left this morning for Santa Gertrudis; Mr. Mock, telegraph operator at El Sauz and Mr. Zilker, of the King Ice Works, accompanied him. We learn that Mr. Zilker will go north and purchase a large new ice machine and also all the necessary paraphernalia to make ice cream by steam. It is probable that the small cans, like those used at Monterrey to freeze ice cream and deliver it at residences, will be introduced."[56]

On another note, romance filled the air. Santiago was engaged to Corina and the family was pleased over the match. The Kings were also looking forward to a wedding. Richard King II was engaged to Miss Pearl Ashbrook. King was so pleased at the prospect of Richard's marriage that on July 15, 1883, he and Henrietta presented him with a Deed of Gift with love and affection to the 40,000-acre, well-watered Rancho Puerta de Agua Dulce. Richard II was now the owner and manager of his own ranching property. By the time of the wedding in December the St. Louis paper announced that the couple would be taking possession of an elegant new home built for the new bride.[57] Santiago must have wondered at the difference in treatment of the two bridegrooms. Mifflin had his land tied up in a corporation, and indeed James was the manager, but that was vastly different from owning a ranch.

Richard II was good-natured and affectionate; he was more interested in farming than ranching and would try out many new techniques and farm crops on his new ranch.[58] Richard's marriage left only Alice at home. She dutifully took care of King when Henrietta was away, but she too had a romantic interest. She continued to see Robert Kleberg on a regular basis when he came to the ranch on business. Both she and her father realized that this young man could well have a permanent place at the Santa Gertrudis.[59]

At a time when Petra should be joyous, what with James's upcoming wedding and the elegant new house being built for her, she was having health problems. She had already expressed to Salomé that she thought the move to Corpus Christi had been bad for her health and that she thought she was better at Los Laureles. It may well have been that Corpus Christi didn't have anything to do with it, but that her cancer was advancing and she was beginning a slow decline. Henrietta, always a good friend, wrote to Mifflin about Petra on September 14. "Dear Friend, As the Captain is very busy this morning I will answer your inquiry for the mail bag as the Captain was abroad in Brownsville at the time. . . . I delivered it to your man from La Parra the Capt. has just returned from Brownsville a day or so is well and sends kind regards—we regret very much to hear of Mrs. Kenedy's continued illness—tell her I think if she could come out here for a while it would benefit her. Please remember us to her and we all hope she may speedily improve."[60]

On November 2, 1883, James married Corina in Hidalgo County, probably at the McAllen ranch.[61] Petra and Mifflin were pleased that James was settling down and they welcomed Corina into the family. James and John McAllen were now brothers-in-law.

John, not to be left behind, was off to New Orleans. It seems that romance was also on his mind. He was courting Miss Stella Turcotte and was hoping to make her his bride. The *Corpus Christi Caller* printed the news on September 16 that the SS *Aransas* left yesterday with the following passengers for

Galveston and New Orleans—Miss A. Vidal, John Kenedy.[62] It was convenient for John to escort Anita Vidal to school at the Incarnate Word Academy in New Orleans. Petra and Mifflin ensured that Adrian's daughter Ana Adrianne, Anita as she was called, had her education provided for and was given any spending money that the nuns deemed appropriate. Anita knew Joe, Rosa, and the family well because after Adrian's death her mother had married Joe's brother J. P. Putegnat. The family must have all enjoyed one another's company before John and Anita sailed for New Orleans.

Joe and Rosa and the family had arrived on August 9 as announced by the paper, "J. L. Putegnat and family of Brownsville are on a visit to our city and are the guests of Capt. M. Kenedy. Mr. Putegnat has remained very close to his business in Brownsville for a number of years, but this summer put his drug store in charge of his son a recent graduate from college and concluded to stir around a little. Mr. P is just down from Monterrey and Saltillo where he has represented Messrs. Clarke & Curtis of Galveston."[63] Petra must have been happy to have the family with her, especially the grandchildren. It was fun for their young children to see Corpus Christi and have a chance to enjoy the various entertainments around town, but most surely to see and visit with their grandmother and other family members.

Sometime in the next month the visit turned tragic when Joe became seriously ill. The October 17 newspaper in Brownsville noted, "we are sorry to learn that Dr. Putegnat is in Corpus Christi seriously ill."[64] Neither Dr. Spohn nor his associates were able to help him, and Joe died on November 10. The Brownsville paper printed the following: "November 10, Joe Putegnat dies." The article said he died at half past eleven o'clock at the residence of Capt. M. Kenedy, that he was born in Mobile, Alabama, and was forty-five years old. They had twelve children with eight surviving, the youngest, Irene, was only nine months old. The Corpus paper ran a Masonic burial notice on November 11. It requested that all Masons in good standing be at the Masonic lodge room at 9:30 to attend the funeral of J. L. Putegnat, who would be buried with Masonic honors.[65]

Mifflin was concerned about his stepdaughter Rosa and the welfare of her family after Joe's death. On the day of Joe's death Mifflin wrote Jim Wells and told him he wanted to help his stepdaughter to start on a clean slate. Rosa returned home with the family and by December the paper was reporting that she and her son had the store ready for Christmas. The article said, "Putegnat today opened one of the most magnificent displays of Christmas goods in the Yznaga building that was ever brought to this frontier. Customers will receive the courteous and polite attention of Mr. Hoyt as salesman. Dolls of all kinds and descriptions, children's tableware, and toy engines run by steam and everything else that can amuse and please children and contribute to their enjoyment of Christmas in any manner, abound in an endless profusion that can only be realized by an actual inspection of the splendid display."[66] Mifflin must have wondered if Joe Jr. and Rosa had heeded his advice after his efforts to give them a new start. The store was housed in the Yznaga's new building. A beautiful young daughter of this wealthy and prominent family would soon become involved with Petra and Mifflin's son Tom.

Mifflin missed an event while Joe was ill that had been planned for a long time. Their congressman was in town to visit Aransas Pass and see how he might familiarize himself with the project so that he could work more intelligently for an increased appropriation at the coming session of Congress. Mr. James Ward, the agent of the Mexican National Railroad Company, arranged transportation for the group of invited businessmen that accompanied the congressman. They left Central Wharf at 7:15 A.M. The paper said that Capt. Kenedy could not attend but with his usual forethought laid in an abundant supply of drinkables and edibles for the occasion. The congressman reported that he would try for a large appropriation in the next session of Congress for the river and the deep harbor. Chowder was served and the group arrived home about 10 P.M. well satisfied with the trip.[67]

Joseph L. Putegnat died in the Kenedy house in Corpus Christi on November 10, 1882, while he and Rosa and the children were on a trip to visit Petra and Mifflin. Courtesy of Jesse (Sam) Thornham, Joe Thornham, McGoohan families, Petra's descendants.

At the end the year, Petra was pleased that James was happily married. In December, Mifflin wrote to James at La Parra and signed the letter "Your affectionate father M Kenedy," and then added, "Ma about same and all join in memories to Corina."[68] Then three days later Mifflin wrote to James to tell him his ambulance had arrived and he would either send it by boat or wanted to know if he would take it by land.[69] John was back in Texas and the Brownsville newspaper reported that on December 11 he left there to return to La Parra.[70] Mifflin was pleased, too, about a new prospective business venture. He had written James Wells in November to tell him that the "sickness of

Mrs. K—and myself also being under the weather, and the sickness and death of J. Putegnat here, has seriously interfered with my business for the last two months." He then laid out the general parameters for the sale of the ranch and how he would work with the London company, but he did not want it known that the ranch was on the market. Mifflin felt that there were people who would frustrate a sale if they could and he believed in keeping his own counsel.[71] In December, Wells informed Mifflin that he had received a letter from the agents Rentfro and Hicks for the London company asking for information on the ranch before their representatives came to Texas to see the property.[72] Mifflin ended the year with the expectation that he might once again sell another ranch at a large profit.

CHAPTER 20

1884:
Farewell to Santiago

Petra's illness was getting worse in 1884, and she was spending most of her time in bed. She seldom could even go downstairs. Mifflin was staying close, taking care of her and seeing to it that she had the best of care. Mifflin was having financial problems, which he shared with his friend Captain King. They continued to support each other in times of need but, like Petra, King also had a sickness growing inside of him.

Management of the ranch challenged Mifflin as his sons' lives had changed dramatically during the year. One child proved irresponsible, another got into trouble with the law again as well as becoming critically ill, and Mifflin had to turn to the third to take charge of the ranch. There were moments of joy, though, as one son married and another blessed them with a grandson.

Mifflin was building the house for Petra and supervising every nail and board that was put up. He consulted her when decisions needed to be made. Together they ordered the china and discussed the furnishings. Mifflin wanted only the best for Petra. She had been his helpmate for thirty years. She was the mother of his six children, and he loved their three surviving sons and one daughter. Petra had also given him a stepfamily. Mifflin referred to them as his children, using "my dear little daughter" for letters to Adrian's daughter Anita Vidal and signing them "Truly affectionately, Your Grandfather, M. Kenedy."[1] The children had been raised as one family, and his stepdaughters had married well. They were established in respected homes up and down the Rio Grande Valley. The combined family members had stood as sponsors for one another's children at baptisms through the years. The girls were devoted to their mother and she to them. This year all the children would be called upon to support the family. Mifflin would need the men to help him hold the business together. Regretfully the first cracks in their unified family would come during this year as the family members began to quarrel. This division would ultimately break Petra's heart. She had spent the last thirty years holding the family together and working to support each child. Petra was determined to make the family cohesive. In her world, family and faith were the two most important things in one's life.

The cattle market declined in 1884. King was supplementing his income by selling horses. He and Mifflin had always had superior saddle stock and were known for offering excellent quality. One of the King Ranch stories relates that "one evening at dusk, a stranger rode up to the Santa Gertrudis commissary and asked to spend the night. He was mounted on a beautiful iron gray stallion; he was hospitably asked to stay. Captain King himself came out to look at the gray horse. He told the stranger that the stallion was one of the finest animals he had ever seen. The gray stood sixteen hands—bigger than the horses the Captain bred. When King had finished walking around the horse admiringly, he told the stranger to make himself at home, to stay awhile. The stranger expressed his thanks and explained that he must leave early the next morning. The captain came out to bid him fair journey and courteously sent a vaquero to put the stranger upon the San Antonio road. When the time came for the vaquero to turn back, the stranger said, 'Get down. I want to change with you. Take this horse back to Captain King and tell him that Jesse James sent this as a gift, with his compliments.' Although they were never sure of the man's true identity, the horse stayed and helped to sire beautiful iron gray horses that were known as the Jesse James horses."[2] Mifflin and King had spent thousands of dollars upgrading both their cattle and horse stock.

The men faced problems similar to the other ranchers when putting their cattle on the trail. In April, both Kenedy and King were gathering their herds. The newspaper reported that Capt. M. Kenedy was preparing to drive 9,000 cattle in three bands of 3,000 and that King was preparing to send more.[3] Mifflin and King ran into trouble on the range. James Kenedy telegraphed Mifflin on April 22 with the news that on the twentieth he had started up the trail hunting for lost cattle and he was going himself with his outfit and was leaving Tom in charge of the ranch.[4] On April 27 the paper reported, "No reliable information can be obtained relative to the loss resulting from the mixing of the herds of cattle near Peña reported in our last issue. It is estimated all the way from 500 to 2,000 head as dead, dying and lost by straying. Captains King and Kenedy are now engaged in shipping their cattle at the rate of thousand a day from Peña Station via the Texas Mexican and International railroads. Mr. U. Lott's herd of 2,500 when last heard from were above Fort Ewell on route in good condition not a head having been lost. Captain Kenedy and Mr. Lott left last Monday for Peña and spent most of the week looking after their cattle interests." Many of the ranchers were shipping cattle over the Texas

Mexican railroad. The paper reported that in May the hide inspector of Nueces County said they had the largest shipment of cattle ever, totaling 6,013 head.[5]

King had other problems to deal with in April besides his cattle stampeding. Robert Kleberg, in Brownsville, wrote to King's daughter, Alice, on April 4, 1884, in San Antonio at the Menger Hotel. He told her that he had received her letter of the twenty-sixth and expressed his love for her. He also mentioned concern for her father's health. He told Alice that her father had paid him the greatest compliment when he told him that he should consider the place (the Santa Gertrudis) "as my home." Kleberg said that of all the interesting places in the world, he would like to go to the Santa Gertrudis. He recalled that when he was there he wanted to get up so he could "hear her sweet low voice bid him good morning." Robert went on to tell her that her "father's iron constitution and unconquerable will would win the fight." He assured her that everybody he met inquired about her father's health and expressed their sympathy for "his long suffering and expressed an earnest wish that he would soon recover."[6]

Alice King took care of her father many times when her mother was away. She later married lawyer Robert Kleberg, who helped Henrietta in running the ranching empire Richard King left. Courtesy Christus Spohn Health System, Corpus Christi, Texas.

Alice was probably in San Antonio with her father to see Dr. Herff, his physician. The prognosis was not good. By April 18, Alice was back at the Santa Gertrudis and Robert was writing her from Corpus Christi. He started the letter as he always did with "My Dear Little Heart," and told her he was busy helping with the sale of Mr. Roger's ranch, he hoped to be at the ranch in a week, and he urged her to take care of herself because the Corpus Christi fever was increasing.[7]

By July, Mifflin's troubles were continuing, too. In despair about the ranch, he wrote his son-in-law Robert Dalzell in Brownsville, "My ranch is left without a head." He went on to say that Tom was in Brownsville and had been for the last two months and that he still couldn't depend on him. He then reminded him that Louisa would say, "I am blowing off."[8] Tom returned to La Parra on July 23, as reported by the *Brownsville Cosmopolitan*.[9] Two days later Mifflin telegraphed Henry Hawley to consult with the caporal and do the best for the ranch and work in harmony with him.[10] Harmony was evidently something Mifflin could not seem to find in his sons and the management of the ranch. Three days later Mifflin telegraphed Tom at La Parra to say that Hawley was in charge of all pastures and livestock, management of all employees, purchase and sale of livestock under the supervision of Mifflin, and approval of all payrolls and ranch accounts.[11] On August 6, Mifflin wrote Hawley that his attorney had told him to put a man at the gate and be sure to keep out intruders. He instructed Hawley to tell Tom to go with one or two men: "I expect him to hold the fort." He wanted Tom to camp at the gate to deter anyone from attempting to enter by force.[12] Kenedy wrote Hawley with another problem on the same day. He told him that some of their lost cattle had been put on King's small pasture. He told him if Tom was still working, to send him, if not, to send his caporal to retrieve the livestock. They would need to work for three days and would need to notify King or his caporal before they started work—and they should leave at once before the rains.[13]

Mifflin then wrote a long letter to Tom with the same information, addressing it to "Dear Son."[14] For someone with no confidence in Tom, Mifflin seemingly expected him to be in two places at the same time and to take care of both exactly as he instructed.

By the end of the month, Mifflin made another decision regarding the ranch's management. On August 23, Mifflin wrote Tom that James's health was declining, and he was sending John to the ranch and placing him in charge. He told Tom that on Monday John and his family would take charge of the ranch.[15] Mifflin evidently developed confidence in John's ability to run the ranch and by October was writing him with detailed instructions for its operation. On October 24, he wrote him to push the branding with all dispatch, look to the fences, put the yearlings at San Pedro if there was water, have men look to the roving cattle, be sure and have hay for winter. He inquired if doña Eulalia had any cattle in the pasture. He also told him that he had an invaluable man in Mr. Hawley and should avail himself of his services.[16] As usual, Mifflin was managing every detail from afar.

Mifflin thought a lot of Mr. Hawley, and in June had instructed James that if he lived on the ranch he should give him $75 a month and furnish him with sugar, coffee, flour, and meat. He thought paying him $100 per month was too much, however. He had also instructed James to keep the five-year-old bulls in hand until their brands peeled off. He wanted a P branded on their jaw and wanted James to select his best two bulls to be placed in the Paistle pasture with about 2,000 of the best cows and heifers. He wanted him to look for quality, not quantity, and to keep the red and red roan but no white cattle.[17] Mifflin was not the type of owner, like King, who rode the range with his vaqueros or who was at the ranch a lot. In fact, he was seldom at the ranch, but he was a "hands-on" owner. He wrote detailed instructions, knew his property and stock, and was always in control. He always looked at the bottom line and what would bring the most profit. Finally, in November, Mifflin gave up his hope that James would recover and return as ranch manager. He wired Francisco Ytúrria, his banker, and told him that James was no longer managing the

Kenedy Pasture Company and therefore had no right to draw on the company funds.[18] He did not give John that right, though.

Overextended, Mifflin was in trouble financially. In August, he wrote to J. H. Stevens that he had "sickness in my family—Shortly after you left Santiago was taken ill with typhoid malarial fever, and complete congestion of the left lung—and came here for treatment, and is still here. He appears the last few days to be improving but is in a very critical condition. His chances are about equal—the rancho is running itself with Hawley and Tom at the helm. Mrs. Kenedy was again prostrated about the same time as Santiago—she is in a very precarious condition—so much so, that it is impossible for me to leave home for an hour—so I have not been able to go to work. . . . Now Mr. Stephens, I have over one hundred thousand dollars due. . . . I cannot afford to take any chances and you must have stock and survey in hand by that date. Things must not fail. I have other payments due about the same time."[19]

Mifflin wrote King in October that his necessities were very urgent, and the means he had at his command would not meet his obligations. He wanted King to send him the balance in his favor at St. Louis as soon as possible. He told King that he was giving him the information in confidence about his money affairs. He did not believe that it was known about the default on the interest of the bonds last July and again on the upcoming January. The failure to pay interest on the bonds meant they had no value as a security and even if he had them he could raise no money on them.[20] With the personal problems Mifflin was having with the family, this was one burden he shared only with his friend King. At the same time he did write Captain Armstrong in Austin to tell him his ranch was for sale and that he would write the next day to give him the price and terms.[21] He followed up on that letter, telling Armstrong he would be glad for him to extend an invitation to Doctor Newton to examine the property. The price of the property was $3.5 million, $15 per head for meat cattle, and $50 per head for saddles and workhorses and mules. The proposition was good until July 1, and he could have the cattle counted by September 1.[22]

Mifflin could not leave Petra and attend the first National Cattleman's Convention, but he was very glad that King was going. Mifflin wrote to him on November 11 that he thought the major thing he would have to face would be how others addressed the role of "Texas Fever" and how it affected the cattle. He told him that the only way it could be combated was by scientific men—veterinary surgeons from the agricultural colleges or the federal department in Washington. He said he thought Dr. Ainsworth of the Army at Laredo had made Texas Fever a study for years and concluded there was no such thing. "I am informed by Spohn who has been in communication with him and says he can do us more good in combating the Texas Fever problem than all the talking cattlemen." He suggested that King see if Spohn could go with him and that Mifflin would go from Collins and meet him where the trains meet. He informed him that Doddridge and Rachel were going as delegates with expenses paid. He also shared that "Mrs. K is about the same and Santiago is no better and in a bad fix."[23]

King not only went to the convention in St. Louis, he played a prominent role. His interest seemed to be in a National Cattle Trail and not in Texas Fever. King offered an ambitious plan for a National Cattle Trail to be authorized by Congress as a fenced passage three to six miles wide with quarantine grounds and watering places along the route all the way from Texas to Dakota. When it looked like congressional subsidy would not happen, he proposed that the cattlemen go together and purchase the land themselves. The proposal did not pass, but it certainly showed the scope of vision with which King and Kenedy approached all their projects.[24]

In January 1884, John began the year much better than his father with his wedding to Marie Stella Turcotte of New Orleans. Maria Stella was short with dark eyes and brown hair. She was beautiful, well educated, and articulate.[25] The Turcottes were good Catholics, which pleased Petra, and were an old and respected French family of New Orleans. The *Corpus Christi Caller* announced: "New Orleans Wedding—Cards are out for the marriage of Mr. Jno. G. Kenedy, of this city to Miss Stella Turcotte of New Orleans at St. Louis Cathedral in the city, Wednesday, January 30, at 5 o'clock P.M. We wish the couple much joy and a long life of happiness. Mr. Kenedy's friends will gladly welcome him and his bride on their return to Corpus." The *Brownsville Reporter* reprinted the following account of the wedding:

THE SON OF A TEXAS CATTLE KING LEADS A NEW ORLEANS BELLE TO THE ALTAR
Kenedy–Turcotte

A happy throng were present yesterday evening to witness the wedding of Mr. John Kenedy, of Corpus Christi, Texas to the charming daughter of Mr. Jos. Turcotte, an old, well-known merchant of this city. Miss Stella was followed to the altar by quite a number of her personal friends who made up a very pretty wedding party. The Cathedral was beautifully illuminated and the ceremony very interesting, after which the bridal party assembled at Mrs. Pepin's residence, on Esplanade Street, where a sumptuous repast was in waiting, and dancing was indulged in until a late hour. Mr. and Mrs. Kenedy will make Texas their home, and will leave in a few days for Corpus Christi, at which point Mr. Kenedy is now interested in business. Mr. Kenedy is well known on this frontier and especially in

John Kenedy, photo found in a locket given to Sarah by Mifflin on October 28, 1886, the year after Petra's death.

Brownville. Together with the numerous friends of the groom in this city the *Cosmopolitan* extends congratulations to the happy couple. We have been informed that it is probable that Mr. Kenedy will make Brownsville his future home.[26]

John's future was definitely uncertain after James dismissed him from the ranch. It appears he was considering utilizing his business degree in either Corpus Christi or Brownsville. Both communities seemed eager to have him. John's choices might have been quite different if James had not become so ill, and if Tom had not continued his irresponsible behavior. John and Stella's

Marie Stella Turcotte Kenedy, the girl from New Orleans who loved the life in the city, moved to the isolated Wild Horse Desert in 1884.

future was at La Parra, and he would continue to build a land and cattle empire like his father and manage it in a cool, calculating manner. John had his father's characteristics and was known as a good, but tough businessman.

Petra was too ill to attend the wedding and Mifflin could not leave her. James was busy at La Parra and in early February wrote Corina that he was busy fencing the lower pasture; he was sending a light wagon to bring her to La Parra.[27] It is doubtful if any of the other members of the family were there. John felt perfectly at home with his good friends the Turcottes and many of the family members would move to Texas later to be with their sister and live either on or near La Parra. Several of them would work for John. Their children were raised alongside John and Stella's children, and the cousins would be very close. This helped Stella's adjustment to Texas. Stella was a sophisticated city girl with expensive tastes and a love of art and music. She was only nineteen when she married and had to create her own world at the isolated La Parra Ranch.[28]

Marie Stella enjoyed speaking French with any French-speaking person around. There were not too many in South Texas and even less at La Parra. The yearning to have a French contact made her affinity with Padre Juanito (Père Jean Bretault, OMI) all the more bonding. He, a Frenchman, was the member of the Cavalry of Christ who visited La Parra on his missionary journeys between Brownsville and Corpus Christi. The bond ultimately prompted Marie Stella to suggest to her daughter, Sarita, when it became apparent there would be no heirs, to bequeath the La Parra ranch house and grounds to the Missionary Society to which Padre Juanito belonged. In keeping with her wishes the property now serves as an Oblate prayer retreat called Lebh Shomea (Listening Heart) House of Prayer.[29]

Before John and Stella arrived in Texas, Petra heard that Nene was sick enough in Brownsville to be reported in the paper on March 8, but by March 22 the paper reported she was considerably better.[30] John and his new bride were back in Corpus Christi on April 10, and the paper extended their congratulations and best wishes.[31] John had returned in time for the social season in Corpus Christi; he introduced Stella to his family and friends.

John's brother-in-law, Dr. Spohn, was planting a large number of trees around his property on the bluff and wrapped them with wire to protect them from the stock running at large.[32] Dr. Spohn was also active in the local gun club; in the weekly shoot at the end of March he came in third.[33] He continued his support of the Episcopal Church, serving on the vestry. Easter morning the Episcopal Church had been filled with flowers and the offertory asked for by the rector produced $100, which went toward retiring the church debt. They had raised $450 for the year to clear the church entirely of indebtedness and the sitting vestry was reelected.[34] Sarah was continuing her involvement in the social scene and had been instrumental in arranging the details for the Leap Year Ball at the beginning of the year.[35] Sarah and Dr. Spohn were well established and respected throughout the community.

The talk of the town in March was the "Monster of the Deep." A huge lobster or crab had been caught; its right pincer measured thirteen inches and it weighed twenty-five pounds.[36] In late April the Presbyterians hosted a picnic. A crowd of young and old assembled at the Texas Mexican railway depot and took the train to Banquete. There they enjoyed the open air and a great day, including the train ride itself.[37] In May everyone in town was

(Left) Dr. Spohn saved Willie Chamberlain's life when a rabid wolf bit him. Dr. Spohn took him to France where Louis Pasteur injected him with the serum he had developed. Courtesy of Raymondville Historical Museum, Texas.

(Right) Sarah Kenedy Spohn took her place in Corpus Christi society as one of its most prominent citizens. Courtesy of Raymondville Historical Museum, Texas.

very appreciative of Captain King's ice works as the temperature rose.[38] June was watermelon time.[39]

Stella would certainly have appreciated the new push for an opera house. The city did not have one and the citizens were beginning to talk about the need.[40] Coming from New Orleans, she must have found it difficult to imagine life without music and traveling entertainers.

The newspaper published the school census in June and the children from eight to sixteen years of age totaled 774.[41] Mifflin knew the importance of a good newspaper for both social news and business promotion. He had taken an interest in the Corpus Christi paper when Eli Merriman started it in 1883. Sometime in 1884 he had bought out Ed Williams's interest in the paper when Ed left for Mexico. Although he owned only a quarter interest, Mifflin, along with his family and their friends, probably received extra attention in the paper's news coverage.[42]

In May, Robert Kleberg was caught in a very difficult situation. He wrote to Alice on May 27 from Corpus Christi that he appreciated her consolation and "as long as I have your approval—your respect and your love—I can stand all else however hard the blow might be." Kleberg defended his client Mr. Collins and was victorious. The problem was that Alice's father, Captain King, had been his opposition. He reported to Alice that Captain King was appealing the decision but had treated him with respect. He also told her that he had visited Captain King's room to try to keep him from drinking too much. He was worried about Captain King's opinion of him. His client, Mr. Collins, had appreciated the awkwardness of the situation and offered him $500. Robert told Alice he just wanted to return the fee and step aside. He did not know if he would be welcomed at the ranch, and Alice advised him not to visit now. He also confirmed that the "town is gay with musical and theatrical performances," and he had "turned down a sailing party for a lovely señorita from Monterrey."[43] A week later, on June 4, Robert was in Austin appearing before the Texas Supreme Court. He wrote Alice that Captain Kenedy told him Captain King had spoken about all the other lawyers in the case but had not said a bad word about him.[44]

The big celebration in town in June was Juneteenth, a large, formal celebration. The paper reported the event, writing that the nineteenth anniversary of emancipation was celebrated with a street parade, "from the courthouse down Mesquite street then over to Belden street to Chaparral[, from] there up Chaparral to Headen's wharf." The procession included mounted Officers of the Day, the Sturtz brass band, the Field Band of Roberts Rifles, and Roberts Rifles. A grand dinner was spread at Headen's wharf, with speeches made by W. H. Leopard, William Mead, Thomas Wilson, and Felix Thompson. Baseball, croquet, and other sports followed, and the celebration ended with a grand ball at Market Hall.[45]

The town was delighted now that they had rapid transit. The British steamship *Alice* arrived at Aransas Pass with 717 packages of bonded goods for Mexico. The goods were rapidly loaded and forwarded to their destination by the Texas Mexican and Mexican National railroad companies and made the remarkable quick transit of twenty-seven days from Liverpool to Nuevo Laredo, Mexico.[46] Kenedy and King had brought international trade to South Texas and Mexico.

John settled into Corpus Christi and by August was moving out to La Parra to take charge. He and Stella then settled into their "steamboat" house on the prairie. Mifflin was turning more to John for assistance and help. John's brother Tom was another story. Tom was good looking, fun to be with, and loved attention from both his male friends and female admirers. He had stayed at Spring Hill only one year and never liked ranching. He worked at the ranch for his father, off and on, but took no real interest in it. He did love fine horses and beautiful women and Brownsville appealed to him much more than Corpus Christi. Tom was also surrounded by family in Brownsville. His recently widowed half-sister, Rosa, whose husband Joe Putegnat had died in November, was there, along with his half-sister María Vicenta and her husband Fred Starck. His other half-sister Luisa and husband Robert Dalzell would soon be back, too. His uncle Elisha Jeff Kenedy and many of Mifflin and Petra's family friends were all in Brownsville. Tom, like his mother, had a Latin heart and had always been more comfortable there.

Tom also enjoyed the company of his extended family, the Putegnats. His half-brother Adrian's widow, Ana Vidal, had married J. P. Putegnat and they were all good friends with William, the other brother. William was in the pharmacy business with Rosa and Joe Jr., and in the spring had been selling raffle tickets yet could not sell all. He turned in the winning ticket that would have paid $15,155. The paper commented that there were many men who wished they had purchased that ticket.[47]

Tragedy seemed to be following the family, and by July William was dead, like his recently deceased brother Joe. He died on July 24 of a lung and respiratory ailment, at forty-one years of age. The newspaper said that few citizens were more popular than Billy Putegnat and that prominent citizens of the two cities followed his remains to their last resting place. The suddenness of his death left a young wife in a weak and fragile condition, expecting a child in the near future.[48] Rosa had been left with a baby nine months old and now this widow was left to bring a child into the world without its father. Tom, Ana, Nene, and Rosa needed to help her, as the family once more underwent tragedy and Petra was too ill herself to be there. Petra needed the family, too, and starting in late summer Mifflin called on Nene and Rosa to begin staying with Petra as her condition worsened.

Luisa and Robert Dalzell had been away, and the community was delighted they were returning. In May, the paper said that it "looked natural again with Captain R. Dalzell on our streets. All our old citizens are delighted to shake the Captain's hand once more."[49] The Dalzells had been in Galveston, where they went after Mifflin sold the steamboat business, and they were glad to be back in Brownsville with their family and friends. Luisa slipped easily into Brownsville life. At the end of December the newspaper mentioned how much they appreciated her bringing a delicious Christmas cake to its offices.[50]

Tom probably inherited his love of horses from his uncle, Elisha Jeff Kenedy. The paper noted in May, "Capt. E. J. Kenedy's fine blooded gray stallion died last night after suffering considerably from what appeared to be botts. This was a very valuable animal and the Captain has everyone's sympathy in his loss."[51] In July, Captain Kenedy consulted with Tom about some horses he wanted to buy. The paper reported,

Yesterday afternoon the reporter in the company with Mr. Tom and Captain Jeff Kenedy and Sheriff Brito, visited the military cemetery to look at a pair of magnificent chestnut colored steeds, weighing about 1,100 lbs. each and in perfect condition. They are one of the finest matches we have seen for a long time. They are three and four years old, the oldest animal being a little the heaviest. When they have reached their full growth they will develop into very speedy animals; even now they travel together to the pole in four minutes. Don Tomás had them out last evening and though a little stiff yet from the long sea voyage in the Harris, their action was perfect and they proved themselves one of the finest matched teams on this frontier—Don Tomás says he is going to keep them here and trot them for the use of baseball and shooting clubs and the editors. The latter element will doubtless like to borrow them for a little trip into the country when some enraged citizen, armed with a double-barreled bootjack is searching for the "man who wrote that article."[52]

It appeared that politics had not changed a lot and if one wanted to encourage votes then one gave back to the community. The use of these fine horses probably went a long way to help Tom in his fledgling political career. How Tom could afford his lifestyle remains an unanswered question. He evidently worked at the ranch during the spring when they were getting the cattle ready for the drives and then came to Brownsville for the summer. Mifflin was paying his top men either $50 or $75 a month, which would not sustain Tom's lifestyle.

Tom wanted to get into politics, and Sheriff Brito would eventually play a large role in Tom's life when Tom would challenge him in a race for sheriff. This year Tom had his eye on the county commissioner's position. He spent the summer involved with baseball games and shooting matches. In June the paper reported that Captain Kenedy's shooting team had a decided victory over Captain Champion and they were not at liberty to say exactly what the losses in wagers were. Tom scored at the top with 88 percent, as did Captain Champion for his team. His uncle Jeff Kenedy was shooting on the opposite team and only shot 60 percent.[53] In July Tom was pitching, and the paper said he pitched well for his baseball team with the other team unable to hit his pitches.[54] Tom served as captain of both the shooting and baseball teams. This was a good way to end up his summer visit, and two days later the paper reported, "Mr. Tom Kenedy left for La Parra yesterday afternoon. Don Tomás while here, made hosts of friends on both sides of the river and everybody is sorry that he has gone away."[55]

Tom returned to La Parra and found Mifflin continuing to change management of the ranch from Tom to Hawley to John because of James's illness. When Tom arrived at the ranch, Mifflin telegraphed that Hawley was in charge.[56] By late August Mifflin put John in charge, and by September 2 Tom was back in Brownsville. The paper reported that day, "Mr. Tom Kenedy arrived here yesterday. The town during his absence has been very dull and we heartily welcome him back."[57] Tom was glad to be back in Brownsville and looking forward to a new social season and his pursuit of a political office. He did, however, have to deal with a problem.

On September 20, 1884, Roberto Tomás Kenedy was born. He was Tom's illegitimate son by a family maid at La Parra named Ramona Gonzáles. He was baptized in 1885 in Brownsville in an interesting circumstance surrounding Tom's marriage to a Brownsville socialite. The same day of Tom's wedding, Ramona appeared at the church with his illegitimate son to request that he be baptized. The priest decided to baptize the baby two days later, on July 31, 1885. The priest was Father Jean Maurel and the baby's sponsor was Apolonia Sustaita.[58]

In 1969, Ramona Gonzáles's family filed a lawsuit seeking to claim some of the Kenedy estate that was in litigation. Sarita Kenedy Garza entered a deposition on May 16, 1969. She only had a first grade education so it was difficult to follow some of her statements. In the statement she said she was Roberto Tomás Kenedy's daughter and her great-grandmother was Petra Vela de Vidal Kenedy. She said her father always went by the Kenedy surname even though his baptism certificate reflected the name Roberto Gonzáles. Sarita said that her father was born in Brownsville and was a member of the Catholic faith. She said that his father was Tomás Kenedy and he had no brothers or sisters. She said that her great-grandfather was Mifflin Kenedy. She said that Ramona died when Roberto was seven or eight and then she was brought to Corpus Christi. She knew nothing about a wedding between her grandmother and Tom Kenedy. The court did rule that Roberto Tomás was not a legitimate child of Tom's and therefore had no right to inherit from the estate.[59]

Tom did not let the baptizing incident stop him in any way. In September 1884 he filled his time with baseball. His team, the Kenedy Nine, was the champion of West Texas and was playing a team in Matamoros.[60] The Matamoros Union team offered the challenge in the paper and Tom's team accepted the invitation in the paper and the acceptance was signed by T. M. Kenedy, Capt. By early October, Tom got his wish and was nominated by the Blue Club for public office. Mifflin and his friends were all Blue Party supporters and Tom had secured their nomination for county commissioner for precinct no. 4.[61] Mifflin was not pleased about Tom's nomination or his determination to enter politics. On October 24, Mifflin telegrammed Tom and said he had "no interest in the political fight in Cameron and I advise you to retire from politics, go to work, and earn an honest living. When the election is over your political friends will have no further use for you, your money gone, your shirt tail out and niggling in the wind, bankrupt and no means to tuck it in and none so poor as to do you—such is the fate of unfledged politicians."[62] Then to make matters worse Tom made the telegram public and Mifflin had to telegram James Wells, Thomas Carson, and Robert Dalzell to apologize for his son's indiscretion. The telegram read, "Telegram to Tom was of a private nature and [he] made a mistake in making it public. He is of age and responsible for his own actions. I regret very much if I have done anything that will embarrass you, as I am in full accord with you and will furnish my portion of the material aid to ensure your success. M. Kenedy."[63] Mifflin did follow up with his promise and sent Carson, who was the mayor of Brownsville, his $500 for the election expenses and he saw to it that his vaqueros voted. On October 31, he telegraphed John at La Parra to "stop the branding and vote every man entitled to vote."[64] Mifflin had fulfilled his political promises, and despite his declaration to Tom that he did not care about Brownsville politics he had written King earlier in the month about trying to secure his support for his son-in-law, Robert Dalzell, for the position of collector of customs for the Port of Brazos de Santiago.[65]

The political scene was a hot one and on the twenty-first of October it was reported that a drunken Red [of the Red Party] fired two shots into the Blue [Party] procession. He was disarmed but the paper feared that if this six-shooter business continued half a dozen people would be killed before the election was held.[66] The newspaper carried a description of the lively celebration on November 11: "Our streets last night were a blaze of lights, every window being illuminated and every house and jacal were ornamented with Chinese lanterns or lights. As the procession passed many points red, blue and Bengal lights were burned and rockets let off. . . . The procession left the court house promptly at 6 P.M. there being about 1,600 men in line. The order of march was as follows: Squad Mounted Police, 4th Inf. Band, Banner, Cleveland and Hendricks . . . Mayor Carson, Elector Wells in carriage, City officials and Council . . . Blue Club band . . . Citizens on foot, Rancheros and citizens on horseback. All the ladies at the ball tonight will be dressed in blue."[67]

The official votes for the county were published two days later and the Blues had won the county; Tom won his race for county commissioner. Tom's political office was secure, but his next race would prove deadly. The newspaper noted that Tom left for Corpus Christi on December 15 with the note that they were sorry to lose him.[68] Tom knew that his brother was critically ill and he was probably traveling to Corpus Christi to be with the family.

Petra and Mifflin were busy with all the family and business problems. Permeating every event and activity was Petra's illness and declining health. Petra and Mifflin were funding Anita Vidal's education at the Ursuline Academy in New Orleans. Mifflin wrote to Anita in March saying that he had gotten her letter four days ago and that her grandmother was, "an invalid when you left here for school and is so yet—at times she has been much worse than at others but just now she is better—she gets down stairs very seldom and has not been out of this house over twice since you left a year ago."[69] Records from the Ursuline Convent show that Anita Vidal attended from 1883 to 1885, graduating in August 1885.[70]

By July, Petra was seriously ill. Mifflin wrote Robert Dalzell that she had taken seriously ill with the same symptoms that had prostrated her this month a year ago. He said that she had become very low-spirited.[71] Petra had tried hard to keep her spirits up but the pain was increasing daily and her strength was being sapped. To Petra, faith had always been her strength and it was to faith that she turned daily. Mifflin had given her a large gold embossed Spanish Bible for her fifty-eighth birthday. He had given it to her as her illness worsened, hoping it would bring her solace. Petra was now approaching her sixtieth birthday and she read often from her Bible. Mifflin made sure she had only the best, from her monogrammed coach to the new home he was building. She wore a large rectangular-cut diamond in a gold setting, which was a gift from Mifflin. Later, the proceeds from the sale of that ring were given to The Driscoll Foundation in Corpus Christi by her grandson's wife, Elena Kenedy, to help fund the Driscoll Children's Hospital.[72] Petra would have highly approved of such a move as she always supported education and children.

Petra also said her rosary daily and wanted to hear about the changes at the church in Corpus Christi. Bishop Manucy preached his farewell sermon on March 16 and then prepared to leave for Mobile, Alabama.[73] The paper reported on June 13, "Bishop Dominicus Manucy to be appointed to Mobile. He came to Corpus Christi Sept. 29, 1875. His diocese stretched from the Rio Grande to the Nueces. His pastoral visits had to be made in private conveyance and undermined his health. Since his arrival he has seen nine new churches and chapels built and four priests ordained and the erection of three large chapels in the country and convents in Rio Grande City and Roma. There are now 40,000 Catholics in the diocese."[74] Bishop Manucy, despite his negative attitude, had served his people well. He had built churches where there were none and had brought thousands into the faith across the Wild Horse Desert. When Bishop Manucy left he appointed Father Jaillet vicar general and administrator. Petra's good family friend, Father Jaillet, was back. He had been their priest through the years and had been through joy and sorrow with all her family. She would need him and his support in the year to come.

Father Jaillet went to work enthusiastically. He reorganized the Altar Society that had been established by Father St. Jean. It rained heavily when he arrived and he realized that the church leaked badly and needed metal shingles. He announced in church service the next Sunday that they needed $1,000 to repair the church and he was putting up the first $500. He always tried to be first in giving. However, when the city required that they pave the sidewalks around the church property, he announced that his purse was very flat. Father Jaillet also cared passionately about education. He always said, "The children of today are the parishioners of tomorrow; hence, they must be brought up in the fundamental truths of our Holy Faith." He encouraged the Sisters of the Incarnate Word Academy to construct a new building. He supervised it for them and it was completed in 1885. He not only taught numbers and religion there but he personally tested the pupils at the end of the school year.[75] The students studied hard because they did not want to disappoint Father Jaillet. Petra and Mifflin supported the school just as they had in Brownsville. Petra could not volunteer because of her illness, but Mifflin saw to it that they provided material gifts.

By August, Petra seemed a little better, and Mifflin telegraphed John at La Parra that she was not so sick as when John left but that he had sent for Nene. He wanted John to remain at the ranch for instructions and to have his horses ready.[76] A little over a week later Mifflin wrote to Rosa, "your mother says if you can possibly do so she wishes you to come to her. Sarah says if you wish to bring two or three of your children she will take care of them. If you can come get the very best conveyance to be had, and come via the San Pedro Gate to La Parra and to Santa Gertrudis—Capt. King will send you in to Collins [now Alice]. Engage your conveyance to Santa Gertrudis. But we will relieve them at La Parra."[77] Mifflin engaged the entire family in Petra's care. Sarah and Dr. Spohn did not have children, so Sarah was offering to help with Rosa's children. Captain King stood by to help also and take them from the Santa Gertrudis to the railroad connection at Collins Station where they could board the train for Corpus Christi. Mifflin also told Rosa that if she could, to bring a woman servant who would make herself generally useful.[78]

Petra went through a period in September and October of feeling better, and Mifflin was able to work with her on furnishing her home. In February, Mifflin had ordered three loads of Austin limestone for the fence at the new house.[79] Then in May, he had written a letter to Mr. Scott in New York about sending him the plans of the serving room, or the room between the dining room and kitchen, and he wanted to install shelves between the door of the butler's pantry and the kitchen door. He wanted a tub to handle the knives, forks, and fine ware in keeping with the balance of the room. He wanted porcelain with grooves connected to the faucets and pipes to drain the water, and he included a diagram so there could be no mistakes.[80]

In June the newspaper reported on the progress of the house. "Messrs. Carroll & Iler, carpenters and builders, are still at work on the fine residence for Capt. Kenedy. When finished this will be one of the strongest, handsomest, most commodious and comfortable residences in the South. A better view is hard to find anywhere in Texas or out of it. Mike Brennan of San Antonio has recently put up around the property a handsome iron fence set in beautiful stone. George Burris, brick mason, John Hall, tinner, and Mike Niland, painter have done considerable on this place, which grows handsomer daily."[81]

On October 6, Mifflin ordered more housewares after consulting with Petra. He again wrote to Mr. Scott and said, "I have not responded to order any china or tableware but since consulting Mrs. K—and having shown her the samples have decided to do so—so please say to Mr. Fernarnds I will take the Dinner, Breakfast, and Tea sets—also one Table Set Glassware—one Dessert Set, one Ice Cream Set, one Chocolate Set—one Glass Fruit Set, . . . will put the monogram of Mrs. K—PVK—on Dinner, Breakfast, and Tea Set—also on Glass Set for table, Dessert Set, Chocolate Set—now in reference to the table set of glass ware, I see no use for water bottles as they look much like a restaurant—neither do I see any necessity for liqueurs." He also wrote on the same day and said he was confirming that he wanted the Watson's moth carpet lining in fifty-yard rolls to go under the carpet. It was made in Erie, Pennsylvania, and he had seen it at Berkman's in New York. He said the tiles had arrived but he thought the ones for the fireplace were rather plain.[82]

Mifflin and his family were interested in art and were known as art collectors, which was rare in the Wild Horse Desert. Many of their paintings hang in the Corpus Christi Museum today. The museum printed this description: "Mifflin Kenedy was a collector of art in addition to being a very successful rancher and businessman. An inventory of his collection, done in 1885, included 68 paintings and prints, mostly of European artists since at the time the greatest art in the world was considered to originate in Europe. It is remarkable that Mifflin Kenedy amassed such a collection, given the relative isolation of South Texas."[83] At the end of October, Mifflin wrote Mr. Swenson in New York that he was sending a box containing three paintings, one of Madam Mairteron, wife of Louis the XIV of France, as the vestal virgin in the sacred fire, by Boucher. The other two were painted by Eugenia Amburell "who is an old French lady now living here." He told him that the Mairteron painting was two hundred years old and he thought it was a valuable painting. The others he felt had little merit but they were highly prized by the old lady. He said that the painting by Boucher had been done during the reign of Louis the XIV, and after his death, Louis XIV's son gave the picture to Louis XV's mistress Madame du Barry, who gave it to her lady of honor Madame de Launay, who gave it to her grandfather. The other two pictures were painted for an exhibition at the Louvre; the artist received medals for them. Mifflin wanted Swenson to put the pictures in proper hands to have them repaired and handsomely framed.[84]

Mifflin continued to write to Anita about her grandmother and of his disappointment in his new daughter-in-law Stella Turcotte Kenedy's action when on a trip to New Orleans. On September 7, Mifflin wrote to Anita in New Orleans and told her that he had received her letter and that her Uncle James and his wife had been in Corpus Christi for some three months. James was in critical condition, having had typhoid malarial fever and congestion of the left lung. His son was born in Corpus Christi. George Mifflin Kenedy was born August 24, 1884,[85] and shortly after, James had gone to Monterrey and Saltillo to see if the climate there would help him. John and Stella were at La Parra, but Stella had taken sick and Dr. Spohn and Sarah had to go by boat to bring her back to Corpus, where she had been for six weeks. Mifflin told Anita, "the old house has been quite a hospital this last year."[86]

He told her how they were all much surprised to learn that Stella had not called on her when she was in New Orleans and that he was disappointed in his daughter-in-law. He said she had received "the greatest attention and kindness from all here, and had a nice house here, furnished, awaiting her return." Mifflin said he asked Stella why she had not called on Anita and her answer was she did not have time. Stella had traveled to New Orleans in the summer arriving back on June 22 on the steamer *Aransas*.[87]

Mifflin shared with Anita that he had not written as much as he should have but he had rheumatism in his right hand. He said he could not write with a pen and was obliged to write with a pencil. Mifflin thought she should stay in school another year and had written her mother but had not gotten her answer yet. He told her that "your grand mia" sends much love and that Anita would hear from her soon. He signed it "Yours affectionately, M Kenedy."[88] Mifflin followed up with the letter he promised in October. He wrote to tell Anita he had mislaid her last letter and had forgotten the name of the sister who took Sister St. Michael's place but he had written to Sister S. Michael and "enclosed his check on Swenson & Sons in New York for $550 today—of this amount he intended to pay a balance of $30.50 on last years' due—$50 for her pocket money and a balance of $450 to be applied on her school account. Her uniforms and any clothing she required and anything that the good sisters may think [it] necessary and proper for her to have." He told her that her grandmother was improving but seldom left her room. Her Uncle Santiago was in

Corpus Christi and was in critical condition, his lungs badly affected. James's wife and child were there also. Mifflin told Anita that her Aunt Nene was there attending her grandmother and they had not been clear of sickness in the house since Anita left. He feared that her Uncle Santiago would not recover. He also told her that his own mother, Sarah, was very low and he might hear of her death at any moment. Mifflin said if his mother lived until November 4 she would complete her ninety-first year. He said that her Aunt Sarah and Uncle Arthur were fine and that her Aunt Rosa had been there.[89]

Mifflin tried to keep the family news circulating and to communicate Petra's and James's conditions to everyone throughout the year. Nene was at Petra's side a good deal during the year; evidently trouble was brewing between her and her husband, Fred. Mifflin wrote his son-in-law that he "can see no necessity for such hasty action. Three or four days can make a great difference. Nene is entitled to some consideration—I advise that you wait for her arrival—will you do so. Answer. M. Kenedy"[90] Whatever the problem, it was very serious. At the beginning of December Mifflin felt it necessary to send Starck a telegram asking that he "not bring our children and wives in this matter and he must be the best judge of how to act and let him know his decision."[91] This situation led to a deep and irrevocable break with Captain Dalzell and led to serious consequences for Starck in the New Year. This split of one family against another brought great distress to a weakened Petra.

Of all the things that happened to Petra and Mifflin in 1884, the worse was Santiago's illness and declining health. At the first of April, James was involved in another shooting incident. This was his third, and this one was in Texas at La Parra Ranch. On April 7, the paper printed this account: "A telegram received by our Sheriff from Mr. James Kenedy at La Parra stated that he, Mr. K., had accidentally shot and killed a man, and asked advice on the premises. Mr. Brito received the telegram today, and it stated that the accident had occurred yesterday. He promptly wired Mr. Kenedy to have a coroner's jury render a verdict and report same and the testimony to him. What the steps our Sheriff will take or has taken in the matter we cannot ascertain as he has gone down to Point Isabel. Nothing further than what we have given has been heard up to 12 P.M. today."[92] The next day the paper printed, "We are truly glad to learn, from sources perfectly reliable, that the killing of a man at La Parra by Mr. James Kenedy, some days since was purely accidental. A full and careful examination by Deputy Sheriff Tomás Treviño entirely exonerates Mr. Kenedy from all blame in the matter. He had at once surrendered himself to the deputy sheriff but was released immediately upon the conclusion of the examination. This is as we surmised in a former issue, and the result gives universal gratification to our people, among whom Captain Kenedy's family are all so well and favorably known."[93] The paper reported on the ninth that James was sick in bed.[94] It seemed that James's health declined after this incident, and it may be that the injuries he received during this fight aggravated his precarious health.

Mifflin was evidently a lot more worried about the consequences of the shooting than the paper was. He wrote a detailed letter to his lawyer, James Wells, so he could defend Santiago. He started the letter by explaining that on Sunday Santiago had accidentally shot a man and killed him and he was giving him all the details. He said that no one saw the killing and he would give him just as near as he could what Santiago told him on his arrival at the ranch, which agreed exactly with what he told others immediately after the killing:

> Santiago arrived at the ranch about five o'clock on horseback from the Barrodas gate, where he had started a drove of cattle for Kansas at 1 P.M. and as is the general custom had his pistol on his belt. He rode into the horse lot or stable and found a strange horse there. He went around to the harness room and found Isaac Hodges and a Mexican in the room named Lorenzo Vega or Vela. Now this man Vega or Vela had been in Tom Kenedy's employ taking care of some stallions for some ten days but had been discharged some four or five days and afterwards Santiago had requested him not to go into this room (harness room) and not into the kitchen (Hodges is the cook). When Santiago found him with Hodges in the harness room he asked Hodges who the horse in the corral belonged to. He answered that Vega or Vela was the man. Santiago said to him that he had told you several times not to put your horse in the stable or come into this room or the kitchen at the house and to leave the ranch. Now take your horse and leave this minute. Santiago said the man looked at him and smiled and Santiago then left the room thinking, he said, to give him time to get away and went around the lot to straighten some trees. I had sent him 300 cherries, willows and mulberrys. While occupied with this he saw Vega come out of Hodges' room and go up to the dwelling house. Santiago waited until he saw Vega return towards the harness room and met him at the door, when Vega entered the door and Santiago said to him, "Cabrón have I not told you several times not to go into the room and leave the ranch." Vega replied, "mas cabrón es usted carajo" ["Damn it, you're more of a bastard than I am"]. Santiago struck at him with his right hand (his left is useless). Vega dodged him and he hit the door casing. Vega hit him in the breast knocking him back—Santiago said his right hand being badly injured, and having little use of his left and finding the man would get the advantage of him drew his pistol with the intention of hitting him over the head.

> He struck out at Vega and in the scuffle at this moment his foot slipped, he fell backwards, his pistol fired, the man made three or four steps further in the house and fell dead. The ball struck back of and a little under the right ear and up and out above the right eye—The ball passed through his head and struck the side of the room in front of the door where his shot was fired some eight feet or more from the floor. The direction of the ball confirms Santiago's account of the affair. When the shot was fired he was in a kneeling or falling position says the latter. He says he did not draw his pistol to shoot, that his hand was benumbed, that he did not cock his pistol that he is aware of and the only way he can account for it is that when he struck or attempted to strike the man he may have cocked it accidentally. Hodges says when Vega went out of the room and to the house he went out into the horse lot to hang up some clothes that he had been washing. That he heard a noise like some scuffling or wrestling he said and went to the door. He saw Vega on the floor and Santiago standing over him. When he saw him he threw up his arms and said, "My God, Isaac, I have killed this man, I did not intend to do it." The next one that got there was Pefaris, a young man that attends to the store, and the next Paris, I believe the mail rider—and the same statement was made to them as to Isaac. He then went to the house and made the same statement to doña Sescuda an old Mex woman—the housekeeper. He then telegraphed Brito and myself saying he had killed a man accidentally. He also sent for Henry Hawley and Tomás Treviño Dept. Sheriff to give himself up—He made the same confession to them—Treviño sent a courier at once for nearest justice of the peace at Punta del Monte but could not be found—Courier returned and then asked Treviño to hold inquest as best he could. . . . I am convinced it was accidental and I have asked Tomás Treviño to send me a copy on inquest. I will forward it to you. I think it is possible that this man Vega or Vela may be one of the men that killed Sheriff Masters in Starr County.[95]

Mifflin must have hurried to the ranch as soon as he heard of the shooting, and, using his analytical mind, reconstructed the story so he could relate it to Wells. There evidently was a grand jury called to investigate the shooting. On September 4, Mifflin wrote to John, his acting manager: "I sent with Isaac Hodges $50 in specie and $100 in currency. Isaac has a strapping big Moke here, who I am certain he shall take down one way or another although I have told him he cannot go—So you will know how to act if he puts in an appearance—now if Isaac goes into the kitchen let him know at once that his friends cannot go there, and coffee drinkers (outsiders) will not be permitted. Treat him kindly and justly but firmly and make him obey instructions. If he will not then let him go. He is very dirty personally and I would not have him about the kitchen unless he will keep clean—He is an important witness in Santiago's case so try and get along with him until that case is decided—I have written Wells to give you the names of the witnesses wanted of the grand jury papers to investigate the case if he wants you to send the jury of inquest at the ranch you will have to do it—no matter how inconvenient—Tom is in Brownsville and will give him the list—Tomás Treviño, Howley, Isaac and the old woman and Ipefano are the most important witnesses—Isaac is the most important"[96] This shooting incident must have hung over the head of Mifflin as well as Petra throughout the year.

In June, Mifflin was dealing with an old land question with his son and with Corina's family. He wrote to James calling him "Dear Son" and signing it "your affectionate father." In the letter he counsels James about buying into the Mesteñas land the McAllens owned. This land and its ownership were highly disputed between the Kenedys and McAllens for years. James evidently wanted to buy a portion of the land and Mifflin told him to wait and see what kind of terms he could get. He told him that he did not think "they would be giving you a figure you would be willing to give. All you can do is to watch the situation, keep them in hand, and see what terms you can make when they make up their minds to sell." He told him that McAllen promised Mifflin he would not sell any portion and would keep the land intact. He said he had failed to do so and the sale he made to Lina and Cantu had complicated the matter. He also told him that it could be a long time before John Young and his mother came to a division and he believed the interest in it was unclear.[97]

By July, Santiago was very ill and could not even sit up.[98] He brought Corina to live with Mifflin and Petra as she awaited the birth of their first child. Corina in later years said that when she first came to stay with Petra she gave her a *metate*.[99] Petra, who was already very ill herself, must have grieved over Santiago and his illness but was happy that Corina had come to stay with them. The two women must have spent time together talking about the baby and Corina and James's plans. Corina also visited with Rosa and Nene and the other family members as they came and went to help Petra. Mifflin's little rental house was filling up. Robert Kleberg was also worried about Mifflin and wrote Alice on July 6, 1884, from Corpus Christi to tell her that he had called on Captain Kenedy. He told her that Kenedy was unwell and so he spent the evening with him. He said he was "suffering from some irritation of the ileus—nothing serious but annoying to him."[100] Mifflin, sick also, had little time to take care of himself because he was so busy taking care of everyone else in his immediate family.

Corina Ballí Kenedy and Georgie Kenedy, after husband and father, James Kenedy, had died. Corina raised Georgie in Laredo after James's death, where she was also a benefactor to the church. Courtesy Mary Margaret McAllen Amberson.

At the end of August, joy filled the little house. On August 24, Corina Ballí Kenedy gave birth to George Mifflin Kenedy at Petra and Mifflin's rented house in Corpus Christi.[101] Petra was filled with joy as she heard the cries of Santiago's son. The sight of Santiago holding his son must have been painful to her. They all knew how ill he was yet they also saw his determination to get well and live to enjoy his family and little son. Mifflin welcomed this young grandson into his family. He now had a Kenedy heir who also carried his name. The new arrival may have been named George after Mifflin's older brother George Fairlamb Kenedy.[102] The family gathered around and shared the joy with Corina and Santiago. For a moment they could forget about the illness that permeated the house.

Petra was surely a help to Corina. She had given birth to fourteen children, in many different conditions. She knew how to take care of babies and she could give this young mother helpful advice. Mainly she offered the mother's touch of listening and supporting and filling those hours with reassurance that the baby would do well and grow up to be all she and Santiago hoped for. Santiago decided to take his health into his own hands after the birth of baby George. He had always been a fighter and had never followed conventional rules. Santiago had a new baby and beautiful wife and he was determined to do anything to try to cure himself. Santiago wasted no time in putting his plan into action. A week and a half after George was born, he left for Laredo, Monterrey, and Saltillo. He felt that the climate would improve his health.

On September 2, Mifflin wrote a letter to Captain Dalzell telling him that Petra was better but was not able to leave her room. He said, "She comes down stairs occasionally but only for a very short time—she spends most of her time in bed—at times she is hopeful, but most of the time she despairs of getting well. I think unless there is some great change in her condition she will go to New Orleans in October for treatment if she is able to travel. James is better or is stronger than he was but in my opinion is no better. His left lung is congested and useless—He seems to think if he can go to Monterrey and Saltillo he will improve—He leaves for Laredo tomorrow morning, and if he finds he can bear the trip will go on to Monterrey in a few days—He goes against my advice."[103]

Mifflin also corresponded with King, asking him for a favor. He needed King to send a conveyance to Collins Station for Rosa. He asked if she could stay the night with King and then requested King forward her to La Parra. There she would meet Nene and "with your permission will avail herself of the same conveyance back to Santa Gertrudis and then on to Collins Station." Mifflin told King that he knew at certain times this might cause him much inconvenience but hoped it will not be so now. He asked him to pardon the liberty that he had taken.[104] Mifflin needed King to help with shuttling the family back and forth from Brownsville to Corpus Christi. He also telegraphed Starck in Brownsville to get the very best conveyance and to get a relay of horses because Rosa was starting home and they were waiting to hear when Nene would start from Brownsville.[105] Rosa was starting home to Brownsville and Nene was leaving Brownsville to take her place in Corpus Christi and they were meeting midway.

Mifflin then wrote John at La Parra that Nene and Irene (Rosa's daughter) were leaving for La Parra the next day and for him to meet them at the San Pedro gate. They would wait at La Parra for Rosa's arrival and she would bring the mail from Santa Gertrudis when King sent her.[106] He then wrote another letter to Captain Dalzell to tell him about the plans and said that Mrs. Kenedy was improving and he hoped it might be permanent.[107]

Mifflin must have felt like he was on a merry-go-round with all the correspondence and people to coordinate. His hand bothered him most of the time and trying to keep up with all the arrangements was taxing to him physically as well as mentally. Mifflin was sixty-six years old and not in the best of health. For the last year he had essentially run a hospital in his home, shuttled family members hundreds of miles across the Wild Horse Desert, managed a cattle empire, struggled with financial difficulties, experienced problems with his sons, and was in the process of building an extraordinary home. He too had an opportunity to be dispirited and despondent, particularly as he watched Petrita fighting the disease that was slowly taking over her body.

Santiago wrote a series of letters to Corina while on his trip that gave a unique insight into the battle he was waging against his illness. Neither Petra nor Santiago was giving in to disease, and each was fighting in a unique way to win the battle for health. Santiago arrived in Monterrey on the seventh of September and told Corina that he was feeling much better and that his appetite was splendid. He said that the cough had almost left and that when he was in Nuevo Laredo, China (Concepción Rodríguez, his half-sister) wanted Corina to come for a visit. He told her that she could go to see her and then he would start back to Laredo and meet her and take her back to Corpus Christi with him. Santiago wanted her to be sure that the trip would not injure her or the baby and if she went she must get a good woman to help her. If she should decide to go, she must telegraph Manuel Rodríguez so he can meet her at the depot, and to have him respond back to her so that there could be no mistake. He wanted to know how she and George Kenedy were getting along. He told her that if she went she must take money and a lunch so that when the train stopped for twenty minutes at Benavides she could have her woman go in and get cups of coffee for them. He then sent his love to Father, Mother, Rosa, and George.[108]

James was obviously lonely and the next day wrote Corina to write him two or three times a day and let him know how she and the baby were doing. He told her he was stopping at a hotel with beautiful gardens near the central part of Monterrey. He acknowledged that the dust on the trail had bothered him and he was taking an herbal tea called ancosvita. He told her that if he was going to be there longer than three weeks he would send for her. He wanted to know if she had gotten a nurse to help take care of the baby and to clean up the house at Santa Anita. He again sent his love to Father, Mother, and Rosa.[109]

In the next week, Santiago wrote nearly every day. Mifflin was taking care of him financially, and on the fourteenth sent Santiago a letter telling him that he was arranging a $1,000 bank draft and that his mother was improving; Corina and the baby were doing well.[110] During the week, Santiago told Corina that he had experienced heavy rains and if she came to join him that she should go to La Parra and then to Santa Anita, and not through Collins Station.[111]

Two weeks later, James's health had declined. He wrote Corina to say he was sorry that he had not written for a few days but he had been sick with a cold, cough, and fever while in Saltillo. He said he was a little better but he didn't think he would be home before the tenth of October. He was at a boarding house with four or five boarders and the lady that ran it was being very kind to him. He said he was getting everything he wished for and it was his own foolishness that had gotten him sick. He wanted her to give Georgie a kiss and to keep looking for a nurse she liked.[112]

Mifflin was also trying to help Santiago out, perhaps trying to manage his affairs. On September 29, Mifflin telegraphed Manuel to see if his business would permit him to go to Monterrey and accompany Santiago as far as Laredo. The same day, he sent a second telegram saying Santiago declined to come home.[113] The next day Santiago wrote Corina that he had been shopping and was sending her some "goodies." He was sending her one hundred pounds of *harina semita* (a type of meal or flour), twenty pounds of chocolate, twenty pounds of *paste demembrilli*, five pounds of *arroz* (rice), and maybe some other things. He also told her that he had picked a bad time to come and that it had rained for three weeks and he should have stayed at home. He says she will get tired of him this winter and that the limestone water was making his bowels loose and it was very weakening. He sent his love to Father, Mother, Nene, and Sarah and the balance of the family and he told her that he would be home between the ninth and twelfth.[114]

James and Corina's son, George Mifflin Kenedy, was baptized on October 3 in Corpus Christi at St. Patrick's by Ferd. Jas. Goebels. The sponsors were David M. Murphy and Petra Kenedy.[115] Petra had made the supreme effort to get out of bed and go to church to be there when this grandchild was baptized into the faith. It was probably Petra's last time in the church she loved. In her weakened state and with the pain she was enduring, she stood proud and tall beside the young mother and child. In this child, she saw the legacy of Santiago being carried forward and her heritage being preserved. Through him and her other children and grandchildren she could see into the future and know that her legacy would live on even after her death. Petra felt blessed that she had been allowed to see him born and that she could share this sacred moment with him and the family. Petra was known in the family as "Petrita" by Mifflin, "Ma" by her children, and "Grand Mia" by her grandchildren.[116] She was the "Mother" of the family. She was the center of their world and through the years gave them strength, love, and faith to carry on in tough times.

Mifflin wrote to King on the ninth and said that Santiago had returned and was sicker than before.[117] Mifflin telegraphed to his sister Mrs. S. (Sarah) J. (Josephine) Thompson in Coatesville, Pennsylvania, on October 14. In the telegram he used his pet name for Petra. He wrote, "Petrita confined to her room, James here in critical condition. Nene, here, husband sick in bed and with all this I can't leave."[118] Mifflin was caught in a real dilemma. His mother was dying and he had his hands full with an ill family and could not go and be by her bedside or see her once more before she died.

Mifflin was having trouble with Starck, and on the eighteenth informed John at La Parra that Starck and the three children were on the way from Brownsville to meet up with Nene who was nursing Petra. He wanted John to send two conveyances to meet them at the Sands and forward them to Collins Station to meet the train. If that was a problem then Starck was to lay over at La Parra.[119] The Starck problem continued and worried Mifflin enough that he had asked him not to "bring in our wives and children into it."

November 4 was Mifflin's mother's birthday, and he wired Jo to wish his mother a happy ninety-first birthday and to send their love and congratulations.[120] Jo wired Mifflin back in three days to let the family know that his mother did complete her ninety-first year and was very weak but comfortable. She felt that she was failing fast.[121] Good news arrived for an old friend on December 21 when King became a grandfather. "Richard King III was born at the ranch house on the Puerta de Agua Dulce. His advent, his name, brought a smile of pride in the grizzled beard of his grandfather."[122] Kenedy and King had shared many joys and troubles through their years together. Now they both could share the knowledge that they had namesakes who could carry on the legacy they had fought so hard to establish.

Robert Kleberg had written Alice from Corpus Christi on December 21 to say he had heard of the birth of Richard III and he hoped that the child would fill the aching void in her good parents' hearts and that he longed to meet the young man. Robert and Alice had experienced some difficulties in the earlier part of the month when Alice wrote to Robert of her parents' hesitation in giving them their blessing to be married. In a letter written on December 1, Robert told her about some very personal information that Captain King had shared with him about his philosophy of marriage and his courtship of Henrietta. King told Robert that he had never shared this information with anyone else. He told Robert about the importance of matrimony in the life of every man and the beneficent influence this step had on his own life, happiness, and success. He shared with him the diffidence and fear with which he had been inspired to win the love of Alice's dear mother and related the little circumstances of his first courtship. He said he had tried to know Henrietta by observing her mother as he thought that was the best way to judge what a daughter would be like. He also told Robert that Alice was just like her mother. He told Alice that he knew how powerful and impetuous her father's love was for her, that in all of his disappointments in his family relations that King had looked to her for his consolation. Robert knew that her father realized how important this step was for her happiness and he was aware of his declining health. Robert concluded the letter by saying how difficult it must be for her parents that he had "asked for that which they prize more than everything else on earth, their little pet." Robert said that he would "never cease to try and prove worthy of their highest respect and esteem," and that his respect and esteem for them had not grown any less because of their apparent reluctance to give their consent to their union. He knew they would never marry without her parents' consent, but "as long as he has her love he will never grow weary in the endeavor." He closed his letter with "good night my own true heart, may heaven bless and protect you and yours—as the sincere prayer of your affectionate lover—Robert J. Kleberg."[123]

As Christmas Eve approached it was quiet and sorrowful in the Kenedy home in Corpus Christi. Everyone surely walked with a light tread and avoided making any loud noises. The house was dark and there was no laughter or celebration of any kind. In the bedroom, Santiago lay dying. He had continued to decline since returning home in October. Mifflin wrote Captain Dalzell that Santiago could speak only in a whisper.[124] Corina was beside herself. Georgie was only three months old. Santiago had spent so little time with him and now he would not be there to help her raise him or watch him grow up. Georgie looked like his mother with big brown eyes; he was a handsome baby. Corina was twenty-five years old and had no idea what her future held. Santiago was slipping away and with him their hopes and dreams. Petra faced this holiday with sorrow and the realization that she was on the brink of losing another son. First it had been Adrian, then Phebe, then Willie, and now Santiago. Petra lifted a prayer for their souls and a special prayer to the Blessed Virgin Mary for Santiago.

The day after Christmas, Mifflin took time out to focus on the new house he was building for his Petrita. He wrote to Mr. Scott telling him that he thinks he has the "finest house in Texas." He said, "Without intending it, I am told and believe that I have the finest house inside Texas. Governor Coke and our Senator at Washington went through it some days ago, and pronounced it. Tile floors are 'simply beautiful.'"[125]

Then Mifflin went on about the things that were not right or that he needed corrected. He thought the windows were too heavy but they would be fine in the winter and they could be stowed in the summer. He was upset that there was no place to hang a hat and he had made a mistake by using brass fireplace fixtures because they tarnish. He said the glass for the fireplace in the main room was taken in transit and so were the gold bronze backs of the hooks and hinges. He thought he should have used silver or heavy nickel for the features.[126]

Mifflin was worried about the mantle in the dressing room because it was plain and the wardrobe ordered for the cross hall upstairs for Mrs. Kenedy was not what he expected. It was to be nine feet wide and the one they sent was only five feet, six inches. Mifflin went on to say, "the front of the wardrobe inside and outside is common except glass in doors. I altered the inside preferring not to send it back. Wardrobes for the bedrooms were not mouse and roach proof so I had them done. You made a mistake in not making the book cases in the library with brass—I wrote you once about making a large drawer for maps—now in place they will have to stay as is." He continued at length about the bells and gongs on the inside and outside doors. He wanted to be able to hear them with the windows closed and he wanted to have different sounds for the front and side entrances. He needed more hooks and round knobs so as not to hurt the clothes.[127]

It was good that Mifflin had a distraction because he had received notice that his mother had died. The Pennsylvania newspaper said, "Mrs. Sarah Kenedy an aged and highly respected resident of Coatesville died on Wednesday evening. She was about 92 years of age."[128] The *Brownsville Cosmopolitan* reported on January 10, 1885, that they had clipped the following article from the *Chester Valley* (Pennsylvania) *Times*, which paid tribute to the late Mrs. Sarah Kenedy "mother of our fellow townsman, Capt. Jeff Kenedy." The article said that she was an excellent woman who had faithfully attended the sick, and administered with impartial tenderness to the poor as well as to the rich.[129]

Death now surrounded Petra and Mifflin. They had lost Mifflin's mother and neither could be there to comfort her or the family in her last days. Now they knew the time was drawing close for the end of Santiago's life. Father Jaillet was near and proved once again to be their dear friend as well as spiritual advisor. He was particularly important to Santiago and in his last few days on the earth, Father Jaillet administered to Santiago and prepared him for death. Death came on Monday, December 29, 1884, at 2:45 P.M. His death certificate listed consumption as cause of death while the church records listed pneumonia. His burial was at Courtalie Cemetery.[130] Mifflin had written that James had typhoid fever. Certainly his lungs had been affected and his death was probably not a pleasant one as his lungs filled with fluid and he could not breathe. The family had been close by during the last few days and helped to make the arrangements for the funeral.

The paper carried a description of his funeral on January 3, 1885: "Died in this City 2:45 P.M. Monday December 29, 1884 James W. Kenedy. The funeral took place last Tuesday at 3:00 from the Catholic Church. He was greatly loved and respected by all that knew him. The funeral services at the altar were rendered by Father Jaillet whose duty he fulfilled but he was also satisfying a duty to friendship. He wanted to offer a soothing balm to the grieving parents.

He spoke of how James complied with his Christian duties and his pious union of his soul with God during the last days of his illness. He felt confident that he was thoroughly prepared to meet the summons of the Supreme Judge. The family could draw consolation from this in their grief. The Reverend Father concluded with the wish that everybody should, in a like manner, prepare for death when it shall come for it will be the precious signal of our deliverance and the beginning of endless happiness."[131] Father Jaillet's message was particularly important to Petra who could receive solace from the thought that Santiago had been forgiven of his sins and she would be with him in heaven. The family was highly respected in Corpus Christi as well as in Brownsville. The Brownsville paper reported that on the announcement of James's death by unanimous request of the entire bar in Corpus Christi the court was adjourned as a mark of respect and sympathy for Captain Kenedy and to enable all who desired to attend the funeral.[132]

Petra, already in fragile health, never recovered from Santiago's death. It was an overpowering grief that she could not throw off. She had always been able to confront adversity when it descended on the family, but this was more than she could handle. She could face her own physical problems with strength but losing this son at the prime of his life was overwhelming. She tried to lend comfort to Corina and to Mifflin. James was similar to the biblical prodigal son. He had caused them a great deal of worry and grief in their life but he had come into the fold and had a family of his own and a new life in front of him. Now he was gone, dying so young, and there was a void that could not be replaced in his mother's heart.

CHAPTER 21

1885:
Goodbye to Petrita

A man must win; a woman must preserve what is won.

The Brownsville newspaper thanked Mrs. Starck on January 2 for her magnificent New Year's jelly cake, made as only she could.[1] Nene was not going to let Luisa get ahead of her in bringing a cake to the paper's employees. Life quickly turned solemn for the two sisters and Petra when Capt. William Kelly recorded in his diary on January 6 that charges had been preferred in the Masonic Lodge headquarters against Fred Starck. The trial was filed for Thursday, January 5. On January 15, Fred Starck was found guilty and expelled from the Lodge.[2] Mifflin wrote to Captain Kelly later in the year saying that the matter had weighed heavily on Petra's mind. He felt that if Dalzell had given him information the trouble could have been avoided. He said that Starck had not wanted to come to Corpus Christi but he had insisted on Starck's doing so. If Starck was in Texas, Mifflin was the "innocent cause." The situation involved several issues: rent collected and not accounted for, and the "Rodríguez business and the intense hatred that Dalzell had for Starck blinded him to everything else." Mifflin said it was entirely a family matter with no outsiders involved, that "if any of the family in Brownsville can gather any consolation from it, they are welcome to it." Further clouding the issue was the fact that the charges were brought against Starck by E. J. Kenedy, Mifflin's brother. Also adding to the scenario was the close and intimate friendship between Captain Kelly and Robert Dalzell, almost certainly assuring Captain Kelly's siding with Dalzell against Starck in the Lodge's accusations.[3] The affair was a "source of great agony to Mrs. Kenedy and she departed this life lamenting the actions and the indiscretion of her family."[4]

Petra's family certainly had its problems, but they were never before spread throughout the community for others to gossip about. Family unity and support had always been of the utmost importance to her, and now in her last days she had to worry about this permanent rift that had developed between the Dalzells and Starcks. Captain Dalzell and Fred Starck had always been on opposite sides, going back to the Civil War. Starck was a Union officer and Dalzell worked with Mifflin for the Confederates, running cotton. They had also been on opposite sides politically, with Starck being a Red party member and Dalzell a Blue. The trouble between them evidently came to a head when Captain Dalzell returned to Brownsville to live permanently. The exact nature of the problem is unclear from the information available but it damaged the Starck marriage and brought Petra unending grief.

In December of 1885, the Lodge had voted to expel Starck, stating that he must leave the city of Brownsville and the jurisdiction of the Lodge on or before the first day of November next, "never to take up your residence here again." Starck had signed papers to that effect and also that he would never again call himself a Mason.[5] Starck appealed and lost, with the proceedings enigmatically discussing the testimony of the party claiming to have been injured as "her and her mother." Perhaps this is the "Rodríguez" to whom Mifflin refers. In the appeal Starck had written that the committee had not gone to the place where the offense was supposed to have happened to see for themselves that the offense could not have been committed without detection, nor were his friends and family interviewed. Starck had several other complaints in the appeal, but all were denied and the expulsion and its conditions stood.[6]

In December Tom had been in Corpus Christi with the family, perhaps to be there at Santiago's death, and at La Parra, but was in Brownsville by January 17. The paper welcomed him, saying "Our town is always more lively and bustling when this prince of good fellows is among us."[7] The paper noted that Tom purchased a "magnificent new buggy and two fine horses," reporting he had the best turnout in this section.[8] During this time, Tom was evidently courting a special young lady. His brothers and sisters had married and now Tom was ready to start a family. The paper again noted on February 7 that Mr. Tom Kenedy had arrived from La Parra Ranch last evening, having made the trip of one hundred miles in ten hours.[9] Tom had a reason to make good time back and forth from the ranch. He was courting and winning the hand of Miss Yrene Yznaga, the pretty young daughter of a prominent Brownsville businessman, Antonio Yznaga, a successful merchant and rancher. Yrene was referred to as "one of the Belles of the Rio Grande."[10]

Tom wrote Petra and Mifflin informing them of his engagement to Yrene. Mifflin wrote an insightful letter in return in which he offered strong fatherly advice to Tom, again expressing his doubts about Tom's ability to be successful and support a wife. Mifflin wrote that he and Petra had known Mr. and Mrs. Yznaga many years and knew they were the best of people; no family on the Rio Grande stood higher in their opinion than the Yznagas, or were more entitled to respect. He said that he and Petra considered Tom fortunate in his acceptance by the family. Mifflin wrote that he took it for granted that Tom had informed Mr. Yznaga of his situation, the state of his affairs, his prospects for the future, and of how he expected to maintain and provide for his family. In the interest of his daughter, Mr. Yznaga had a right to know and no doubt had conferred with Tom on the subject.[11]

Mifflin then told Tom that when a woman marries, she has the right to expect all the comforts she leaves behind when she leaves her parental home. Mifflin asked Tom if he was prepared to give the woman of his choice such a home, to examine his situation fully, and not deceive himself or the woman who had accepted him, trusting in his honor and good faith. Mifflin felt that if Tom had done all of these things and informed Mr. Yznaga of his indebtedness it would give him much pleasure to see Tom married, but to not count on the family for help.[12]

It seemed that indebtedness might be a way of life for Tom, and Mifflin was concerned. Prior to his wedding, with Mifflin out of town, Tom went to James Wells and borrowed $1,000 to cover his wedding and honeymoon expenses.[13]

Petra was surely pleased at Tom's choice. The Yznaga family was one of the leading Mexican families in South Texas. Mifflin's association with don Antonio Yznaga went back to at least 1867. In October of that year Captain Kenedy and don Antonio had been named coexecutors of J. Alexander Werbiskie's will.[14] Yznaga's daughter was beautiful and wealthy, and smitten with Tom. Tom was Petra and Mifflin's first born. He was good looking, with dark eyes and a merry disposition that affected all those around him. He had grown up during the lean years in Brownsville when the family was first getting established. He was surrounded with conflict through the Cortina years and the Civil War. He spent four years in Pennsylvania with his brothers, but the Quaker surroundings seemed to have had no bearing on either James or Tom. Tom's nature reflected the gay life of the border, the fandangos, the music, and the "let life come as it may" attitude. Tom married four months after Petra's death. Even though Petra did not live long enough to attend the ceremony, she must have felt hopeful that Tom would settle down and take on the responsibility of supporting his family.

The day before the wedding the newspaper ran the following: "Mr. Thomas M. Kenedy, son of Capt. Mifflin Kenedy will be married, at the pro-cathedral in this city at 6 o'clock Friday morning, to Miss Yrene, the lovely daughter of Mr. A. J. Yznaga of this city. The wedding will be one of the social

Tom Kenedy and Yrene Yznaga on their wedding day, July 29, 1885. The wedding was described as the social event of the year. Courtesy Raymondville Historical Museum, Texas.

events of the season."[15] The paper recorded the wedding the next day, on July 29, 1884, in great detail, indicating that it was indeed the social event of the season. The cathedral, decorated with flowers and blazing with lights, was crowded at the 6 A.M. ceremony. The beautiful bride wore a brocaded satin dress covered with bead embroidery and wore a veil with orange blossoms. The groomsmen and bridesmaids were Judge Forto and Miss Kingsbury; Mr. Antonio J. Yznaga and his sister, Miss Juanita; Mr. R. M. Dalzell; his sister

Miss Irene and Mr. J. L. Putegnat and his sister Miss Lulu. Little Misses Sunie Putegnat, Olivia Yznaga and Mamie Dalzell were also in attendance. The ceremony was solemnized by Father Lorenzo.[16]

After the services the bridal party and their immediate friends went to Miller's Hotel for a sumptuous wedding breakfast with the health of the newly wedded couple being toasted in sparkling wine. The bridal party then crossed the river, went to the end of the track in front of the customs house at Matamoros to a waiting train, and after the last farewells left on their wedding trip to Saltillo. The news article included a listing of the wedding presents, saying they were numberless and most costly with the more portable articles and especially the jewels being taken on the trip.[17] There was no representation from Tom's sister Vicenta Starck's family, from his sister Concepción's family, or from John and Stella. Their families are also not listed on the gift list. Mifflin's bridal gift was the Brownsville land he gave for their home.

Three legal documents reflected what happened to Tom and Yrene during their brief marriage. In the first document, Mifflin Kenedy gave to Yrene as a wedding gift lots 10, 11, and 12 of block 53 in the city of Brownsville, located at Eighth and Levee Street. They later built their house there.[18] The second document was dated April 2, 1886, and was an agreement between Tom Kenedy and Martin Hanson to build a two-story house with specifications to be furnished by Charles Carroll of Corpus Christi. Martin was to be paid $6,800 in U.S. currency and $1,000 in Mexican currency. Tom had turned to the same architect who built his father's house in Corpus Christi. The house was to be a grand one, although not as grand as his father's. It was about 6,000 square feet with twenty-six rooms, including two music rooms. It had a double brick water closet, a coach house, and a stable in the back built of brick, with an iron railing. The property was enclosed with a six-foot-high brick fence that was 217 feet long.[19]

Petra did not live long enough to hear about this house, but she also did not have to experience the tragedy that occurred there. In July of 1887, Yrene, who was pregnant with their first child, was walking down the uncompleted stairs of the house when she tripped and fell. The fall killed her and the unborn child.[20] Another story was that Yrene was hanging curtains and fell off the ladder. The third legal document verifies the timing of the story. On July 9, 1887, Tom sold the house to Yrene's parents, don Antonio and Juana, for one dollar, with the provision that they would assume the debt. The personal items went with the house. The Yznagas lived in the house for years and later sold it to the Rentfros for $410,000.[21] Tom would die tragically a few years later, but Petra never knew about Tom's death; she died thinking that the future was bright for her wayward son.

In 1888, Tom ran for sheriff against Sheriff Brito, who had held the position for a long time. Things were getting pretty tense between the two. One night Tom, looking for Sheriff Brito, walked into the saloon and slammed his .30–30 carbine down on the bar and demanded to see Brito, who owned the bar. He was not there, and Tom was convinced to leave.[22] In the meantime, Tom, after Yrene's untimely death, was courting Elvira María Esparza, who was estranged from her husband José Esparza, a Brownsville deputy. Sheriff Brito, hoping to get rid of his competition, inflamed José Esparza against Tom in order to incite a fight. It worked, and on Tom's thirty-fifth birthday, as he was returning from Matamoros and a night of celebrating with his friends and Elvira, Esparza ambushed him on the pier and killed him. Frank Ytúrria said that Esparza fled to Mexico and escaped. He also said that Captain Kenedy sent Frank and George Putegnat to find him, kill him, and bring his head back in a sack for the Captain.[23] George Putegnat wrote an account of that trip and confirmed that he did travel into Mexico to find Esparza. They found him tied to a tree by Mexican officers. The officers asked Frank and George to identify the man, and when they did, the officers handed Putegnat a pistol. George declined the offer to kill Esparza, and said he wanted to bring him back to Brownsville for trial. They said they would bring Esparza to Brownsville. Putegnat left Mexico to tell Mifflin that they had caught him and he was being returned for trial. Evidently Esparza found the means to bribe the officers and escaped. He later returned to Texas and lived on a ranch outside of Brownsville. Sheriff Brito was assassinated four years later. Frank Ytúrria said, "no one knows exactly who ordered Brito's assassination. But the guy everyone knew did it was Mifflin Kenedy's pistolero, Herculano Berber."[24]

The house Tom Kenedy built for Yrene Yznaga, which he sold to her parents after her death. Brownsville Historical Association.

Before Petra's death, she and Mifflin received disturbing news about their close friend Richard King. He knew he was mortally sick, but it was difficult for the captain to think of leaving Santa Gertrudis ranch. It had been his life, built from a vast unoccupied prairie with the sweat of his brow and his undaunted spirit. Henrietta and Alice finally convinced him to travel to San Antonio to place himself under the care of Dr. Ferdinand Herff. On February 25, when he left the ranch, his last instructions were to tell Jim Wells in a letter to keep on buying land and to never let a foot of the Santa Gertrudis get away. "It took a man on a good horse a whole week of steady riding to circuit the fence of the Santa Gertrudis. Out there on the miles and miles of grass there were more than forty thousand head of cattle branded with the running W. There were nearly seven thousand horses, there were twelve thousand sheep."[25] Captain King was leaving an enormous legacy that no livestock tally, no warranty deeds, and no set of facts or figures could accurately describe. It would have been a hard time for Captain King. It was roundup season, "when the great steers on the wild spring-steel legs came clattering their horns through the thickets, when scores of shouting centaurs rode in the dust to the bellowing music of the gathered herds."[26]

Mifflin was as close to King as a brother, and yet he could not be with him. He knew his dear friend was traveling to San Antonio and knew his condition was grave, but the situation was similar to the time of his mother's death. He could not get away.

Shortly after James's death, Corina had asked if she and little Georgie could live on La Parra. Mifflin wrote to John and asked him if it would be all right and suggested putting them up in a little house on the property. At the time of James's death he had virtually nothing. In his bank account was $303.72.[27]

Mifflin wanted Petra to live in the house he had built for her, and she was determined not to be the "third person" to die in the "hut." Her son-in-law Joe Putegnat had died there, and also her son Santiago. Mifflin pushed the workmen hard to complete the grand house because he knew Petra's time was short. Mifflin admired Petra's courage and knew it had been tested through the years by all the trials and tribulations that she had overcome. He described her courage in a letter to his son-in-law Robert Dalzell when he wrote that Petra had always had a great desire to keep her infirmity a secret. When anyone called, she made an effort to appear cheerful and much better than she actually was.[28] Petra was about to face a short but difficult journey—the one to the new house.

On the morning of February 26, 1885, Mifflin carefully prepared her beautiful monogrammed coach. The servants placed heated bricks wrapped in cloths at her feet to keep her warm. The seat was cushioned with blankets and pillows for comfort. Mifflin instructed the coachman to drive the horses slowly and carefully. Nene was there to help Petra dress. Mifflin and Nene helped Petra down the stairs of the rented house to the coach. Then very slowly they drove her across the street and through the wrought iron gate and up the driveway to her new home. Her Italian style home was 108 feet long and sixty-eight feet wide, with a lofty sixty-five-foot tower that rose from the front of the house. A wrought iron fence surrounded the house; servants' quarters and a carriage house were in the back. Petra must have gazed in awe at the magnificent structure. Mifflin had talked about it and had shared many

The Kenedy Mansion that Mifflin built for his Petrita and into which she moved February 26, 1885, before she died on March 16, 1885. Raymondville Historical Museum, Texas.

details with her. Now she was viewing the house in its grandeur. It truly dominated any other structures on the bluff and would as long as it stood.

Petra was helped from the coach and, on Nene's arm, followed Mifflin as he showed her the beautiful home he had built for his Petrita. First they walked around the grounds and then slowly and laboriously climbed the front steps; Mifflin showed off his doorbell, fixtures, and beautiful glass and wood door with the etched letters MK. The house that Petra then entered was indeed one of the finest in the South. When she stepped inside the doorway, she was greeted with elegance. Mifflin had walnut, oak, mahogany, cherry, pine, and cypress brought from all over the world to finish the interior. There were more than two hundred gas burners casting halos of light, creating a setting of warmth and opulence. The library's floor was of fine tile and carpet. The handsome beautifully carved staircase was of polished mesquite wood. Etched glass transoms and elegant furniture had been placed in each room. The magnificent dining room had a table set with the china monogrammed with her initials that they had chosen together.[29]

Upstairs, the family bedrooms and sitting rooms all faced the water. The bedrooms were large and comfortable; the bathrooms were large, with big mirrors and running hot water from the ceramic hand-painted fixtures. When Petra undressed, her clothes would have gone into the wardrobe that had been redone, under Mifflin's instructions, so the interior would be right. Petra had a large mahogany bed and was surrounded by the steam heat's warmth. Mifflin, knowing Petra's determination, later told Robert Dalzell that "it was her last effort and she threw all her strength and energy into it."[30]

Petra must have thought of the many houses they had lived in through their lifetime together. Their first house had been on Elizabeth Street in Brownsville, and then they fled to Matamoros during the Civil War while the Union army occupied the house. After the war, they reclaimed the house, but it was never the same. Their next house was their home at Los Laureles. Petra had loved the house there and all the frenzied activity of the ranch. She had enjoyed the ranch community and felt at home on the Wild Horse Desert. Then they had lived in the little rented house in Corpus Christi.

The house would have been quiet the next week, what with everyone trying not to disturb Petra's rest. The family stayed close by to see to anything she needed. On March 8, Mifflin entered Petra's bedroom to tell her that something bad had happened again. He told her that John and Stella had lost their newborn child. It was a little girl named Anne and her death resulted from a breech delivery. She was buried in the Corpus Christi cemetery.[31] Mifflin wrote to his sister Jo about their lot and the loss of the baby.[32] Once again Petra suffered with her son and his wife at the loss of an infant child. Petra had now lost seven children and several grandchildren. She understood the grief that accompanied such a loss and surely said an extra prayer for little Anne's soul.

In the next few days, Petra's pain worsened and she became delirious, drifting in and out of consciousness. Mifflin wrote his sister Josephine that in these last few weeks it had been necessary to prescribe morphine to try to keep her comfortable.[33] Mifflin had hoped to take Petra to New Orleans in the middle of October, if she could stand the trip, to see if she could be helped there.[34] This was at about the same time Santiago returned from Saltillo, more ill than when he left. Petra, like any mother, was not about to leave her son as he faced his own death, so she stayed in Corpus to be with him and delayed her own treatment.

By the time the New Year arrived and Santiago had passed on, it was too late for her to travel to New Orleans. Mifflin did the next best thing. On March 13, the renowned Dr. Herff arrived by special train to examine Petra. This same doctor was treating Captain King for cancer in San Antonio. Dr. Herff examined Petra under anesthesia and consulted with three other doctors. His prognosis was that her case was hopeless, that the uterine cancer had spread throughout her body. Dr. Herff came in to tell Petra personally after he had completed his examination. He explained that there was nothing he could do to help her, and he advised against surgery, saying her chance of survival was slim. He said she may recuperate a little, but realized she was in constant pain and recommended the morphine.[35] He explained that there was nothing he could do to help her and that death was not far away; she should make her plans.[36]

Petra and Mifflin discussed what should be done next. Petra made it clear from the time the doctor departed that she would move forward with her own plans for her funeral. She wanted to spare her children and Mifflin the task of making those difficult decisions. Although it was hard for her to concentrate because of the medication, she managed to tell Nene and Sarah how she wanted to be dressed. She also gave them instructions for the burial and then called for Mifflin. She spoke to him directly about how she wanted to be buried on the right side of Santiago. Mifflin told his Petrita that he would see to it that all her wishes were granted and especially that she would rest on this earth beside Santiago.

Mifflin Kenedy in a rocking chair.

Mifflin then called Father Jaillet, who came and administered the last rites. He and Petra had been through many trials, tribulations, and joys together. He had watched their children grow up and ministered to their needs; he had been there even to baptize the next generation. He had recently conducted the difficult service of James's burial. Petra and Mifflin had always been there for him as financial sponsors, now in two churches, and also as good friends. After he had administered the rites he stayed for a while in the room and watched Petra's labored breathing. He knew her time was short and he felt for her family. Mifflin had been strong, but he had endured such heartache during the last few months. Once Petra was gone, his life would be empty and the children would have lost their anchor. She was a strong woman whose faith had never wavered. Father Jaillet knew that Petra would be in the hands of God but he worried what would happen to the family after her death.

This photograph made in 1875 may show a grieving Petra dressed in black after Willie's death. She is perhaps wearing a cameo of his portrait at her neck. This photograph also portrays a much thinner and older looking Petra, perhaps a consequence of her dangerous surgery the year before. Courtesy Corpus Christi Museum of Science and History.

    Her surviving children were all successful, each in his or her own way. Sarah and Dr. Spohn were well established in Corpus Christi and although they did not have any children yet, they were still young. Dr. Spohn was considered one of the finest surgeons in Texas and even, some said, in the United States.[37] John and Stella had just been through the heartbreak of losing a child, but Stella had been saved and there was time for them to have other children.

John was successfully running La Parra for Mifflin and it looked like the arrangement was working well for both of them. Tom had finally found happiness with Yrene, and it looked like his future was secure in Brownsville at last. Luisa was happily married to Captain Dalzell and Petra knew they would be fine, but she did worry a great deal about Nene and her trouble with Fred. She only wished she could mend the damage that had been done between those two families. Rosa was doing well after Joe's death, and Joe Jr. was looking after his mother. Concepción and Manuel were established and raising a family. Mifflin, Petra knew, would face lonely times.

On March 12, Petra became delirious and again drifted back and forth into unconsciousness.[38] Three days later, the morning of March 15 dawned crisp and cool. On a day Mifflin should have been sharing the joy and pride of their new house being the subject of the *Corpus Christi Caller*'s lead article, he could not share that pride with Petra. The paper ran an elaborate spread with three pictures of their new home.[39] Mifflin would have wished he and Petra could sit together and share their mutual joy in their new surroundings. She had not been out of bed since he had brought her to the new house; she was now in and out of a drug-induced coma to help her combat the pain in her last hours.

The house was in a deathwatch on March 16. The family in Corpus Christi gathered in the house and took turns sitting with Petra. Petra had received the last rites and everything had been done for her that could be done to make her comfortable. At dusk, Petra took her last breath on this earth and was at peace with her God.

When Petra died she had thirty-two grandchildren and only one, James's son George, was Mifflin's. The rest came from her union with Luis Vidal. These heirs proudly trace their heritage back to Petra, as the "Mother" of their family. Petra's legacy is also carried out through the two Catholic charitable organizations her children with Mifflin created. Combined, the assets of these two charitable groups represent a fortune between $500 million to $1 billion, including a 440,000-acre oil-rich ranch.[40] Petra's strong convictions and religious faith were passed on to all her children.

The sparks that flew when Mifflin and Petra blended their two cultures and personalities created a legacy that has changed the face of South Texas and created a lasting gift to the state and millions of its citizens. Once again,

> "There is a woman at the beginning of all great things."
> —Lamartine

Epilogue

A week after Petra's death Mifflin wrote to his son-in-law Robert Dalzell expressing his great loss: "I did not think her departing was so near. Dr. Herff told me she would last some months. It seems to me I cannot grasp the situation. I can hardly believe she has gone."[1] Mifflin had one more death to attend—that of his best friend Captain King. Richard King died in San Antonio on April 14, a month after Petra's death, with Mifflin and King's family at his bedside. Mifflin returned with the family to Santa Gertrudis and then went home to his big house in Corpus Christi.[2]

Mifflin remained close to the King family. Standing in for his departed friend, he gave Alice away in marriage to Robert Justus Kleberg.[3] Robert Kleberg in turn continued to serve as both a good friend and legal counsel to Captain Kenedy. He visited him in August of 1885 to help him with his business affairs and wrote in a letter to Alice about how worried Captain Kenedy was about settling his affairs with his children and his wife's children.[4] He continued advising Captain Kenedy on his business affairs.

Throughout the years that Mifflin lived after Petra's death, he continued to honor her. In 1893 he had a stained glass window placed on the east wall of the chancel of the Brownsville Immaculate Conception Church in her honor.[5] On the anniversary of her death he arranged for an elaborate requiem mass to be said for her in Brownsville, Texas. He wrote Father Jeffreys and told him that he felt "her name would be remembered when all her contemporary women will be forgotten." He said, "I desire to pay her all the honours that the church can bestow and make the mass as solemn and impressive as possible."[6]

By August Mifflin began settling Petra's estate. Mifflin wrote Dalzell that Petra had died intestate because it would have been expensive to go through the courts, and a division of the property would have been bad for him. He settled with each of the children—both Petra's with Luis and Petra's with him—for $50,000 for their interest in Petra's estate, with either promissory notes or deeds to land and real estate. He had no cash settlements.[7] Intestate law said that the surviving spouse received one-half of the deceased's half of the community property, and the children split the other half equally.[8] Thus

EPILOGUE

Mifflin Kenedy took great interest in his three grandchildren and heirs. Shown here with Sarah, Georgie, and John Jr.

Mifflin would be doling out $350,000 in promissory notes and/or deeds to land and real estate, which made Petra's total estate worth $700,000. The settlements with Petra's heirs would be disputed for the next seventy-five years on whether they were fairly dealt with in the settling of their mother's estate. Mifflin lived to see John's two children born, who, along with George, gave him every reason to believe there would be direct heirs to inherit his and Petra's empire. It was not to end the way he thought it would.

The Big House at La Parra, with twenty-six rooms, was built around the beginning of World War I. It took five years to construct. After John and Marie Stella moved into the Big House, John Jr. and Elena moved into the original "steamboat" house. There was also a beach house on Baffin Bay, five miles east of the ranch headquarters, where materials for construction of the original house and for the Big House were offloaded from barges and carried by ox cart to the construction site.

During his lifetime, Mifflin continued to oversee the development of La Parra and saw his successful San Antonio and Aransas Pass Railroad bought by Southern Pacific Railroad in 1892.[9] He had spent his life transporting commodities through the Rio Grande Valley by mule trains, carts, trail drives, steamboats, and railroads. He was one of the most successful entrepreneurs of the nineteenth century.

Two years after Petra's death, in 1887, Mifflin adopted Carmen Morell as his daughter. She was the daughter of José Morell, a Monterrey merchant and Mifflin's longtime friend and business associate. The reason he gave for the adoption was to pay back an old debt to Morell. This adoption entitled Carmen to a full 25 percent of his estate, equal to the portion of his natural heirs.[10] Through the years there has been speculation as to whether Carmen was indeed a natural daughter of Mifflin's, born out of wedlock, or a mistress to him. After the adoption she moved into the mansion in Corpus Christi and managed the house; her sisters were frequent visitors. After Mifflin's death in 1895 she stayed on in the house until her death four years later in 1899. John Kenedy Sr. bought out her one-fourth interest in his father's estate from her sisters. Her relatives—she had no children—filed suit in 1997 claiming that she had been defrauded, but the claim was dismissed.[11]

Of Mifflin's children, Tom, James, Willie, and Phebe were already deceased at the time of his death. James's wife, Corina Ballí Kenedy, never remarried and raised their son George in Laredo. She and George were also generous to the Catholic Church. George inherited one-fourth of Mifflin's estate. Corina's life changed drastically after George's death and she became desperate for money, writing John Kenedy Sr. frequently, requesting assistance. She died almost destitute in 1932. George Kenedy, as he was growing up, stayed both at La Parra and in Laredo with his family. He was close to his cousins Johnny and Sarita. He also became a favorite nephew of John McAllen and spent summers at the Santa Anita with McAllen and his son James. George married twice, first to Sofia Rivadulle and later to Beatrice Samano.[12] He died in 1920 of tuberculosis, like his father James, and was buried in the Kenedy family plot in Brownsville, Texas.

John Kenedy Jr. who married Elena Suess, was fun-loving and cared little for ranching.

The next oldest living, John Gregory Kenedy Sr., married Marie Stella Turcotte in 1884, and they lived at La Parra the rest of their lives. They had two children. John managed and expanded the Kenedy Pasture Company and became one of the wealthiest cattle raisers in Texas.[13] He and his wife contributed to the Catholic Church to provide money for bishops' residences, Oblate missionaries, Spring Hill College, and also gave their Corpus Christi home to the church and the land for the new Corpus Christi Cathedral. Marie Stella first initiated the idea of leaving their ranching headquarters at La Parra to the church.[14]

Sarah Josephine Kenedy married Dr. Arthur Spohn and continued to live in Corpus Christi and travel the world. They never had children. After Carmen Morell's death, Sarah moved into the mansion that Mifflin had built for Petra and entertained there until her death of a heart attack while getting ready for a party.[15]

John Sr. and Marie Stella's children were John Gregory Kenedy Jr. and Sarah Josephine Kenedy, often called Sarita. John Gregory Kenedy Jr. married Elena Seuss of Saltillo, Mexico. They also lived on La Parra in the original steamboat house. They had no children. After John Jr., Sarita, and her husband Arthur East died, only Elena was left on the large La Parra Ranch. When Elena died she put her half interest in La Parra into The John G. Kenedy Jr. Charitable Trust with the direction to fund missionary, educational, charitable, and religious purposes.[16] There is still dispute over the settlement of the estate and a lawsuit that claims John Kenedy Jr. fathered an illegitimate child named Ann Fernandez. Her descendants are hoping to prove a right to the Kenedy Fortune.[17]

Sarah Josephine Kenedy (Sarita) married Arthur East and they also lived at La Parra. Sarita took an active role in ranching and managing the ranch. She had no children either. She formed a close friendship with Brother Leo, a Trappist monk, that led to a nearly twenty-year court battle over her will and the distribution of her estate. Sarita had decided to follow Marie Stella's wishes, and emulating Petra, leave her half of the ranch to the Catholic Church, especially recognizing the Oblate fathers and the service they rendered to all the ranches throughout South Texas. Upon her death, Sarita's will left the balance to the John G. and Marie Stella Kenedy Memorial Foundation in honor of her parents. She also willed the big house to the Missionary Oblates of Mary Immaculate, "providing the main building is used for some religious purpose."[18] Her will was challenged by the Catholic Church, her cousins the Turcottes and Easts, and Petra's descendants from Luis Vidal.

Petra's children with Luis Vidal and their descendants signed documents settling their rights to their portion of their mother's estate before oil and gas were discovered on La Parra and associated ranches, thus they were excluded from the vast wealth that accumulated in later years.[19] These families, however, have spread out over the Wild Horse Desert and beyond to make their own names and fortunes.

Luisa Vidal, who married Robert Dalzell, continued to live in Brownsville where the two built a large home. Luisa's daughter Mayme married Robert Hefley, one of the founders of the Dr. Pepper Bottling Co.[20]

EPILOGUE

Elena Kenedy, awarded by the Vatican, Pope Pius XII on March 13, 1942, The Equestrian Order of the Holy Sepulcher of Jerusalem. This is the highest papal honor awarded to a woman. Note the Jerusalem Cross on the robe.

Rosa Vidal married Joseph L. Putegnat, and after his death continued to live in Brownsville and help her son with the pharmacy her husband had started. She remained close to her half brothers and sisters, and the day Mifflin Kenedy died she was at La Parra visiting John; she accompanied him to Corpus Christi upon hearing of Mifflin's death.[21]

Anita Vidal, Adrian's daughter, married Louis Tom Cowen. She had been

Arthur East, who married Sarita, was from a nearby ranching family and was a quiet reserved man.

left out of the first settlement, and Mifflin later settled with her as Adrian's heir. She lived and raised her family in Brownsville.[22]

Concepción Vidal and Manuel Rodríguez lived in Nuevo Laredo, where he served as mayor for three years. They lived very well until the Mexican Revolution, when in 1914 the soldiers burned most of Nuevo Laredo and Concepción and Manuel lost nearly everything they had.[23]

Vicenta (Nene) Vidal Starck and her children, without Fred, moved into the big house with Mifflin until Carmen moved in. Then she returned to

Sarita was often seen dressed as a cowgirl. She was most at home out on the range with vaqueros working cattle. Courtesy of Raymondville Historical Museum.

Sarita Kenedy, also awarded the Equestrian Order of the Holy Sepulcher of Jerusalem.

Brownsville. Fred Starck left Brownsville and died in California. Nene lived with her daughter Lillian and husband Frank Rabb and, like her mother, also died of cancer.[24] Frank Rabb purchased Palm Grove Plantation in the late 1880s, which is now owned by the National Audubon Society.[25]

Today Petra and Mifflin's heritage, their family and friends, are celebrated in the Kenedy Ranch Museum, a program of the John G. and Marie Stella Kenedy Foundation in Corpus Christi. The museum is located in Sarita,

EPILOGUE

Texas, in the building that originally served as the Kenedy Pasture Company headquarters. It is open to the public and the family's rich story is told in vivid murals and artifacts.

Petra's legacy is the loving memory of children and descendants and the blending of two cultures, and the fortune that established the John G. and Marie Stella Kenedy Memorial Foundation and The John G. Kenedy Jr. Charitable Trust. It is a legacy left through her devotion to her family and her church.

Notes

Endnotes with "GG" preceding a number are all from the George Getchow Documents, copied from the vault at the Big House at La Parra and given to the King Ranch Archives and produced in Litigation, Cause No. C-291-93-D, *Manuel de Llano, Blanca A. de LL. de Aguilar, Martha Dell de Olivera, Carmen de Llano, Fernando de Llano and Josephina de Llano v. The John G. and Marie Stella Kenedy Memorial Foundation, John G. Kenedy Jr. Charitable Trust, Exxon Corporation, Exxon Company U.S.A., Exxon Exploration Co. and Mobil Oil Company,* in the District Court, Hidalgo County, Texas, 206th Judicial District.

Endnotes with "Lbook" and identified as "Letter press book" are all from the George Getchow Documents copied from the vault at the Big House at La Parra and given to the King Ranch Archives and produced in Litigation, Cause No. C-291-93-D, *Manuel de Llano, Blanca A. de LL. de Aguilar, Martha Dell de Olivera, Carmen de Llano, Fernando de Llano and Josephina de Llano v. The John G. and Marie Stella Kenedy Memorial Foundation, John G. Kenedy Jr. Charitable Trust, Exxon Corporation, Exxon Company U.S.A., Exxon Exploration Co. and Mobil Oil Company,* in the District Court, Hidalgo County, Texas, 206th Judicial District.

Preface

1. Francis E. Abernethy, ed., *Between the Cracks of History: Essays on Teaching and Illustrating Folklore,* Publications of the Texas Folklore Society, 55 (Denton: University of North Texas Press, 1997), vii.

Prologue

1. Américo Paredes, *With His Pistol in His Hand: A Border Ballad and Its Hero* (Austin: University of Texas Press, 2000), 11.
2. Randolph B. Campbell, *Gone to Texas: A History of the Lone Star State* (New York: Oxford University Press, 2003), 190–91.
3. Homero Vera, "Gregorio Vela—Rancher," *El Mesteño,* 6, no. 1 (Winter–Spring 2003): 52, 54, and 48, respectively.
4. Requiem Mass reported in *Brownsville Herald,* March 17, 1885, GGII 008734.
5. Ibid.
6. Jovita González, "Social Life in Cameron, Starr, and Zapata Counties" (master's thesis, University of Texas, 1930), 11, and 21–22, quoting Archivo General de la Nación, Mexico, Historia, Inspección de Nuevo Santander, 1757, 55, 64.
7. Andrés Tijerina, *Tejano Empire: Life on the South Texas Ranchos* (College Station: Texas A&M University Press, 1998), 12.

8. Donald E. Chipman and Harriett Denise Joseph, *Notable Men and Women of Spanish Texas* (Austin: University of Texas Press, 1999), xii.

9. Ibid., xii and xii–xiii.

10. Ibid., xii–xiii.

11. Ana Carolina Castillo Crimm, "Petra Vela and the Kenedy Family Legacy," in *Tejano Epic: Essays in Honor of Felix D. Alamaraz, Jr.*, ed. Arnoldo De Leon (Austin: Texas State Historical Association, 2005), 44–45; Vera, "Gregorio Vela—Rancher," 52.

12. Chester County Will Abstract—1840–1844. 10054 will bi. 18, 1.

13. Eleanor Morton, ca. 1930, *The Village Record*, n.d., n.p.

14. E-mail from Steve Harding, designer of the Kenedy Ranch Museum, August 26, 2002.

15. Harding e-mail, February 6, 2002.

16. Father Francis Kelly Nemeck, OMI, La Parra, in conversation and from his research.

17. Requiem Mass reported in *Brownsville Herald* on March 17, 1885.

18. Bruce Cheeseman letter of December 2, 2005, to the authors.

19. Andrés Sáenz, *Early Tejano Ranching: Daily Life at Ranchos San José and El Fresnillo*, ed. and intro. Andrés Tijerina (College Station: Texas A&M University Press and the University of Texas Institute of Texan Cultures at San Antonio, 1999), xii.

Chapter 1, 1823–54

1. Ana Carolina Castillo Crimm, "Petra Vela and the Kenedy Family Legacy," in *Tejano Epic: Essays in Honor of Felix D. Alamaraz, Jr.*, ed. Arnoldo De León (Austin: Texas State Historical Association, 2005), 46.

2. Laurence A. Duaine, *With All Arms: A Study of a Kindred Group* (Austin: Nortex Press, 2004), 22.

3. Thomas H. Naylor and Charles W. Polzer, eds., *The Presidio and the Militia on the Northern Frontier of New Spain, Volume One: 1570–1700* (Tucson: University of Arizona Press, 1986), 298; Diana Hadley, Thomas N. Naylor, and Mardith K. Schuetz-Miller, eds., *The Central Corridor and the Texas Corridor, 1700–1765* (Tucson: University of Arizona, 1997), 89, n. 15.

4. Duaine, *With All Arms*, 214.

5. Ibid. The mining records and all of the old records were in Cerralvo because at first it was the capital city. Most of these records were lost during the Indian revolt. There were twenty-seven mines in the area, and with the loss of records the mines were also lost. The Indians hid the mines extremely well as only five of them have been found. Conan T. Wood, "Cerralvo as the Mother City of the Lower Rio Grande Valley," speech given to the Lower Rio Grande Valley Historical Society, copy in Lon C. Hill Memorial Library, Harlingen, Texas.

6. David J. Weber, *The Spanish Frontier in North America* (New Haven, Conn.: Yale University Press, 1992), 20, 23.

7. Duaine, *With All Arms*, 228 and 224.

8. Ibid., 248.

9. Ibid.

10. Homero Vera, "Gregorio Vela—Rancher," *El Mesteño* 6, no. 1 (Winter–Spring 2003), 58; Duaine, *With All Arms*, 307–308.

11. Duaine, *With All Arms*, 307. In another record it was an "enormous" poisonous snake. She was buried to the ringing of bells, and don Juan gave twice the required fee.

12. Ibid., 7, 63.

13. Mary Margaret Amberson, James A. McAllen, and Margaret H. McAllen, *I Would*

Rather Sleep in Texas: A History of the Lower Rio Grande Valley and the People of the Santa Anita Land Grant (Austin: Texas State Historical Association, 2003), 2.

14. Andrés Tijerina, *Tejano Empire: Life on the South Texas Ranchos* (College Station: Texas A&M University Press, 1998), xxi.

15. Duaine, *With All Arms,* 304 and 309.

16. Vera, "Gregorio Vela—Rancher," 47–48.

17. Armando C. Alonzo, *Tejano Legacy: Rancheros and Settlers in South Texas, 1734–1900* (Albuquerque: University of New Mexico Press, 1998), 3.

18. Information provided by Homero Vera from the Matamoros 27 Abril 1842 census Exp. 1 Caja 7 No. de Inventarion 34 Fojas Utiles 7 Padron de Vecinos del Ayuntamiento del 1 (Primer) Cuartel de la Sección del Oriente Plaza Hidalgo Poniente. Veleño was apparently originally denounced for four leagues, thus the difference in the price paid for the two different ranches. Homero Vera e-mail, July 19, 2006, to authors.

19. Vera, "Gregorio Vela—Rancher," 48, 52.

20. John Kenedy Sr., deposition given in Corpus Christi, Texas, June 11, 1905. Deposition Exhibit 5, District Court Records, Corpus Christi, Texas. GG II 010101–010105.

21. Vera, "Gregorio Vela—Rancher," 52. These were *agostadero de ganado mayor* (grazing lands for major livestock: cattle, horses, mules). The *agostadero* Santa Teresa consists of 1,329 acres in Jim Hogg County and 7,527 in Starr County, abstracts JH-328 and S-220.

22. Alonzo, *Tejano Legacy,* 36.

23. Vera, "Gregorio Vela—Rancher," 48. Armando Alonzo states that historians have not placed much emphasis on the impact of Indian raids on the older frontier communities as a reason for settling in the towns, *Tejano Legacy,* 309, n. 46.

24. Jovita González, "Social Life in Cameron, Starr, and Zapata Counties" (master's thesis, University of Texas at Austin, 1930), 59–60.

25. Randolph B. Campbell, *Gone to Texas* (New York: Oxford University Press, 2003), 190.

26. Alonzo, *Tejano Legacy,* 11.

27. Ibid., 44, 66, and 113.

28. Homero Vera research from court records in Mier, in e-mail to authors July 13, 2006.

29. Ibid.

30. Decree granted by Jose Feliciano Ortiz, magistrate of the first hall of the Supreme Court of Justice of that state, May 24, 1826.

31. Vera, "Gregorio Vela," 48; Mier Church Baptism Records, 1767–1880, University of Texas at Brownsville.

32. Antonio Ma. Guerra, *Mier in History, A Translation and Reprint of Mier en la Historia by Antonio Ma. Guerra, 1953,* trans. José María Escobar and Edna Garza Brown (San Antonio: Munguia Printers, 1989), 57.

33. Information provided by Homero Vera from the Mier Municipal Archives.

34. Amberson, McAllen, and McAllen, *I Would Rather Sleep in Texas,* 341; Frances Vick interview with Donald Chipman, Professor Emeritus of History, University of North Texas, May 2, 2006, concerning Petra Kenedy's letter to Salomé Ballí.

35. Vera, "Gregorio Vela—Rancher," 66. Homero Vera, phone interview with Jane Monday, July 2006.

36. Homero Vera phone interview with Jane Monday, July 2006.

37. Arnoldo De León, *The Tejano Community, 1836–1900* (Albuquerque: University of New Mexico Press, 1982), 5.

38. Alonzo, *Tejano Legacy,* 43.

39. Jovita González and Eve Raleigh, *Caballero: A Historical Novel* (College Station: Texas A&M University Press, 1996), 36.

40. According to Bill Moreau, retired civil engineer and former owner of East Texas Engineering and Surveying firm, a vara is 2.777 feet, or one can divide a vara by .36 to arrive at footage.

41. De León, *The Tejano Community*, 7. See also Alonzo, *Tejano Legacy*, 119–20.

42. Alonzo, *Tejano Legacy*, 121.

43. De Leon, *The Tejano Community*, 7.

44. Crimm, "Petra Vela and the Kenedy Family Legacy," 47.

45. Lieutenant W. H. Chatfield, *Twin Cities of the Border: Brownsville, Texas, and Matamoros, Mexico, and the Country of the Lower Rio Grande* (New Orleans: E. P. Bradao, 1893), 31, 32. See also Catholic Archives of Texas, Austin.

46. Information provided by Homero Vera from the Matamoros 27 Abril 1842 census Exp. 1 Caja 7 No. de Inventarion 34 Fojas Utiles 7 Padron de Vecinos del Ayuntamiento del 1 (Primer) Cuartel de la Sección del Oriente Plaza Hidalgo Poniente.

47. Homero Vera interview June 29, 2006, with Jane Monday.

48. Information provided by Homero Vera from the Matamoros 27 Abril 1842 census Exp. 1 Caja 7 No. de Inventarion 34 Fojas Utiles 7 Padron de Vecinos del Ayuntamiento del 1 (Primer) Cuartel de la Sección del Oriente Plaza Hidalgo Poniente.

49. Information provided by Homero Vera from the Matamoros 27 Abril 1842 census.

50. Crimm, "Petra Vela and the Kenedy Family Legacy," 48–51.

51. Ibid., 47; Chatfield, *Twin Cities of the Border*, 31, 32.

52. Crimm, "Petra Vela and the Kenedy Family Legacy," 50.

53. E-mail, November 26, 2005, from Father Francis Kelly Nemeck, La Parra.

54. John Kenedy, deposition, GGII 010101–010105.

55. Vera, "Gregorio Vela—Rancher," 49.

56. Crimm, "Petra Vela and the Kenedy Family Legacy," 47 n. 8, 49–50, 47 n. 8 and Homero Vera, and 50 respectively.

57. Arnoldo De León, *They Called Them Greasers* (Austin: University of Texas Press, 1983), 79.

58. Requiem Mass reported in *Brownsville Herald* on March 17, 1885, Corpus Christi Library.

59. Amberson, McAllen, and McAllen, *I Would Rather Sleep in Texas*, 78.

60. Ibid.

61. Ibid., 76–79.

62. Requiem Mass reported in *Brownsville Herald*, March 17, 1886, Corpus Christi Library.

63. Gen. Thomas J. Green, *Journal of the Texian Expedition against Mier* (New York: Harper and Brothers, 1845), 109.

64. Requiem Mass reported in *Brownsville Herald* on March 17, 1885; also, John Martindale Heaner private papers.

65. Green, *Journal of the Texian Expedition against Mier*, is now in the possession of the OMI order of Oblates in San Antonio, Texas.

66. Crimm, "Petra Vela and the Kenedy Family Legacy," 51.

67. Caleb Coker, ed., *The News From Brownsville: Helen Chapman's Letters from the Texas Military Frontier, 1848–1852* (Austin: Texas State Historical Association, 1991), 116–17.

68. Gilberto M. Hinojosa, *A Borderlands Town in Transition: Laredo, 1755–1870* (College Station: Texas A&M University Press), 109.

69. Translated by Homero Vera from a letter received from Ana Carolina Crimm and given to Jane Monday. Copied from the Archivo Militar, Mexico D.F., Mexico.

70. E-mail from Homero Vera, Kenedy Ranch Museum, Sarita, Texas, October 5, 2005.

71. Interview by author Jane Clements Monday with Rosita Putegnat, Petra Kenedy's great-granddaughter, July 2001, Houston, Texas.

72. 1850 Census, Texas—Cameron, Starr, and Webb Census, vol. XII, no. 3, September 1995, 150.

Chapter 2, 1823–54

1. Luis Holton, Coatesville, PA, January 17, 1943, GGII 010103.

2. Chester County Will Abstract—1840–44. 10054 will bi. 18, 1. Chester County Will Abstract, 1064–65.

3. E-mail from Father Francis Kelly Nemeck, La Parra Ranch.

4. Newspaper article from the Chester County Historical Society, March 18, 1895. Kenedy Family Vertical File, Raymondville Historical Museum, Historical and Community Center; J. Smith Futhey and Gilbert Cope, *History of Chester County Pennsylvania* (Luis H. Everts, 1881), 305.

5. Newspaper articles, Chester County Historical Society, from Barbara J. Rutz, researcher.

6. Robert L. Dyer, "Steamboating on the Missouri River with an Emphasis on the Boonslick Region," *Boone's Lick Heritage* 5 (June 1997), Boonslick Historical Society's Quarterly Magazine, Boonslick, Boonville, Mo.

7. Chester County Will Abstract, 1840–44, 1064–65.

8. Barbara J. Rutz, researcher, Chester County Archives and Records Services, West Chester, Pa., letter to Jane Monday, March 2003.

9. Newspaper article from the Chester County Historical Society, March 18, 1895.

10. Harry P. Owens, "Sail and Steam Vessels Serving the Apalachicola-Chattahoochee Valley," *Alabama Review* (July 1968), 203.

11. Tom Lea, *The King Ranch* (Boston: Little, Brown, 1957), 2; Dick Frost, *King Ranch Papers: An Unauthorized and Irreverent History of the World's Largest Landholders* (Chicago: Aquarius Rising Press, 1985), 18. The 1850 Census lists Richard King as having been born in New York, but in the 1860 and 1870 Censuses he is listed as born in Ireland. His children have listed next to their names that their father was foreign born.

12. Daniel D. Arreloa, *Tejano South Texas* (Austin: University of Texas Press, 2002), 197; Arnoldo De León, *Tejano Community, 1836–1900* (Dallas: Southern Methodist University Press, 1997), xii–xiii.

13. Mary Margret McAllen Amberson, James A. McAllen, and Margaret H. McAllen, *I Would Rather Sleep in Texas: A History of the Lower Rio Grande Valley and the People of the Santa Anita Land Grant* (Austin: Texas State Historical Association, 2003), 82–83.

14. Ibid., 86, and 90–91.

15. K. Jack Bauer, "Mexican War," in *The New Handbook of Texas*, 6 vols., ed. Ron Tyler, Douglas E. Barnett, Roy R. Barkley, Penelope C. Anderson, and Mark F. Odintz (Austin: Texas State Historical Association, 1996), 695–97.

16. Amberson, McAllen, and McAllen, *I Would Rather Sleep in Texas*, 98.

17. John Ashton, "Kenedy, Mifflin," in *The New Handbook of Texas*, 1064–65; Lea, *The King Ranch*, 9.

18. *American Flag*, October 1, 1846; Leroy Graf, "Economic History of the Lower Rio Grande Valley, 1820–1875," (PhD diss., Harvard University, 1942); Don Graham, *The Kings of Texas: The 150 Year Saga of an American Ranching Empire* (New Jersey: John Wiley, 2003), 31.

19. H. T. Nance, "Steamboating on the Rio Grande," *Successful Attitudes* (Fall 1988): 18 (Brownsville Historical Association).

20. Caleb Coker, ed., *News from Brownsville: Helen Chapman's Letters from the Texas Military Frontier, 1848–1852* (Austin: Texas State Historical Association, 1992), 6–7.

21. Lea, *The King Ranch*, 34–35.

22. Ibid., 39.

23. Coker, *News from Brownsville*, 173.

24. Lea, *The King Ranch*, 42–43.

25. Dave Dawley, "*A Shared Experience*'s Historical Survey—Steamboats on the Rio Grande," available at http://www.rice.edu/armadillo/Past/Book/Part2/steambot.html, accessed October 20, 2006.

26. Lea, *The King Ranch*, 42.

27. Ibid., 43, 45.

28. Lea, *The King Ranch*, 159; Alicia A. Garza and Christopher Long, "Brownsville, Texas," in *The New Handbook of Texas*, 1:776.

29. Milo Kearney, ed., *More Studies in Brownsville History* (Brownsville: Pan American University at Brownsville, 1989), 126.

30. Graf, "Economic History of the Lower Rio Grande Valley, 1820–1875," 276.

31. Lea, *The King Ranch*, 56.

32. James Heaven Thompson, "A Nineteenth-Century History of Cameron County, Texas" (master's thesis, University of Texas at Austin, 1965), 76–77.

33. Jerry Thompson, *Cortina: Defending the Mexican Name in Texas* (College Station: Texas A&M University Press, 2007), 37.

34. Frank C. Pierce, *A Brief History of the Lower Rio Grande Valley* (Edinburg, TX: New Santander Press, 1998), 123.

35. Johnnie Mae De Maur, "The History of Kenedy County" (master's thesis, Texas College of Arts and Industries, 1940), 17.

36. Pat Kelley, *River of Lost Dreams* (Lincoln: University of Nebraska Press, 1986), 45, and 42; Lea, *The King Ranch*, 56–59.

37. Amberson, McAllen, and McAllen, *I Would Rather Sleep in Texas*, 114.

38. Nance, "Steamboating on the Rio Grande," 18.

39. Kelley, *River of Lost Dreams*, 54.

40. Lea, *The King Ranch*, 62.

41. Coker, *News from Brownsville*, 173.

42. 1850 Census, Rio Grande Valley, Cameron, Starr, Webb, 572–73, November 7, 1850.

43. Amberson, McAllen, and McAllen, *I Would Rather Sleep in Texas*, 108.

44. Lea, *The King Ranch*, 73.

45. John Salmon Ford, *Rip Ford's Texas*, ed. Stephen Oates (Austin: University of Texas Press, 1963), 74.

46. Amberson, McAllen, and McAllen, *I Would Rather Sleep in Texas*, 116–17.

47. Ibid., 117–18.

48. Ibid.

49. De León, *Tejano Community*, 17.

50. Coker, *News from Brownsville*, 221, and 236.

51. Robert B. Vezzetti, ed., *Tidbits, A Collection from the Brownsville Historical Association and the Stillman House Museum*, n.p., n.d., 15.

52. Coker, *News from Brownsville*, 145.

53. Letter to E. G. Stillman from Harbert Davenport, June 6, 1940, Brownsville Historical Association.

54. Interview with Alexander Stillman by Jane Monday and Frances Vick in Brownsville, Texas, March 16, 2006.

55. E-mail from Priscilla Rodriguez, executive director, Brownsville Historical Association, February 21, 2006; Lea, *The King Ranch,* 140. In the Stillman House today a small tube-shaped lamp, resting on a delicate metal stand, sits on the sewing table in the parlor. If Charles had courted Betsy in Brownsville he may have encountered such a lamp. When a suitor went courting, the father would appraise the young man, pour the proper amount of oil into the lamp to burn at the measured amount of time, and then light the wick. When the supply of oil was exhausted and the flame burned out, it would be time for the gentleman to leave, hopefully to return another evening.

56. John Mason Hart, "James Stillman," in Vezzetti, ed., *Tidbits,* 113.

57. Amberson, McAllen, and McAllen, *I Would Rather Sleep in Texas,* 109.

58. Thompson, "A Nineteenth Century History of Cameron County, Texas," 74–75.

59. Stephen Michaud and Hugh Aynesworth, *If You Love Me You Will Do My Will* (New York: W. W. Norton, 1990), 52.

60. Ford, *Rip Ford's Texas,* 467; Coker, *News from Brownsville,* 168.

61. Michaud and Aynesworth, *If You Love Me, You Will Do My Will,* 52.

62. Ford, *Rip Ford's Texas,* 467

63. *Brownsville Daily Cosmopolitan,* March 17, 1866.

64. E-mail from Francis Kelly Nemeck, OMI, La Parra, February 21, 2005.

65. Amberson, McAllen, and McAllen, *I Would Rather Sleep in Texas,* 126.

66. Ibid., 127.

67. Ibid., 341; Petra Vela de Kenedy to Salomé, April 26, 1883, from Corpus Christi, Texas. McAllen Family Archives from Ella Howland Archives, Laredo, Texas.

68. Minnie Gilbert, "Don Pancho Ytúrria and Punta del Monte," in *Rio Grande Round-Up: A Story of Texas Tropical Borderland Valley By-Liners, Book III* (Mission, Tex.: Border Kingdom Press, 1980), 52.

69. Jovita González and Eve Raleigh, *Caballero: A Historical Novel* (College Station: Texas A&M University Press, 1996), 29.

70. Mifflin to Mr. Scott of New York, GGII 0020201.

71. Jonathan Day Folder, Corpus Christi District Courthouse Records, Corpus Christi Warehouse; Amberson, McAllen, and McAllen, *I Would Rather Sleep in Texas,* 219.

72. Requiem Mass, GGII 008734.

73. Lea, *The King Ranch,* 126, and 437.

74. Ford, *Rip Ford's Texas,* 461.

75. Andrés Tijerina, *Tejano Empire: Life on the South Texas Ranches* (College Station: Texas A&M University Press, 1998), 117.

76. González and Raleigh, *Caballero,* 257.

77. Jovita González, "Social Life in Cameron, Starr, and Zapata Counties" (master's thesis, University of Texas at Austin, 1930), 68.

78. Lea, *The King Ranch,* 91–92.

79. Ibid., 93–94.

80. Murphy Givens, "King Ranch Absorbed Older Bobedo Ranch," *Corpus Christi Caller-Times,* December 20, 2006.

81. Chauncey D. Stillman speech, in Vezzetti, ed., *Tidbits,* 64–67; Lea, *The King Ranch,* 115–16.

82. Bruce Cheeseman, "History of the Rincón de Los Laureles," February 1992, provided to Jane Monday, March 2000.

83. Vezzetti, ed., *Tidbits*, 67.

84. Annals of the First Monastery of the Incarnate Word and Blessed Sacrament in American—Brownsville, Texas. Incarnate Word Archives, Corpus Christi, Texas, 5.

85. Sister Mary Xavier Holworthy, Incarnate Word and Blessed Sacrament, Corpus Christi, Texas, 1945, in *Diamonds for the King*, Brownsville Historical Association, 17.

86. Ibid., 19.

87. Annals of the First Monastery of the Incarnate Word and Blessed Sacrament in American—Brownsville, Texas. Incarnate Word Archives, Corpus Christi, Texas, 6.

88. Ibid.

89. Jonathan Day Folder, Corpus Christi District County Records, Marriage Certificate of Mifflin Kenedy and Petra Vela de Vidal.

90. Day Folder, Corpus Christi District County Records Marriage Certificate. Sacramental Records of Immaculate Conception Cathedral, vol. 1, page 32, #42.

91. Armando C. Alonzo, *Tejano Legacy: Ranchers and Settlers in South Texas, 1734–1900* (Albuquerque: University of New Mexico Press, 1998), 115-16.

92. Day Folder, Corpus Christi District County Records Marriage Certificate. Sacramental Records of Immaculate Conception Cathedral, vol. 1, page 32, #42.

93. Day Folder, Corpus Christi District County Records Marriage certificate; Interview with Patricia Reneghan, great-granddaughter of Petra, July 2001, Seguin, Texas.

94. Certificate of Baptism of Thomas Mifflin Kenedy at St. Mary's Church, record at Immaculate Conception Church, Brownsville, Texas, vol. 1, page 145, #92.

95. Crimm, "Petra Vela and the Kenedy Family Legacy," 49.

Chapter 3, 1855–60

1. M. Patricia Gunning, *To Texas with Love: A History of the Sisters of the Incarnate Word and Blessed Sacrament* (Austin: Von Boeckmann-Jones, 1971), 72.

2. *Brownsville Herald*, March 17, 1886, Corpus Christi Library.

3. Gunning, *To Texas with Love*, 76–79; Requiem Mass reported in *Brownsville Herald*, March 17, 1886. Also in the private papers of John Martindale Heaner.

4. Gunning, *To Texas with Love*, 81–83, and 85.

5. *100 Years of Service*, Centenary Souvenir of the Sisters of the Incarnate Word and Blessed Sacrament, Brownsville, Texas, Brownsville Historical Association, 31.

6. Ibid.; Family interview with Patricia Reneghan in Seguin, Texas, author Jane Monday, July 2001.

7. Gunning, *To Texas with Love*, 75.

8. Milo Kearney and Anthony Knopp, *Boom and Bust: The Historical Cycles of Matamoros and Brownsville* (Austin: Eakin Press, 1991), 88.

9. *American Flag*, January 9, 1850.

10. Gunning, *To Texas with Love*, 75.

11. Mifflin Kenedy to Captain John Wilson, June 10, 1865, given to Jane Monday by Bruce Cheeseman.

12. Kingsbury Papers: Gilbert D. Kingsbury Lectures, Reports, and Writings, Vol. II 1855–1867, Center for American History, University of Texas, Austin.

13. 1860 Census, Cameron County, Texas, City of Brownsville p. 268 taken June 13, 1860.

14. Jerry Thompson, "Mutiny and Desertion on the Rio Grande: The Strange Saga of Captain Adrian J. Vidal," *Military History of Texas and the Southwest* 14, no. 3 (1975): 166.

15. Captain A. J. Vidal, January 2, 1863 to Henry Miller, Brownsville Historical Association.

16. Mary Margret McAllen Amberson, James A. McAllen, and Margaret H. McAllen, *I Would Rather Sleep in Texas: A History of the Lower Rio Grande Valley and the People of the Santa Anita Land Grant* (Austin: Texas State Historical Association, 2003), 162. Kingsbury was a writer who also went by the name of Franklin F. Fenn.

17. Kingsbury Papers.

18. Ibid.; Arnoldo De León, *They Called Them Greasers* (Austin: University of Texas Press, 1983), 15.

19. Kingsbury Papers.

20. Arnoldo De León, *The Tejano Community, 1836–1900* (Dallas: Southern Methodist University Press, 1997), 132.

21. Mifflin Kenedy to his sister Josephine, GGII 0020113; Mifflin Kenedy to Richard King, GGII 0020193; Mifflin Kenedy to John Kenedy, GGII 0020098; Mifflin Kenedy to Fred Starck, GGII 0020094.

22. Interview with Bruce Cheeseman by Jane Monday, March 2000.

23. Jerry Thompson, "Vidal, Adrian J.," in The Handbook of Texas Online, http://www.tsha.utexas.edu/handbook/online/.

24. Jerry Thompson, "Mutiny and Desertion on the Rio Grande," 167.

25. Ibid., 161.

26. Ibid., 167.

27. Robert B. Vezzetti, ed., *Tidbits, a Collection from the Brownsville Historical Association and the Stillman House Museum*, n.p., n.d., 3–6.

28. "The Neale Family of Brownsville," *The Brownsville Herald*, 1934, Brownsville Historical Association.

29. *New Orleans Daily True Delta*, March 10, 1850; Milo Kearney and Knopp, *Boom and Bust*, 70–74.

30. De León, *The Tejano Community*, 18.

31. Ibid., xii–xiii.

32. James Heaven Thompson, "A Nineteenth Century History of Cameron County, Texas" (master's thesis, University of Texas, 1965), 60.

33. Vezzetti, ed., *Tidbits*, 5.

34. Interview with Chula T. Griffin by author Jane Monday.

35. De León, *The Tejano Community*, 122.

36. Interview with Chula T. Griffin by author Jane Monday.

37. Jerry Thompson and Lawrence T. Jones III, *Civil War And Revolution on the Rio Grande Frontier* (Austin: Texas State Historical Association, 2004), 21.

38. Susan Seeds and Janis Hefley, from family recipes passed down from Luisa's daughter, Petra's granddaughter.

39. Mary Josephine Dalzell Hefley was Luisa's daughter. The family called her Mayme. This recipe was in Mayme's handwriting. Janis Hefley and Susan Seeds are sisters and descendants of Mayme and Petra.

40. Amberson, McAllen, and McAllen, *I Would Rather Sleep in Texas*, 182–83, and 177.

41. De León, *The Tejano Community*, 133–34.

42. Chula T. Griffin interview with author Jane Monday.

43. Correspondence from Rosa Maria Swisher, Concepción's great-granddaughter to Jane Monday, May 30, 2006.

44. Jovita González and Eve Raleigh, *Caballero: A Historical Novel* (College Station: Texas A&M University Press, 1996), 80, and 87–88.

45. Amberson, McAllen, and McAllen, *I Would Rather Sleep in Texas,* 158–59.

46. Tom Lea, *The King Ranch* (Boston: Little, Brown, 1957), 437.

47. John Salmon Ford, *Rip Ford's Texas,* ed. Stephen Oates (Austin: University of Texas Press, 1963), 461.

48. 1872 depositions taken in Brownsville from Santiago Alvarez, Anseno Longorio, Juan Miguel Longoria, Santos Longoria, Tomás Sandoval, and Vitterian Sandoval, who had all worked at San Salvador de Tule when Mifflin owned it, 1872, GGII 007000–007171.

49. Daniel D. Arreola, *Tejano South Texas* (Austin: University of Texas Press, 2002), 66; Lea, *The King Ranch,* 124.

50. Roberto M. Villarreal, "The Mexican-American Vaqueros of the Kenedy Ranch: A Social History" (master's thesis, Texas A&I University, 1972), 2–3.

51. Lea, *The King Ranch,* 116.

52. Ibid., 117.

53. Charles H. Harris III and Louis R. Sadler, *The Texas Rangers and the Mexican Revolution* (Albuquerque: University of New Mexico Press, 2004), 75.

54. Lea, *The King Ranch,* 118–19.

55. Jane Clements Monday and Betty Bailey Colley, *Voices from the Wild Horse Desert: The Vaquero Families of the King and Kenedy Ranches* (Austin: University of Texas Press, 1997), 48.

56. Homero Vera, "Cruillas, Nuevo Santander/Tamaulipas," *El Mesteño* 6, no. 1 (2003): 41.

57. Lea, *The King Ranch,* 123.

58. De León, *The Tejano Community,* 55.

59. Kearney and Knopp, *Boom and Bust,* 85–86.

60. Lea, *The King Ranch,* 127–28.

61. St. Mary's Church of Brownsville Baptismal Records, Brownsville, Texas, vol. 1, p. 191, #137.

62. St. Mary's Church of Brownsville Baptismal Records, 55–56, and 138.

63. Ibid., 132–33.

64. Ibid., 134.

65. Lea, *The King Ranch,* 136; 138.

66. Bruce Cheeseman correspondence with authors, December 2, 2005.

67. Robert Wright, OMI, *The Oblate Cavalry of Christ* (Oblate Heritage Series, OMI General Postulation Rome, Italy, 1998), 26–27.

68. Cynthia L. Vidaurri, "Texas-Mexican Religious Folk Art in Robstown, Texas," in *Hecho en Tejas: Texas-Mexican Folk Arts and Crafts,* ed. Joe S. Graham (Denton: University of North Texas Press, 1991), 233–34.

69. Kearney and Knopp, *Boom and Bust,* 86; Wright, *The Oblate Cavalry of Christ,* 26–27; Vezzetti, ed., *Tidbits,* 82.

70. St. Mary's Church of Brownsville Baptismal Records, Brownsville, Texas, vol. 1, page 191, #137.

71. Lea, *The King Ranch,* 141.

72. Ibid., 141–42.

73. Fax from Steve Harding of Steve Harding Design, Inc., February 6, 2002, containing information on registration and sketches of the brands from Homero Vera.

74. Lea, *The King Ranch*, 403.

75. Ibid., 140-41.

76. Chester County Will Abstract from Pennsylvania; Gregorio Vela's death certificate, Vera, *El Mesteño*, "Gregorio Vela—Rancher," 47-48.

77. Lea, *The King Ranch*, 143.

78. Ibid., 143, and 145.

79. Milo Kearney, ed., *More Studies in Brownsville History* (Brownsville: Pan American University at Brownsville, 1989), 163-66; Vezzetti, ed., *Tidbits*, 142-46.

80. Interview with Chula T. Griffin by author Jane Monday.

81. De León, *The Tejano Community*, 7-8.

82. Lea, *The King Ranch*, 147.

83. Ibid.

84. Caleb Coker, ed., *The News from Brownsville: Helen Chapman's Letters from the Texas Military Frontier, 1848–1852* (Austin: Texas State Historical Association, 1991), 365.

85. Kingsbury Papers.

86. Shirley Brooks Greene, *When Rio Grande City Was Young: Buildings of Old Rio Grande City* (Edinburg: Pan American University, 1987), 10-11.

87. Bernard Doyon, OMI, *The Cavalry of Christ on the Rio Grande, 1849–1883* (Milwaukee: Bruce Press, 1956), 73.

88. "Memory of Eleven Pioneers Honored in Catholic Diamond of City Gardens," *Corpus Christi Caller-Times*, October 8, 1936, Corpus Christi Library, Corpus Christi, Texas.

89. Lieutenant W. H. Chatfield, *The Twin Cities of the Border and the Country of the Lower Rio Grande*, Centennial Oration by the Hon. William Neal (New Orleans: E. P. Brandad, 1893), 14.

90. Vezzetti, ed., *Tidbits*, 17.

91. Kearney and Knopp, *Boom and Bust*, 99-100.

92. Ibid.; Vezzetti, ed., *Tidbits*, 17.

93. Vezzetti, ed., *Tidbits*, 17.

94. Chester County Will Abstract 1064-65; Sacramental Records of Immaculate Conception Cathedral, vol. 2, page 128, #213, Baptized June 21, 1859, born April 22, 1859.

95. Leroy P. Graf, "The Economic History of the Lower Rio Grande Valley, 1820–1875" (PhD diss., Harvard University, 1942), 253.

96. Graf, "The Economic History of the Lower Rio Grande Valley," 253.

97. Lea, *The King Ranch*, 158-9.

98. Vezzetti, ed., *Tidbits*, 59-60.

99. Ibid., 29.

100. Ibid., 29-30.

101. Ibid., 33.

102. Ibid., 30.

103. Ibid.

104. Kingsbury papers.

105. Slave schedule in the Rio Grande Valley, County of Cameron, Starr, Webb, October 5, 1850; Slave schedule, Brownsville, County of Cameron, State of Texas, June 14, 1860; Slave schedule, Starr County; Slave schedule in the County of Nueces, June 23, 1860.

106. Amberson, McAllen, and McAllen, *I Would Rather Sleep in Texas*, 174–76.

107. James Heaven Thompson, "A Nineteenth Century History of Cameron County, Texas," 63.

108. Vezzetti, ed., *Tidbits*, 81–82.

109. Kearney, *More Studies in Brownsville History*, 87.

110. From the Sacramental Records of Immaculate Conception Cathedral, vol. 2, page 128 #211 (John Gregory), #212 (Sarah Josephine), #213 (William). Given the common belief at the time of the importance of infant baptism, it is puzzling that Petra would have waited so long, especially for the first two, and even more especially given the threat of infant death posed by the yellow fever epidemic of 1858. Father Francis Kelly Nemeck, e-mail to authors, November 29, 2005; Roberto Mario Salmon, "San Román, José," in The Handbook of Texas Online. San Román had partnered with John Young and Charles Stillman on steamboating on the Rio Grande but sold out to M. Kenedy & Co.

111. Andrés Tijerina, *Tejano Empire: Life on the South Texas Ranchos* (College Station: Texas A&M University Press, 1998), 55–56.

112. Hale to Walworth, letter July 14, 1850, GG II 019249.

113. Lovenskiold to Captain King, GG II 019253.

114. De León, *The Tejano Community*, 45.

115. Amberson, McAllen, and McAllen, *I Would Rather Sleep in Texas*, 164–65.

116. Américo Paredes, *A Texas-Mexican Cancionero: Folksongs of the Lower Border* (Austin: University of Texas Press, 1976), 23; Lea, *The King Ranch*, 160; Amberson, McAllen, and McAllen, *I Would Rather Sleep in Texas*, 164.

117. James Heaven Thompson, "A Nineteenth Century History of Cameron County, Texas" (master's thesis, University of Texas at Austin, 1965), 47.

118. Américo Paredes, *Folklore and Culture on the Texas-Mexican Border* (Austin: University of Texas Press, 1993), 9.

119. Américo Paredes, *"With His Pistol in His Hand"* (Austin: University of Texas Press, 1958), 140.

120. Paredes, *Folklore and Culture on the Texas-Mexican Border*, 9.

121. Américo Paredes, "The Mexican Corrido: Its Rise and Fall," in *Madstones and Twisters*, ed. Mody Boatright et al. (Dallas: Southern Methodist University Press, 1958), 104–105; Paredes, *Folklore and Culture on the Texas-Mexican Border*, 9; Américo Paredes, "Folklore and History," in *Singers and Storytellers*, ed. Mody Boatright et al. (Dallas: Southern Methodist University Press, 1961), 62; Paredes, *A Texas-Mexican Cancionero*, 48.

122. Amberson, McAllen, and McAllen, *I Would Rather Sleep in Texas*, 164.

123. Paredes, *"With His Pistol in His Hand,"* 32.

124. Lea, *The King Ranch*, 161.

125. Gunning, *To Texas with Love*, 85.

126. Jerry Thompson, *Cortina: Defending the Mexican Name in Texas* (College Station: Texas A&M University Press, 2007), 57.

127. Thompson, *Cortina*, 59–62.

128. Ibid., 28.

129. Ibid., 40–41.

130. Amberson, McAllen, and McAllen, *I Would Rather Sleep in Texas*, 165–66; Lea, *The King Ranch*, 162; Thompson, "Defending the Mexican Name in Texas," 63.

131. Walter Prescott Webb, *The Texas Rangers: A Century of Frontier Defense* (Austin: University of Texas Press, 1980), 182.

132. Ibid., 183.

133. Thompson, *Cortina*, 81–82.

134. Ibid., 62.

135. Lea, *The King Ranch*, 162–63.

136. Pierce, *A Brief History of the Lower Rio Grande Valley*, 155.

137. John Mason Hart, *Revolutionary Mexico: The Coming and Process of the Mexican Revolution* (Berkeley: University of California Press, 1997), 116.

138. T. R. Fehrenbach, *Lone Star: A History of Texas and the Texans* (New York: American Legacy Press, 1968), 507.

139. E. Basse to William Hale, provided by Bruce Cheeseman to Jane Clements Monday.

140. Kingsbury papers.

141. Mifflin Kenedy's lead vest is available for viewing at the Raymondville Historical Museum, Raymondville, Texas.

142. Amberson, McAllen, and McAllen, *I Would Rather Sleep in Texas*, 168.

143. Thompson, *Cortina*, 86–87.

144. Ibid., 91.

145. Depositions: Regarding the loss of cattle to rustlers along the Rio Grande, 1872, GGII 007000–007171.

146. Ibid.; GGII 000955.

147. Ibid.

148. Webb, *The Texas Rangers*, 181–82.

149. J. Walworth to Wm. G. Hale, December 11, 1859, transcription from Bruce Cheeseman.

150. Thompson, *Cortina*, 94–95.

151. Thompson, "A Nineteenth Century History of Cameron County, Texas," 50.

152. Ford earned the nickname of "Rip" because he fought in the Mexican War and had to notify families of the death of a loved one and included the words Rest In Peace.

153. Lea, *The King Ranch*, 165.

154. Thompson, *Cortina*, 112.

Chapter 4, 1860–62

1. 1860 Census Cameron County, City of Brownsville, M653 Roll: 1289, 268 taken June 13, 1860.

2. Robert B. Vezzetti, ed., *Tidbits, A Collection from the Brownsville Historical Association and the Stillman House Museum*, n.d., 154.

3. Tom Lea, *The King Ranch* (Boston; Little, Brown, 1957), 168–69.

4. Vezzetti, ed., *Tidbits*, 119.

5. Lea, *The King Ranch*, 171.

6. Ibid., 174.

7. John Day Folder, Death and Marriage Records, Corpus Christi Court Records, Corpus Christi District Warehouse, Corpus Christi, Texas.

8. Ibid.

9. Rosa Maria Swisher, Laredo, Texas, to Jane Monday, June 2006.

10. Ibid..

11. Ibid.

12. 1860 Census Cameron County, Texas, City of Brownsville; Family interview with Rose Swisher in 2005 by author Jane Monday; John Day folder; Family Genealogical Records, Corpus Christi District Courthouse Records.

13. *American Flag,* April 16, 1860.

14. Lea, *The King Ranch,* 173.

15. Bruce Cheeseman communication to authors, in their possession.

16. Bruce Cheeseman, "Rincón Santa Gertrudis Land Grant," given to Jane Monday.

17. Ibid., 174

18. Ibid.

19. Interview with Mary Margaret Amberson by Jane Monday by phone, May 2006.

20. Kingsbury papers, Gilbert D. Kingsbury Lectures, Reports, and Writings, Vol. II 1855–67, Barker American History Center.

21. John Henry Brown, *Indian Wars and Pioneers of Texas* (Austin: L. E. Daniel, 189?), 582.

22. John Day Folder, Corpus Christi Court Records, Family Genealogical Records, Corpus Christi District Warehouse, Corpus Christi, Texas.

23. Ibid.

24. *Tidbits,* Vezzetti, ed., 97.

25. Kingsbury papers, 1861 Account Book, Brownsville, Texas Post Office, Center for American History, University of Texas, Austin, Texas.

26. Mary Margret McAllen Amberson, James A. McAllen, and Margaret H. McAllen, *I Would Rather Sleep in Texas: A History of the Lower Rio Grande Valley and the People of the Santa Anita Land Grant* (Austin: Texas State Historical Association, 2003), 185 and 186.

27. John Day Folder, Corpus Christi Court Records, Family Genealogical Records, Corpus Christi District Warehouse, Corpus Christi, Texas

28. Arnoldo De León, *Tejano Community, 1836–1900* (Dallas: Southern Methodist University Press, 1997), 148.

29. Kenedy Family Plot at Buena Vista Cemetery in Brownsville, Texas.

30. There is conflicting data on Luisa's birth date. She was listed as eighteen in 1860 but her death certificate indicates she was born in 1840 not 1842. Her gravestone also lists her birth date as 1840, making her twenty in 1860 not eighteen.

31. Jovita González and Eve Raleigh, *Caballero: A Historical Novel* (College Station: Texas A&M University Press, 1996), 255-56.

32. Robert Dalzell's obituary, "Dalzell Passes Away," *Brownsville Daily Herald,* April 26, 1910.

33. Mifflin Kenedy to Richard King, October 9, 1884, GGII 0020173 and GGII 0020174; GGII 0020116-0088346.

34. Amberson, McAllen, and McAllen, *I Would Rather Sleep in Texas,* 201.

35. Stephen A. Townsend, *The Yankee Invasion of Texas* (College Station: Texas A&M University Press, 2006), 3-4.

36. Lea, *The King Ranch,* 179; Amberson, McAllen, and McAllen, *I Would Rather Sleep in Texas,* 188-89.

37. Lea, *The King Ranch,* 180-1.

38. James Heaven Thompson, "A Nineteenth Century History of Cameron County, Texas" (master's thesis, University of Texas, 1965), 90, 96.

39. Townsend, *The Yankee Invasion of Texas,* 9; Lea, *The King Ranch,* 182.

40. Townsend, *The Yankee Invasion of Texas*, 5; Marilyn McAdams Sibley, "Charles Stillman: A Case Study of Entrepreneurship on the Rio Grande, 1861–1865," in Vezzetti, ed., *Tidbits*, 100–103.

41. Bruce Cheeseman, GGII 019179

42. Day Folder, Family Genealogical Records, Corpus Christi District Warehouse, Corpus Christi, Texas.

43. Milo Kearney, ed., *More Studies in Brownsville History* (Brownsville: Pan American University at Brownsville, 1989), 193.

44. Joseph Kleiber Letterpress Book—January 21, 1862, Center for American History, Kingsbury Papers, letter August 3, 1862, to Postmaster General, the Honorable Montgomery Blair, GGII 200207.

45. *Fort Brown Flag*, July 31, 1862.

46. Amberson, McAllen, and McAllen, *I Would Rather Sleep in Texas*, 195–96.

47. Stillman to King, March 11, 1862, GGII 002068.

48. Vezzetti, ed., *Tidbits*, 126.

49. Lea, *The King Ranch*, 183.

50. Amberson, McAllen, and McAllen, *I Would Rather Sleep in Texas*, 188.

51. Ibid., 219.

52. Miller Hotel letter from Capt. A. J. Vidal, Brownsville Historical Association.

53. Thompson, "A Nineteenth-Century History of Cameron County, Texas," 89.

54. Rosita Putegnat interview with George N. Putegnat, January 31, 1956, given to author Jane Monday.

55. Certificate of Marriage of J. L. Putegnat and Rosa Vidal, Immaculate Conception Church, Brownsville, Texas, GGII 008270. There is conflicting information on Rosa Vidal's birth date. Her baptismal certificate indicates she was born in 1844 but earlier information had her birth date as September 24, 1841; GGII 008270 documents.

56. Family interview with Rosita Putegnat, who was one hundred years old in 2001, in Houston, Texas, by Jane Monday.

Chapter 5, 1863

1. Mary Margret McAllen Amberson, James A. McAllen, and Margaret H. McAllen, *I Would Rather Sleep in Texas: A History of the Lower Rio Grande Valley and the People of the Santa Anita Land Grant* (Austin: Texas State Historical Association, 2003), 231.

2. M. Patricia Gunning, *To Texas with Love: A History of the Sisters of the Incarnate Word and Blessed Sacrament* (Austin: Von Boeckmann-Jones, 1971), 86.

3. John Kenedy Sr., deposition given in Corpus Christi, Texas, June 11, 1905, in his handwriting, Deposition Exhibit 5, District Court Records, Corpus Christi, Texas.

4. Ibid.

5. Tom Lea, *The King Ranch* (Boston: Little, Brown, 1957), 456 n. 54.

6. Drew E. VandeCreek, Cairo, Illinois—History, Mark Twain's Mississippi River, available at http//dig.lib.niu.edu/twain/culturaltourism/cairo-history.html, accessed October 24, 2006.

7. Ed Max, comp., *Waynesburg and Honey Brook Township in the Civil War*, printed for the Chester County Historical Society, n.d., 101.

8. *The Village Record*, Coatesville, Pennsylvania, May 25, 1864.

9. Ibid.

10. John Kenedy Sr., deposition given in Corpus Christi, Texas, June 11, 1905. Deposition Exhibit 5, District Court Records, Corpus Christi, Texas.

11. John Kenedy Sr., deposition.

12. *Union Paper,* Coatesville, Pennsylvania, May 14, 1866; *Union Paper,* July 14, 1866.

13. Civil War Prisoner/Prison Research Web site, http://www.angelfire.com/ny5/elmiraprison. In Elmira Prison Camp OnLine Library, Gallery 19, on this site the bag used in the tunnel digging is identified as the extra shirt of J. P. Putegnat and the two stones he picked up on the way out are shown with two photographs of Putegnat, one just after he reached home.

14. Amberson, McAllen, and McAllen, *I Would Rather Sleep in Texas,* 197.

15. Kingsbury letter written March 13, 1863, Vol. 1–2R72, Center for American History, University of Texas, Austin, Texas.

16. Milo Kearney, ed., *More Studies in Brownsville History* (Brownsville: Pan American University at Brownsville, 1989), 170.

17. Amberson, McAllen, and McAllen, *I Would Rather Sleep in Texas,* 210.

18. Lea, *The King Ranch,* 197.

19. *Rio Grande Round-Up, A Story of Texas Tropical Borderland,* Valley By-Liners Book III (Mission, Tex.: Border Kingdom Press, 1980), 132. Also Lea, *The King Ranch,* 201.

20. Kearney, ed., *More Studies in Brownsville History,* 195.

21. John Mason Hart, *Revolutionary Mexico: The Coming Process of the Mexican Revolution* (Berkeley: University of California Press, 1989), 113–15.

22. Kearney, ed., *More Studies in Brownsville History,* 207.

23. *Rio Grande Round-Up,* 132.

24. Stephen A. Townsend, *The Yankee Invasion of Texas* (College Station: Texas A&M University Press, 2006), 5–6.

25. Ibid., 7.

26. Ibid., 9.

27. Ibid.

28. Robert B. Vezzetti, ed., *Tidbits, a Collection from the Brownsville Historical Association and the Stillman House Museum,* n.p., n.d., 126–27.

29. Jerry Thompson, "Mutiny and Desertion on the Rio Grande: The Strange Saga of Captain Adrian J. Vidal," *Military History of Texas and the Southwest* 12, no. 3 (1975), 161.

30. Rosita Putegnat interview with George N. Putegnat, January 31, 1956, given to author Jane Monday.

31. Thompson, "Mutiny and Desertion on the Rio Grande," 163.

32. Amberson, McAllen, and McAllen, *I Would Rather Sleep in Texas,* 219.

33. Ibid., 218.

34. Jerry Thompson, *Cortina: Defending the Mexican Name in Texas* (College Station: Texas A&M University Press, 2007), 161–62.

35. Lea, *The King Ranch,* 204–205.

36. Arnoldo De León, *They Called Them Greasers* (Austin: University of Texas Press, 1983), 55.

37. Ibid., 55.

38. Jerry Thompson and Lawrence T. Jones III, *Civil War And Revolution on the Rio Grande Frontier* (Austin: Texas State Historical Association, 2004), 30.

39. Lea, *The King Ranch,* 202–204.

40. Thompson, "Mutiny and Desertion on the Rio Grande," 162.

41. Ibid., 163.
42. Ibid., 162–63.
43. Ibid., 163.
44. "The Mexican Adventure," account of the murder of Jeff Barthelow by Adrian Vidal as reported in an 1891 edition of a Laredo newspaper, copied by Elizabeth Winn, June 8, 1997. See also *Houston Tri-Weekly Telegraph,* November 12, 1863, quoting the *Brownsville Fort Brown Flag,* October 30, 1863; Lea, *The King Ranch,* 204–205; Thompson, *Cortina,* 164.
45. "The Mexican Adventure," account of the murder of Jeff Barthelow by Adrian Vidal.
46. Thompson, "Mutiny and Desertion on the Rio Grande," 164.
47. Thompson, *Cortina* 164.
48. Lea, *The King Ranch,* 206–207.
49. Thompson, *Cortina,* 164.
50. Lt. W. H. Chatfield, *The Twin Cities of the Border and the Country of the Lower Rio Grande,* Centennial Oration by the Hon. William Neal (New Orleans: E. P. Brandad, 1893), 16; Lea, *The King Ranch,* 207.
51. Chatfield, *Twin Cities of the Border,* 15.
52. Lea, *The King Ranch,* 208.
53. Thompson, "A Nineteenth-Century History of Cameron County, Texas," 96.
54. Amberson, McAllen, and McAllen, *I Would Rather Sleep in Texas,* 222–23.
55. Ibid., 221.
56. Baptismal Records of Immaculate Conception Church, Brownsville, Texas, vol. 3, December 26, 1863, page 14, #152.
57. Gunning, *To Texas with Love,* 86.
58. Father Francis Kelly Nemeck, e-mail to authors, December 1, 2005.
59. Rev. P. F. Parisot, *The Reminiscences of a Texas Missionary* (San Antonio: Johnson Bros. Printing Co., 1899), 101–102, 105.
60. Father Francis Kelly Nemeck, e-mail to authors, December 1, 2005.
61. Amberson, McAllen, and McAllen, *I Would Rather Sleep in Texas,* 226.
62. Vezzetti, ed., *Tidbits,* 103.
63. Amberson, McAllen, and McAllen, *I Would Rather Sleep in Texas,* 225.
64. William Neale, Brownsville Historical Association article from their archives.
65. Amberson, McAllen, and McAllen, *I Would Rather Sleep in Texas,* 225.
66. Lea, *The King Ranch,* 210.
67. Américo Paredes, *"With His Pistol in His Hand"* (Austin: University of Texas Press, 1958), 12. See also Amberson, McAllen, and McAllen, *I Would Rather Sleep in Texas,* 225; Charles W. Goldfinch, "Juan N. Cortina 1824–1892, A Re-Appraisal" (master's thesis, University of Chicago, 1949), 67.
68. Lea, *The King Ranch,* 214; Townsend, *Yankee Invasion of Texas,* 32.
69. Paredes, *"With A Pistol in His Hand,"* xi.
70. Thompson, "Mutiny and Desertion on the Rio Grande," 165–66.
71. Miller Hotel Ledger page for November and December 1863, Brownsville Historical Association.
72. Bruce S. Cheeseman, "Let us have 500 good determined Texans": Richard King's Account of the Union Invasion of South Texas, November 12, 1863, to January 20, 1864," *Southwestern Historical Quarterly* (July 1997): 90–91. Kineños, King's men, were the vaqueros who worked the King Ranch.
73. Lea, *The King Ranch,* 216–17.

74. Hiram Chamberlain to Edward F. Gray, January 1, 1864, published under the title "Report of the Raid on King's Ranch" in the Houston newspaper, *The Tri-Weekly Telegraph*, February 1, 1864. It has been reported erroneously that Captain King knew the raid was coming and left thinking his family would be safe if he was not there. However, letters written between November 12, 1863, and January 20, 1864, were discovered in the National Archives in Washington, in Record Group 109, Confederate Papers Relating to Citizens or Business Firms, and show without a doubt that King had been gone for several days prior to the raid, which contradicts the oral tradition and family history that King had been warned of the raid. See Cheeseman, "Let us have 500 good determined Texans," 77–95.

75. Lea, *The King Ranch*, 219.

76. Cheeseman, "Let us have 500 good determined Texans," 93.

77. Baptismal Records of Immaculate Conception Church, Brownsville, Texas, vol. 2.

Chapter 6, 1864–65

1. Mary Margret McAllen Amberson, James A. McAllen, and Margaret H. McAllen, *I Would Rather Sleep in Texas: A History of the Lower Rio Grande Valley and the People of the Santa Anita Land Grant* (Austin: Texas State Historical Association, 2003), 213–14, 216, 221.

2. Tom Lea, *The King Ranch* (Boston: Little, Brown, 1957), 220–21.

3. Amberson, McAllen, and McAllen, *I Would Rather Sleep in Texas*, 228.

4. Nannie M. Tilley, ed., *Federals on the Frontier: The Diary of Benjamin F. McIntyre, 1862–1864* (Austin: University of Texas Press, 1963), 298.

5. John Salmon Ford, *Rip Ford's Texas*, ed. Stephen Oates (Austin: University of Texas Press, 1963), 347–48.

6. Ibid., 348.

7. Bruce S. Cheeseman, ed., *Maria von Blücher's Corpus Christi: Letters from the South Texas Frontier, 1849–1879* (College Station: Texas A&M University Press, 2002), 141.

8. Sister Mary Xavier Holworthy, "History of the Diocese of Corpus Christi, Texas" (master's thesis, St. Mary's University of San Antonio, 1939), 100.

9. Tilley, *Federals on the Frontier*, 295.

10. Ibid., 296.

11. Amberson, McAllen, and McAllen, *I Would Rather Sleep in Texas*, 229.

12. Ibid.

13. The newspaper article quoted in a letter that Max Dreyer has on October 27, 1890, from A. A. Champion, GGII 008180.

14. Certificate of Marriage, Immaculate Conception Church, Brownsville Texas, H. P. (Vela) 103, PUT 224, GGII 008200.

15. Lea, *The King Ranch*, 220, and 224.

16. Ford, *Rip Ford's Texas*, 234.

17. Lea, *The King Ranch*, 225.

18. Kingsbury Papers 1858–72, Vol. I–2R72, Center for American History, University of Texas, Austin, Texas.

19. Ford, *Rip Ford's Texas*, 351.

20. Joe Kleiber Collection, letter written April 16, 1864, Joseph Kleiber Letterpress original, J. K. Wells collection secured for the University of Texas Library by J. Evetts Haley.

21. Michael W. Hamilton, descendant of Vicenta Vidal Starck and Petra, letters in possession of Hamilton.

22. Military records of Fred Starck, in possession of Michael W. Hamilton, Starck descendant.

23. Tilley, *Federals on the Frontier*, 365.

24. Ibid., 311.

25. Contributed by Michael W. Hamilton, fourth generation descendant of María Vicenta Vidal Starck.

26. Tilley, *Federals on the Frontier*, 323–24.

27. Rosita Putegnat interview with Jane Monday.

28. Jerry Thompson, "Mutiny and Desertion on the Rio Grande: The Strange Saga of Captain Adrian J. Vidal," *Military History of Texas and the Southwest* 12, no. 3 (1975): 166.

29. Ibid.

30. Ibid., 166–67.

31. Tilley, *Federals on the Frontier*, 359; A. A. Champion to Max Dreyer on October 27, 1890, GGII 008180.

32. Ibid., 346.

33. Ford, *Rip Ford's Texas*, 237.

34. Lea, *The King Ranch*, 226.

35. Jerry Thompson, *Cortina: Defending the Mexican Name in Texas* (College Station: Texas A&M University Press, 2007), 167.

36. Ibid., 166.

37. Thompson, "Mutiny and Desertion on the Rio Grande," 167.

38. Tilley, *Federals on the Frontier*, 325–26.

39. Ibid., 354.

40. Ford, *Rip Ford's Texas*, 470; Lea, *The King Ranch*, 225–26.

41. Lea, *The King Ranch*, 226, 228.

42. Tilley, *Federals on the Frontier*, 372.

43. Ibid., 374.

44. Ibid., 374.

45. Ibid., 80–81.

46. Military records of Fred Starck, in possession of Michael W. Hamilton; Gravestone in the Starck Family Plot, Brownsville Old Cemetery.

47. Lea, *The King Ranch*, 228.

48. Ibid., 234.

49. Ford, *Rip Ford's Texas*, 371.

50. Ibid., 371–72.

51. Ibid., 376.

52. Lea, *The King Ranch*, 231–32.

53. Ford, *Rip Ford's Texas*, 250.

54. Leroy P. Graf, "The Economic History of Lower Rio Grande Valley, 1820–1875" (PhD diss., Harvard University, 1942), 489.

55. John Mason Hart, *Revolutionary Mexico: The Coming Process of the Mexican Revolution* (Berkeley: University of California Press, 1989), 113.

56. Mifflin Kenedy to Richard King, February 2, 1865, GGII 0191180.

57. Mifflin Kenedy to Richard King, February 3, 1865, GGII 0191180.

58. Ibid.

59. Mifflin Kenedy to Richard King, February 3, 1865, GGII 018861–64.

60. Ibid.

61. Mifflin Kenedy to Richard King, February 6, 1865, GGII 002045-003479.
62. Mifflin Kenedy to Richard King, February 15, 1865, GGII 002045.
63. Mifflin Kenedy to Richard King on March 27, 1865, GGII 002045-003479.
64. Mifflin Kenedy to Richard King, March 31, 1865, GGII 002045-003479.
65. John Kenedy Sr., deposition given in Corpus Christi, Texas, June 11, 1905. Deposition Exhibit 5, District Court Records, Corpus Christi, Texas.
66. Amberson, McAllen, and McAllen, *I Would Rather Sleep in Texas*, 262.
67. Mifflin Kenedy to Hale, April 21, 1865, GGII 019181.
68. Lea, *The King Ranch*, 234-35.
69. Thompson, *Cortina*, 203.
70. Amberson, McAllen, and McAllen, *I Would Rather Sleep in Texas*, 269-70.
71. *Village Record,* November 2, 1936.
72. Mifflin Kenedy to Richard King, GGII 002045-003479.
73. Lea, *The King Ranch*, 237-38.
74. Mifflin Kenedy to Richard King, June 29, 1865, GGII 002045-003479
75. Robert B. Vezzetti, ed., *Tidbits, a Collection from the Brownsville Historical Association and the Stillman House Museum*, n.p., n.d., 20.
76. Ford, *Rip Ford's Texas*, 397.
77. Lea, *The King Ranch*, 239.
78. Ford, *Rip Ford's Texas*, 403.
79. Lea, *The King Ranch*, 240.
80. Richard King to Reuben Holbein, May 3, 1865, GGII 019263.
81. Lea, *The King Ranch*, 243.
82. Mifflin Kenedy to Richard King, May 15, 1865, GGII 019264.
83. Mifflin Kenedy to Hale, May 15, 1865, GGII 019264.
84. Mifflin Kenedy to Richard King, May 16, 1865, GGII 019182.
85. Mifflin Kenedy to Charles Stillman, May 31, 1865, GGII 019198.
86. Thompson, *Cortina*, 211.
87. Consultation by Jane Monday with Bruce Cheeseman, March 2000. Letter courtesy of Bruce Cheeseman and in possession of author Jane Monday.
88. Kenedy Family Vertical File, Max Dreyer, Raymondville Historical Museum and Community Center, Raymondville, Texas.
89. Mifflin Kenedy to J. W. Lock & Co. at Camargo, June 10, 1865, per "Alamo," GGII 008202.
90. Rosa Marie Swisher, Petra descendant, to Jane Monday, May 30, 2006.
91. Michael W. Hamilton, Petra descendant, gave this story in an interview in San Antonio, March 2006.
92. Interview with Max Dreyer, a descendant of Elisha Jeffrey Kenedy, Mifflin Kenedy's brother, in Raymondville, Texas, February 2000.
93. Harbert Davenport to S. L. Gill, January 20, 1953, GGII 008181.
94. Mifflin Kenedy to Hiram Chamberlain Jr., June 13, 1865, GGII 019264.
95. Interview by Jane Monday with Chula T. Griffin, Tour Guide for Brownsville Cemetery Tours, Brownsville Historical Association, August 2001.
96. Rosa Marie Swisher to Jane Monday, May 30, 2006.
97. Mifflin Kenedy to Anita Vidal, October 16, 1884, GGII 0020116-17.
98. Father Francis Kelly Nemeck, e-mail to authors December 1, 2005, 1:41 P.M. The plot where Adrian's grave is located is enclosed by a wrought iron fence, and measures some thirty

by thirty feet. This plot and surrounding plots are reasonably well kept. This was probably the original Kenedy/Vidal plot, and Phebe Ann and William were originally buried here also. Sometime between 1876 and 1885, Phebe Ann and William's remains were transferred to the new Kenedy plot in Brownsville's Buena Vista Cemetery. Some time afterward, James and his son, George, were buried in the new plot, next to each other, while Thomas and his wife, Yrene, were buried also in the new plot, next to each other. Sometime in the mid-1900s, Sarita Kenedy East had the remains of her grandparents, Petra and Mifflin, transferred from a Corpus Christi cemetery to rest side by side in Buena Vista Cemetery.

99. Mifflin Kenedy to William Hale, July 1865, GGII 019169.
100. Mifflin Kenedy to Messrs. Robinson, July 5, 1865, GGII 019160.
101. Mifflin Kenedy to Hiram Chamberlain Jr., 1865, GGII 019161.
102. Mifflin Kenedy to Messrs. Robinson, 1865, GGII 019164.
103. Lea, *The King Ranch*, 239.
104. Ibid., 243-44.
105. August 17, 1865, birth of Ana Adrianne Vidal, GGII 008200.
106. Baptism of George Mifflin Putegnat, Putegnat Papers, Patricia Reneghan Collection.
107. Mifflin Kenedy to James Richardson, 1865, GGII 019182.
108. Richard King to Major General Giles Smith, September 15, 1865, GGII 019183.
109. Mifflin Kenedy to Major General Giles Smith, September 16, 1865, GGII 019183.
110. Major E. P. Durell to Major General Giles Smith, November 29, 1865, GGII 008274.
111. Ytúrria to Major General Giles Smith, August 31, 1865, GGII 008232.
112. Mifflin Kenedy to Charles Stillman, October 19, 1865, GGII 019183.
113. Mifflin Kenedy in Matamoros to Captain L. G. Aldrick at Natchez, Mississippi, April 7, 1866, from Bruce Cheeseman to author Jane Monday, March 10, 2000.
114. Richard King's Petition for a Pardon, October 7, 1865, GGII 019245.
115. Amberson, McAllen, and McAllen, *I Would Rather Sleep in Texas*, 280.
116. Ibid., 281.

Chapter 7, 1866

1. Mary Margaret McAllen Amberson, James A. McAllen, and Margaret H. McAllen, *I Would Rather Sleep in Texas: A History of the Lower Rio Grande Valley and the People of the Santa Anita Land Grant* (Austin: Texas State Historical Association, 2003), 282.
2. Bagdad, Brazos, and Clarksville Folder, Stillman Historical Museum, Brownsville, Texas. The statue of St. Joseph with the Christ Child resides in the Immaculate Conception Cathedral in Brownsville, Texas, and is one of the earliest statues brought from the Daprato Company in Italy, circa 1860. It is an exceptional example of wood carving from this company.
3. Tom Lea, *The King Ranch* (Boston: Little, Brown, 1957), 244.
4. Ibid., 249.
5. Amberson, McAllen, and McAllen, *I Would Rather Sleep in Texas*, 296-97.
6. J. Lee Stambaugh and Lillian J. Stambaugh, *The Lower Rio Grande Valley of Texas* (San Antonio: The Naylor Company, 1954), 138-40. See also Lawrence F. Hill, "The Confederate Exodus to Latin America," *Southwestern Historical Quarterly* 39, no. 2 (October 1935): 100-134; no. 3 (January 1936): 160-99; no. 4 (April 1936): 309-25; Alexander Watkins Terrell, *From Texas to Mexico and the Court of Maximilian* (Dallas: The Book Club of Texas, 1933), 1-88.
7. Hill, "The Confederate Exodus to Latin America," 114.
8. Stambaugh and Stambaugh, *The Lower Rio Grande Valley of Texas*, 139-40.

9. Mifflin Kenedy to Captain L. G. Aldrich, April 7, 1866, GGII 019183.

10. Mifflin Kenedy to Aldrich, GGII 019183; Amberson, McAllen, and McAllen, *I Would Rather Sleep in Texas,* 279.

11. Mifflin Kenedy to Robert Dalzell, April 13, 1866, GGII 019223–019242.

12. Robert B. Vezzetti, ed., *Tidbits, a Collection from the Brownsville Historical Association and the Stillman House Museum,* n.p., n.d., 25.

13. Mifflin Kenedy to Wm. Robinson, April 9, 1866, GGII 019184.

14. Mifflin Kenedy to Charles Stillman, April 10, 1866, GGII 019266.

15. John Salmon Ford, *Rip Ford's Texas,* ed. Stephen Oates (Austin: University of Texas Press, 1963), 470.

16. Mifflin Kenedy to Mrs. Sarah Kenedy, April 9, 1866, GGII 007615–007614.

17. Sister Mary Xavier Holworthy, "History of the Diocese of Corpus Christi, Texas" (master's thesis, St. Mary's University of San Antonio, 1939), 100.

18. Rev. P. F. Parisot, *The Reminiscences of a Texas Missionary* (San Antonio: Johnson Bros. Printing Co., 1899), 109.

19. Ibid.

20. Holworthy, "History of the Diocese of Corpus Christi, Texas." Today the belfry tower rises eighty-eight feet in the air and houses four bells—the bell from the original chapel first built before the main church was built, plus the three bells given by Mifflin Kenedy. The bells are still rung today "with the same clarity and beauty" as in the early years, daily at noon, before Sunday Masses, and on special occasions.

21. M. Patricia Gunning, *To Texas with Love: A History of the Sisters of the Incarnate Word and Blessed Sacrament* (Austin: Von Boeckmann-Jones, 1971), 87.

22. Mifflin Kenedy to Charles Worthington, June 16, 1866, GGII 0020558-9.

23. T. M. Balsiones to F. Cummings, Customs Inspector, June 26, 1886, GGII 019225-37.

24. Amberson, McAllen, and McAllen, *I Would Rather Sleep in Texas,* 288.

25. Ford, *Rip Ford's Texas,* 404.

26. Américo Paredes, *Folklore and Culture on the Texas-Mexican Border* (Austin: University of Texas Press, 1993), 9.

27. Amberson, McAllen, and McAllen, *I Would Rather Sleep in Texas,* 341.

28. Américo Paredes, "On Gringo, Greaser, and Other Neighborly Names," in *Singers and Storytellers,* ed. Mody C. Boatright, Wilson M. Hudson, and Allen Maxwell (Dallas: Southern Methodist University Press, 1961), 286.

29. Amberson, McAllen, and McAllen, *I Would Rather Sleep in Texas,* 284.

30. Interview by Mark Twain to the *Chicago Tribune,* July 9, 1886, available at www.twainquotes.com.

31. Mifflin Kenedy to Charles Stillman, April 2, 1866, GGII 019266.

32. Article written in Coatesville paper on March 18, 1895, about Mifflin Kenedy, furnished by Chester County Historical Society, Barbara J. Rutz Researcher, Chester County Historical Society, provided to Jane Monday, March 9, 2003.

33. Interview by authors with John Martindale Hearen, descendant of María Vicenta, in Brownsville, Texas, March 14, 2006.

34. Article written in Coatesville paper on March 18, 1895 about Mifflin Kenedy.

35. Leroy P. Graf, "The Economic History of Lower Rio Grande Valley, 1820–1875" (PhD diss., Harvard University, 1942), 476.

36. Richard King to General Getty on September 16, 1866, in possession of Texas A&M at Corpus Christi, Special Collections and Archives, Mary and Jeff Bell Library.

37. Amberson, McAllen, and McAllen, *I Would Rather Sleep in Texas,* 293.
38. Mifflin Kenedy to Richard King, September 23, 1866, GGII 019184.
39. Amberson, McAllen, and McAllen, *I Would Rather Sleep in Texas,* 293.
40. Ibid., 285–86.
41. Mifflin Kenedy to F. J. Parker, September 6, 1866, GGII 018491.
42. Mifflin Kenedy to Richard King, October 27, 1866, GGII 019185.
43. Mifflin Kenedy to Richard King, October 28, 1866, GGII 019185.
44. Mifflin Kenedy to Richard King November 2, 1866, GGII 019185.
45. Mifflin Kenedy to Richard King November 4, 1866, GGII 019186.
46. Lea, *The King Ranch,* 323.
47. Mifflin Kenedy to Richard King, November 18, 1866, GGII 019186.
48. Putegnat Family Papers given to Jane Monday by family descendant Patricia Reneghan, March 2001.

Chapter 8, 1867–68

1. Mary Margaret McAllen Amberson, James A. McAllen, and Margaret H. McAllen, *I Would Rather Sleep in Texas: A History of the Lower Rio Grande Valley and the People of the Santa Anita Land Grant* (Austin: Texas State Historical Association, 2003), 292.
2. Ibid., 295–96.
3. John Salmon Ford, *Rip Ford's Texas,* ed. Stephen Oates (Austin: University of Texas Press, 1963), 465.
4. John Kenedy, deposition given in Corpus Christi, Texas June 11, 1905. Deposition Exhibit 5, Court Records, Corpus Christi, Texas
5. Amberson, McAllen, and McAllen, *I Would Rather Sleep in Texas,* 423–29.
6. Ibid., 290.
7. John Day Folder, Corpus Christi Court Records, Corpus Christi District Warehouse, Family Genealogical Records.
8. Arnoldo De León, *The Tejano Community, 1836–1900* (Dallas: Southern Methodist University Press, 1997), 148.
9. Rev. P. F. Parisot, *The Reminiscences of a Texas Missionary* (San Antonio, Tex.: Johnson Bros. Printing, 1899), 111.
10. M. Patricia Gunning, *To Texas with Love: A History of the Sisters of the Incarnate Word and Blessed Sacrament* (Austin: Von Boeckmann-Jones, 1971), 88–90.
11. Ibid.
12. Ibid.; Parisot, *Reminiscences of a Texas Missionary,* 113.
13. Gunning, *To Texas with Love,* 88–90.
14. *The Daily Ranchero,* November 13, 1867, Corpus Christi Library, Corpus Christi, Texas.
15. *New York Times,* October 1867, reprinted from the *Brownsville Courier.*
16. Putegnat Family Bible, provided by Patsy Reneghan, Seguin, Texas, to author Jane Monday, July 2001.
17. Gunning, *To Texas with Love,* 86.
18. Parisot, *Reminiscences of a Texas Missionary,* 113.
19. Tom Lea, *The King Ranch* (Boston: Little, Brown, 1957), 251.
20. Gunning, *To Texas with Love,* 86; Amberson, McAllen, and McAllen, *I Would Rather Sleep in Texas,* 290.
21. Amberson, McAllen, and McAllen, *I Would Rather Sleep in Texas,* 296.

22. Bruce S. Cheeseman, *Perfectly Exhausted with Pleasure: The 1881 King-Kenedy Excursion Train to Laredo* (Austin, Tex.: W. Thomas Taylor, 1992), 15.

23. Lea, *The King Ranch*, 253.

24. Immaculate Conception Church, Brownsville, Texas; Baptismal Records, vol. 3, p. 409, no. 667.

25. Immaculate Conception Church, Brownsville, Texas; Baptismal Records, Book III, p. 452, no. 107.

26. Gunning, *To Texas with Love*, 93–94.

27. Ibid.

28. Lieutenant W. H. Chatfield, *The Twin Cities of the Border and the Country of the Lower Rio Grande* (New Orleans: E. P. Brandao, 1893), 17.

29. Parisot, *Reminiscences of a Texas Missionary*, 114–15.

30. Ibid., 113–115.

31. Amberson, McAllen, and McAllen, *I Would Rather Sleep in Texas*, 303.

32. Bruce Cheeseman interview with author Jane Monday, March 2000.

33. Amberson, McAllen, and McAllen, *I Would Rather Sleep in Texas*, 302.

34. Lea, *The King Ranch*, 253–54.

35. Bruce Cheeseman, "History of the 'Rincón de Los Laureles,'" paper given to author Jane Monday, March 2000.

36. Ibid.

37. Ibid.

38. Ibid.

39. Paper written in 1992 by Bruce Cheeseman, Archivist of King Ranch for ranch management on the history of the Laureles headquarters site. Obtained from Bruce Cheeseman in 2000.

40. Mifflin Kenedy, 1872 deposition, GGII 000979.

41. Ashton, "Laureles Ranch," 105.

42. Fax from Steve Harding of Steve Harding Design, Inc., February 6, 2002, containing information on registration and sketches; Lea, *The King Ranch*, 257.

43. Lea, *The King Ranch*, 255.

44. Ibid., 254.

45. Mifflin Kenedy to Major von Blücher, June 14, 1866, Texas A&M University of Corpus Christi Library in Special Collections and Archives, Mary and Jeff Bell Library.

46. Bruce S. Cheeseman, ed., *Maria von Blücher's Corpus Christi: Letters from the South Texas Frontier, 1849–1879* (College Station: Texas A&M University Press, 2002), 186.

47. Roberto Mario Salmon, "José San Ramón," The Handbook of Texas Online, Texas State Historical Association, www.tsha.utexas.edu/handbook/online.

48. Certified deed copy from Petra Vela de Kenedy and husband to Andrés Vela and Others, Starr County. See Brooks County Clerk Records, Book of Deeds, Transcribed Records of Starr County, Book 7, 354–55; the original transcription is in the Starr County Book of Deeds, Book Y, 469. The Land Grant title for Gregorio's Santa Teresa land grant is in Brooks County Transcribed Records of Starr County, Book 1, 75–76, the original transcription in Starr County Book of Deeds is in Book B, 217–21.

49. John Martindale Heaner, May 15, 2006, to author Frances Vick. See also Texas General Land Office Publication, *Guide to Spanish and Mexican Land Grants in South Texas*.

50. Louis Holton Researcher, January 17, 1948, GGII 010105.

51. Patrick J. O'Connell, *The Kenedy Family at Spring Hill College* (Mobile, Ala.: privately published, 1986–87), 16.

52. Father Kelly Nemeck, e-mail January 15, 2006, to the authors.
53. O'Connell, *Kenedy Family at Spring Hill College*, 16.
54. Ibid., 11.
55. Ibid., 4.
56. Ibid.
57. Catholic Diamonds publication, Incarnate Word Archives, Corpus Christi, Texas.
58. O'Connell, *Kenedy Family at Spring Hill College*, 5.
59. Ibid., 6.
60. Ibid., 5–6.

Chapter 9, 1869–71

1. John Salmon Ford, *Rip Ford's Texas*, ed. Stephen Oates (Austin: University of Texas Press, 1963), 468.
2. Mifflin Kenedy, deposition, August 20, 1872, GGII 000979.
3. Ford, *Rip Ford's Texas*, 466.
4. Mifflin Kenedy, deposition, August 20, 1872, GGII 000958, GGII 000959, GGII 000960, GGII 000961, GGII 000962.
5. Ibid.
6. John Ashton, "Laureles Ranch," in *The New Handbook of Texas*, 6 vols., ed. Ron Tyler, Douglas E. Barnett, Roy R. Barkley, Penelope C. Anderson, and Mark F. Odintz (Austin: Texas State Historical Association, 1996), 268.
7. Tom Lea, *The King Ranch* (Boston: Little, Brown, 1957), 257.
8. Ibid., 259.
9. Ibid., 271–72.
10. Bobby Cavazos, *The Cowboy from the Wild Horse Desert: A Story of the King Ranch* (Houston: Larksdale, 1999), 19.
11. Lea, *The King Ranch*, 271.
12. Ibid., 271–72.
13. Ibid., 266–67.
14. Ford, *Rip Ford's Texas*, 467.
15. Dora Mae Kelley, "Early Hidalgo Transportation," *Daily Review*, December 7, 1952, centennial edition. Pan American University Library, Edinburg, Texas, pages unnumbered; Rosita Putegnat Interview.
16. Kelley, "Early Hidalgo Transportation."
17. *Century of Conflict*, GGII 008735.
18. *Mobile Times*, February 5, 1869.
19. Patrick J. O'Connell, *The Kenedy Family at Spring Hill College* (Mobile, Alabama: privately published, 1986–187), 8–9.
20. O'Connell, *The Kenedy Family at Spring Hill College*, 10.
21. Ibid.
22. Baptism records at Church of the Immaculate Conception, vol. 4, 104, #321.
23. Robert B. Vezzetti, ed., *Tidbits, a Collection from the Brownsville Historical Association and the Stillman House Museum*, n.p., n.d., 106–107.
24. Mary Margaret McAllen Amberson, James A. McAllen, and Margaret H. McAllen, *I Would Rather Sleep in Texas: A History of the Lower Rio Grande Valley and the People of the Santa Anita Land Grant* (Austin: Texas State Historical Association, 2003), 308.

25. Roberto M. Villarreal, "The Mexican-American Vaqueros of the Kenedy Ranch" (master's thesis, Texas A&I University, 1972), 5.
26. Américo Paredes, *With His Pistol in His Hand* (Austin: University of Texas Press, 1971), 31; Walter Prescott Webb, *The Texas Rangers* (Cambridge, Mass.: Houghton Mifflin, 1935), 14.
27. Paredes, *With His Pistol in His Hand,* 24.
28. Villarreal, "The Mexican-American Vaqueros of the Kenedy Ranch," 19; Homero Vera, "Don Esteban Cisneros and Doña Eulalia Tijerina de Cisneros," *El Mesteño* 4, no. 43 (2001): 4.
29. Ibid.
30. O'Connell, *The Kenedy Family at Spring Hill College,* 11.
31. Ibid., 8–11.
32. Amberson, McAllen, and McAllen, *I Would Rather Sleep in Texas,* 304–305.
33. Lea, *The King Ranch,* 256.
34. Amberson, McAllen, and McAllen, *I Would Rather Sleep in Texas,* 308.
35. Ibid., 308–309.
36. 1870 Census, Corpus Christi, Duval County, August 1, 1870, Mifflin Kenedy, Line 2, Series M593 Roll: 1600, page 98.
37. Lea, *The King Ranch,* 261–62.
38. Ibid.
39. Audrey Simmons, "The Story of Clarksville and Bagdad," Brownsville Historical Association, 99.
40. Lea, *The King Ranch,* 263.
41. Ibid., 265.
42. Ibid., 268–69.
43. David Montejano, *Anglos and Mexicans in the Making of Texas, 1836–1986* (Austin: University of Texas Press, 1987), 54.
44. Lea, *The King Ranch,* 249–50; Dorothy Abbott McCoy, "James B. Wells," in *Rio Grande Round-Up: A Story of Texas Tropical Borderland,* Valley By-Liners Book III (Mission, Tex.: Border Kingdom Press, printed by Eakin Publications, Burnet, Texas, 1980), 133–34. See also Amberson, McAllen, and McAllen, *I Would Rather Sleep in Texas,* 296–97.
45. Putegnat family papers, Reneghan Family Bible, given to Jane Monday by Patricia Reneghan.
46. Amberson, McAllen, and McAllen, *I Would Rather Sleep in Texas,* 309.
47. Marriage Records at the Church of Immaculate Conception, Brownsville, Texas.
48. Putegnat family papers given to Jane Monday by Patricia Reneghan.
49. Lea, *The King Ranch,* 263.
50. Ibid., 264.
51. Amberson, McAllen, and McAllen, *I Would Rather Sleep in Texas,* 316.
52. Ibid.
53. Putegnat Family Records given to Jane Monday by Patricia Reneghan.

Chapter 10, 1872–74

1. Bruce Cheeseman, letter to Jane Monday and Frances Vick, December 2, 2005.
2. Joseph Kleiber to Humphrey Woodhouse, May 6, Joseph Kleiber Letterpress Book, October 11, 1860 to July 10, 1877, Center for American History, University of Texas, Austin, Texas.
3. Joseph Kleiber to Humphrey Woodhouse, May 13, Joseph Kleiber Letterpress Book, October 11, 1860 to July 10, 1877, Center for American History, University of Texas, Austin, Texas.

4. Joseph Kleiber to Humphrey Woodhouse, April 27, Letterpress Book, October 11, 1860 to July 10, 1877, Center for American History, University of Texas, Austin, Texas.

5. Tom Lea, *The King Ranch* (Boston: Little, Brown, 1957), 297.

6. Ibid., 298.

7. Murphy Givens, "The Cattle Queen of Texas," *Corpus Christi Caller Times*, "Storybook Mansions," Wednesday May 10, 2000.

8. Lea, *The King Ranch*, 307.

9. Ibid., 320–21.

10. Joe S. Graham, *El Rancho in South Texas* (Denton: University of North Texas Press, 1994), 40–41.

11. Ibid.

12. Givens, "The Cattle Queen of Texas."

13. Ibid.

14. Ibid.; Robert B. Vezzetti, ed., *Tidbits, a Collection from the Brownsville Historical Association and the Stillman House Museum*, n.p., n.d., 87.

15. John Ashton, "Laureles Ranch," in *The New Handbook of Texas*, 6 vols., ed. Ron Tyler, Douglas E. Barnett, Roy R. Barkley, Penelope C. Anderson, and Mark F. Odintz (Austin: Texas State Historical Association, 1996), 296.

16. Alexander Stillman interview, March 2000, with authors.

17. Bruce Cheeseman, "History of Laureles Headquarters," paper given to Jane Monday, March 2000, 2.

18. Lois E. Myers, "He Couldn't Get along without A Wife: A Women's View of Married Life in Victoria County, 1877–1881," *South Texas Historical Journal* 1, no. 1 (Spring 1988): 17.

19. Johnnie Mae de Mauer, "The History of Kenedy County" (master's thesis, Texas College of Arts and Industries, Kingsville, 1940), 5.

20. Frost Woodhull, "Ranch Remedios," in *Man Bird, and Beast*, ed. J. Frank Dobie (Austin: University of Texas Press, 1930), 18, 43–44.

21. Ibid., 64.

22. John G. Bourke, "The Folk-Foods of the Rio Grande Valley," in *Southwestern Lore*, ed. J. Frank Dobie (Dallas: Southern Methodist University Press, 1965), 95.

23. Leon Guinn, "Paisano Tracks," in *Coyote Wisdom*, ed. J. Frank Dobie, Mody C. Boatright, and Harry H. Ransom (Dallas: Southern Methodist University Press, 1965), 268.

24. Woodhull, "Ranch Remedios," 54, 57.

25. Guinn, "Paisano Tracks," 268.

26. Woodhull, "Ranch Remedios," 53.

27. Patrick J. O'Connell, *The Kenedy Family at Spring Hill College* (Mobile, Ala.: privately published, 1986–87), 10. Sarah attended Ursuline Academy from 1868 to 1874, Assistant Ursuline Archivist, Sylvia Probst, June 14, 2006, to Jane Monday.

28. E-mail, August 10, 2001, from "Drovers Mercantile," using *Ellsworth Reporter* and Harry E. Chrisman, *The Ladder of Rivers* (Denver: Sage Books, 1962).

29. John Mason Hart, *Revolutionary Mexico: The Coming Process of the Mexican Revolution* (Berkeley: University of California Press, 1989), 123.

30. Lea, *The King Ranch*, 267.

31. Ibid., 266–69.

32. Mary Margret McAllen Amberson, James A. McAllen, and Margaret H. McAllen, *I Would Rather Sleep in Texas: A History of the Lower Rio Grande Valley and the People of the Santa Anita Land Grant* (Austin: Texas State Historical Association, 2003), 317.

33. Lea, *The King Ranch,* 274; Amberson, McAllen, and McAllen, *I Would Rather Sleep in Texas,* 320.
34. Lea, *The King Ranch,* 276.
35. Amberson, McAllen, and McAllen, *I Would Rather Sleep in Texas,* 321.
36. Depositions regarding the loss of cattle to rustlers along the Rio Grande River, GGII 000957–979.
37. J. Frank Dobie, *A Vaquero of the Brush Country* (Boston: Little, Brown, 1943), 57.
38. Depositions regarding the loss of cattle to rustlers along the Rio Grande River, GGII 000957–979.
39. Homero Vera, e-mail to authors, July 2006.
40. Amberson, McAllen, and McAllen, *I Would Rather Sleep in Texas,* 326.

Chapter 11, 1873

1. Mary Margaret McAllen Amberson, James A. McAllen, and Margaret H. McAllen, *I Would Rather Sleep in Texas: A History of the Lower Rio Grande Valley and the People of the Santa Anita Land Grant* (Austin: Texas State Historical Association, 2003), 328.
2. Tom Lea, *The King Ranch* (Boston: Little, Brown, 1957), 277.
3. Arnoldo De León, *Tejano Community, 1836–1900* (Dallas: Southern Methodist University Press, 1997), 18.
4. Sister Mary Xavier, IWBS, *A Century of Sacrifice: The History of the Cathedral Parish* (Corpus Christi, Tex.: n.p., 1953), 1–3.
5. *Nueces Valley* newspaper, January 18, 1873, Corpus Christi Public Library, Corpus Christi, Texas, Microfilm #5.
6. *Nueces Valley* newspaper, January 18, 1873.
7. Ibid., February 1, 1873.
8. Ibid., February 15, 1873.
9. Bruce Cheeseman, "The King Spohn Family Friendship: A Productive Partnership Embodying Heritage, Hope & Leadership," speech given to Spohn Health System executives at a corporate retreat in Santa Fe, New Mexico. Given to Jane Monday, March 2000.
10. Cheeseman, "The King Spohn Family Friendship."
11. *Nueces Valley* newspaper, February 22, 1873.
12. Mifflin Kenedy from Holbein, February 28, 1873, GGII 002045–03479.
13. *Nueces Valley* newspaper, March 15, 1873.
14. Ibid., March 1, 1873.
15. Richard King to Mifflin Kenedy, March 21, 1873, GGII 002045–03479.
16. Ibid.
17. *Nueces Valley* newspaper, March 22, 1873.
18. Ibid., March 22, 1873.
19. Ibid., April 12, 1873.
20. Jerry Thompson and Lawrence T. Jones III, *Civil War and Revolution on the Rio Grande Frontier* (Austin: Texas State Historical Association, 2004), 8–9; *Nueces Valley* newspaper, April 12, 1873.
21. Richard King to Mifflin Kenedy, May 2, 1873, GGII 002048–002089.
22. *Nueces Valley* newspaper, May 24, 1873.
23. Richard King to Mifflin Kenedy, June 7, 1873, and July 5, 1873, GGII 002048–002089.
24. *Nueces Valley* newspaper, June 14, 1873.

25. Max Dreyer interview, Raymondville, Texas, March 2000, with Jane Monday.
26. *Corpus Christi Caller,* June 1873, Corpus Christi Library, Corpus Christi, Texas.
27. *Nueces Valley* newspaper, July 5, 1873.
28. Ibid., July 12, 1873.
29. Ibid.
30. Lea, *The King Ranch,* 324.
31. *Nueces Valley* newspaper, July 26, 1873.
32. Ibid., August 2, 1873.
33. Unpublished bound copies of King, Kenedy Co. Correspondence, 1873 #0539, Corpus Christi Museum, Corpus Christi, Texas. Transcribed by Lillian Embree. Unless otherwise noted, all letters from Kelly are from this source.
34. William Kelly to Joseph Cooper, August 13, 1873.
35. William Kelly to Joseph Cooper, September 3, 1873.
36. William Kelly to Captain Kenedy, September 14, 1873. Ibid. #0539.
37. William Kelly to Captain Kenedy, September 18, 1873, GGII 006457–006471.
38. William Kelly to Captain Kenedy, September 28, 1873.
39. William Kelly to Joseph Cooper, October 13, 1873.
40. Charles W. Monday Jr., MD, Board Certified General Surgeon, interview with authors, May 2006.
41. William Kelly to Captain Kenedy, October 5, 1873.
42. William Kelly to Richard King, October 8, 1873.
43. Lea, *The King Ranch,* 300.
44. William Kelly to Captain Kenedy, September 28, 1873.
45. William Kelly to Joseph Cooper, October 13, 1873.
46. William Kelly to Mifflin Kenedy, October 8, 1873.
47. William Kelly to Captain Kenedy, September 14, 1873.
48. A *resaca* can also be shallow freshwater lakes that are made when rivers change course. Resaca Lake is a natural oxbow lake, formed when the Rio Grande flooded its banks and changed course, leaving behind a "loop" of riverbed. E-mail from Homero Vera, July 2006.
49. William Kelly to Captain Kenedy, October 5, 1873.
50. Ibid.
51. William Kelly to Captain Kenedy, October 8, 1873.
52. William Kelly to Richard King, October 8, 1873.
53. William Kelly to Captain Kenedy, October 19, 1873.
54. William Kelly to Captain Kenedy, September 27, 1873.
55. William Kelly to Captain Kenedy, November 2, 1873.
56. Arnoldo De León, *They Called Them Greasers* (Austin: University of Texas Press, 1983), 58.
57. William Kelly to Captain Kenedy, November 2, 1873.
58. William Kelly to Captain Kenedy, November 3, 1873.
59. Ibid.
60. William Kelly to Captain Kenedy, November 9, 1873.
61. William Kelly to Captain Kenedy, November 7, 1873.
62. William Kelly to Captain Kenedy, November 16, 1873.
63. William Kelly to Holbein, November 19, 1873.
64. William Kelly to Captain Kenedy, November 19, 1873.
65. William Kelly to Captain King, December 7, 1873

66. William Kelly to Captain Kenedy, December 7, 1873.
67. William Kelly to Captain Kenedy, December 14, 1873.
68. William Kelly to Captain Kenedy, November 16, 1873.
69. William Kelly to Captain King, December 7, 1873.
70. William Kelly to Captain Kenedy, November 23, 1873.
71. William Kelly to Captain Kenedy, December 14, 1873.
72. William Kelly to Captain Kenedy, December 23, 1873.
73. William Kelly to Hiram Chamberlain, November 9, 1873.
74. Amberson, McAllen, and McAllen, *I Would Rather Sleep in Texas,* 328.

Chapter 12, 1874

1. Mary Margaret McAllen Amberson, James A. McAllen, and Margaret H. McAllen, *I Would Rather Sleep in Texas: A History of the Lower Rio Grande Valley and the People of the Santa Anita Land Grant* (Austin: Texas State Historical Association, 2003), 328.
2. J. Frank Dobie, *A Vaquero of the Brush Country* (Boston: Little, Brown, 1943), 49.
3. John Kenedy, deposition, GGII 010101–010105.
4. Patrick J. O'Connell, *The Kenedy Family at Spring Hill College* (Mobile, Ala.: privately published, 1986-187), 12.
5. William Kelly to Holbein at Santa Gertrudis, January 2, 1874, unpublished bound copies of King, Kenedy Co. Correspondence, 1874, Corpus Christi Museum, Corpus Christi, Texas. Transcribed by Lillian Embree. Unless otherwise noted, all letters from Kelly are from this source.
6. Richard King to Mifflin Kenedy, February 27, 1874, GGII 002295.
7. Richard King to Mifflin Kenedy, March 5, 1874, GGII 002096–000349.
8. William Kelly to Richard King, March 4, 1874.
9. William Kelly to Messrs. Perkins Swenson & Co., May 7, 1874.
10. William Kelly to Mifflin Kenedy, January 18, 1874.
11. William Kelly to Senator Russell, February 4, 1874.
12. William Kelly to Joseph Cooper, February 28, 1874.
13. William Kelly to Mifflin Kenedy, January 1874.
14. William Kelly to Joseph Cooper, April 15, 1874; William Kelly to Senator Russell, February 4, 1874.
15. William Kelly to Francisco Ytúrria, April 26, 1874, Kenedy Log Book of 1874, 289-94, Corpus Christi Museum; Kelly to Russell, February 4, 1874.
16. Richard King to Mifflin Kenedy, April 11, 1874, GGII 002096–000349.
17. William Kelly to Bernardo Ytúrria, May 2, 1874.
18. William Kelly to Robert Dalzell, May 8, 1874, GGII 007593–007598.
19. William Kelly to Joseph Cooper, May 8, 1874.
20. Putegnat Family Tree, from Putegnat Family Interview, Seguin, Texas, 2003.
21. William Kelly to Messrs. Perkins Swenson & Co., November 11, 1874.
22. Jeremiah Galvan to King Kenedy Co., August 11, 1874.
23. Mifflin Kenedy to Stephen Powers, September 17, 1874, Center for American History, Powers Papers, University of Texas, Austin, Texas.
24. William Kelly to Manuel Rodríguez, June 20, 1874.
25. William Kelly to Mifflin Kenedy, January 20, 1874.
26. William Kelly to Senator Russell, February 4, 1874.
27. William Kelly to Mifflin Kenedy, February 22, 1874.

28. William Kelly to Senator Russell, March 1, 1874.
29. William Kelly to Senator Russell, March 22, 1874.
30. William Kelly to Joseph Cooper, April 4, 1874.
31. William Kelly to Mifflin Kenedy, March 4, 1874.
32. Richard King to Mifflin Kenedy, March 5, 1874, GGII 002096-000349.
33. Richard King to Mifflin Kenedy, March 13, 1874, GGII 002096-000349.
34. Richard King to Mifflin Kenedy, March 17, 1874, GGII 002096-000349.
35. William Kelly to Richard King, April 12, 1874.
36. Richard King to Mifflin Kenedy, May 1, 1874, GGII 002096-000349.
37. Richard King to Mifflin Kenedy, May 9, 1874, GGII 002096-000349.
38. Mifflin Kenedy to Mr. Jesus Sina, April 20, 1874.
39. Diary of Joseph Almond, Corpus Christi Library, Reserved Archives.
40. Richard King to Mifflin Kenedy, July 12, 1874, GGII 002096-000349.
41. Mifflin Kenedy to Richard King, September 1874, GGII 0020433.
42. Stephen Powers from Mifflin Kenedy, September 17, 1874, GGII 002096-000349 and Center for American History, Powers Papers, University of Texas, Austin, Texas.
43. William Kelly to Messrs. Coleman, Mathis, & Dalton, 1874.
44. William Kelly to Messrs. Coleman Mathis & Fulton, October 9, 1874.
45. Mifflin Kenedy to Robert Dalzell, November 9, 1874, GGII 002045-00349.
46. Tom Lea, *The King Ranch* (Boston: Little, Brown, 1957), 301.

Chapter 13, 1875

1. Willie Kenedy to Mifflin Kenedy, January 1, 1875, GGII 002444-002507.
2. Patrick J. O'Connell, *The Kenedy Family at Spring Hill College* (Mobile, Ala.: Published privately by Spring Hill College, 1986-87), 14.
3. John Kenedy, deposition, Exhibit 5, GGII 013737-013750.
4. Jane Quinn, *Minorcans in Florida: Their History and Heritage* (San Augustine, Fla.: Mission, 1975), 183.
5. Father Kelly Nemeck e-mail of December 10, 2005 to the two authors; Bernard Doyon, OMI, *The Cavalry of Christ on the Rio Grande, 1849–1883* (Milwaukee: Bruce Press, 1956), 139-40.
6. Andrés Tijerina, *Tejano Empire: Life on the South Texas Ranchos* (College Station: Texas A&M University Press, 1998), 117.
7. Ibid., 118.
8. Rev. P. F. Parisot, OMI, *The Reminiscences of a Texas Missionary* (San Antonio, Tex.: Johnson Brothers Printing, 1899), 115-16.
9. Quinn, *Minorcans in Florida*, 187-88.
10. Joe Graham, ed., *Ranching in South Texas: A Symposium*. "Los Padres Rancheristas: The 19th Century Struggle for Mexican-American Catholicism in South Texas," Jose Roberto Juarez, July 22, 1994.
11. Tijerina, *Tejano Empire*, 124.
12. Ibid., 125
13. David Montejano, *Anglos and Mexicans in the Making of Texas, 1836–1986* (Austin: University of Texas Press, 1987), 43-44.
14. Armando C. Alonzo, *Tejano Legacy: Rancheros and Settlers in South Texas, 1734–1900* (Albuquerque: University of New Mexico Press, 1998), 177.

15. Ibid., 178.
16. Ibid., 179, 181.
17. Frank Cushman Pierce, *A Brief History of the Lower Rio Grande Valley* (Edinburg, Tex.: New Santander Press, 1998), 108–109.
18. Tom Lea, *The King Ranch* (Boston: Little, Brown, 1957), 308.
19. Ibid., 310, 314, 320.
20. Richard King to Mifflin Kenedy, February 1, 1875, GGII 002048–002089.
21. Richard King to Mifflin Kenedy, February 3, 1875, GGII 002048–002089.
22. Lea, *The King Ranch*, 301–304
23. Richard King to Mifflin Kenedy, January 25, 1875, GGII 002048–002089.
24. Chuck Parsons and Marianne E. Hall Little, *Captain L. H. McNelly: Texas Ranger* (Austin: State House Press, 2001), 167.
25. Ibid., 168.
26. Ibid., 169.
27. Ibid., 170.
28. Walter Prescott Webb, *The Texas Rangers: A Century of Frontier Defense* (Austin: University of Texas Press, 1980), 15.
29. Lea, *The King Ranch*, 281.
30. Ibid., 278.
31. Ibid., 280.
32. Parsons and Hall Little, *Captain L. H. McNelly, Texas Ranger*, 184.
33. Lea, *The King Ranch*, 194.
34. Ibid., 281–82.
35. Mary Margret McAllen Amberson, James A. McAllen, and Margaret H. McAllen, *I Would Rather Sleep in Texas: A History of the Lower Rio Grande Valley and the People of the Santa Anita Land Grant* (Austin: Texas State Historical Association, 2003), 330.
36. Richard King to Mifflin Kenedy, May 1, 1875, GGII 002251.
37. Richard King to Mifflin Kenedy, May 4, 1875, GGII 002248.
38. Lea, *The King Ranch*, 280.
39. Parsons and Hall Little, *Captain L. H. McNelly*, 199–200.
40. Frances T. Ingmire, *Texas Ranger Service Records, 1847–1900*, vol. 2 (St. Louis, Mo.: Ingmire Publications, 1982),
41. Telegram from Richard King to Mifflin Kenedy, November 22, 1875, GGII 002048–002089.
42. Parsons and Hall Little, *Captain L. H. McNelly*, 239–40.
43. Amberson, McAllen, and McAllen, *I Would Rather Sleep in Texas*, 331–32.
44. Ibid., 332.
45. L. H. McNelly to Mifflin Kenedy, GGII 01849–020592.
46. Richard King to Mifflin Kenedy, January 21, 1875, GGII 002048–002089; Richard King to Mifflin Kenedy, March 5, 1875, GGII 002048–002089.
47. Richard King to Mifflin Kenedy, February 5, 1875, GGII 002226.
48. Richard King to Mifflin Kenedy, January 25, 1875, GGII 002226.
49. Mifflin Kenedy to Stephen Powers, February 7, 1875, GGII 0020363–65.
50. John Salmon Ford, *Rip Ford's Texas*, ed. Stephen Oates (Austin: University of Texas Press, 1963), 470; Lea, *The King Ranch*, 336.
51. Mifflin Kenedy to Stephen Powers, May 26, 1875, GGII 0020368.
52. Mifflin Kenedy to Stephen Powers, August 27, 1875, GGII 0020374.

NOTES TO PAGES 234–242

53. J. J. Gomila to Stephen Powers, September 22, 1875, GGII 0020378.
54. Mifflin Kenedy to Stephen Powers, October 22, 1875, GGII 0020359; Wm. M. Perkins, D. L. Kernion, B. A. Shepherd are listed at Perkins & Co. in New Orleans at http://www.rootsweb.com/~usgenweb/la/lafiles.htm, Louisiana division, Main Branch, New Orleans Public library, *1861 New Orleans City Directory*.
55. Mifflin Kenedy to Stephen Powers, November 24, 1875, GGII 0020384.

Chapter 14, 1876

1. Mary Margaret McAllen Amberson, James A. McAllen, and Margaret H. McAllen, *I Would Rather Sleep in Texas: A History of the Lower Rio Grande Valley and the People of the Santa Anita Land Grant* (Austin: Texas State Historical Association, 2003), 333.
2. Tom Lea, *The King Ranch* (Boston: Little, Brown, 1957), 295.
3. John Salmon Ford, *Rip Ford's Texas*, ed. Stephen Oates (Austin: University of Texas Press, 1963), 412.
4. Amberson, McAllen, and McAllen, *I Would Rather Sleep in Texas*, 334.
5. L. N. McNelly to Captain Kenedy, April 19, McAllen Family Archives.
6. Amberson, McAllen, and McAllen, *I Would Rather Sleep in Texas*, 334–35.
7. Ford, *Rip Ford's Texas*, 413–14.
8. Lea, *The King Ranch*, 293.
9. *Corpus Christi Caller*, January 26, 1876, Corpus Christi Library.
10. Mifflin Kenedy to Stephen Powers, February 8, 1876, GGII 0020389.
11. Mifflin Kenedy to Stephen Powers, February 26, 1876, GGII 0020393.
12. *Corpus Christi Caller*, February 29, 1876, Corpus Christi Library.
13. Mifflin Kenedy to Stephen Powers, March 14, 1876, GGII 0020397.
14. Richard King to Mifflin Kenedy, March 28, 1876, GGII 002045-003479.
15. *Corpus Christi Caller*, March 19, 1876, Corpus Christi Library.
16. Mifflin Kenedy to Stephen Powers, March 29, 1876, GGII 020400-1.
17. *Corpus Christi Caller*, February 8, 1876, Corpus Christi Library.
18. *Corpus Christi Caller*, March 2, 1876, Corpus Christi Library.
19. Catholic Diamond Publication, Catholic Archives, Corpus Christi, Texas.
20. *Corpus Christi Caller*, March 5, 1876, Corpus Christi Library.
21. *Corpus Christi Caller*, April 29, 1876, Corpus Christi Library.
22. *Corpus Christi Caller*, May 24, 1876, Corpus Christi Library.
23. Lena Henrichson, *Pioneers on the Nueces* (San Antonio, Tex.: The Naylor Company, 1963), 99.
24. Putegnat Family records and Day Folder in Corpus Christi District Court Records.
25. Lieut. W. H. Chatfield, *The Twin Cities of the Border and the Country of the Rio Grande* (New Orleans: E. P. Brandao, 1893), 14.
26. *Corpus Christi Caller*, July 5, 1876, Corpus Christi Library.
27. Patrick J. O'Connell, *The Kenedy Family at Spring Hill College* (Mobile, Ala.: Published privately by Spring Hill College, 1986–87), 14.
28. Metairie Cemetery Association, New Orleans Records, #16–50.
29. *Corpus Christi Caller*, November 26, 1876, Corpus Christi Library.
30. Frank Wagner, "Perry Dodddridge," in The Handbook of Texas Online, http://www.tsha.utexas.edu/handbook/online/index.html.
31. *Corpus Christi Caller*, November 26, 1876, Corpus Christi Library.

32. *Corpus Christi Caller,* October 3, 1876, Corpus Christi Library.

33. Grace Dunn Vetters, "Dr. Arthur Edward Spohn and Spohn Hospital," Corpus Christi Library, Nueces County Historical Commission, GGII 008843.

34. Telegram from Mifflin Kenedy to Stephen Powers, November 10, 1876, GGII 0020404-5.

35. *Corpus Christi Caller,* November 26, 1876, Corpus Christi Library.

36. J. L. Allhands, "Uriah Lott," in The Handbook of Texas Online, http://www.tsha.utexas.edu/handbook/online/index.html.

Chapter 15, 1877–78

1. J. L. Allhands, *Uriah Lott* (San Antonio, Tex.: The Naylor Co., 1949), 15-16.

2. John Mason Hart, *Revolutionary Mexico: The Coming and Process of the Mexican Revolution* (Berkeley: University of California Press, 1987), 140.

3. Roberto M. Villarreal and Alicia Villarreal-Wallach, *Atanasia* (Riviera, Tex.: Vamos, 1997), 1.

4. Mifflin Kenedy to Stephen Powers, February 4, 1877, GGII 0020258; Mifflin Kenedy to Stephen Powers, December 14, 1877, GGII 0020281.

5. Mifflin Kenedy to Stephen Powers, February 4, 1877, GGII 0020258.

6. Mifflin Kenedy to Stephen Powers, May 10, 1877, GGII 0020262.

7. John Kenedy, deposition, GGII 010101-010105.

8. Mary Margaret McAllen Amberson, James A. McAllen, and Margaret H. McAllen, *I Would Rather Sleep in Texas: A History of the Lower Rio Grande Valley and the People of the Santa Anita Land Grant* (Austin: Texas State Historical Association, 2003), 336.

9. Ibid., 338-39.

10. Roberto M. Villarreal, "The Mexican American Vaqueros on the Kenedy Ranch: A Social History" (master's thesis, Texas A&I University, 1972), 21.

11. Ramon F. Adams, *Come an' Get It: The Story of the Old Cowboy Cook* (Norman: University of Oklahoma Press, 1952), 123.

12. Jane Clements Monday and Betty Bailey Colley, *Voices from the Wild Horse Desert* (Austin: University of Texas Press, 1997), 32.

13. Amberson, McAllen, and McAllen, *I Would Rather Sleep in Texas,* 340.

14. J. Frank Dobie, *Cow People* (Austin: University of Texas Press, 1964), 219-22.

15. Mifflin Kenedy to Father Jeffers, January 14, 1886, GGII 019363-4.

16. Sister Mary Xavier, IWBS, *A Century of Sacrifice: The History of the Cathedral Parish* (Corpus Christi, Tex.: n.p., 1953), 27-28.

17. Putegnat Family Papers, from Patricia Reneghan, to Jane Monday.

18. Mifflin Kenedy to Stephen Powers, August 5, 1877, GGII 002068.

19. Tom Lea, *The King Ranch* (Boston: Little, Brown, 1957), 293. See also Chuck Parsons and Marianne Hall Little, *L. H. McNelly, Texas Ranger, The Life and Times of a Fighting Man* (Austin: State House Press, 2001), 300-301.

20. Mifflin Kenedy to Stephen Powers, October 7, 1877, GGII 0020269-70.

21. Mifflin Kenedy to Stephen Powers, October 31, 1877, GGII 0020276-7.

22. Edward Downey to Richard King, January 23, 1878, GGII 002045, GGII 003479.

23. "Life on the Bluntzer Farm Round 1880," *Cuero Record,* November 18, 1953.

24. Andrés Tijerina, *Tejano Empire: Life on the South Texas Ranchos* (College Station: Texas A&M University Press, 1998), 59.

NOTES TO PAGES 252–264

25. Ibid., 98–99.
26. Ibid., 43–44.
27. Jane Clements Monday and Betty Bailey Colley, *Voices from the Wild Horse Desert: The Vaquero Families of the King and Kenedy Ranches* (Austin: University of Texas Press, 1997), 148–51.
28. Amberson, McAllen, and McAllen, *I Would Rather Sleep in Texas,* 348–49.
29. Ibid., 347–50.
30. Lea, *The King Ranch,* 337–38.
31. Mifflin Kenedy to Stephen Powers, March 2, 1878, GGII 0020283.
32. Mifflin Kenedy to Stephen Powers, April 28, 1878, GGII 0020283 and June 7, 1878, GGII 0020293–96.
33. Harry Sinclair Drago, *The Legend Makers: Tales of the Old-Time Peace Officers and Desperadoes of the Frontier* (New York: Dodd, Mead, 1975), 76.
34. Ibid., 77.
35. Earle R. Forrest, "Dora Hand, The Dance Hall Singer of Old Dodge City," *The Westerners Brand Book,* Los Angeles Corral, Book Number 7, 50.
36. Denis McLoughlin, *Wild and Woolly: An Encyclopedia of the Old West* (Garden City, N.Y.: Doubleday, 1975); GGII 008912.
37. Drago, *The Legend Makers,* 77.
38. Ibid.
39. Ibid., 77–78.
40. Ibid., 78.
41. Ibid., 78–79.
42. Ibid., 79.
43. Ibid.
44. Ibid., 79–80.
45. Ibid.
46. Ibid.
47. Ibid., 80–81.
48. Nyle H. Miller and Joseph W. Snell, *Why the West Was Wild* (Norman: University of Oklahoma Press, 2003), 311–12.
49. Forrest, "Dora Hand," 52–53.
50. Ibid., 53–54.
51. Mifflin Kenedy to Stephen Powers, November 8, 1878, GGII 008855–010169.
52. J. J. Cocke to Mifflin Kenedy, November 14, 1878, GGII 0020306–9.
53. Mifflin Kenedy to Stephen Powers, November 25, 1878, GGII 008910–008913.
54. Mifflin Kenedy to Stephen Powers, December 17, 1878, GGII 008910–008913.

Chapter 16, 1879–80

1. Chester County Historical Association, West Chester, Pennsylvania.
2. Michael W. Hamilton, private papers, descendant of Petra and Vicenta Vidal Starck.
3. Mifflin Kenedy to Stephen Powers, January 20, 1879, GGII 0020349.
4. J. J. Gomila to Stephen Powers, August 14, 1879, GGII 0020322.
5. Telegrams from Mifflin Kenedy to Stephen Powers, August 15, 1879, GGII 0020322 and August 16, 1879, GGII 0020323.

6. Mifflin Kenedy to Stephen Powers, September 21, 1879, GGII 0020349.

7. Bruce S. Cheeseman, *Perfectly Exhausted with Pleasure: King Kenedy Excursion* (Austin: W. Thomas Taylor, 1992), 22.

8. David Montejano, *Anglos and Mexicans in the Making of Texas, 1836–1986* (Austin: University of Texas Press, 1987), 90–91.

9. Tom Lea, *The King Ranch* (Boston: Little, Brown, 1957), 337.

10. *Semi-Weekly Ledger,* April 4 and 17, 1880, Corpus Christi Library, GGII 019875.

11. *Galveston Daily News,* June 13, 1880, GGII 019875.

12. *Galveston Daily News,* September 21, 1880, GGII 019875, GGII 019876.

13. *Semi-Weekly Ledger,* June 18, 1880, Corpus Christi Library, GGII 019875.

14. *Galveston Daily News,* September 2, 1880, GGII 019875.

15. *Galveston Daily News,* December 31, 1880, GGII 019876.

16. Mifflin Kenedy to Stephen Powers, September 20, 1880, GGII 0020351.

17. 1880 Census, University of Texas-PanAm, Edinburg, Texas. Cameron Co., Hidalgo Co., Starr Co., Webb Co., Zapata Co., T009, 1294, 1311, 1327, 1332, 1334.

18. Ibid.

19. Ibid.

20. Mifflin Kenedy to Richard King, July 29, 1880, GGII 019511, GGII 009553

21. Jane Clements Monday and Betty Bailey Colley, *Voices from the Wild Horse Desert: The Vaquero Families of the King and Kenedy Ranches* (Austin: University of Texas Press, 1997), 109.

22. Arnoldo De León, *Tejano Community, 1836–1900* (Dallas: Southern Methodist University Press, 1997), 145–46.

23. "Bits of History," *Corpus Christi Caller,* December 16, 1992.

24. Coleman McCampbell, *Saga of a Frontier Seaport* (Dallas: South-West Press, 1934) 39–40.

25. *Semi-Weekly Ledger,* June 16 and June 23, 1880, Corpus Christi Library.

26. Ibid., November 3, 1880.

27. Ibid., August 12, 1880.

28. Ibid., October 17, 1880.

Chapter 17, 1881

1. Mifflin Kenedy to John Kenedy, August 8, 1892, GGII 01307–013730.

2. Christopher Long, "Corpus Christi, Texas," *The New Handbook of Texas* (Austin: Texas State Historical Association, 1996), 332.

3. *San Antonio Express,* January 5, 1881, GGII 020002.

4. *Semi-Weekly Ledger,* Corpus Christi, January 19, 1881, GGII 020005.

5. Ibid, January 16, 1881, GGII 020004.

6. Ibid., February 27, 1881, GGII 020015.

7. Bruce S. Cheeseman, *Perfectly Exhausted with Pleasure: The 1881 King-Kenedy Excursion Train to Laredo* (Austin, Tex.: Book Club of Texas, 1992), 27.

8. Ibid., 28.

9. Ibid.

10. Ibid.

11. John Kenedy from Edward Chamberlain in San Antonio saying he had gone to try to buy the ring back but Mrs. Lott had sold it. April 12, 1881, GGII 017527–017578.

12. Sister Mary Xavier, IWBS. *A Century of Sacrifice* (Corpus Christi, Tex.: n.p., 1953), 28.

13. Father P. F. Parisot, *The Reminiscences of a Texas Missionary* (San Antonio, Tex.: Johnson Bros. Printing, 1899), 122–33.

14. Parisot, *Reminiscences of a Texas Missionary*, 126.

15. Ibid., 129.

16. Ibid., 130–31.

17. Tom Lea, *The King Ranch* (Boston: Little, Brown, 1957), 351–52.

18. Ibid., 351–52.

19. *Galveston Daily News*, January 23, 1881, GGII 020006.

20. Robert M. Villarreal, "The Mexican-American Vaqueros of the Kenedy Ranch: A Social History" (master's thesis, Texas A&I University, 1972), 22–23.

21. *Semi-Weekly Ledger*, January 26, 1881, GDII 020006.

22. Ibid.

23. Robert J. Kleberg to his parents, July 24, 1881, Texas A&M–Corpus Christi Library, Special Collections and Archives, Mary and Jeff Bell Library.

24. Long, "Corpus Christi, Texas."

25. July 29, 1881, Newspaper, GGII 019554–019595.

26. July 1881, Newspaper, GGII 02002–020036.

27. John Kenedy, deposition, GGII 010101–010105.

28. John Salmon Ford, *Rip Ford's Texas*, ed. Stephen Oates (Austin: University of Texas Press, 1963), 469.

29. Mifflin Kenedy to Stephen Powers, October 19, 1881, GGII 019554–019595.

30. Mifflin Kenedy to Stephen Powers, October 29, 1881, GGII 018491.

31. Mifflin Kenedy to Stephen Powers and James Wells, October 29, 1881, GGII 018491.

32. Cheeseman, *Perfectly Exhausted with Pleasure*, 28.

33. Ibid.

34. *Semi-Weekly Ledger*, January 2, 1881, GGII 020002.

Chapter 18, 1882

1. See Jane Clements Monday and Betty Bailey Colley, *Voices from the Wild Horse Desert: The Vaquero Families of the King and Kenedy Ranches* (Austin: University of Texas Press, 1997), 30. The kineños called Richard King "El Cojo"—the lame one—because of his limp. The story was that King was bitten by a rattlesnake and one of the kineños treated it with kerosene. From then on King walked with a limp. Tom Lea, *The King Ranch* (Boston: Little, Brown, 1957), 353–54.

2. Lea, *The King Ranch*, 353–54.

3. John Henry Brown, *Indian Wars and Pioneers of Texas* (Austin, Tex.: L. E. Daniel, 189–?); "A Sweet Memory of Captain M. Kenedy," Carmen Morell Kenedy, Corpus Christi Library, 1895.

4. John Salmon Ford, *Rip Ford's Texas*, ed. Stephen Oates (Austin: University of Texas Press, 1963), 469–70.

5. Brown, *Indian Wars and Pioneers of Texas*, 232–33.

6. Ibid.

7. 1882 Ledger Book of the Kenedy Pasture Co., Corpus Christi Museum.

8. Robert M. Villarreal, "The Mexican-American Vaqueros of the Kenedy Ranch: A Social History" (master's thesis, Texas A&I University, 1972), 43.

9. Father Francis Kelly Nemeck, e-mail to Jane Monday on June 15, 2006.

10. Jane Quinn, *Minorcans in Florida: Their History and Heritage* (St. Augustine, Fla.: Mission Press, 1975), 192–98.

11. Harbert Davenport, "Stephen Powers," The Handbook of Texas Online, www.tsha.utexas.edu/handbook/online.

12. Mifflin Kenedy to James Wells, February 12, 1882, GGII 019596–019633.

13. Lea, *The King Ranch*, 338.

14. Ibid., 339.

15. Ibid.

16. Bruce Cheeseman to the authors, December 2, 2005.

17. Mifflin Kenedy to James, May 19, 1882, LBook-1, Letter press book, 1882–1885, Box 22.

18. Mifflin Kenedy to James Kenedy, June 9, 1882, LBook-1, Letter press book, 1882–1885, Box 22.

19. Mifflin Kenedy to James Kenedy, June 12, 1882, LBook-1, Letter press book, 1882–1885, Box 22.

20. Mifflin Kenedy to James Kenedy, July 1, 1882, LBook-1, Letter press book, 1882–1885, Box 22.

21. Mifflin Kenedy to Fred Starck, July 3, 1882, LBook-1, Letter press book, 1882–1885, Box 22.

22. Mifflin Kenedy to James Kenedy, July 7, 1882, LBook-1, Letter press book, 1882–1885, Box 22.

23. E. Mallory to James Kenedy, July 14, 1882, LBook-1, Letter press book, 1882–1885, Box 22.

24. *Galveston Daily News*, "A Texas Stock Rancho—The Kenedy Pasture the Largest in the United States," July 17, 1882, Corpus Christi Library.

25. James Kenedy to James Wells, November 11, 1882, Wells papers, Center for American History, University of Texas, Austin, Texas, Box 2H203 (1883–1884).

26. E. Mallory to James Kenedy, October 6, 1882, Kenedy Pasture Co., LBook-1, Letter press book, 1882–1885, Box 22.

27. James Kenedy to James Wells, November 11, 1884, GGII 019460, LBook-1, Letter press book, 1882–1885, Box 22.

28. Villarreal, "The Mexican American Vaqueros of the Kenedy Ranch," 11.

29. Mifflin Kenedy to James Kenedy, November 24, LBook-1, Letter press book, 1882–1885, Box 22.

30. Sister Mary Xavier, IWBS, *A Century of Sacrifice* (Corpus Christi, Tex.: n.p., 1953), 31.

31. Teal Cooprerco to Mr. Hicks, Wells, and Rentfro in Brownsville, LBook-1, Letter press book, 1882–1885, Box 22.

32. Mifflin Kenedy to S. M. Swenson Sons, New York, December 12, LBook-1, Letter press book, 1882–1885, Box 22.

33. Mifflin Kenedy to James Kenedy, December 15, LBook-1, Letter press book, 1882–1885, Box 22. "La Parra" refers, first, to a 23,000-acre Spanish land grant by the same name. Mifflin placed the headquarters of the Kenedy Ranch on the highest sand dune (some 27 feet above sea level) in the middle of that 23,000 acres. Even though Mifflin picked out the spot, he never actually lived there. The Kenedy Ranch (owned and operated by the Kenedy Pasture Co.) comprised of ten or twelve Spanish land grants (La Atravesada being one of them) and ultimately came to about 440,000 acres. By extension, then, the entire Kenedy Ranch is also referred to as "La Parra." Therefore, "La Parra" sometimes refers to the northeast division of the Kenedy Ranch (the 23,000-acre tract), and "La Parra" sometimes refers to the entire ranch (the whole 440,000 acres). This was true in Mifflin's time, and it is still true today. Father Francis Kelly Nemeck, e-mail December 12, 2005, to the authors.

34. Mifflin Kenedy to James Kenedy, December 15, 1882, LBook-1, Letter press book, 1882–1885, Box 22.

35. Mifflin Kenedy to James Kenedy, December 21, 1882, LBook-1, Letter press book, 1882–1885, Box 22.

Chapter 19, 1883

1. Murphy Givens, "Corpus Christi's Downtown Area in 1883," *Corpus Christi Caller*, August 2, 2000, Corpus Christi Library.
2. *Corpus Christi Caller*, January 28, Corpus Christi Library.
3. "Excursion to Ingleside," *Corpus Christi Caller*, August 12, Corpus Christi Library.
4. "Oyster Season," *Corpus Christi Caller*, October 28; *Corpus Christi Caller*, November 25 and December 9, Corpus Christi Library.
5. *Corpus Christi Caller*, November 1883, Corpus Christi Library.
6. Bruce Cheeseman, in conversation with authors.
7. *Corpus Christi Caller*, November 4, Corpus Christi Library.
8. *Brownsville Cosmopolitan*, December 26, Corpus Christi Library.
9. *Corpus Christi Caller*, March 18, Corpus Christi Library.
10. *Corpus Christi Caller*, June 10, Corpus Christi Library.
11. Tom Lea, *The King Ranch* (Boston: Little, Brown, 1957), 354–55.
12. E. Mallory to Tom Kenedy, March 2, GGII 019312–019376.
13. Mifflin Kenedy to James Kenedy, January 11, GGII 019634–019698.
14. Ibid.
15. Mifflin Kenedy to Ytúrria, January 14, GGII 019634–019698.
16. Mifflin Kenedy to John Kenedy, January 22, GGII 019634–019698.
17. *Corpus Christi Caller*, January 28, Corpus Christi Library.
18. Telegram from Mifflin Kenedy to John Kenedy, March, GGII 019634–019698.
19. 1883 Kenedy Pasture Co. Ledger Book, Corpus Christi Museum.
20. Mifflin Kenedy to James Kenedy, August 24, GGII 019634–019698.
21. Mifflin Kenedy to Fred Starck, January 18, GGII 019634–019698.
22. Telegram from Mifflin Kenedy to J. L. Putegnat, January 19, GGII 018490–020572.
23. *Corpus Christi Caller*, March 11, Corpus Christi Library.
24. Mifflin Kenedy to John McAllen, April 14, GGII 019634–019698.
25. Mary Margaret McAllen Amberson, James A. McAllen, and Margaret H. McAllen, *I Would Rather Sleep in Texas: A History of the Lower Rio Grande Valley and the People of the Santa Anita Land Grant* (Austin: Texas State Historical Association, 2003), 341.
26. Petra Vela Kenedy to Salomé Ballí McAllen on April 26, 1883, from Corpus Christi, Texas. McAllen Family Archives from Ella Howland Archives, Laredo, Texas.
27. Ibid.
28. Mrs. Groesbeck to Mifflin Kenedy, November 12, 1883, GGII 018503–06.
29. Mason Carr to Mifflin Kenedy, December 5, GGII 018501.
30. James Wells to Mifflin Kenedy, March 1, GGII 002045–003479.
31. E. Mallory to John Kenedy, March 2, GGII 002045–003479.
32. *Corpus Christi Caller*, March 4, Corpus Christi Library.
33. Lea, *The King Ranch*, 355.
34. Murphy Givens, "Corpus Christi History," *Corpus Christi Caller*, August 19, 1998, Corpus Christi Library.

35. GGII 002045-003479.
36. Lea, *The King Ranch*, 356.
37. Ibid.
38. Ibid., 357
39. Mrs. Henrietta King to Mifflin Kenedy, May 2, GGII 002218.
40. Richard King to Mifflin Kenedy, May 3, GGII 002217.
41. Richard King to Mifflin Kenedy, May 15, GGII 002213.
42. Richard King to Mifflin Kenedy, June 30, GGII 002175.
43. Richard King to Mifflin Kenedy, June 6, GGII 002096-00349.
44. Richard King to Mifflin Kenedy, June 12, GGII 002096-00349.
45. Mifflin Kenedy to James Kenedy, June 15, GGII 019634-019698.
46. Mifflin Kenedy to James Kenedy, June 22, GGII 019634-019698.
47. Mifflin Kenedy to James Kenedy, June 24, GGII 019634-019698.
48. Richard King to Mifflin Kenedy, July 9, GGII 002189.
49. Lea, *The King Ranch*, 358.
50. *Corpus Christi Caller*, July 6, GGII 007327.
51. Richard King to Mifflin Kenedy, July, GGII 002096-000349.
52. Mifflin Kenedy to James Kenedy, June 30, GGII 019634-019698.
53. Richard King to James Kenedy, August 17, GGII 002180.
54. Richard King to Mifflin Kenedy, September 25 and October 26, GGII 002096-000349.
55. *Corpus Christi Caller*, October 7, Corpus Christi Library.
56. *Brownsville Cosmopolitan*, September 7, Corpus Christi Library.
57. Lea, *The King Ranch*, 358.
58. Ibid., 359.
59. Ibid., 359-60.
60. Mrs. Henrietta King to Capt. M. Kenedy, September 14, GGII 002169.
61. Information from Mary Margaret Amberson from Hidalgo Co. Marriage Record—vol. D, 20.
62. *Corpus Christi Caller*, September 16, Corpus Christi Library.
63. *Corpus Christi Caller*, August 9, Corpus Christi Library.
64. *Brownsville Cosmopolitan*, October 17.
65. *Corpus Christi Caller*, November 11, Corpus Christi Library.
66. *Brownsville Cosmopolitan*, December 10, 1883.
67. *Corpus Christi Caller*, November 11, Corpus Christi Library.
68. Mifflin Kenedy to James Kenedy, December 15, GGII 019634-019698.
69. Mifflin Kenedy to James Kenedy, December 18, GGII 019634-019698.
70. *Brownsville Cosmopolitan*, December 11, 1883.
71. Mifflin Kenedy to James Wells, November 18, 1883, GGII 018508.
72. James Wells to Mifflin Kenedy, December 1883, GGII 019634-019698.

Chapter 20, 1884

1. Mifflin Kenedy to Ana Adrianne Vidal, September 26, 1886, GGII 008339.
2. Tom Lea, *The King Ranch* (Boston: Little, Brown, 1957), 361-62.
3. *Corpus Christi Caller*, April 16, 1884, Corpus Christi Library.
4. James Kenedy to Mifflin Kenedy, April 22, 1884, GGII 020087-020246.

5. *Corpus Christi Caller*, May 14, 1884, Corpus Christi Library; *Corpus Christi Caller*, April 27, Corpus Christi Library.

6. Robert Justus Kleberg to Alice Gertrudis King, April 4, 1884, Texas A&M University at Corpus Christi Library in Special Collections and Archives, Mary and Jeff Bell Library.

7. Robert Justus Kleberg to Alice Gertrudis King, April 9, 1884, Texas A&M University at Corpus Christi Library in Special Collections and Archives, Mary and Jeff Bell Library.

8. Mifflin Kenedy to Robert Dalzell, GGII 0020090–91.

9. *Brownsville Cosmopolitan*, July 23, Corpus Christi Library.

10. Mifflin Kenedy to Henry Hawley, July 25, GGII 020163.

11. Mifflin Kenedy to Tom Kenedy, July 28, GGII 020087–020246.

12. Mifflin Kenedy to Henry Hawley, August 6, GGII 020162.

13. Mifflin Kenedy to Henry Hawley, August 8, GGII 020168.

14. Mifflin Kenedy to Tom Kenedy, August 8, GGII 020171.

15. Mifflin Kenedy to Tom Kenedy, August 23, GGII 020087–020246.

16. Mifflin Kenedy to John Kenedy, October 24, GGII 0020120.

17. Mifflin Kenedy to James Kenedy, June 13, GGII 0020147.

18. Telegram from Mifflin Kenedy to Francisco Ytúrria, November, GGII 02087–02046.

19. Mifflin Kenedy to J. H. Stevens, August 14, GGII 0020088.

20. Mifflin Kenedy to Richard King, October 9, GGII 0020106.

21. Mifflin Kenedy to Capt. John Armstrong, October 19, GGII 002046.

22. Mifflin Kenedy to Capt. John Armstrong, May 25, 1884, GGII 0020246.

23. Mifflin Kenedy to Richard King, November 11, GGII 0020131.

24. Lea, *The King Ranch*, 364.

25. Jane Monday interview with Patsy Reneghan.

26. *Times Democrat*, January 31, reprinted from *Brownsville Reporter*, February 9, 1884, Corpus Christi Library.

27. James Kenedy to Corina Kenedy, February 16, GGII 008881–008913.

28. Jane Monday interview with Patricia Reneghan.

29. Father Francis Kelly Nemeck e-mail December 18, 2005, to the authors.

30. *Brownsville Cosmopolitan*, March 8, and 22.

31. *Corpus Christi Caller*, February 10, Corpus Christi Library.

32. Ibid., March 9.

33. Ibid., March 30.

34. Ibid., April 20.

35. Ibid., January 7.

36. Ibid., March 23, 1884.

37. Ibid., April 22.

38. Ibid., May 14.

39. Ibid., June 1.

40. Ibid., May 14.

41. Ibid., June 8.

42. May Segret Decker, "A Biography of Eli T. Merriman" (master's thesis, Texas A&I University, 1942).

43. Robert Kleberg to Alice King, May 27, Texas A&M University at Corpus Christi Library in Special Collections and Archives, Mary and Jeff Bell Library.

44. Ibid., June 4.

45. *Corpus Christi Caller,* June 22, Corpus Christi Library.
46. Telegram from Mifflin Kenedy to Francisco Ytúrria, November, GGII 0020113.
47. *Daily Cosmopolitan,* April 2, Brownsville, Jernigan Library, Texas A&M at Kingsville, AND3-Reel 3.
48. Ibid., July 25.
49. Ibid., May 5.
50. Ibid., December 26.
51. Ibid., May 25.
52. Ibid., July 22.
53. Ibid., June 24.
54. Ibid., July.
55. Ibid., June 24.
56. Mifflin Kenedy to Tom Kenedy, July 28, GGII 020087–020246.
57. *Daily Cosmopolitan,* July 28; *Daily Cosmopolitan,* September 2, from Jernigan Library, Texas A&M at Kingsville, AND3-Reel 3.
58. Baptismal Register, Immaculate Conception Church, Brownsville, Texas, p. 171, no. 413.
59. Sarita Kenedy Garza, deposition, sworn May 29 in Galveston County. The deposition was part of the Raul Treviño v. Edgar Turcotte law suit of Kenedy County, Texas, filed in Nueces County, Texas May 16, 1969, District Court Records, Corpus Christi, Texas.
60. *Daily Cosmopolitan,* September 10, Jernigan Library, Texas A&M at Kingsville, AND3-Reel 3.
61. Ibid., October 6.
62. Telegram from Mifflin Kenedy to Tom Kenedy, October 24, GGII 0020223.
63. Mifflin Kenedy to James Wells, October 24, GGII 020087–020246.
64. Mifflin Kenedy to John Kenedy, October 31, GGII 020087–020246.
65. Mifflin Kenedy to Richard King, October 5, GGII 0020106.
66. *Daily Cosmopolitan,* October 21, Jernigan Library, Texas A&M at Kingsville, AND3-Reel 3.
67. Ibid., December 15.
68. Ibid.
69. Mifflin Kenedy to Ana Adrianne Vidal, March 7, GGII 008335–008346.
70. Letter from Sylvia Probst, assistant to Sr. Joan Marie Ayock, OSU, archivist, Ursuline Convent, Archives and Museum, June 14, 2006.
71. Mifflin Kenedy to Robert Dalzell, July 23, GGII 020087–020246.
72. Last Will and Testament of Elena S. Kenedy, filed January 20, 1983, in Kenedy County Corpus Christi District Court House Records. The ring was not found in the safe upon opening after Elena Kenedy's death.
73. Most Rev. Dominic Manucy, 1875–85, Catholic Archives, Corpus Christi, Texas.
74. *Corpus Christi Caller,* June 13, Corpus Christi Library.
75. Most Rev. Dominic Manucy, 1875–85, Catholic Archives, Corpus Christi, Texas.
76. Telegram from Mifflin Kenedy to John Kenedy, August 1, GGII 0020157.
77. Telegram from Mifflin Kenedy to Rosa Putegnat, August 10, GGII 0020173 and GGII 0020174.
78. Ibid.
79. *Corpus Christi Caller,* February 21, Corpus Christi Library.
80. Mifflin Kenedy to C. R. Scott of New York, May 16, GGII 0020201.
81. *Corpus Christi Caller,* June 29, Corpus Christi Library.

82. Mifflin Kenedy to Mr. Scott, October 6, GGII 0020202–3.
83. Art Collection, Corpus Christi Museum of Science and History, Corpus Christi, Texas.
84. Mifflin Kenedy to Swenson, October 28, GGII 0020236–38.
85. Mifflin Kenedy to Anita Vidal, September 7, GGII 008336–38; Birth certificate was filed in Cameron County, Mary Margaret Amberson, 1880–90 Cameron County Birth Records.
86. Mifflin Kenedy to Anita Vidal, September 7, GGII 008336–38.
87. Ibid.
88. Ibid.
89. Mifflin Kenedy to Anita Vidal, October 16, 1884, GGII 0020116–0088346.
90. Mifflin Kenedy to F. E. Starck, October 16, GGII 0020097.
91. Mifflin Kenedy to F. E. Starck, December 2, GGII 0020087–020246.
92. *Daily Cosmopolitan,* Brownsville, April 6, Jernigan Library, Texas A&M at Kingsville, AND3–Reel 3.
93. Ibid., April 7.
94. Ibid., April 9.
95. Mifflin Kenedy to James Wells, April 13, 1884, GGII 019460.
96. Mifflin Kenedy to John Kenedy, September 4, 1884, GGII 0020092.
97. Mifflin Kenedy to James Kenedy, June 13, 1884, GGII 0020147.
98. Mifflin Kenedy to Harry Hawley, July 25, 1884, GGII 020087–020246.
99. A metate is a stone block with a concave surface used for grinding corn and other grains or peppers. It was an essential part of any new home and may have been handed down for several generations. Homero Vera, South Texas Historian, to Jane Monday by interview, May 26, 2006. Corina Ballí Kenedy to John G. Kenedy, January 15, 1895, GGII 009724–009726.
100. An ileus is an intestinal obstruction causing colic, vomiting, and toxemia.
101. George's birth certificate, GGII 008970–008976.
102. Day Folder, Kenedy History, Corpus Christi Warehouse.
103. Mifflin Kenedy to Robert Dalzell, September 2, GGII 0020090.
104. Mifflin Kenedy to Richard King, September 4, GGII 0020193.
105. Mifflin Kenedy to F. E. Starck, September 5, GGII 0020094.
106. Telegram from Mifflin Kenedy to John Kenedy, September 5, GGII 0020098.
107. Mifflin Kenedy to Robert Dalzell, September 5, GGII 0020101.
108. James Kenedy to Corina Kenedy, GGII 00881–008913.
109. James Kenedy to Corina Kenedy, September 8.
110. Mifflin Kenedy to James Kenedy, September 14, GGII 0020102.
111. James Kenedy to Corina Kenedy, September 12 and 17.
112. James Kenedy to Corina Kenedy, September 24.
113. Mifflin Kenedy to Manuel Rodríguez, GGII 002014.
114. James Kenedy to Corina Kenedy, September 30.
115. Baptismal Registry, Corpus Christi, GGII 008970–008976.
116. Letters GGII 008335–38; GGII 008346; GGII 0020113; GGII 0020120.
117. Mifflin Kenedy to Richard King, October 9, GGII 0020106.
118. Mifflin Kenedy to his sister Sarah Josephine Kenedy Thompson, GGII 0020113.
119. Mifflin Kenedy to John Kenedy, October 18, GGII 0020214.
120. Mifflin Kenedy to Sarah Josephine Kenedy Thompson, November 4, GGII 0020087–020246.
121. Telegram from Sarah Josephine Kenedy Thompson to Mifflin Kenedy, GGII 020087–020246.

122. Lea, *The King Ranch*, 366.

123. Robert Kleberg and Alice King, Texas A&M University at Corpus Christi Library in Special Collections and Archives, Mary and Jeff Bell Library.

124. Mifflin Kenedy to Robert Dalzell, December 24, GGII 020087–020246.

125. Mifflin Kenedy to C. R. Scott, December 26, GGII 020087–020246.

126. Ibid.

127. Ibid.

128. Chester County newspaper, *The Village Record,* December 26, 1884, provided by Barbara J. Rutz, researcher for Chester County Historical Society.

129. *Brownsville Cosmopolitan,* January 10, 1885, Corpus Christi Library.

130. St. Patrick Internment Book, Catholic Cathedral Archives, Corpus Christi, Texas.

131. *Corpus Christi Caller,* January 3, 1885, McAllen Family Archives.

132. Ibid.; *Daily Cosmopolitan,* Brownsville, December 31, from Jernigan Library, Texas A&M at Kingsville, AND3-Reel 3.

Chapter 21, 1885

The epigraph quote is from Laurence A. Duaine's *With All Arms: A Study of a Kindred Group* (Austin, Tex.: Nortex Press, 2004), 223.

1. *Daily Cosmopolitan,* Brownsville, Texas, January 2, 1885.

2. Captain William Kelly's Diary, January 6, provided by Chula Griffin from the Brownsville Historical Association, Brownsville, Texas, and GGII 007955; William Kelly Diary, January 15, GGII 007955.

3. *Daily Cosmopolitan,* Brownsville, Texas, Captain William Kelly's obituary, January 29, 1921, documented his close friendship with Capt. Robert Dalzell.

4. Mifflin Kenedy to William Kelly, October 16, 1885, GGII 019459–019510.

5. Z. E. Coombes, of Dallas, Grand Master, T. W. Hudson, of Houston, Grand Secretary, *Proceedings in the Fiftieth Annual Communication of the M.W. Grand Lodge of Texas Held at the City of Houston Commencing on the Second Tuesday in December,* A.D. 1885, A. L. 5885 (Houston: W. H. Coyle, Printer, Stationer and Lithographer, 1886), 132–34.

6. A. J. Rose, of Salado, Grand Master, T. W. Hudson, of Houston, Grand Secretary, *Proceedings in the Fifty-First Annual Communication of the M.W. Grand Lodge of Texas, Held at the City of Houston, Commencing on the Second Tuesday in December,* A.D. 1886, A. L. 5886. (Houston: Smallwood, Dealy & Baker, Printers and Book Binders, 1887), 125–29, 248–49.

7. *Daily Cosmopolitan,* Brownsville, Texas, January 6, 1885.

8. Ibid., January 17, Jernigan Library, Texas A&M at Kingsville, AND3-Reel 3.

9. *Ibid.,* February 7.

10. John S. Yznaga, "The Yznaga Family in South Texas Valley," October 1, 1993, GGII 006447–007834, GGII 008657.

11. Mifflin Kenedy to Tom Kenedy, GGII 006805–006982.

12. Ibid.

13. Tom Kenedy to James Wells, GGII 018490–020572.

14. J. B. Wells Collection, 1837–1926: Box 2H330, Center for American History, University of Texas, Austin, Texas.

15. *Daily Cosmopolitan,* Brownsville, Jernigan Library, Texas A&M at Kingsville, AND3-Reel 3.

16. Ibid., July 29, 1885.

17. Ibid.
18. Legal documents about Tom Kenedy's marriage, Yznaga Family, GGII 006447–007834.
19. Ibid.
20. Interview with Rosita Putegnat, and GGII 008612.
21. Yznaga, "The Yznaga Family in the South Texas Valley," October 1, 1993, GGII 006447–007834.
22. George Putegnat, March 6, 1981, Putegnat Family Papers, Patricia Reneghan Collection.
23. Stephen Michaud and Hugh Aynesworth, *If You Love Me You Will Do My Will* (New York: W. W. Norton, 1990), 53–54.
24. Paper written and signed by George W. Putegnat, March 6, 1981, Putegnat Family Papers.
25. Tom Lea, *The King Ranch* (Boston: Little, Brown, 1957), 367.
26. Ibid., 368.
27. Mifflin Kenedy to John Kenedy, GGII 006457–006471, and Francisco Ytúrria about money, GGII 006651.
28. Mifflin Kenedy to Robert Dalzell, March 22, 1885, GGII 020247–020251.
29. Mifflin Kenedy to C. R. Scott, GGII 0020122.
30. Mifflin Kenedy to Robert Dalzell, March 22, 1885, GGII 020247–020251.
31. Francis Kelly Nemeck, OMI, "Three Generations of Kenedys: A Mosaic," unpublished paper, furnished to Jane Clements Monday by Father Francis Kelly Nemeck.
32. Oblate Archives, #479-84-85, La Parra Ranch, Lebh Shomea, Sarita, Texas.
33. Mifflin Kenedy to Jo Kenedy Thompson, GGII 021087–02046.
34. Ibid.
35. Ibid. Also, Oblate Archives #479-84-85, Lebh Shomea, Sarita, Texas.
36. Mifflin Kenedy to Robert Dalzell, GGII 020087–020246
37. Bruce Cheeseman, "The King-Spohn Family Friendship," 9.
38. Mifflin Kenedy to Robert Dalzell, March 22, 1885.
39. *Corpus Christi Caller,* March 15, 1885, Corpus Christi Library.
40. *Austin American-Statesman,* September 27, 2005, B3.

Epilogue

1. Mifflin Kenedy to Robert Dalzell, March 24, 1885, GGII 020087–020246.
2. Tom Lea, *The King Ranch* (Boston: Little, Brown, 1957), 368–70.
3. Mona D. Sizer, *The King Ranch Story* (Dallas: Republic of Texas Press, 1999), 144.
4. Robert Kleberg to Alice King, August 24, 1885; Robert Kleberg to Alice King, August 21, 1885.
5. "A Preservation Plan for the Immaculate Conception Cathedral," Catholic Archives of Texas, Austin, Texas.
6. Mifflin Kenedy to Father Jeffreys, January 11, 1886, GGII 021087–02046.
7. GGII 012362–012344.
8. Jean A. Stuntz, *Hers, His, and Theirs: Community Property Law in Spain and Early Texas* (Lubbock: Texas Tech University Press, 2005), 138.
9. Mary Margaret McAllen Amberson, James A. McAllen, and Margaret H. McAllen, *I Would Rather Sleep in Texas: A History of the Lower Rio Grande Valley and the People of the Santa Anita Land Grant* (Austin: Texas State Historical Association 2003), 432–33.
10. GGII 012362–012344.

11. GGII 010170–1011962.
12. Amberson, McAllen, and McAllen, *I Would Rather Sleep in Texas*, 342–45.
13. John Henry Brown, *Indian Wars and Pioneers of Texas* (Austin: L. E. Daniell, 1896), 232.
14. GGII 016358–016361.
15. GGII 008819–008854.
16. Last Will and Testament, filed January 20, 1983, in Kenedy Co., Corpus Christi Court House records.
17. *Dallas Morning News*, March 29, 2006, 4A.
18. Father Francis Kelly Nemeck, "Three Generations of Kenedys," unpublished paper.
19. GGII 008031.
20. Interview with descendants of Luisa, Susan Seeds, and Janis Hefley.
21. GGII 008244–008310.
22. GGII 008121–008226.
23. Interview with descendant Rosa Marie Swisher.
24. Interview with descendants Michael Hamilton and Marty Heaner.
25. Todd Williams, "Rabb Ranch, An Oasis of Palms," *The Armadillo*, September 15, 1982.

Bibliography

LETTERS, MANUSCRIPTS, AND ARCHIVAL COLLECTIONS

George Getchow Documents copied from the vault at the Big House at La Parra and given to the King Ranch Archives and produced in Litigation, Cause No. C-291-,93-D, *Manuel de Llano, Blanca A. de LL. de Aguilar, Martha Dell de Olivera, Carmen de Llano, Fernando de Llano and Josephina de Llano v. The John G. and Marie Stella Kenedy Memorial Foundation, John G. Kenedy Jr. Charitable Trust, Exxon Corporation, Exxon Company U.S.A., Exxon Exploration Co. and Mobil Oil Company,* in the District Court, Hidalgo County, Texas, 206th Judicial District.
Box #2 GGII 000314–GGII 002044
Box #3 GGII 002045–GGII 003479
Box #5 GGII 006447–GGII 007834
Box #6 GGII 007836–GGII 008854
Box #7 GGII 008855–GGII 010169
Box #8 GGII 010170, GGII 010963–GGII 011762
Box #9 GGII 011763–GGII 013268
Box #10 GGII 013269–GGII 014763
Box #11 GGII 014764–GGII 016131
Box #12 GGII 016132–GGII 018489
Box #13 GGII 018490–GGII 020572
Box #14 GGII 020573–GGII 022395
Box #22 LBOOK 1 Press Book [1882–1885]
LBOOK 2 Press Book [1885–1887]
LBOOK 3 Press Book [1887–1888]
LBOOK 4 Press Book [1888–1890]
LBOOK 5 Press Book [March–December 1890]
LBOOK 6 Press Book [1890–1891]
LBOOK 8 Press Book [1891–1893]
LBOOK 9 Press Book [January–September 1894]
LBOOK 10 Press Book [1894–1895]

Almond, Joseph. Diary of Corpus Christi Library, Reserved Archives.
Annals of the First Monastery of the Incarnate Word and Blessed Sacrament in American—Brownsville, Texas. Incarnate Word Archives, Corpus Christi, Texas.

Bagdad, Brazos, and Clarksville Folder, Stillman Historical Museum, Brownsville, Texas.

Chester County Will Abstract—1840–1844, Chester County, Pennsylvania.

Chester County Historical Society, Newspaper article from March 18, 1895. Kenedy Family Vertical File, Raymondville Historical Museum, Raymondville, Texas.

Cooper, Joseph & Co. 1867–1868, Correspondence. Corpus Christi Museum of Science and History.

Day, John. Folder, Corpus Christi Court Records, Corpus Christi District Warehouse, Corpus Christi, Texas.

Family Genealogical Records, Corpus Christi District Courthouse Records. Corpus Christi District County Records, Marriage Certificate of Mifflin Kenedy and Petra Vela de Vidal.

Kelly's diary, Captain William. Brownsville Historical Association, Brownsville, Texas.

Kenedy Family Vertical File, Raymondville Historical Museum, Raymondville, Texas.

Kenedy, James. Letters to Corina Ballí Kenedy. McAllen Family Archives.

Kenedy Papers, Contractors of River Transportation Correspondence 1869–1873. Corpus Christi Museum of Science and History.

Kenedy Pasture Company Letters. Corpus Christi Museum of Science and History.

King, Kenedy & Co., 1867–1872, Book of Correspondence. Corpus Christi Museum of Science and History.

King, Kenedy & Co., 1873, Correspondence. Corpus Christi Museum of Science and History.

King, Kenedy & Co., 1874, Correspondence. Corpus Christi Museum of Science and History.

King, Kenedy & Co., Documents concerned with cargo from wrecked schooner "Annie," 1873. Corpus Christi Museum of Science and History.

King, Kenedy & Co. Log Book. Transcript of 1873, 1874, 1875. Corpus Christi Museum of Science and History.

Kingsbury Papers, Gilbert D. Kingsbury Lectures, Reports, and Writings, vol. 2, 1855–1867, Barker American History Center, Center for American History, University of Texas, Austin.

Kleiber, Joseph. Letter Press Book, October 11, 1860–July 10, 1877. Center for American History, University of Texas, Austin.

Powers, Stephen, Papers. Center for American History, University of Texas, Austin.

Simmons, Audrey. "The Story of Clarksville and Bagdad," Brownsville Historical Association.

Swisher, Rosa Maria. Letter to Jane Monday.

Texas A&M University at Corpus Christi, Library in Special Collections and Archives, Mary and Jeff Bell Library.

Wells, J. B., Collection. 1837–1926. Box 2H330. Center for American History, University of Texas at Austin.

Books

100 years of Service, Centenary Souvenir of the Sisters of the Incarnate Word and Blessed Sacrament, Brownsville, Texas, Brownsville Historical Association.

Abernethy, Frances E. *Between the Cracks of History: Essays on Teaching and Illustrating Folklore.* Denton: University of North Texas Press, 1997.

Acosta, Teresa Palomo, and Ruthe Winegarten. *Las Tejanas: 300 Years of History.* Austin: University of Texas Press, 2003.

Adams, Ramon F. *Come An' Get It: The Story of the Old Cowboy Cook.* Norman: University of Oklahoma Press, 1952.

Allhands, J. L. *Uriah Lott.* San Antonio, Tex.: Naylor, 1949.

Alonzo, Armando C. *Tejano Legacy: Rancheros and Settlers in South Texas, 1734–1900.* Albuquerque: University of New Mexico Press, 1998.

Amberson, Mary Margaret McAllen, James A. McAllen, and Margaret H. McAllen. *I Would Rather Sleep in Texas: A History of the Lower Rio Grande Valley and the People of the Santa Anita Land Grant.* Austin: Texas State Historical Association, 2003.

Arreloa, Daniel D. *Tejano South Texas.* Austin: University of Texas Press, 2002.

Boatright, Mody C., and Donald Day. *Backwoods to Border.* Dallas: Southern Methodist University Press, 1967.

———, Wilson M. Hudson, and Allen Maxwell, eds. *Madstones and Twisters.* Dallas: Southern Methodist University Press, 1958.

———, Wilson M. Hudson, and Allen Maxwell, eds. *Singers and Storytellers.* Dallas: Southern Methodist University Press, 1961.

Bourke, John G. "The Folk-Foods of the Rio Grande Valley." In *Southwest Lore,* ed. J. Frank Dobie. Dallas: Southern Methodist University Press, 1965.

Brown, John Henry. *Indian Wars and Pioneers of Texas.* Austin: L. E. Daniell, 189?.

Campbell, Randolph B. *Gone to Texas: A History of the Lone Star State.* New York: Oxford University Press, 2003.

Cavazos, Bobby. *The Cowboy from the Wild Horse Desert: A Story of the King Ranch.* Houston: Larksdale, 1999.

Chatfield, Lieutenant W. H. *The Twin Cities of the Border: Brownsville, Texas and Matamoros, Mexico, and the Country of the Lower Rio Grande.* New Orleans: E. P. Brandao, 1893.

Cheeseman, Bruce S. *Perfectly Exhausted with Pleasure: King Kenedy Excursion.* Austin, Tex.: W. Thomas Taylor, 1992.

———, ed. *Maria von Blücher's Corpus Christi: Letters from the South Texas Frontier, 1849–1879.* College Station: Texas A&M University Press, 2002.

Chipman, Donald E. *Spanish Texas, 1519–1821.* Austin: University of Texas Press, 1992.

———, and Harriett Denise Joseph. *Notable Men and Women of Spanish Texas.* Austin: University of Texas Press, 1999.

Chrisman, Harry E. *The Ladder of Rivers.* Denver: Sage Books, 1962.

Coker, Caleb, ed. *The News from Brownsville: Helen Chapman's Letters from the Texas Military Frontier, 1848–1852.* Austin: Texas State Historical Association, 1991.

Coombes, Z. E., Grand Master. Proceedings in the Fiftieth Annual Communication of the W. M. Grande Lodge of Texas Held at the City of Houston, Commencing on the second Tuesday in December, A.D. 1885, A. L. 5885. T. W. Hudson of Houston, Grand Secretary. Houston: W. H. Coyle, Printer, 1886.

Crimm, Ana Carolina Castillo. "Petra Vela and the Kenedy Family Legacy." In *Tejano Epic: Essays in Honor of Felix D. Almaraz, Jr.*, ed. Arnoldo De León. Austin: Texas State Historical Association, 2005.

De León, Arnoldo. *The Tejano Community, 1836–1900.* Dallas: Southern Methodist University Press, 1997.

———. *They Called Them Greasers.* Austin: University of Texas Press, 1983.

———, ed. *Tejano Epic: Essays in Honor of Felix D. Almaraz, Jr.* Austin: Texas State Historical Association, 2005.

Dobie, J. Frank. *Cow People.* Austin: University of Texas Press, 1964.

———. *Happy Hunting Ground.* Dallas: Southern Methodist University Press, 1925.

———. *Southwestern Lore.* Dallas: Southern Methodist University Press, 1965.

———. *Texas and Southwestern Lore.* Dallas: Southern Methodist University Press, 1967.

———. *A Vaquero of the Brush Country.* Boston: Little, Brown, 1943.

———, ed. *Man, Bird, and Beast.* Austin: University of Texas Press, 1930.

———, Mody C. Boatright, and Harry H. Ransom, eds. *Coyote Wisdom.* Dallas: Southern Methodist University Press, 1965.

Doyon, Bernard, OMI. *The Cavalry of Christ on the Rio Grande, 1849–1883.* Milwaukee: Bruce Press, 1956.

Drago, Harry Sinclair. *The Legend Makers: Tales of Old-Time Peace Officers and Desperadoes of the Frontier.* New York: Dodd, Mead, 1975.

Duaine, Laurence A. *With All Arms: A Study of a Kindred Group.* Austin, Tex.: Nortex Press, 2004.

Fehrenbach, T. R. *Lone Star: A History of Texas and the Texans.* New York: American Legacy Press, 1968.

Ford, John Salmon. *Rip Ford's Texas,* ed. Stephen Oates. Austin: University of Texas Press, 1963.

Forrest, Earle R. "Dora Hand, The Dance Hall Singer of Old Dodge City." *The Westerners Brand Book.* Los Angeles Corral.

Frost, Dick. *King Ranch Papers: An Unauthorized and Irreverent History of the World's Largest Landholders.* Chicago: Aquarius Rising Press, 1985.

Futhey, J. Smith, and Gilbert Cope. *History of Chester County, Pennsylvania.* Philadelphia: Louis H. Everts Press of J. B. Lippincott, 1881.

Gilbert, Minnie. "Don Pancho Ytúrria and Punta del Monte." In *Rio Grande Round-Up: A Story of Texas Tropical Borderland.* Valley By-Liners, Book 3. Mission, Tex.: Border Kingdom Press, 1980.

Goldfinch, Charles W. "Juan N. Cortina, 1824–1892, A Re-Appraisal." Master's thesis, University of Chicago, 1949; published in *Juan N. Cortina: Two Interpretations*. New York: Arno Press, 1974.

González, Jovita, and Eve Raleigh. *Caballero: A Historical Novel*. College Station: Texas A&M University Press, 1996.

Graham, Don. *The Kings of Texas: The 150-Year Saga of an American Ranching Empire*. New Jersey: John Wiley, 2003.

Graham, Joe S. *Ranching in South Texas: A Symposium*. Kingsville: Texas A&M University–Kingsville, 1994.

———. *El Rancho in South Texas: Continuity and Change from 1750*. Denton: University of North Texas Press, 1994.

Green, General Thomas J. *Journal of the Texian Expedition against Mier*. New York: Harper and Brothers, 1845.

Greene, Shirley Brooks. *When Rio Grande City Was Young: Buildings of Old Rio Grande City*. Edinburg, Tex.: Pan American University, 1987.

Guerra, Antonio Ma. *Mier in History, A Translation and Reprint of Mier en la historia, 1953*. Trans. José María Escobar and Edna Garza Brown. San Antonio, Tex.: Munguia Printers, 1989.

Guinn, Leon. "Paisano Tracks." In *Coyote Wisdom*, ed. J. Frank Dobie, Mody C. Boatright, and Harry H. Ransom. Dallas: Southern Methodist University Press, 1965.

Gunning, M. Patricia. *To Texas with Love: A History of the Sisters of the Incarnate Word and Blessed Sacrament*. Austin, Tex.: Von Boeckmann-Jones, 1971.

Hadley, Diana, Thomas N. Naylor, and Mardith K. Schuetz-Miller, eds. *The Central Corridor and the Texas Corridor, 1700–1765*. Tucson: University of Arizona Press, 1997.

Harris, Charles H., III, and Louis R. Sadler. *The Texas Rangers and the Mexican Revolution*. Albuquerque: University of New Mexico Press, 2004.

Hart, John Mason. *Revolutionary Mexico: The Coming Process of the Mexican Revolution*. Berkeley: University of California Press, 1989.

Henrichson, Lena. *Pioneers on the Nueces*. San Antonio, Tex.: Naylor, 1963.

Hinojosa, Gilberto M. *A Borderlands Town in Transition: Laredo, 1755–1870*. College Station: Texas A&M University Press, 1983.

Ingmire, Frances. *Texas Ranger Service Records, 1847–1900, Vol. II*. St. Louis, Mo.: Ingmire Publications, 1982.

Kearney, Milo, and Anthony Knopp. *Boom and Bust—The Historical Cycles of Matamoros and Brownsville*. Austin, Tex.: Eakin Press, 1991.

———, ed. *More Studies in Brownsville History*. Brownsville, Tex.: Pan American University at Brownsville, 1989.

Kelly, Pat. *River of Lost Dreams: Navigation on the Rio Grande*. Lincoln: University of Nebraska Press, 1986.

Lea, Tom. *The King Ranch*. Boston: Little, Brown, 1957.

Max, Ed, comp. *Waynesburg and Honey Brook Township in the Civil War*. Chester County Historical Society. n.p., n.d.

McCampbell, Coleman. *Saga of a Frontier Seaport*. Dallas: South-West Press, n.d.

McLoughlin, Denis. *Wild and Woolly: An Encyclopedia of the Old West.* Garden City, N.Y.: Doubleday, 1975.

Michaud, Stephen, and Hugh Aynesworth. *If You Love Me You Will Do My Will.* New York: W. W. Norton, 1990.

Miller, Nyle H., and Joseph W. Snell. *Why the West Was Wild.* Norman: University of Oklahoma Press, 2003.

Monday, Jane Clements, and Betty Bailey Colley. *Voices from the Wild Horse Desert: The Vaquero Families of the King and Kenedy Ranches.* Austin: University of Texas Press, 1997.

Montejano, David. *Anglos and Mexicans in the Making of Texas, 1836–1986.* Austin: University of Texas Press, 1987.

Naylor, Thomas H., and Charles W. Polzer, eds. *The Presidio and the Militia on the Northern Frontier of New Spain, Vol. 1: 1570–1700.* Tucson: University of Arizona Press, 1986.

O'Connell, Patrick J. *The Kenedy Family at Spring Hill College.* Mobile, Ala.: Published privately by Spring Hill College, 1986–87.

Paredes, Américo, *Folklore and Culture on the Texas-Mexican Border.* Austin: University of Texas Press, 1993.

———. "Folklore and History." In *Singers and Storytellers,* ed. Mody C. Boatright, Wilson M. Hudson, and Allen Maxwell. Dallas: Southern Methodist University Press, 1961.

———. "The Mexican Corrido: Its Rise and Fall." In *Madstones and Twisters,* ed. Mody C. Boatright, Wilson M. Hudson, and Allen Maxwell. Dallas: Southern Methodist University Press, 1958.

———. "On Gringo, Greaser, and Other Neighborly Names." In *Singers and Storytellers,* ed. Mody C. Boatright, Wilson M. Hudson, and Allen Maxwell. Dallas: Southern Methodist University Press, 1961.

———. *A Texas-Mexican Cancionero: Folksongs of the Lower Border.* Austin: University of Texas Press, 1976.

———. *With His Pistol in His Hand: A Border Ballad and Its Hero.* Austin: University of Texas Press, 2004.

Parisot, Father P. F. *The Reminiscences of a Texas Missionary.* San Antonio, Tex.: Johnson Bros. Printing, 1899.

Parsons, Chuck, and Marianne E. Hall Little. *Captain L. H. McNelly: Texas Ranger, The Life and Times of a Fighting Man.* Austin, Tex.: State House Press, 2001.

Pierce, Frank Cushman. *A Brief History of the Lower Rio Grande Valley.* Menasha, Wisc.: Collegiate Press/George Banta Publishing, 1917.

Quinn, Jane. *Minorcans in Florida: Their History and Heritage.* St. Augustine, Fla.: Mission Press, 1975.

Rio Grande Round-Up, A Story of Texas Tropical Borderland, Valley By-Liners Book III. Mission, Tex.: Border Kingdom Press, 1980.

Rose, A. J., Grand Master, and T. W. Hudson, Grand Secretary. *Proceedings in the Fifty-First Annual Communication of the M. W. Grand Lodge of Texas.* Houston: Smallwood, Dealy and Baker, Printers and Book Binders, 1887.

BIBLIOGRAPHY

Sáenz, Andrés. *Early Tejano Ranching.* Ed. Andrés Tijerina. College Station: Texas A&M University Press, 1999.

Sizer, Mona D. *The King Ranch Story.* Dallas: Republic of Texas Press, 1999.

Stambaugh, J. Lee, and Lillian J. Stambaugh. *The Lower Rio Grande Valley of Texas.* San Antonio, Tex.: Naylor, 1954.

Stillman, Chauncey Devereux. *Charles Stillman, 1810–1875.* New York: C. D. Stillman, 1956.

Stuntz, Jean A. *Hers, His, and Theirs: Community Property Law in Spain and Early Texas.* Lubbock: Texas Tech University Press, 2005.

Terrell, Alexander Watkins. *From Texas to Mexico and the Court of Maximilian.* Dallas: Book Club of Texas, 1933.

Thompson, Jerry. *Cortina: Defending the Mexican Name in Texas.* College Station: Texas A&M University Press, 2007.

———, and Lawrence T. Jones III. *Civil War and Revolution on the Rio Grande Frontier.* Austin: Texas State Historical Association, 2004.

Thrapp, Dan L. *Encyclopedia of Frontier Biography,* vol. 2. Lincoln: University of Nebraska Press, 1988.

Tijerina, Andrés. *Tejano Empire: Life on the South Texas Ranchos.* College Station: Texas A&M University Press, 1998.

Tilley, Nannie M., ed. *Federals on the Frontier: The Diary of Benjamin F. McIntyre, 1862–1864.* Austin: University of Texas Press, 1963.

Townsend, Stephen A. *The Yankee Invasion of Texas.* College Station: Texas A&M University Press, 2006.

Tyler, Ron, Douglas E. Barnett, Roy R. Barkley, Penelope C. Anderson, and Mark F. Odintz, eds., *The New Handbook of Texas.* 6 vols. Austin: Texas State Historical Association, 1999.

Vezzetti, Robert B., ed. *Tidbits, A Collection from the Brownsville Historical Association and the Stillman House Museum.* N.p., n.d.

Vidaurri, Cynthia L. "Texas-Mexican Religious Folk Art in Robstown, Texas." In *Hecho en Tejas: Texas-Mexican Folk Arts and Crafts,* ed. Joe S. Graham. Denton: University of North Texas Press, 1991.

Villarreal, Roberto M., and Alicia Villarreal-Wallach. *Atanasia.* Riviera, Tex.: Vamos, 1997.

Webb, Walter Prescott. *The Texas Rangers: A Century of Frontier Defense.* Austin: University of Texas Press, 1980.

Weber, David J. *The Spanish Frontier in North America.* New Haven, Conn.: Yale University Press, 1992.

West, John O. *Mexican-American Folklore.* Little Rock, Ark.: August House, 1988.

Westerners Brand Book, Los Angeles Corral, Book Number 7.

Winkler, John. *The First Billion: The Stillmans and the National City Bank.* New York: Vanguard Press, 1934.

Wright, Robert, OMI. *The Oblate Cavalry of Christ.* Rome, Italy: Oblate Heritage Series, 1998.

Xavier, Sister Mary (Holworthy), IWBS. *A Century of Sacrifice: The History of the Cathedral Parish, Corpus Christi, Texas, 1853–1953.* 1953.

———. *Father Jaillet, Saddlebag Priest.* Nueces-Duval County Historical Commission. San Diego, Tex.: Grunweld Printing, 1996.

———. *History of the Diocese of Corpus Christi,* 1939.

Journals

Cheeseman, Bruce S., "Let Us Have 500 Good Determined Texans": Richard King's Account of the Union Invasion of South Texas, November 12, 1863, to January 20, 1864." *Southwestern Historical Quarterly,* July 1997.

Dyer, Robert L. "Steamboating on the Missouri River with an Emphasis on the Boonslick Region." *Boone's Lick Heritage* 5, no. 2, June 1997.

Hill, Lawrence F. "The Confederate Exodus to Latin America." *Southwestern Historical Quarterly,* 39, issue 2, October 1935; issue 3, January 1936; issue 4, April 1936.

Kelley, Dora Mae. "Early Hidalgo Transportation." *Daily Review,* December 7, 1952, Centennial edition. Pan American University Library, Edinburg, Texas, n.p.

Myers, Lois E. "He Couldn't Get along without A Wife: A Women's View of Married Life in Victoria County, 1877–1881." *South Texas Historical Journal* 1, no. 1. Spring 1988.

Owens, Harry P. "Sail and Steam Vessels Serving the Apalachicola-Chattahoochee Valley." *Alabama Review,* July 1968.

Thompson, Jerry. "Mutiny and Desertion on the Rio Grande: The Strange Saga of Captain Adrian J. Vidal." *Military History of Texas and the Southwest* 12, no. 3. 1975.

Vera, Homero. "Don Esteban Cisneros and Dona Eulalia Tijerina de Cisneros." *El Mesteño* 4, no. 43. April 2001.

———. "Gregorio Vela—Rancher." *El Mesteño* 6, no. 1. Winter–Spring 2003.

Williams, Todd. "Rabb Ranch, An Oasis of Palms." *The Armadillo,* September 25, 1982.

Unpublished Material

Blown, Reverend Edward Harold, OMI. "The Putegnat Family." Rio Grande City, Texas, December 1969.

Cheeseman, Bruce. "History of the Rincón de Los Laureles." Paper.

———. "The King Spohn Family Friendship: A Productive Partnership Embodying Heritage, Hope and Leadership." Speech given to Spohn Health System Executives.

———. "Rincon Santa Gertrudis Land Grant." Paper.

Decker, May Segret. "A Biography of Eli T. Merriman." Master's thesis, Texas A&I University, 1942.

De Mauer, Johnnie Mae. "The History of Kenedy County." Master's thesis, Texas College of Arts and Industries, August 1940.
González, Jovita. "Social Life in Cameron, Starr, and Zapata Counties." Master's thesis, University of Texas at Austin, 1930.
Graf, Leroy P. "The Economic History of the Lower Rio Grande Valley, 1820–1875." PhD diss., Harvard University, 1942.
Hamilton, Michael. Private family papers.
Heaner, John Martindale. Private family papers.
Holworthy, Sister Mary Xavier. "History of the Diocese of Corpus Christi," Master's thesis, St. Mary's University of San Antonio, 1939.
———. Incarnate Word and Blessed Sacrament, Corpus Christi, Texas, 1945. *Diamonds for the King*. Brownsville Historical Association.
Minner, Sister Jeanne Francis. "The Early Development of Education in Corpus Christi, Texas 1846–1909." Master's thesis, Catholic University of America, Washington, D.C., 1950.
Morales, Maria E. "The History of La Parra Ranch in Kenedy County, Texas." Paper. Texas A&M University–Kingsville.
Nemeck, Father Francis Kelly. "The Big House." Unpublished paper.
———. "Jean Bretault, OMI." Unpublished paper.
———. "The Kenedy Family Chapel." Unpublished paper.
———. "The Kenedy-Turcotte-Lytton Cemeteries." Unpublished paper.
———. "Three Generations of Kenedys." Unpublished paper.
———. "Three Generations of Turcottes." Unpublished paper.
Putegnat, George N. to Rosita Putegnat, January 31, 1956. Transcript given to Jane Monday.
Putegnat, George. "Frontier Episodes," March 6, 1981.
———. "The Putegnat Family, 1848–1955."
Putegnat family papers and Reneghan Family Bible, given to Jane Monday by Patricia Reneghan.
Thompson, James Heaven. "A Nineteenth-Century History of Cameron County, Texas." Master's thesis, University of Texas, 1965.
Villarreal, Robert M. "The Mexican-American Vaqueros of the Kenedy Ranch: A Social History." Master's thesis, Texas A&I University, 1972.
Wood, Conan T. "Cerralvo as the Mother City of the Lower Rio Grande Valley." Speech given to the Lower Rio Grande Valley Historical Society, copy in Lon C. Hill Memorial Library, Harlingen, Texas.

Newspapers

American Flag
Austin American-Statesman
Brownsville Courier
Brownsville Daily Cosmopolitan

Brownsville Fort Brown Flag
Brownsville Herald
The Corpus Christi Caller-Times
Cuero Record
The Daily Ranchero
Galveston Daily News
Houston Tri-Weekly Telegraph
Mobile Times
New Orleans Daily True Delta
The New York Times
Nueces Valley
San Antonio Express
Semi-Weekly Ledger
Times Democrat
Union Paper, Coatesville, Pennsylvania
The Village Record, Coatesville, Pennsylvania

Interviews and Correspondence

Amberson, Mary Margaret, to Jane Monday by telephone, May 2006.
Cheeseman, Bruce, letter to Jane Monday and Frances Vick, December 2, 2005.
———, to Jane Monday, March 2000, letter from Mifflin Kenedy to Aldrick.
Chipman, Donald E., to Frances Vick concerning Petra Kenedy's letter and Spanish Colonial Texas.
Dreyer, Max, to Jane Monday in Raymondville, Texas, March 2000.
"Drovers Mercantile," e-mail, August 10, 2001, using *Ellsworth Reporter* and Harry E. Chrisman *The Ladder of Rivers* (Denver: Sage Books, 1962).
Griffin, Chula, to Jane Monday, May 2000.
Hamilton, Michael, to Jane Monday and Frances Vick concerning María Vicenta and Fred Starck, March 2006.
Heaner, John Martindale, to Jane Monday and Frances Vick concerning María Vicenta, Fred Starck, and the Vela land grants, March 2006.
———, to author Frances Vick May 15, 2006. See also Texas General Land Office Publication, *Guide to Spanish and Mexican Land Grants in South Texas.*
Monday, Charles Jr., MD. Board Certified General Surgeon, to Jane Monday and Frances Vick concerning Petra Kenedy's illness and surgery for a goiter, April 2006.
Nemeck, Father Francis Kelly, OMI, e-mail January 15, 2006, to authors.
———, e-mail December 10, 2005, to authors.
———, e-mail December 1, 2005, to authors.
———, e-mail February 21, 2005, to Jane Monday.
———, e-mail February 22, 2005, to Jane Monday.
Probst, Sylvia, assistant to Sr. Joan Marie Aycock, OSU, archivist, Ursuline Convent, Archives and Museum.

Putegnat, Rosita, to Jane Monday concerning the Putegnat family and Petra Vela de Vidal Kenedy, July 2001, Houston, Texas.

Reneghan, Patricia, to Jane Monday concerning Putegnat family and Petra Vela de Vidal Kenedy, July 2001, Seguin, Texas.

Stillman, Alexander, to Jane Monday and Frances Vick concerning the house at Los Laureles, April 2006.

Swisher, Rose, to Jane Monday concerning Rodriguez family and Petra Vela de Vidal Kenedy, by telephone and correspondence, 2005, and May 30, 2006.

Vera, Homero, e-mail to authors, July 2006.

———, e-mail to Jane Monday, October 5, 2005.

Census, County, and Church Documents

1850 Census, Rio Grande Valley, Cameron, Starr, Webb, 572–73, November 7, 1850.

1850 Census, Texas—Cameron, Starr, and Webb Census, vol. 12, no. 3, September 1995, 150.

1860 Census, Cameron County, Texas, City of Brownsville p. 268 taken June 13, 1860.

1870 Census, Corpus Christi, Duval County, August 1, 1870, Mifflin Kenedy, Line 2, Series M593 Roll: 1,600 pages, page: 198.

1880 Census, University of Texas–PanAm, Edinburg, Texas. Cameron Co., Hidalgo Co., Starr Co., Webb Co., Zapata Co., T009, 1294, 1311, 1327, 1332, 1334.

1850 Slave schedule in the Rio Grande Valley, County of Cameron, Starr, Webb, October 5, 1850.

1860 Slave schedule, Brownsville, County of Cameron, State of Texas, June 14, 1860.

1860 Slave schedule, Starr County; Slave schedule in the County of Nueces, June 23, 1860.

Cameron County Birth Records, 1880–1890.

Catholic Archives of Texas, "A Preservation Plan for the Immaculate Conception Cathedral," Austin, Texas.

Catholic Diamond Publications, Catholic Archives, Corpus Christi, Texas.

Chester County Will Abstract—1840–1844. 10054 will bi. 18, 1.

Chester County Archives and Records Services, West Chester, Pennsylvania.

Diocesis de Matamoros, A. R., Parroquia de Nuestra Senora del Refugio, Santa Iglesia Catedral, Book of Baptisms Numero 7, Foja 6 Partida 37.

District Court Records, Corpus Christi, Texas. Sarita Kenedy Garza deposition, sworn in Galveston County, part of the Raul Trevino v. Edgar Turcotte lawsuit of Kenedy County, Texas, filed in Nueces County, Texas, May 16, 1969.

Immaculate Conception Cathedral, from the Sacramental Records, vol. 2, page 128, #211 (John Gregory), #212 (Sarah Josephine), #213 (William).

Immaculate Conception Church, Certificate of Baptism of Thomas Mifflin Kenedy at St. Mary's Church, record at Brownsville, Texas, vol. 1, page 145, #92.

———, Certificate of Marriage of J. L. Putegnat and Rosa Vidal, Brownsville, Texas.

———, Brownsville, Texas; Baptismal Records, vol. 3, page 409, #667.
———, Brownsville, Texas; Baptismal Records, Book III, p. 452, #107.
Matamoros 27 Abril 1842 Census Exp. 1, Caja 7, No. de Inventarion 34, Fojas Utiles 7. Padron de Vecinos del Ayuntamiento del 1 (Primer) Cuartel de la Sección del Oriente Plaza Hidalgo Poniente.
Mier Church Baptism Records, 1767–1880, University of Texas at Brownsville.
St. Mary's Church of Brownsville, Baptismal Records, Brownsville, Texas, vol. 1, page 191, #137.
———, Baptismal Records, Brownsville, Texas. Certificate of Baptism of Thomas Mifflin Kenedy at St. Mary's Church, record at Immaculate Conception Church, Brownsville, Texas.
St. Patrick Interment Book, Catholic Cathedral Archives, Corpus Christi, Texas.

Index

Alamo, 133
Alhambra saloon, 254, 257
Allen, A. C., 228
Alonzo, Armando, 11
Alvarado, Francisco, 115
Alvarado, Ignacio, 248–49
Alvarado, Ramón, 298
Alvarado, Victor, 298
Amberson, Mary Margaret McAllen, 39, 40
American and Mexican Emigrant Company, 143
Ampudia, Gen. Pedro de, 21
Andrade y Castellanos, Manuela, 18, 19
Anglo Americans: authority over land titles, 35; initial incursions into northern Mexico, 1–2; pay differential vs. Tejanos, 265; as raiders, 184, 198, 227; targeting of Tejanas for marriage, 35, 39, 40; vaqueros as teachers of cowboys, 57; vigilante violence by, 230, 231. *See also* cultures, Mexican and Anglo
Armstrong, Capt. James B., 55, 208
Army, U.S.: desertion of Fort Brown, 72; post-Civil War attack on Bagdad, 141; relief of Brownsville from Cortina, 78; and river supply contracting, 29, 30–31, 33, 60. *See also* Union Army
art collectors, Kenedys as, 322–23
Ashbrook, Pearl (Mrs. R. King II), 301

Bagdad, Mexico: Civil War growth of, 91, 94, 101; Cortina's defense against French, 118–19; French takeover of, 125–26; illustration, 90; Union soldiers' attack on, 141
Ballí de la Garza, María Salomé, 39–40, 53, 154–55, 275
bandit attacks: Anglo raids on Tejano ranches, 184, 198, 227; and chaos in Mexico, 140; McNelly's crackdown on, 230–33; Nuecestown attack, 229–30; and post-Reconstruction politics, 215; on railroad investors, 245; on ranches, 56, 151, 168, 171–72, 183–84, 195–98; on Taylor's wagon train, 27, 29; testifying in Washington on, 236; and travel dangers, 173–74, 175–76; vigilante response, 227, 230–31
banking, informal nature of, 51, 53
Banks, Gen. Nathaniel P., 104, 108
Barthelow, Jeff, 105–6
Bee, Gen. Hamilton P., 94, 101, 103–5, 107–8
Belden, Samuel, 31, 32, 65
Benavides, Col. Santos, 112, 119
Berber, Herculano, 341
black beans, drawing of, 21, 59
blockade of Rio Grande, Union, 88–92, 94, 101–3, 112, 128
blockade running, 127–28, 132
Blücher, Felix von, 166–67
Blücher, Maria von, 118
Blue Party, 183
Boca del Rio, Mexico, 103
border conflicts, Rio Grande: and Mexican-American War, 27–30; Mexican government responses, 236–37; post-Civil War, 130, 139–40, 141, 229. *See also* bandit attacks; Cortina, Juan Nepomuceno
Botica del León, 96–97, 204, 302–3
Bourland-Miller Commission, 35
Brackenridge, George, 111
brands, ranch, 60, *61*, 165, 172, 200
Brazos Santiago, Texas, 90–91
breeding operations, 219–20, 276–77, 306
Bretault, Fr. Jean, 313
Brito, Sheriff, 317, 340–41
Brownsville, Texas: Centennial celebration, 240–41; Civil War chaos, 103–18, 125, 128; community structure, 51–55; Cortina's occupation of, 72–78; cultural mosaic, 37–39, 50–52; daily life for Petra and Mifflin, 52–55; duel in, 252–53; economic decline of, 171; ethnic tensions in, 226–27; expulsion of Starck from, 336; great fire of 1857, 64–66; initial lawlessness in, 37–38; Kings' home in, 34, 62; Mifflin's properties in, 64; Petra and

Brownsville, Texas (*continued*)
Mifflin's wedding, 7; Petra's attachment to, 272–73; Petra's move to, 22–23; Petra's shift of focus from, 215–16; politics of, 72, 153, 177–78, 183, 203, 209–12, 317, 319; pre-Civil War growth of, 30–31, 34, 67–68; Protestant churches in, 38–39; Putegnat pharmacy, 96–97, 204, 302–3; and Reconstruction, 153–62; social life for upper class, 145; Tom's attachments to, 315–16; weather disasters, 155–59, 206, 266–67; yellow fever epidemics, 68, 155, 159, 186. *See also* Church of the Immaculate Conception; Missionary Oblates of Mary Immaculate; Sisters of the Incarnate Word and Blessed Sacrament
Brownsville-Point Isabel railroad, 185–86, 202
Brownsville Town Co., 66–67

Caballero, 40, 54, 87
Cabrera, Tomás, 76, 78
Canales, Gen. Servando, 126, 151, 237
Canby, Maj. Gen. E. R. S., 177
Carvajal, Gen. José, 75
Catholic Church: anti-Catholicism from Anglos, 226; in Brownsville, 45, 57, 59, 69–71, 84, 88, 116, 118, 121, 137, 141, 147, 159–61; in Corpus Christi, 219, 250, 282–83, 287, 291, 320–21; importance of faith in hard times, 80; ministering to rural faithful, 59–60, 225–26, 275–76, 291; Petra's devotion to, 15, 41, 45, 57, 71, 168, 282–83, 320; Protestant competition, 38–39; requiem for Willie, 249–50. *See also* charity work; Missionary Oblates of Mary Immaculate; Sisters of the Incarnate Word and Blessed Sacrament
cattle. *See* drives, cattle; ranching; thievery, cattle
Cavazos, José Narciso, 31
Cavazos, Savas, 237
Celaya, Simon, 185, 208
Centennial celebrations, 240–41
Cerralvo, Mexico, 7, 9
Chamberlain, Bland, 280
Chamberlain, Henrietta (Mrs. R. King), 33–34, 35, 37, *37*, 40, 57–58. *See also* King, Henrietta
Chamberlain, Hiram: arrival in Brownsville, 33; death of, 152; and King's courtship of Henrietta, 37, 57; on King's move to Santa Gertrudis, 84; Protestantism of, 38–39; and Union raid on Santa Gertrudis, 115
Champion, 27
Chapman, Helen, 30, 33–34, 35, 37, 63–64
Chapman, Maj. William, 30, 31, 33, 55, 59
charity work: in Brownsville, 71, 147–48, 160–61; in Corpus Christi, 250, 272, 282–83, 287, 291, 321; foundation and trust, 5, 6, 352; legacy to children of, 291, 313, 351–52; Petra's dedication to, 3, 43, 47, 57, 320
Chavero, Ana Marie de (Adrian's wife) (daughter-in-law), 119, 186–87, 188
Cheeseman, Bruce, 189
children: during Brownsville fire, 65–66; charity legacy to, 291, 313, 351–52; close ties among, 97; and dangers of ranch life, 64; education of, 23, 42–43, 46–47, 98–100, 168–69, 179; eve of Civil War status, 80; expansion of family in 1870s, 245; fire at Spring Hill College, 176–77; home environment for, 44–45; legacy after Mifflin and Petra, 351–57; Mifflin's fondness for step-children, 83, 136, 305; natural/illegitimate status, 22–23, 45; Petra's devotion to, 41, 44–45, 49, 66, 88, 305; Petra's moral legacy to, 43; Petra's separation from, 98–100, 271, 272–73; religious training of, 169, 204; rifts among, 305; status at Petra's death, 346–47. *See also individual children's names*
Chipman, Donald, 3
Chisolm Trail, 191–92
cholera epidemics, 22, 31
chuck wagons, 247
Church of the Immaculate Conception, Brownsville: bells for, 147–48; building of, 57, 59, 69–71, *70*, *72*; welcome for bishop, 226
Civil War: blockade of Rio Grande, 88–92, 94, 101–3, 128; and Brownsville, 103–18, 125, 128; drought during, 90, 117–18; ending of, 128–29; King's and Mifflin's support for Confederacy, 112, 113, 115–16, 119–20; profiteering during, 90, 102–3, 112–13, 120, 127; stresses for Petra, 88, 121, 129–30, 140; Texas secession, 86–87. *See also* cotton trade; Vidal, Adrian
Clark, Jack (Jap), 265, 298
coach, Petra's, 174–76, 268–69
Coatesville, Pennsylvania, 4–5, 99–100, 128–29, 150–51
Cobos, Gen. José María, 108
Coke, Gov. Richard, 215, 230
Collins Station, 265
Colonel Cross, 30, 31
Comanche, 32
Comisión Pesquisidora de la Frontera del Norte, 197–98
Confederate Army: Adrian's career in, 94, 100–101, 103–4; Ford's role in, 86, 94, 108, 117, 124–25, 129; and French Intervention War, 129; King as officer in, 119; Mexico as refuge for, 101, 122; Putegnat's career in, 100–101
Conservatives vs. Separatists on land status, 35

INDEX

convent. *See* Sisters of the Incarnate Word and Blessed Sacrament
Corpus Christi, San Diego and Rio Grande narrow gauge railway, 273
Corpus Christi, Texas: beginnings of family focus on, 169–70; Catholic Church in, 219, 250, 282–83, 287, 291, 320–21; Centennial celebrations, 240–41; charity work in, 250, 272, 282–83, 287, 291; growth of, 171, 270, 303; and Kenedy family, 200–201, 218–19, 270–71, 272–73, 289, 290; Kenedy Mansion, 279, 291–92, 305, 321–22, 333–34, 342–44; as opportunity for Mifflin, 273; social life of, 289–91; Spohn-Kenedy marriage, 241–42; Tex-Mex railway deal, 274–75; wool market in, 278
Corpus Christi Caller, 314
Corpus Christi-Laredo Railroad. *See* Texas Mexican (Tex-Mex) Railway
corridos (narrative folksong), 73
Cortina, Juan Nepomuceno (Cheno): and Adrian, 67, 73–74, 108, 124; as cattle thief, 184–85, 187–88, 196, 197, 229; as folk hero, 49, 66–67, 73; hatred of King, 199; influence of, 215; loss of land to Stillman, 31; machinations during Civil War, 104–5, 107, 108, 112, 117, 118–19, 120, 121, 126–27; Mexican government's shutdown of, 236–37; occupation of Brownsville, 72–78; portrait, 67; raid on Mifflin's ranch, 7
Cortina War, 74–78
Corvette, 29, 30
cotton trade: establishment of, 88–91, 94; King's and Mifflin's roles in, 112, 113, 115–16, 119–20; post-Civil War decline of, 141–42; post-Civil War protection of, 129, 130–32; profiteering from, 102–3, 127; renewal of, 125; Stillman's role, 89, 90, 91, 111, 128; success of, 112–13; Union attacks on, 115–16, 119
Couincell, City Marshal J. L., 195
cowboys, 57, 192, 247–48, 265
Cowen, Ana Adrianne (née Vidal) (granddaughter), 353–54. *See also* Vidal, Ana Adrianne
Cowen, Louis Tom, 353–54
credit services, Kenedy and King's control of, 167
Cruillas, Mexico, 57
cultures, Mexican and Anglo: Adrian's adjustment problems, 47–50; Anglo Protestant treatment of children, 44–45; blending in Brownsville, 37–39, 50–52, 54; entertainment traditions, 17–18, 63, 73; holidays on Los Laureles Ranch, 268; Mexican community structure, 6, 9–11, 13, 15, 17–18, 44–45, 71–72;

Mexican vs. Anglo-American labeling, 149–50; Petra's contribution to, 2, 4, 17–18, 170, 173–74, 295; sons' adjustment to Quaker community, 99; women's roles and rights, 3–4, 18, 19–20, 22, 40. *See also* ethnic tensions; language issues; marriage; Tejanas; Tejanos
Cummings, Frank, 183

Dalzell, Julia (granddaughter), 154
Dalzell, Luisa (Louisa) Vidal de (daughter), 218, 316, 352. *See also* Vidal, Luisa
Dalzell, Mary Josephine (granddaughter), 240
Dalzell, Robert Mifflin (grandson), 89–90
Dalzell, Capt. Robert (son-in-law): courtship and marriage of, 84, 87–88; defense of Brownsville from Cortina, 75; and family rift with Starck, 324, 336–37; legacy of, 352; political activities, 153, 319; portrait, 86; raiding of house lumber from, 140; return to Brownsville, 316; in steamboat business, 145, 162, 218
Dana, Gen. N. J. T., 111, 112, 113
Davenport, Harbert, 78
Davis, Allen, 241
Davis, Gov. Edmund J., 101, 104, 112, 183
Davis, Henry, 31
Denver & Rio Grande Railroad, 274
Díaz, Gen. José de la Cruz Porfirio, 84–85, 196, 236, 246
diseases and public health: cholera, 22, 31; Corpus Christi's challenge, 270; smallpox, 118; yellow fever, 68, 155, 159, 186, 206, 207
Dobie, J. Frank, 215, 248
Doddridge, Perry, 241
Doddridge, Rachel, 241
Dodge City, Kansas, James's killing of Dora Hand in, 254, 257–60, 261–62
Domenece, Abbé, 3
Downey, Edward, 45, 177, 202, 218, 222, 233
dress customs, Tejano, 54–55, 83, 87
drives, cattle: challenges of, 276, 306; daily life on, 192, 247–49; organization of, 228–29, 237–38, 246–47, 251, 254, 277, 285; profitability of, 172; rail replacement of, 265, 306–7; scope of, 190–91; trails, **191**, 191–92
drought: during Civil War, 90, 117–18; hardships for ranches, 276, 277, 280, 289, 292; and river trade, 55
Dubuis, Bishop Claude Marie, 160–61
Duff, Col. James, 104, 106–7
Dunn, J. B., 227
Durell, Maj. E. P., 137–38
Dye, Mayor George, 111

Earp, Wyatt, 257, 259
East, Arthur, 352, *354*
East, Sarah Josephine (Sarita) (née Kenedy) (granddaughter), 39, 313, 352, *355, 356*
economics: Brownsville's decline, 171; Brownsville's structure, 51–52; Civil War's effect on, 88, 101; post-hurricane depression, 159; stock market crash (1873), 207. *See also* ranching; steamboat business
education: children's, 23, 42–43, 46–49, 98–100, 161, 168–69, 177, 179; Mifflin's, 24; Petra's, 16
Ellsworth, Kansas, shooting of James in, 195
Escandón, José de, 2
Escobedo, Gen. Mariano, 151
Esparza, José (Tom's assassin), 341
Espíritu Santo land grant, 238
ethnic tensions: Adrian's killing of rancher, 105–6; and Adrian's resignation from Union Army, 121–22; Anglo appropriation of Tejano land, 2, 73, 178–79, 227–28; Anglo prejudice against Tejanos, 48, 225; anti-Catholicism from Anglos, 226; and King's defense of ranch, 199–200; and Mexican raids on San Antonio, 20–22; Petra's prejudices, 149–50, 295; and Tejanos in Confederate Army, 94, 104; vigilante killings in Nuecestown, 229–30; wagon train massacre, 27

family, importance of, 5, 6, 15. *See also* children
fandango (dancing), 17–18, 101
federal government and law enforcement for ranches, 173, 183–84, 195–98, 200. *See also* government contracts for river trade
fencing of range, 165–66, 184–85, 189–90, 193, 202, 265
fires: Brownsville, 64–66, 108; Spring Hill College, 176–77
Fisher, William S., 21
Fitch, Capt. John, 42, 228
Floyd, Lt. D. H., 203–4
foods, Mexican traditions, 17, 52–53, 252
Ford, John "Rip": and Adrian, 122–24; on Brownsville politics, 183; Civil War role, 86, 94, 108, 117, 124–25; on Cortina, 75, 126; and Cortina's capture, 237; and family in Matamoros, 120; on Imperialists vs. Juaristas, 149; influence with Union Army, 130–31; and last battle of Civil War, 129; on Mifflin, 146, 153–54; on Mifflin's courtship of Petra, 39; and Mifflin's initiation into ranching, 40; resourcefulness of, 78; on security of ranches, 184, 236
Fort Brown: during Civil War, 101, 105, 118, 125; Cortina's takeover of, 74; establishment of, 31; hurricane damage, 266–67; post-hurricane rebuilding of, 161–62; U.S. Army desertion of, 72; and war profiteering, 102; yellow fever epidemic at, 68
fortune seekers: and Brownsville's growth, 50; Civil War profiteering, 90, 102–3, 112–13, 120, 127; post-Mexican War, 31
Francisco Ballí and Company, 53
Fremantle, Col. A. J. L., 101
French Intervention War: Adrian's role in, 124, 126–27, 132–33, 135–36; beginnings, 89; Confederate soldiers' participation in, 129; Cortina's role in, 108, 118–19, 124, 126; French takeover of river trade, 125–26; and lawlessness on border, 139–40; and Matamoros, 117; principals' sympathies in Civil War, 111; withdrawal of French, 149, 150
Fryer, B. E., 260, 261

Galvan, Jeremiah, 65, 89, 161, 208, 217, 218
Galveston, Texas, steamboating in, 218
García, Margarita (marriage witness/godparent), 45, 60
García, María Antonia (Petra's great-grandmother), 10
García, María Josefa (Petra's godparent), 16
Garrettson, Fannie, 254, 259
Garza, Juan, 103
Garza, Remigio, 103
Garza, Santos, 103
Garza, Sarita Kenedy, 318
Gause, Jonathan, 24
Glavecke, Adolphus, 74–75, 153
godparents *(padrinos)*, 16, 71–72
Gonzáles, Ramona, 318
González, Jovita, 3, 17, 40, 54, 87
Goodrich, Elizabeth (Betsy) (Mrs. Charles Stillman), 37, 42
Gould, Jay, 273–74
government contracts for river trade: growth of, 30–31; loss of, 55; M. Kenedy & Co.'s manipulation of, 33; Mexican War supplies, 29; post-war development of, 142, 145; pre-Civil War successes, 60
Grampus, 32
Grant, Gen. Ulysses S., 130, 196
Green, Thomas J., 21
Greer, Capt. John, 204
Gregory, Capt. William S., 41–42, 56, 163
Groesbeck, Mrs., 296

Hale, William, 233–34
Hand, Dora (Fannie Keenan), 254, *256*, 257–60
Hawley, Henry, 307–8

INDEX

Hayes, Pres. Rutherford B., 237
Haynes, Col. John L., 104, 108, 122
Headley, Alexander, 232
healer, Petra as, 22, 194, 260–61
Heintzelman, Maj. Samuel P., 78
herbal remedies, 194
Herff, Dr. Ferdinand, 307, 341, 344–45
Herron, Gen. Francis J., 117, 118, 125
hide and cattle laws, 208–9
Hodges, Isaac, 325, 326
holidays on Los Laureles Ranch, 268
homes: big house at La Parra, 350, *350;* Concepciòn and Manuel's, 83; Kenedy Mansion in Corpus Christi, 279, 291–92, 305, 321–22, 333–34, 342–44; Kings' Brownsville house, 34, 62; Los Laureles additions, *163–66,* 193; Petra's childhood, 17; restoration of ownership after Civil War, 137–38, 143; "steamboat" house at La Parra, *281, 282;* Stillmans' in Brownsville, *43;* Tom and Yrene's, 340, *341*
Horrocks, James, 145
horses: Jesse James's horse, 306; King's loss of, 228; sale of, 219–20; Tom Kenedy's love of, 316–17; Vela, 9
hurricanes, 155–59, 266–67

ice business, King's, 300, 314
Imperialists vs. Juaristas, 105, 111, 117, 132–33, 135–36, 139–40. *See also* French Intervention War
Incarnate Word School for Girls, 46–47. *See also* Sisters of the Incarnate Word and Blessed Sacrament
Indians: and Gregorio Vela's death, 20; raid on convent, 43; raids on ranches, 13, 56, 63; raids on upper-Rio Grande communities, 30; tragedy of situation for, 63–64
inheritance of, 15
inheritance of land: Cortina's, 31; and disposition of descendants, 351; disputes over, 15, 352; and La Atravesada Ranch, 178–79; Mexican women's right to, 3; Petra's estate, 15–16, 22–23, 348–49
I Would Rather Sleep in Texas (Amberson), 40

Jaillet, Fr. Claude, 320–21, 334–35, 345
James, Jesse, 306
John G. and Marie Stella Kenedy Memorial Foundation, 6, 352
John G. Kenedy, Jr. Charitable Trust, 6, 352
Joseph, Harriett Denise, 3
Journal of the Texian Expedition against Mier (Green), 21
Juárez, Pres. Benito, 89, 118, 126, 127, 196

Juaristas vs. Imperialists, 105, 111, 117, 132–33, 135–36, 139–40. *See also* French Intervention War

Keenan, Fannie (Dora Hand), 254, 257–60
Kelley, Mayor Jim, 254, 257–59
Kelly, Jim, 195
Kelly, Capt. William, 204, *205,* 209–12, 216–18, 336
Kenedy, Corina Ballí Treviño de (daughter-in-law): birth of Georgie, 328–29; courtship and marriage of, 294–95, 301; and death of James, 333; land dispute, 327; later life and death of, 351; portrait, *328;* request to live at La Parra, 342
Kenedy, Elena (née Seuss), 352, *353*
Kenedy, Elisha Jeffers (Mifflin's brother): attempt to rescue Adrian, 133, 135; and charges against Starck, 336; and fight against Cortina, 75; and horses, 316–17; as Mifflin's business partner, 80, 146; portrait, *134;* youth of, 26
Kenedy, George Fairlamb (Mifflin's brother), 328
Kenedy, George Mifflin (grandson), 323, *328,* 328–29, 331, 333, 351
Kenedy, James Walworth (Santiago/Spike) (son): accidental shooting at La Parra, 324–27; baptism of, 60; birth of, 58; character of, 292; courtship and marriage of, 294–95, 301; Dora Hand affair, 254, 257–60; education of, 98–100, 168, 169, 177; Ellsworth incident, 195; final health decline, 308–9, 323–24, 327, 329, 330–32, 333, 334–35; home at La Parra, 282; love of ranching, 58, 194–95; portraits, *182, 255;* ranch operations, 251, 281, 284–86, 287–88, 292–94, 312; return from Pennsylvania, 154; as Texas Ranger, 232, 233, 237
Kenedy, John Gregory, Jr. (grandson), *351,* 352
Kenedy, John Gregory (Gregorio) (son): baptism of, 71; birth of, 62; character of, 223, 292; courtship and marriage of, 301–2, 310–13; education of, 98–100, 161, 168, 169, 177, 179; on ending of Civil War, 128–29; home at La Parra, 282; legacy of, 351–52; loss of child, 344; in New Orleans, 215–16; on Pennsylvania stay, 100; portraits, *130, 181, 311;* ranch operations, 281, 292–94, 308, 311–12, 315; return from Pennsylvania, 154
Kenedy, John (Mifflin's father), 24, 25, *25*
Kenedy, John William (Willie) (son): baptism of, 71; birth of, 66; character of, 223–24; death of, 241; education of, 168, 169, 177, 179; portrait, *224;* requiem for, 249–50

Kenedy, María Petra Vela de: ancestry of, 7, 9–12; baptism of, 16; beauty of, 39; birth of, 7; and Brownsville, 34, 52–55; character of, 39, 44–45, 173–74; charitable work of, 3, 43, 47, 57, 320; and children's deaths, 87, 241, 335; Civil War stresses, 88, 121, 129–30, 140; coach for, 174–76; and Corpus Christi, 218–19, 270–73, 287; courtship and marriage to Mifflin, 7, 39–41, 45; cultural contribution of, 2, 4, 17–18, 170, 173–74, 295; death of, 344–46; devotion to children, 41, 44–45, 49, 66, 88, 305; devotion to church, 15, 41, 45, 57, 71, 168, 282–83, 320; education of, 16; and family cohesion, 5, 15, 97; family legacy of, 42, 43, 351–57; family role of, 41, 268, 331; final health decline of, 305, 309, 316, 320, 321, 329; and fire in Brownsville, 65–66; as healer, 22, 194, 260–61; and Henrietta King, 62; illnesses, 206–8, 234–35, 272, 301; and La Parra mansion, 342–44; Latin American relocation program, 142–43; on leaving Brownsville, 215–16; on Lee King's death, 297; letter to Salomé de McAllen, 294; and Luis, 18–20, 22; in Matamoros, 18–19, 129–30; in Mier, 13, 17; and Mier Expedition, 20–22; Mifflin's devotion to, 261, 269, 320, 348; mothering experience of, 328–29; overview, 1–6; pejorative labeling of Anglos, 149–50; Pennsylvania trip, 150–51; portraits, *8, 44, 95, 242, 346;* property legacy, 22–23, 40–41, 167, 235, 348–49; as rancher, 16–17, 60, *61,* 169, 193–94, 201, 203, 220, 294; requiem mass for, 348; summary of Vidal children, 18; and Tex-Mex railway deal, 275; youth and social context, 17–18. *See also* children

Kenedy, Marie Stella (née Turcotte) (daughter-in-law), 323, 344, 351–52. *See also* Turcotte, Marie Stella

Kenedy, Mifflin: and Adrian, 47–48, 133, 135–36; and Brownsville, 34, 52–55; and Carmen Morell, 350–51; character of, 5, 27, 49, 55–56, 64, 89, 146, 190, 287; charitable work of, 71, 147–48, 160–61, 321; Civil War role of, 89, 112, 113, 115–16, 119–20; and Corpus Christi, 273; and Cortina, 75–77; cotton trade role of, 89, 112, 113, 115–16, 119–20; courtship and marriage of, 7, 39–41, 45; and Dalzell, 87–88, 145; devotion to Petra, 261, 269, 320, 348; education of, 24; family roles of, 324, 329–30, 331–32; financial difficulties, 309; fondness for step-children, 83, 136, 305; illnesses of, 327, 329–30; and King, 5, 27, 59, 127–28, 151, 152, 163–64, 297–300, 329; at King/Kleberg wedding, 348; La Parra home building, 291–92; loyalty to Confederacy, 112; and McNelly, 231; micromanagement style, 291–92, 308, 333–34; monopolistic trading practices, 29–34, 55, 66, 142, 185, 190; and mother, 146–47; overview, 2, 4–5; pardon for war activities, 138–39, 143–44; Pennsylvania trips, 263, 284; and Petra's death, 346–47, 348; political influence of, 72, 149, 153–54, 209–11, 219, 270, 286, 319; portraits, *28, 96, 114, 144, 243, 345, 349;* on Powers's death, 283; and railroad developments, 186, 190, 217–18; Robb Commission testimony, 196–97; and Santiago's Dodge City adventure, 260, 261–62; socioeconomic status, 80; and Tom, 318–19, 338; and war profiteering, 102; youth of, 24–27. *See also* property holdings; ranching; steamboat business

Kenedy, Phebe Ann (daughter), 84, 87
Kenedy, Phebe Ann (Mifflin's sister), 25–26
Kenedy, Roberto Tomás, 318
Kenedy, Sarah Josephine (Mifflin's sister), 25–26, 99–100, 332
Kenedy, Sarah Josephine (Mrs. Spohn) (daughter): baptism of, 71; birth of, 64, 66; courtship and marriage of, 241–43; death of, 352; education of, 168–69, 179, 221; and family cohesion, 97; and Petra's death, 346; portraits, *180, 239, 314;* and social scene in Corpus Christi, 272, 313
Kenedy, Sarah Josephine (Sarita) (Mrs. East) (granddaughter), 39, 313, 352, *355, 356*
Kenedy, Sarah Starr (Mifflin's mother): final illness and death, 324, 332, 334; and Kenedy boys' move to Coatesville, 99–100; and Mifflin, 146–47; Mifflin's financial support for, 167; and Mifflin's origins, 25; portrait, *26*
Kenedy, Thomas Mifflin (Tomás) (son): baptism of, 45; birth of, 44; character of, 292, 307, 315–16, 318, 338; courtship and marriage of, 337–39; death of, 341; education of, 98–100, 168, 169; and horses, 316–17; political career, 317, 318–19, 340–41; portraits, *339;* ranch operations, 215, 220, 281, 307–8, 318; return from Pennsylvania, 154
Kenedy, Yrene Yznaga de (daughter-in-law), 337–39, *339*
Kenedy Mansion, Corpus Christi, 279, 291–92, 305, 321–22, 333–34, 342–44
Kenedy Pasture Co., 280–81
Kenedy Ranch, scope of, 281–82. *See also* La Parra Ranch
Kenedy Ranch Museum, 356–57

INDEX

Keralum, Fr. Pierre Yves, 59, 60
King, Alice Gertrudis (Mrs. R. Kleberg), 204, 301, 307, *307*, 332–33, 348
King, Ella Morse, 204
King, Henrietta María (Nettie), 62, 84, 115, 152, 204
King, Henrietta (née Chamberlain): courtship and marriage of, 33–34, 35, 37, 40, 57–58; and dangers of remote ranches, 63; hiring of Kleberg, 284; and Lee's death, 297; and Petra, 62; portrait, *37*
King, Kenedy & Co., 145, 171, 190, 204, 206, 216–18. *See also* steamboat business
King, Pearl (née Ashbrook), 301
King, Richard: and Alice/Kleberg courtship, 332–33; background of, 27; in Brownsville, 34, 62; character of, 27; and Cortina, 78, 199; cotton trade role, 112, 113, 115–16, 119–20; courtship and marriage of, 33–34, 35, 37, 40, 57–58; death of, 348; dedication to ranching, 55–56, 229, 287, 300, 341; final health decline of, 305, 307, 341–42; financial difficulties, 297–300, *298*; horse breeding and selling, 219–20, 306; illnesses, 216, 280, 292; and Kleberg, 284, 314–15; and McNelly, 231, 250; and Mifflin, 5, 27, 59, 127–28, 151, 152, 159–60, 163–64, 297–300, 329; murder accusation against, 179, 182; near-drowning of, 267; pardon for war activities, 143–44; political influence of, 72, 209–11, 219; portraits, *28, 112;* and R. E. Lee, 62–63; and railroad development, 217–18; Robb Commission testimony, 196; slave ownership by, 69; and Spohn, 201; and steamboat business, 29–34, 127–28, 149, 208; and Texas Rangers, 178; trust in men, 248–49; and Union raid on Santa Gertrudis, 116; vigilantism accusations against, 227; and war profiteering, 102; and Wells, 283–84. *See also* property holdings; ranching
King, Richard II, 84, 204, 248, 301
King, Richard III, 332
King, Robert E. Lee, 116, 296–97
King, Thomas B., 34
King Ice Works, 300, 314
Kingsbury, Gilbert, 48
Kingsbury, Robert, 101
Kinney, Col. Henry L., 200
Kleberg, Alice Gertrudis (née King). *See* King, Alice Gertrudis
Kleberg, Robert Justus: courtship and marriage of, 301, 307, 332–33, 348; on King and ranch, 277; and legal case against King, 314–15; as legal counsel for King, 284; on Mifflin's stress level, 327; on social life in Corpus Christi, 279
Kleiber, Joseph, 120, 185, 190

La Atravesada Ranch, 178
Lady Gay Theatre, 254
La Gloria, Rancho, 11
land. *See* property holdings
land grants, Spanish-Mexican: and additions to La Parra, 281–82; administration of, 11, 13; 1852 summary of, **36**; Espíritu Santo, 238; Las Mesteñas, 154; Porción 57, **14**; Puerta de Agua Dulce, 229, 301; Rincón de Los Laureles, 162–63; Rincón de Santa Gertrudis, 229; San Martín Grant, 40; San Salvadore del Tule, 56; Vela family interests, 4, 9–11, 167. *See also* Los Laureles Ranch; Santa Gertrudis Ranch
language issues: Adrian's adjustment problems, 48; Anglo traders' need for Spanish, 31; challenges for Petra, 151, 272; and land exploitation of Mexicans, 179; and Petra's devotion to heritage, 295; and sons in Pennsylvania, 100
La Parra Ranch (Grapevine Ranch): accidental shooting at, 324–27; boundary disputes at, 293, 294, 296; homes at, *281,* 282, 350, *350;* Mifflin's attempts to sell, 287, 288, 303–4, 309; Mifflin's management through sons, 281, 284–88, 292–94, 307–9, 311–12, 315, 318; purchase of, 278, 280–82; scope of, 285–86
Laredo, Texas, 30, 273
Las Mesteñas land grant, 154
Las Rucias, Texas, 124–25
Latin American relocation for Southerners, 142–43
lawsuits and Brownsville businesses, 233
Lea, Tom, 40, 41, 297
Lebh Shomea (Listening Heart) House of Prayer, 313
Lee, Gen. Robert E., 62–63, 128–29
Lerdo de Tejada, Pres. Sebastian, 236
Lewis, Capt. G. K. (Legs), 56, 58–59
Lincoln, Pres. Abraham, 88, 129
Lipan Indians, 30
Litteral, Pvt., 105
Loma Alto Ranch, 229
López, Albino, 117
Los Federales Ranch, 276
Los Laureles Ranch: acquisition of, 162–65; branding, 165, 172, 200; cattle up-breeding, 276–77; challenges of running, 220–21; establishment of, 171–72, 193; fencing of, 165–66;

Los Laureles Ranch (*continued*)
isolation of, 235; Mifflin and Petra's work on, 201, 203; and move to Corpus Christi, 272; new owners' handling of, 294; safety and security challenges, 173–74, 245; sale of, 280; status of (1870 and 1880), 183–84, 267–68; Stillman's acquisition of, 41–42
Lott, Uriah, 159, 234, 244, 264, 274–75
Lyons, Gene, 195

M. Kenedy & Co.: cotton shipping during Civil War, 89–91, 94, 125; dissolution of, 145; establishment of, 32; loss of boats to Union, 112; monopolistic practices of, 33, 34, 55; pre–Civil War development, 60; and putting out of Brownsville fire, 65. *See also* steamboat business
McAllen, John: and cattle theft problem, 153; hosting of bishop, 275; marriage of, 88; ranching operations, 294; on Reconstruction politics, 178, 183; and Young land dispute, 154–55
McAllen, Salomé Ballí Young de, 39–40, 53, 154–55, 275
McCampbell, John S., 199
McClane, John, 230–31
McClernand, Gen. John A., 120, 121
McNelly, Capt. Leander, 230–33, 236, 250
Magnolia Mansion, Corpus Christi, 192
Magruder, Gen. John Bankhead, 129, 143
Major Brown, 30
Mallory, E., 291
Mallory, Fannie (Mrs. J. H. C. White), 291
Manucy, Bishop Dominicus Matthew: arrival of, 225; and Corpus Christi church, 250, 287, 291; departure of, 320; ministry to rural faithful, 275–76, 291; praise for Petra, 282; prejudices of, 225, 226
marriage: land acquisition through, 35, 39, 40; Mexican views on parenthood and, 22–23, 45; and Petra's social status in Mexico, 18, 19–20; religious complications in, 39; Tejano practices in remote areas, 225–26
Masonic Lodge, expulsion of Starck, 336
Masterson, Bat, 257, 259
Matamoros, Mexico: and Brownsville, 38; as Civil War refuge, 89, 98, 117, 120, 129–30; as Confederate supply base, 101; hurricanes, 266–67; illustration, *102;* and Juaristas, 118, 151–52; origins of, 18; Petra's move to, 18–19
Maxan, Nestor, 179, 182, 252–53
Maximilian, Emperor of Mexico, 126, 143, 149
Mejía, Gen. Tomás, 126

Mexican-American War (1846–1848), 27, 29, 200
Mexicans. *See* Tejanos
Mexico: and bandit attacks in Texas, 140; and cattle raiding problem, 184, 185, 197–98; challenges of being next to U.S., 246; as Confederate refuge, 101, 122; early Anglo incursions into, 1–2, 20–22, 59; lack of assistance against Cortina, 76; northern ranching communities, 8–11, *12,* 13, **14,** 15–16; as patriarchal society, 40; politics of, 84–85, 196, 236, 246; post-Imperialist chaos in, 149–50; property and social status in, 10–11; support for Tex-Mex railroad, 236–37, 245–46; women's status in, 3–4, 18, 19–20, 22. *See also* French Intervention War; *specific towns and cities*
Mier, Mexico, 2, 3, 11, 13, 16–17, 20–22
Mier Expedition, 20–22, 59
Miller, Charles, 65
Miller, Henry, 63, 65, 153
Miller Hotel, 63, *91*
mining, Stillman's venture, 37
Missionary Oblates of Mary Immaculate: and education in Brownsville, 42–43; Jaillet, 320–21, 334–35, 345; Kenedy family's support for, 57, 352; Keralum, 59, 60; lack of respect from bishop for, 225; Lebh Shomea House of Prayer, 313; ministry to rural faithful, 59–60, 225–26, 275–76, 291; support for Kenedys, 7, 39, 45, 313, 320–21, 334–35, 345; Unionists' mistrust of, 110, 118; Verdet, 7, 39, 45, 46, 64. *See also* Church of the Immaculate Conception; Parisot, Fr. Pierre
monopolistic trading practices, King, Kenedy, and Stillman, 29–34, 55, 66, 142, 185, 190
Montgomery, Col. W. W., 101, 104
Moorhead, Josiah, 153
Morell, Carmen (Mifflin's adopted daughter), 350–51
Mussina, Jacob, 31
Mustang, 112–13

National Cattleman's Convention, 309–10
National Cattle Trail, 310
National City Bank of New York, 37, 145, 246
National Railway System of Mexico, 246
Native Americans. *See* Indians
natural/illegitimate children, 22–23, 45
Neale, William, 108, 111, 177
Newel, Rev. Fr. C., 45
newspapers, wealthy's support for, 314
Noakes, Thomas John, 230
Nueces County, 200
Nueces River, 11, 118

INDEX

Nuecestown, Texas, 229–30
nuns. *See* Sisters of the Incarnate Word and Blessed Sacrament

Oblate order. *See* Missionary Oblates of Mary Immaculate
O'Donnell, James, 32
oil reserves on Kenedy Ranch, 347
Olive, Print, 195

padrinos (godparents), 16, 71–72
Page, Samuel H., 230
Palmer, Gen. William Jackson, 274
Palmer-Sullivan Co., 273
Palm Grove Plantation, Brownsville, 193, 356
Paradez, Tomás, 162–63
pardons, post-Civil War, 138–39, 143–44
Paredes, Américo, 2, 112
Parisot, Fr. Pierre: bandit attack on, 140; and French withdrawal from Mexico, 150; fundraising for church organ, 69, 71; and ministry to rural faithful, 275; portrait, *142*; and post-Civil War border chaos, 141; post-hurricane church recovery, 161; Unionists' mistrust of, 110–11; at Vidal/Kenedy weddings, 119, 121; and yellow fever epidemic, 68
Partisan Rangers, Adrian's, 122, 124
patriarchal society, Mexico as, 40
Peña, Miguel de la, 252–53
Peña, Niceforo, 197
Penascal Raid (1874), 227
Pennsylvania: and Civil War's end, 128–29; and Mifflin's origins, 4–5; Mifflin's real estate assistance to mother, 167; Mifflin's visits to, 263, 284; Petra's trip to, 150–51; sons' time in, 98–100
Perkins Swenson & Co., 216
pharmacy, Putegnat, 96–97, 204, 302–3
Pierce, Leonard, 118, 126
politics: of Brownsville, 72, 153, 177–78, 183, 203, 209–12, 317, 319; and Corpus Christi's growth, 303; Dalzell's participation in, 153, 319; and Diaz in Mexico, 84–85, 196, 236, 246; end of Reconstruction, 215; Ford's influence, 130–31; and Jim Wells, 253; and land acquisition in Texas, 35; Mifflin and King's influence on, 72, 149, 153–54, 209–11, 219, 270, 286, 319; and payoffs to Mexican government, 237; and Powers, 250–51; Putegnat's career in, 83; and railroad development, 210–12, 216–17; South Texas, 208–12; and Stillman, 32; Tom Kenedy's career in, 317, 318–19, 340–41; and Walworth, 72, 83

Polk, Pres. James, 27
pontoon bridge across Rio Grande, *110*
Porción 57, **14**
porciones (Spanish land grants), 11. *See also* land grants, Spanish-Mexican
Powers, Stephen: and business politics, 250–51; City Council position, 153; death of, 282–83; as defender of Mifflin and King, 233; defense of Brownsville against Cortina, 75; as opposition, 217; and pardon attempt for Cortina, 187; portrait, *283*; as Stillman's lawyer, 33; and taking of lands from Tejanos, 227
profiteering, Civil War, 90, 102–3, 112–13, 120, 127
property holdings: Anglo takeover of Tejano lands, 2, 73, 178–79, 227–28; in Brownsville, 64, 340; Civil War confiscation of, 112; claims on Kenedy fortune, 318–19; and Cortina's crusade against Anglos, 31, 66–67; disputes over land, 154–55, 327; final disposition of, 352; hurricane damage, *157*; King's and Mifflin's ranch purchases, 40–42, 165, 227–28, 229, 238; marriage as acquisition tool, 35, 39, 40; and Mifflin's and Petra's compatibility, 5; post-Civil War restoration of, 137–39, 148–49; and R. King & Co., 59, 83–84, 131–32, 162–67, 182–83; and railroad developments, 234, 243–44, 246, 263–65; and social standing in Mexico, 10–11; title issues, 34–35, 83–84, 178–79, 220; Vela ranches, 8–11, *12*, 13, **14**, 15–16, 55, 167; and water supplies, 276, 278. *See also* inheritance of land; land grants, Spanish-Mexican; La Parra Ranch; Los Laureles Ranch; Santa Gertrudis Ranch
Protestants vs. Catholics, 38–39
public health problems. *See* diseases and public health
Puerta de Agua Dulce, Rancho, 229, 301
Putegnat, Ana Marie Chavero de (daughter-in-law), 186–87, 188. *See also* Vidal, Ana Marie Chavero de
Putegnat, Edward (grandson), 240
Putegnat, George Mifflin (grandson), 137
Putegnat, Irene (granddaughter), 302
Putegnat, John Peter (grandson), 177, 187
Putegnat, John Peter III (grandson), 188
Putegnat, John Peter (Pierre) (son-in-law), 94, 96, 100–101, 186–87
Putegnat, Joseph Louis (grandson), 116
Putegnat, Joseph Luke (son-in-law): as Confederate supporter, 177–78; courtship and marriage of, 94, 96–97; death of, 302; defense against Cortina, 75; drugstore operation, *92*;

Putegnat, Joseph Luke (*continued*)
pharmacy business, 96–97, 204; political career of, 83; portrait, *303;* social life in Brownsville, 145
Putegnat, Mary Louise (granddaughter), 158–59, 160, 218
Putegnat, Rosa Eliza (granddaughter), 152, 155
Putegnat, Rosa Vidal de (daughter): birth of, 19; as caregiver for Petra, 316, 321, 329; courtship and marriage of, 94, 96; and death of husband, 302–3; legacy of, 353; portrait, *93;* social life in Brownsville, 145; youth of, 46
Putegnat, Rosita (great-granddaughter), 121
Putegnat, Susan Catherine (granddaughter), 250
Putegnat, William, 100–101, 140, 316
Putegnat, William (grandson), 186

Quakerism, 4–5, 24, 99

R. King & Co., 59, 83–84, 131–32, 162–67, 182–83
Rabb, Frank, 193, 356
Rabb, John, 191, 192
Rabb, Lillian (granddaughter), 356
Rabb, Martha, 191, 192
raiding of ranches. *See* bandit attacks; thievery, cattle
railroad development: access property in Brownsville, 234, 243–44, 246, 263–64; Brownsville–Point Isabel, 185–86, 202; in Corpus Christi, 273, 315, 350; effect on cattle operations, 265, 306–7; map of, **264**; and Mifflin's many responsibilities, 263–64; and political battles, 210–12, 216–17; vs. steamboat business, 142, 152, 185–86, 190, 204, 206, 208–13; Stillman's connections, 37; weather challenges for, 221. *See also* Texas Mexican (Tex-Mex) Railway
Ramireño, Rancho, 105–6
Ramirez, Gertrudis Salinas de, 19
Ramirez, José Antonio (Petra's great-grandfather), 15
Ramirez, Col. Juan Nepomuceno, 19
Ramirez, María Catarina Vela de (Petra's great-grandmother), 15
Ramirez, María Gertrudis (Petra's grandmother), 15
ranching: brand registration, 60, *61*, 165, 172, 200; breeding operations, 219–20, 276–77, 306; challenges of, 220–21; Civil War losses, 144; and control of cattle trade, 185; cowboys, 57, 192, 247–48, 265; daily life, 202–3, 251–52, 265–66, 268–69; fencing of range, 165–66, 184–85, 193, 202, 265; hide and cattle laws, 208–9; horses, 219–20, 228, 306, 316–17; and hospitality, 260–61; Indian raids, 13, 56, 63; King's and Kenedy's holdings, 2, 265, **266**; King's and Mifflin's purchases, 40–42, 165, 227–28, 229, 238; King's dedication to, 55–56, 229, 287, 300, 341; King's innovations and success, 189–90; King's rebuilding efforts, 201, 202–3; La Atravesada, 178; land acquisition methods, 227–28; Loma Alto, 229; Los Federales, 276; market ups and downs, 88, 151, 207, 245, 306; Mifflin's introduction to, 40, 55–57; and Mifflin's many responsibilities, 263–64; oil reserves, 347; Petra as rancher, 16–17, 60, *61*, 169, 193–94, 201, 203, 220, 294; political support for, 208–9; postwar restoration of, 145–46, 151; Puerta de Agua Dulce, 229, 301; R. King & Co. partnership, 59, 83–84, 131–32, 159–60, 182–83; railroad effects on, 265, 306–7; Ramireño, 105–6; safety and security challenges, 56, 60, 63, 64, 151, 168, 171–74, 195–98, 200, 203–4, 224–25, 236, 286, 287–88; San Salvadore del Tule, 56, 77, 80, 83, 197; Santa Rosa, 111; Santa Teresa, 3, 4, 11, *12*, 13, **14**, 197; Santiago's love of, 58, 194–95; sheep, 56, 229, 278; and tallow production, 185; and Texas Fever, 309–10; Vela ranches, 8–11, *12*, 13, **14**, 15–16, 55, 167; Veleño, 3, **14**, 40–41, 55, 167; weather challenges, 221–22, 266–67, 276, 277, 280, 289, 292; Ytúrria Ranch, 40. *See also* drives, cattle; La Parra Ranch; Los Laureles Ranch; Santa Gertrudis Ranch; thievery, cattle
Rankin, Melinda, 47
real estate. *See* property holdings
Reconstruction: and Brownsville's recovery, 153–62; business/property recovery, 136–37, 141–46, 148–49, 151; ending of King and Mifflin's ranching partnership, 131–32, 159–60, 182–83; Ford's role in, 131; Mexican chaos during, 149–50, 151–52; pardons for Mifflin and King, 138–39, 143–44; and political changes, 177–78, 183
Red Party, 183
religion: and Brownsville's cultural mosaic, 37–39; children's training in, 169, 204; and death of infants, 87; home altars, 60; and lack of slaves in Kenedy household, 69; and marriage complications, 45; Petra and Mifflin's contrasting backgrounds, 4; Protestant/Catholic competition for souls, 47; Quakerism, 4–5, 24, 99. *See also* Catholic Church
Republicans in Texas during Reconstruction, 183
Reséndez, María Josefa (Petra's mother), 16

INDEX

Richardson, Capt. James J., 56, 115, 173, 179, 182
Rincón de Los Laureles, 162–63. *See also* Los Laureles Ranch
Rincón de Santa Gertrudis, 229. *See also* Santa Gertrudis Ranch
Rio Grande Female Institute, 47
Rio Grande Railroad Co., 185–86, 263–64
Rio Grande Railway (RGRC), 234. *See also* Texas Mexican (Tex-Mex) Railway
Rio Grande (Río Bravo): abortive plan to open, 33; Anglo settlement along, 1–2; drying up of, 218; Petra's ancestors' settlement of, 11; pontoon bridge, *110;* scoping of for river trade, 30–31; Union blockade of, 88–92, 94, 101–3, 112, 128. *See also* steamboat business
river trade. *See* steamboat business
roads and trails (1850s), **51**
Robb, Thomas, 196
Robb Commission, 196–97
Rock, H. S., 209
Rockefeller, William, 37
Rodríguez, Alfredo (grandson), 240
Rodríguez, Concepción Vidal de (daughter), 19, 46, *81,* 83, 145, 354
Rodríguez, Manuel (son-in-law), *82,* 83, 267, 354
Rogers, C. M., 192
Roma, Texas, 30–31
Rowe, E. D., 98–99
Ruiz, Manuel, 107
Russell, Maj. William J., Jr., 208, 217, 219

Sabinitos, Rancho de, 15
sailing life, Mifflin's early, 24
St. Ange, Mother, 156–57
St. Joseph College/Academy, Brownsville, 154, 159, 161
St. Mary's Catholic Church, Brownsville, 7
St. Patrick's Church, Corpus Christi, 287, 320–21
Salinas, Gertrudis, 19
Salinas, Gen. Juan Flores, 232
San Antonio and Aransas Pass Railroad, 350
Sandoval, Jesus, 231
San Martín Grant, 40
San Román, 145
San Román, José: buyout of, 204, 206; Civil War move to Matamoros, 89; as godparent, 71; Mifflin's questions about loyalty of, 203; political and business troubles, 212–13; as steamboat business partner, 55; and weather damage to railroad, 208
San Salvadore del Tule Ranch, 56, 77, 80, 83, 197
Santa Anita, Rancho, 39

Santa Gertrudis Ranch: as Civil War refuge, 89; consolidation of, 80, 83; cotton trade role, 102; daily life on cattle drive, 248–49; development of, 56; drought hardships, 280; fires at, 277; hospitality of, 101; King's acquisition of, 41; King's attempt to sell, 298; King's family move to, 84; layout of, 229; R. King & Co. partnership, 59, 83–84, 131–32, 159–60, 182–83; Robert E. Lee's visits to, 63; scope of, 341–42; Union attack on, 113, 115–16
Santa Rosa Ranch, 111
Santa Teresa, Rancho, 3, 4, 11, *12,* 13, **14**, 197
Scott, Gen. Winfield, 29
Sedgewick, Gen. Thomas, *110*
Separatists vs. Conservatives on land status, 35
Seuss, Elena (Mrs. J. G. Kenedy, Jr.), 352, *353*
Shears, Robert, 73, 74, 153
sheep ranching, 56, 229, 278
Sheridan, Maj. Gen. Philip Henry, 130, 142
shipping by steamboat. *See* steamboat business
Sisters of the Incarnate Word and Blessed Sacrament: Civil War adventures, 109–10; convent school, 42–43, 46–47; Corpus Christi convent, 321; Cortina's sparing of, 74; and hurricane, 156–57, 160–61; Indian raids on, 43; and Petra's charity work, 43; post-war recovery, 148
Slaughter, Gen. James E., 128
slavery, 69
smallpox epidemic, 118
social life: bride's trousseau, 87; in Brownsville, 145; in Corpus Christi, 238–39, 278–79, 289–91, 313–14, 315; daily activities, 52–53; holidays on Los Laureles Ranch, 268; and hosting military during Civil War, 101; Petra and Mifflin's style, 62, 269
social status: in Brownsville, 51–52; Mexican structures, 4, 9–11, 13, 15–16, 18, 19–20, 22
Society of Friends, 4–5, 24, 99
Somervell, Alexander, 21
Specht, Frank, 196
Spohn, Dr. Arthur E. (son-in-law): arrival in Corpus Christi, 162, 200–201; building of reputation, 238–40; charitable work of, 313; courtship and marriage of, 241–43; Episcopal Church background of, 313; legacy of, 352; portraits, *314;* and social life in Corpus Christi, 272, 279; status at Petra's death, 346; treatment of Petra, 206–7
Spohn, Sarah Josephine (née Kenedy) (daughter), *239,* 272, 313, *314,* 346, 352. *See also* Kenedy, Sarah Josephine
Spring Hill College, Alabama, 168, 169, 176–77, 179

Stansbury, R. N., 35
Starck, Daisy (granddaughter), 263
Starck, F. J. C. (grandson), 125
Starck, Frederick Edward, Jr. (grandson), 154, 160
Starck, Maj. Frederick Edward (son-in-law): and Adrian, 124; charity work in Brownsville, 291; courtship and marriage of, 120–21; death of, 356; expulsion from Brownsville, 336–37; and family divisions, 177–78, 324; and Fr. Parisot, 110; local political role, 153, 250–51; portrait, *122;* and smallpox epidemic, 118; troubles of, 332; unpopularity with soldiers, 122, 125
Starck, Lillian (granddaughter), 193
Starck, María Vicenta Vidal de (Nene) (daughter): birth of, 22; as caregiver for Petra, 284, 316, 329; courtship and marriage of, 120–21; departure from Brownsville, 125; illness of, 313; legacy of, 354, 356; marital troubles, 324, 332; as Petra's caregiver, 261; portrait, *121;* youth of, 46
Star of Philadelphia, 24
steamboat business: Brownsville's decline in control of, 171; Dalzell's role in, 145, 162, 218; financial difficulties of, 202; French takeover of river trade, 125–26; in Galveston, 218; government contracts, 29, 30–31, 33, 55, 60, 142, 145; illustration, *38;* irregularities by Kenedy and King, 149, 208; Kelly's role, 204, 206; King, Kenedy & Co., 145, 171, 190, 204, 206, 216–18; King's role in, 29–34, 127–28, 149, 208; M. Kenedy & Co., 32, 60, 65, 112, 145; Mifflin's and King's styles in, 127–28; Mifflin's early experience in, 24–27; monopolistic practices in, 29–34, 55, 66, 142, 185, 190; moving out of, 159, 216–18; post-Civil War developments, 136–37, 141–46, 148–49, 152, 212–13; pre-Civil War development of, 55, 60; vs. railroads, 142, 152, 185–86, 190, 204, 206, 208–13; Stillman's role in, 32, 37, 142, 145; Walworth's role in, 31; weather disasters, 159, 206, 221–22. *See also* cotton trade
Steel, Adj. Gen. William, 215
Steele, Maj. Gen. Frederick, 131
Stevens, J. Henry, 228–29, 277
Stillman, Charles: Brownsville home of, *43;* on chaos of Civil War, 107; cotton trade role of, 89, 90, 91, 111, 128; courtship and marriage of, 37; founding of National City Bank of New York, 37, 145; initial land appropriations, 31; and Mifflin's acquisition of Los Laureles, 163–64; mining venture, 37; move to New York, 171; as Petra's neighbor in Matamoros, 18–19; portrait, *42;* and railroad development, 37, 142, 217; ranching operations, 41–42; slave ownership by, 69; steamboat business role of, 32, 37, 142, 145; and war profiteering, 102, 103
Stillman, Cornelius, 162, 164
Stillman, Elizabeth (Betsy) (née Goodrich), 37, 42
Stillman, James, 37, 145, 246
Stock Raisers Association, 185
Strong, Lt. Richard, 131
Swisher, Rosa Maria (descendant through Concepción Vidal de Rodríguez), 54, 136

tallow factories on ranches, 185
Tamaulipas No. 2, 149, 159
Taylor, Capt. Richard, 107
Taylor, Gen. Zachary, 27, 29, 30, 200
teaching career, Mifflin's, 24
Tejada, Pres. Sebastián Lerdo de, 196
Tejanas as marriage targets for Anglos, 35, 39, 40
Tejanos: and Anglo prejudice, 48, 225; Anglo raids on ranches of, 184, 198, 227; assimilation vs. cultural preservation, 27, 50–51; in Confederate Army, 94, 104; dress customs, 54–55, 83, 87; faith practices, 225–26; foods, 17, 52–53, 252; importance of land to identity, 11; Kenedy Ranch families, 286; loss of lands to Anglos, 2, 34–35, 73, 178–79, 227–28; pay differential vs. Anglo workers, 265; political participation in Texas, 72; and post-Texas Revolution raids, 20–22; ranching life of, 251–52; resentment of Texas Rangers, 232; social culture, 17–18
telegraph line, 218
Texas Fever, 309–10
Texas Land & Cattle Co., Ltd., 280
Texas Longhorn cattle, 190
Texas Mexican (Tex-Mex) Railway: cattle shipment business, 306–7; company establishment, 274; completion of, 273–75; and Corpus Christi's growth, 219, 289; illustration, *274;* land for, 264–65; Lott's role in, 234, 244, 264, 274–75; Mexican support for, 236–37, 245–46; Mifflin and King's investment in, 234; plans for, 216–17, 216–18; starting ceremony, 244
Texas Rangers, 56, 77–78, 106, 178, 184, 230–33
Texas Revolution (1836), 13
Texas Volunteers. *See* Confederate Army
thievery, cattle: economic impact of, 171–72, 173, 187–88, 228; and hide and cattle laws, 209; lack of U.S. government protection, 173, 183–

INDEX

84; McNelly's retrievals from Mexico, 232–33; Mexican government's response, 184, 185, 197–98; and Mifflin's City Council duties, 153; ranchers' efforts against, 184–85, 195–96, 213–14; revolutionary respite in, 237; vigilante actions against, 227
Thornton, Jesse, 218
Tijerina, Eulalia, 178–79, 286
Tilden, Lt. Bryan P., Jr., 30
titles, land, 34–35, 83–84, 178–79, 220
Tobin, Capt. W. G., 77–78
trails, **51**, *191*, 191–92
transportation in South Texas, **51**. *See also* railroad development; steamboat business
travel, hazards of, 175–76, 204
Treaty of Guadalupe Hidalgo, 6, 29
Treviño, Abelardo, 84, 119
Treviño, Corina Ballí (James's wife) (daughter-in-law), 294–95, 301. *See also* Kenedy, Corina Ballí Treviño de
Treviño, Dolores, 84
Treviño, Felícitas (Mrs. F. Ytúrria), 40
Treviño, Manuel, 84–85, 120
Treviño Garza, Mariano, 208, 213
Troy, 32
Turcotte, Arnaud, 216
Turcotte, Marie Stella (Mrs. J. G. Kenedy) (daughter-in-law), 216, 301–2, 310–13, *312*. *See also* Kenedy, Marie Stella
Turcotte, William, 216

U.S. Army. *See* Army, U.S.
Union Army: Adrian's career in, 104, 105–7, 108, 113, 119, 121–24; attack on Santa Gertrudis Ranch, 113, 115–16; blockade of Rio Grande, 88–92, 94, 101–3, 112, 128; occupation of Brownsville, 108–16; post-war attack on Bagdad, 141; Starck's career in, 122, 124, 125
Ursuline Convent, New Orleans, 168–69

Vallecillo mines, 37
vaqueros of northern Mexico, 57. *See also* cowboys
Vega/Vela, Lorenzo, 325–26
Vela, Andrés (Petra's uncle), 167
Vela, Francisco (Petra's ancestor), 7, 9
Vela, Isidro, 104
Vela, José Gregorio (Petra's father), 4, 11, 13, 15, 16, 20
Vela, José Nicodemus (Petra's grandfather), 11, 15
Vela, Lázaro (Petra's great-grandfather), 10, 11, 13
Vela, María Antonia García de (Petra's great-grandmother), 10

Vela, María Catarina (Petra's great-grandmother), 15
Vela, María Gertrudis Ramirez de (Petra's grandmother), 15
Vela, María Josefa Reséndez de (Petra's mother), 16
Vela, María Petra. *See* Kenedy, María Petra Vela de
Veleño, Rancho, 3, **14**, 40–41, 55, 167
Verdet, Fr. Jean Marie Casimir, 7, 39, 45, 46, 64
Vidal, Adrian (son): birth of, 22; character of, 49–50, 94, 104; Confederate Army career, 94, 100–101, 103–4; and Cortina, 67, 73–74, 108, 124; courtship and marriage of, 119; cultural adjustment problems, 47–50; death of, 132–33; desertion from Union Army, 121–24; education of, 47–49; as Juarista, 124, 126–27, 132–33, 135–36; letter to Miller Hotel, *92;* and Miller Hotel, 63; Ramireño incident, 105–7; Union Army career, 104, 105–7, 108, 113, 119
Vidal, Ana Adrianne (Anita) (Mrs. Cowen) (granddaughter), 137, 302, 320, 353–54
Vidal, Ana Marie Chavero de (daughter-in-law), 119, 186–87, 188
Vidal, Concepción (Conchita) (daughter), 19, 46, *81*, 83, 145, 354
Vidal, Juana (daughter), 23
Vidal, Luisa (Louisa) (daughter): birth of, 23; courtship and marriage of, 84, 87; family recipes, 53; legacy of, 352; move to Galveston, 218; and Petra's charity legacy, 43; portrait, *85;* return to Brownsville, 316; youth of, 46
Vidal, Col. Luis (father of Petra's Mexican children), 6, 20, 22
Vidal, Luis (son), 23
Vidal, Manuela Andrade y Castellanos de, 18, 19
Vidal, María Vicenta (Nene) (daughter), 22, 46, 120–21, *121*, 125. *See also* Starck, María Vicenta Vidal de
Vidal, Petra Vela de. *See* Kenedy, María Petra Vela de
Vidal, Rosa (daughter), 19, 46, 83, *93*, 94, 96. *See also* Putegnat, Rosa Vidal de
Vidal, Vidal (son), 23
vigilante attacks, 227, 230–31
Villarreal, Roberto, 178
Vinton, Lt. Jack, 105

Walworth, Capt. James: death of, 128, 131; King and Kenedy's political support for, 72; official withdrawal from steamboat business, 145; as ranching partner, 59, 83; as steamboat business partner, 31

water supplies: and Civil War, 118, 130; as primary consideration in land acquisition, 276, 278, 280; and ranching, 56, 289
water transportation, *51*. *See also* steamboat business
wealth, influence of, 131, 258–59, 314. *See also* politics
weather: disasters of, 155–59, 206, 208, 221–22, 266–67; end of drought in 1856, 60. *See also* drought
Webb, Walter Prescott, 178
Webb and Miller Hotel, 63, *91*
Wells, James B., 227, 253, 283–84, 296
Werbiski, Alexander, 153
West & Chenery, 142
Western Trail, 191–92
Wharf Stock and Ship Channel Co., 273
White, Fannie (née Mallory), 291
White, J. H. C., 291
Wild Horse Desert: beauty of, 201; challenges for ministering priests, 225–26; dangers of, 183–84; drought problems, 118; plants of, 194; taming of, 230–33; Tejano settlement of, 6. *See also* ranching
Woll, Gen. Adrian, 20
women: Mexican vs. Anglo roles for, 3–4, 18, 19–20, 22, 40; Petra's cultural contributions, 2, 4, 6, 17–18, 170, 173–74, 295; Tejanas as marriage targets for Anglos, 35, 39, 40
Woodhouse, H. E.: complaints about river trade monopoly, 185; payments to Mifflin for land access, 234, 244; river trade losses, 212–13; and shipping competition, 206, 217, 218; and stolen hide shipments, 209

yellow fever epidemics, 68, 155, 159, 186, 206, 207
Young, John J., 39, 55, 69, 154
Young, Salomé Ballí de, 39–40, 53, 154–55, 275
Ytúrria, Felícitas Treviño de, 40
Ytúrria, Francisco, 40, 51, 75, 283, 341
Ytúrria Ranch, 40
Yznaga, Antonio, 337
Yznaga, Yrene (Tom's wife) (daughter-in-law), 337–39

ISBN-13: 978-1-58544-614-8
ISBN-10: 1-58544-614-9